FINANCIAL MANAGEMENT

HARVARD BUSINESS REVIEW EXECUTIVE BOOK SERIES

Executive Success: Making It in Management

Survival Strategies for American Industry

Managing Effectively in the World Marketplace

Strategic Management

Catching Up with the Computer Revolution

Financial Management

Marketing Management

Using Logical Techniques For Making Better Decisions

FINANCIAL MANAGEMENT

DWIGHT B. CRANE
Editor

JOHN WILEY & SONS
New York • Chichester • Brisbane • Toronto • Singapore

This publication is designed to provide accurate and authoritative information in regard to the subject matter covered. It is sold with the understanding that the publisher is not engaged in rendering legal, accounting, or other professional service. If legal advice or other expert assistance is required, the services of a competent professional person should be sought. *From a Declaration of Principles jointly adopted by a Committee of the American Bar Association and a Committee of Publishers.*

Library of Congress Cataloging in Publication Data:

Main entry under title:

Financial management.

(Harvard business review executive book series)
Includes indexes.
1. Corporations—Finance—Addresses, essays, lectures. I. Crane, Dwight B., 1937– . II. Series.
HG4026.5.F57 1983 658.1'5 83–1112
ISBN 0–471–87598–8

Printed in the United States of America

10 9 8 7 6 5 4 3 2 1

Foreword

For sixty years the *Harvard Business Review* has been the farthest reaching executive program of the Harvard Business School. It is devoted to the continuing education of executives and aspiring managers primarily in business organizations, but also in not-for-profit institutions, in government, and in the professions. Through its publishing partners, reprints, and translation programs, it finds an audience in many languages in most countries in the world, occasionally penetrating even the barrier between East and West.

The *Harvard Business Review* draws on the talents of the most creative people in modern business and in management education. About half its content comes from practicing managers, the rest from professional people and university researchers. Everything *HBR* publishes has something to do with the skills, attitudes, and knowledge essential to the competent and ethical practice of management.

This book consists of 36 articles dealing with what executives need to know about corporate finance and investment decisions. Neither abstruse nor superficial, the articles chosen for this volume are intended to be usefully analytical, challenging, and carefully prescriptive. Every well-informed business person can follow the exposition in its path away from the obvious and into the territory of independent thought. I hope that readers can adapt these ideas to their own unique situations and thus make their professional careers more productive.

KENNETH R. ANDREWS, Editor
Harvard Business Review

Contents

Part Six Pension Fund Management 383

Part Seven New Developments in Financial Markets 425

Introduction

A study of *Harvard Business Review* issues published over the past several years reveals a considerable amount of information concerning corporate finance and investment decisions. Chief financial officers and other executives have explained their approaches to dealing with important financial issues. Academicians have described new theoretical developments and explained their relevance. And financial consultants have provided suggestions for solving key management problems.

Given this wealth of material, two objectives were used to guide the selection of articles for this book. The first objective was to provide a reference source with useful information about each of the major financial topics—working capital management, capital investment decisions, and others. The second purpose was to provide a review of recent developments in financial research and of current thinking about financial management problems. Furthermore, articles of both types were selected to provide a blend of practical advice and food for thought that will challenge financial decision makers.

It is clearly an appropriate time to pull together available thinking on financial decision making, not because all the important problems have been solved, but because so much has happened over the last two decades. The environment in which financial decisions are made has changed dramatically, posing serious problems on the one hand but providing new opportunities as well. At the same time, financial research has proceeded apace. Admittedly, new financial theory is not as earthshaking as some of the recent economic and political events, but some important lessons have emerged nonetheless.

Changes in the Environment

Inflation has been one of the most important forces driving developments in the U.S. economy and financial markets over the past several years. Going back to the 1960s, which business manager, investor, or public official correctly anticipated the inflation that the United States would experience?

Since then, all these parties plus the public at large have had to adjust to a new reality of soaring prices.

One significant result of the inflation was higher interest rates. Another was a shift in the conduct of monetary policy. The new policy attempted to control the growth of monetary aggregates rather than emphasize stable interest rates. As this policy worked to slow inflation, the economy weakened and interest rates became more volatile. Some success on the inflation front had been achieved by mid-1982, but interest rates remained stubbornly high, stock prices were low, and the economy was far from strong. It was also important that few, if any, observers believed the inflation problem had been permanently solved.

The implications of all this for corporate financing decisions were quite straightforward. With weak stock prices, selling new equity was expensive to most corporations. Debt was available and used by firms, but traditional long-term fixed-rate debt was expensive. It was difficult to attract investors to these instruments because they had been badly burned by inflation and rising rates in the past few years, and they had serious concerns about the future direction of rates. The natural result was rising debt ratios on corporate balance sheets, with a large share of the debt short term.

The asset side of corporate balance sheets posed similar concerns, particularly in new plant and equipment investment. Some observers argued strongly that there was an underinvestment in these assets, thus contributing to a relatively slow productivity growth and a weaker competitive position for U.S. firms in the world economy. Several phenomena may have contributed to this problem. One theory is that U.S. managers are too concerned about short-term profit performance. Another is that firms set target rates of return or hurdle rates on new investments that are too high. Still another is that concerns and uncertainty about the future environment have discouraged investment.

All of these arguments have some merit. Focusing here on the environment, developments over the past several years have complicated capital investment decisions that were already complex, particularly those that had strategic implications for firms. Inflation, for example, increased both the cost of external financing and the amount required for corporate expansion. More important for several industries, competition from non-U.S. corporations grew significantly. Reflecting the growing strength of their home countries, Western European and Japanese companies expanded their international outreach. Thus U.S. companies began to face more competition at home and in other geographic markets, causing a loss in domestic market share in some industries and a declining U.S. share of world exports.

The Oil Price Shocks

Industries in the United States and other countries were also greatly affected by the dramatic increase in oil prices that began in 1973–1974. Not all the news was bad because some companies, such as firms involved in oil exploration, clearly benefited from higher oil prices. For others, however, the adjustment to a world of high oil prices was more painful. Firms that relied heavily on energy or other oil-related inputs for their production process had to contend with a significantly higher cost structure. Others had to adapt to shifting consumption patterns induced by high oil prices. Still others were faced with declining exports to countries weakened by the need to import expensive oil.

Oil importing countries were forced to adopt new and usually restrictive economic policies to change domestic consumption patterns. Even with these actions, many countries had to significantly increase their external borrowing, particularly after the second round of price increases in the late 1970s. High interest rates added to their growing debt burden and compounded the economic difficulties experienced by many third world and other countries.

Massey–Ferguson, a large Canadian corporation that experienced considerable financial distress in the early 1980s, provided an illustration of how high oil prices could squeeze both revenues and expenses of some corporations. The company produced diesel engines in the United Kingdom that were used in farm equipment to be sold in other countries, many of which were developing or newly industrialized countries. Because of the availability of North Sea oil, the British pound was a relatively strong currency. This made the United Kingdom a high-cost location for production, because salaries and other expenses were obviously paid in pounds. Unfortunately, these expensive engines were then to be sold to several countries with oil-induced balance of payments problems and weakened currencies—not an attractive combination. Although this oversimplification does not do justice to Massey–Ferguson's strategy and situation, it provides an example of how a dramatic upward shift in oil prices was a contributor to higher manufacturing costs and lower revenue at the company.

Developments in the Financial Markets

The implications of the massive transfer of financial assets from oil-importing to oil-exporting countries spilled over in an important way into the international financial markets, especially the Euromarkets. The Eurodollar market that developed in London in the early 1960s grew considerably over the succeeding decade. However, it remained a market that intermediated funds primarily between depositors and borrowers that were located in Western European and other developed countries. United States banks and corporations, for example, were major borrowers in the Eurodollar market during the 1973–1974 credit crunch in the United States.

In the aftermath of the oil price shocks, the nature and size of the Euromarket changed dramatically. It became the major vehicle for recycling petrodollars from oil-exporting to oil-importing countries. In the seven-year period from 1974 through 1981, the volume of bank lending in the Eurocurrency market increased sixfold to reach $133 billion. The volume of new international bond issues increased by a similar magnitude, totaling $45 billion in 1981.

As the Euromarket developed in the 1970s, it also expanded to include other major currencies, a result of the increased economic strength of Japan and Western European countries and the renewed importance of their currencies. In addition, the Euromarket spread geographically to key financial centers around the world.

This growth of the Euromarkets resulted in a major breaking down of geographic and institutional barriers in the international financial markets. Twenty years earlier a corporate borrower desiring U.S. dollars would get them in the United States and would deal with a U.S. financial institution, either a commercial bank for short-term funds or an investment bank for long-term funds. By the early 1980s, the same borrower could obtain dollars in any of several locations around the world and could choose from a large number and variety of financial institutions, or in some situations, even bypass an intermediary altogether. Similar alternatives were available for other key currencies, and for investing funds as well as borrowing. Thus the options available to sophisticated corporations were greatly enhanced by developments in the international markets, as was their ability to reduce costs or improve returns by operating across financial markets.

Fortunately for U.S. business firms, the breaking down of barriers and the growth in financial alternatives also proceeded rapidly in the domestic capital markets. This resulted from several factors including a growing sophistication of business firms, high level of competition in the marketplace, and a trend toward deregulation of financial institutions.

These changes led to an increase in direct access to the financial markets. Borrowing by nonfinancial firms in the commercial paper market grew rapidly, spurred in part by a relatively high prime rate in the mid-1970s. Once firms "discovered" the paper market, they tended to continue using it. In addition, more firms bypassed intermediaries and went directly to lenders with private placements of debt. Deregulation was also playing a major role in improving companies' access to the market in 1982. The SEC put a shelf-registration rule, Rule 415, into effect for a nine-month trial period beginning in March 1982. This rule allowed companies to register all the securities they planned to issue over a two-year period. After this registration had been cleared, the company could sell some of these securities "off the shelf" at any time, picking an underwriter on a competitive basis at the time of the sale. As of mid-1982 it wasn't known whether the new rule would be maintained after the trial period, but it seemed likely that some relaxation of earlier rules would be continued.

This increased competition among financial institutions broadened the options available to corporate borrowers. The presence of foreign banks was a key factor, for a growing number of them established themselves in the U.S. market and then competed to gain a market position. But perhaps the more significant long-term trend that emerged was a blurring of the distinction among financial institutions. Commercial banks moved toward investment banks as they strengthened their domestic merchant banking activities, such as private placement and merger and acquisition activities. Securities firms, on the other hand, entered the "retail banking" business. Merrill Lynch led the way with their Cash Management Account, and other major firms followed suit.

The insurance industry was not left out as insurance firms entered the securities business through acquisitions. In the early stages of these acquisitions it was not clear how much cumulative advantage could be achieved through the combination of these businesses. In August 1982, however, it was interesting to note that Prudential announced a reorganization related to its Bache acquisition. One weakness in the product line of securities firms was their inability to lend money except through margin accounts. Perhaps Prudential found a way to deal with this product line gap and gain some synergy. In its reorganization, Prudential put a lending group, Pru Capital, next to Bache under the same senior executive.

The blurring of distinctions among financial institutions put pressure on regulation and legislation that had previously staked out territories for each. Numerous observers were forecasting changes in legislation, such as a repeal or a revision of the Glass–Steagall Act, which separated commercial and investment banking. The pressure for change was real and not all of it was coming from competitors who wanted to broaden their domain. Other sources included consumers and corporations that were benefiting from the new competitive environment. Another source was the thrift industry, which was in serious trouble because of its narrow historical mission and the resulting burden of low interest rate mortgages. How fast changes would occur was not known, but pressure from several sources argued that something needed to be done.

It is interesting to note that inflation, which had a major impact on corporate investment and financing decisions, was also a driving force in developments in financial institutions. Inflation and the high interest rates it spawned encouraged consumers to look for new ways to save so that they could earn market rates of interest. Money market funds were formed to respond to this need and later provided the means for brokerage firms to get into the "retail banking" business. Commercial banks were faced with the loss of "core" demand and savings deposits and were forced to pay market rates of interest on a larger and larger share of their funds. Thus, with rising interest costs, and also higher operating costs because of inflation, commercial banks searched for more fee income in the traditional territory of investment bankers. Perhaps the interinstitutional competition would have occurred anyway with the passage of time, but inflation and the pressure it brought certainly provided a strong incentive for change.

Trends and Implications of Financial Research

Just as the environment changed, the nature of research in finance shifted significantly in the last two decades, although it would be stretching the point to say that the two trends were very closely related. In the early days of finance as a topic of academic inquiry, the subject was treated in an institutional manner; that is, writers in the field described the institutions and institutional arrangements involved in carrying out the financial function of corporations. Things changed in the late 1950s and early 1960s as researchers devoted more effort to developing models and procedures to be used by firms to do more complete analysis and make better decisions. This research adopted the viewpoint of corporate managers, addressing issues about how they could better manage financial matters to achieve their own objectives.

Although work of this kind continued, a new stream of research began in the mid-1960s and came to dominate the academic finance literature. This research focused on the behavior of financial markets and the implications of this behavior for business firm decisions. As seen by typical corporate financial officers, this work tended to be quite "academic" and frequently unreadable. Some of it was not easy reading to fellow academics. Nonetheless, some important information and lessons emerged.

Perhaps the most basic lesson is that the financial markets are relatively efficient. The idea of efficiency is often misunderstood, particularly by managers of investment portfolios who believe they have a superior approach to making money. But the idea is simple. The stock market, for example, is efficient in the sense that, first, information about companies and the economy is widely dispersed throughout the investment community and, second, this information is quickly reflected in stock prices. Fortunately, there are portfolio managers who work hard to achieve high returns. Because these managers actively seek out information and execute trades based on what they learn, prices incorporate new data quickly.

What does this mean for corporate financial decisions? One implication is easy to believe and is consistent with the way corporate officers typically manage their business. Because the financial markets are relatively efficient, corporations are much more likely to earn attractive returns for their shareholders by devoting resources to product decisions, that is, the asset side of the balance sheet. Financing decisions certainly require thoughtful attention and they can be an important part of corporate strategy. However, a plan that requires a financial officer to regularly outguess the bond and stock markets is not likely to be successful.

A second important implication of market efficiency is that the stock market is not fooled, for very long at least, by actions that manipulate earnings per share but do not affect the cash flow of the corporations. The theory underlying the financial market research suggests that it is cash flow that matters to shareholders, not reported earnings, and the evidence supports this theory. Various studies have shown that the market "sees through" accounting changes and other actions, such as stock dividends, which do not increase the cash flow available to shareholders. This conclusion has an important bearing on the evaluation of acquisitions and other major capital investment decisions. There is a natural concern about how these decisions will affect earnings per share in the near term. Financial market research, however, indicates that a longer-term perspective, which pays attention to the value of the cash flows that will be generated by the investment, would be more useful.

The research also has implications for how these cash flows should be valued. Some firms select a target rate of return based on a historical rate of return of the firm or a return desired by management, perhaps with some adjustment for the perceived riskiness of the investment project. This target rate is then used to obtain a value for the project and decide if it is worthwhile.

Capital market research would agree with this basic procedure, but would say the target rate should reflect the rates of return available to investors and creditors on projects of similar risk, not a historical return on company assets, for example. The logic is that if corporations are to continue to attract new funds for investments, cash flows from those investments must provide returns at least as good as other alternatives in the marketplace. There is ample evidence of what happens to the share price of corporations that retain and invest shareholder funds at below-market rates of return.

It is interesting and important to note that in some cases the risk-adjusted rate of return desired by the financial markets may actually be lower than internally set rates. This results from the fact that shareholders can and do diversify risk by holding shares in more than one company. Thus the risk they bear from a capital investment made in one of their companies is frequently less than the risk perceived by the manager whose career is on the line. This poses an important dilemma for companies. Rates set high enough to make managers feel comfortable may in fact lead to an underinvestment in the future of the company.

Financial managers reading these ideas for the first time may find that the results of financial market research when explained this way are still "academic." However, the issues involved are not unimportant. If, as has been alleged, U.S. industry is underinvesting in new capital, partly as a result of evaluating investment using horizons that are too short and target rates of return that are too high, then financial market research provides some food for thought that is particularly timely.

Structure of the Book

The articles included in this book are grouped around the traditional topics of finance. Working Capital Management, the first topic, has been significantly affected by developments in the environment. Inflation and high interest rates have made management of cash and other elements of working capital more important. At the same time, improved technology for moving funds, new banking services, and better information systems have helped corporations make progress. Articles in Part 1 report this progress, both domestically and internationally, and they provide some advice to corporations wishing to improve their management of cash and accounts receivable.

The second topic, Management of Foreign Exchange Exposure, has also become increasingly significant to U.S. companies as they have expanded internationally. Furthermore, it has become more difficult as a result of the move to floating exchange rates in 1971 and the subsequent fluctuation in currency values. Authors of the three articles in Part 2 suggest new systems to measure foreign exchange exposure and provide ideas for management of the risk. In their suggestions, all the authors adopt a view consistent with the financial research discussed above. They believe the risk to be managed is not the risk of changes in reported earnings (i.e., accounting risk), but rather the economic risk arising from the fact that cash inflows and cash outflows over time are in different currencies.

Articles in Part 3, Financing the Corporation, deal with a range of topics including estimation of external financing needs, deciding the appropriate amount of debt, and dealing with financial intermediaries. Perhaps the most controversial topic concerns the issue of how much debt is correct. One set of articles on this topic adopts a management or internal view and suggests a procedure that managers can use to analyze how much debt their company can handle in adversity. Another article adopts more of an external view of companies, that is, the perspective of credit and equity security holders, and it provides a summary of what recent financial research has to say about the debt question.

The most important implications of the capital market research of the past several years have primarily concerned investment decisions. The nature of this research and its implications are spelled out in Part 4, Making Good Investment Decisions. However, this part is not just theoretical. One article, for example, describes a practical capital-budgeting system and two other articles provide advice on a particularly critical investment area—investments made to gain market share.

Two other investment topics are included as separate Parts—Mergers and Acquisitions, and Pension Fund Management. Articles on mergers in Part 5 describe procedures that can be used to screen and evaluate target companies. Particular emphasis is placed on the need to look for ways to create value with the acquisition, where value derives from economies of scale or another source of synergy that improves the cash flow of the combined firms. As pointed out in the capital market research, investors can easily diversify their own portfolios. Thus mergers for the sake of diversification per se seldom lead to higher stock prices of acquiring firms.

Pension fund contributions are not usually thought of in the same manner as capital investments, but they have many common features, such as the need to decide how much to invest. Articles in Part 6 provide advice on this and other aspects of pension funds including the assumptions underlying a pension plan and management of the funds.

Finally, the major changes in the financial environment that have occurred over the last several years have created new needs for both suppliers and users of funds. It is not surprising that the financial markets have developed new instruments and new organizational forms to respond to the evolving needs of the marketplace. Floating rate notes and sophisticated project financing techniques are but two examples of the innovations that have occurred. Articles in Part 7, New Developments in Financial Markets, discuss several of these innovations and provide some thoughts about the future.

PART ONE
WORKING CAPITAL MANAGEMENT

AN OVERVIEW

United States corporations are correctly thought of as sophisticated managers of liquid assets. Their treasurers began years ago to take out "sharp pencils" to pare down demand deposit balances, as bankers reluctantly noted. These days pencils are no longer adequate to the task. Computerized services and new techniques for moving funds are provided by banks and used by firms to manage cash very efficiently.

In spite of these technological improvements, not all firms have moved full force to take advantage of available options. Part of the reason is that senior managers are more concerned about other aspects of their business. For example, the potential profit improvement from more efficient use of cash is not always seen as significant compared with the changes in established relationships and disruptions in operating procedures that might be required. A 10% or other reduction in non–interest-bearing deposits provides only a one-time improvement in profits when these funds are invested, not a continuing profit growth as sales from a new product might provide.

Incentives have been substantially changed, however, as the prime rate and other short-term rates have reached high levels such as those experienced in the early 1980s. Banks are also contributing to better use of cash as they compete for market position and for income by marketing cash management seryices. Thus Searby's article, "Use Your Hidden Cash Resources," provides a useful reminder of the techniques and approaches that can be used to improve cash management. His message is basic, but important: Look for opportunities to speed up the receipt of cash and to slow down disbursements. For international firms, Dyment's message in "International Cash Management" is exactly the same. The difference is that the cash management problem is made more complex because cash is received and disbursed in different countries and currencies. He has some helpful suggestions for dealing with this complex problem.

Another area of working capital management, accounts receivable, is also receiving important attention in the early 1980s as high interest rates and a weak economic environment have combined to increase the cost and credit risk involved in lending to customers. In their article, "Better Way to Monitor Accounts Receivable," Lewellen and Johnson describe a useful way to track the quality of outstanding receivables. As they explain, some of the more standard quality measures are subject to distortions as sales levels change over time.

Stancill shares companies' concern with the quality of their receivables, but lest they become too concerned, he provides an important reminder that credit extension is a key factor in supporting sales and profits of a company. In his article, "Is Your Bad Debt Expense Too Low?," Stancill suggests an approach to establishing credit standards that includes the expected profitability of good accounts as well as the probability and cost of bad accounts. As with other quantitative approaches to management problems, full implementation of Stancill's approach would be difficult. But careful thinking about the credit extension problem in the way he describes could lead to better decisions.

1

Use Your Hidden Cash Resources

FREDERICK WRIGHT SEARBY

"Companies searching for additional cash sources or profit improvement would do well to remember Dashiell Hammett's Maltese falcon and first take a look close to home," says this author, who offers clues to implement the tough-minded changes needed to reduce costs and free corporate cash reserves for profitable uses. Not only can clerical costs be minimized, but, more important, the heretofore unrecognized potential in the corporation's cash gathering and disbursing systems can be tapped for business growth. Cash management, moreover, represents a real opportunity for commercial banks looking for a significant new service to offer their corporate customers.

Mystery story buffs and Humphrey Bogart fans alike will remember Dashiell Hammett's superb tale *The Maltese Falcon*, later made into a suspenseful movie. The title object in Hammett's story was a foot-high gold statue of a bird, encrusted from head to foot with precious stones. Painted over with black enamel to disguise its value, the falcon had been passed from hand to hand for centuries. Few of its possessors even guessed its true value, and none was perceptive enough to scratch its enameled surface to bare the treasure underneath.

Hammett's story provides a moral for today's top management and senior financial officers. For most companies have in their own possession a treasure of which they are unaware. They have failed to look beneath the surface of a familiar, everyday reality—the company's own cash gathering and disbursing system—little suspecting the wealth it may conceal.

To be sure, the high interest rates of the past two years have stimulated many companies to whittle down some of their cash balances or take another look at the length of their receivables. By and large, however, these belt-tightening efforts have been carried out piecemeal by individual departments.

Only in rare cases has a chief executive, perceiving the profit potential in reducing his company's fallow cash assets, set in motion an across-the-board, multidepartmental review of cash gathering and disbursing processes. Yet, where this has happened, the results have often been astonishing. Consider these recent examples:

☐ A major oil company reduced the cash in its gathering and disbursing system by 75%, providing over $25 million for marketing and refining expansion.

☐ A large railroad that showed cash balances of only $9 million drew a total of $17 million out of its cash gathering and disbursing system to help finance a major equipment acquisition program.

☐ A leading insurance company that showed cash balances of $8 million discovered an additional $18 million which could be profitably extracted and put to work.

Solely by tapping the previously unrecognized potential in its cash gathering and disbursing systems, each of the first two companies avoided substantial outside financing at an unfavorable time, without weakening its working capital position or its relationships with outside financial institutions, and saved approximately $1 million in interest charges. The insurance company in the third example profited by a sizable expansion of its loan portfolio.

The recurring savings to manufacturing companies with $100 million or more in assets from much less spectacular cash balance reductions—say, 20% of cash deposits held at year-end 1967—would be about $144 million annually, assuming that the $2.4 billion thus released was invested at 6%.

Reasons for Dormancy

Why has such a substantial resource lain dormant, like the treasure of the Maltese falcon, in so many companies? There are at least three reasons:

1. *Accounting treatments usually understate the size of cash balances.* A substantial portion of the cash available seldom appears as cash on a company's balance sheet, if indeed it appears at all. The two principal sources of this hidden cash are (a) receipts by an agency of the company that have not yet reached a dispersing bank (cash-in-transit), and (b) cash in a bank on which checks have been drawn but not charged to a company bank account (float). Such items thus understate the true amount of money to be managed and explain the paradox of the railroad and the insurance company mentioned above that were able to withdraw more cash than their cash balances showed.

2. *Scorekeeping practices of the financial function hinder imaginative*

cash management. Frequently, the treasurer or other financial officer most able to improve cash management processes is evaluated primarily by his ability to produce funds on short call and to obtain the prime rate on commercial bank loans. Obviously, both of these factors are important to the financial health of a company. However, the first measurement can encourage money managers to maintain unnecessarily large reserve balances or excessive standby lines of credit which require sizable compensating balances with commmercial banks. As for the second measurement—the rate at which money can be borrowed—it is almost always calculated at the simple interest rate, masking the true cost of borrowing when compensating balances are required by the lending bank, as they usually are.

For example, if the treasurer must maintain a 20% compensating balance to obtain the current prime rate of, let us say, 6% on a commercial bank line of credit, then the company's true cost is not 6%, but 7.5%.

3. *Corporate management has not come to grips with the substance of its cash gathering and disbursing processes.* Frequently in the past, top management has shied away from examining the company's cash processes because of their assumed complexity, preferring to leave "technical details" to the bank officers and the company's accountants—none of whom is concerned with more than a fraction of the total picture. Instead of using a cash management system designed to free cash resources for other uses, such a company is operating with a conglomeration of processes and procedures that have evolved piecemeal in response to various historical circumstances, practices, and pressures. Today, however, more and more companies are reclaiming the initiative in cash management and applying the same systematic, problem-solving approaches here that they use elsewhere in their businesses.

Basically, the process of "finding" interest-free funds within the company merely entails thorough fact gathering and analysis. But the opportunities thus identified almost always involve making tradeoffs among mutually related variables. This calls for careful analysis of the overall, interrelated, long-term profit impact of alternative decisions on the system as a whole. Moreover, some of the improvement opportunities fall in the controller's domain, while others are in the province of the treasurer—a split of responsibility that underscores the need for top management attention. Effective cash management, therefore, requires the concerted attention of talented personnel whose top management sponsorship and direction gives them the authority to cross organization lines.

Interwoven Opportunities

In real life, a company's cash gathering and cash disbursing activities are two sides of an interwoven system in which changes to one must be evaluated for their impact on the other. For the purposes of this article, however, it will be useful to consider cash gathering and cash disbursing opportunities separately.

Exhibit 1 illustrates a total cash management control system covering 85 to 90% of the expected cash flow for a typical company and shows in visual form how the various facets of cash management fit together.

Cash Gathering

An obvious but easily overlooked way to speed incoming cash is getting bills to customers earlier. Consider these examples:

☐ Simply by installing and enforcing standards, a Midwestern oil company cut several days off the time branch offices were taking to process retail customers' credit card invoices and forward them to the home office. In the home office further time was saved by mechanizing the invoice-processing operation and eliminating an auditing step that turned out to be costing more than the errors it was intended to uncover. Altogether, the company has saved $150,000 annually by taking these steps to speed up the mailing of its bills.

☐ American Telephone & Telegraph Company is working on two ways of speeding its billing processes: computerized processing of receivables and billing through customers' banks. For most of the 350,000,000 collect and credit calls handled annually by the Bell System's 1,500 U.S. operating offices, an operator writes a ticket, which is then mailed to one of 108 local accounting offices that prepare customer bills. But in the area served by Southern Bell, where 100,000 credit and collect calls are made daily, the same call records are now collected in 11 computer centers and transmitted at high speed over existing telephone lines to a processing center in Atlanta, where the billing data are swiftly sorted and relayed to the proper accounting offices, again over telephone lines. The system has cut a day or more from receivables, which in this one area alone will release cash assets conservatively estimated at $200,000 a year. AT&T expects to extend the system nationwide within a few years.

AT&T is also trying out an automatic bill payment plan under which the customer authorizes his bank to pay drafts drawn on his account by a Bell company. Along with the usual bill, AT&T's computer-based accounts receivable processes automatically produce a draft which is presented directly to the customer's bank for payment. In addition to speeding collection of AT&T receivables, this plan reduces the customer's cost of administering accounts payable.

☐ Smaller companies have speeded up their billing in simpler, but no less effective, ways. A well-known shipping company found it had been losing from 2 to 13 working days in billing to various classes of customers, partly because data required for bill preparation were re-

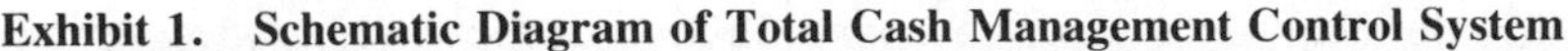

Exhibit 1. Schematic Diagram of Total Cash Management Control System

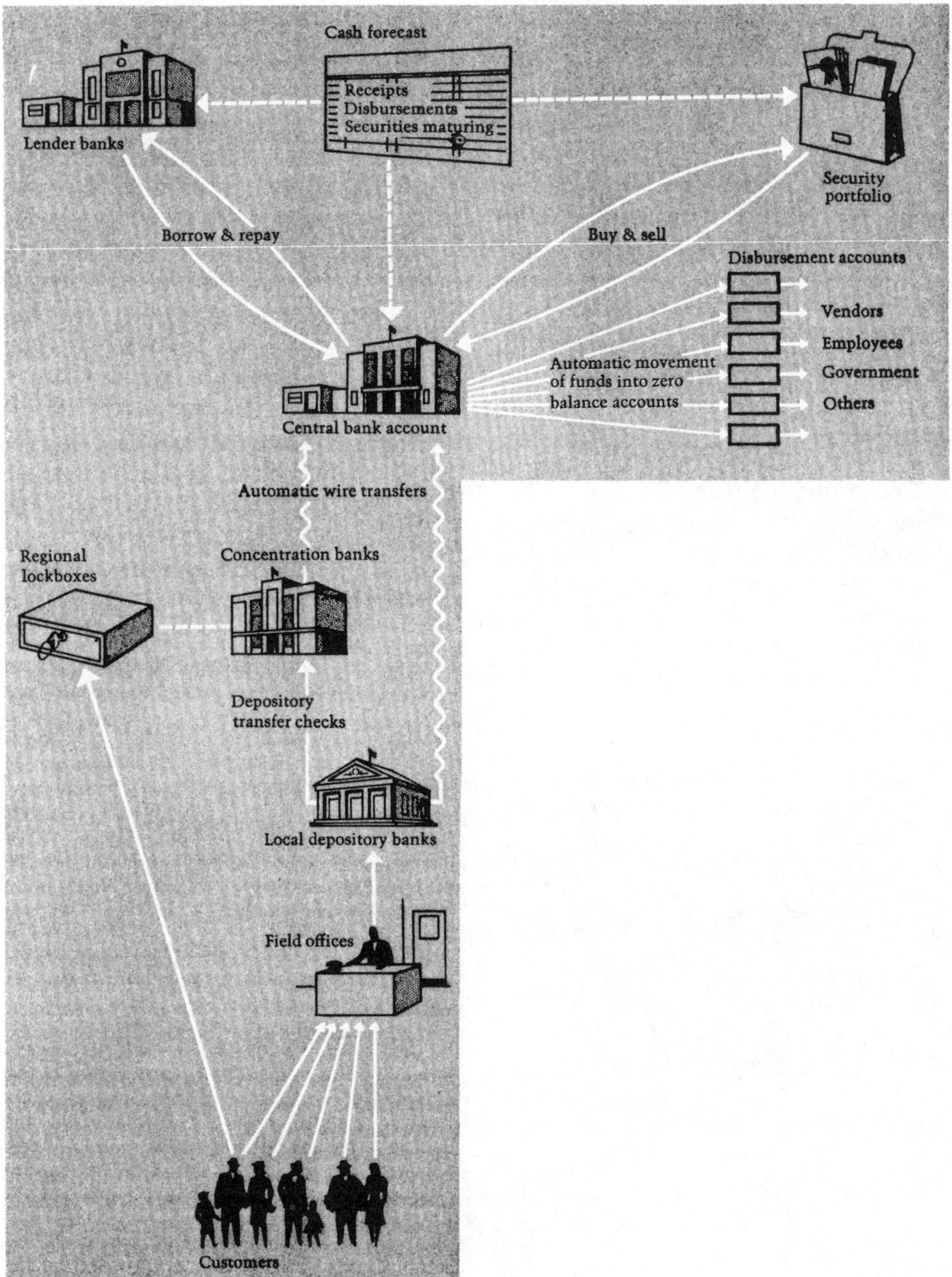

ceived unnecessarily late, and partly because a few accounting supervisors did not appreciate the time value of money. By improving the flow of data and installing elementary controls, the company was able to free \$400,000 that had been tied up in receivables.

From the time the customer puts his check in the mail, the financial manager has four important opportunities: (1) to cut down cash-in-transit time; (2) to minimize "uncollected funds"—that is, recently deposited checks drawn on other banks and not yet credited to the company's account; (3) to reduce balances in collection banks and speed the movement of funds to disbursing locations; and (4) to optimize the balances necessary to compensate banks for depository and movement services.

The financial manager can avail himself of four principal devices for accelerating his company's inward cash flow: depository transfer checks, wire transfers, lockboxes, and relocation of gathering banks.

Depository Transfer Checks. Used to move funds to concentration or disbursing banks, depository transfer checks are nonnegotiable, usually unsigned, and payable only to a single company account in a specific bank.

In a representative situation shown in Exhibit 2, the company's local agent deposits his day's receipts in a local bank and immediately mails a depository transfer check for the same amount to a designated concentration bank. Receiving the depository transfer check in the next day's mail, the

Exhibit 2. Use of Depository Transfer Checks

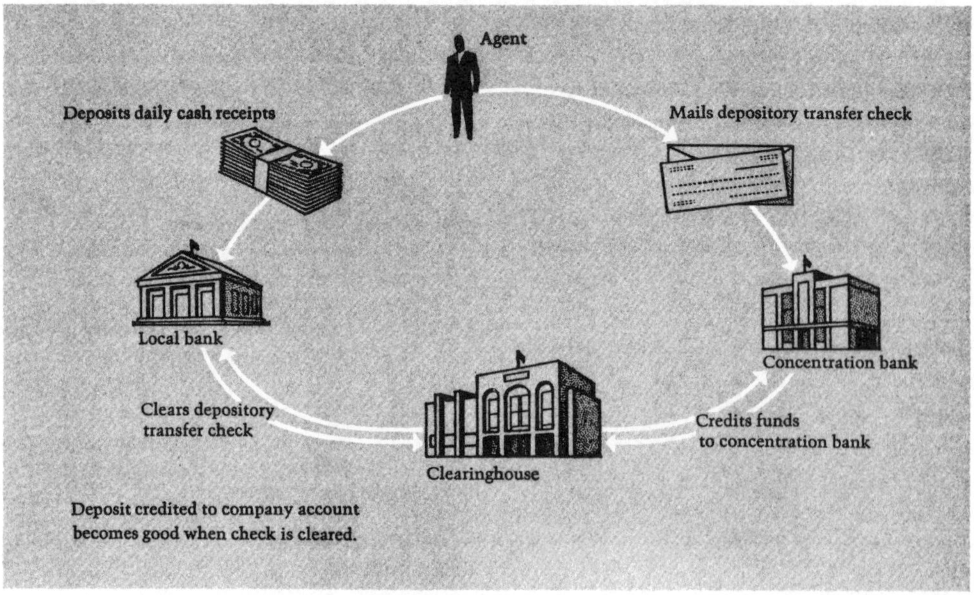

concentration bank puts it into collection that same day, either through the Federal Reserve System or by forwarding it directly to the local depository bank.

Installing lockboxes can also require major changes in accounting and control systems if cash receipts have to be processed at different locations.

Selection of Gathering Banks. Frequently, the cash gathering system can be made more effective by selecting more advantageously located banks for use as local depositories or concentration points.

A concentration bank—as well as the local depository bank, if possible—should meet five criteria:

1 The bank should be in the Federal Reserve city that is serving the collection area.
2 It should be on the bank wire system.
3 It should receive 90% of deposited checks one day after they are mailed.
4 Its check availability schedule should average less than one and a half days for normal deposits.
5 Its service charge, earnings allowance rate, and reserve requirements should be competitive.

Many large industrial companies use several cash gathering systems, depending on the size, regularity, type, and origin of their receipts, as well as on the availability of bank services.

By use of this device, funds received at field points are moved directly into concentration banks without requiring action first by headquarters' financial officers. And, although anyone in the local organization may issue a depository transfer check, since the check is nonnegotiable, it cannot be misapplied.

Depository transfer checks cost only 5 to 10 cents apiece, but they are not so fast as wire transfers and may offer no advantage when more than a day is required for mailing or clearing.

Wire Transfers. Available in approximately 60 U.S. cities, wire transfers are the fastest way to move money between banks. On order, a bank will transfer a specified amount of a customer's funds by telegram to a designated bank. The funds are considered collected on receipt of the wire notice.

Frequently, a bank is given standing instructions to wire transfer routinely any funds above a stated bank balance to a specified bank. In this case the movement of funds is automatic, while balances are held at the level necessary to compensate the bank fairly for its services.

Wire transfers require that both the sending and the receiving banks have access to the bank wire system. And, of course, they are uneconomical unless the value of having money available as early as possible exceeds the extra cost of the wire transfer (the price is generally about $1.50 a transfer). In general, wire transfers for amounts under $2,000 are not practical.

Lockboxes. Cash gathering can often be expedited by having remittances mailed directly to a post office box that is opened by a bank. The use of lockboxes speeds the collection of checks as well as the movement of remittances, since the checks are deposited before, rather than after, the accounting is done. On occasion, however—especially where only checks for small amounts are involved—the cost of a lockbox may outweigh its benefits. One company, for example, found that by using a lockbox it could speed up remittances from its customers by an average of three days. But the average remittance was only $5, whereas the additional per-check cost of a lockbox was two cents, or eight times the incremental value of receiving the money three days early—$.0025 (i.e., $5 × .06 × 3 ÷ 356, where 6% represents the value of money). Wisely, the company kept on making local deposits. But it did start using depository transfer checks to move customer remittances to gathering banks. They may use, for example, alternative combinations of the four devices just mentioned, tailoring the appropriate cash gathering system for each area in the light of such factors as mailing time statistics for the area, and local bank availability schedules, service charges, earnings allowances, and reserve requirements. Exhibit 3 shows how one company selected appropriate cash gathering systems for different areas.

Cash Disbursing

The principal opportunities available to the financial manager for improving his company's disbursing procedures and freeing more funds for investment include synchronizing transfers with clearings, delaying check mailings, and eliminating field working funds.

Synchronizing Transfers with Clearings. Financial managers recognize that the funds actually available in banks are generally greater than the balances shown on the company's books. This difference (float) is caused by the delay between the time a check is written and its clearing by the bank—due to mailing time, handling by payee, and normal collection time. Exhibit 4 shows the sizable amount of float which built up in one oil company's royalty disbursing account.

If a financial manager can accurately estimate the size of float and predict when checks will clear, he can maintain a negative book balance and invest the float. He does not have to reimburse the disbursement account until shortly before the checks are presented for payment. Often, he can synchronize transfers into disbursement accounts with check clearings if an accurate clearing projection has been developed.

One device that may help the financial manager forecast and control float is the zero balance account. Under this system, no balance is maintained

Exhibit 3. Alternative Retail Cash Gathering Systems, Company X

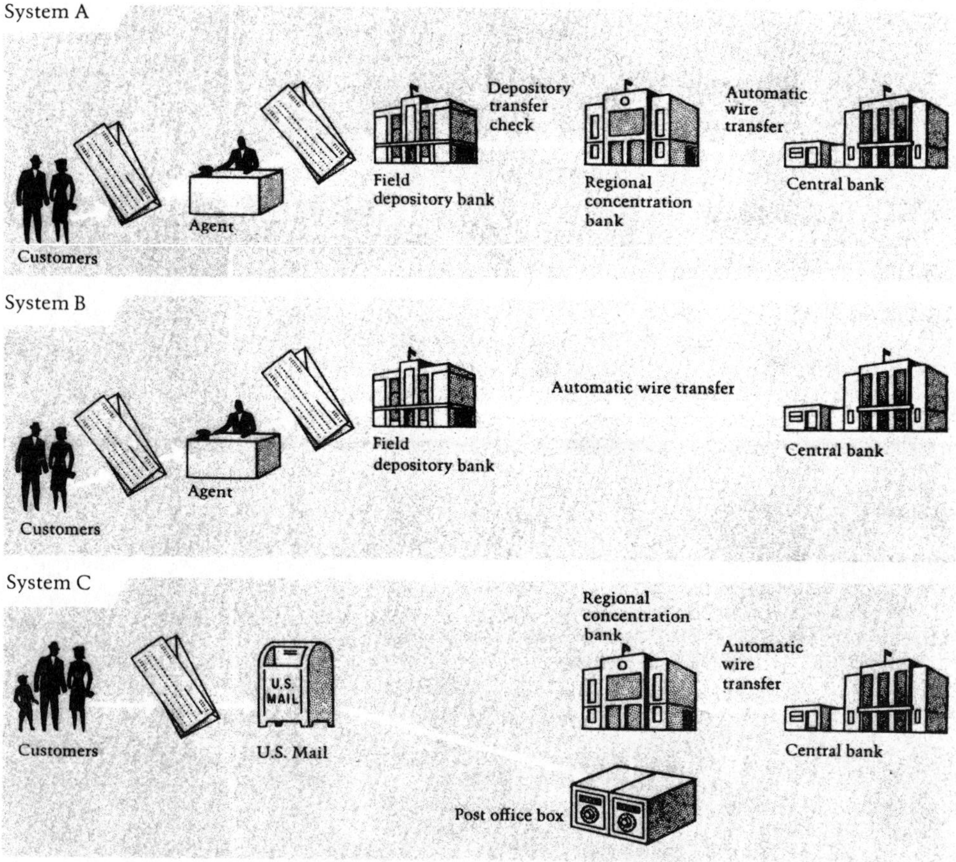

System A

Customers
Agent
Field depository bank
Depository transfer check
Regional concentration bank
Automatic wire transfer
Central bank

System B

Customers
Agent
Field depository bank
Automatic wire transfer
Central bank

System C

Customers
U.S. MAIL
U.S. Mail
Post office box
Regional concentration bank
Automatic wire transfer
Central bank

in the disbursing accounts. Instead, all funds are held in a single general account, and the bank is authorized to transfer funds from the general account into each zero balance account as disbursement checks actually clear. In this way the forecasting and control problem is centralized in the single general account.

Some money managers may be reluctant to have a consistently negative book balance position at disbursing banks. This problem can be overcome by realigning the disbursing system so that major portions of the check float are generated at the banks that require the largest compensating balances. When this is done, the float balances at these important banks usually are sufficient to cover the compensation needs, while the book balances can be held at a small positive figure.

Delaying Check Mailings. Without the loss of prompt-payment discounts, credit rating, or supplier goodwill, substantial free credit and cost savings

Exhibit 4. Actual Funds Available While Company Y's Books Showed Zero Balances

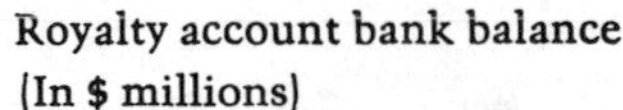

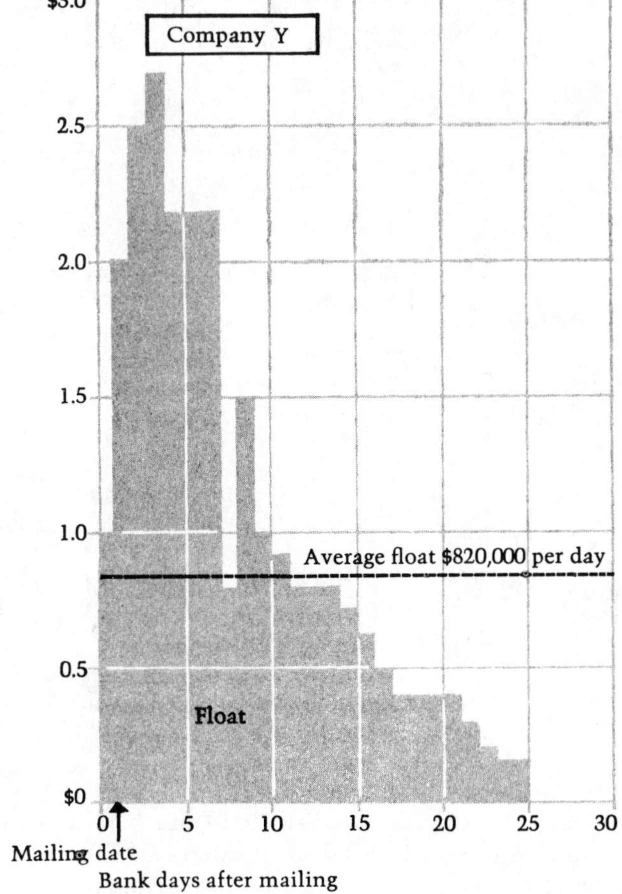

can often be realized from better timing of accounts payable. For example, input data can be date-coded to trigger printing by computer and mailing on the latest possible date. (In many states, payments mailed on the discount expiration date legally qualify for the discount.) Nondiscount suppliers, such as transportation companies or joint venture partners, can be paid at the latest possible date that is consistent with legal and competitive conditions.

The oil company referred to in Exhibit 4 not only found ways to minimize its royalty payment float, but was also able to delay its royalty check mailings each month. Following a thorough study, this company discovered that it was sending out $10 million in oil royalty payments each month 12 days ahead of industry practice and 15 days ahead of legal requirements in most states. On the basis of an analysis of mailing times, the company began coding its oil royalty accounts so as to release computer-printed checks an average of 12 days later than before. The recurring savings to the company from this relatively easy change were $237,000 a year (i.e., $10,000,000 × 12/365 × 12 × .06, with the first 12 representing the number of days; the second 12, the number of months; and 6%, the value of money).

Eliminating Field Working Funds. Many companies maintain small bank balances in field locations for convenience in paying small local bills. In total these funds frequently create unnecessarily large cash balances because of "cushions" maintained for contingencies. For example, one company with a large marketing organization in 25 states reduced its cash balances $3 million by substituting draft payments and a centralized disbursement account for field working funds.

Draft payment plans and centralized field disbursement accounts are two devices which can be used to improve field disbursing procedures. Payments to local vendors can be made with drafts drawn by themselves on a designated bank. Limits can be set on the amount of drafts, and payment may be refused. Among the advantages of drafts are that cushions are eliminated, because funds are not needed until the draft is presented; one reimbursement per day covers all drafts; bank service charges for cashing drafts are lower than for checks; and clerical costs of preparing checks and maintaining individual working funds are eliminated.

However, some of the disadvantages are that many smaller banks do not accept drafts; their use requires the cooperation of suppliers; and drafts may reduce the company's float. Alternatively, a centralized, zero-balance account can be maintained to pay local vendors. Checks are issued locally but drawn on the central account. The checks can be coded to show the disbursing location and purpose, and the bank can provide periodic listings, by code and amount, of the checks that have cleared.

This system also eliminates working fund cushions and the clerical costs of maintaining individual working funds. Furthermore, check float is centralized in a single account, simplifying the control problem.

Impact on Banks

Better corporate cash management has obvious portents for commercial banks. Sometimes, such as in the case of a receivables reduction, its effects are confined to a shifting of deposits from one company to another. At other times, say, when a company begins using automatic wire transfers to reduce cash-in-transit, the result is a shift of deposits from one bank to another bank. Overall, however, there can be no doubt that the systematic analysis and overhauling of cash management systems as described in this article will reduce (and, in fact, are currently reducing) the amount of interest-free demand deposits available to commercial banks.

How are the banks reacting to all this? Naturally enough, many are reluctant to initiate a process that in the short run results in a partial drying up of their traditional source of raw material, and in the long run may well require substantial changes in "product line" and pricing policies.

Positive View

Increasingly, however, most of the nation's biggest and most farsighted banks are taking a positive approach. Recognizing the legitimacy of their customers' concern with the profit improvement opportunities concealed in their cash management systems, these banks are taking the view—a real sign, perhaps, of the much-heralded marketing revolution in banking—that the long-term health of their institutions depends on how well they serve the best interests of their customers. And they know that this means more than simply adding new services. It means being willing to drop old services—and to look for new and more flexible pricing practices.

In fact, many banks are working actively with large corporate customers to help them design more effective cash gathering and disbursing systems—thereby, not surprisingly, strengthening greatly their working relationships with these customers. In at least one case, the bank in question inherited some of the customers' deposits from other banks less eager to assist in improving cash management, emerging with only slightly lower overall deposits. But even those whose deposits have been substantially drawn down have found themselves, thanks to their new and deeper knowledge of their customers' businesses, in a far better competitive position to develop profitable new business.

Summary

Companies searching for additional cash sources or profit improvement would do well to remember Dashiell Hammett's Maltese falcon and first take a look close to home.

The opportunities for capital generation or for profit improvement in cash management are often impressive. For a company representing the mean of *Fortune's "500,"* for example, even a day's reduction in cash-in-transit would be worth well over $100,000 in recurring annual savings. For a small company, the dollar figure will be smaller but relatively no less significant. (Company managers can estimate, on a rough basis, the value of reducing a day's cash-in-transit by dividing their sales by 365 and multiplying the result by 6%. The resulting figure, of course, represents not the cash freed up, but the savings recurring annually from the cash freed up.) And this, as we have seen, is only one of a number of ways of freeing idle funds. In other words, it is only a fraction of the total opportunity.

To take advantage of the total opportunity, all that is needed to begin with is a systematic, tough-minded examination of cash processes to uncover profit opportunities such as those indicated by the systems listed in the Appendix to this article.

Once these opportunities are identified and the savings targets are established, the financial manager can proceed, with top management's support and encouragement, to implement the changes needed to reduce costs and free corporate cash reserves for profitable uses. Some of these may be independent, such as closing out inactive accounts; others may be interdependent, such as modifying cash collection procedures and setting cash balance minimums at concentration banks.

A company can expect both immediate and long-range benefits from appraising its cash handling practices and capitalizing on the unveiled potential. Not only can clerical costs in cash gathering and disbursing be minimized, but, more important, large sources of funds can be tapped for business growth.

Appendix. Systems Chosen

Description	Used Where	Effect on Field and Home Office Operations
Local cash receipt and deposit	Payments made on locally maintained accounts receivable	200 field locations mail their deposits to new, relocated regional banks
Depository transfer check to regional concentration bank	Average local receipts less than $2500 per day or . . .	Regional banks receive mail overnight from 90% of locations
Automatic wire transfer to disbursing bank	Wire transfer not available	Intransit cash reduced by $750,000
Local cash receipt and deposit	Payments made on locally maintained accounts receivable	Can be used in 20 field locations controlling 50% of deposits
Automatic wire transfer to central bank	Average local receipts exceed $2500	Intransit cash reduced by $1,250,000
Direct mailing of checks to regional post office box cleared by concentration bank	Payments made on centrally maintained credit card receivables	Two regional lockboxes established
Automatic wire transfer to central bank		Intransit cash reduced by $800,000 Home office clerical costs reduced by $25,000 per year

2
International Cash Management

JOHN J. DYMENT

As holding cash for international transactions has become ever more risky and costly, a number of companies have developed various techniques to reduce the amount they keep on hand. In this article, the author draws on the experiences of these companies to aid other managements in analyzing their cash receipt and disbursement systems and their relationships with banks. He concludes by describing the duties entailed in managing cash that crosses national borders.

In recent years, as interest rates have risen throughout the world and foreign exchange rates have continued to fluctuate, many companies have looked for ways to conserve their resources by practicing international cash management:

- A company with sales of $500 million discovered that changes in its invoicing procedures and cash transfer methods could reduce its requirement for liquid assets by 20%.
- A company near the top of the *Fortune "500"* saved more than $1 million by reducing by one day the time that it took to transfer intercompany and interplant cash.
- A French soft goods manufacturer that imported raw materials and then sold the finished products throughout Europe undertook a study to find ways to conserve cash. The company's management found it was able to free the French franc (FF) equivalent of $3.5 million in funds and to reduce interest and bank charges by $500,000 by improving its cash management procedures.

The manufacturer's target average bank balance, which had been $1 million, is now zero. The rest of the $3.5 million saved has come from simply speeding up the movement of money from customers and delaying the time that money paid to suppliers is debited to its accounts. Neither the company's customers nor its suppliers are affected by this change in timing, which simply moves money fast through the international banking system.

It is not difficult to determine if there are opportunities in your company to achieve significant savings by improving cash management, but the analysis must be objective and thorough. It calls for a careful examination of three distinct elements of cash management: cash receipts, cash disbursements, and bank deposits and loans.

The objectives of the analysis should be to identify delays and determine whether liquid assets can be used either to save interest expense or to earn interest income. Let us examine the sort of changes that can be profitably made under each of these systems.

Obviously, some of the potential sources of savings that I will look at apply to cash handling procedures both within a country and among countries, but in this article I will omit techniques of a purely domestic nature that have been adequately covered in other articles on cash management.[1]

Cash Receipts

In going over its cash receipts system, a company may find savings in one or more of four areas: invoice dates and payment terms, changes in the currency of sales, arrangements with "concentration" banks, and flexibility toward new developments.

Check Invoice Dates and Payment Terms

One of the easiest things to check is whether invoice dates, which form the basis for permitted payment time periods, are the same as shipping dates and whether the terms of payment and discount are no more generous than competition requires.

One company uncovered a number of unexpected differences when it checked some of its invoice dates against their shipping dates. Although procedures called for invoices to be prepared the same day as shipments were made, management found that, whenever the computer system had problems that caused delays, an invoice bore the date of preparation, which was by then one or two days after the date of shipment. By simply changing this procedure to backdating its invoices, the company has been able to save $10,000 per year. Similarly, other companies have found that their invoicing procedures do not allow for correct dating when shipments are made from distant manufacturing plants.

The management of a French-based company asked people in its commercial department whether sales would suffer if customers were granted a 2% instead of a 3% discount for prompt payment. Responses indicated that sales would not change significantly. The 1% reduction resulted in savings of $24,000 per year. Wholesale credit terms in the same company allowed for payment in 60 days. However, the definition of when the 60 days began differed. Some customers who had not been given specific guidelines counted from the end of the month, others from the end of a fortnight, and still others from some other date. A policy was established to start counting from the end of a fortnight. Expected savings: $40,000.

Change in the Currency of Sales

Before the days of floating currencies, it did not matter so much which currency was specified in a sales contract as long as it was fully convertible and there was little chance of devaluation before collection. Now, companies are finding that, where permitted under foreign exchange control rules, they can often specify a change in currency that will be acceptable to the customer. This change inconveniences the customer somewhat but helps the supplier avoid the risk of losing his profit from an adverse movement of the customer's currency.

Sometimes the reverse situation occurs when the customer's currency is preferred to one's own or there is a significant difference in the interest rates and invoices may be discounted or used as loan collateral.

For example, a French manufacturer has found he can both save cash and protect profits earned on his sales in Germany against a French franc decline by using a new sales company registered in Germany. Instead of invoicing customers directly, he invoices the sales company, which reinvoices the customer. Clerical work is all done in Paris. The sales company then borrows an amount equal to its invoices in Deutsche marks, converts it to francs, and pays the manufacturer. The current interest rate is only 8% in Germany, whereas in France it is 12% for this type of financing. In addition, a risk of loss from foreign exchange fluctuations is eliminated because the company's debt in Deutsche marks equals customers' receivables, which are also in Deutsche marks.

Use of Concentration Banks

Sometimes companies fail to realize that a check must clear in the country on whose currency it is drawn. The delays caused by this requirement are considerable. They can be overcome by using a bank in each country of sale to collect, clear, convert, and transfer receipts locally. Often management has thought about such arrangements when dealing over great distances but has then overlooked them when dealing with locations close by.

For example, the distance from Paris to Brussels is about the same as from New York to Boston or Washington—a few hours by car or train, less than an hour by plane. A French manufacturer had Belgian customers mail their Belgian franc checks to Paris for deposit and conversion. Analysis showed, however, that the average time from mailing to having usable funds in Paris was 13 days. To reduce this delay, the manufacturer opened a new bank account in Brussels, and Belgian customers now pay directly to that account. The balance of cleared funds is transferred to Paris each week. The average delay is 9 days—3 in Belgium for mailing and clearing, 4 for the average time in the concentration bank, and 2 for conversion and receipt in Paris.

In addition to freeing cash that represents four days' sales, the charge has led to a saving in transfer costs. Formerly, 100 checks a week were transferred at a cost of FF 7 per check plus FF 5 for exchange cost—a total of FF 1,200, or $250 per week. After the change, there was one transfer and conversion, costing only FF 12, or $2.50 per week.

Concentration banks can also accumulate funds in a hard currency from sales to customers in soft currency countries. For instance, customers of European companies trading in South America can be asked to purchase a bank draft in U.S. dollars (since U.S. dollars are more readily available in South America than European currencies) and send it to a lockbox account in a New York bank. The funds can be cleared in New York without delay and are then available for conversion and transmission to the European company's headquarters any time they are needed.

Bank Negotiations. Even when companies use a concentration bank, however, they are sometimes surprised at unexpected delays in international transfers. The reasons given include the mail, inexplicable administrative delay, central bank clearance, and incomplete documentation. Meanwhile, the company account in the sending country has been debited, and the bank in the receiving country has not been credited.

One European company's transfers from a major customer took 12 days from the time they were debited to the customer in Rome to the time they were credited to its own account in Paris. The delay occurred because the customer's bank did not have a direct relationship with the company's principal bank in Paris. New arrangements with different banks resulted in transfers that credited the company's Parisian account the same day its customers' accounts were debited in Rome.

The company also discovered that transfers from a branch in Germany by banker's check took nine days from the time of debit to the time of credit in Paris. After negotiations, the bank (with some reluctance) agreed to telegraph credit in Paris the same day as the debit was recorded in Germany.

Post Office Transfers. In many countries, the post offices offer very useful services to individuals and small businesses by transferring funds between countries. Companies may routinely use these popular services, for the delay of perhaps three days within a country and six days between countries seems small.

When large sums are involved, however, prompt transfer arrangements with banks are preferable. Despite their initial statements on the great difficulty of achieving it, banks can provide same-day credit between countries.

Challenge Inflexible Thinking

Countries with national branch banking systems, such as Canada, Switzerland, and the United Kingdom, provide the greatest flexibility for efficient cash management. In Canada, for example, a branch may be opened in a new mining site or at a construction development in the far north with a portable safe, a card table, and some forms, and can provide almost all services offered in downtown Toronto, including credit of payments to any account anywhere in the country and foreign exchange conversion at daily updated rates. Although the United States lacks branch banking, computer networks among corresponding banks have enabled U.S. banks to come very close to matching branch banking countries' systems for transferring money between major cities.

Nevertheless, in most countries outside North America, flexibility and speed are the exception rather than the rule. This service is slow in part because of two factors: (1) dominance within a country by a few large banks that lack the competition to encourage them to question and modify their traditional practices; and (2) national banking laws and regulations that control currency movements.

Nevertheless, with imagination, proper and persistent negotiation, and the use of contacts as high up in the bank as possible, many things at first considered impossible do get done.

For example, a government-owned bank in Western Europe was indifferent about a retailer's receipt transfers and unable to see how it could help the company overcome its problems with them. The company's stores normally mailed cash to the central office, which took three days, and checks to customers, which required 16 days to clear the post and the bank. The retailer began simultaneous negotiations with two other banks that had also been nationalized but that still remained competitive. What one thought possible was used to persuade either the other banker or the company's original one to make a better offer.

Now the retailer is able to deposit cash in a branch of any one of the three anywhere in the country and receive credit for that amount *the same day* at the company's head office banks. Moreover, it also receives credit at the head office two days later for checks drawn on local banks and seven days later for checks drawn on nonlocal banks. As a result, the retailer saves $50,000 per year in interest costs.

To take another example, consider a European company that does business in a West African country. The host country's procedures delayed the company's legally authorized bank transfers by an average of five months. Investigation showed it took only six weeks to receive payment when financed by a letter of credit. Even though it was dealing with its own branch, the company adopted letters of credit for all imports and realized both a $26,000 interest saving and a significant reduction in its exposure to loss from devaluations.

Cash Disbursements

Several of the foregoing recommendations for receipts are appropriate for disbursements as well. If a company can move money faster through the banking system, it can hang on to its cash longer and still pay its important suppliers on time. However, the reverse strategy—choosing an instrument that takes a long time to clear—can be useful in many instances.

Pay by Check

Unless a foreign supplier has specified another form of payment, a check drawn on a parent company bank will take just a few days by mail to get to the supplier and be credited to the parent company's account on his books, but it can take 7 to 10 days more to be returned to the country of origin and be cleared.

One European company changed from paying most foreign suppliers by bank transfers to paying by checks. The transfers took two days to clear, the checks 12 days. The annual saving was $46,000.

But carrying this strategy a step further and selecting a disbursing bank some distance from suppliers is risky. Recently a U.S. company paid a London commodity trader for more than $500,000 of grain by a check drawn on a bank in northern Scotland. That was the last time the company did so, however, because within minutes of receiving the check, the trading firm spotted the ploy, and news of it spread throughout the staff and probably to many in other trading companies. Earning a reputation as a "fast operator" can harm a company, especially in a business that depends on confidence in a high standard of conduct.

Despite the risk of creating a poor image, selective payment of suppliers using distant banks is a growing practice.

Take Discounts for Prompt Payment

Despite the very high effective interest cost, it is surprising how often companies fail to take the cash discounts that are offered for prompt payment. In one company, administrative procedures made it difficult to get disbursing checks issued on time. In another, those in the manufacturing plants believed that additional working capital was not available and that the savings were insignificant in comparison with their total budget.

In the first case, the company discovered that most of its suppliers were not carefully checking to see whether the discount was correctly taken. It could pay any time up to 30 days, still take the discount, and never hear about it. Extended terms were then worked out with the few suppliers who did object. In the second case, no one had calculated that losing the 2%-net, 10-day discount was an effective annual interest cost of more than 36%, for the bills were paid in 30 days anyway. Management simply instructed all its plants to take all discounts and thereby saved an estimated $44,000.

Seek Ways to Net and Consolidate

Netting payments against receipts need not be limited to intercompany transactions. If a major international supplier is also a customer, netting can save transaction and conversion costs as well as the cost of having funds tied up in the banking system for the time in transit. Netting, of course, also reduces exposure to foreign exchange fluctuations.

Sometimes a company may be supplied from several different points by the same supplier. Transaction and administrative costs may be reduced by requiring the supplier to consolidate his accounts so that one payment to a central location is made each month.

Bank Deposits and Loans

Before looking at opportunities for saving by improving the management of short-term borrowings, let us examine the need for positive cash balances. Management should look at the top left-hand corner of its company's balance sheet, at the first line that reads "Cash." Is there anything there? If so, does management know why?

Some years ago, the chairman of an international insurance group became dissatisfied with the explanations of why his company's balance sheet showed $11 million in cash. He knew that compensating balances, the need for business contacts, and day-to-day cash requirements required substantial balances, but he thought the total should be a lot less than $11 million.

He was right. He needed no more than $5 million, and if the principal banks had not required large compensating balances in their U.S. accounts to support a line of credit, the required balance would have been close to zero. The cuts he did achieve were by (1) eliminating inactive accounts, (2) precisely compensating banks for services and loan agreements, and (3) making transfers to special accounts on a more timely basis or eliminating such transfers entirely.

I will discuss each of the three points just mentioned in the sections that follow. But, first, company management should ask itself: Why should there be any uninvested cash at all?

Unrestricted Cash

Outside the United States, usury laws are not especially strict, so most banks can charge the effective interest rate on a loan directly. Thus a company needs little, if any, cash for compensating balances to help pay for loans.

What about day-to-day cash needs? The true need is usually far less than expected. By keeping enough cash on hand to pay current bills and to allow for uncertainties in receipts, a company will find that its actual cash balances vary but almost always stay above zero.

If a company invests in short-term time deposits that earn, say, 7% and it pays 9% on short-term loans, then it should invest in the time deposits even if it must borrow for a time as a result. A profit will be earned if the period of time for which money is borrowed is less than seven-ninths of the period of time over which money is earned. For example, $1,000 invested at 7% earns $70 in one year, and $1,000 borrowed at 9% costs $70 in seven-ninths of a year. So borrowing for less than seven-ninths of a year will leave a profit on the invested funds.

The best decision, therefore, is to invest a good portion of bank balances in short-term investments, even if that results in borrowing via overdrafts or daily notes at an increased rate for certain periods of time. The optimum amount that should be invested can be determined with the aid of a short computer program using forecasted daily bank balances. If forecasting daily balances is too uncertain, an analysis of a recent, but representative, period can give a useful approximation of the optimum investment amount.

To illustrate this phenomenon, consider the example illustrated in Exhibit 1. It shows daily bank balances for a 22-day period, during which a company could earn 7% on short-term bank deposits and borrow at 9%. To complicate it slightly, let us assume that borrowing must be done by issuing $5,000 notes, which are retired on the day that enough cash is available to do so. The optimum strategy would have been to invest $180,000 in short-

Exhibit 1. Comparison of Actual Bank Balances with Optimum Investment in Time Deposits Over a 22-Day Period

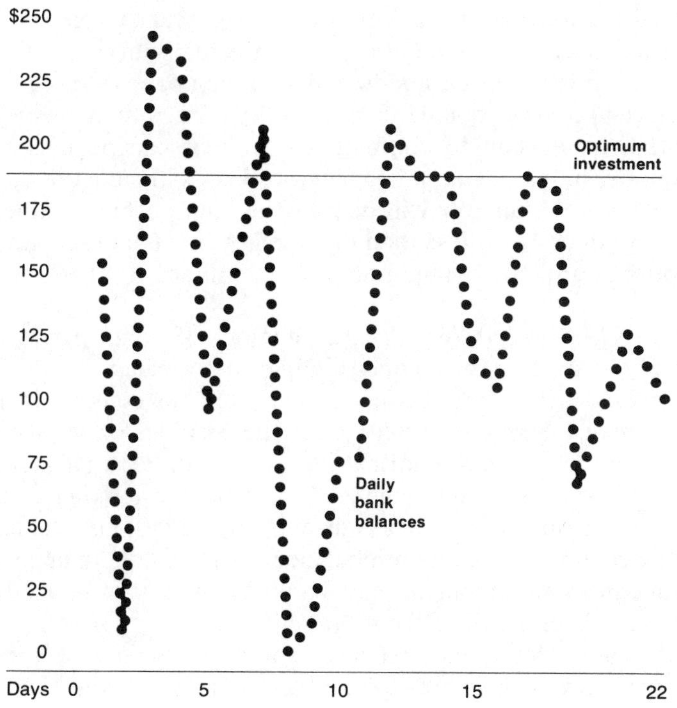

term securities; $759 in interest would have been earned, and $373 in interest would have been paid, for a net profit of $386.

Note that only if the company's year-end happens to coincide with four of these 22 days will its balance sheet show a positive balance of unrestricted cash. *Most companies will find they hold too much uninvested cash.*

Now let us consider each of the three principal reasons for having too much cash on hand: balances in dormant accounts, overcompensation for credit lines of other services, and money set aside unnecessarily early for major payments.

Eliminate Inactive Accounts. There seems to be some natural law stipulating that it is easier to open a new bank account than to close an old one. This trend is particularly noticeable in international operations, where the first point of contact for doing business in a new location may be a bank and a deposit is required to start off. Over the years, various banking needs are discovered, and other accounts are opened. But although a company's needs change, the old accounts normally remain and become dormant, the original reason, or even who authorized it, being forgotten.

A useful exercise is to call for a listing of *all* bank accounts with their current and average balances, along with some measure of activity. It is likely that the large number so listed will surprise most executives. The cost for all but the most active accounts should be justified.

If the reason for a given account is reciprocal or referred business, how much has been received and how much is likely to be received? What is the profit on this business, and how does it compare with the company's current marginal cost of capital? If the quantity of reciprocal business cannot be estimated, a decision to continue an account can be backed into by calculating how much business is needed to justify the cost of carrying the account. Usually the answer will be that the relationship is either worth a lot more or produces a lot less than the breakeven amount, even though the exact amount is difficult or impossible to determine.

Compensate More Precisely. A large number of companies watch their books closely to see that the compensating or other balances are in line with company policy. The banks being compensated, of course, do not know what the company books say; they judge the earnings on an account from the bank balances, which are normally greater than book balances because of the "float" of outstanding checks. In addition to looking at the wrong balance figures, companies often consider only month-end values and fail to take into account the intramonth balances. The custom in many countries is not to show intramonth balances on bank statements, although the banks' computers may keep track of them.

Where policy-determined balances should be maintained, it is neither a difficult nor a time-consuming clerical job to get a reasonable estimate of the average bank balances for the largest accounts, whether intramonth balances are shown or not. I know of no case where such an analysis has not revealed that some banks have been overcompensated.

Check Timing on Large Transfers. For every country a company operates in, it will have at least one account for payroll purposes, probably an account from which periodic tax and dividend payments are made, and, if construction is undertaken, probably one from which progress payments will have to be made from time to time. The amount required for each account is usually predictable, so there is little need to have funds transferred early or to gradually accumulate. Yet both do happen.

For instance, a company in the entertainment industry had a German subsidiary which, to provide for royalty payments, routinely accumulated large balances in bank accounts that paid no interest. At the same time, subsidiaries in other countries were financing their growth with heavy bank borrowings. Obviously, better use could have been made of the funds.

Interest Rates

A company conducting business around the world has many more financing and banking options available than does a company that operates only in the United States. Without realizing it, a company may agree to a form of financing at a significantly higher cost in one location than is readily available to it elsewhere.

For example, banks in some countries customarily deduct interest on short-term loans in advance; that is, company management can credit its account with the amount borrowed less the full interest for the period borrowed. One company that usually borrowed several million dollars for 90 days at a time found that it could lower its effective interest cost if it borrowed the same amount for only 30 days and renewed the loan twice thereafter, even though the stated interest rate was the same because of the practice of deducting interest in advance.

Moreover, banks differ in practices and terms concerning the timing for loans. Some banks may charge interest for 30 days, but the company has use of the funds for only 27, whereas others charge for 30 days and loan the funds for 30 days. Some deduct interest payments in advance, so the company pays interest on funds it never sees, and some base annual rates on a 360-day year, whereas others use a 365-day year. Given all of these variations, comparisons obviously become very difficult, and a computer program may be needed to simulate the cost of the options and determine the lowest cost plan for current cash forecasts.

The International Cash Manager

I have described a number of ways in which companies can improve their international cash management. Although every company faces a unique set of circumstances, my experience leads me to believe that a company can usually find better ways of handling its international transactions if it assigns that responsibility to one person.

Of course, cash that crosses borders usually crosses organizational lines as well. This situation makes assigning the responsibility for international cash management to one person appear difficult, but it can be and should be done. Fortunately, the specific functions that the international cash manager should control can be precisely defined, and the continuing value of the position can be objectively evaluated. Such an evaluation should make it clear to the general managers in various countries why the extra reporting, negotiating time, and use of their banking contacts is worthwhile.

Chief Responsibilities

The functions of an international cash manager should include negotiating and selecting banking services, clearing intercompany transfers, and monitoring exposures to losses on foreign exchange fluctuations. I will conclude by briefly describing each of these three functions.

Banking Services. Too often the cash and bank credit resources that are surplus in one country are not used to help others. A company in Germany may have surplus cash and a line of credit that permits it to borrow at 7%, whereas in France the same company may have a subsidiary that is short of cash and currently borrowing money at 12%. Exhibit 2 gives some idea of the range of rates that are available to companies for borrowing or lending as short-term funds.

At the time the rates in Exhibit 2 were in effect, it would appear to have benefited a company to borrow in Germany or the Netherlands and to put those funds into time deposits in France. Of course, international finance is not as simple as that. There are transaction and currency conversion costs,

Exhibit 2. Annual Commercial Bank Rates (mid-February 1978)

	Interest Cost to Borrow ½% over Prime Rate	Interest Earned on Three-Month Time Deposits
Belgium	9.25%	6.50%
France	11.85	10.88
Germany	6.75	3.19
Italy	17.00	9.00
Japan	5.00	3.25
The Netherlands	7.25	5.38
Switzerland	7.75	3.75
United Kingdom	8.00	7.13
United States	8.50	6.85

limits to the amounts available, and risks of loss on foreign exchange fluctuations that must be taken into account.

Therefore, international cash managers need to have access to a good deal of information, including forecasts of cash requirements. They should also be able to speak with authority when dealing with banks, and so they should be given the authority to make the final selection of the banking services and arrangements for international cash movements.

Intercompany Transfers. Another useful service the international cash manager can perform is to cut down the actual cash movements by acting as a clearinghouse for intercompany transfers. For instance, if a subsidiary in country A owes $100,000 to another subsidiary in country B, and B owes $50,000 to a subsidiary in country C, while the one in C owes $50,000 to the one in A, three transfers totaling $200,000 can be reduced to one (A to B) of $50,000, with the rest offset by internal journal entries. Of course, such netting is possible only where foreign exchange controls do not prevent the transfer of funds.

Foreign Exchange Exposure. It is surprising how many companies simply do not know what their foreign exchange exposure is. Intercompany accounts, for example, are seldom identified in internal balance sheets by the currency in which they are due. After currency rates have already changed, it is sometimes discovered that a profit has been created in a high-tax country and a loss in a low-tax country. The result is a net tax increase, which could have been avoided by better management of the choice of currencies in which these intercompany transactions took place.

The international cash manager may take any of the following actions to reduce an exposed position:

- ☐ Net or match intercompany balances, as previously described.
- ☐ Borrow locally, and convert the currency to offset net asset positions or the anticipation of receipts.
- ☐ Buy local currency, and deposit it to offset net borrowed positions or the anticipation of disbursements.
- ☐ Buy or sell a foreign exchange contract for later delivery of the currency owed or owned.
- ☐ Change the currency of invoicing.

A project to improve international cash management should start by determining the time delays experienced in international transfers. Wherever delays occur, they should be challenged. Through discussions with banks and using the points I have cited here as examples of what can be achieved, new and better ways to manage international transactions can be discovered.

Note

1. See, for example, Sanford Rose, "More Bang for the Buck: The Magic of Electronic Banking," *Fortune*, May 1977, p. 202, which describes several cash management techniques for operations in the United States.

3

Better Way to Monitor Accounts Receivable

WILBUR G. LEWELLEN AND ROBERT W. JOHNSON

After reviewing the methods companies commonly use to monitor receivables and pointing out the flaws they contain, the authors describe a much more effective approach. Focusing attention on the critical variables—the ongoing flow of receipts from sales made in a given month—the authors present a reporting format that flags changes in the pattern of this flow and allows the executive to trace these changes to their sources.

When a warning signal flashes on the instrument panel of his aircraft, the skilled pilot immediately questions whether the signal mechanism is faulty or whether the airplane is indeed in trouble. The financial executives charged with overseeing the management of accounts receivable for their company face a similar problem. When the reporting device they use to monitor collection experience flashes a warning, they confront a dilemma: Is the monitoring device defective, or are accounts receivable in fact moving out of control? Just as the pilot may endanger his passengers if he responds to a false signal light, so may the financial executive compromise the profitability of one's company by the reactions to an erroneous credit indicator. Equally dangerous, of course, is the warning signal that fails to operate when it should.

It is our contention that most of the procedures now widely used for monitoring the management of accounts receivable are, by their very nature, misleading and capable of frequent errors—of both omission and commission. We shall show how commonly used control mechanisms may signal improvement or deterioration in the status of accounts receivable when there actually has been no change in the rate of customer payments. We will also show that the same faulty control mechanism that permits such false signals can also fail to flash a warning when one *is* needed. We shall then go on to suggest an alternative analytical framework that does provide meaningful and reliable information for managers.

Collection Experience

As a starting point, it is necessary to specify exactly what is meant by the term "collection experience" as it applies to an enterprise that sells to customers on credit. It seems to us logical to define that notion simply as the rate at which remittances for credit sales are received over time; that is, the chronological pattern according to which the receivables created during a given interval are converted into cash. If we take a month to be our standard unit of account, the issue is the liquidation rate for each month's new credit sales. A *constant* collection experience—receivables "in control"—denotes a situation wherein the fractions of credit sales still uncollected as time passes follow a stable and predictable pattern from month to month. To illustrate:

Suppose a company finds that, say, 90% of the credit sales made during a month always remain outstanding at the end of that month, 60% always remain outstanding at the end of the following month, and 20% always are still uncollected at the end of an additional month, but all are liquidated within the succeeding 30 days. If, for instance, we assume that the company in question has $100,000 of credit sales in January of a particular year, the receivables—and collections—generated by those sales would be as shown in Exhibit 1.

Likewise, another $100,000 of credit sales in February would give rise to a set of collections and receivables running from February to May; March's sales would affect events until June; and so on throughout the year. The total of collections and receivables attributable to the various individual months would combine to produce, at any stage, aggregates for the company as a whole.

Exhibit 1. Collection Experience of Hypothetical Company for January Sales (in thousands of dollars)

Month	Collections during Month	Receivables Outstanding at End of Month
January	$10	$90
February	30	60
March	40	20
April	20	0

Reasons for Failure

The concept of collection experience, therefore, refers to nothing more than this standard notion of the rate of account conversion into cash—and will be used in just that sense here as we consider whether the usual techniques for assessing a company's receivables provide accurate signals about customer payment patterns. We shall examine with some care the two most common criteria—days' sales outstanding and aging of accounts receivable.

(A critical discussion of other systems may be found in the Appendix to this article.)

Days' Sales Outstanding

A widely used index of the efficiency of credit and collections is the collection period, or number of days' sales outstanding in receivables (DSO). It is calculated for any point in time by dividing the recent average dollar sales volume per day into the dollar amount of receivables outstanding at that time. The equivalent reciprocal index, called receivables turnover, is simply DSO divided into 360 days. Thus, if receivables "turn over" six times a year, the collection period is necessarily 60 days. Our comments therefore apply to both measures of credit circumstances.

The manifest unreliability of these measures can be seen by examining the signals flashed to the credit manager of a company whose collection experience is stable, but whose monthly sales vary over time. Consider the hypothetical case earlier described, wherein the percentages of receivables still uncollected for a given month's credit sales consistently follow a 90%–60%–20% sequential end-of-month pattern—in short, a fixed and definite rate of customer payments. Exhibit 2 indicates the effect on the DSO calculation of three sales profiles under this steady collection experience:

1 Level sales for three months at $60,000 per month.
2 Rising sales for the next three months at $30,000, $60,000, and $90,000, respectively.
3 A declining sales profile of $90,000, $60,000, and $30,000.

Thus, in all three situations, *total* sales for the calendar quarter are identical. Only their distribution differs.

Exhibit 2 reveals the collection period the credit manager would record at the *end* of each of the three quarters. Clearly, the signals are both misleading and capricious. They are sensitive not only to the sales pattern observed, but also to the sales-averaging period selected. Indeed, the choice of averaging period virtually determines the nature of the signals.

If, for example, the most recent 30 days were chosen for computing average daily sales, then it would appear that collection experience had improved for the company during April through June, as compared with January through March, because the collection period had fallen from 51 to

Exhibit 2. Days' Sales Outstanding (DSO) with Varying Sales Patterns and Varying Averaging Periods (dollar figures in thousands)

		Receivables Outstanding at End of Quarter		Sales per Day if Averaging Period is Most Recent			Reported End-of-Quarter Collection Period, if Averaging Period is		
Month	Sales	% of Sales	Dollar Amount	30 Days	60 Days	90 Days	30 Days	60 Days	90 Days
January	$60	20	$ 12						
February	60	60	36						
March	60	90	54						
			$102	$2	$2.0	$2	51 days	51 days	51 days
April	$30	20	6						
May	60	60	36						
June	90	90	81						
			$123	$3	$2.5	$2	41 days	49 days	62 days
July	$90	20	$ 18						
August	60	60	36						
September	30	90	27						
			$ 81	$1	$1.5	$2	81 days	54 days	41 days

41 days. Similarly, as the sales pattern of July through September unfolded, the DSO figure would climb to 81 days and generate concern that remittances were slowing significantly. Throughout, however, the rate of customer payments is *invariant*, by stipulation. The problem lies entirely with the monitoring device.

Comparable ambiguities prevail for any averaging period. If 90 days were selected instead, the chronological sequence of erroneous signals would simply be reversed. Balances at the end of the second quarter would indicate 62 days' sales outstanding and imply a deterioration in collections, but, by the end of the third quarter, an apparent improvement to 41 days would be reported.

Thus, no single averaging period will consistently yield a correct appraisal where there are fluctuations in sales. In fact, within any given sales interval, even the *direction* of the signal depends on the averaging period chosen.

It should be emphasized that these observations do not rely for their validity on sales variations as sharp as those depicted in Exhibit 2. Milder increases and decreases in volume would merely moderate—not eliminate—the discrepancies identified. Moreover, 60 days cannot be recommended as a kind of "happy medium" averaging period that can be counted on to minimize the extent of potential errors. This interval looks relatively good here only by accident. Consider, for example, the DSO figures based on the most recent 60 days' sales that would emerge if the sales for April and May, or July and August, were reversed.

Insuperable Difficulties. Despite a vague awareness of the existence of problems of this sort, it has been argued in the literature that valid comparisons of DSO figures may be made if the calculations pertain to the same point in a company's seasonal sales cycle from year to year, or that comparisons among companies are legitimate so long as the same date is utilized in the computations for each.[1] We cannot agree. Intertemporal or intercorporate reliability of such an index can be counted on only if the credit sales patterns involved for the months preceding the analysis point are *literally* identical. This condition is, of course, unlikely.

An added difficulty is the fact that a mechanism that transmits false signals about nonexistent changes in collection experience may also fail to send the *true* warning when needed. To illustrate:

Suppose that during the April to June period in Exhibit 2, customer payments slow down in such a way that the pattern of successive end-of-month uncollected balances becomes 60%–80%–95% instead of 20%–60%–90%. Receivables at the end of June would then amount to $152,000. A 30-day-sales averaging period for the DSO calculation would suggest 51 days' sales outstanding—matching the value for the end of March, and concealing the underlying deterioration in payment patterns. The financial executive would be lulled into believing that credits and collections are in control when actually they are not.

Aging of Receivables

Another common device for monitoring receivables is the "aging" criterion. Again, however, we must ask how dependable this monitoring method is when sales can vary from month to month.

The aging schedules in Exhibit 3—derived as of the end of each calendar quarter from the data in Exhibit 2—show that rising sales (Quarter 2) create an impression of improved customer payment patterns, whereas falling sales (Quarter 3) produce a schedule that suggests a deterioration in collections. This is understandable when one recognizes that the most recent month's sales always dominate the calculations. Thus, the proportion of total receivables in accounts less than 30 days old will naturally be relatively high in a period of rising sales and low in a period of falling sales—even when, as is the case here, the payment profile is completely stable.

This will result in a continual series of spurious warning signals being flashed to the credit manager simply in response to normal sales fluctuations. Only during the unusual intervals when sales are level from month to month will the indicator be of any potential use.

Even at that, the aging schedule suffers from an inherent deficiency. It is difficult to interpret meaningfully any figures that are contributed from

Exhibit 3. Reported Receivables Aging Schedules (dollar figures in thousands)

Age of Account	Receivables Outstanding at End of Quarter[a]	Percent of Total
End of Quarter 1		
(March 31)		
60–90 days	$ 12	12%
30–60 days	36	35
0–30 days	54	53
	$102	100%
End of Quarter 2		
(June 30)		
60–90 days	$ 6	5%
30–60 days	36	29
0–30 days	81	66
	$123	100%
End of Quarter 3		
(September 30)		
60–90 days	$ 18	22%
30–60 days	36	45
0–30 days	27	33
	$ 81	100%

[a]Figures from Exhibit 2.

differing sources but are constrained to add up to 100%. The fact that, say, 30% of a company's receivables outstanding a. a point in time are under 30 days old and 70% are 30 to 60 days old may not mean that there is an extraordinarily large number of overdue accounts and that receivables are out of control. It could merely be that an unusually—and desirably—high percentage of rapid payments were made on the most recent month's sales, leaving very few of them outstanding and raising the apparent weight of old accounts. The latter, however, may be no greater than normal in relation to the original sales that created them.

From the aging proportions per se there is no way of detecting this phenomenon, and erroneous conclusions could easily be drawn by management. Any criterion according to which the role of one element is automatically affected by changes in the others embodies this defect.

Adjusting for the Biases

One response to the foregoing observations might be that it would be possible to live with the distortions inherent in the various procedures described, so long as the credit manager is aware of the general nature and direction of the relevant biases. Again, we would demur.

In the illustrations cited, we have employed rather basic patterns of progressive increases and decreases in sales. While one might conceivably develop some rule-of-thumb adjustment allowances to handle the effects of such simple changes in volume, it would be much more difficult—if not impossible—to compensate correctly for all the peculiar, nonsystematic variations in sales confronted in actual practice. Even if the *direction* of the distortion were known, the *extent* would still be an issue—and would still be obscured. For example:

Suppose that in a period of rising sales it turns out that the collection period has lengthened from 40 days to 50 days. The financial executive would have to know whether that is more or less than the "normal" result for the specific monthly sales growth rate being experienced.

An Effective Tool

The central difficulty with the two most commonly used monitoring devices (as well as those discussed in the Appendix) is that, in one form or another, the view taken of collection experience is conceptually inappropriate. Either collections or balances are *aggregated* in the calculations, making it impossible to detect changes in remittance rates for particular components of credit sales.

If aggregation is the problem, *dis*aggregation is the key to its solution. The remittance rates for each individual component of sales should be identified and separated out if the data are not to be confounded by external influences, such as sales variations.

Can this be done? Fortunately, there is an analytical technique that meets the need. It involves nothing more than casting up the periodic receivables status report in the same form as the basic definition of "collection experience" with which we began our discussion, that is, balances outstanding as a percentage of the respective *original* sales that gave rise to those balances. In this fashion, customer payment rates are automatically traced to their source, and the appraisal of collection success is rendered independent of sales patterns and of the impact of changes in relative account composition. A typical report—prepared as of the end of each calendar quarter for our illustrative situation—is offered in Exhibit 4.

Not surprisingly, this record of the ratio of receivables balances to original sales indicates that the collection rate on accounts has been perfectly stable throughout the period in question. Exactly 90% of the most recent month's, 60% of the next most recent month's, and 20% of the third most recent month's credit sales show up as outstanding at each point in time examined. (These figures do not—and will not, except by accident—sum to 100%, because they do not purport to describe the makeup of a fixed total. Each is calculated according to a *different* sales base.)

The same answer would emerge at the end of every one of the nine months tabulated, and will persist under any conceivable sales pattern we

Exhibit 4. Uncollected Balances as Percentages of Original Sales (dollar figures in thousands)

Month of Origin	Sales during Month	Receivables Outstanding at End of Quarter	Percentage Outstanding (receivables/ sales)
January	$60	$ 12	20%
February	60	36	60
March	60	54	90
		$102	
April	$30	$ 6	20%
May	60	36	60
June	90	81	90
		$123	
July	$90	$ 18	20%
August	60	36	60
September	30	27	90
		$ 81	

might stipulate, so long as customer payment rates are in fact stable. Conversely, any deviation in those rates for any of the relevant sales intervals would be immediately detected and would not be concealed by aggregation or changes in other collections.

Accurate Analysis

To illustrate the improvement from a management standpoint, consider a simple example:

Suppose the group of customers to whom merchandise was sold during February happen to be slow payers and remit for only 15% of their purchases during the month following the month of sale, rather than the 30% figure which has been normal. In that case, balances at the end of March would be as shown in Exhibit 5, instead of as portrayed in Exhibit 4. Since only the figure for February would show up as out of line with past experience in the status report, the problem could be tracked to its source without difficulty.

Of equal importance, an acceleration of the payments on other months' sales would not obscure the analysis by exerting offsetting effects. Assume, for instance, that collections on credit sales originally made during January are simultaneously higher than normal, amounting to fully 55% of original balances during March rather than the usual 40%. Those extra receipts would neutralize the concurrent decline attributable to the customers from February and put total receivables back at $102,000 as of the end of March (Exhibit 6).

Exhibit 5. Effect on Percentages Outstanding of Slow Payment on February Sales (dollar figures in thousands)

Month	Sales during Month	Receivables Outstanding at End of Quarter	Percentage Outstanding (receivables/ sales)
January	$60	$ 12	20%
February	60	45	75
March	60	54	90
		$111	

Nonetheless, the credit executive could see from the report that changes *have* occurred even though the totals are "normal." He would not be lulled into thinking that payment patterns have remained stable—as would be indicated by, say, a DSO calculation—and could institute policy changes before it is too late to prevent some unpleasant surprises. In particular, if the shift in collection rates persists, then, as sales begin to rise, the increase in the funds commitment necessary to support receivables could be anticipated.

Value in Forecasting

The virtues of the framework we propose are, in fact, as notable in the context of forecasting funds requirements as in the contemplation of changes in policy. It may often be that the financial executive cannot do much about a slowdown in customer payment patterns without adversely affecting profitability. Competitive conditions—or the simple undercapitalization of many customers—may render it impossible to tighten terms and raise standards of acceptability without a substantial loss of revenue. Whatever the constraints, the need to project receivables balances for budgeting purposes is always present, and it is clear that the usual techniques leave a great deal to be desired. To illustrate:

Exhibit 6. The Combined Effect of Fast Payment on January Sales and Slow Payment on February Sales (dollar figures in thousands)

Month	Sales during Month	Receivables Outstanding at End of Quarter	Percentage Outstanding (receivables/ sales)
January	$60	$ 3	5%
February	60	45	75
March	60	54	90
		$102	

Consider the forecasts that would be made by the credit manager of a company whose sales and collection experience has for some time been steady, as in the January to March period in Exhibit 2. Assume that total sales in the upcoming calendar quarter are predicted to be $180,000 again, but that they follow the monthly pattern of April through June.

If the executive were monitoring receivables in terms of DSO—with a 90-day-sales averaging period—he would see 51 days' sales outstanding consistently, and would therefore use that standard to forecast balances. Because total sales anticipated for the next 90 days just match those experienced during the most recent 90, the DSO prediction would simply be for $102,000 in receivables outstanding as of the end of June. Given the 90%–60%–20% uncollected balance sequence that actually prevails, however, receivables would turn out to be $123,000 instead—an error that could be uncomfortable.

If sales of $180,000 were then forecasted for the third quarter, $102,000 in outstanding accounts would once more be the DSO-based estimate for the end of September, but $81,000 would turn out to be the actual figure. Comparable mistakes would—or could, depending on the circumstances—occur from use of the other techniques described earlier and in the Appendix, because none really gets at the rate of customer payments in a meaningful way.

Only by ascertaining that the normal uncollected balance profile is 90%–60%–20% (i.e., collections are 10%–30%–40%–20%) can one disentangle the independent effects of remittance rates and sales patterns and thereby achieve an accurate forecast. Accuracy, of course, is important not only to the credit executive but also to the company's banker, who may be confronted with a working-capital loan request based in large part on receivables predictions.

Tracking Flows Over Time

The parameters of the model, for forecasting purposes, are easily obtained from past data. Ordinarily, a simple record of historical end-of-month balances (like that shown in Exhibit 4), broken down into percentages of original monthly sales for, say, the most recent two years, will suffice. This number of observations should provide a reasonably good indication of the trend, or lack thereof, of payment patterns.

The analysis might resemble the one presented in Exhibit 7, where it appears that the fraction of sales made in a given month that are uncollected at the end of that same month has varied from 86% to 97% during the year considered; the fraction still on the books 30 days later has ranged from 54% to 73%; and the proportion after another 30 days has been between 17% and 39%. (Balances for four, five, or more months might also be shown if customers took longer to pay.)

Whether tabulated in this manner or plotted on a graph, the indicated percentages summarize very quickly and conveniently for management the company's ongoing collection experience. A continual updating of the record will then keep the appraisal current.

Exhibit 7. Status Report on Receivables Outstanding as a Percentage of Original Sales

	Month											
	J	F	M	A	M	J	J	A	S	O	N	D
Percentages outstanding for 1970 from sales of:												
Same month	90%	89%	91%	95%	97%	93%	86%	92%	91%	90%	91%	90%
One month before	60	62	59	68	73	69	59	54	62	63	61	60
Two months before	20	19	18	35	37	33	23	20	17	21	22	20
Percentages outstanding for 1971 from sales of:												
Same month	90%	91%	90%	93%	96%	96%	89%	91%	90%	88%	89%	90%
One month before	60	61	59	70	72	68	57	62	59	61	61	60
Two months before	20	22	21	33	39	33	19	18	21	20	19	20

Note: To ascertain the payment flows for one month's original sales, see the numbers in a descending left-to-right diagonal pattern. Thus the sequence 89%–62%–21%, singled out for July–August–September of 1971, refers to balances originating in July's sales as they remain outstanding as of the end of three successive months.

It would appear, in the situation shown in Exhibit 7, that remittance rates *are* fairly stable; no secular trend is evident in the 24 months examined. On the other hand, it seems characteristic for payments to slow down during April, May, and June of each year before returning to the "normal" pattern of roughly 90%–60%–20%. Additional data for earlier years might be collected to confirm this interpretation. Various standard statistical techniques, including regression analysis, could be applied to test rigorously whether a trend is present, as judged by whether the more recent percentages tabulated differ significantly—in the statistical sense—from those of earlier periods.

Alternatively, and less formally, a simple moving average of perhaps the last six months' percentages at each of the three levels could be maintained and compared with the corresponding averages for the same intervals one and two years earlier. Or, if no seasonal variations were apparent, a comparison of *any* successive six-month intervals would do. Note that seasonality in *sales* is not the issue. That effect has been factored out by the percentage calculations. Indeed, as is obvious, the volume of sales need not be recorded in the receivables status report. Only payment patterns are of concern.

The average collection experience suggested by these calculations would then be used in forecasting receivables balances, given monthly sales estimates from the company's marketing department. Thus, the average end-of-month outstanding balance percentages listed in Exhibit 7 for July through December of 1970 and 1971 are 90%, 60%, and 20%; and for April through

June of both years, 95%, 70%, and 35%. Projections of balances for 1972 would logically be based on these relationships.

Whatever the evidence for the particular company involved, and whatever the preferred averaging technique, the percentages displayed provide the financial executive with an effective tool *both* for detecting changes in remittance rates and for forecasting.

Control Limits

As far as policy is concerned, the signal to management that something has happened with customer payments would be either an affirmative statistical significance test, of the kind just described, or a deviation of the moving average greater than a specified tolerance limit. To illustrate:

The credit manager might establish a rule that a 5% change in the most recent six-month outstanding balance averages in comparison with the averages for the preceding six months, or for the corresponding period a year earlier, would be reason to consider a revision in credit policy. Thus, if the July to December 1971 end-of-month receivables averages come out to a 95%–65%–25% profile, whereas 1970s July to December figures were 90%–60%–20%, that might well be grounds for reexamining sales terms and credit standards. In fact, a 5% increase or decrease even in *one* of the three percentages in the profile could suggest the need for action. Alternatively, an observation of three consecutive monthly percentage deviations (other than seasonal) of 5% above or below the average at that position in the profile over the preceding 6 or 12 months might trigger the manager's attention.

A potential increase in bad debts in particular might be foreshadowed by a rise in the percentages at the tail end of the receivables schedule, or the appearance of balances for an additional end-of-month interval. For instance, the profile might begin to change to 90%–60%–20%–3%; the last figure could represent not merely slow payers, but prospective default cases.

It should be emphasized that a below-average outstanding balance tendency can be as important to management as an upward shift. A general acceleration in remittance rates may indicate that credit guidelines or collection practices are becoming too stringent, and that many legitimate customers are in fact being excluded.

Concluding Note

No single measure of deviation will fit every company's circumstances and tastes for "fine tuning" credit policy. Purely random fluctuations in the relevant percentages may be much larger for one company than for another. The important thing is to organize the detection and control of collection experience around an analytical framework that provides input information useful to the decision process.

We believe the scheme outlined in this article meets that requirement far better than any other currently available. It does not mix together receivables originating in different sales periods; and it is the only procedure that is not distorted by changes in sales patterns.

Appendix. Deficiencies of Other Systems

In this article we have described the shortcomings of the best-known approaches used by management to monitor accounts receivable. Here we describe some variations of these approaches that are familiar to many businesspeople, and point out their deficiencies.

Average Age of Receivables

Some companies employ a receivables-monitoring device that summarizes, in a single number, the information contained in the aging schedule. This number or index is the so-called average age of receivables. It is typically calculated with the assumption that the average duration of outstanding accounts that are less than 30 days old is exactly 15 days, that the average for those 30 to 60 days old is 45 days, and so on, for as many categories as are relevant. The product of these figures times the proportions of each age segment in the total, when summed, yields a global average age measure of overall balances. By this criterion, the schedules depicted in Exhibit 3 would imply that an average account was 32.8 days old as of the end of Quarter 1. The computation would be:

$$
\begin{array}{rl}
.12 \times 75 \text{ days} = & 9.0 \text{ days} \\
+\ .35 \times 45 \text{ days} = & 15.8 \text{ days} \\
+\ .53 \times 15 \text{ days} = & 8.0 \text{ days} \\
\hline
\text{Total} \qquad = & 32.8 \text{ days}
\end{array}
$$

Similarly, an average account would be 26.8 and 41.8 days old, respectively, as of the close of Quarters 2 and 3.

The signals given by "average age" must, of course, coincide with those given by the complete aging schedule—and can only incorporate the same shortcomings.

Relative Changes

Another technique often followed compares the periodic changes in the level of receivables to the concurrent changes in the level of sales. The misleading signals that result are in the same direction as those generated by collection period methods, and they occur for the same reason: rising (falling) sales necessarily produce quarter-end receivables that are large (small) relative to the sales for the entire quarter, despite a constant collection experience for each individual monthly bloc of credit sales.

Exhibit A. Distribution of Collections by Age of Account (dollar figures in thousands)

	March		June		September	
Age of Account (in days)	Collections	Percent of Total	Collections	Percent of Total	Collections	Percent of Total
0–30	$ 6	10.0%	$ 9	17.7%	$ 3	4.0%
30–60	18	30.0●	18	35.3●	18	24.0●
60–90	24	40.0●	12	23.5●	36	48.0●
90–120	12	20.0●	12	23.5●	18	24.0●
	$60	100.0%	$51	100.0%	$75	100.0%

Percentage Collections

It has also been argued that the collection/balance ratio should be used by management. For example:

> A further means of checking upon the quality of a firm's credit and collections policies is the preparation of periodic reports to show what percentage of customers' balances on the books at the beginning of each period is collected during that period.[2]

The reliability of this scheme can be tested by comparing the results it would show for the nine-month sales pattern for our standard illustration. If we assume that the company's sales for the last several months of the preceding fiscal year were steady at $60,000 per month, the ratio of monthly collections to beginning-of-month receivables for January through September would vary from 54% to 68%. Since these indexes can fluctuate so widely even under conditions of no change in customer payment rates, their usefulness as inputs to credit policy decisions is in serious question.

Aging of Collections

Finally, the distribution of monthly collections by age of account involved has been suggested as a possible monitoring device.[3] Exhibit A presents such a breakdown for March, June, and September of our example. Examination of the data would lead the credit manager to believe that collections were speeding up in the vicinity of June, since a larger percentage of collections are in the 0 to 30 day and 30 to 60 day age groups than was true three months earlier. Similarly, the credit manager would become concerned that collections were slowing in September because the percentage distribution of receipts shifted back toward the 60 to 90 day and 90 to 120 day categories.

This distortion, of course, is nothing more than the normal result of rising and falling monthly sales volumes. Payment rates being stable, the higher the proportion of more recent sales, the heavier will be the weight of collections on recent accounts compared to total collections—and vice versa for a declining sales pattern. The financial executive might, in consequence, be led to undertake "remedial" action that could be detrimental to profitability when in fact no revisions are warranted.

Notes

1. See, for example, Pearson Hunt, Charles Williams, and Gordon Donaldson, *Basic Business Finance*, 4th ed. (Homewood, Illinois, Richard D. Irwin, 1971), p. 62.

2. R. P. Kent, *Corporate Financial Management*, 3rd ed. (Homewood, Illinois, Richard D. Irwin, 1969), p. 194.

3. H. Benishay, "Managerial Controls of Accounts Receivable: A Deterministic Approach," *Journal of Accounting Research,* Spring 1965, p. 114.

4

Is Your Bad Debt Expense Too Low?

JAMES McNEILL STANCILL

In establishing credit standards for accounts receivable, it is important to consider the expected profitability of good accounts, as well as the probability and cost of bad accounts. Stancill presents an approach that works toward this objective.

An executive who deals with finances in his or her company, if asked the question in the title of this article, probably would say that it's a ridiculous question. How can your bad debt expense be too low? Or, to put it another way, how can you be too restrictive in your credit-granting approach?

The answer is, of course, that, if the company's profit is the measuring stick, it *is* possible to be too restrictive in granting credit. But for many managers, a bad debt is something entirely different from some "objective" measure, such as net income. To them a bad debt is an insult to their pride. I have seen managers—maybe you have too—who fly into a rage at the realization that collection from a customer is unlikely. "Why that devil promised he'd pay me!" a manager will cry. Or "I'll never get caught like that again!"

Now don't get me wrong; I am not in favor of bad debts. But credit losses are a fact of business life. I suggest that there is an optimal bad debt expense that maximizes net income. To understand this optimality look at this hypothetical example:

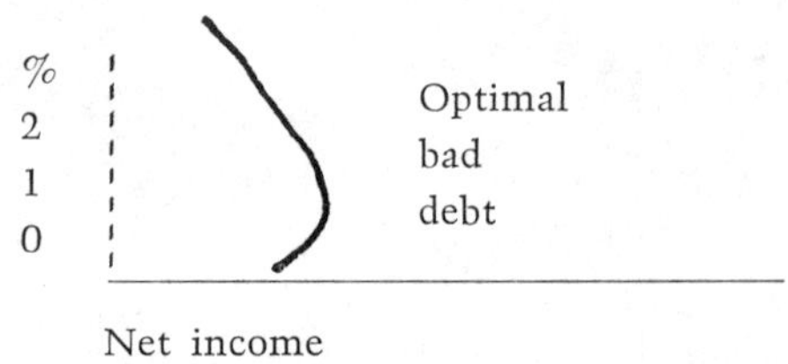

This chart looks like Arthur Laffer's tax chart: too high or too low a tax rate will result in less tax revenue to the government. In this case, however, too much laxness in granting credit or too much strictness will both result in less net income for a given volume of sales.

In an analytical sense the credit-granting problem may be expressed as follows:

Grant credit if

$$\text{Expected gain} > \text{Expected loss.}$$

where the expected gain is equal to the seller's gross profit, G (sales minus cost of goods sold), multiplied by the probability of collection, P. The expected loss equals the cost of goods sold, C (for that marginal transaction), multiplied by the probability of not collecting, or 1 − P. Thus:

Grant credit if

$$G(P) > C(1 - P).$$

Assume a sale, S, of $1,000 with a cost of goods sold of $700, a gross profit of $300, and a probability of collection of .9. This would be the decision rule:

Grant credit if

$$\$300(.9) > \$700(1 - .9)$$
$$\$270 > \$70.$$

Slow-Pay Factor

Now, this model assumes that the customer will pay on time. Often a business will make sales deliberately to slow-pay accounts. To show sales to "slow pays" but without getting unduly technical, one has only to add a slow-pay factor to the decision rule. Thus:

Grant credit if

$$G(P) - i(t)S > C(1 - P) + i(t)S.$$

The expression i(t)S should be read as some interest rate, i, for the expected period of slow pay, t, multiplied by S—that is, the face amount of the invoice. The interest rate should be the opportunity cost of tying up the amount of the invoice for the extra time. A cash-rich company might put this "extra" money into money market securities and earn a pretax 8% per year. A cash-poor company that is borrowing to finance its receivables might save the interest it would otherwise be paying—say, 10% up to possibly 36% per annum.

Taking 18% as an example of the yearly opportunity cost and assuming a mean slow-pay period of two months, you can derive a slow-pay factor of 2/12 of 18%, or 3%. Incorporating the 3% factor into the equation gives you this:

Grant credit if

$$\$300(.9) - .03(\$1{,}000) > \$700(1 - .9) + .03(\$1{,}000)$$
$$\$270 - \$30 > \$70 + \$30$$
$$\$240 > \$100.$$

Some sellers earning meager gross profits might have numbers like the following:

$$S = \$1{,}000$$
$$C = \$900$$
$$G = \$100$$
$$i(t) = .03$$
$$P = .90$$

Or to put it in decision rule form:

Grant credit if

$$\$100(.9) - .03(\$1{,}000) > \$900(1 - .9) + .03(\$1{,}000)$$
$$\$90 - \$30 > \$90 + \$30$$
$$\$60 \not> \$120$$

Since the left side is not greater than the right side, the supplier should refuse credit unless one is confident that the account, if it pays at all, will pay on time. In that case it's a toss-up whether to grant credit.

Probability of Payment

At this point the astute reader may say, "Yes, but how do you figure out the probability that the customer will pay?" This is a good question.

If aggregate data on particular groups of customers are unavailable to give the credit department a clue about this customer, the department must rely, of course, on what it can find out about him—general condition, financial characteristics, and cash flow sufficiency.

One neglected ingredient in the prognosis is the amount of credit the seller is extending; you can reduce his probability of payment by giving him too much credit. It's important that the sellers, once they have extended credit to a certain customer, reconsider (P) when the amount of credit extended is to be increased.

Instead of trying to gauge precisely the probability of payment, the supplier may estimate this type of customer's bad debt percentage and compare that number with the critical probability of collection ($\hat{P}$) necessary to make the decision rule balance—that is, make the left side equal the right. It can be shown that in the simple decision rule model,

$$G(P) > C(1 - P),$$

the left side will equal the right if the probability of collection, P, is equal to the creditor's percentage cost of goods sold. That is,

$$\hat{P} = C/S,$$

where $\hat{P}$ is the critical (minimum) probability of collection in a prospective transaction before the customer "deserves" credit. Thus, in my first example, $\hat{P}$ = \$700/\$1,000 = .70.

As long as the probability of collection from a prospect is at least 70%, the company should sell to him (assuming that the loss, if it occurs, would not be disastrous). In my second example, the company has an anemic gross profit and must be extremely careful of its credit risk. In this example,

$$\hat{P} = \$900/\$1{,}000 = .90.$$

Inclusion of a slow-pay factor raises $\hat{P}$ somewhat.

All this simply means that if sellers have a hefty gross profit percentage, they should be more liberal in granting credit than if they are operating with a slim gross profit. Only after noting the expected gross profit in the particular transaction should they make a decision as to the credit worthiness of potential customers.

Obviously, if they were quite certain that the customer wouldn't pay, they would be foolish to sell to the account, irrespective of the gross profit percentage. (Incidentally, the use of an international or domestic letter of credit can raise (P) to a virtual certainty. Through this medium the customer substitutes his bank's credit for his own.)

How many credit managers are charged to consider gross profit in the decision to give credit? Often managers are accused of not doing their job if the bad debt expense goes up. But granting credit may be a way of raising net income, and isn't that the point?

PART TWO
MANAGEMENT OF FOREIGN EXCHANGE EXPOSURE

AN OVERVIEW

International corporations face two kinds of foreign exchange exposure—accounting (or translation) exposure and economic exposure. A considerable amount of attention has been focused on the first kind of risk because managers are naturally concerned about the implications of currency fluctuations for reported profits. There has also been significant controversy about the best way to report the effects of changes in currency values, as the Financial Accounting Standards Board and others have tried to sort out a variety of thorny issues.

Unfortunately, no matter how the reporting issues are resolved, there are certain to be differences between accounting risk and economic risk. The economic risk stems from the fact that cash outflows for a foreign investment, for example, might be in one currency while inflows are in another. Changes in the values of such assets and liabilities for reporting purposes do not always match fluctuations in economic value. Thus it is possible that a change in relative currency values would affect currently reported profits without affecting the economic value of a foreign investment over the longer term. Similarly, it is possible to take hedging actions that would stabilize reported profits, but that at the same time would increase economic exposure to changes in currency values.

All three of the authors in Part 2 take the position that although translation risk is an understandable concern of managers, it is economic exposure that matters in the longer run. Prindl looks at the implications of a shift in concern from translation risk to economic risk and provides some suggestions on how to manage economic risk in "Guidelines for MNC Money Managers." He points, for example, to the need for anticipatory rather than historical reporting systems and to the need for more centralized control over economic exposure. Hagemann describes such an anticipatory system. He proposes a planning and foreign exchange management system that concentrates on future flows of foreign currencies rather than reported values of foreign assets and liabilities. This exposure management system is described in his article, "Anticipate Your Long-Term Foreign Exchange Risks." Finally, Serfass' position is stated in the title of his article, "You Can't Outguess the Foreign Exchange Market." He describes the approach he takes as a chief financial officer to minimize his company's economic exposure to foreign exchange risk.

5

Guidelines for MNC Money Managers

ANDREAS R. PRINDL

The state of world financial markets and their implications for the managers of multinational companies are well known. But what is not so well known is the actual financial response of the MNCs to the unpredictable exchange markets and growing credit restrictions in most countries. In practice, the MNCs have severely curtailed their aggressive financial policies by taking generally covered positions and ensuring continued credit availability in place of ephemeral exchange gains. The author discusses these positive changes and offers guidelines for companies that face similar financial problems.

Financial management in international corporations has long been complicated by problems of communications, time differences, and distance. Adding to these standard impediments are the more important regulatory constraints imposed by exchange control authorities, central banks, and tax systems. Together, they bring about the fragmented structure that characterizes multinational enterprises. Individual affiliates are, in effect, walled off from other group members by this array of regulatory barriers; the liquidity and foreign exchange management of the group cannot be treated as a global function. Foreign expansion can mean isolation of units for internal reasons as well, due to the split into divisional and functional responsibilities.

The currently unpredictable markets, floating rates, and credit restrictions in many countries have exacerbated these traditional problems. As a result, many U.S. and European companies are finding it necessary to reassess their reporting and control systems and to revamp their financial management policies. This has led to changes in reporting elements that will allow a more flexible response before events, to more centralization, and to more conservative policies toward exchange risk and the availability of credit.

In this article, I shall review the responses of some international companies to today's markets and describe ways in which these companies have augmented their internal information systems, strengthened their control techniques, and tried to lessen the impact of their fragmentation. I shall then show why these are positive changes and conclude with guidelines for companies with similar financial management problems.

Anticipatory Strategy

Most corporate reporting systems are built on a historical time frame, the result of a traditional accounting bias toward depicting only present and immediately past periods. However, with continuous turbulence in financial markets and the uncertainty of internal flows in a period of global economic slowdown, historically oriented reports are no longer adequate. Thus many multinational companies are now building elements into their internal reporting requirements that attempt to anticipate (1) future cash flows within the group, (2) future exchange exposure positions, and (3) the effects of exchange exposure on all company operations and entities, not just the consolidation effect.

None of these elements can be identified in standard accounting/consolidation reports, but all three are critically important in today's conditions.

Internal Information Systems

A major U.S. consumer products company has installed a global monthly and quarterly cash forecasting system to complement its annual budget planning, with both the monthly and quarterly forecasts broken down by currency and prepared on a rolling basis. A Swedish multinational now requires cash forecasting by currency weekly for four weeks and monthly 13 months forward, as well as a daily phone call to the parent from each Swedish division about short-term cash requirements, surpluses, and expected exchange conversions. These rolling forecasts, expanding on a more static planning structure, are typical of numerous similar efforts.

Proper anticipation of future trends and probable risks, as long as the magnitude and direction of change are accurate, helps a company analyze the possible impact of fluctuating interest and exchange rates on all corporate operations. Forecasting, in one sense, is nothing new; nearly every company has a yearly planning exercise. But such forecasts are usually sales and profit oriented and do not include currency items or sufficient liquidity data to assist the treasurer in creating an anticipatory strategy.

Better internal forecasting is complemented by newly created data banks that compile information on external market and regulatory constraints. Ignoring these constraints can be risky, often bringing detailed scrutiny of all transactions after a breach of regulations is disclosed. It can also be costly, because several countries levy material fines for contravening intercompany credit-term requirements. The rules constraining each financial technique can be logically broken down into generic types; continual updating of changes in these regulations is possible through subsidiaries or through commercial banks offering such services.

Many multinationals have also expanded their use of computer programs for financial decisions. This is not surprising, given the massive amounts of complex data and the degree of uncertainty a corporation must consider. In the United States, a number of companies have installed computer programs to identify more quickly their aggregate and individual exposure positions. One chemical company, for instance, has established a program that consolidates the balance sheets of its 100-plus subsidiaries by currency (over 25 currencies are involved) and prepares varied types of exposure reports. It can obtain printouts of:

- ☐ Group aggregate exposure by currency for six periods forward.
- ☐ Group currency exposure in each currency by individual location.
- ☐ Group currency exposure in each currency by balance-sheet category.
- ☐ Aggregate hedges, with rates and maturities, and other off-balance-sheet items.
- ☐ Each subsidiary's current exposure and that for six periods forward.
- ☐ Each subsidiary's local currency balance-sheet breakdown.

Data, which arrive by telex monthly from the company's subsidiaries, are optically read into the computer and stored until required. The whole array of reports can be run out in about four minutes at a cost of $8 to $10.

Many corporations also now use simple simulation models. These models allow a company to make assumptions—the classic "what if" situation—about future exchange rates and to apply these to its current and projected positions. Such limited simulation models do not normally predict future events, but are useful in sensitivity analysis; they provide an inexpensive way to test the effect on profits, taxes, or liquidity of any single future change. Because only one-point estimates are involved, the absolute accuracy of future predictions is not mandatory, and such models can quickly and economically be run many times using different assumptions.

More extensive linear programming of economic scenarios, or full-scale simulation of one company to achieve optimal financial management, has not been as successful. A number of companies have spent massive amounts of time and money trying to "model the world." Their experience has been that the actual mathematical input is relatively straightforward, but that insurmountable problems arise in predicting future exchange and interest rates.

At present, it is difficult to obtain future rate predictions from outside sources: Most observers would agree that attempts to predict short-term rates in today's market are dubious and even dangerous. Economic factors are irrelevant in very short-term movements and offer little guidance in the key time period (3 to 12 months forward) for decision making.

In the absence of both adequate narrow-band rate forecasts and knowledge about spot rate/interest rate correlations between countries, all full-scale modeling approaches, even by the largest, most sophisticated companies, have so far failed.

The renewed drive toward better and more anticipatory reporting has been complemented by the U.S. Treasury's reporting requirements for international companies based in the United States and by the recently announced accounting changes of the Financial Accounting Standards Board (FASB) concerning translation of foreign currency items. The U.S. Treasury has required, starting from the company's status as of March 31, 1975, that each U.S.-based company with a certain level of foreign assets and liabilities, or consolidating subsidiaries abroad, regularly report its position in nine currencies. Data on foreign exchange transactions and forward contracts are included.

It is fair to say that the information required by the Treasury is critical for and should be available in the company's finance department in any case; any company that finds it hard to supply that data to the Treasury has, without doubt, a poor reporting system.

The FASB requirements can be found in its Statement No. 8 on Foreign Currency Translations. Basically, they call for the adoption of a single accounting convention for foreign currency items by all U.S. companies, the elimination of exchange reserves, and the valuation of outstanding forward contracts at closing date. In anticipation of these requirements, a number of U.S. companies have already changed over to the monetary/nonmonetary or "temporal" method recommended by the FASB. In many cases, this will bring material changes in reported results of companies previously using different conventions.

Transaction Exposure

Analysis of standard financial statements, no matter how well detailed, does not provide an answer to the question, "What is actually at risk in any particular company?"

Thus not all of the accounting exposure reported by a company will have a real impact. A multinational company may consolidate a number of asset or liability items at different closing rates, items that will never be converted or that will be renewed and maintained indefinitely. As ongoing elements in a subsidiary's financial structure, these items have no tax effect when restated in terms of a parent balance sheet; they can be seen as permanent features of the group abroad, as long as affiliates are not liquidated. Losses on their translation in the United States, the United Kingdom, and other countries where consolidated accounts are published provide no tax offsets.

(Liquidity considerations are likewise affected by nonfinancial constraints such as institutional requirements and backstop availability of credit, which themselves vary over time.)

Meaning of Exchange Risk

Many accounting conventions, even after the changes imposed by the FASB, have little connection with the actual operating effects of possessing, or having commitments in, foreign currency. This has, correctly, brought about a reexamination of the meaning of *exchange risk*.

The term *accounting risk* indicates that the publicly stated value of the company's assets, equity, and/or income may be negatively affected by exchange rate movements. Although no actual changes in the company may have occurred, its image may seem endangered and its stock market appeal diminished. Some finance executives fear that even their ability to raise loans or equity is put into question.

Certainly, there is a risk that a company with large translation losses appears less well managed than competitors in the same economic position that have borrowed only their own currency or covered all their translation risk.

Other finance executives now see translation losses as ephemeral, depending on their own stockholder structure and perception of risk. These losses can then be seen more as an embarrassment or, depending upon how they arise, as an unavoidable cost of doing business. (One company recently told me that pure translation losses in its balance sheet up to $5 million in any year would not be a matter for concern.) A company may be envisioned as a permanent on-going entity where realized profits and remitted dividends are more material factors. In management where the conservation of assets is predominant, economic effects on operations, financial structure, and realized profits now outweigh the possible reporting effects.

Sensitivity to this economic exposure is apparently beginning to counterbalance the traditional bias of U.S. companies to cover only translation risk. In the chemical industry, reporting systems now often divide inventory into that which has a world price (and thus is not locally exposed if held by a subsidiary) and into that where local factors set the price.

Other companies have required new details on intercompany items. These were previously neglected under the assumption that "intercompany items wash out in consolidation." Not only is that a very doubtful assumption per se, but it also ignores the very real economic impact of intercompany exposure on any one subsidiary.

Economic effects of exchange risk involve not only short-term conversions, but also the future sales and cash flows of subsidiaries in countries where the local currency has sharply depreciated or appreciated relative to other currencies. The original factors underlying the investment decision abroad—productivity, availability of labor and finance, low rates of inflation and taxation—can themselves be affected by exchange-rate movements. Price controls may follow a devaluation; local labor availability and the supply of loanable funds may be restricted. The entire validity of a foreign subsidiary may be at stake; here economic exposure affects the whole financing and planning function of the company. Therefore, exchange risks of all kinds must be coordinated with planning and budgeting, with the direct investment decision, and with debt structure.

Conservative Attitude

The reporting system changes discussed earlier and a better awareness of all aspects of risk have resulted in a generally more conservative attitude, which, again, I believe to be a positive development. This conservatism can be seen both in a general increase in hedging transactions of all kinds and in an expanded use of forward markets. Fortunately, the advent of floating rates has neither curtailed the ability to hedge most convertible currencies up to one year nor substantially increased the costs of doing so.

Companies that were formerly more aggressive in maintaining open positions are rethinking their posture. The technique of "exposure netting"—that is, taking or leaving exposed positions in two currencies that are expected to offset each other—has dwindled considerably. (And no wonder, because the same unpredictability of exchange-rate movements that has inhibited computer simulation mitigates against this technique.) Most companies are focusing not on the optimization of earnings from exchange gains, but on eliminating unacceptable risks more consistently.

The expanded use of forward markets has also altered certain traditional international money-management techniques. Netting, or book offsetting, of intercompany accounts to save conversion costs is curtailed when the underlying commitments have been covered forward. This coverage has reduced and even stopped certain netting programs.

Leading/lagging, to the extent it is practiced, distorts traditional cash management systems used to accelerate cash flows and affects netting practices as well. A concern about protecting credit relationships has similarly inhibited the export acceleration programs of more than one multinational, which are more concerned with keeping credit lines—present and future—than in squeezing out the last day of float or penny of cost from the banking system. All the foregoing implies a natural shifting in the selection of international money-management techniques from time to time.

Finance Centralization

A casual reading of executive advertisements for international treasurers or their equivalents attests to the expansion of treasury department capabilities, both in the United States and in Europe. (In fact, the U.S. concept of treasurer, not traditional in Europe, is being developed on that continent; companies such as Azko, Fisons, GKN, and Cadbury Schweppes all have created and staffed a treasurer position.) The title "International Treasurer" or "Assistant Treasurer—International" is becoming more widespread in the United States, usually implying the addition of personnel and/or a split in the treasurer/assistant treasurer's position into domestic and international functions. The result is a necessary centralization of financial decision making, because only a central point can see all risks and all alternatives of a multinational group.[1]

The trend seen in the late 1960s of pulling back European headquarters staff has been reversed. Many U.S. companies—among them Chrysler, Tenneco, Universal Oil Products, Honeywell, and CBS—have created or strengthened a European treasury function. This alleviates many problems in local communications, and, equally important, it helps to strengthen the global finance function. Despite all the personnel implications, this centralization is absolutely necessary.

The development of a European (or other regional) headquarters augments this process, although, on the surface, it would appear not to. In the best cases, the financial headquarters is an integral part of the parent treasury with direct reporting responsibility. In some instances, the European treasurer is also an officer of the U.S. parent with appropriate signing authority. Both sides make risk and rate projections; these are hammered into one policy by weekly exchanges of ideas and tactics and by frequent personal visits or interchanges.

Structural changes sometimes promote centralization as well. The use of intermediary companies to achieve central coordination of risks and flows is receiving more study. Full reinvoicing intermediaries, for example, offer major flexibility in financial management, although they may be difficult and costly to establish. A current innovation is the confirming house technique, recently adopted by two U.S. companies in the United Kingdom, which allows all export receivables of a group to be purchased and funded by a single intermediary. Trading exchange exposure of a group can be concentrated in such an entity, with funding unmatched as to maturity and currency. Because they derive from a single entity, the results are both hedging flexibility and simplified information flows.

It is outside the scope of this article to discuss the personnel implications of such centralization. The best companies clearly see that they are not dealing with improved data and systems alone but with a range of local managers as well. These managers may see their role diminished, their contribution downgraded, or their development thwarted. Local input and expertise remain highly valuable; the continued participation and encouragement of staff abroad and frequent personal or telephone contact must complement centralization.

I should note in passing that tax considerations are critical to, and apparently now better coordinated with, finance decisions of all kinds. There have been cases in the past where a hedging strategy was designed without taking into consideration the impact of taxes. This is clearly unwise, because taxes are a predominant component of exposure management. Tax strategy, if carried out correctly, is essential to a company's financial structure, and international money management should not ignore or endanger tax planning.

Credit Availability

Many companies are also taking a more conservative attitude in liquidity management. The availability of credit has taken on new importance, because of continuing tightness in several markets, to global credit limits imposed by banks, and to the feeling that in an uncertain world it is best to ensure sufficient borrowing power no matter what contingencies arise. A conservative attitude has been particularly noticeable in those companies trying to line up credit facilities in advance of requirements; many became willing to pay commitment fees, rather than rely on lines of credit. Because these fees in the Eurodollar and other domestic markets now average ½ to ¾% per annum, there is not an immaterial cost involved.

This anticipatory response parallels that in the area of exchange risk. Liquidity management is affected and restricted by the same factors. Its disposition is controlled and limited by exchange control barriers, barriers that are more likely to increase than decrease. Funds held in different locations cannot be considered interchangeable, and there is still no mechanism to create an international pool of funds in one company.

International liquidity management directly embodies the fragmentation of the multinational company; the approach devised by companies to deal with liquidity constraints is again a centralized one, based on better reporting systems. Normally, the new role of "Assistant Treasurer—International" will encompass both liquidity and exchange management. This management role is aided by the fact that the reporting system used for liquidity management will include virtually all necessary data for the review of hedging decisions. Indeed, detailed liquidity/cash budgeting is an integral part of the exchange-management mechanism.

For example, a Canadian affiliate of an international group may have surplus funds for three months. It can leave them in local currency time deposits, place them in U.S. dollars at a lower yield, or put them in sterling deposits at a higher rate. Assuming that the creditworthiness of deposit institutions is equal, such a liquidity management decision cannot be made on the basis of interest spreads or the Canadian affiliate's position alone.

Even if the subsidiary takes the most conservative course, leaving funds in local deposits, this action has an effect on the parent. Because such subsidiaries cannot easily know either the other dollar or pound commitments of the group or its overall cash needs and investment requirements, local liquidity management is likely to fall increasingly under centralized financial management—which is the main theme of this article.

As a result, exchange risks are becoming better integrated with liquidity management. Both deal with the monetary assets of the company and its underlying sales functions, as well as with inventory, credit management, and borrowing facilities. The structured borrowing/investment policy in liquidity management is the converse of the hedging/risk acceptance policy in its sister area. Together, they form the conceptual core of global working-capital management; success in either is essential for success in the other. Both are now dependent on a centralized and anticipatory approach, which is being adopted by many companies, although they allow decentralized policies in research, marketing, and production.

Concluding Note

To summarize the tenets of this article, the international corporation should:

- ☐ Make financial management anticipatory, based on a perception of future risks and opportunities.
- ☐ Review and strengthen its reporting systems, particularly forecasting elements, to allow such a response.
- ☐ Centralize control over exposure risk and liquidity utilization as far as possible.
- ☐ Cover economic, transactional exposure generally and translation risk when the maximum potential losses are considered to be unacceptable by defined corporate criteria.
- ☐ Analyze and make financial decisions on an after-tax basis.
- ☐ Ensure availability of credit in uncertain markets on an individual subsidiary basis, even if this involves certain additional costs.
- ☐ Look skeptically at exchange-rate forecasting that provides one-point or very narrow-band estimates of future spot rates, and look just as skeptically at massive computer simulation programs that claim to simplify the decision-making process. The future rate uncertainty level is such that both seemingly facile approaches are of little value, although computer programs for efficient identification of risks and simple sensitivity analysis may be useful.
- ☐ Coordinate exchange-risk management closely with liquidity management, since both have common goals and are equally affected by environmental and structural constraints.
- ☐ Be aware of the nonfinancial implications of financial strategy, particularly the personnel effects of centralization and the necessity of dealing with an array of governmental and institutional contacts.

Implementation of international financial management along these lines allows a structured approach to an increasingly complex and critical area and leads to optimal development of international money management within the company. A more consistent approach, if adopted by most multinationals, could not only benefit the organizations themselves but could also contribute to more orderly markets in general.

Note

1. This point is treated at length in the excellent article by Robert K. Ankrom, "Top-level Approach to the Foreign Exchange Problem," *HBR*, July-August 1974, p. 79. For portrayals of other corporation's exchange-exposure management, see also Newton H. Hoyt, Jr.'s "The Management of Currency Exchange Risk by the Singer Company," *Financial Management*, Spring 1972, p. 13; and Eugene L. Schotanus's "A Strategy for Coping with Exchange Risks," *Management Accounting*, January 1971, p. 45.

6

Anticipate Your Long-Term Foreign Exchange Risks

HELMUT HAGEMANN

The floating exchange rate system has now been in existence for several years; yet only recently have a few companies begun to factor its effect into their long-range planning. Starting from the point at which they first make an investment that will entail doing business internationally, these companies are now worrying less about what their exposure will be for the next few months as identified by their accounting systems and are looking instead at what it will be over the next few years. They are also looking beyond foreign exchange gains and losses incurred by individual subsidiaries to the more fundamental question of preserving the corporation's overall earnings position. After discussing these aspects of long-term foreign exchange management, the author explains the system that one large multinational corporation has set up to enable it to cover its risks on an ongoing basis.

In recent years, drastic fluctuations in exchange rates have repeatedly taken corporate directors of finance by surprise. Lacking timely information and handicapped by inadequate and inefficient accounting systems, many companies have been confounded by the speed and complexity of developments whose underlying causes and financial implications they did not fully understand.

Every industrial country has its quota of companies that have been bruised either lightly or severely by the vagaries of the foreign exchange market, but the greatest number of battle-scarred veterans are unquestionably to be found in West Germany. Many West German manufacturers are highly dependent on exports and therefore especially vulnerable to exchange rate fluctuations. And, of course, as the strongest major currency in Europe, the deutsche mark has undergone revaluations in the past five years that have brought its dollar value from DM 3.65 to a low of DM 2.23 and back to DM 2.60, wreaking havoc with the plans and projects of most of Germany's exporters.

Nor have heavy losses resulting from inept management of foreign exchange risks been confined to unsophisticated companies. In 1974 alone, Volkswagen, the world's fourth largest automaker, lost more than $310 million, mainly as a result of DM revaluation. More recently, ITT announced that in the third quarter of 1976 its foreign exchange losses amounted to 33.5% of its total profits. And 3M booked a loss amounting to 20.5% of its $85.2 million profits in the third quarter of 1976.

Says the finance director of a large German exporter, "We've always covered our foreign exchange risks, but we still took a terrible beating on the revaluation. The worst of it is that we don't even know how to assess the real impact of these movements on our profitability."

In the same vein, the president of a large multinational corporation feels that "today we're paying for our past neglect of possible shifts in exchange rates. These changes have inflated our profits in some countries and caused us big losses in others. They've obsoleted all our resource, production, and logistic strategies and thrown a tremendous risk-management responsibility on the finance function—which unfortunately doesn't seem quite able to cope."

With different rates of inflation in different countries, exports increasing faster than production, corporate overseas investment increasing faster than total capital investment, and no end in sight to the pattern of essentially unpredictable exchange rate adjustments, the problem—and the penalty for those who fail to solve it—is rapidly gaining in gravity. Increasingly, foreign exchange movements pose a serious threat to the earning power of many corporations. It has become clear that a better approach to identifying foreign exchange risks and finding effective ways to deal with them is needed.

It is against this background that a few sophisticated companies have begun to take a new long-term approach to the management of foreign exchange risks, an approach that appears to hold considerable promise for any manufacturing company deriving a substantial share of its volume from overseas sales. It is applicable in principle to the operations of a company selling its goods anywhere in the world outside its home base, regardless of where the goods are manufactured. Although new in practical application, this approach is based on easily understood financial concepts and principles and can be explained without reference to the technical intricacies of day-to-day dealings on the world's foreign exchange markets.

Basic Characteristics

The purpose of long-term foreign exchange management is *not* to cover a given foreign exchange exposure through dealings on the forward markets, but to minimize and, if possible, eliminate such exposures before they become critical and therefore too costly to cover. A long-term approach differs from conventional approaches in the following three important respects.

Longer Time Horizon

Accepted current methods of covering foreign exchange risks normally use a time horizon of three to six months. However, because of production and investment commitments, foreign exchange risks may actually arise as much as five years before they are reflected in the accounting system. With a three- to six-month time horizon, therefore, coverage operations will often come too late. Once a currency is under serious pressure, the forward coverage costs become exorbitant, frequently exceeding the probable foreign exchange loss.

Take the example of, say, a Japanese auto manufacturer. As Exhibit 1 shows, the company produces a car in January for export to the United States and sells it in April for $3,000, which it will collect three months later in July. This company's accounting system would identify a foreign exchange exposure only during the three months when the figure of $3,000 in accounts receivable would appear on its books. Losses due to a devaluation of the dollar between January and April would, for accounting purposes, be defined as losses on regular transactions, not as foreign exchange losses.

Exhibit 1. Risks in Home Investment and Production

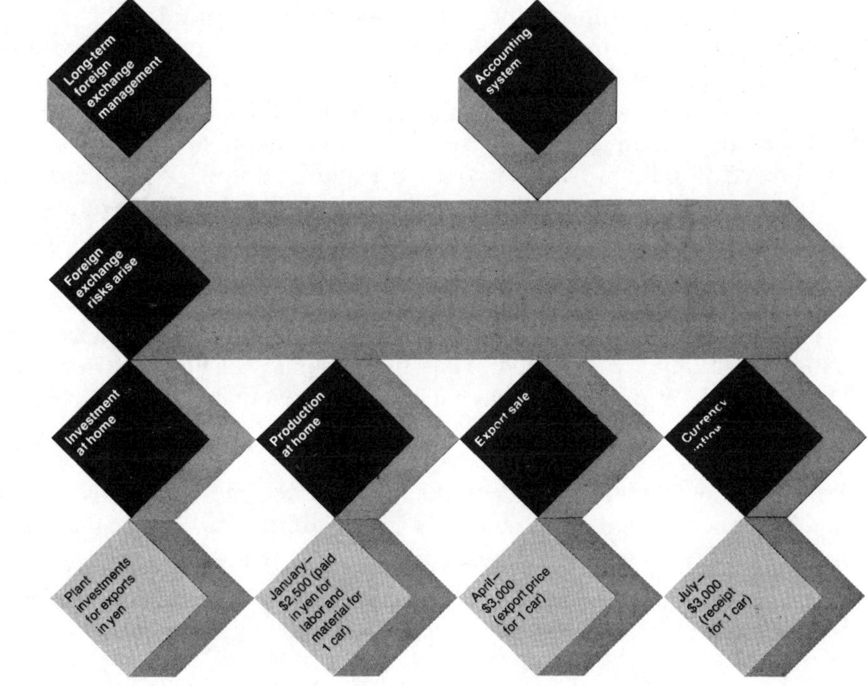

Yet that is exactly what they are, because the company committed itself in January to the export sale. To have risked the loss of its U.S. markets by stopping its exports or to have raised its final selling price in line with the devaluation would not have been realistic options. In effect, the company was locked into the exposure at least from the time the car came off the assembly line.

Indeed, the company actually incurred exchange risks considerably earlier—from the point at which it invested in production facilities to supply foreign markets. (In fact, domestic facilities that supply foreign markets commonly entail a much greater risk than do foreign facilities, because material and labor cannot be paid for in the same currency for which the products are sold. The point seems obvious; yet few companies even consider covering such risks when they invest at home.)

Thus the first key characteristic of a longer-term approach to foreign exchange management is that it does not rely on the accounting system. Risks are "managed" from the time the investments are made until the final receipts from sales of the product are received.

Dynamic Orientation

To identify the foreign exchange exposure, it is not enough, as some companies have recognized, simply to compare foreign assets and liabilities (however defined) on a given date—whether by the current or noncurrent method or the monetary or nonmonetary method.[1] Rather, the *flows* of foreign currencies arising from transactions affecting these assets and liabilities over an appropriate period of time must be considered.

For example, if an Italian company has assets of 10 million French francs that mature in two years and liabilities of 10 million French francs that mature in one year, its franc assets and liabilities are exactly in balance. But foreign exchange risks still exist in both years, since there will be an outflow of 10 million francs in one year and an inflow of 10 million francs in the next. If the franc is revalued in the first year and devalued in the second, the company will have incurred exchange losses on both its assets and its liabilities.

Many assets and liabilities translate into currency flows over time, and it is the difference between inflows and outflows that define a company's exposure in any given period. Thus the dynamics of time is a second vital characteristic of proper foreign exchange management.

Preservation of Earnings

Finally, under the new approach the financial manager's objective concerning foreign exchange management is entirely different. Rather than seeking to minimize *reported* foreign exchange losses, the financial manager tries to preserve the earning power of the company as a whole through exchange rate fluctuations. For example, suppose a U.S. company has to repay a loan of 10 million French francs in 1978 and expects export sales to France of 10 million francs during the same year. Only the liability, not the expected income, will be shown on the books. Assuming that the export estimates are reliable, it should not be necessary to cover that loan, because the export receipts can be used to repay it. In other words, there is no foreign exchange risk if the export sales are realized.

Yet from an accounting point of view, the financial manager is still in an awkward position. If the franc should revalue by 10%, his or her liabilities will result in an accounting loss of 1 million francs, whereas the increased dollar value of the French sales receipts will be identified not as foreign exchange gains, but as additional profit on regular transactions.

If, therefore, financial managers merely want to safeguard the interest of their own department, they will make sure to cover the 10 million franc liability, even if their expected export receipts from France are 10 million francs or considerably more. If they are to protect the earning power of the company as a whole, however, they need to take a more systematic approach, which can only be implemented with fuller understanding and support on the part of top management.

Systematic Steps

Recently a few large companies have successfully put into practice this more fundamental approach to foreign exchange management. Although their programs differ in detail, they all include these same three basic steps: (1) estimate net exposure; (2) estimate range of exchange rates; and (3) cover risks.

Estimate Net Exposures

"Net exposure" is the difference between estimated inflows and outflows of a foreign currency over a specified period or periods—not only those already known or contracted (from maturing receivables and payables, loan repayments, and interest and dividend payments), but also those that are expected or can reasonably be foreseen on the basis of the company's short- and long-term plans (from forecasted export sales, material purchases from abroad, planned investments in other countries, capital issues in other currencies, and equity increases in foreign subsidiaries).

To calculate the overall net exposure, the parent and each subsidiary estimate their expected inflows and outflows of each currency for the period or periods in question. Rather than allowing each subsidiary to cover its risks on its own, with attendant high coverage costs, management then consolidates all these estimates for the corporation as a whole. Instead of imposing this step as a requirement, companies with partially decentralized financial management have found it possible to achieve central control of foreign exchange exposure by giving subsidiaries concrete incentives to cover their risks only with the parent.

For a manufacturing company, the time horizon for estimating net exposure might be five years, broken down into cumulative 30-day, 60-day, and 90-day estimates; 6-month, 9-month, and 12-month estimates; two-year, three-year, and four-year estimates; and estimates for all flows after five years. The periods cited are arbitrary, but the principle involved is simple—a series of staged forecasts for successively longer time periods, up to some reasonable limit. Obviously, a higher degree of precision is both possible and desirable for the first year; for subsequent years, rough estimates suffice.

Since inflows and outflows of any given currency may be subject to significant uncertainties, it is also helpful to consider the probable upper and lower limits of variation from the projected values in estimating net exposures. The object is to develop an approximate picture of net exposure positions in the major currencies involved, so that the company can move early to reduce its exposure through decisions on currency denominations, maturities of loans, repayment schedules, and the like.

Logically, then, the impact a given decision (for example, on a plant investment or a long-term purchase contract) will have on the company's net exposure becomes an important input to that decision. Currently, foreign exchange risks associated with investment projects are specified—if at all—only for the individual projects; but what is important is the extent to which each investment will increase or decrease the overall net exposure of the company.

For example, in analyzing alternative production sites for one of its major components, one American company discovered that building a plant in West Germany instead of in the United States would substantially reduce its overall net exposure over the next five years. The DM inflow from the company's present exports of finished products to Germany would in fact then be offset by DM payments for investment outlays in Germany and the subsequent purchase of components by the U.S. plants. Had the project been evaluated by itself, building the plant in Germany would have appeared, on the basis of foreign exchange risk, much less desirable than building it in the United States.

Of course, there are many other factors a company has to consider besides foreign exchange risks when it makes its final investment decisions. For instance, product market strategies, raw material supplies, availability of qualified personnel, differences in the investment climate of various countries, and regulations concerning profit and capital transfers may be far more important considerations than the risks associated with possible fluctuations in foreign exchange rates.

Only the combined assessment of all these factors and their probable influence on the company's future profitability will lead to sound investment decisions.

Estimate Range of Exchange Rates

As William D. Serfass points out in Article 7, the pursuit of speculative profits on the foreign exchange markets is a pastime about as rewarding as Russian roulette for corporate money managers. Informed guesses of the likely range (not necessarily direction) of long-term future exchange rate movements do, however, serve a vital purpose: that of providing a rough idea of the range of possible gains or losses that may result, given a particular net exposure.

To take an obvious example, a U.S. company ought to be less concerned about its exposure in Canadian dollars than, say, half that same exposure in English pounds. By computing the upper and lower limits of the probable gains or losses, the financial manager can predict and possibly forestall threats to a company's financial health arising from excessive exposure in volatile currencies.

Over the shorter term (three to six months), these same estimates provide a necessary basis for weighing the cost of forward coverage against the risks of leaving the net exposure uncovered. Note that it may at times be preferable to accept these risks. Since the costs of coverage are primarily determined by the differences in short-term interest rates among countries, rather than by expectations concerning exchange rate movements, coverage may be attractive at some times, yet prohibitively costly at others.

Of course, specific exchange rate movements are difficult if not impossible to predict, but a company can at least reduce its undesirable net exposure positions well in advance, decreasing its vulnerability to exchange rate swings.

Cover Risks

Having highlighted its principal future foreign exchange risks, the company can now devise means of coverage. Basically these reduce to two techniques:

- ☐ Buying or selling particular currencies on the forward market to cover estimated net exposures in those currencies at particular future periods.
- ☐ Influencing individual components of expected currency inflows or outflows so as to reduce or eliminate estimated net exposures. This may mean changing the company's financial plans, such as by substituting a loan in another currency for a local loan, or its operating plans, such as by reducing exports to a certain country, purchasing more material from abroad, or expanding or curtailing capital investment in a particular country.

Since the forward market is essentially confined to short-term (up to 12 months) contracts, longer-term foreign exchange risks can usually be reduced only by changing the net exposure—and this frequently has the advantage of enabling the company to avoid undertaking large-scale coverage operations on the forward market.

For example, a European chemical company bought a large factory from an American contractor for $64 million, agreeing to pay for it in U.S. dollars. A large outflow of dollars was in prospect for the first year, followed by increasing inflows of dollars from sharply rising exports. Covering the risk of the resulting net exposure during the first two years would have been extremely costly.

However, the company found that it could significantly reduce this net exposure by reducing its local bank loan and negotiating a loan of $50 million with a foreign bank. The proceeds of the loan were used for paying the U.S. contractor, while interest and loan repayments helped to offset the risks of dollar-denominated exports, as shown in Exhibit 2. This operation entailed no additional costs; indeed, the interest rate on the dollar loan at that time was slightly lower than on the local capital market. And because the loan was carried on the books of a foreign subsidiary that was subject to a higher tax rate, income taxes could also be reduced.

As a rule, the chief financial executive will wish to explore the choices available to him for altering the net exposure without affecting basic strategic or operating decisions. Should it appear that serious imbalances in net exposures will persist after available financial measures have been exhausted, top management might even consider revising its operating plans accordingly.

Although the ability of financial managers to influence operating plans is generally limited, it is one of their major responsibilities to identify and highlight the foreign exchange risks associated with existing operating plans, so that these risks are properly entered into the overall evaluation of alternative strategies and plans.

Management System

Systems embodying the concept of foreign exchange management I have described in this article will inevitably differ from company to company in terms of organization and in the degree of computerization involved. Their principal elements can, however, be seen in the system (shown in Exhibit 3) that is being successfully used by a large international company. With this system, the company's financial managers go through the following cycle:

Long-Term Financial Plans. Based on the operating plans of the divisions, the parent and subsidiaries develop long-term financial plans for five years. As part of the cash flow projection, the subsidiaries also submit their estimates of major foreign currency flows above a certain level, which is deliberately set high because of the enormous uncertainty involved. This confines the planning work to significant flows and avoids burdening the smaller subsidiaries with unnecessary paperwork.

Exhibit 2. Net Exposure Coverage Operation

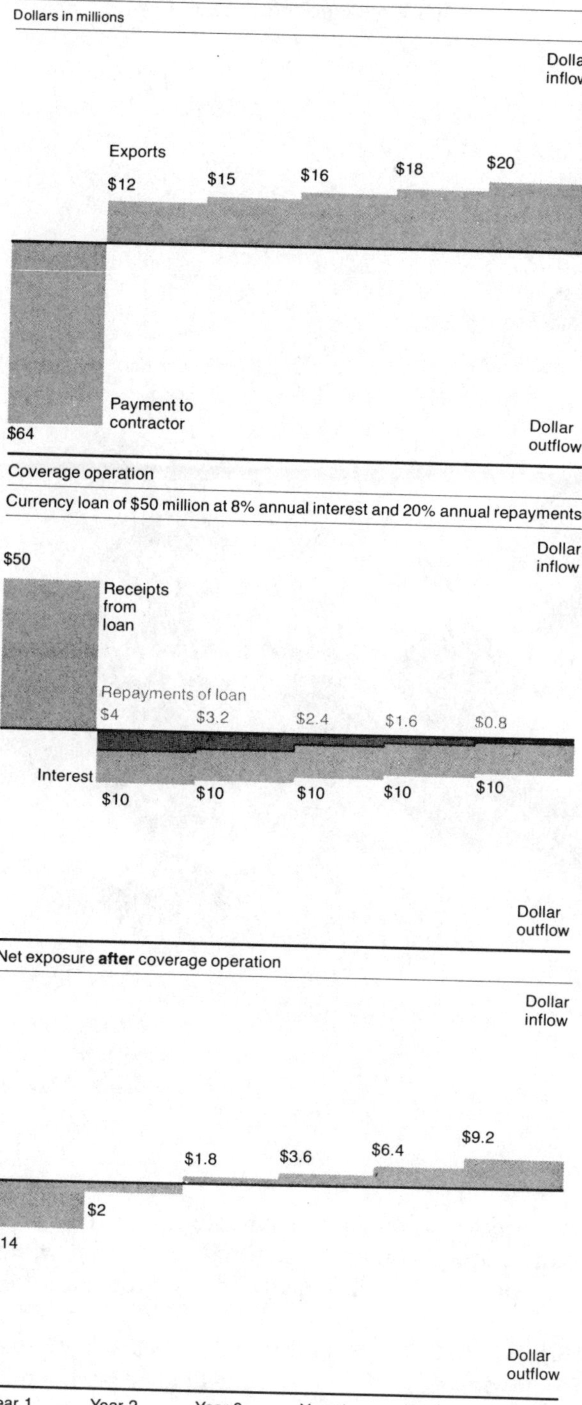

Exhibit 3. System for Foreign Exchange Management

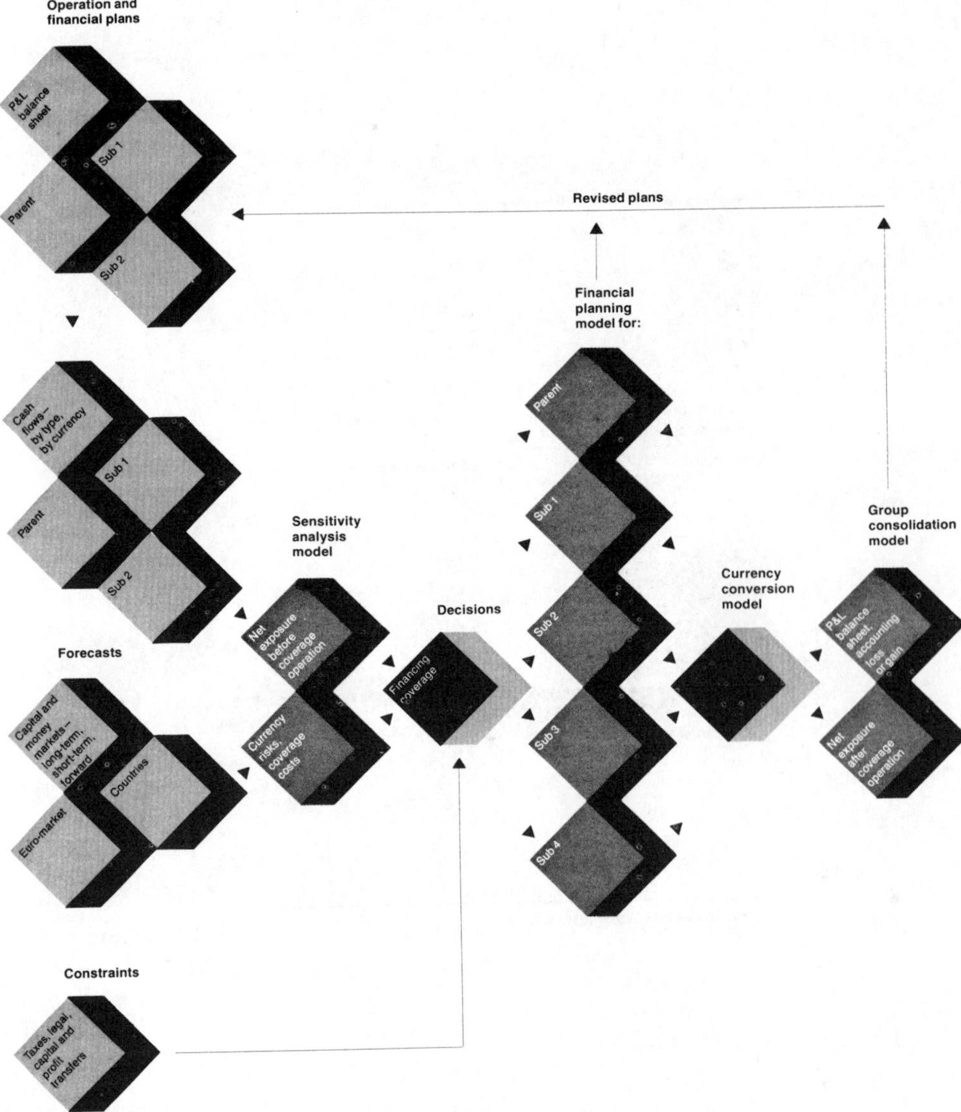

Those in corporate finance consolidate all currency flows of the subsidiaries and the parent company, netting out the intercompany flows to derive the net exposure in each major currency for the total corporation.

Analysis of Capital, Tax, and Regulatory Outlook. With the support of the larger foreign subsidiaries, the corporate finance staff analyzes trends in major capital and foreign exchange markets to identify interest rate differentials between various capital markets and estimates the upper and lower limits of possible exchange rate movements.[2] For many currencies the estimated ranges will be very wide, signaling high risk if significant differences between currency inflows and outflows are anticipated.

Since financing and coverage decisions are subject to tax and legal regulations and constraints on capital and profit transfers, such constraints are carefully analyzed for each country, taking possible changes into account.

Sensitivity Analysis. A sensitivity analysis model is used to calculate the effects of different rates of devaluation or revaluation on the profitability of the corporation and to test the impact of uncertainties in the estimates of each component of the net exposure. This model also shows the balance sheet and P&L statements for the total corporation, the parent, and each subsidiary for five years, highlighting the change in earnings after taxes due to exchange rate movements as well as foreign exchange losses or gains as defined by the accounting system. Corporate management can quickly see which subsidiaries are highly vulnerable to foreign exchange risks and how taxes and the degree of self-financing will be affected in each subsidiary if no specific counter measures are taken.

Coverage Decisions. Having identified the major areas of foreign exchange risk, the corporate finance staff proceeds to develop measures for reducing the net exposure in particular currencies and years. Because they are highly interdependent, coverage and financing measures have to be worked out simultaneously and integrated into the financial plans of the corporation. All measures are thoroughly discussed with the subsidiaries affected and checked against legal and tax regulations or restrictions.

Adjustments of Financial Plans. The individual measures are then integrated into the financial plans of the parent and the subsidiaries. Adjustments are calculated with a financial planning model in local currencies and discussed with local management.

Currency Conversion and Group Consolidation. The financial plans of the individual subsidiaries are converted from local currency into the home currency of the parent, using a "currency conversion model." The plans are then consolidated on the basis of standard accounting rules for the total corporation with the aid of a "group consolidation model." At the same time, the net exposure is recalculated for all major currencies to reflect the changes due to the coverage decisions. If the net exposure turns out to be still too high in certain currencies or periods, another round of adjustments is necessary.

Losses Avoided

In practice, the company has found this system to be a powerful tool to avoid excessive foreign exchange losses. Experience suggests, however, that such a system can be useful only if it is applied by imaginative financial managers who see beyond the boundaries of their own organizational units.

Notes

1. Robert K. Ankrom, "Top-level Approach to the Foreign Exchange Problem," *HBR*, July-August 1974, p. 79.

2. See Martin Murenbeeld, "Economic Factors for Forecasting Foreign Exchange Rate Changes," *Columbia Journal of World Business*, Summer 1975.

7
You Can't Outguess the Foreign Exchange Market

WILLIAM D. SERFASS, JR.

In these days of fluctuating currency values, a company trading or manufacturing abroad is acting dangerously if it fails to protect itself against shifts in the value of the dollar. It can do this by hedging in foreign exchange forwards. As a company whose overseas business accounts for a large share of its total sales ($60 million), HMW Industries, Inc. must have this protection. Here a top executive of this Stamford, Connecticut company describes the foreign exchange management program by which it reduces the risks inherent in dealing in many currencies.

American businesspeople who speculate in foreign currencies are courting disaster. The cases of Franklin National Bank of New York and Herstatt Bank of West Germany, whose foreign exchange losses precipitated their collapse, are well known. And recall the recent experience of some "experts" in the foreign exchange field:

- ☐ Union Bank of Switzerland, an institution with an impeccable reputation, swallowed losses of approximately $150 million.
- ☐ A Swiss branch of Lloyds Bank, one of the bluest of the blue-chip British banks, suffered losses of $75 million from unauthorized dealings in foreign exchange.
- ☐ Michele Sindona, the Italian financier, saw his substantial financial interests in Italy, Switzerland, and Luxembourg wither because of overextension in the foreign exchange market. The Vatican, acting on his advice, lost $60 million in that market.

If the "gnomes of Zürich" and other international bankers, who employ sophisticated specialists to carry out their international monetary operations, can't beat the foreign exchange market, how can American businesspeople? The answer is, they can't, so they shouldn't try.

Corporate executives involved in domestic and foreign manufacturing, selling, exporting, and importing are well aware of the financial impact that floating currencies can have on their businesses. They know that rates fluctuate, sometimes widely and dramatically in short periods. This problem presents a corporation with the responsibility of developing methods to eliminate or at least reduce vulnerability to changing money values.

So what should a company do to reduce its exposure in world markets? It should hedge—within the corporate structure, if it is a multinational corporation, and through the use of foreign exchange forwards, if it has no transnational assets and liabilities. Hedging within the corporate structure can be accomplished by balancing worldwide net transactions of each currency and by shifting expenses through transfers of liquid assets from one currency to another. The remaining net exposure can then be balanced within the foreign exchange forward market, as I shall explain.

Consider the experience of my company, HMW Industries. It consists of three businesses—Time Computer, Inc., which manufactures, sells, and exports the Pulsar, a solid-state wristwatch; Wallace Silversmiths, Inc., which produces sterling flatware and sterling and plated hollowware; and Hamilton Technology, Inc., which makes high-precision metal products and which imports and sells automated parts-making machinery. Our sales in the last fiscal year totaled $60 million. We depend proportionately more on foreign and precious metals trade than do much larger companies.

In dealing with foreign exchange currencies and precious metals trade, we follow these guidelines: (1) we do not speculate; (2) we protect our budgeted costs; and (3) if we believe that temporary distortions in exchange rates exist, we suspend or accelerate our established programs.

Commodity Price Protection

Although wavering exchange rates are a recent phenomenon, the problems they create are similar to those any fluctuating commodity creates. Many U.S. businesspeople have gained experience in hedging through the markets for commodities such as wheat, corn, and copper. The mechanisms for reducing the risk of foreign currency fluctuations are generally available to companies—through the foreign forwards market—just as futures dealings are in many commodities.

The principles of a well-developed commodities hedging program can be used in hedging in many foreign currencies. The costing aspects of dealing with fluctuating rates are like the techniques used in determining standard costs and setting overhead rates. In currency hedging, predetermined standard costs and foreign exchange rates (similar to overhead rates) are used as price setters and as elements of cost to be measured periodically for comparison with results.

Let's look at one commodity to see how materials trade resembles foreign exchange. A major cost at HMW is the sterling silver that Wallace Silversmiths uses. In 1974, silver prices fluctuated between \$3.90 and \$6.70 an ounce, and 1975 prices ranged from \$3.90 to \$5.70 an ounce.

At various times during the year, Wallace promotes its sterling flatware at discount prices. When these programs are planned, we must furnish our customers with printed price literature so that they can promote the discounted merchandise with their retail customers. Suppose that, at the point of planning a promotion, the spot price of silver is \$4.50 per ounce, that silver must be purchased for manufacture three months later, that the three-month futures price is \$4.60, and that list prices have previously been determined according to a silver cost of \$5 per ounce.

Suppose we recalculate the cost of the product at the \$4.60 futures price level. Taking into consideration the lower gross-profit percentages and the higher gross-profit dollars anticipated from the promotion, the subsidiary can then establish the promotion price. With a list price of \$150 per place setting at \$5 silver, the lower promotional price—at \$4.60 silver and lower gross-profit percentage—will be expressed as an amount under the list price, for example, as "30% off."

When we determine the promotion price and the silver costs, we "lock in," through purchase of futures contracts, the price of the raw silver quantities needed to fulfill the promotion. Because silver prices often fluctuate 15 to 20 cents an ounce daily, forward market protection during a promotion period eliminates the risk of chaotic price changes and unexpected profit reduction, which might oblige us to terminate the promotion abruptly.

HMW can use similar futures commitment methods in establishing more stable list prices at which products are normally sold during the year.

Foreign Exchange Protection

After HMW establishes the operating plan for a particular year, each subsidiary estimates its month-by-month requirements for the entire year in every foreign currency used in the company's international trade. In each currency, the subsidiary considers spot exchange rates, forward contract rates, HMW's present forward exchange position, timing, and anticipated receipts and disbursements. We then forecast an average exchange rate.

We allow our subsidiaries to arrive at different average exchange rates. HMW tries to avoid standardizing or making every subsidiary's exchange rate uniform. The requirements of each subsidiary vary in accordance with the amount and timing of its foreign currency activity. Although we review the overall net requirements at the corporate level and adjust our exchange programs on a net basis, the subsidiaries operate on their predetermined average rates. (Other companies, of course, may want to take a more standardized approach; it's a matter of individual discretion.)

These net cash flows indicate points at which imbalances may exist either in receipts or disbursements. Excess receipts can be covered by short sales, whereas excess disbursements can be covered by purchases of forward contracts.

We base selling prices on these foreign currency cost inputs. Our objective over each year is then to average out at a rate approximating that used in determining the prices in the operating plan.

HMW sells Pulsar watches in 52 countries. Our foreign subsidiary—Pulsar S.A., in Geneva—establishes our prices in Swiss francs. As we collect Swiss franc receivables, we accumulate resources to liquidate Swiss franc liabilities. Balancing franc receipts against franc disbursements and trying to match them to reduce the exposure to exchange variations, we prepare long-range forecasts monthly.

In addition to balancing receipts and disbursements monthly in each medium of exchange, we sometimes cross-balance between two or more currencies. This technique is especially appropriate for dealing with currencies in the European "snake." (Germany, France, Belgium, Denmark, and the Netherlands maintain their cross rates within 2¼% of each other and float as a group against other currencies. This controlled "wiggle" effect gives rise to the name "snake agreement.") For example, we may match French franc receivables against German deutsche mark liabilities and cover the net result in the forward exchange market. While such a move still exposes us somewhat, the cost of forward contracts fully hedging both currencies may not warrant the protection received, if we consider the rather limited exposure we get from these controlled currency spreads.

Long-Term Contracts

An HMW subsidiary—Hamilton Technology—is the exclusive U.S. distributor for Mikron Haesler, a Swiss manufacturer of highly sophisticated, multistage, automatic, precision parts-making machines. After delivery to the United States, these machines are assembled, customized, and tooled by Ham Tech. The contract for sale involves commitment on our part to purchase the machinery in Swiss francs and to collect the gross price from our customer in dollars. The whole procedure takes 12 to 24 months. Here is the sequence:

- ☐ Obtain a request for a quotation from a customer.
- ☐ Obtain a quote from Mikron to determine our landed cost in Swiss francs.
- ☐ Determine the cost of our U.S. tooling, customizing, general and administrative expenses, and our profit.

- ☐ Quote to the customer a dollar price, after the Swiss franc costs are translated into the prevailing forward exchange rate at the estimated time of payment.
- ☐ Receive the award, usually 60 to 120 days after the price quotation.
- ☐ As much as six months later, receive goods from Switzerland, assemble, and tool.
- ☐ Make payment to Mikron in Swiss francs.
- ☐ Deliver goods to the customer, and then receive final payment.

How does HMW protect itself from adverse exchange fluctuations? If we commit ourselves to a forward exchange contract at the time of the bid and receive no award, we will be in a long position with no outstanding commitment. On the other hand, making no foreign exchange commitment might put the profitability of the contract in jeopardy if the exchange rate changes unfavorably before we pay Mikron. To reduce our exposure, we take two steps:

1 We insert in the bid an escalation clause calling for a price adjustment to offset any forward market currency fluctuations up to the time of the award date.
2 At the time of the award, we make a commitment for a forward exchange contract in Swiss francs and base it on the estimated payment date of the supplier's invoice.

Inasmuch as the cost of the equipment represents a substantial portion of the total contract cost, we have been able to lock in that cost through our foreign exchange commitments. Thus we considerably narrow the risk involved in realizing the estimated contract profit.

No business decision that involves two currencies can eliminate the speculative element; even sitting back and doing nothing introduces a degree of speculation for a company with business abroad. If it has foreign currency liabilities it does not protect, the company is speculating that the dollar will not weaken by the time it must pay those liabilities. Conversely, if it decides not to hedge its receivables in a foreign nation, the company is speculating that this particular nation's currency will not weaken before the receivable is collected. Corporate management must determine exposure, weigh the risk, and implement the best method of protection.

Each quarter, our economist reviews with us our precious metals and foreign currency positions and requirements for one year forward. Then management formulates its policy and implements it by issuing instructions to maintain or increase our foreign exchange forwards positions. We generally do not sell out previously established positions. In addition, we consult the economist weekly about current developments that may necessitate modifying our programs.

What do these programs mean to HMW?

1 What is most important, they reduce our susceptibility to short- or intermediate-term foreign currency fluctuations.
2 The programs give us a firmer costing base from which prices can be determined.
3 These programs give us reaction lead time to adjust prices; we can avoid the panic of short-term currency spirals.

There is a cost to all these programs—the premium paid for the "insurance." Another but less obvious cost is in the substantial management time required to evaluate the facts, form opinions, and formulate programs. The cost of doing nothing, however, can be far more expensive. And even more expensive is a hopeless attempt to outguess the currency and the precious metals speculators.

PART THREE
FINANCING THE CORPORATION

AN OVERVIEW

Financing decisions start with an estimation of the funds that will be needed over some reasonable period of time. These estimates can be obtained through typical financial planning procedures, but the process is complicated somewhat by an inflationary environment. In "Measuring Company Growth Capacity during Inflation," Rappaport presents a framework for thinking about this issue. In particular, this article focuses managers' attention on the amount of funding required to maintain productive capacity during an inflationary period.

After determining external financing needs, a key question is how much of this need should be met with debt. Two important facts are well known. First, debt is normally the cheapest form of long-term financing for corporations that can use the tax deductibility of interest. Second, a company can go too far in using debt, thus hampering management with restrictive covenants, depressing its stock price because of increased risk, and exposing the company to risk of failure if an adverse economic environment develops. Unfortunately, neither of these facts is much help in estimating the point at which a company has an appropriate amount of debt. Companies have obviously learned to live with this situation by adopting target debt ratios that reflect industry practice, desired bond ratings, and other concerns of senior management.

Three articles in Part 3 offer some advice on the issue of how much debt. Donaldson is the author of two of them, "New Framework for Corporate Debt Policy" and "Strategy for Financial Emergencies." In the first article, he provides an approach to be used in assessing the uncertainty of corporate cash flows, which in turn influences the amount of debt that can be appropriately handled. Donaldson suggests in his second article a way for corporations to do formal contingency planning to be better prepared to deal with the uncertainties of future environments. In the third article of this group, "How Much Debt Is Right for Your Company?," Piper and Weinhold summarize recent theoretical developments on the debt capacity issue. A key argument for "more debt" in earlier theoretical work was the tax deductibility of interest to the corporation. More recent work looks at returns to holders of corporate securities and pays attention to the tax status of these security holders. Debt becomes less beneficial to the extent that corporate bonds are held by taxable investors.

Because there are limits to debt capacity, companies must sometimes consider new equity issues. Management is frequently held back, however, by concerns that their shares are currently undervalued in the equity market. On the other hand, if the stock is really undervalued, why not repurchase shares? Piper and Fruhan ("Is Your Stock Worth Its Market Price?") provide an objective method for estimating the economic value of a company's shares that can be used to provide a more informed basis for actions by the company.

The last two articles in Part 3 provide advice for selecting and dealing with financial institutions when it is time to obtain financing. In "How to Negotiate a Term Loan," Arnold provides some insights on how banks view a potential borrower and then suggests a way for companies to forge a strategy for dealing with the bank. Logue and Rogalski conducted a study to answer the question in their title, "Does It Pay to Shop for Your Bond Underwriter?" Their results suggest that the industry was very competitive on pricing, so that an investment banker could be selected primarily on the basis of more subjective factors such as quality of service. (Subsequent events would confirm the very competitive pricing, but "shelf-registration" of securities was being tested during 1982. Under this new procedure, a large block of securities could be registered with the SEC and then securities could later be pulled off this "shelf" for sale without going through a complicated underwriting process. During this transition period, active searching for the best price probably paid off for some companies.)

8

Measuring Company Growth Capacity During Inflation

ALFRED RAPPAPORT

A financial statement based on historical costs does not, of course, provide an adequate economic picture of a business during a time of inflation. But neither does the replacement cost information recently prescribed by the SEC, the author of this article asserts. He advocates the use of a distributable funds measure for more effective management control systems. "Distributable funds" is defined as the maximum amount that the company can pay out to its stockholders during the fiscal period without impairing its business capability. Distributable funds thus represent the total amount made available during the period for dividends and expansion of business capacity. The components of distributable funds are aftertax income during the fiscal period, a cost increase provision for productive capacity, any change in working capital required, and any change in debt capacity. A company's distributable funds depend on return on sales, growth in sales, net working capital requirements, the rate of cost increases in productive capacity, dividend payout percentage, and the company's target debt-equity ratio. The recommended approach enables management to assess the effects of its operating, investment, financing, and dividend decisions on corporate performance.

> The failure of conventional financial reporting to reflect the impact of inflation on corporate earnings . . . obscures the fact that business is simply not accumulating and retaining the resources required to meet the challenges facing it. Put differently, it contributes to misleading the American public into believing that corporate earnings are so thoroughly

Author's note. I gratefully acknowledge the helpful comments of a number of people, particularly John C. Burton. This article was written during my tenure as the 1977–1978 Coopers & Lybrand Research Fellow at the Graduate School of Management, Northwestern University.

> adequate for all legitimate corporate purposes as to justify substantial additional reallocation of a portion of those earnings to social purposes.. . .
>
> The economic reality is that American business overall is not generating and retaining funds adequate even to replace existing capacity and continue operations at present levels; on the contrary, some businesses may actually be distributing their capital and be in the process of unconscious liquidation.

So said Harold M. Williams, chairman of the Securities and Exchange Commission, in a speech to The Conference Board.[1] My purpose in this article is to introduce a performance measurement approach that enables top management to obtain a better understanding of its performance in an inflationary environment as well as in an environment of price stability. This measurement establishes a sound basis for assessing whether a business is in fact distributing its capital and unconsciously liquidating.

I shall show that this distributable funds approach gives insights into the current economics of a business not provided by either historical-cost financial statements or the recent SEC-mandated replacement-cost disclosure. Although the Financial Accounting Standards Board (FASB) and the SEC might wish to assess the merits of the statement of distributable funds as a supplementary disclosure for external reporting purposes, any such consideration should be preceded by a period of experimentation and by careful evaluation of the expected benefits compared with the costs of compliance.

Physical Capital Approach

The recent SEC ruling on disclosure of the estimated cost of replacing inventories and productive capacity at the end of the fiscal year, as well as the cost of sales and depreciation expense computed on the basis of estimated replacement cost during the year, is based on the physical capital concept of capital maintenance. This concept holds that a business earns no income until it makes provision to replace the productive capacity of existing assets. According to the FASB, "The general procedure to maintain physical capital is to value assets, such as inventories, property, plant, equipment, and some intangibles, at their current replacement costs and to deduct expenses, such as cost of goods sold, depreciation, and the like, valued at replacement cost from revenues to measure periodic earnings."[2]

Although this approach deals with the problems of "inventory profits" (i.e., increases in costs between the acquisition and the sale of inventory) and underdepreciation encountered under conventional reporting, replacement-cost income calculated under the physical capital approach suffers as a measure of distributable funds because:

- ☐ It is based on the assumption that maintaining existing productive capacity is the appropriate corporate objective. In an economy characterized by increasing product turnover and corporate diversification, maintaining existing productive capacity is rarely the optimal way of preserving and enhancing the earning power of the business. Enlightened executives continually seek opportunities to redeploy capital from unsatisfactorily profitable existing operations to more promising investment opportunities.

- ☐ It neglects working capital, which is an essential element of the company's continuing capacity to produce goods and services.
- ☐ It fails to account for debt, which generally is used to finance part of productive capacity.

The distributable funds approach addresses each of these limitations as well as the shortcomings of conventional historical-cost statements. To accomplish this, I introduce the concept of business capacity maintenance. This concept is based on the idea that a going concern has distributable funds available only after it makes provision to maintain that portion of its operating capability financed by equity. Distributable funds represent the maximum amount that the company can distribute to its stockholders during a period without impairing its business capacity.

In contrast with physical or productive capacity, business capacity includes not only productive facilities, but also the company's net working capital requirements as an essential element of its ability to make and sell a certain volume of products and services. The business capacity maintenance concept also recognizes that going concerns frequently discontinue some products while introducing new products and expanding into new markets. Because the price changes for depreciable assets may differ, separate provision must be made for productive capacity that management plans to replace and for capacity not expected to be replaced at the end of its economic life. Finally, the business capacity concept recognizes that part of a company's operating capability is ordinarily financed by debt.

In brief, the distributable funds approach accounts for the higher cost of conducting business, the funds required to operate at a larger sales volume than last period, and the possibility of financing a portion of the company's needs via debt.

Business capacity is the foundation for future earning power. Calculation of the distributable funds can provide managers and investors with a sound basis for assessing the future earning and dividend potential of the company.

Case of GSM Corporation

The amount of distributable funds made available during the period is affected not only by the profitability of operations, but also by whether the company (1) is operating in an inflationary environment, (2) plans to replace all its existing productive capacity or partially redeploy its capital to other product-market sectors, (3) is experiencing sales growth and therefore needs more working capital, and (4) has undergone a change in debt capacity.

To see how a statement of distributable funds is developed, consider the case of GSM Corporation, which is based on a composite of capital-intensive manufacturers.

GSM's statement of income (Exhibit 1) reports a 10% growth in sales and net income for 1978 over 1977. The aftertax return on sales for both years was 6%. The statement of financial position (Exhibit 2) reflects a rather strong current position and a debt-equity ratio of .50, which is average for GSM's industry. GSM's return on equity for both years was 18%. The statement of changes in financial position (Exhibit 3) shows that operations, coupled with an increase in long-term debt, provided sufficient financial resources for the company's expanded working capital needs, a dividend payout of 50% of net income, and capital expenditures substantially greater than depreciation.

A review limited to GSM's financial statements might lead an investor or securities analyst to believe that the company is growing and enjoying economic vitality. In fact, however, GSM is distributing its capital, not growing. The statement of distributable funds (Exhibit 4) discloses that its distributable funds deficits for 1978 and 1977 were $2,247,500 and $1.85 million, respectively. To illustrate how the distributable funds amount is determined, I shall review each item in Exhibit 4 in turn.

Exhibit 1. Statement of Income (year ended December 31)

	1978	1977
Sales	**$110,000,000**	$100,000,000
Costs and other expenses		
Costs of goods sold (exclusive of depreciation)	**79,950,000**	72,600,000
Selling, general, and administrative expenses	**6,550,000**	6,000,000
Depreciation	**7,700,000**	7,000,000
State, local, and miscellaneous taxes	**1,100,000**	1,000,000
Interest and other expenses on debt	**1,500,000**	1,400,000
Total	**$ 96,800,000**	$ 88,000,000
Income before taxes	**$ 13,200,000**	12,000,000
Provision for taxes on income	**6,600,000**	6,000,000
Net income	**$ 6,600,000**	$ 6,000,000
Cash dividends	**$ 3,300,000**	$ 3,000,000

Exhibit 2. Statement of Financial Position (at year-end)

	1978	1977
Current assets		
Cash	**$ 1,100,000**	$ 1,000,000
Receivables, less allowance for losses	**16,500,000**	15,000,000
Inventories	**26,400,000**	24,000,000
Total	**$44,000,000**	$40,000,000
Current liabilities	**11,000,000**	10,000,000
Net working capital	**33,000,000**	30,000,000
Property, plant, and equipment—net[a]	**22,000,000**	20,000,000
Total	**$55,000,000**	$50,000,000
Long-term debt	**$18,400,000**	$16,700,000
Stockholders' equity	**36,600,000**	33,300,000
Total	**$55,000,000**	$50,000,000

[a]Gross amounts are $44,000,000 and $40,000,000 for 1978 and 1977, respectively.

Exhibit 3. Statement of Changes in Financial Position

	1978	**1977**
Financial resources were provided		
From operations		
Net income	**$ 6,600,000**	$ 6,000,000
Depreciation	**7,700,000**	7,000,000
Total	**$14,300,000**	$13,000,000
From other sources		
Increase in long-term debt	**1,700,000**	1,500,000
Total	**$16,000,000**	$14,500,000
Financial resources were used for		
Capital expenditures	**$ 9,700,000**	$ 8,800,000
Dividends	**3,300,000**	3,000,000
Increase in net working capital	**3,000,000**	2,700,000
Total	**$16,000,000**	$14,500,000

Exhibit 4. Statement of Distributable Funds

	1978			1977		
Net income after taxes			**$6,600,000**			$6,000,000
Funds required for increases in costs of productive capacity						
Depreciation expense (at current replacement cost) for productive capacity expected to be replaced (see Exhibit 5)	**$11,550,000**			$10,500,000		
Less historical-cost depreciation	**5,775,000**			5,250,000		
Additional depreciation		**$5,775,000**			$5,250,000	
Depreciation expense (at current price levels) for productive capacity not expected to be replaced (see Exhibit 6)	**$ 5,197,500**			$ 4,550,000		
Less historical-cost depreciation	**1,925,000**			1,750,000		
Additional depreciation		**$3,272,500**		$2,800,000		
Total		**$9,047,500**			$8,050,000	
Funds required for increase in net working capital		**2,300,000**			1,600,000	
Less funds available via increased debt capacity		**2,500,000**			1,800,000	
Total			**$ 8,847,500**			$ 7,850,000
Distributable funds			**$(2,247,500)**			$(1,850,000)
Distributable funds			**$(2,247,500)**			$(1,850,000)
Less dividends			**3,300,000**			3,000,000
Funds available for expansion			**$(5,547,500)**			$(4,850,000)

The statement begins with net income after taxes, to which should be added deferred income taxes, if any, since they are treated as an increase in distributable funds. Net income is followed by the "funds required for increases in costs of productive capacity" section, which considers the impact of cost increases on cost of goods sold and on depreciation.

The "inventory profits" amount is already part of the SEC disclosure requirement. This figure represents an inflation adjustment to the cost of goods sold while the increase in required working capital adjusts for required increases in inventory levels—that is, cost of goods *not* sold. I make this distinction to show the reader that there is no "double counting" in making provision for changes in both required working capital and inventory profit.

For companies using either the first-in, first-out (FIFO) or the average-cost method of inventory costing, inventory profit can be estimated by taking the difference between the historical cost and the replacement cost of inventory at the time it is sold. Companies using the last-in, first-out (LIFO) method of inventory costing charge the most recent costs incurred to cost of goods sold, thereby in most cases reducing the amount and significance of inventory profits. GSM uses LIFO and reported no inventory profit for 1978 and 1977.

The depreciation expense (at current replacement cost) for productive capacity expected to be replaced is shown in Exhibit 5. At the end of 1978, GSM management estimated that of its gross fixed assets of $44 million, it expected that $33 million would be replaced.

The 1978 depreciation expense on the facilities expected to be replaced amounted to $5.775 million on a historical-cost basis. (For ease of exposition, I have assumed that the guideline lives used to calculate depreciation expense, which the Internal Revenue Service prescribes, closely approximate the assets' economic life as estimated by GSM management. In some industries, the estimated economic life is considerably greater than guideline life. When this is the case, the historical-cost depreciation should be calculated on the basis of estimated economic lives, rather than guideline lives, before multiplying it by the ratio of replacement cost to historical cost.)

GSM estimated its ratio of replacement cost (with current technology) to historical cost to be 2.0, thus yielding a replacement-cost depreciation expense of $11.55 million, or a provision of $5.775 million above historical-cost depreciation. This is a reasonable figure for a capital-intensive company. In an analysis of 10-K replacement-cost numbers of 175 companies in 21 industries, Arthur Young & Co. reported an average ratio of 1.68. The steel industry had a ratio of 2.21, metal manufacturing 1.98, petroleum refining 2.08, utilities 2.16, heavy equipment 1.59, soaps and cosmetics 1.46, beverages 1.64, airlines 1.54, and retailers 1.33.[3]

Any such ratio estimate necessarily is subjective, but it should be based on the least expensive approach consistent with minimum reliability standards.[4] In many companies, this may call for a combination of methods including indexing, appraisals, and direct pricing.

Exhibit 5. Depreciation Expense (at current replacement cost) for Productive Capacity Expected to be Replaced

	1978	1977
Facilities expected to be replaced	**$33,000,000**	$30,000,000
Facilities not expected to be replaced	**11,000,000**	10,000,000
Property, plant, and equipment—gross	**$44,000,000**	$40,000,000
Depreciation expense on facilities expected to be replaced	**$ 5,775,000**	$ 5,250,000
Multiplied by ratio of replacement cost to historical cost	**× 2.0**	× 2.0
Equals depreciation expense for productive capacity expected to be replaced	**$11,550,000**	$10,500,000

In developing a distributable funds statement, a company must make provision not only for cost increases in productive capacity it expects to replace, but also for that part of its capacity it will not replace, as explained earlier. This is necessary because during inflationary periods the purchasing power of a company's investment dollar is eroding, albeit at different rates that depend on the industrial sectors in which management contemplates redeploying its investment. If management is uncertain about where to deploy its investment in productive capacity, a "total economy" index such as the GNP price deflator can serve as the price change index. If it has more concrete investment plans, of course, a more specific index would be appropriate.

GSM management estimates that 25% of its 1978 gross fixed assets, or $11 million, will not be replaced. The 1978 depreciation expense on these facilities was $1.925 million. GSM plans to remain in the manufacturing sector and has chosen an industrial plant and equipment price change index.

The calculation of depreciation expense for productive capacity not expected to be replaced appears in Exhibit 6. Of the $11 million of facilities not expected to be replaced as of the end of 1978, assume that $6 million was purchased in 1955, when the industrial plant and equipment index was 100, and $5 million was acquired in 1960, when the index was 120. Adjustment of these historical costs to the 1978 index level yields a total index-adjusted cost of $29 million. This amount divided by the total acquisition cost ($11 million) of retained facilities establishes GSM's price change index to be 2.7.

This index is then applied to the historical depreciation expense of these facilities to obtain the depreciation expense at current price levels of $5,197,500. The additional $3,272,500 of depreciation is recorded in the state-

Exhibit 6. Depreciation Expense (at current price levels) for Productive Capacity Not Expected to Be Replaced

1. Acquisition Date	2. Industrial Plant and Equipment Index	3. Acquisition Cost	4. Ratio of 1978 to Year-of-Acquisition Index	5. Index-Adjusted Cost (3 × 4)
1955	100	$ 6,000,000	290/100	$17,400,000
1960	120	5,000,000	290/120	12,100,000
1978	290			
		$11,000,000		$29,500,000

$$\text{Price change index} = \frac{\text{Index-adjusted cost}}{\text{Acquisition cost}} = \frac{\$29{,}500{,}000}{\$11{,}000{,}000} = 2.7$$

	1978	1977
Depreciation expense on facilities not expected to be replaced	**$1,925,000**	$1,750,000
Multiplied by price change index for industrial plant and equipment	**× 2.7**	× 2.6
Equals depreciation expense (at current price levels) for productive capacity not expected to be replaced	**$5,197,500**	$4,550,000

ment of distributable funds as part of the funds required for increases in costs of productive capacity.

As a business expands or otherwise changes its operations, adequate working capital is no less an integral part of its capacity than is physical capacity. So any increases in net working capital requirements must be deducted in arriving at the distributable funds figure.

To demonstrate this point, assume that a company is at its target capital structure and that there is no change in debt capacity during the period; it is operating in a noninflationary environment, it plans to replace all of its existing productive capacity, and it distributes all its earnings as dividends. If the company's required working capital level has increased during the past year, it does not have the resources to sustain operations at current levels because it has paid out its entire earnings as dividends. To raise working capital to the level required by the most recent period's operations, the company is compelled to either increase its debt beyond the stipulated target level, thereby taking on more financial risk, or issue additional stock.

Working capital requirements may rise from one period to the next for a number of reasons, including higher sales volume, a change in the product mix, or changes in credit and inventory policies. Care is necessary in trying to measure changes in net working capital requirements; the actual change in net working capital from last year to this year ($3 million at GSM) may not yield a good measure of the rise or decline in the funds required.

There are two reasons for this. First, the end-of-the-year balance sheet figures may not reflect the average or normal needs of the business during the year. Second, both the accounts receivable and inventory balance sheet amounts may overstate the magnitude of the funds committed by the business. To estimate the additional funds required, two items should be considered: (1) an increased inventory investment in variable cost terms; and (2) a receivable investment in terms of the variable cost of the product delivered to generate the receivable rather than the absolute dollar amount of the receivable.

In each case, the amount reflects what the company must disburse in cash to carry these items.

For purposes of simplification let us assume that GSM's year-end working capital levels are normal for the year. Then I calculate the $2.3 million required for the 1978 increase in net working capital. To calculate the funds required for the increase in inventory level, multiply the increase in units of inventory by the current variable manufacturing cost. The 1978 variable cost of goods sold, $79.95 million (see Exhibit 1), is derived in Exhibit 7. During 1978 there was an increase of 1,400,000 units of inventory with a variable manufacturing cost of $1.50 per unit, yielding required funds of $2,100,000.

The amount of funds required for the increase in accounts receivable is calculated as:

Exhibit 7. Calculation of Variable Cost of Goods Sold in 1978

Beginning inventory, LIFO (variable manufacturing component)—22 million units @ $1.00	$ 22,000,000
Variable manufacturing costs of goods produced—54.7 million @ $1.50	82,050,000
Total goods available—76.7 million units	$104,050,000
Less ending inventory, LIFO (variable manufacturing component)—22 million units @ $1.00 = $22,000,000 + 1.4 million units @ $1.50 = $2,100,000	24,100,000
Variable cost of goods sold—53.3 million units @ $1.50	$ 79,950,000

$$\text{Increase in accounts receivable} \times \frac{\text{Variable cost of goods sold}}{\text{Sales}}$$

$$= \$1{,}500{,}000 \times \frac{\$\ 79{,}950{,}000}{\$110{,}000{,}000} = \$1{,}100{,}000$$

The $2,300,000 increase in funds required in net working capital can then be summarized as:

Cash	$ 100,000
Accounts receivable	1,100,000
Inventories	2,100,000
Current liabilities	(1,000,000)
	$2,300,000

In GSM's case, each dollar of higher sales requires approximately 23 cents of funds for net working capital, or $2.3 million in 1978 for the $10 million sales increase over 1977.

Considering Debt Capacity

Most companies in part finance their operations with debt capital, and this, of course, must be taken into account in determining the distributable funds. Distributable funds become available only after business capacity has been maintained. The maintenance of business capacity, in turn, includes establishing a target level of financial risk, that is, the risk associated with financing the company's operations.

Estimating a company's debt capacity at some target level of financial risk involves an element of subjectivity. Debt capacity is not only related to debt-equity ratios, but may well be conditioned by interest coverage, cash flow to total debt ratios, strength of collateral, industry outlook, company operating characteristics, and company management. Nonetheless, financial executives should be able to estimate within a reasonable range how much more debt the company can incur without jeopardizing either its borrowing rate or its bond rating.

It is important to recognize that the funds available via increased debt capacity represent the change in that capacity during the fiscal period while the company kept the target level of financial risk constant. This means that the year-to-year change in the actual level of long-term debt is a good measure of funds available only if the company is operating at its target debt level at the end of each year.

Based on debt-equity ratios, cash flow, and value of collateral considerations, as well as discussions with the principal bond-rating services, GSM figured that the funds available via increased debt capacity were $2.5 million and $1.8 million for 1978 and 1977, respectively. The company increased its long-term debt in 1978 to $1.7 million; thus of the $2.5 million increase in funds available, \$1.7 million had been used by the end of 1978 and \$800,000 remained available.

Even after taking into account the increase in debt capacity, GSM reported deficits for distributable funds—\$1.85 million in 1977 and \$2,247,500 in 1978. Clearly the company was paying dividends at the risk of liquidating its business capacity. In 1978 GSM paid out \$3.3 million from a \$2,247,500 deficit in distributable funds, thus causing a shortfall of \$5,547,500 in funds available for expansion of business capacity.

The GSM example clearly demonstrates that neither earnings growth nor additions to fixed assets give compelling evidence that a company has maintained its business capacity during the year. GSM's higher costs of productive capacity, coupled with an increase in its working capital requirements, have led it into partial liquidation of its business capacity.

Interdependent Elements

Why should management concern itself with and monitor distributable funds? The distributable funds approach provides a sound approximation of the total dollar amount made available during the period for dividends and expansion of business capacity. Business capacity, in turn, provides the basis for future earning power and hence returns to stockholders. Although periodic fluctuations in business capacity can be expected, of course, large or frequent distributable funds deficits could signal an erosion of business capacity and threaten the company's earning power—if not its very survival.

The distributable funds analysis presented here is no substitute for a well-conceived strategic plan; it serves as a supplement and a check for economic reasonableness on the company's various product-market strategies and its strategic plan. Moreover, it provides a check on the internal consistency of the company's operating, investment, financing, and dividend plans.

The distributable funds (DF) measurement is defined as:

$$DF = P(S + \triangle S) - (C - 1)(N)(S + \triangle S) - W\triangle S + P(S + \triangle S)(1 - D)L$$

where P = net income after taxes as a percent of sales
S = total sales of last period
$\triangle S$ = increase in this period's sales over last period
W = rate of additional net working capital required for each additional dollar of sales
C = inflation-adjusted productive capacity to historical-cost productive capacity
N = rate of historical-cost depreciation per dollar of sales
D = target dividend payout percentage
L = target debt-to-equity percentage

The four terms on the right-hand side of the equation are, respectively, net income after taxes, the cost increase provision for productive capacity, the change in working capital required, and the change in debt capacity. (Inventory profits may be incorporated in the working capital coefficient, W, and C represents the weighted average or composite inflation coefficient for all productive capacity, whether or not it is to be replaced.)

The company's distributable funds therefore depend on return on sales, sales growth, net working capital requirements, the rate of cost increases in productive capacity, the historical-cost depreciation per dollar of sales, the target dividend payout percentage, and the target debt-equity ratio. Because the rate of cost increase in productive capacity and depreciation per dollar of sales presumably are elements over which management can exercise little control, the company's distributable funds depend on how management decisions and policies affect the remaining five variables.

The four graphs in Exhibit 8 show how these variables are interdependent. In each graph, sales growth, aftertax profit to sales, and the inflation coefficient are treated as variables. The historical-cost depreciation per dollar of sales (N) in all cases is 5%. Each graph shows the range of the composite inflation coefficient (C) from 1.0 to 2.4.

These graphs enable the managers to assess (1) the likelihood, in light of the operating, investment, financing, and dividend assumptions imbedded in the corporate plan, that the company will generate distributable funds; and (2) the sensitivity of distributable funds to changes in operating, investment, financing, and dividend policies.

Consider Graph A. Suppose the company's plans call for a 50% dividend payout rate (D) and a debt-equity ratio (L) of .5. Working capital requirements are projected at 30 cents per dollar of increased sales (W), and the composite inflation coefficient (C) is projected to continue at about 2.2, the level of the recent past.

At a projected aftertax return on sales of 6% and a sales growth rate of 10%, the company's plan has, no doubt unknowingly, set the forces in place for generating distributable funds deficits. Graph A shows that for an assumed inflation coefficient of 2.2 and a 6% return on sales, the maximum affordable sales growth to achieve a distributable funds breakeven point is 5%. As another way of looking at it, if the company wants to grow at 10%, to avoid distributable funds deficits it must increase its return on sales to 7%. This kind of graph enables management to assess the trade-offs between sales growth and profitability on sales.

In addition, the sensitivity of distributable funds to cost increases in productive capacity can be easily tested. For example, if the inflation coefficient were reduced from 2.2 to 1.8, at a 6% return on sales the company could grow at a rate of 13% instead of 5%.

Graph B shows the sensitivity of a distributable funds breakeven to changes in working capital requirements. This graph is identical to Graph A except that working capital requirements are projected at only 20 cents

Exhibit 8. Interaction of Variables in Measuring Distributable Funds

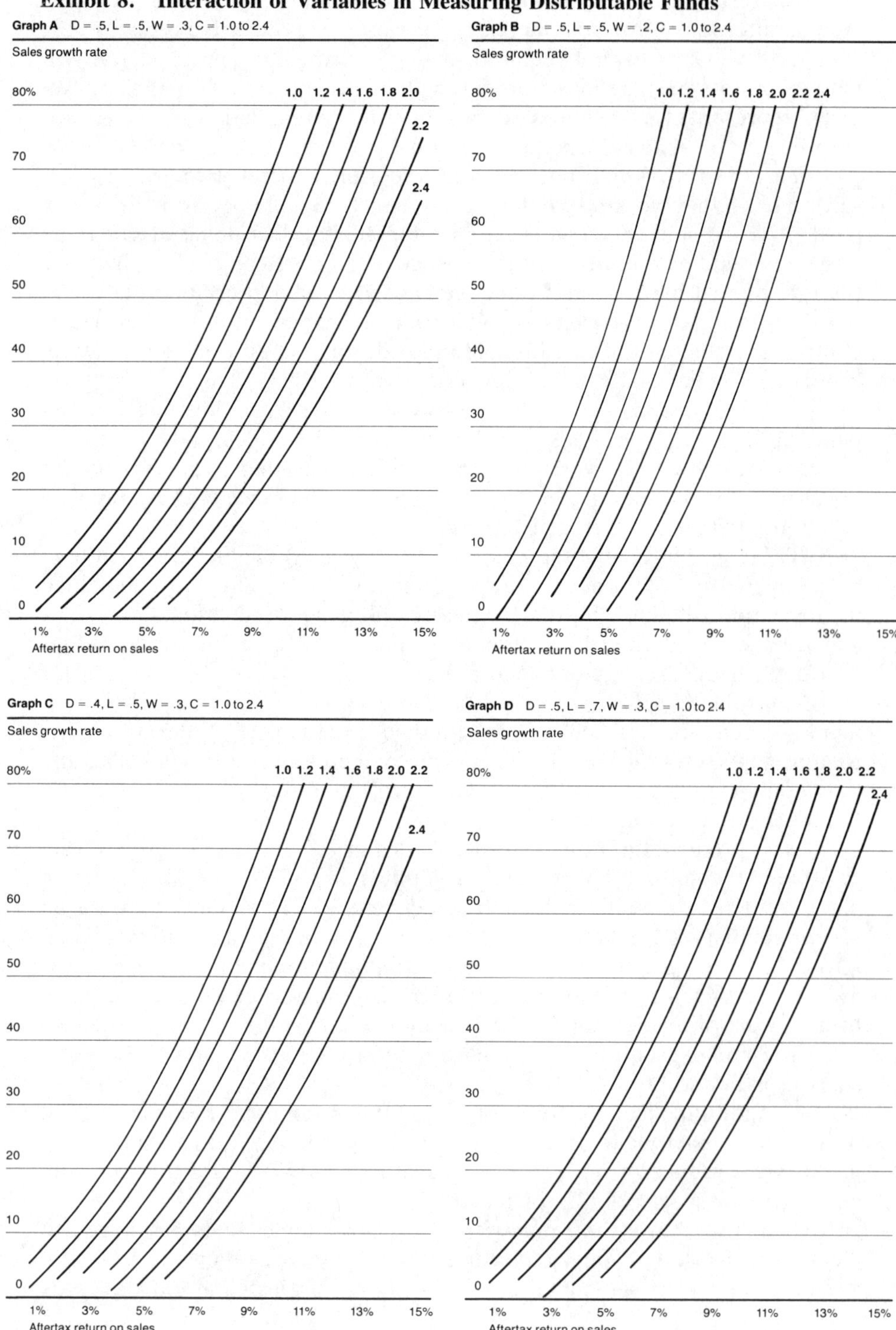

per dollar of added sales. The benefit of effective working capital management is quite apparent. By reducing the needed working capital requirements 10 cents per dollar of sales, the company boosts affordable sales growth rate from a modest 5% to more than 8%.

Graph C departs from the base case in only one respect—the dividend payout ratio is reduced from .5 to .4. Graph D increases the debt-equity ratio from .5 to .7. Managers may wish to test for themselves the sensitivity of the distributable funds breakeven point to these changes in dividend and financing policies.

Better Financial Control

It is essential that corporate management, as well as investors and the government, understand the effects of inflation on the capital invested in a business and on its earning power. Managers and investors need this information in their respective resource allocation roles; government needs the information to assure itself that its taxation policies do not tax at levels that impair capital formation and discourage investment. The task of developing useful and reliable measurements of the effects of inflation is extraordinarily complex, but it must be accomplished if we are to be well-informed decision makers.

The distributable funds approach I have presented enables management to assess the effects of its operating, investment, financing, and dividend decisions on corporate performance. It enables management to see which business units provide distributable funds and which use them. It is also a particularly useful statement for the outside director who wants to know whether the company is really growing. The concept of distributable funds is compatible with the strategic planning approach of most companies. Moreover, the cost of developing distributable funds statements is minimal for companies already subject to the SEC's replacement-cost disclosure rules.

For all of these reasons the distributable funds approach should prove to be a useful addition to more effective financial control systems.

Notes

1. Harold M. Williams, "Inflation, Corporate Financial Reporting and Economic Reality," New York, December 13, 1977.

2. *An Analysis of Issues Related to Conceptual Framework for Financial Accounting and Reporting: Elements of Financial Statements and Their Measurement,* FASB Discussion Memorandum, December 2, 1976 (Stamford, Conn., Financial Accounting Standards Board), p. 134.

3. "Inflation Accounting Is Here to Stay," *Business Week*, December 26, 1977, p. 109.

4. For a discussion of whether companies should add a "catch-up" depreciation charge to replace underdepreciated assets during inflation, see Richard F. Vancil and Roman L. Weil, "Current Replacement Cost Accounting, Depreciable Assets, and Distributable Income," *Financial Analysts Journal*, July-August 1976, p. 39.

New Framework for Corporate Debt Policy

GORDON DONALDSON

Gordon Donaldson's analysis of how many companies haphazardly established their debt capacity, and his careful explanation of what he considered a better way, strikes a chord among corporate administrative and financial officers. The article is a valuable guide, a stimulus to rational thought about building a debt policy from the ground up.

- ☐ Why are many common rules of thumb for evaluating a company's debt capacity misleading and even dangerous?
- ☐ Why is outside experience and advice of limited value as a guide to top management's thinking about debt capacity?
- ☐ What approach will enable management to make an independent and realistic appraisal of risk on the basis of data with which it is already familiar and in terms of judgments to which it has long been accustomed?

The problem of deciding whether it is wise and proper for a business corporation to finance long-term capital needs through debt, and, if so, how far it is safe to go, is one that most boards of directors have wrestled with at one time or another. For many companies the debt-capacity decision is of critical importance because of its potential impact on margins of profitability and on solvency. For *all* companies, however large and financially sound they may be, the decision is one to be approached with great care. Yet, in spite of its importance, the subject of corporate debt policy has received surprisingly little attention in the literature of business management in recent years. One might infer from this either that business has already developed a reliable means of resolving the question or that progress toward a more adequate solution has been slow.

In my opinion, the latter inference is closer to the truth. The debt-equity choice is still a relatively crude art as practiced by a great many corporate borrowers. It follows that there is a real opportunity for useful refinement in the decision-making process. However, there is little evidence, at present, of serious dissatisfaction with conventional decision rules on the part of those responsible for making this decision. Over the past three years I have been engaged in sampling executive opinions on debt policy, and I have found little indication of the same kind of ferment as is going on with regard to capital-budgeting decisions.

The primary purpose of this article, therefore, is to stimulate dissatisfaction with present-day conventions regarding debt capacity and to suggest the direction in which the opportunity for improvement lies. I intend to show that the widely used rules of thumb that evaluate debt capacity in terms of some percentage of balance sheet values or in terms of income statement ratios can be seriously misleading and even dangerous to corporate solvency. I also intend to develop the argument that debt policy in general and debt capacity in particular cannot be prescribed for the individual company by outsiders or by generalized standards; rather, they can and should be determined by management in terms of individual corporate circumstances and objectives and on the basis of the observed behavior of patterns of cash flows.

The question of corporate debt capacity may be looked at from several points of view—for example, the management of the business concerned, its shareholders or potential shareholders, and, of course, the lender of the debt capital. Because each of these groups may, quite properly, have a different concept of the wise and proper limit on debt, let me clarify the point of view taken in this article. I intend to discuss the subject from the standpoint of the management of the borrowing corporation, assuming that the board of directors that will make the final decision has the customary mandate from the stockholders to act on all matters concerning the safety and profitability of their investment.

For the reader who ordinarily looks at this problem as a lender, potential stockholder, or investment adviser, the analysis described in this article may appear at first sight to have limited application. It is hoped, however, that the underlying concepts will be recognized as valid regardless of how one looks at the problem, and they may suggest directions for improvement in the external as well as the internal analysis of the risk of debt.

Nature of the Risks

In order to set a background for discussing possible improvements, I will first describe briefly certain aspects of conventional practice concerning present-day decision rules on long-term debt. These observations were recorded as a part of a research study which sampled practice and opinion in a group of relatively large and mature manufacturing corporations. The nature of this sample must be kept in mind when interpreting the practices described.

Hazards of Too Much Debt

The nature of the incentive to borrow as an alternative to financing through a new issue of stock is common knowledge. Debt capital in the amounts normally approved by established financial institutions is a comparatively cheap source of funds. Whether it is considered the cheapest source depends on whether retained earnings are regarded as "cost free" or not. In any case, for most companies it is easy to demonstrate that, assuming normal profitability, the combination of moderate interest rates and high levels of corporate income tax enables debt capital to produce significantly better earnings per share than would a comparable amount of capital provided by an issue of either common or preferred stock. In fact, the advantage is so obvious that few companies bother to make the calculation when considering these alternatives.

Under these circumstances it is apparent that there must be a powerful deterrent that keeps businesses from using this source to the limits of availability. The primary deterrent is, of course, the risks that are inevitably associated with long-term debt servicing. Although it is something of an oversimplification to say that the debt decision is a balancing of higher prospective income to the shareholders against greater chance of loss, it is certainly true that this is the heart of the problem.

When the word *risk* is applied to debt, it may refer to a variety of potential penalties; the precise meaning is not always clear when this subject is discussed. To most people, however, risk—so far as debt is concerned—is the chance of running out of cash. This risk is inevitably increased by a legal contract requiring the business to pay fixed sums of cash at predetermined dates in the future regardless of the financial condition at that time. There are, of course, a great many needs for cash—dividends, capital expenditures, research projects, and so on—with respect to which cash balances may prove inadequate at some future point.

Too Little Cash

The ultimate hazard of running out of cash, however, and the one that lurks in the background of every debt decision, is the situation where cash is so reduced that legal contracts are defaulted, bankruptcy occurs, and normal operations cease. Since no private enterprise has a guaranteed cash inflow, there must always be *some* risk, however remote, that this event could occur. Consequently, any addition to mandatory cash outflows resulting from new debt or any other act or event must increase that risk. I have chosen to use the term *cash inadequacy* to refer to a whole family of problems involving the inability to make cash payments for any purpose important to the long-term financial health of the business; *cash insolvency* is the extreme case of cash inadequacy. It should be emphasized that although debt necessarily increases the chances of cash inadequacy, this risk exists whether the company has any debt or not, so that the debt-equity choice is not between some risk and no risk, but between more and less.

Conventional Approaches

Observation of present-day business practice suggests that businesspeople commonly draw their concepts of debt capacity from one or more of several sources. Thus, they sometimes—

1. *Seek the counsel of institutional lenders or financial intermediaries (such as investment bankers).* Most corporate borrowers negotiate long-term debt contracts at infrequent intervals, whereas the lender and the investment banker are constantly involved in loan decisions and so, presumably, have a great deal more experience and better judgment. Further, it is apparent that unless the lender is satisfied on the question of risk, there will be no loan. Finally, banks and insurance companies have a well-established reputation for being conservative, and conservative borrowers will take comfort from the fact that if the lender errs, it will likely be on the safe side.
2. *See what comparable companies are doing in this area of financial management.* Every business has an idea of those other companies in or out of the industry that are most like themselves so far as factors affecting risk are concerned. Since this is an aspect of corporate policy which is public information, it is natural that the debt-equity ratios of competitors will be carefully considered, and, lacking more objective guides, there will be a tendency to follow the mode and reject the extremes. This approach has an added practical appeal; group norms are important in the capital market's appraisal of a company's financial strength. If a company is out of line, it may be penalized—even though the deviation from the average may be perfectly appropriate for this company.
3. *Follow the practices of the past.* There is a very natural tendency to respect the corporation's financial traditions, and this is often apparent with regard to debt policy. Many businesses take considerable pride in "a clean balance sheet," an *Aa* rating, or a history of borrowing at the prime rate. It would border on sacrilege to propose a departure that would jeopardize these cherished symbols of financial achievement and respectability! The fact that these standards have apparently preserved corporate solvency in the past is a powerful argument for continuing them, particularly if the implications of a change cannot be precisely defined.
4. *Refer to that very elusive authority called "general practice," "industry practice," "common knowledge," or, less respectfully, "financial folklore."* Remarkable as it seems in view of the great diversity among companies classified as industrials, there is widespread acceptance of the belief that an appropriate limit to the long-term borrowing of industrial com-

panies is 30% of capitalization (or, alternatively, one-third). The origin of, or rationale for, this particular decision rule has been obscured by the passage of time, but there is no doubt that it has become a widely honored rule of thumb in the decisions of both borrowers and lenders.

Fallacy of Double Standard

Without denying the practical significance of some of the considerations that have led businesspeople to follow these guides in formulating debt policy, it must be recognized that there are serious limitations inherent in using them (separately or as a group) as the *only* guides to appropriate debt capacity.

First, consider the practice of accepting advice from the lender. As the lender views the individual loan contract, it is one of a large number of investments that make up a constantly changing portfolio. When negotiated it is only one of a stream of loan proposals that must be acted on promptly and appraised in terms of the limited information to which generalized standards are applied. The nature of the risk to the lender is necessarily influenced by the fact that this loan is only a small fraction of the total sum invested and that intelligent diversification goes a long way to softening the impact of individual default. Further, even when default occurs, all may not be lost; in time the loan may be "worked out" through reorganization or liquidation.

All this is small comfort to the borrower. The individual loan that goes sour—if it happens to be *one's* loan—is a catastrophe. There are few businesspeople who can take a lighthearted attitude toward the prospect of default on a legal contract with the associated threat of bankruptcy. To most, this is viewed as the end of the road. Also, it is important to recognize that although lenders need only be concerned about servicing their own (high priority) claims, the borrowers must also consider the needs that go unsatisfied during the period prior to the time of actual default when debt servicing drains off precious cash reserves.

This is not to imply that the lender is insensitive to individual losses and their effect on the business concerned; but it does mean that risk to the lender is not the same thing as risk to the borrower, and, consequently, the standards of one are not necessarily appropriate for the other. The lender's standards can at times be too liberal—as well as too conservative—from the borrower's point of view.

Some will argue that, as a practical matter, the borrower must accept the debt-capacity standards of the lender, else there will be no contract. However, this implies that there is no bargaining over the upper limit of the amount that will be supplied, no differences among lenders, and/or no shopping around by borrowers. Although all institutional lenders do have absolute limits on the risks they will take (even at a premium interest rate), there is often some room for negotiation if the borrower is so disposed. Under some circumstances there may be valid reasons for probing the upper limits of the lender's willingness to lend.

Lessons of Experience

The second source of guidance mentioned is the observed practices of comparable businesses. This, too, has its obvious limitations. Even assuming strict comparability—which is hard to establish—there is no proof that the companies concerned have arrived at their current debt proportions in a deliberate and rational manner. In view of the wide variations in debt policy within any industry group, there can be little real meaning in an industry average. And what happens if every member of the group looks to the other for guidance? The most that can be said for this approach to debt policy is that the company concerned can avoid the appearance of being atypical in the investment market so far as its capital structure is concerned. But, as in most areas of business, there is a *range* of acceptable behavior, and the skill of management comes in identifying and taking advantage of the limits to which it can go without raising too many eyebrows.

Even a company's own direct experience with debt financing has its limitations as a guide to debt capacity. At best, the evidence that a particular debt policy has not been a cause of financial embarrassment in the past may only prove that the policy was on the conservative side. However, if assurance of adequate conservatism is the primary goal, the only really satisfactory policy is a no-debt policy.

For companies with some debt the experience of past periods of business recession is only partial evidence of the protection a particular policy affords. In most industries, the period of the past 20 years has produced a maximum of four or five periods of decline in sales and earnings. This limited recession experience with the behavior of cash flows—the critical consideration where debt servicing is involved—can be misleading because cash flows are affected by a variety of factors and the actual experience in any single recession is a somewhat unique combination of events that may not recur in the future. Thus the so-called test of experience cannot be taken at face value.

Inescapable Responsibility

In summing up a criticism of the sources from which management commonly derives its debt-capacity standard, there are two aspects that must be emphasized. Both of these relate to the practice of relying on the judgment of others in a situation where management alone is best able to appraise the full implications of the problem. The points I have in mind are as follows:

1. In assessing the risks of running out of cash because of excessive fixed cash obligations, the special circumstances of the individual firm are the primary data that the analyst has to work with. Management has obvious advantages over outsiders in using these data because it has free and full access to them, the time and incentive to examine them thoroughly, and a personal stake in making sensible judgments about what it observes. Even the judgments of predecessors in office are judgments made on information

that is inadequate when compared to what management now has in its possession—if only because the predecessor's information is now 10 to 20 years old. (Subsequently, we will consider how management may approach an independent appraisal of risk for the individual business.)

2. The measurement of risk is only one dimension of the debt-capacity decision. In a free enterprise society, the assumption of risk is a voluntary activity, and no one can properly define the level of risk that another should be willing to bear. The decision to limit debt to 10%, 30%, or any other percentage of the capital structure reflects (or should reflect) both the magnitude of the risk involved in servicing that amount of debt *and* the willingness of those who bear this risk—the owners or their duly authorized representatives—to accept the hazards involved.

In the last analysis, this is a subjective decision that management alone can make. Indeed, it may be said that a corporation has defined its debt policy long before a particular financing decision comes to a vote; it has done this in its choice of the people who are to make the decision. The ensuing decisions involving financial risk will reflect their basic attitudes—whether they see a situation as an opportunity to be exploited or a threat to be minimized.

A most interesting and fundamental question comes up here—one that underlies the whole relationship between management and the shareholder; namely, does management determine the attitude toward risk bearing that the stockholders must then adopt, or vice versa? This is part of the broader question of whether management should choose those financial policies that it prefers and attract a like-minded stockholder group (taking the "if they don't like it, they can sell out" approach) or by some means or other determine the attitudes and objectives of its present stockholder group and attempt to translate these into the appropriate action.

I do not propose to pass judgment on this difficult problem in the context of this article. The fact is, by taking one approach or the other—or some blend—management *does* make these decisions. With respect to risk bearing, however, one point is clear: Responsible management should not be dealing with the problem in terms of purely personal risk preferences. I suspect that many top executives have not given this aspect the attention it deserves.

Reasons for Current Practice

Having considered the case for a debt policy that is internally rather than externally generated, we may well ask why so many companies, in deciding how far to go in using OPM (other people's money), lean so heavily on OPA (other people's advice). The answer appears to be threefold:

1 A misunderstanding of the nature of the problem and, in particular, a failure to separate the subjective from the objective elements.

2 The inherent complexity of the objective side—the measurement of risk.
3 The serious inadequacy of conventional debt-capacity decision rules as a framework for independent appraisal.

It is obvious that if a business does not have a useful way of assessing the general magnitude of the risks of too much debt in terms of its individual company and industry circumstances, then it will do one of two things. Either it will fall back on generalized (external) concepts of risk for "comparable" companies, or it will make the decision on purely subjective grounds—on how the management "feels" about debt.

Thus, in practice, an internally generated debt-capacity decision is often based almost entirely on the management's general attitude toward this kind of problem without regard for how much risk is actually involved and what the potential rewards and penalties from risk bearing happen to be in the specific situation. The most obvious examples are to be found in companies at the extremes of debt policy that follow such rules as "no debt under any circumstances" or "borrow the maximum available." (We must be careful, however, not to assume that if a company has one or another of these policies, it is acting irrationally or emotionally.)

One of the subjects about which we know very little at present is how individual and group attitudes toward risk bearing are formed in practice. It is apparent, however, that there are important differences in this respect among members of any given management team and even for an individual executive with regard to different dimensions of risk within the business. The risk of excessive debt often appears to have a special significance; a person who is a "plunger" on sales policy or research might also be an arch-conservative with regard to debt. The risk of default on debt is more directly associated with financial ruin, regardless of the fundamental cause of failure, simply because it is generally the last act in a chain of events that follows from a deteriorating cash position.

There are other bits of evidence that are possible explanations for a Jekyll-and-Hyde behavior on risk bearing in business:

- Debt policy is always decided at the very top of the executive structure, whereas other policies on sales or production involving other dimensions of risk are shaped to some degree at all executive levels. The seniority of the typical board of directors doubtless has some bearing on the comparative conservatism of financial policy, including debt policy.
- There is also some truth in the generalization that financial officers tend to be more conservative than other executives at the same level in other phases of the business, and to the extent that they may tend to prefer to minimize risk per se, regardless of the potential rewards from risk bearing.

What Is a Sensible Approach?

The foregoing is, however, only speculation in an area where real research is necessary. The point of importance here is that, whatever the reason may be, it is illogical to base an internal decision on debt policy on attitudes toward risk *alone*, just as it is illogical to believe that corporate debt policy can be properly formulated without taking these individual attitudes into account.

For the purposes of a sensible approach to corporate debt policy we need not expect management to have a logical explanation for its feelings toward debt, even though this might be theoretically desirable. It is sufficient that managers know how they feel and are able to react to specific risk alternatives. The problem has been that in many cases they have not known in any objective sense what it was that they were reacting to; they have not had a meaningful measure of the specific risk of running out of cash (with or without any given amount of long-term debt).

It is therefore in the formulation of an approach to the measurement of risk in the individual corporation that the hope for an independent appraisal of debt capacity lies.

Inadequacy of Current Rules

Unfortunately, the conventional form for expressing debt-capacity rules is of little or no help in providing the kind of formulation I am urging. Debt capacity is most commonly expressed in terms of the balance sheet relationship between long-term debt and the total of all long-term sources, viz., as some percent of capitalization. A variation of this ratio is often found in debt contracts that limit new long-term borrowing to some percentage of net tangible assets.

The alternative form in which to express the limits of long-term borrowing is in terms of income statement data. This is the *earnings coverage* ratio—the ratio of net income available for debt servicing to the total amount of annual interest plus sinking fund charges. Under such a rule, no new long-term debt would be contemplated unless the net income available for debt servicing is equal to or in excess of some multiple of the debt servicing charges—say, three to one—so that the company can survive a period of decline in sales and earnings and still have enough earnings to cover the fixed charges of debt. As we will see shortly, this ratio is more meaningful for internal formation of policy but also has its limitations.

Now, let us go on to examine each type of expression more closely.

Capitalization Standard

Consider a company that wishes to formulate its own debt standard as a percent of capitalization. It is apparent that in order to do so the standard must be expressed in terms of data that can be related to the magnitude of the risk in such a way that changes in the ratio can be translated into changes in the risk of cash inadequacy, and vice versa. But how many executives concerned with this problem today have any real idea of how much the risk of cash inadequacy is increased when the long-term debt of their company is increased from 10% to 20% or from 20% to 30% of capitalization? Not very many, if my sample of management information in this area has any validity. This is not surprising, however, since the balance sheet data on which the standard is based provide little direct evidence on the question of cash adequacy and may, in fact, be highly unreliable and misleading.

Although we do not need to go into a full discussion here of the inadequacies of relating the principal amount of long-term debt to historical asset values as a way of looking at the chances of running out of cash, we should keep in mind the more obvious weaknesses:

1 There is a wide variation in the relation between the principal of the debt and the annual obligation for cash payments under the debt contract. In industrial companies the principal of the debt may be repaid serially over the life of the debt contract, which may vary from 10 years or less to 30 years or more. Thus the annual cash outflow associated with $10 million on the balance sheet may, for example, vary from $500,000 (interest only at 5%) to $833,000 (interest plus principal repayable over 30 years) to $1.5 million (interest plus principal repayable over 10 years).

2 As loans are repaid by partial annual payments, as is customary under industrial term loans, the principal amount declines and the percent of capitalization ratio improves, but the annual cash drain for repayment *remains the same* until maturity is reached.

3 There may be substantial changes in asset values, particularly in connection with inventory valuation and depreciation policies, and as a consequence, changes in the percent of capitalization ratio that have no bearing on the capacity to meet fixed cash drains.

4 Certain off-the-balance-sheet factors have an important bearing on cash flows that the conventional ratio takes no cognizance of. One factor of this sort that has been receiving publicity in recent years is the payments under leasing arrangements.

(Although various authorities have been urging that lease payments be given formal recognition as a liability on balance sheets and in debt-capacity calculations, there is no general agreement as to how this should be done. For one thing, there is no obvious answer as to what the capitalization rate should be in order to translate lease payments into balance sheet values. In my opinion this debate is bound to be an artificial and frustrating experience—and unnecessary for the internal analyst—since, as will be discussed later, it is much more meaningful to deal with leases, as with debt, in terms of the dollars of annual cash outflow rather than in terms of principal amounts. Thus a footnoting of the annual payments under the lease is entirely adequate.)

Earnings-Coverage Standard

The earnings-coverage standard affords, on the surface at least, a better prospect of measuring risk in the individual company in terms of the factors that bear directly on cash adequacy. By relating the total annual cash outflow under all long-term debt contracts to the net earnings available for servicing the debt, it is intended to assure that earnings will be adequate to meet charges at all times. This approach implies that the greater the prospective fluctuation in earnings, the higher is the required ratio (or the larger the "cushion" between normal earnings and debt-servicing charges).

This standard also has limitations as a basis for internal determination of debt capacity:

1. The net earnings figure found in the income statement and derived under normal accounting procedures is *not* the same thing as net cash inflow—an assumption that is implicit in the earnings-coverage standard. Even when adjustments are made for the noncash items on the income statement (depreciation charges), as is commonly done in the more sophisticated applications, this equivalence cannot safely be assumed. The time when it may be roughly true is the time when we are least concerned about the hazards of debt, that is, when sales are approximately the same from period to period. It is in times of rapid change (including recessions) that we are most concerned about debt burden, and then there *are* likely to be sharp differences between net income and net cash flow.
2. The question of what the *proper* ratio is between earnings and debt servicing is problematical. In a given case should the ratio be 2 to 1 or 20 to 1? If we exclude externally derived standards or rules of thumb and insist that a company generate its own ratio in terms of its own circumstances, how does it go about doing it? Perhaps the best that could be done would be to work backward from the data of past recessions, which would indicate the low points of net earnings, toward a ratio between this experience and some measure of "normal" earnings with the intention of assuring a one-to-one relationship between net earnings and debt servicing at all times. However, if this is the way it is to be done, the estimate of minimum net earnings would itself provide the measure of debt capacity, and it would be unnecessary to translate it into a ratio. Further, as already noted, there are hazards in a literal translation of past history as a guide for the future. And what of the case where the company has experienced net losses in the past? Does this mean that it has no long-term debt capacity? If a net loss is possible, *no* ratio between normal net earnings and debt servicing, however large, will assure the desired equality in future recessions.

The earnings-coverage standard does not appear to be widely used by industrial corporate borrowers as a basis for formulating debt policy. Where it is used, it appears either to derive from the advice of institutional lenders or investment bankers or merely to reflect the borrower's attitude toward risk bearing. Its use does not seem to indicate an attempt to measure individual risk by some objective means.

A More Useful Approach

Granted the apparent inadequacies of conventional debt-capacity decision rules for purposes of internal debt policy, is there a practical alternative? I believe there is, but it must be recognized immediately that it rests on data that are substantially more complex than what the conventional rules require, and involve a considerably larger expenditure of time and effort to obtain and interpret. However, in view of the unquestioned importance of the debt-equity decision to the future of individual businesses, and in view of the fact that, as will be shown later, the data have a usefulness that goes well beyond the debt-capacity decision, there is reason to give this alternative serious consideration.

The basic question in the appraisal of the magnitude of risk associated with long-term debt can be stated with deceptive simplicity: What are the chances of the business running out of cash in the foreseeable future? How are these chances changed by the addition of X thousands of dollars of annual interest and sinking fund payments?

First, it is necessary to specify whether our concern is with "running out of cash" in an absolute sense (cash insolvency) or merely with the risk of cash inadequacy, that is, running out of cash for certain purposes considered essential to management (e.g., a minimum dividend on common stock). We can consider both of these possibilities, but let us focus for the moment on the ultimate hazard, the one commonly associated with excessive debt—the chance of complete depletion of cash reserves resulting in default on the bond contract and bankruptcy.

There are, of course, a variety of possible circumstances under which a company might have its cash reserves drained off. However, considering the problem from the point of view of mature, normally profitable, and reasonably well-managed companies, it is fair to say that the primary concern with debt is with what might happen during a general or industry recession when sales and profits are depressed by factors beyond the immediate control of management. Thus, when experienced business executives wish to instill the proper respect for the hazards of too much debt in the minds of aggressive young people eager for leverage, they will recount harrowing tales of disaster and near-disaster in the early 1930s.

Refocusing on Problem

The data we seek are information on the behavior of cash flows during the recession periods. As internal analysis of risk must therefore concern itself not with balance sheet or income statement ratios but directly with the factors that make for changes in cash inflow and outflow. Further, because we are dealing with the common denominator of all transactions, analysis must inevitably take into account *all* major influences on cash flow behavior. In short, the problem is a companywide problem. All decisions involving cash should be included, and where cash solvency is at stake, there can be no meaningful boundaries on risk except those imposed by the corporate entity itself.

Therefore, it is somewhat artificial to think in terms of "the cash available for debt servicing," as the earnings-coverage standard does, as if it were an identifiable hoard when a number of needs equally as urgent are competing for a limited cash reserve. Consequently, the problem to which this article was originally addressed—determining the capacity to bear the incremental fixed charges of long-term debt—is in reality a much more general one: viz., the problem of *determining the capacity to bear incremental fixed cash outflows for any purpose whatever.*

Assessing Key Factors

The analysis that is proposed in this article as a way of resolving this problem can be only briefly summarized here. It includes:

1. *Identification.* At the outset, it is important to identify the primary factors that produce major changes in cash flow with particular reference to contractions in cash flow. The most significant factor will be sales volume; many of the other factors will be related in greater or lesser degree to sales. However, to cite the example of another major factor, cash expenditures for raw materials, the relationship to sales volume in a downswing is not at all an automatic one since it also depends on:

- ☐ The volume of finished-goods inventory on hand at the onset of the recession.
- ☐ The working relationship between finished goods on hand, work scheduled into production, and raw-materials ordering.
- ☐ The level of raw-materials inventory.
- ☐ The responses of management at all levels to the observed change in sales.

For most factors affecting cash flow there will be a degree of interdependence and also a range of independent variation, both of which must be identified for the purpose of the analysis.

2. *Extent of refinement desired.* Obviously, the list of factors affecting cash flow that are to be give separate consideration could be lengthy depending on the degree of refinement desired; and the longer the list, the greater the complexity of the analysis. It is therefore essential to form a judgment in advance as to how far refinement in the analysis can or should be carried in view of the objectives of the analysis. It is possible for this

cash flow analysis to range all the way from simple and relatively crude approximations to the other extreme of involved mathematical and statistical formulas and even to the programming of recession cash flows on a computer.

In their simplest form, cash flows can be considered in terms of accounting approximations derived from balance sheet and income statement data. Thus, for example, sales revenues might be adjusted for changes in accounts receivable to derive current cash inflow, and cost of goods sold could be converted into expenditures for goods actually produced by adjusting for changes in inventory levels. However, the hazard of simplification is that important changes may be obscured by combining factors that at one time may "net each other out" and at some other time may reinforce each other. For instance, changes in dollar sales are produced by changes in product mix, physical volume, and price.

Here is where internal analysts have a major advantage. Experience tells them what factors should be given separate treatment, and they have access to the data behind the financial statements so they can carry refinement as far as they wish. Ideally, the analysis should be in terms of cash and not accrual accounting information; that is, it should be in terms of cash receipts (not dollar sales) and cash expenditures for raw materials received (not an accounting allocation for raw materials according to the number of units sold).

3. *Analysis of behavior*. Given a list of all major factors affecting cash flow, the next step is to observe their *individual* behavior over time and in particular during recessions. The objection raised earlier to using historical evidence as a guide to debt capacity was that, as usually employed, it is an observation of the *net* effect of change in all these factors on particular occasions—an effect which can be seriously misleading. But if management takes the individual behavior of these factors into account, the problem is minimized to a point where it can be disregarded.

Past experience in a company with an established position in its industry commonly leads its management to the sensible conclusion that, although it is theoretically possible for the physical volume of sales, for example, to contract to zero in a recession period, in practice there are reasons why this is highly unlikely to occur. These reasons relate to fundamental and enduring forces in the economy, the industry, the competitive position of the company, consumer buying habits, and so on. Thus past experience will suggest a range of recession behavior which describes the outside limits of what recession can be expected to do in the future.

These limits I wish to refer to as the *maximum favorable limit* and the *maximum adverse limit* (referring to the effect on cash flows and the cash position). By combining the evidence contained in historical records and the judgment of management directly involved in the making of this history, we can describe these limits of expected behavior for all factors affecting cash flow. It will be part of our analysis to do so, taking careful account of interdependent variation for reasons given earlier.

4. *Expected range of recession behavior.* On the basis of such informed observation it may be concluded, for example, that the recession contraction in physical volume of sales is not expected to be less than 5% nor more than 25% of the sales of the period immediately preceding the recession. These are the maximum favorable and maximum adverse limits of sales for the company in question. It may also be concluded that the recession is not expected to last less than one year nor more than three years and that no more than 40% of the contraction will be concentrated in the first year of the recession. Naturally, our interest focuses on the maximum *adverse* limit, since we are attempting to assess the chances of running out of cash. By setting such boundaries on the adverse recession behavior of a major factor influencing cash flows we are beginning to set similar boundaries on the recession behavior of the cash flows themselves.

At this point a question presents itself that has major implications for the subsequent character of the analysis: Is it possible to say anything meaningful about the behavior of sales volume or any other factor *within* the limits that have just been described?

Probability Analysis

It is possible that there may be some historical evidence in the company on the comparative chances or probabilities of occurrence of sales contractions of, say, 5 to 11%, 12 to 18%, 19 to 25% (or any other breakdown of the range), but the statistical data are likely to be sketchy. It is perhaps more likely that management might, on the basis of experience, make some judgments such as, for example, that the contraction is most likely—say, five chances out of ten—to fall in the 12 to 18% range; that the chances of its falling in the 5 to 11% range are three chances out of ten; and that the chances of falling in the 19 to 25% range are two chances out of a possible ten.

If this kind of information can be generated for all factors affecting cash flow, then it is possible to come up with a range of estimates of the cash flow in future recession periods based on all possible combinations of the several factors, and for each estimate a numerical measure of its probability of occurrence. The whole set collectively will describe all anticipated possibilities. By totaling the separate probabilities of those combinations of events exhausting the initial cash balance, we can describe in quantitative terms the overall chances of cash insolvency. Ideally we want to know that the chances of cash insolvency, as described by this process of analysis of cash flows, are, say, 1 in 20 or 1 in 50.

Problems to Surmount

However, in order to measure precisely the risk of cash insolvency, we need estimates of probability that are within the expected range of behavior and not just the limits of behavior. There are important practical problems that stand in the way of obtaining this type of information and conducting this type of analysis:

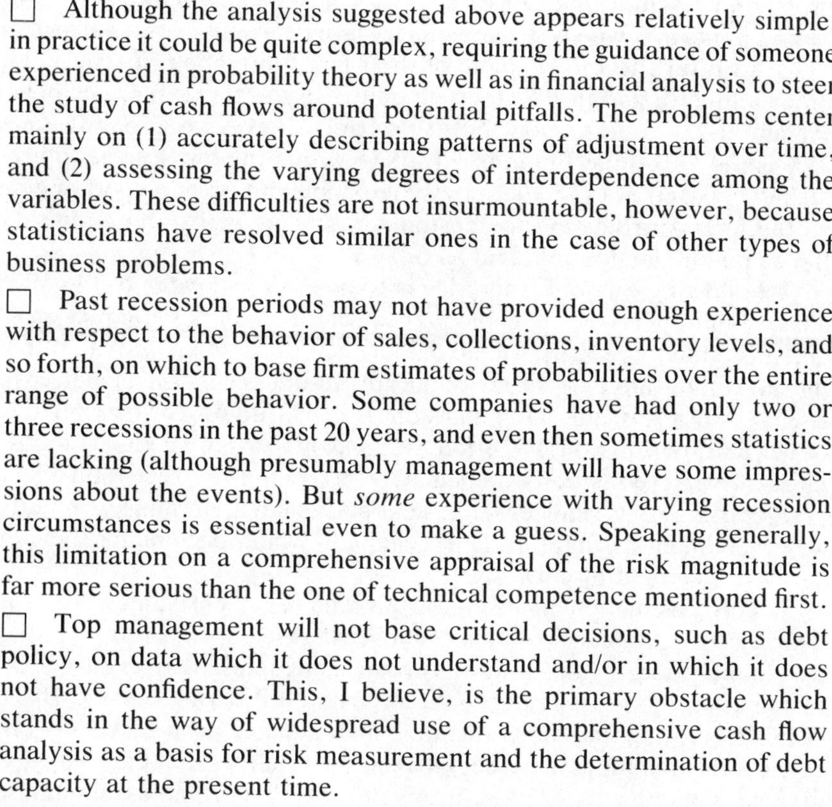

- ☐ Although the analysis suggested above appears relatively simple, in practice it could be quite complex, requiring the guidance of someone experienced in probability theory as well as in financial analysis to steer the study of cash flows around potential pitfalls. The problems center mainly on (1) accurately describing patterns of adjustment over time, and (2) assessing the varying degrees of interdependence among the variables. These difficulties are not insurmountable, however, because statisticians have resolved similar ones in the case of other types of business problems.
- ☐ Past recession periods may not have provided enough experience with respect to the behavior of sales, collections, inventory levels, and so forth, on which to base firm estimates of probabilities over the entire range of possible behavior. Some companies have had only two or three recessions in the past 20 years, and even then sometimes statistics are lacking (although presumably management will have some impressions about the events). But *some* experience with varying recession circumstances is essential even to make a guess. Speaking generally, this limitation on a comprehensive appraisal of the risk magnitude is far more serious than the one of technical competence mentioned first.
- ☐ Top management will not base critical decisions, such as debt policy, on data which it does not understand and/or in which it does not have confidence. This, I believe, is the primary obstacle which stands in the way of widespread use of a comprehensive cash flow analysis as a basis for risk measurement and the determination of debt capacity at the present time.

Because the method is complex (particularly in contrast to the customary rules of thumb) and because the judgments on probabilities and other aspects of the analysis may appear—and may in fact be—tenuous, management may well be unwilling to use the results, particularly when corporate solvency is at stake.

However, when all this is said, the fact remains that much of present-day practice is seriously inadequate, and there is an urgent need for a more meaningful approach to the problem, particularly as far as the borrower is concerned. Thus there is a strong incentive to explore the opportunities for partial or approximate measures of the risk of cash insolvency within the general framework suggested by the comprehensive analysis. One such approach is that to be described. Its aim is to produce an indicator of risk magnitude that can be derived from more conventional and less complex data in which management has confidence.

Analysis of Adverse Limits

The new approach focuses on the expected *limits* of recession behavior and in particular on the maximum adverse limit. It is based on the assumption that although management may be unable to assess with confidence the probabilities within the range, it usually has strong opinions as to the expected limits and would be prepared to base decisions on such expectations. Thus, to return to the example of the sales contraction, management may be unwilling to assign the "betting odds" to the three intervals between a 5% and a 25% contraction, but it probably does have strong feelings that 25% is the "absolute" limit of adversity within the foreseeable future. This feeling is based not merely on past statistics, but on an expert appraisal of all the facts surrounding the customer's buying habits and circumstances, the competitive situation, and so on.

Following this procedure leads to a set of estimates of the maximum adverse limit of recession behavior covering each factor affecting cash flow, and it is a comparatively simple matter then to come up with an estimate of the maximum adverse behavior in any future recession of net cash flow itself—in terms of the minimum dollars of net inflow (or maximum dollars of net outflow), period by period. Making similar judgments as to the maximum adverse conditions immediately preceding the recession—including prerecession cash balances—it is next possible to determine whether, under such maximum assumptions, the company would become insolvent and, if so, how soon and by how much.

This calculation in itself will give management some "feel" for the nearness or remoteness of the event of cash insolvency. It may demonstrate, as I have done in the case of certain companies, that even under these maximum adverse assumptions the company still has a positive cash balance. If this is so, the amount of this minimum balance is an objective judgment of the total amount of incremental fixed cash charges that the company could assume without *any* threat of insolvency. Making some assumptions about the nature and the terms of the debt contract, this figure could be converted into the principal amount of additional debt that could be assumed with the expectation of complete safety.

Suppose, on the other hand, that the maximum adverse assumptions produce a negative cash balance, indicating the possibility of insolvency under certain adverse conditions. This does not mean that the long-term debt is excluded (except for those managements for whom any action that creates or increases the risk of insolvency, no matter how small it may be, is intolerable). The more likely response will be that, provided the chances are "sufficiently remote," the company is fully prepared to run the risk.

Thus we are back to the problem of assessing the magnitude of the risk and the extent to which it would be increased by any given amount of debt. As a means of gaining a more precise impression of the chances of insolvency at the adverse end of the range of recession behavior, without going through the formal process of assigning probability values, I suggest that a second adverse limit be defined for each of the factors affecting cash flow. This will be called the *most probable adverse limit*. It reflects management's judgment as to the limit of *normal* recession behavior, as opposed to the maximum adverse limit, which includes all possibilities, however remote.

Modes and Ranges

A visual representation of these two adverse limits of behavior is shown in Exhibit 1. Assuming experience and expected behavior are somewhat normally distributed about a mode (i.e., the value of most frequent occurrence), there will be:

1 A range of values clustered around this point, where most of past experience has been concentrated and where "bets" as to what the future is likely to bring will also be concentrated.
2 Extremes at either end of the range representing events that have a relatively small chance of happening.

It will be seen that the most probable limit cuts off the extreme "tail" of the frequency distribution in a somewhat imprecise and yet meaningful way. In setting the limits of expected sales contractions, for example, management would be saying that while sales *could*, in its judgment, contract as much as 25%, a contraction is *not likely* to exceed, say, 20%. This 20% is then the most probable adverse limit. While my terms may be new to businessmen, the distinction described is one which is commonly made and one on which judgments as to risk are often based.

From the data on the most probable adverse limits of the various factors affecting cash flow, the most probable adverse limit of recession *net* cash

Exhibit 1. Example of Maximum and Most Probable Limits of Recession Behavior

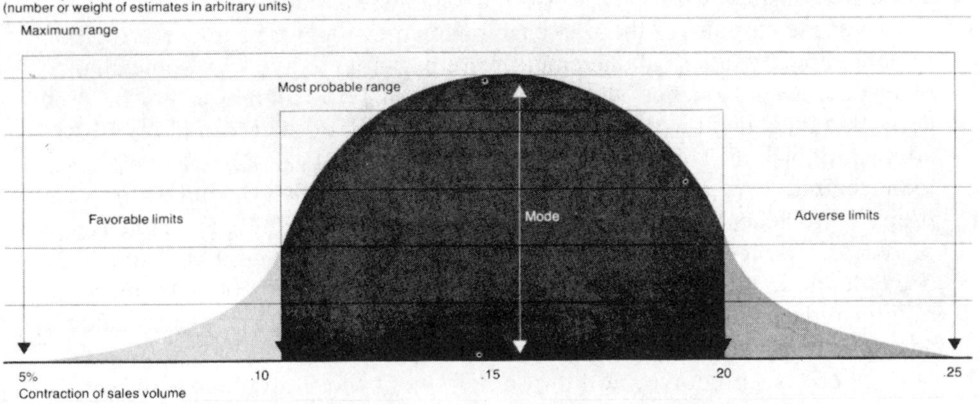

flows would be calculated and, from this, the most probable minimum recession cash *balance*. This last figure reflects management's best judgment as to the adverse limit of what is "likely to happen" as opposed to what "could happen" to net cash flows.

Guidelines for Policy

At this point it should be noted that, when considering cash flows from the point of view of solvency, the list of possible expenditures would be stripped down to those which are absolutely essential for continuity of corporate existence and for the generation of current income. (We will presently bring into consideration other less mandatory expenditures such as dividends and capital expenditures.) Thinking in these terms, suppose the recession cash flow analysis indicates that under the maximum adverse assumptions the minimum cash balance would be negative, say, a deficit of \$1.5 million. Suppose further that under the most probable adverse assumptions the minimum recession cash balance is a surplus of \$3 million. How are these estimates to be interpreted as a guide to corporate debt capacity?

First, it is obvious in this example that management's expectations about the factors governing cash flow include the possibility that the company could become insolvent without any additional debt. However, this possibility is considered to have a relatively remote chance of occurrence since when the analysis is restricted to the most probable limit of recession behavior, the company is left with a positive minimum cash balance. The amount of this balance is a rough measure of the *total amount of additional fixed cash outflows (e.g., debt charges) that could be incurred without creating the threat of insolvency* in the event of normal recession conditions. Thus:

If the likely limit of the recession is expected to be two years, the company could stand additional debt servicing of \$1.5 million per year of recession. This sum can be readily converted into an equivalent principal amount. Assuming a 20-year term loan repayable in equal annual installments and bearing 5% interest, an additional debt of approximately \$15 million could be considered safe under ordinary recession conditions.

Let me emphasize that the cash balance would not be taken as a guide to debt capacity unless management were prepared to live with some chance of insolvency—a chance which would obviously be increased by the new debt. If management were not so inclined, it would reject debt or alternatively adopt a debt limit somewhere between zero and \$15 million. In any case, management would not increase debt *beyond* \$15 million unless it were prepared to accept the chance of insolvency within the most probable range of recession experience. Because of the way the most probable limit has been defined, the chances of insolvency would be expected to increase rapidly and substantially if debt were to exceed \$15 million by any significant amount.

There is, of course, nothing sacred about the \$15 million limit set by management's judgment on the limits of normal recession experience. There is no reason why some managements would not increase debt capital substantially above this figure, assuming the funds were available. Such a step depends entirely on the willingness to bear the financial risks and on the potential rewards for such risk bearing. The foregoing type of analysis does, however, perform the essential function of alerting management to the range of debt beyond which risks may be expected to increase substantially.

Practical Advantages

It is now apparent that the analytical approach proposed here produces a criterion stated in terms of *the number of dollars of debt servicing* that are acceptable within management's concepts of risk bearing at a given point in time. The criterion is derived entirely from within and is completely independent of external judgments or rules of thumb. Although it is admittedly crude and approximate when compared with the theoretical ideal of risk management, I believe it to be meaningful and useful in practice and, in this as in other respects, superior to the conventional forms for expressing debt limits.

It must be added, however, that because the recommended analysis is partial and approximate, those who adopt it must use it as they use current decision rules. That is, they must use it as a general guide and not as a precision instrument. For most managements this will be entirely adequate.

Better Decision Making

One of the real advantages of this approach to debt capacity is that it raises—and answers—a much broader question. As previously indicated, the analysis is actually concerned with the capacity to assume additional fixed cash outflows of any kind, and whatever capacity is demonstrated is not confined to debt servicing. Thus, if it is concluded from the example just given that the company in question can stand an additional outflow in recessions totaling $3 million, the first decision to be made by management is *how to use this capacity*.

There are a variety of ways in which the capacity may be used: to cover payments under a lease contract, to maintain a continuous research program, to stabilize employment, to pay a regular dividend in good times and bad, and so on. These are all competing uses for whatever capacity exists. With the information that the cash flow analysis provides, management now can begin to assign priorities and have some idea of how far it can hope to go in realizing its objectives. If debt servicing is given top priority, then the data have been a means of defining debt capacity.

It is because the proposed analysis has much broader significance than the question of debt (important as that question may be) that I believe the expenditure of time, effort, and money required to generate the data needed is well justified for the individual corporation. The analysis provides information that lies at the base of a whole range of financial and other decisions and has continuing significance. Moreover, most corporate treasurers have the staff and the basic data to undertake a careful and detailed study of the behavior of factors affecting cash flow.

Testing for Cash Adequacy

Up to this point the analysis of cash flow has been discussed in terms of cash solvency. As indicated earlier, this means that attention is confined to outflows that are vital to survival. It was also indicated, however, that the risk of insolvency was part of a broader family of risks, described as the risk of cash inadequacy.

In discussing the question of solvency with management we often find that although there are certain expenditures that *could* be slashed to zero in an emergency, there is a reluctance to take action that would put management in a position of having to do so. These are expenditures which must be treated as mandatory for policy reasons, because management believes that to interrupt them would be detrimental to the long-term interest of the corporation. Among the best examples of such expenditures are certain minimum payments for research, for capital assets, and for preferred and common dividends.

This situation can readily be incorporated into the type of analysis outlined earlier. I refer to the method for doing this as the *test for cash adequacy* as opposed to the test for cash solvency. As soon as management has defined the "irreducible minimum" for these expenditures under recession conditions, they are merely added to the outflows of the previous analysis; then the figure generated for the maximum adverse or most probable adverse recession cash balance is the balance which remains over and above such payments. To return to the example previously used:

The effect would be to wipe out all or some portion of the most probable minimum balance ($3 million) or to add to the maximum adverse deficit ($1.5 million). Thus, if the irreducible minimum is considered to be two years of common dividends at $500,000 a year plus $1 million of minimum capital expenditures, the result would be to cut the most probable balance back to $1 million. The capacity to assume additional fixed cash outflows is thereby substantially reduced. Obviously, management in this case is giving priority to the dividend and capital expenditures over debt leverage—or over any other use for the funds on hand.

One of the benefits of such an analysis is to make management's priorities explicit, to recognize their competing character, and to make possible a reevaluation of their relative importance to the company.

Making separate tests for cash solvency and cash adequacy serves another important purpose. Most discussions of the hazards of debt imply that the danger is the risk of insolvency, and this danger is usually treated with proper respect. However, our analysis may demonstrate that within the range of management's expectations there is little or no risk of insolvency, but a substantial risk of cash inadequacy, particularly if large amounts of long-term debt are added.

If, in the past, management has been setting limits on debt in terms of an assumed risk of insolvency and now finds that the only significant risk is that of inability to meet certain minimum dividend payments and the like, it may well be disposed to assume a greater magnitude of risk and take on more debt. A management which would reject the risk of insolvency if it exceeded a chance of 1 in 50 might be prepared to accept a risk of abandoning cash dividends for a year or two if the chance did not exceed, say, 1 in 20.

In short, once management knows the *kind* of risk it is taking, it may begin to draw distinctions between one form of contingency and another and not operate on the general assumption that the only concern is that of possible insolvency. Better information is thus a prerequisite for better decisions.

Reappraising Present Rules

Assuming management can, by the means described, come up with an independent appraisal of its long-term debt capacity, what does this imply for existing decision rules obtained from external sources or inherited from the past? Does it mean that they will be ignored completely? The answer is likely to be no. Debt policy cannot be made in a vacuum. It must take account of the lenders' willingness to lend and also of the reactions of equity investors who make judgments on the risks inherent in the corporation.

One of the first results of the analysis, therefore, is to reappraise existing debt-capacity decision rules. To illustrate:

Suppose a company has been assuming, as many do, that it can safely incur long-term debt up to a maximum of 30% of capitalization. This rule can be translated into its equivalent of dollars of annual debt-servicing charges and directly compared with the results of the recession cash flow analysis. In view of the fact that the rule probably has been derived from external sources, it is likely that the annual debt servicing that it permits either exceeds or falls short of the amount of cash flow indicated by the internal analysis.

In view of the approximate nature of the analysis, however, this is not likely to cause a change in debt policy unless the amount of the variation is substantial. It is also possible, of course, that the existing decision rule and the cash flow analysis will produce the same result—in which case the existing rule will appear verified. But this cannot be known in advance of the analysis, and in any case the data have been converted into a form that is much more meaningful for the purposes involved.

Such a comparison gives a measure of management's attitude toward the risk that is implicit in the existing decision rule (although management probably had no clear idea of what the risk magnitude was at the time the rule was established).

The results of the cash flow analysis can also be compared with the lender's concept of debt capacity—if different from that of the corporation.

Although lenders are often reluctant to make statements on the outside limits of what they will lend, they will, from time to time, give indications of what they consider an appropriate capital structure for a given industry and company. If the borrower's appraisal of his capacity exceeds that of the lender, he may well decide to push the latter to the limit of his willingness to lend. Without good cash flow data, many borrowers appear reluctant to argue their case aggressively, probably because of uncertainty about where the safe limit lies.

The results can also be related to other aspects of the debt-capacity question, such as the requirements for an A bond rating or the risk expectations of equity investors that appear to be implicit in some price-earnings ratio (assuming this can be determined). Once again, the comparison is between whatever unused debt capacity is indicated by the internal analysis and the standards imposed by external considerations with the aim of probing the acceptable and useful upper limits of long-term debt.

I have carried out this type of analysis for a sample of companies in different industries and made comparisons with existing debt-capacity standards of both the corporations themselves and their lending institutions. The data strongly indicate that there are, in fact, major inconsistencies between managements' explicit expectations regarding recession cash flows and the expectations that are implicit in accepted ratios of debt capacity. The evidence is by no means adequate to make any safe or meaningful generalization about the overall character of industrial debt policy. Nevertheless, among the large and mature corporations that are the basis of the study the evidence seems to suggest:

- ☐ Either the risks of debt have been significantly overrated by a substantial number of firms.
- ☐ Or some managements tend to be unusually conservative toward this aspect of corporate risk.

Future Trends

The trend of economic events in the past 20 years suggests that there is both a need and an opportunity for a more refined approach to the debt-equity choice in corporate structures. As the specter of the depression of the 1930s has faded into the past and confidence in our capacity to avoid a repetition of extreme economic stagnation has grown, a new generation of corporate executives has shown increasing willingness to use long-term debt financing as a source of funds for consolidation and expansion.

As long as long-term debt is avoided or kept to minor proportions, crude decision rules providing wide margins of safety are quite adequate. As the proportions of debt increase, however, the need for a sharper pencil and a more careful analysis grows. This need is further reinforced by the increase in other kinds of fixed cash commitments such as lease payments and the noncontractual but nonetheless vital steady flows required for research, dividends, and the like. Greater stability in the economy over an extended period is likely to encourage a variety of rigidities in cash outflows, and simple rules of thumb are inadequate to cope with the problems these present.

Along with the increasing need for improved analysis has come a greater capacity to carry out this analysis. This improvement derives both from better data and from improved techniques of processing and analyzing data. Financial executives today have access to far more data on cash flows and the factors behind cash flows than they did 20 years ago—far more, in fact, than many are actually putting to use. They also have access to more sophisticated approaches to the analysis of complex data and to machines which can reduce it to manageable proportions. As time goes on and financial management becomes increasingly familiar with these tools of analysis and more aware of the opportunities they afford, the current reluctance to adopt a more complex analytical framework is bound to diminish.

But there is one hitch. However sophisticated the financial officer may be in the newer techniques, there is little merit in serving up a diet of financial data to the board of directors, as a basis for the financial decision, which is too rich for their current digestive capacity. It is for this reason that I have not attempted in this article to convert the reader to a full-scale internal analysis of risk and its components. Rather, I have taken on the more modest objective of alerting top management to four key points bearing on the debt-capacity decision:

1 Although external sources of advice can and should be consulted as an aid to decision making, the question of debt capacity is essentially an internal one to be settled by management with reference to its individual circumstances and individual preferences.
2 Current rules of thumb regarding debt capacity are seriously inadequate as a framework for this decision.
3 The answer lies in a knowledge of the behavior of cash flows and in having a useful measure of the capacity to assume incremental fixed cash outflows.
4 Management needs approaches that will enable it to approximate its debt capacity within the context of data with which it is already familiar and in terms of judgments to which it has long been accustomed. The approach described in this article meets these criteria.

By accepting and acting on these points, management would take an important step forward toward debt-equity decisions in which borrowers and lenders alike could have greater confidence.

Retrospective Commentary (1978)

Twenty-two years have gone by since I undertook the study of corporate debt policy on which the book *Corporate Debt Capacity*[1] and the related

HBR article were based. The timing of these publications coincided with the advent of a new generation of corporate administrative and financial officers who were free of the anxiety-ridden experience of the 1930s and who were supported by a rising buoyancy in the business environment that did not run its full course until the early 1970s. In many companies investment opportunity was beginning to press on traditional financing decision rules, and the managements of these companies were therefore receptive to the thought that these rules were open to question and independent evaluation.

In retrospect, it seems to me that the use of the phrase *debt capacity* in the title of the book suggested a significant change in attitude with respect to the use of debt: from that of a burden to be minimized to that of a resource to be exploited. Indeed, I have been charged at times with a share of the blame for an excessive use of debt by corporations in the 1960s, with its inevitable day of reckoning in the 1970s.

I think that charge overstates both the influence and the responsibility. It is sobering to think, however, that the use of debt by individuals and corporations may be subject to periodic excesses if it is not held in check by those who are in a position to influence it.

How would the article differ from the original if it were written today? Certain developments of the past 16 years have had major significance for the issue of corporate debt policy. One of these is the extraordinary series of events—political, social, and economic—during this period.

They remind us that our human and economic environment is as volatile and as unpredictable as it has ever been. The suggestion that nations are now better able to understand and therefore to manage their economies—and thus economic and business risk is on the decline—is hard to sell these days. The unexpected continues to happen: Who predicted an era of recession *and* inflation? Who predicted (or who believed) the extraordinary consequences of OPEC?

This experience, not lost on corporate managers, has resulted in a sharp swing toward caution and conservatism in financial and fiscal policy in business as well as in government affairs. Corporate financial goals and policies are showing strong signs of concern for solvency in preference to dramatic growth rates in sales and profits.

As the 1962 article made plain, debt policy is the result of perceived risks *and* attitudes toward risk bearing, and both have undergone significant change. I pointed out at the time that any debt involves some incremental risk, but an article today on this topic would undoubtedly put more emphasis on the use of the proposed analysis for protection against downside risk than for upside opportunity. (It was, in fact, that concern which led me in 1969 to write a book and an *HBR* article on the use of debt and other financial reserves as part of a strategy for financial mobility.[2]) It was an idea whose time had not yet come; it would have much more relevance today.

Along with the changes in the objective and subjective elements of risk associated with debt financing, which in the 1970s have led to more caution in the use of debt, changes were also taking place in the theory of capital markets that perceived less benefit to the stockholder from the use of a leveraged capital structure than had been assumed. The hypothesis that a sophisticated portfolio manager, functioning in an efficient capital market, could duplicate the investment and financing options of the corporation—and he would therefore deny an equity premium to the corporation simply because it chose to finance with debt—has become accepted doctrine in schools of business during the past decade. How far this thinking has permeated the younger generation of business managers is hard to tell.

Certainly, a disenchanted investing public, burned by the collapse of the equity markets and the excesses of the 1960s (most notably the EPS game of certain conglomerates projecting an image of unending growth), was receptive to a theory that suggested that value was less a function of individual managerial decisions than it was of fundamental industry risks and returns. And yet, as the French say, the more things change, the more they remain the same. Despite some dramatic business failures, the last recession showed only a very modest rise in the number of business bankruptcies. Although business is more cautious, it continues to finance with substantial amounts of debt. There is little evidence of a flight from debt securities by investors—quite the contrary. The organizational and practical benefits of debt remain for the manager and, given the tax advantage, for the stockholder also.

But so, also, does the fundamental risk. Thus, it seems to me, the primary message of the 1962 article remains as important as ever: The capacity to assume long-term, fixed-cash commitments is a critical and scarce resource affecting both corporate solvency and strategic expenditure policies. Debt servicing is one such commitment, and the decision on how much debt to use and how much to reserve should not be left to chance or to generalized rules of thumb.

A careful study of the particular industry and company cash flow characteristics will improve the manager's ability to anticipate the levels of risk associated with various debt contracts. With better information on risk magnitudes, the new conservatism in risk bearing will assume a more meaningful focus.

Notes

1. *Corporate Debt Capacity* (Boston, Division of Research, Harvard Business School, 1961).

2. *Strategy for Financial Mobility* (Boston, Division of Research, Harvard Business School, 1969); "Strategy for Financial Emergencies," *HBR*, November-December 1969, p. 67.

10
Strategy for Financial Emergencies

GORDON DONALDSON

When a company is forming a financial plan for a certain period ahead, too seldom does it consider what it would do if an unanticipated event, such as a competitor's new product, caused a sudden adverse change in the flow of funds. The author explains how management can improve its information system and procedures for estimating the likelihood of unfavorable events, take inventory of the assets it possesses for countering them, and work out an appropriate strategy.

Modern management concepts place great emphasis on an orderly approach to the future. In the financial area this is reflected in detailed plans with near and distant horizons and in comprehensive budgetary controls.

As the central integrating document for corporate strategy and action, the financial plan must do more than include the best available information about the economic and competitive environment in which the business operates and establish targets for sales and profits to be achieved by certain dates. It must also promote the coordination of resources and efforts to reach these target positions, and form the basis for measuring performance as the future unfolds.

It is inherent in the planning function that there should be moments at regular intervals when a business pauses and thinks about the uncertainties of the future. But it is also inherent in the management function that planning is followed by action that cuts through the uncertainties, sets a course for the business, and makes a commitment that prejudges the future.

Thus most planning in its present form is largely an exercise in converting an unknown future into a known—and therefore manageable—future. Once financial goals are established, they must be met regardless of the environment, and rewards and penalties are set accordingly.

But despite the aura of precision surrounding the financial plan, any manager will readily admit that there are many possible events within the planning horizon that can prevent the plan from being realized: action of a competitor on price or product, technological change, business recession, government interference, wildcat strike, social unrest, even termination or outbreak of war—to mention the more obvious. The manager will acknowledge that these events can occur with little or no warning.

Faced with the conflict between a "certain" plan and an uncertain and often hostile environment, the customary response is: When the unexpected happens, make a new plan. In other words, when the unknown becomes known, management assesses its impact on previous plans and creates a new "certainty" that incorporates the new information.

In this approach the only limitation for dealing with uncertainty is the organization's capacity to generate and adapt to new plans. Of course, if the changes are modest, the variances allowed within the annual planning cycle will take care of them. But if the changes are major, they may require interruption of the normal planning cycle.

The question I raise here is whether current business planning is doing all it can to handle the problem of the unforeseen event. I believe that in one area at least, the area of managing the flow of funds, more can be done to deal with it than merely being willing to prepare a new plan.

In fact, planning as it is commonly practiced today tends to build in rigidities that work *against* quick and effective response to the unexpected event. What some would call contingency planning, or what I think of as a strategy for financial mobility, should be brought into the open for a careful review.

Managing the Funds Flow

Every business has objectives that guide policy and in their most basic form include survival, profitability, and growth. Growth objectives that are central to our philosophy of successful management may be expressed in a variety of ways—sales, profits, market share, geographical coverage, product line—but they are all contingent on a continuous flow of funds affording management the means to implement decisions.

So, although the primary financial responsibility from an ownership viewpoint may be to maximize value, the financial executive's primary managerial responsibility is to preserve the continuity of the flow of funds so that no essential decision of top management is frustrated for lack of corporate purchasing power.

Considered in these terms, the task of financial management involves anticipating the pattern of release of funds from, and commitment of funds to, various specialized uses, identifying points where a surplus or deficiency of liquid funds may be expected, and taking action to employ the surplus or cover the deficit.

Although it demands considerable technical expertise, this task would not be a difficult one even with highly irregular flows were it not for the factor of uncertainty. It is the need arising with little warning and great urgency that tests the financial officers' mettle. Their job is to relieve the chief executive of this concern and to provide the solution regardless of who is to blame for the lack of foresight—even if it is the chief executives themselves.

I indicated previously that the formal financial plan provides for the expected event, for a matching of expected inflows and expected outflows. This is the easy part. The formal plan gives no hint of how the company is prepared to deal with any of several changes that could take place in the inflows or outflows within the planning period (say, one to five years).

Some may argue that there can be no such thing as a plan or a strategy for dealing with the unexpected need for funds because the unknown is, by definition, unplannable. This point of view is persuasive if we imagine an event that has never before entered our experience. Most "unexpected" events resulting in a need for funds, however, have happened before—either to us or to another, similar business—and are therefore "known" to some degree. We are aware that there is some chance of their occurring.

That the event has not been incorporated into the formal plan simply means that its probability of occurrence at the time the plan was formed was not high enough to be treated as a certainty.

So I maintain that an event that is in some degree knowable is in some degree plannable. In thinking about a strategy of response to the unexpected need for funds—a strategy of financial mobility—I find it helpful to divide the approach into three stages, which I shall discuss in sequence:

1 *Maximizing the resource of time.* The search for and use of information concerning the future requires a significant change from current planning techniques.
2 *An inventory of the resources of financial mobility.* Here also I shall suggest a new approach which breaks away from the traditional inventory of assets and includes providing for unexpected needs.
3 *The elements of a strategy for employing the resources of mobility when the unexpected occurs.*

Buying Time

Consider the case of a company that for years has been selling 25% of its output to one customer. Suppose that this customer suddenly announces her decision to make rather than buy the product in the future and to begin immediately to reduce her orders. The company naturally faces an immediate and substantial decline in funds inflow.

This setback would not have been a severe financial problem if the company had received notification early enough to find substitute sales volume or scale down its outflows in an orderly manner. So the problem of the unexpected need for funds is not that it happens, but that the company has had insufficient time for the response necessary to bring the flows into balance again.

The objective of an organized information search into the future is to maximize the resource of time for a response. Obviously, the more time available, the less the disruption of other funds flows, and the lower the cost of the necessary reallocation of funds.

Many businesspeople would read the term *information search* as a fancy substitute for "forecasting" and would therefore think of it as a part of the regular planning routine. In most companies, however, forecasting is limited to the effort to establish the most probable course of events, which then becomes the basis for management's targets and controls.

Unless there is clear evidence that it will occur during the planning period, an event such as the loss of a major customer is unlikely to affect the formal forecast. That possibility may simply remain a lingering worry to the president and the senior executives.

Contingency Analysis

But merely to fret from time to time about contingencies that could have major financial consequences is not enough. To "know thy adversary," the executive should undertake an explicit contingency analysis.

Of course, financial officers could worry about many things if they were so inclined. At any given time, however, there are one or more key contingencies about which they need as much information as possible so as to develop a strategy for dealing with them should they occur.

Unfortunately, formidable psychological barriers to a serious and open approach to contingency analysis often exist in companies. The effort to gain and maintain a commitment to the targeted sales and profit levels is so strong that top management discourages objective consideration of possible events causing the company to fall short of its target. In an atmosphere of enthusiasm and dedication to a goal, contingency analysis may appear as negative, unconstructive excuse-making that borders on disloyalty.

The usual result is to drive contingency planning "underground"; it is carried out only in the minds of those with whom responsibility rests. What goes on in the mind of the chief financial officer is not bad planning simply because it is informal and not put down on paper. But such planning is denied the great benefits of group thinking and detailed analysis.

So I make a plea for bringing financial contingency analysis into the open, where it can receive more thorough and systematic exploration. There are ways of doing this to avoid interference with the proper commitment to established goals. Even though the company may remain determined to achieve a 10% growth in sales this year, someone can in good conscience examine, say, the likely effect of a business recession on sales, profits, and funds flows.

Considering those primary contingencies that have current significance can provide a better understanding in two directions:

1 It sharpens judgment as to the event's chances of occurrence. Periodic review and updating of data on the contingency may permit an earlier response and more time to act. It is often good business judgment to respond to a contingency before it becomes a certainty; management does not wait until the day a strike vote is taken to begin building inventory.
2 It provides better understanding before the event of the potential impact of contingencies on cash or funds flows. For certain clear-cut eventualities, such as the outcome of a lawsuit, the financial effect will be obvious. However, for more complex events that affect cash flows in many ways and over long periods of time, such as a recession, a formal analysis may be the only way to understand the problem.

Unfortunately, the methodology of conventional financial forecasting is not suited to this purpose, and this is unquestionably a primary reason why financial officers typically do not take formal contingency analysis seriously. The cost in time and effort of examining in detail several sets of assumptions about the future, when only one (if that) will come to pass, quickly dampens any enthusiasm for the idea.

The accounting data on which forecasting is based are inherently static and were never intended to describe or explain patterns of change over time; they merely describe what happened between two specific points in time. Thus, forecasting based on these data is an unwieldy point-to-point projection limited to assumptions about those two points in time.

Simulating the Future

We badly need a dynamic forecasting tool that can explore a range of alternatives quickly and accurately so that management can obtain a reliable answer to any "what if" question it feels is important at the moment.

Suppose the question is: What if we have an industrywide or countrywide recession in the second quarter of 1970? In attempting an answer to this question in specific financial terms, one is immediately faced with a multitude of assumptions that have to be made regarding changes in volume of sales (their magnitude and timing), product mix, prices, how soon the recession is recognized and how rapid the response, and what action is taken on inventory levels, employment, capital expenditures, administrative overhead, marketing expenditures, and so on.

To make only one or two sets of assumptions—as conventional forecasting does—is virtually meaningless. What we need, rather, is an understanding of how each of these variables is likely to change over time, how they affect each other, and how they ultimately affect cash flows and profits.

Then and only then can we hope to understand the full implications of the events of the recession as it begins to emerge, and to act more quickly and confidently to balance cash flows and protect profits.

In this connection I am impressed with the potential of a computer model of the company's funds flow system designed so that it can generate cash or funds flow statements, income statements, balance sheets, and related analyses for any desired time horizon and for any set of assumptions.[1] This dynamic analytical tool must be able to answer such questions as:

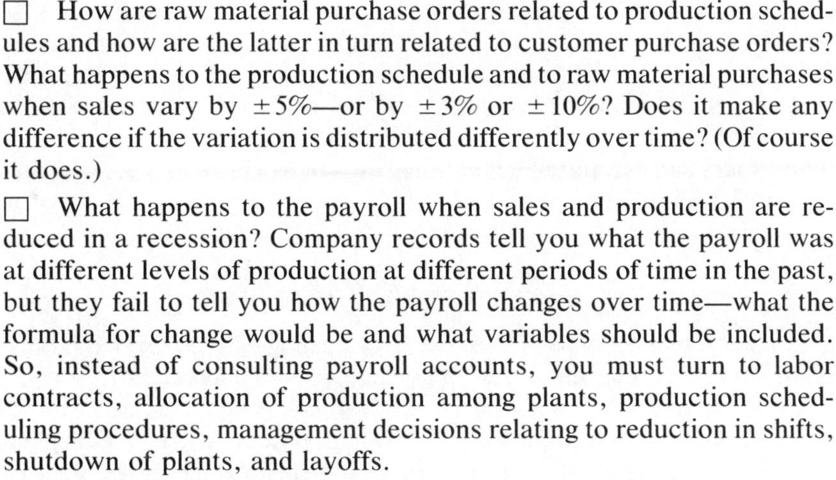

☐ How are raw material purchase orders related to production schedules and how are the latter in turn related to customer purchase orders? What happens to the production schedule and to raw material purchases when sales vary by ±5%—or by ±3% or ±10%? Does it make any difference if the variation is distributed differently over time? (Of course it does.)

☐ What happens to the payroll when sales and production are reduced in a recession? Company records tell you what the payroll was at different levels of production at different periods of time in the past, but they fail to tell you how the payroll changes over time—what the formula for change would be and what variables should be included. So, instead of consulting payroll accounts, you must turn to labor contracts, allocation of production among plants, production scheduling procedures, management decisions relating to reduction in shifts, shutdown of plants, and layoffs.

This is information management should have for general planning purposes as well as contingency analysis, and it is information that financial research can provide. It should be noted that these questions do not relate to what the future *will* be but what the future *could* be, and this is the essential departure from conventional forecasting. They are questions relating to several periods in sequence, not just one.

The answers incorporate management's judgments on such matters as where and how production should be scaled down, as well as facts such as the limits placed by the contract with the union.

Contemplating the initial investment necessary in such an information system may stop some executives from considering it any further. The initial description of how the various elements of cash or funds inflow and outflow change over time—the factors that determine change and the boundaries of change—is time consuming and expensive. It involves the building of a whole new information system, because accounting records are of limited value for this purpose.

But, when completed, such a computer model can simulate the financial consequences of any contingent event with greater reliability than conventional methods, and do it within minutes and at very low incremental cost. This kind of financial simulation need not be confined to a computer model, but it is the most efficient way of systematically building up the data and the only way of obtaining a broad capability of use.

In pencil-and-paper simulation one has to be much more selective in predetermining the critical assumptions so as to restrict the analysis to the most significant outcomes. I have done this kind of analysis without the help of a computer, as well as with a computer model, and the job has been made easier by following management's judgments to identify and focus on the boundaries or limits of change rather than on the full range of adverse effects.

Again using the example of a possible business recession, analysis could be confined to an examination of the cash and profit profile of a serious recession—say, a 20% drop in sales over two years—and how certain key assumptions about the business environment and the timing and magnitude of management responses (e.g., layoff of direct labor), if varied, would affect that profile. A business that has not faced a serious business recession for many years can get a lot of educational benefit from this exercise—in advance of the real thing.

Inventory of Resources

The next step in developing a strategy for dealing with financial contingencies is an inventory of the resources available to management in covering an unexpected deficit in funds flows.

A rough approximation of this list undoubtedly exists in every financial officer's mind. The full range of alternatives, however, goes well beyond the financial domain, and therefore a good case can be made for a more formal and explicit review by the entire top management team. At the least, this resource position should be reported regularly to the chief executive.

To most managers a report of financial resources means the asset side of the balance sheet. But this is definitely not the list of resources we want, for it is largely, if not entirely, an itemization of purchasing power that has been committed to specialized use in the past. What we need is an estimate of the purchasing power *available for commitment* in the future.

In this context, the statement that the labels become reversed—assets become "liabilities" and liabilities become "assets"—is not far from the truth. Among the conventional assets even cash may be quite unavailable to meet new needs because it is locked into current transactions, whereas the liability "bank loans" may be of great potential significance to future needs. So we need a different, action-oriented document related to the uncertainties of the future.

Many companies are accustomed to making projections in terms of pro forma income statements and balance sheets that tell them what their financial condition will be one year hence if things work out as planned. Such statements are useful from the "score-keeping" viewpoint, but they are of little use in telling how to play the game, particularly when events do not turn out according to plan.

Exhibit 1 presents one format for the document designed to be a data base for a strategy of mobility. On the left-hand side is a checklist of possible resources for covering a funds flow deficit. Across the top are headings that differentiate among resources as to the time necessary to put funds to use. I shall comment on these categories in turn and then provide some figures to show how a company can use the form as a basis for devising its strategy.

Uncommitted Reserves

These are resources which, with the possible exception of cash, are not measured on the conventional balance sheet. They represent an estimate of funds available either internally or externally that the company's formal financial plan has not committed to use in the foreseeable future. So in this

Exhibit 1. Form for Inventory of Resources of Financial Mobility for Three Time Horizons

Resources	Available for Use Within		
	One Quarter	One Year	Three Years
I. Uncommitted reserves			
Instant reserves			
Surplus cash	$		
Unused line of credit	$		
Negotiable reserves			
Additional bank loans			
Unsecured	$		
Secured	$		
Additional long-term debt		$	
Issue of new equity		$	
II. Reduction of planned outflows			
Volume-related			
Change in production schedule	$		
Scale-related			
Marketing program		$	
R&D budget		$	
Administrative overhead		$	
Capital expenditures		$	
Value-related			
Dividend payments		$	
III. Liquidation of assets			
Shutdown		$	
Sale of unit			$
	$ →	$	
		$ →	$
Total resources			$

sense the definition of a resource is not a question of ownership but, rather, of availability.

It should also be noted that since external reserves must be negotiated, the numbers contain an element of uncertainty and judgment that is unnerving to a conventional accountant. With all their uncertainties, however, these are the relevant numbers for future management action.

The uncommitted reserves are subdivided into "instant" and "negotiable" reserves. Instant reserves consist of free cash balances, including of course marketable securities, and/or the unused portion of a negotiated line of credit. They represent a unique mobility resource because they are immediately available with complete certainty and are generally unrestricted as to use.

The instant reserve is in a very real sense a time-equivalent; it buys the time necessary to activate other resources. A free cash balance may be translated into the capacity to sustain a cash deficit of a certain size for a certain number of days or weeks. Here "money is time"—the counterpart of the information search I described earlier, which, if successful in providing the breathing space for a response to an unexpected need, becomes a substitute for an instant reserve. "Time is money," in other words.

The size of the instant reserve is a matter of judging the probable magnitude of the unexpected cash deficit and the time necessary to bring other resources into play to cover the deficit.

The time it takes to negotiate a term loan may be a matter of a few weeks or less. An instant reserve of $1 million enables a company to stand a maximum daily deficit of $50,000 for 20 days without recourse to other alternatives. This is a reference point whose adequacy can be judged in terms of the contingent need. If the funds are to be found internally, the time required may be a lot longer and $1 million will buy much less protection.

The category of negotiable reserves covers the range of contract forms, from short-term bank loans to new issues of equity, whereby a company obtains the use of external funds. All involve the consent of a second party and consequently are subject to varying degrees of uncertainty.

Nevertheless, it is possible and indeed essential that corporate contingency planning have the benefit of the most up-to-date and most authoritative estimates of what funds might be forthcoming from these sources. In this connection, it may be necessary to be more specific in identifying the contingencies for which the estimate is being made, because some negotiable reserves depend in part at least on the purpose for which the funds are intended.

It will be apparent that the amount potentially available from some of these sources also depends on whether other sources have been previously employed—long-term debt, for instance, would be contingent on the short-term debt outstanding. The estimates must be sequential and take this interdependence into account.

Perhaps the most uncertain of all negotiable reserves are the proceeds of new issues of common equity. The two extremes of zero and infinity may be suggested by considerations of maintaining control of the company, on the one hand, and an optimistic view of the stock market, on the other.

Under reasonably favorable market conditions, however, the company can expect to issue a certain amount of equity capital, and it should turn its efforts to determining the constraints in advance—considerations of the trends in per-share earnings, the capacity of the market to absorb it, control of the company, and so forth.

Reduction of Outflows

The second broad category of the resources of mobility concerns efforts to revise existing commitments on outflows of funds over the planning period. When an unexpected need arises, it may be desirable to substitute it for one or more of the planned outflows in the existing budget, rather than draw down uncommitted reserves.

Much depends on the nature and urgency of the need, the state of the business's reserves, and the circumstances at the time. In any case, the substitution, if it is a major one, will of course involve some internal negotiation with the members of the management group whose plans for expenditure are to be cut back.

This category can be subdivided into three classes of expenditure: (1) those relating to volume of operations, such as direct labor; (2) those that are functions of the general scale of operations, such as advertising or research and development; and (3) those I call "value-related," meaning expenditures not directly related to the company's product or service but made to improve shareholders' wealth (e.g., dividends).

Among these three classes of expenditure the scale-related outflows usually provide the largest potential resource of mobility, because their expenditure horizons usually have some flexibility. The other two classes may be available under certain circumstances. Volume-related expenditures can be cut back with greatest effect when the unexpected need coincides with a period of declining sales.

Some members of management may object to the whole idea of budget cuts as an element of a strategy of financial mobility. They may reason that, once made, a plan should be carried out, and it is the function of financial reserves to insulate the budget from the shock of the unexpected need. This argument is most likely to come from those executives whose budgets are most vulnerable.

It is a fact of corporate life, however, that a reallocation of planned outflows is a common and necessary part of the response to contingent needs by most businesses. And for good reasons:

- ☐ The appearance of new and unexpected demands for funds can and should change priorities, for any new information changes our view of the future to some extent. For example, new marketing and product development expenditures forced by the action of competition may reduce the profitability of certain products that formerly had a satisfactory return.
- ☐ Defending the remaining financial reserves may be more important than defending the budget.

At this point of crisis, business behavior is not always very rational. Internal and external reserves can sink to dangerous levels while the usual expenditures flow out unchecked. (Is this because it is easier to negotiate with an external source such as a banker than to negotiate with your own management team?) Thus:

One company of my acquaintance emerged from World War II with a very strong cash position and financial structure but a weak competitive position. Instead of facing up to a major overhaul and reallocation of funds flows in its traditional business, the company consumed all of its surplus cash and borrowing power in an effort to buy the profitability of other industries through acquisitions. Unfortunately, this merely postponed the day when, because of a shortage of cash and deteriorating profits, the company had to institute drastic revisions of its capital and operating budgets.

So-called idle reserves are vulnerable when they should not be, and the instant reserve is particularly visible and vulnerable. It is the nature of a justifiable reserve to be idle in the sense that military reserves are idle. The role of the instant reserve is to protect against the completely unexpected and urgent need. Every business needs some such capacity. So long as some advance notice of a need is available—affording a grace period to activate other sources, including budget revisions—the instant reserve should never be used.

So if budget revisions are to play some role in contingency planning, the financial officer must make an advance estimate of the funds that can be released. Obviously, this is a delicate and judgmental issue. The available amounts depend heavily on circumstances, including how recent was the last round of belt-tightening.

With specific contingencies in mind, however, the judgments can be made. Every manager knows of soft spots in the capital budget, for example. A manager can make judgments as to how short the expenditure horizon can be before it begins to hurt sales, quality, delivery schedules, and, not least, management and worker morale.

The mental exercise involved in this analysis is a very useful one if undertaken in the right spirit, and an unhurried examination *before* an emergency need arises is better than a hasty response later under pressure.

Liquidation of Assets

The last major category of expenditure is the liquidation of nonfinancial earning assets (not the liquidation of marketable securities, which are classed with cash as an instant reserve.)

There is, I think, good reason to question the liquidation of assets as a part of contingency planning and action. The decision to phase out a portion of the business should be based on long-range considerations of alternative use of the resources. Also, as a practical matter the funds released from liquidation of earning assets are usually very uncertain in their timing and amount.

On the other hand, there is a common tendency to postpone the decision to divest as long as the investment is contributing something to profits or sales. With the possibility that new information and unexpected needs may change basic priorities, the liquidation of earning assets should be retained as a potential resource of mobility even though it will be rarely used.

The inventory of resources should identify those earning assets that are separable from the main business, without damage to its earning power, and are lowest in earning potential among all corporate investments. An estimate of their liquidation value would be necessary in any case to evaluate the return on investment by which their desirability as an investment was being judged.

Sample Inventory of Resources

A simple illustration of what the inventory of resources for unexpected needs might look like is given on the left side of Exhibit 2. This is the hypothetical Majestic Company's inventory as of September 30, 1969, looking ahead one year. Under the formal financial plan, gross outflows of funds for the year are expected to be $6.25 million, and gross inflows are expected to fall short of this amount, leaving a funds flow deficit of $350,000. The company plans to make it up by the use of a negotiated line of credit.

The inventory indicates that Majestic at present has no free cash reserve and no remaining long-term debt capacity. There is some short-term debt capacity represented by the negotiated credit line and management's judgment that on a secured basis the company could borrow an additional $300,000 from banks. Majestic is gradually reducing its preferred stock and has no intention of using preferred stock in the future. Under favorable market conditions and for certain needs it is prepared to raise up to $300,000 in a common stock issue.

A review of planned outflows has indicated that a modest cutback in the production schedule would save $74,000 in planned expenditures without sacrificing expected sales volume. Any larger cutback would depend on a decline in sales volume below the predicted level.

Reductions in marketing expenditures and administrative overhead are possible because of the inherent flexibility of expenditures not closely tied

Exhibit 2. Inventory of Resources of Mobility of Majestic Company as of September 30, 1969, with One-Year Horizon

Projected gross expenditures (October 1, 1969–September 30, 1970)	$6,250,000
Projected deficit of receipts	$ 350,000
Projected source of funds	
Bank line of credit	$ 350,000

	Sources of Mobility in Funds Flows, September 30, 1969		Pro Forma Position, September 30, 1970	
I. Uncommitted reserves				
Instant reserves				
Surplus cash	0		0	
Unused line of credit	$350,000		0	
Total instant		$ 350,000		0
Negotiable reserves				
Additional bank loan (secured)	$300,000		$450,000	
Additional long-term debt	0		0	
Preferred stock	0		0	
Issue of common stock	$300,000		$300,000	
Total negotiable		$ 600,000		$ 750,000
Total reserves		$ 950,000		$ 750,000
II. Reduction of planned outflows				
Volume-related				
Change in production schedule	$ 74,000		$ 74,000	
Scale-related				
Marketing	$ 84,000		$ 84,000	
Administrative overhead	$ 70,000		$ 70,000	
Capital expenditures	$100,000		$ 50,000	
Value-related				
Dividend payments	$ 50,000		$ 50,000	
Total reduction in outflows		$ 378,000		$ 328,000
III. Liquidation of assets				
Sale of land		$ 50,000		$ 50,000
Total resources		$1,378,000		$1,128,000

to sales volume and the fact that several years of rising expenditure have produced some "fat" that can usefully be melted away under financial pressure.

The rather large sum attributed to capital expenditures reflects the fact that this happens to be a year of unusually high capital outlays. Provided these planned expenditures have not been translated into construction contracts or purchase orders at the time an unexpected need looms, Majestic can reduce the budget by as much as $100,000 and still protect "essential" expenditures.

Finally, the company is too small to permit separating and liquidating any parts of the business without disintegrating the whole business. The company does, however, have some land held for plant expansion, and this could yield $50,000.

These resources total $1.378 million. Considering that the components of this resource position are in large part themselves contingent on circumstances, needs, and bargaining position, the amount may not be as large as it looks. This is obviously a judgment to be made at the highest level in the organization, where the responsibility for inadequate funds flows rests.

Pro Forma Position. The right-hand side of Exhibit 2 takes the analysis one step further by developing a pro forma resource position for the end of the one-year planning period. It shows the effects of the financial plan and of events as they are now expected to occur. The most significant change is the disappearance of the $350,000 line of credit which Majestic plans to commit to use this year.

Although the total resource position will not change greatly, the anticipated consumption of the company's instant reserves should be a signal for action *now* (not then). All other resources will take some time to activate; and on the principle that a company should always have some instant reserves against the completely unexpected need, management should immediately begin converting the negotiated reserves or reallocating budgeted flows to restore the minimum instant reserve.

This example illustrates a principal objective of a formal analysis of the company's capacity for mobility. It is to provide the basis for a top management review of the issue of contingent strategy, of the alternatives open, of the effect of company plans on the capacity to absorb financial shocks, and of the need for action before pressures of circumstances make action difficult or costly. It enables nonfinancial management to see more clearly the nature and extent of the resources limiting its actions and to realize the interrelationship between financial reserves and budgeted flows.

Not all financial officers will endorse the desirability of communication with the whole top management team. Some will prefer to keep financial contingency planning an exclusive and somewhat secret affair; they have the squirrel instinct and tuck their acorns away in many places well out of sight against a long, cold winter of need. Most of them, however, will see contingency planning as a group responsibility, of which financial contingency planning is one part, and will see benefit in a document that aids communication and promotes a common focus.

Strategy for Response

Assuming that the kinds of analysis I suggested earlier have produced both a picture of the financial impact of the prospective contingent needs considered to be critical for the business and a measure of the resources available to meet those needs, the next and final question concerns a strategy incorporating unexpected as well as expected events into a single overall corporate plan.

The strategy sets out the *sequence* in which the resources of financial mobility are to be brought into play as unplanned needs emerge. It also takes into account the *adequacy* of these resources, now and at the end of the planning period, both in total amount and in distribution among specific resources.

Sequence of Response

With regard to sequence of use in times of an unplanned deficit in funds flows, business practice seems to follow different patterns.

One observed pattern can be described as "the line of least resistance." When an unexpected need arises, the financial officer turns to the resource most completely under his control, most predictable, and involving the least disturbance to the status quo of the business. If the need is large or persistent, he turns successively to other resources down the line of increasing difficulty of negotiation and uncertainty.

His objective of containing financial shocks within the financial sector—that is, within the range of resources under his control—leads to covering the deficit out of surplus cash or short-term bank loans, or reallocating certain flexible, value-related financial outlays. That may seem commendable from the viewpoint of the operating managers, and in some circumstances it may be the right thing to do.

On the other hand, this approach can have the effect of consuming all the company's highly mobile reserves before the top executives have been alerted to the situation. Later they are confronted with an urgent need for a change in budget priorities without adequate time for consideration or orderly response.

Depending on the lead time available for meeting an unexpected need and its probable duration and magnitude, a better way to do it might be called "following the line of greatest resistance"—beginning the process of activating the resources with the *longest* lead time for negotiation or with the *greatest* uncertainty of availability as early as possible. This refers both to external negotiation, such as medium- or long-term borrowing, and internal negotiation on funds, such as those tied up in inventory or in the capital budget.

Another business practice is what might be called the "key resource" approach, which involves basing the strategy for contingencies on one principal resource, such as cash reserve or short-term borrowing capacity. Some companies have been able to survive contingent needs for many years on just such a strategy.

The fault in this approach lies in the fact that the various forms that a contingent need can take—in its distribution over time, in its impact on the company, in its urgency—call for matching it with a variety of resources of mobility, not just one.

There is a parallel here with the old financial dictum that the duration of a source of funds should match the duration of the use of the funds in the company. It can also be said that the timing and urgency of the need should be matched by the time required to activate the source of funds and the certainty of availability.

Companies that hold large reserves of cash as a regular practice are the most obvious examples of this "key resource" approach. Companies that maintain large reserves of borrowing power over extended periods of time also employ this approach, although its presence is less apparent because the balance sheet does not show it so readily.

Both groups may compound the error of holding instant reserves against all contingencies by assuming that the amount of the reserve must be the total of all contingencies, although the probability of all the contingencies occurring at the same time is very remote. To put it another way, the same sum of uninvested funds can serve more than one contingency need.

The opposite of the large liquid-reserve strategy is the no liquid-reserve strategy, in which all available resources become fully employed in specialized use, including short- and long-term borrowing power. In recent years this approach has become the more prevalent of the two extremes, as a defensive, depression-schooled generation of top management has given way to an aggressive new generation accustomed to a more consistent trend of growth in sales and profits and obsessed with keeping resources fully employed in order to maximize ROI.

With this changing of the guard has come greater emphasis on forecasting as a substitute for defensive reserves of idle funds. The "new look" in corporate finance is the balance sheet showing high leverage and near-zero cash balances. This strategy carries the latent danger of exposing the operations quickly to the full shock of any unexpected funds flow deficits, since the only ways open to cover a deficit are a change in budget priorities or the liquidation of existing earning assets. Financial mobility becomes synonymous with organizational mobility.

Range of Resources. All the strategies I have described so far seem to me to have inherent flaws in their logic and shortcomings in practice. Ideally, a sound strategy for dealing with financial contingencies would be based on the availability of a range of resources of mobility, although not necessarily the full range suggested in Exhibit 1. The range of resources means a range in the speed and certainty with which these resources can be directed into new uses.

Financial flexibility depends only in part on "idle" reserves; the strategy includes the potential diversion of other resources in varying degrees of specialized (and profitable) use. The plan encompasses guidelines to the sequence in which these resources will be brought into play.

Now the resources listed in Exhibit 1 may be roughly classified as follows:

- Active resources
  - Liquidation of earning assets.
  - Reduction of planned outflows.
- Passive resources
  - Negotiable reserves.
  - Instant reserves.

The active resources are employed in profit-generating activities, whereas the passive resources are currently inactive. From the viewpoint of minimizing dislocation of corporate plans and earning power, one might assume that it would be good strategy to try to contain the effects of the need with use of the passive resources. I maintain, however, that the passive reserves should be the minimum necessary for contingency planning, and the instant reserves in particular should be the minimum essential for urgent needs that demand instant response.

If this is so, then it is unwise to use the instant reserve when the nature of the need does not demand instant response. Since a strategy for financial mobility is aimed at a "portfolio" of risks—at a range of contingent needs varying in urgency and time available for response—it should be based on a portfolio of resources that coincides (approximately) with the portfolio of needs in certainty of availability and in time required to activate.

The strategic objective is to match as closely as possible any unexpected cash deficit with the resource most comparable in certainty and timing. For example:

☐ Suppose that information is received that estimates on a plant under construction are in error and cash outflows required four months from now will be 10% higher than expected. The financial executive should immediately begin to bring into play the *least* liquid resource that can be activated in four months' time.

If, as the time approaches, the resource in question is responding more slowly than expected and will not produce the funds needed, or if the error in cost of construction proves to be 15% instead of 10%, the resources that require less time to activate and that are more certain will be employed. If there is a choice among resources to match the need, the one used would be the one that causes the least dislocation of corporate plans and earning power.

I recognize that this approach has some practical problems. Much depends on the financial officer's bargaining strength both internally and externally. This in turn depends on the visibility of the new need and the sense of urgency present, as well as the company's apparent financial strength at the time.

In regard to financial strength, greater emphasis on future cash flows and formal contingency analysis and planning as a part of top management's information system should foster acceptance of the proposed strategy. Unfortunately, in many companies operating management's attention is so focused on the record of sales and profits that it takes a history of declining sales and profits to persuade top echelons to accept budget adjustments as part of cash-flow management. In the meantime the delays in response inevitably consume key reserves.

A strategy that suggests the nature and sequence of resources to be used should also deal with their restoration after they have been used. If it has been necessary to use up the company's instant reserves, steps should be taken immediately after the need has passed to restore the cash balance or repay the short term bank loan by a reallocation of other resources.

If the response was a budget cut in capital expenditures, advertising, or maintenance, the cut should be restored as soon as possible—unless the crisis turns out to be an opportunity to eliminate unproductive or unnecessary outlays.

One company I know of, which frequently faces significant cyclical swings in demand with little or no advance warning, follows a regular practice of replenishing its diminished cash reserve with short-term borrowing, then restoring short-term debt capacity with a medium-term loan. Then, as time permits, it restores medium-term borrowing power by a reallocation of internal flows.

In all such action the objective is to obtain a balance in the resources of mobility. A formal inventory of resources will keep the question of balance before top management.

Adequacy of Reserves

This brings us to difficult questions about the size of the various resources of mobility: How large should the instant reserve and the reserve of negotiable debt be? The decision can never be wholly objective, since we are dealing with judgment as to the risk of running out of cash, and this depends in part on attitudes toward risk taking. There is, however, a rational approach to the decision as well as an instinctive one.

I mentioned previously that if it were not for uncertainty, all available resources would be fully invested. Some resources are held in reserve because new circumstances may confront the company so suddenly that it has insufficient time to readjust the planned outflows and the existing investment and to restore the balance. So the size of the reserve must be measured in terms of the magnitude of the contingent need and the time necessary to integrate the new investment (need) with existing investments.

Let us return to the case of the loss of a major customer. Assume that there is a distinct chance of losing 25% of sales volume suddenly. The practical effect of this is that *for a time* the company will have overinvested in inventory and plant and will have overhead expenditures out of line with the new lower volume of business. Depending on the situation, this could mean a net outflow of cash to operations rather than a net inflow from operations while the work force, inventory, and so on are being scaled down, or until new sales revenues are found to replace the old. Changes in budgeted outflows are obviously necessary, but that takes time, even on a crash basis.

For this contingent need a reserve of short-term borrowing power seems in order, and the amount required is of course directly related to the magnitude of the need and the time necessary to adjust to the new level of inflows and outflows. The adjustment would not be complete, however, until the loan has been repaid and the reserve of borrowing power restored to a level consistent with new contingent needs.

If this line of reasoning is correct, it follows that *there is no simple formula* for determining the size of debt and cash reserves. The amount is unique to a particular company at a particular time, judged in terms of the specific contingencies that it takes seriously. The amount will change as the contingent needs change. It is in part a function of the other resources of mobility at management's disposal and of the speed with which management can make the required adjustments.

In rejecting rules of thumb on cash balances—an area of financial management where rules of thumb have a long and honored tradition—I recognize that cash balances serve several purposes, only one of which is the contingent need. Some rules of thumb, such as those relating the cash level to the sales level, rightly recognize a connection with the volume of transactions. They also have the not unimportant virtue of being simple and objective, and for that reason are easier to defend than a number resulting from complex analysis.

But cash balances that are a part of contingency planning must be related to the other resources of mobility and to the specific needs for which these resources are held, and the decision cannot be left to the whim of an unreasoned guideline.

If Flexibility Is Lacking. A company's reserves should be large enough so that the changes in budgeted flows required by new information can be accomplished without a shock to the organization. If, because of past economy drives, very little flexibility remains in the budgeted flows, then a greater burden for mobility must rest on the uncommitted reserves, and they should be larger as a consequence.

There will be circumstances where, with all the resources of mobility counted, the total capacity for response to the unexpected need is extremely low. The company then faces a harsh pair of alternatives: (1) accept the exposure to contingency risks, with their threat to the continuity of the business; or (2) take measures to liquidate some segment of the business assets in order to provide the desired mobility. This may be the kind of pressure necessary to initiate action on excessive inventories, a marginal product line, or a weak division.

I recall the case of a company that for the first time undertook a comprehensive review of its financial mobility. When the board of directors received a report that highlighted the almost total absence of the resources I have been discussing, a long-standing debate on whether to sell a major division and get out of that line of business was quickly concluded, and within three months the division was sold.

The issues at stake were, of course, more than those of finance. But the decisive consideration was the company's realization that it lacked the capacity to reallocate financial resources in support of the growth sectors of the business and at the same time meet opportunities or adversities as they arose. The action wrought a radical change in the company's financial structure and provided a substantial capacity to meet unexpected needs, a capacity that it made good use of in later years.

Conclusion

Uncertainty has always been a part of business experience, and yet current planning techniques and the philosophy of management by goals and objectives seem remarkably insensitive to unexpected change. We may be entering a period where business uncertainties will increase as the nation attempts to readjust its commitments abroad and attack major social and economic problems at home. If so, the need for formal planning to cope with an unexpected deficit in funds flows takes on greater importance at this time.

In this article I have suggested three steps in a strategy for dealing with financial emergencies around which a new approach to the problem can be organized.

The first has to do with the company's information system and the way in which it processes data about the likely course of events in the future. Management should examine in detail any contingencies it is concerned about, so it can understand their financial implications in advance for quicker identification and more rapid and confident response. This calls for an analytical capability beyond normal forecasting procedures. A cash-flow computer model has the ideal capability for providing this kind of analytical flexibility. If a company's resources do not permit such an investment, a pencil-and-paper analysis of a limited range of assumptions about the contingent need can serve the purpose of identifying, in advance of the actual event, its likely financial consequences and their nature, magnitude, and timing.

The second step in an orderly approach to contingency planning is the preparation of an inventory of the resources of financial mobility. Unlike the conventional list of assets on a balance sheet, these are the full range of alternatives open to a business in meeting an unexpected deficit in funds flows. The resources will include instant and negotiable reserves, a reallocation of certain budgeted flows, and the liquidation of idle and earning assets. A serious effort to take inventory may reveal cases of overprotection or underprotection as well as gaps in the range of alternatives and too much dependence on one resource.

The third step—and the most difficult one—is formulation of a strategy for dealing with the unknown. This requires some judgments about the size and distribution of resources and particularly about the sequence in which they will be employed as contingent needs emerge. Obviously, the strategy must be tailored to the contingencies and the company's circumstances.

A good strategy will encompass the full range of resources and will recognize that unexpected needs having different lead times for response and different degrees of urgency call for different resources that match the need in speed and certainty of supply. A good strategy will endeavor to minimize the allocation of resources to a passive (nonprofit-producing) role, at the same time providing a capacity for fast response when the need is sudden and urgent or when it is essential to buy time to permit a basic reallocation of resources.

Note

1. See George W. Gershefski, "Building a Corporate Financial Model," *HBR*, July-August 1969, p. 61.

11
How Much Debt Is Right for Your Company?

THOMAS R. PIPER and WOLF A. WEINHOLD

It has long been conventional wisdom that, whatever its troubling side effects, the aggressive use of financial leverage pays off in higher company values. Two decades of finance-based research, which the authors summarize here, qualify that wisdom substantially. Corporate and personal tax rates, which, of course, vary from situation to situation, significantly affect the attractiveness of debt. So, too, do the hidden costs of higher leverage, which include the restrictions it places on a company's flexibility in adapting financial policies to strategic goals. To assist companies in building an optimal capital structure, the authors outline a series of questions for CFOs to ask themselves before they establish a debt policy.

A decade of high inflation has trapped many chief financial officers between severe financing needs and weakened balance sheets. The overall deterioration in corporate financial health has been stunning (see Exhibit 1). Hard-pressed during the 1970s to supply inflation-mandated additions to working capital and to meet the increased cost of new plant and equipment, CFOs leveraged every new dollar of equity with some $3½ of debt. Having piled so much new debt onto their balance sheets, they now face sharply higher interest payments as a percent of pretax profits. Worse, since much of that debt is short term, they also face volatile swings in interest rates and heightened refinancing risks.

This deterioration has not gone unobserved. Of a sample of 430 companies with a debt rating of A in 1972, 112 had been downgraded by 1981 and only 39 had received higher ratings. Nor is it apparent that these financial pressures will soon ease. Continuation of inflation at a 10% annual rate will

Exhibit 1. Selected Ratios of Well-Being for Nonfinancial Corporations (average of year-end values)

	Liquid Assets/ Short-Term Debt	Long-Term Debt/Short-Term Debt	Net Addition to Debt/Net Addition to Equity	Interest Paid as Percentage of Pretax Profits
1956–60	1.90	3.95	1.32	7.4%
1961–65	1.54	3.87	1.48	9.5%
1966–70	.96	3.38	2.98	17.7%
1971–75	.80	3.18	3.69	33.4%
1976–80	.70	2.82	3.33	31.7%

Source: Henry Kaufman, "National Policies and the Deteriorating Balance Sheets of American Corporations" (New York, Salomon Brothers, February 25, 1981). Address before the Conference Board's 1981 Financial Outlook Conference.

drive up external financing needs and interest expenses as existing low-cost debt matures and must be refinanced at today's high rates.

CFOs therefore often find themselves in conflict with operating managers, who are eager to fund product-market strategies aimed at protecting competitive advantage. Especially in companies for which equity financing is unacceptable and in which operating management—concerned primarily with production, sales, and marketing—is the dominant force, there is great pressure to leverage the company with an even greater percentage of debt. What is the CFO to do? Is such leveraging worth fighting over?

By way of answer, this article summarizes two decades of research on the use of debt by companies with equity-financing alternatives. The major finding is that debt financing has in practice a far lower payoff than many CFOs believe. As a result, some of the assumptions of corporate financial policy are due for a careful rethinking.

We also outline a process by which CFOs can arrive at a sensible debt policy, a policy that protects against short-term vagaries in the capital markets, enhances the company's value (the total economic value of its debt and equity), recognizes its strategic position, and—not least important—can be understood by senior management.

The Appeal of Debt Financing

Discussion of this subject typically begins with an effort (like that in Exhibit 2) to demonstrate debt's favorable impact on a company's return on equity.

Exhibit 2. Debt Financing and the Return on Equity (aftertax cost of debt is 5%)

Assumed Aftertax Return on Capital	Debt as Percentage of Total Capital	Aftertax Return on Book Equity
12.5%	0%	12.5%
12.5	10	13.3
12.5	30	15.7
12.5	50	20.0
12.5	70	30.0

But this enhancement of return on equity is not without cost. It raises fixed interest expenses and thus shifts a company's break-even point upward toward the expected sales level. More important, it boosts the volatility of earnings and, by extension, of share price. Absolute profits at the low end of the sales range are much lower when a company uses debt financing than when it uses all equity, but its increase in profits at the upper end of the sales range is much greater in percentage terms. The reverse is also true: As sales fall toward the low end of the range, the percentage decline in profits is much greater too. Thus the greater the reliance on debt, the more a high level of sales increases profits—and the more a low level reduces them. As research by Robert Hamada has shown, 21 to 24% of the nondiversifiable risk (price volatility) of common stocks can be explained by the added financial risk a company takes on by using debt and preferred stock.[1]

Of course, equity investors ultimately care about such volatility. Traditional financial theory assumes, however, that they will not become concerned about the increased risk until the amount of a company's debt grows sufficiently large to threaten it with bankruptcy. If the theory is right, moderate use of debt—enough to leverage earnings but not enough to make investors aware of the heightened risk—pays off in a higher value for the company.

Effects of Taxation

This traditional theory was challenged by Franco Modigliani and Merton Miller in their landmark article of 1958. In their view, were there no taxes or transaction costs, debt financing would have no impact on a company's value.[2] For every uptick in financial leverage, equity holders would immediately demand a higher return as compensation for the increased risk.

Modigliani and Miller's reasoning becomes clear if we compare, for example, the total funds available for distribution to a company's suppliers of capital under two very different capital structures: one that is all equity; the second, half equity and half debt paying 10%. Total distributable funds (or EBIT, earnings before interest and taxes) are $1,000 in each case on a capital base of $4,000. As Exhibit 3A shows, in a world without taxes the decision to use debt does not affect a company's value.

Furthermore, if the securities of the company with 50% debt exceed in value those of the other business, investors would profit from selling their high-priced shares and using the proceeds, plus an equivalent amount of personal borrowing, to buy shares in the company with no debt. These arbitrage activities will soon correct any mispricing of the securities and drive them back to equivalence.

This fiscal Garden of Eden is a wonderful illusion, of course; it does not really exist. Corporate taxes are here to stay, and they have a great impact on a company's capital structure. Exhibit 3B shows that, in a world of corporate taxes, the decision to use debt increases the funds our sample company can distribute to its suppliers of capital by $96 ($616 versus $520) over what it could return to them with an all-equity capital structure. The source of this largesse is obvious: the Internal Revenue Service. By making the interest cost of debt tax deductible, the IRS provides a subsidy equal to the company's marginal tax rate (assumed to be 48%) times its interest expense ($200), or $96.[3] But this is not all, for there are personal income taxes to consider, which greatly complicate the choice between debt and equity. The complication arises from uncertainty about what tax rates to assume. If, for example, all investment income were taxed at the same personal rate, debt financing would remain just as attractive as before. Exhibit 3C extends our company example to show that, if both interest and dividend income were taxed at a 50% personal rate, a capital structure of 50% debt would still enhance the company's total distributable funds—here by $48 ($308 − $260).

In the real world, of course, interest and dividends are not taxed alike. Furthermore, much of the return on equity comes in the form of capital gains, which are taxed only when the underlying shares are sold, and then at but 40% of the rate on interest income. For companies that pay no dividends and whose shareholders never sell their stock, the effective personal tax rate on equity income is zero.

In practice, these differences in personal tax rates carry a great deal of weight in capital-structure decisions. Think of a situation in which the effective tax rate on returns from debt is 35% and on returns from equity, 0%. As Exhibit 3D suggests, debt financing becomes much less attractive than in our previous examples, for the use of debt enhances total distributable funds by only $26 ($546 − $520)—as opposed to $48 (when all personal income is taxed at the same rate) and $96 (when no personal taxes exist).

Exhibit 3. Impact of Debt on Total Distributable Funds

A			B		
Equity	$4,000	$2,000	Equity	$4,000	$2,000
Debt	0	2,000	Debt	0	2,000
Capital	**$4,000**	**$4,000**	**Capital**	**$4,000**	**$4,000**
EBIT	$1,000	$1,000	EBIT	$1,000	$1,000
Interest	0	200	Interest	0	200
PBT	$1,000	$ 800	PBT	$1,000	$ 800
Tax	0	0	Tax	480	384
PAT	**$1,000**	**$ 800**	**PAT**	**$ 520**	**$ 416**
Distribution			**Distribution**		
Dividends	$1,000	$ 800	Dividends	$ 520	$ 416
Interest	0	200	Interest	0	200
Total	**$1,000**	**$1,000**	**Total**	**$ 520**	**$ 616**

C			D		
Equity	$4,000	$2,000	Equity	$4,000	$2,000
Debt	0	2,000	Debt	0	2,000
Capital	**$4,000**	**$4,000**	**Capital**	**$4,000**	**$4,000**
EBIT	$1,000	$1,000	EBIT	$1,000	$1,000
Interest	0	200	Interest	0	200
PBT	$1,000	$ 800	PBT	$1,000	$ 800
Tax	480	384	Tax	480	384
PAT	**$ 520**	**$ 416**	**PAT**	**$ 520**	**$ 416**
Distribution			**Distribution**		
Dividends	$ 520	$ 416	Dividends	$ 520	$ 416
Personal Tax	260	208	Personal Tax	0	0
Aftertax	**$ 260**	**$ 200**	**Aftertax**	**$ 520**	**$ 416**
Interest	$ 0	$ 200	Interest	$ 0	$ 200
Personal Tax	0	100	Personal tax	0	70
Aftertax	0	100	Aftertax	0	130
Total	**$ 260**	**$ 308**	**Total**	**$ 520**	**$ 546**

Debt Policy and Corporate Value

The impact of debt financing on total distributable funds influences, in turn, a company's value. The Appendix shows this influence at work. If, for example, a company in the 48% bracket were to substitute $1,000 of debt for $1,000 of equity and if the personal tax rate were 35% on debt income and 10% on equity, the value of the company should increase by .28 times the amount of the debt ($1,000), or $280.

These calculations suggest a few general observations. Note, first, that a company's exact payoff from debt financing depends on the particular tax rates of both company and investors and is, consequently, difficult to define. Note also that when the personal tax rate on equity is much lower than that on interest income (a condition that is currently built into the U.S. tax codes), the payoff is likely to be less than traditional financial theory would predict. Finally, note that for a company with no taxable income to shelter, using debt financing actually *reduces* its value!

Empirical studies have, in general, shown that—because of the tax deductibility of interest—debt financing leads on average to an addition to company value equal to some 10 to 17% of the addition to debt.[4] A company that switched from an all-equity capital structure to one that included $10 million of debt would therefore see its value rise by $1 million to $1.7 million.

The Problems with Debt

Now, these aggregate findings seem to argue for a company's raising its level of debt as much as possible. According to Modigliani and Miller, however, the

> existence of a tax advantage for debt financing . . . does not necessarily mean that corporations should at all times seek to use the maximum possible amount of debt in their capital structures.. . .[T]here are, as we pointed out, limitations imposed by lenders, as well as many other dimensions in real-world problems of financial strategy which are not fully comprehended within the framework of static equilibrium models.. . .These additional considerations, which are typically grouped under the rubric of "the need for preserving flexibility," will normally imply the maintenance by the corporation of a substantial reserve of untapped borrowing power.[5]

This flexibility is important as a defense against financial distress and its attendant costs, which include, but are not limited to, the costs of potential bankruptcy. (Indeed, in most cases, bankruptcy costs are rather small. For example, out-of-pocket bankruptcy costs for railroads amounted to only 3 to 5% of their past market yalue.[6]) Far more significant is the likelihood that aggressive use of debt will make it difficult to raise necessary funds quickly on acceptable terms. And, obviously, liquidity constraints can lead to altered operating and product-market strategies that in turn may reduce a company's market value.

Managers fearful of incurring liquidity constraints or of violating debt covenants will usually trim strategic expenditures, be unaggressive in exploiting market and investment opportunities, and base operating policies on the low end of a range of sales forecasts. At the same time, competitors are more likely to mount an attack, for an aggressive financial strategy often renders a company less capable of responding vigorously to market conditions.

Problems may also arise with the hidden "agency" costs of monitoring the loan covenants, indenture agreements, property mortgages, and performance guarantees that accompany debt financing. Especially for highly leveraged growth companies, agency costs may become prohibitive as debt approaches 20 to 30% of capital at market value. The specter of financial distress reminds lenders that a substantial portion of that value reflects future investment opportunities, which are meaningful only if the company continues to prosper. Providers of debt capital are usually willing to lend against tangible assets or future cash flows from existing activities but not against intangible assets or uncertain growth prospects. For most companies, the implicit costs of financial distress brought on by too much debt—lost opportunities, vulnerability to attack, suboptimal operating policies, and inaccessibility to debt capital—loom larger than the threat of bankruptcy. Furthermore, as the level of debt rises as a percentage of total capital, so does the probability that a company, especially if it has high depreciation charges, will have insufficient income to enjoy fully the tax deductibility of its interest expense.

Establishing a Sound Debt Policy

CFOs do, naturally, pay attention to these various considerations, but their main responsibility must be to balance a company's financial needs with its ability to obtain financing. It is their job to preserve continuity in the flow of funds so that no strategically important program or policy ever fails for lack of corporate purchasing power. And they must protect this continuity of funds even during turbulent capital markets or bad times for the company.

Accordingly, CFOs must rely on traditional suppliers of capital. The delays involved in developing new institutional sources, especially when conditions are difficult, make the timely pursuit of strategy impossible. CFOs should, of course, constantly attempt to broaden their range of financing alternatives, but they must realize that critically important programs require well-established sources of capital that are reliable even in adversity.

Questions to Ask

The critical measure of a company's overall financial health is, as Exhibit 4 suggests, the degree of fit between its strategic goals and operating policies and its ability to raise funds. More particularly, its debt policy must ensure access to funds on a timely basis from traditional suppliers of capital. How can CFOs formulate a sensible and successful debt policy for their companies—one that they can sell with confidence to the rest of top management? We suggest that they begin by asking themselves the following questions:

1. *What are the company's real financing requirements?*

How much additional money will it have to raise during the next three to five years to carry out its portfolio of product-market strategies? What is the likely duration of that need? Can it be deferred without incurring large organizational or opportunity costs?

2. *What are the special characteristics of that financing in terms of currencies, maturities, fixed versus floating rates, special takedown or prepayment provisions, ease of renegotiation, and the like?*

3. *What segments of the capital markets will the company tap for each type of finance needed?*[7]

4. *What are the lending criteria used by each of the target sources of capital?*

An analysis of these criteria, which differ considerably from lender to lender, will suggest a target capital structure for the company.[8] The appropriate level of debt in that structure will vary in turn from company to company with differences in industry, quality of management, sales volatility, competitive position, profitability, and so on. For example, companies with high operating and competitive risk might try to offset it with low financial risk; in contrast, companies with low operating and competitive risk are much freer to use high levels of debt.

In practice, many companies express their target debt level as that which will result in a bond rating of A or higher. Their concern for an A rating reflects three major considerations: first, companies rated below A have been unable at times to raise funds in the public bond market on

Exhibit 4. Corporate Financial System

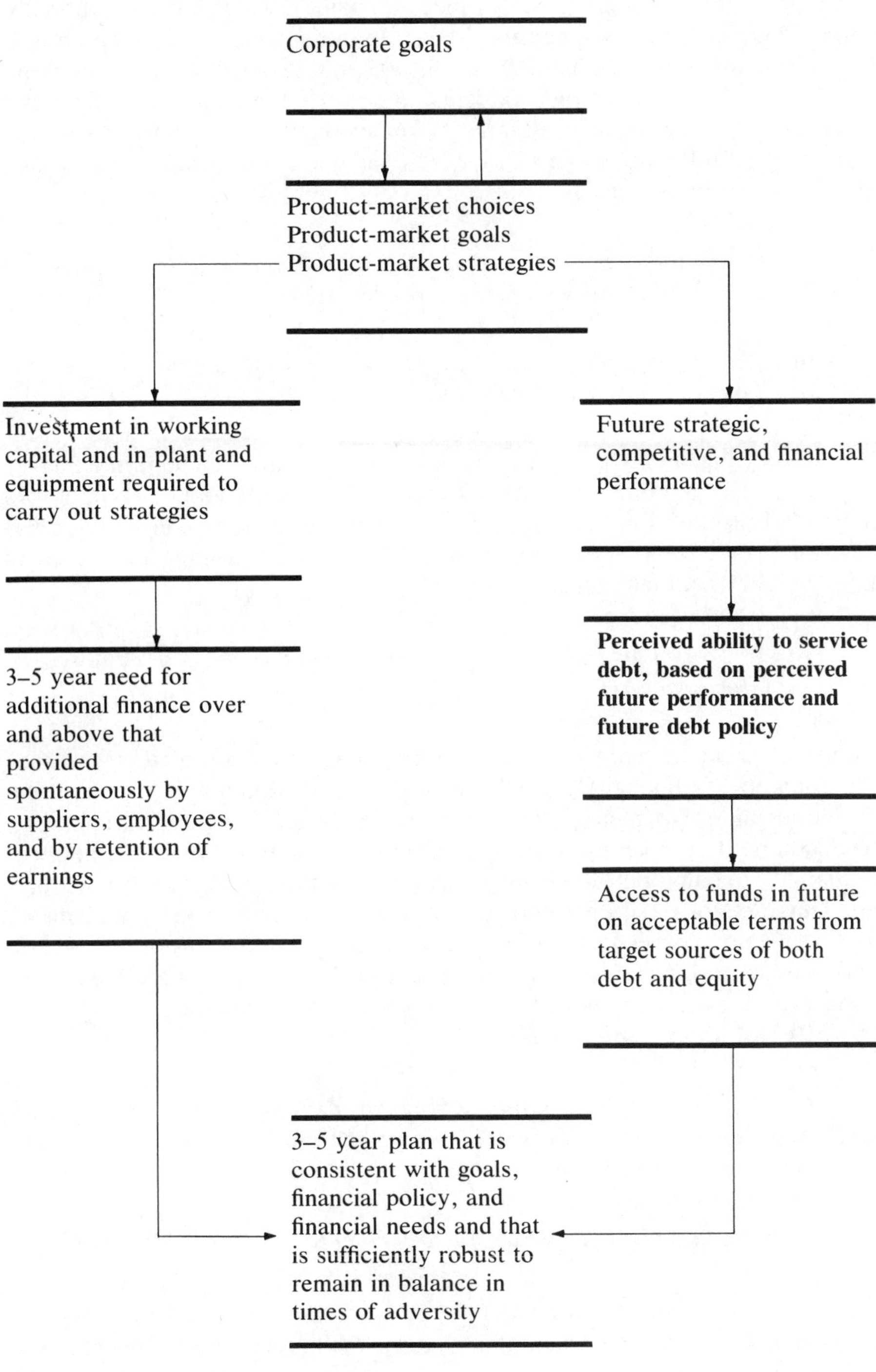

acceptable terms; second, life insurance companies, which have traditionally been a source of debt finance for BBB rated companies, are vulnerable to a sudden reduction in loanable funds should policyholders decide to borrow against the cash value of their policies; and third, companies need financial reserves to protect against adversity. For example, since the Ford Motor Company hit difficulties in 1979, its debt has been downgraded three times in less than three years.[9]

5. *Could the company comply with all loan covenants, as reflected in its pro forma financial statements, in good times and bad?*

6. *Will the company's debt policy allow a flow of funds to all strategically important programs even during adversity?*

Specifically, against what scenarios of adversity is management most eager to protect itself? If bad times hit, what are the company and its competitors most likely to do? Furthermore, in each of these scenarios, how much additional finance would the company need? How much warning would it have? How would its target sources react?[10]

7. *Will the company be competitively vulnerable if it achieves its target capital structure?*

This danger can take any of several forms: attack by a competitor who sees the company as financially weak; management's adoption of conservative operating and investment policies—to the detriment of the company's long-term competitive position—because of worries about a shortfall of finance; or inability to find funds for strategically important programs during adversity and thus loss of position to competitors who are able to get financing. A loss of even one percentage point in profitability, if it continues for 10 years, will more than offset the estimated gain of 4% in the per-share value of a company's equity that, as Exhibit 5 shows, results from an increase in debt from 20% of book value to 40%.

8. *What are the implications of the new debt policy for existing bondholders and shareholders, the latter in terms of earnings per share, dividends per share, and market price?*[11]

9. *Can the new debt policy be implemented?*

Can the funds needed during the next five years be raised in a manner consistent with the target capital structure? Will management be willing to

Exhibit 5. Theoretical Wealth-Creation Opportunities through the Capital-Structure Decision

Line	Debt as Percent of Book Capital		
	0%	**20%**	**40%**
1 Debt	$ 0	$ 200	$ 400
2 Book equity	1,000	800	600
3 Total book capital	$1,000	$1,000	$1,000
4 EBIT/book capital	30%	30%	30%
5 EBIT(line 3 × line 4)	$ 300	$ 300	$ 300
6 Interest(line 1 × 10%)	0	20	40
7 Profit before tax(line 5 − line 6)	$ 300	$ 280	$ 260
8 Profit after tax	$ 150	$ 140	$ 130
9 Value of company[a]	$1,000	$1,040	$1,080
10 Value of debt(line 1)	0	200	400
11 Value of equity(line 9 − line 10)	$1,000	$ 840	$ 680
12 Number of shares[b]	100	80.8	63
13 Value per share	$ 10	$ 10.40	$ 10.80
14 Percent increase in value per share		+4%	+4%

[a]The market value of the company at 0% debt is assumed to equal the book value. The market value is assumed to rise by an amount equal to 20% times the change in the dollar amount of debt, in line with the theoretical impact of corporate and personal taxes. This analysis omits the cost of financial distress.

[b]The number of shares reduced through the repurchase of shares in an amount equal to the change in the amount of debt divided by the market value per share at the new capital structure.

raise funds in that manner? If not, is management prepared to change its product-market strategies or dividend policy?

The CFO's Responsibility

Answers to this set of questions can help CFOs arrive at sound decisions regarding capital structure and effectively communicate them to other top managers. Although much research supports the belief that some substitution of debt for equity will boost a company's value, no simple formulas exist for calculating the optimal level. But limits to the payoff from using debt do indeed exist. In theory, as we have seen, a growth in debt from 20 to 40% of book capital will increase the per-share value of a company's stock by only 4% or so—not counting the expected costs of financial distress (see Exhibit 5). The problem for CFOs is therefore to identify the point at which the incremental risks of financial distress more than offset the incremental benefits of the interest tax shield.

Financial statements of many American companies, however, reveal a heavier reliance on debt than is justified by the payoff from the tax deductibility of interest. Why so? Because under certain conditions a CFO may be inclined to push a company's capital structure beyond its optimal balance point. Among these conditions are the following:

- ☐ The company is privately held and is precluded either from raising new equity or from raising it at an acceptable price. Here the alternative to debt financing is to forgo projects that are strategically important.
- ☐ The CFO overestimates the payoff from debt financing by confusing the high returns from borrowing at a low fixed rate before an unexpected surge in interest rates with the payoff from the tax deductibility of interest.
- ☐ The CFO fails to understand the theoretical basis for wealth creation through debt financing at the company level or to take account of both corporate and personal taxes.

Other, more general, considerations may also be involved:

- ☐ Less effort and time are required to bring out a debt issue than an equity issue. DuPont, for instance, once raised several billion dollars of financing by telephone in one afternoon.
- ☐ Earnings-per-share growth is often an important measure of managers' performance and an important influence on their compensation. Thus, to heighten EPS growth by increasing financial leverage may seem to them an attractive policy.
- ☐ Many managements strive to avoid interference or control by outside suppliers of capital.[12] Low debt levels may help them avoid onerous restrictive covenants; but in a world of inflation-induced financing needs, dependence on the equity markets may appeal even less than the covenants do. Further, distrustful of the equity market's rationality in setting prices and concerned for the volatility of their company's stock, managers remember that leveraging with debt raises the rate of sales growth that can be financed without the sale of new equity.

An unleveraged company earning a 15% return on capital after taxes and reinvesting 60% of its earnings can finance nominal sales growth of 9% per year without the sale of new equity (see Exhibit 6). With inflation at 9%, real growth is zero. In contrast, were the same company leveraged with debt equal to 40% of book capital, it could fund nominal sales growth of 13% per year and real sales growth of 4%. It would also need to seek new equity less often and so could tap the market on more favorable terms.

Exhibit 6. Financial Leverage and Sustainable Sales Growth

Line		Debt as Percentage of Book Capital	
		0%	**40%**
1	Total book capital, beginning of year	$1,000	$1,000
2	Debt	$ 0	$ 400
3	Book equity	$1,000	$ 600
4	EBIT/book capital	30%	30%
5	EBIT	$ 300	$ 300
6	Interest (line 2 × 10%)	0	40
7	Profit before tax	$ 300	$ 260
8	Tax at 50%	150	130
9	Profit after tax	$ 150	$ 130
10	Dividends (line 9 × 40%)	60	52
11	Earnings reinvested	$ 90	$ 78
12	Equity, end of year (line 3 + line 11)	$1,090	$ 678
13	Increase in equity (line 11 ÷ line 3)	9%	13%
14	Increase in liabilities consistent with no change in liabilities to equity	9%	13%
15	Increase in equity plus liabilities	9%	13%
16	Increase in assets that can be financed without equity sale (line 15)	9%	13%
17	Increase in nominal sales consistent with a stable sales-to-assets ratio[a]	**9%**	**13%**
18	Rate of inflation (assumed)	9%	9%
19	Increase in real sales that can be financed without sale of new equity	**0%**	**4%**

[a]The percent increase in nominal sales that can be financed without sale of new equity (assuming a constant ratio of total liabilities to equity and a constant ratio of sales to total assets) is equal to the nominal return on common equity (book equity at the beginning of the year) times the percentage of earnings retained in business.

Especially given the many-sided appeal of debt financing, good two-way communication between CFOs and the rest of top management is essential. Major mistakes in capital-structure decisions often follow from (1) undue emphasis on but one of the many determinants of an appropriate debt policy; (2) failure to give sufficient consideration to the volatility of lenders' attitudes; (3) failure to test the debt policy in advance for its viability in times of adversity; or (4) the tendency of operating managers to push CFOs during buoyant times toward higher debt levels than are prudent.

As too many businesses have learned the hard way, the time to build financial reserves is when things are going well. Correcting an unduly aggressive use of debt is always painful, but especially so if that adjustment must be made under duress. To avoid such agonizing retrenchments—that is, to plan for a steady flow of capital (and to secure management's commitment to that plan)—is the central professional challenge and responsibility of today's CFO.

Notes

1. Robert S. Hamada, "The Effect of the Firm's Capital Structure on the Systematic Risk of Common Stocks," *Journal of Finance*, May 1972, p. 435.

2. Franco Modigliani and Merton Miller, "The Cost of Capital, Corporation Finance, and the Theory of Investment," *American Economic Review*, June 1958, p. 261.

3. See Modigliani and Miller, "Corporate Income Taxes and the Cost of Capital: A Correction," *American Economic Review*, June 1963, p. 433.

4. Ronald W. Masulis, "A Model of Stock Price Adjustments to Capital Structure Changes," Working Paper, UCLA, September 20, 1980; Modigliani and Miller, "Some Estimates of the Cost of Capital to the Electric Utility Industry, 1954–57," *American Economic Review*, June 1966, p. 333.

5. Modigliani and Miller, "Corporate Income Taxes and the Cost of Capital," p. 442.

6. Jerold B. Warner, "Bankruptcy Costs: Some Evidence," *Journal of Finance*, May 1977, p. 337.

7. See Jay O. Light and William L. White, *The Financial System* (Homewood, Ill., Richard D. Irwin, 1979) for a full discussion of the forces influencing the rules that govern decisions in the major institutions and the impact of such rules on pricing of securities in financial markets.

8. See Morton Backer and Martin L. Gosman, "The Use of Financial Ratios in Credit Downgrade Decisions," *Financial Management*, Spring 1980, p. 53. Their three-year study explores the marked differences in the financial ratios various lenders use to assess creditworthiness.

9. See also *Standard & Poor's Ratings Guide*, edited by Karl Sokoloff and Joan Matthews (New York, McGraw-Hill, 1979), for a discussion of the rate-setting process.

10. For an excellent discussion of the need to develop a comprehensive financial and operating plan to meet sudden adversity, see Gordon Donaldson's Article 10, "Strategy for Financial Emergencies," in this book.

11. For a discussion of the determinants of share prices, see Article 12, "Is Your Stock Worth Its Market Price?," by Thomas R. Piper and William E. Fruhan, Jr.

12. See Gordon Donaldson, "Self-Sustaining Growth: A Study of the Financial Goals of the Mature Industrial Corporation," Working manuscript, October 1981.

Appendix

Table A. Impact of Financial Leverage on Company Value

Assume a company with expected constant earnings before interest and taxes out to infinity and with a policy of distributing all of its earnings as dividends. If the company has no debt, then the operating earnings available to investors as dividends are equal to EBIT $(1-T_c)$, and investors will have, for purposes of consumption (after payment of personal taxes), an amount equal to EBIT $(1-T_c)(1-T_{pe})$, where T_c is the company's tax rate on a marginal dollar of income and T_{pe} is the shareholders' tax rate on a marginal dollar of income in the form of dividends.

Equation 1:
Funds available for consumption after payment of all taxes = EBIT $(1-T_c)(1-T_{pe})$.

Assume a company similar in all respects to the one just described except that it leverages itself with debt, D, borrowed at an interest rate, i, from investors who are taxed on interest income at a rate T_{pi}. The company is able to distribute to its suppliers of capital an amount equal to $(EBIT - iD) \times (1-T_c) + iD$, and the investors will have, for purposes of consumption (after payment of personal taxes), an amount equal to $(EBIT - iD) \times$

Equation 2:

$$\frac{[(1-T_{pi}) - (1-T_c)(1-T_{pe})]\, iD}{i\,(1-T_{pi})}$$

$$= [1 - \frac{(1-T_c)(1-T_{pe})}{(1-T_{pi})}]D.$$

Thus,

Equation 3:

$$V_l = V_u + [1 - \frac{(1-T_c)(1-T_{pe})}{(1-T_{pi})}]\, D,$$

where

V_l = value of a leveraged company.
V_u = value of an unleveraged company.

$(1-T_c)(1-T_{pe}) + iD(1-T_{pi})$. This is equal to EBIT $(1-T_c)(1-T_{pe})$ − $iD(1-T_c)(1-T_{pe}) + iD(1-T_{pi})$. The first term is identical to the funds available for consumption from an unleveraged company.

Thus the value of a leveraged company, V_l, is equal to the value of an unleveraged company, V_u, plus the present value of an annual flow equal to $iD[(1-T_{pi}) \times (1-T_c) \times (1-T_{pe})]$. The appropriate discount rate is the rate for flows of equal risk, adjusted for personal taxes, or $i(1-T_{pi})$. The present value of an annual flow of $iD[(1-T_{pi}) - (1-T_c)(1-T_{pe})]$ to infinity, at a rate equal to $i(1-T_{pi})$, is

T_c = corporate tax rate on a marginal dollar of earnings.

T_{pe} = personal tax rate on equity returns.

T_{pi} = personal tax rate on interest income from corporate debt.

D = dollar amount of debt.

Table B. Increase in the Company Value from Use of Debt (derived from Equation 3 above)

	Corporate tax rate of 48%			Corporate tax rate of 0%		
Personal tax rate on equity returns	Personal tax rate on debt returns			Personal tax rate on debt returns		
	T_{pi} = 0%	or **35%**	or 50%	T_{pi} = 0%	or 35%	or 50%
T_{pe} = 0%	.48D	.2D	(.04D)	0	(.54D)	(D)
or **10%**	.53D	**.28D**	.06D	.1D	(.38D)	(.8D)
or 20%	.58D	.36D	.17D	.2D	(.23D)	(.6D)

12

Is Your Stock Worth Its Market Price?

THOMAS R. PIPER and WILLIAM E. FRUHAN, JR.

Given todays's stock market conditions, few executives of corporations whose shares are in public hands would claim that the market is overvaluing their stock. Indeed, many lament the days in the early 1970s when price-earnings multiples were generally in the teens and higher. How can you determine if the stock market is misvaluing your stock? One way is through use of a dividend valuation model. It uses as its basis a company's fundamental determinants of value, including its prospects for profitability and its long-run investment opportunities. The result may not differ from Wall Street's estimate of your stock's value, but the model has many uses anyway as an aid to financial planning.

Valuation of a company and its common stock is an important part of financial management. In a publicly owned company especially, valuation inevitably enters discussions of the following:

- The prospect of selling new equity.
- The timing of new equity issues.
- The pricing of acquisitions and divestitures.
- The company's vulnerability to an unwanted takeover bid.
- The advisability of a stock repurchase program.

Unfortunately, the discussions often break down as managers try to reconcile today's price-earnings ratios with those prevailing in the 1960s and early 1970s. The sharp decline in P-E multiples has invalidated the old benchmarks of fair value. The confusion about the reasonableness of today's share prices can lead executives to conclude, erroneously, that their company's stock is grossly undervalued and therefore they should defer an equity issue or initiate a large stock repurchase plan.

In this article we review the evidence on the efficiency of U.S. capital markets and consider the implications of market efficiency for the corporate financial manager's ability to second-guess the market. We outline the limitations and dangers of commonly employed valuation methods and encourage the reader to use as one approach a method that recognizes the fundamental determinants of value: (1) the company's future, long-run profitability; (2) its future, long-run investment opportunities; (3) the risk-free rate of interest in the economy; and (4) the additional return that investors seek as compensation for the company's operating and financial risk that cannot be "diversified away" via the ownership of a portfolio of stocks.

Market Efficiency

When economists say that the stock market is efficient, they mean that information is widely and cheaply available to investors and that security prices reflect all relevant and ascertainable information. The agent in this efficiency is the large population of professional investors, each trying to achieve an excess return of ½% or 1%. (The importance of an incremental return of ½%, incidentally, should not be underestimated. In the pension portfolio management business, for example, an incremental return of 50 basis points can reduce annual retirement plan costs by roughly 10%. Those who earn superior returns gain new clients.)

These investors, and analysts too, quickly process new information about a company or an industry, resulting in a rapid adjustment of the stock price—possibly so rapid that no one can extract any huge gains. In a perfectly efficient market, because all publicly available information is embedded in the market price, an analyst cannot identify mispriced securities by reviewing this information.

There is some evidence of periodic breakdown in market efficiency for certain stocks, caused in part by restrictions on short selling and by the reluctance of investment managers to hold portfolios that differ greatly from those of competing portfolio managers. The competitive and personal risks of betting against other managers *and* of being wrong apparently outweigh the possible benefits from the pursuit of contrary investment. Putting it another way, one's job is probably safe as long as one's relative performance is *reasonably* good.

There is also evidence that sometimes insiders hold information that gives them profitable market-timing opportunities. The most celebrated case centered on a major discovery of silver, zinc, and copper near Timmins, Ontario, by Texas Gulf Sulphur in 1964. Some members of management allegedly profited from transactions in Texas Gulf stock prior to announcement of the find.

But the concept of an efficient market is both appealing intellectually and remarkably well supported by the facts.[1] The concept provides the financial manager in a publicly owned enterprise with a good starting point for thinking about security prices. Unless a person has a very good reason to believe to the contrary, it is advisable to assume that the market price is neither more nor less than fair value. Outguessing the market should be seen for what it is: a task becoming more difficult as the number of sophisticated professional investors has increased. A decision that the market is giving the wrong value to a stock should be supported either by information not previously considered by investors or by evidence of a breakdown in the valuation process.

An example of the analysis we alluded to, and represented schematically in Exhibit 1, may be helpful. In mid-1978 the management of Digityme, a medium-sized specialty chemical company, was convinced that the stock

Exhibit 1. Analysts' and Company Management's Rationales on Determination of Proper Stock Price

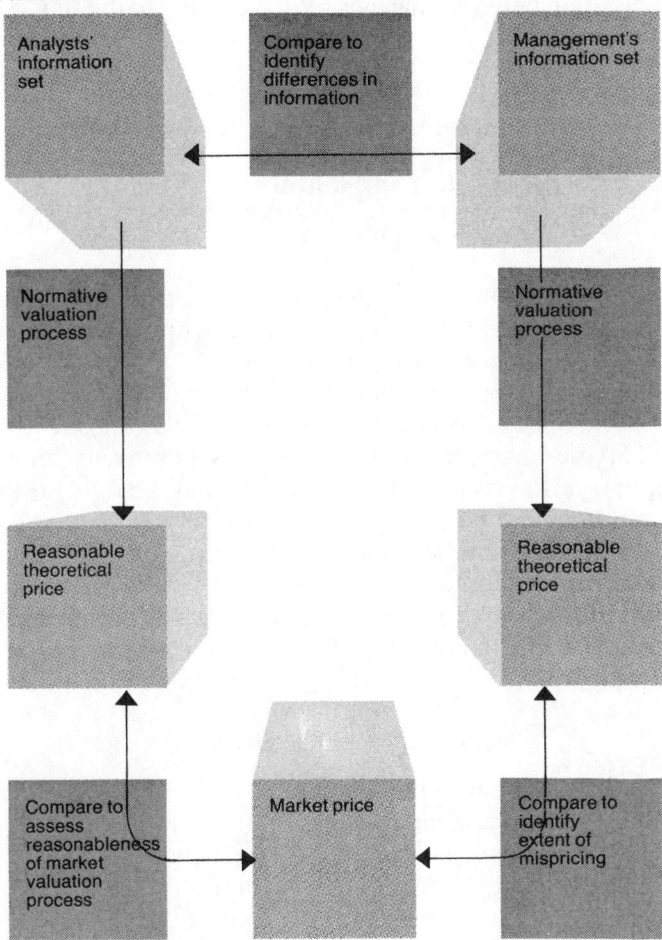

was undervalued. The company's price-earnings ratio had tumbled from the high 30s, during the 1970 to 1973 period, to 8. A large share repurchase program at a 17% premium over the market seemed certain to benefit the remaining shareholders and reduce the risk of an unfriendly takeover. Management decided first, however, to identify the source of the mispricing and quantify its magnitude.

Examination of the publicly available information raised doubts about any undervaluation. Other medium-sized technology-based companies had suffered similar revaluations during the 1970s. Furthermore, the shares seemed reasonably priced on the basis of the consensus forecasts of respected analysts who followed the stock. Their valuation process, as reflected in the market price, seemed sound.

Fortunately, Digityme management had made a full assessment of the prospects for the various divisions. It had also examined the appropriateness of generally accepted accounting principles to its situation. This analysis identified a wide gap between management's forecast of the return on equity and that of the "Street":

Street estimate	15%
Management estimate	
Before accounting adjustments	18%
After such adjustments	25%

According to the internal forecast, the stock was undervalued by 35 to 45%. Management, having found that it had no quarrel with the analysts' valuation process in arriving at a theoretical price (consonant with the steps in Exhibit 1), decided that the gap lay in the information that the two sides had available. As a result, the company resolved to repurchase shares aggressively.

The Digityme example illustrates three requirements for successful second-guessing of the market. First, management must avoid the trap of equating a low P-E multiple (on a historical basis) with evidence of undervaluation. Second, the company must monitor the leading analysts' perceptions for significant variations from its own forecasts. Third, the company must be able to translate these forecasts into estimates of economic value. It is to the matter of valuation processes that we now turn.

Valuation Methods

Intuition tells us that a company's economic value depends on its prospects for profitability, its future ability to reinvest funds in the business, its riskiness, and the return available from a risk-free benchmark (the standard is Treasury Bills). It is not surprising, for example, that IBM sells at a substantial premium over its book value, whereas Boston Edison sells at a substantial discount from book value (see the last column of Exhibit 2).

Exhibit 2. Comparison of IBM and Boston Edison financial characteristics (in percent)

	Return on Book Equity		Dividend Payout Ratio			
	1975–79	1980	1975–79	1980	Estimated Cost of Equity	Market Value as a Percent of Book Value
IBM	21	24	55	60	16	225
Boston Edison	8.8	11	152	73	15	65

A glance at the performance of each explains the pricing. IBM has been very successful at reinvesting a substantial percentage of its earnings at high returns. Investors will pay a premium over book value in recognition of IBM's ability to earn above-market returns. In contrast, Boston Edison's business requires heavy reinvestment of funds at low returns. Its stock is priced accordingly at a discount.

What a financial executive needs is a valuation method that (1) uses explicit assumptions about his or her company's future performance, the relative riskiness of its common stock, and the risk-free rate of interest, and (2) estimates the value of a company's stock based on these assumptions. Book value as a measure of economic value ignores the key roles of profitability and reinvestment opportunities, and is therefore of little help. Liquidation value is appropriate, obviously, only if the management plans to dissolve the enterprise. Recognizing these deficiencies, analysts in corporations, investment banking firms, and brokerage houses are turning increasingly to a long-time friend, the dividend valuation model, as a method of valuation.[2]

Dividend Valuation Model

What the long-term determinants of stock prices are is not mysterious. The decision to purchase common stock is quite like the decision by a company to invest in inventory or receivables or in plant and equipment. In return for an initial outlay, the investor hopes to receive a cash return in the form of dividends or profit on sale of the stock, or both. The value of the stock equals the present value of the future cash inflows discounted at the investor's required return (the cost of equity).

Suppose a company currently earns an 8% return on its book equity of $10 per share and pays out one-half of its net income as dividends. It expects to continue this pattern of profitability and earnings reinvestment indefinitely. The company's operations are not highly cyclical and its debt is moderate. Investors, recognizing the low risk, "require" only a 13% return on their investment.[3] This represents a 4% risk premium over the 9% return available from risk-free U.S. government bonds. Exhibit 3 shows the data affecting dividend growth. (See the Appendix for a discussion of forecasting a dividend stream.)

Obtaining an 8% return on book value and retaining half of its earnings, the company will show EPS and dividend per share growth of 4% per year. The present value of a dividend stream that grows at a constant rate to infinity is equal to today's dividend rate divided by the investor's cost of equity less the growth rate of dividends per share. This present value (discount rate, 13%) is \$4.44 per share. In other words, the economic value of the stock is \$4.44—which, assuming an efficient market, would be the market value of the stock.

In requiring forecasts of profitability and reinvestment rates far into the future, the dividend valuation model makes great demands on management. Nevertheless, it is useful to have a valuation method that focuses on the fundamental determinants of value. This focus may result in better forecasts and in a greater appreciation of the degree of uncertainty involved in the price assessment. The dividend valuation model also eliminates dependence on relative valuation and allows an estimate of absolute value.

An estimate of absolute value is important for maintaining a semblance of rationality when the market seems wildly irrational—as in the "two-tier" market of the early 1970s when growth stocks sold at very high price-earnings ratios. Within that group, the P-E multiple of one company seemed no more or less outrageous than those of others.

One of those market darlings was Avon Products, whose price had been bid up to \$140, or 60 times earnings, by early 1973 on the basis of its outstanding earnings record. Over the previous decade Avon's per-share net had grown at a compound annual rate of 17%.

Could Avon keep up the pace? Despite its lofty market premium, the company was showing familiar signs of aging—a gradual decline in profit-

Exhibit 3. Future Dividend Stream of Sample Company

	1	2	3 = 1 × 2	4	5 = 3 × 4	6	7 = 5 × 6	8 = 3 − 5
Year	Beginning Book Equity	Return on Book Equity	Earnings per Share	Div. Payout Ratio	Div. per Share	Present Val. Factor 13%	Present Value	Retained Earnings
1	\$10.00	8%	\$0.80	50%	\$0.40	.885	\$0.35	\$0.40
2	10.40	8	0.83	50	0.42	.783	0.33	0.41
3	10.81	8	0.86	50	0.43	.693	0.30	0.43
4	11.24	8	0.90	50	0.45	.613	0.28	0.45
5	11.69	8	0.94	50	0.47	.543	0.26	0.47
			+4%/year		+4%/year			

ability and in its ability to reinvest a high percentage of earnings. Its return on equity had slipped from 37% in 1965 to 33% in 1972, and its dividend payout rate had crept up from 55% in 1965 to 63% in 1972.

An article in *Fortune* at the time suggested that the debate over the "true" valuation of growth stocks be resolved by use of the dividend valuation model. For Avon the author postulated a steadily declining growth rate and a steadily rising dividend rate for the maturing company. Applying to the projected dividend stream a discount rate suitable to the riskiness of the stock (14%), he calculated its value at only $42.50![4]

Perhaps some of this reasoning on absolute value sank in with investors. Avon's stock, which had already slipped from a February 1973 high of $140 to $102 at the time of publication of the article—partly on account of disappointing earnings gains in the second quarter of 1973—collapsed along with the rest of the market, reaching a low of $19 in the fall of 1974. It then recovered and has traded in a range of $30 to $60 for the past five years.

Recently, management of a rapidly expanding computer company was pondering the timing of an equity issue. Its share price, along with the prices of other technology stocks, had run up sharply. The stock was selling at 12 times estimated 1981 earnings and almost 5 times book value. Management found it difficult to forecast performance—which contributed to the uncertainty over timing.

The chief financial officer broke the impasse by estimating what the company would have to do to merit the current market price. When confronted with the required future profitability and reinvestment rate, the CEO quickly decided to instruct the underwriter to proceed with the offering. The range of numbers produced by the company's forecasts fell below those necessary to warrant the value that the market placed on the shares.

A Short-Cut Approach to Valuation

Book value alone provides very little insight into the true value of a stock; it is disconcerting to see the frequency with which stocks are cited as "cheap" or "undervalued" because they are selling at less than book value. Often an examination of the company's performance in fundamental terms readily explains the low market valuation.

The company may be a "cash trap"—meaning that it cannot earn an adequate return on its book equity, but it continues to reinvest much of its earnings at this inadequate return. Boston Edison is an example of a company caught in a hostile regulatory environment and unable to earn an adequate return. The market sees Boston Edison as a cash trap and prices its shares accordingly.

Book value fails to reflect how much a company is earning on its capital. It is possible, however, to develop a matrix of market value-book value ratios that incorporates the three determinants of value: (1) the reinvestment rate, (2) the return earned on equity capital, and (3) the return that investors require.

The matrix tables are developed by calculating dividends per share for a certain set of assumptions and discounting them to their present value at the company's cost of equity. The present value is then divided by the beginning book value to arrive at the market value-book value ratio. For example, the ratio for the sample company shown in Exhibit 3 is .44 ($4.44 ÷ $10).

These matrices (Exhibit 4) are rather rigid in their assumption that, for example, the return on equity or the reinvestment rate will remain constant for 5, 10, or 20 years. They do, however, offer a quick method of determining the reasonableness of a particular ratio of market price to book value. They confirm that the stock of IBM, which seems able to reinvest 30 to 40% of its earnings at returns that are 7 to 9% greater than its cost of equity, should sell at a substantial premium to book value. Boston Edison's market value-book value ratio of .65 seems appropriate in view of heavy reinvestment of earnings at returns that are 3 to 5% less than the returns that its shareholders require.

The examples of IBM, Boston Edison, and Avon are not unique. A study of 1,448 companies indicates that the pricing suggested by the dividend valuation model is fairly consistent with the actual market value-book value ratios as of December 31, 1975 for their common shares.[5] Exhibit 5 shows the ratios. A company whose return on equity averaged, say, between 8% and 11.9% during the previous 10-year period, and whose reinvested earnings averaged between 20% and 39%, had a market value-book value ratio of .7.

Exhibit 4. Market Value-Book Value Ratios Based on Cost of Equity of 15%

30 % of earnings reinvested

Years in which returns will continue†	Future return on book equity 10 %	15 %	20 %	25 %	30 %
5	.8	1.0	1.2	1.4	1.6
10	.7	1.0	1.3	1.7	2.0
20	.6	1.0	1.4	2.0	2.6
30	.6	1.0	1.5	2.2	3.0

70 % of earnings reinvested

Years in which returns will continue	Future return on book equity 10 %	15 %	20 %	25 %	30 %
5	.8	1.0	1.2	1.5	1.7
10	.7	1.0	1.4	2.0	2.7
20	.5	1.0	1.8	3.1	5.4
30	.4	1.0	2.2	4.6	10.0

IBM ○ Boston Edison ●

*It is necessary to calculate a set of tables for each cost of equity figure. The theoretical ratio of market value to book value changes as the cost of equity assumption is changed.

†The company is assumed to earn a return on book equity equal to its cost of equity after the initial 5-, 10-, 20-, or 30-year period.

Exhibit 5. Median Market Value-Book Value Ratios for 1,488 Stocks as of December 31, 1975

Percentage of Earnings Reinvested	Average Rate of Return on Common Equity, 1966–75				
	2% to 7.9%	8% to 11.9%	12% to 17.9%	18% to 24.9%	25% and over
19% or less	.4	.4	1.2	1.4	NMF[a]
20% to 39%	.3	.7	1.0	NMF	3.7
40% to 59%	.4	.7	1.1	2.2	4.6
60% to 79%	.4	.7	1.0	1.9	NMF
80% to 119%	.4	.7	1.0	2.1	NMF
120% to 159%	.4	.7	1.5	3.0	NMF
160% and more	.4	.6	1.9	NMF	NMF

[a]Not a meaningful figure.

Not surprisingly, the study identified a number of companies whose market prices differed significantly from the expected prices based on the dividend valuation model. The discrepancies undoubtedly resulted in part from (1) distortions in the reported profitability due to accounting practices or inflation; (2) opportunities for significant enhancement of value through recapitalization or sale of assets; or (3) forecasts for profitability and reinvestment different from historical levels. However, these discrepancies point to the importance of careful analysis of the fundamentals rather than to a flaw in the valuation model.

An Old and Dangerous Friend

Price-earnings ratios cannot be ignored. They are a part of most discussions on whether a stock or an acquisition is cheap or dear. They are part of our internal filters, our baggage, built up by years of thinking about share prices in price-earnings terms. Indeed, they are useful if approached with care and recognition that they can be very misleading.

The reasonableness of a company's P-E ratio often is tested by one of four methods:

1. *Comparison of today's P-E ratio with its average level of the past five to ten years.* Even in today's environment, executives balk at investment bankers' recommendations to sell new equity at P-E ratios of five to seven. The executives recall too fondly the multiples of 13 to 18 that prevailed in the 1960s.

Wishful thinking may cause a company's management to overlook the real reasons for a decline in the ratio and make the dangerous choice to defer issuing new equity. Most stocks have suffered, of course, from the increase in interest rates from 5% in 1965 to double digits today, as lenders have attempted to protect their real returns in the face of inflation. The cost of equity for a company of average risk in the S&P industrial index of 400 stocks has risen accordingly from an estimated 9% in 1965 to about 15% at this writing.

An increase in the discount rate from 9% to 15% substantially reduces the present value of a stream of dividends, and this reduction is reflected directly in the P-E ratio. Exhibit 6 sets out the history.

A key issue is whether, in the future, growth in the company's earnings and dividends will offset the rise in the discount rate resulting from the higher inflation rate. This, naturally, depends on management's ability to raise product prices and nominal profitability to levels consistent with the higher nominal cost of equity.[6]

2. *Comparison of today's P-E ratio, expressed as a percent of the P-E ratio for a broad market index, with its average level of the past 5 to 10 years.* Analysts generally try to neutralize factors that influence markets by comparing a stock's current price-earnings ratio as a percent of the ratio of, say, the S&P 400 (in the case of the stock of a manufacturer) with the same relationship for the past 5 to 10 years. This neutralizes such factors as the rise in interest rates. It does not, however, recognize differences among companies in their ability to raise product prices and nominal profitability in order to offset higher rates of inflation.

This approach, furthermore, fails to adjust for situations in which a company's fundamentals are suffering. For example, Xerox's P-E ratio as a percent of the P-E of the S&P 400 is at a historical low today. But this does not mean that Xerox stock is cheap relative to the market. Although still a very profitable company, Xerox clearly does not warrant the same *relative* P-E ratio today that it commanded in 1965. Its ability to reinvest earnings in high-return projects has weakened, as evidenced by a decline in its return on book equity from 31% to 18% and by an increase in its dividend payout ratio from 20% to 35%.

The Xerox case, of course, is not unusual; a maturing company can expect a substantial decline in its price-earnings ratio. In Exhibit 7 we have charted this experience for a typical, although hypothetical, company. As

Exhibit 6. Financial Data of Standard & Poor's Industrial Index, 1960–1980

	1960	1965	1970	1975	1976	1977	1978	1979	1980
Market value	$62	$99	$101	$101	$120	$105	$107	$121	$161
Earnings per share	$3.39	$5.51	$5.43	$8.55	$10.68	$11.57	$13.12	$16.08	$16.15[a]
P-E ratio	18	18	19	12	11	9	8	8	10
10-year Treasury bonds	4%	4%	8%	7%	7%	7%	8%	9%	12%

[a]Twelve months ended September 30, 1980.

Exhibit 7. Impact of Changing Fundamentals on P-E Ratio of Hypothetical Company

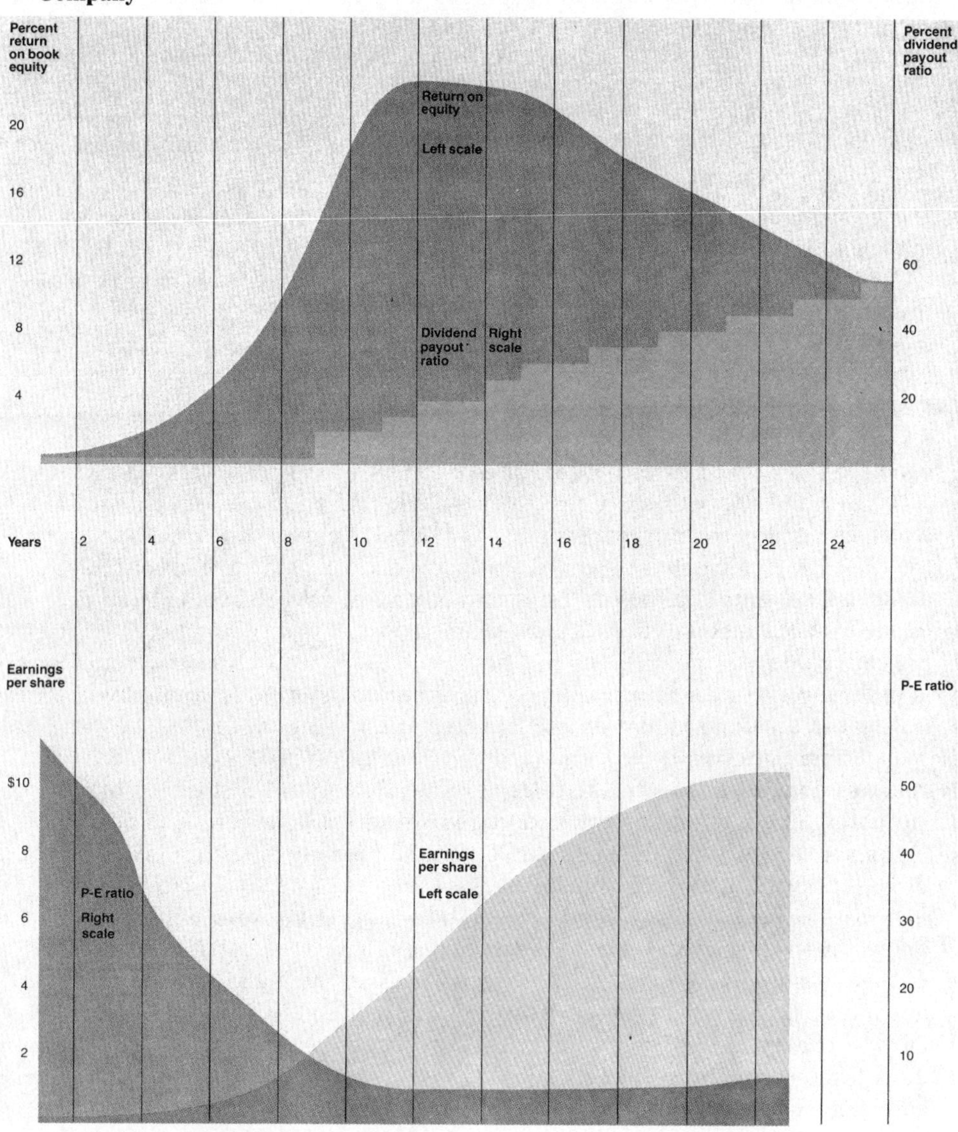

its return on equity flattens and then descends, its dividend payout ratio ascends along with its earnings. The decline of its P-E ratio anticipates the paths of the return-on-equity measure and the dividend payout ratio.

3. *Comparison of today's P-E ratio with those of comparable companies.* Another method of testing the reasonableness of a P-E ratio is to set it alongside the ratios of companies that are as comparable as possible in fundamental valuation terms—profitability, reinvestment opportunities, nondiversifiable operating characteristics, and financial risk.

Inasmuch as analysts use this approach widely, it is important for management to understand the pricing of a stock at a given moment. The approach has a built-in problem, however, because it may lead analysts (and investors) into the very trap that snared the unsuspecting buyer of growth stocks in 1972 and 1973—when the P-E ratios of entire groups of "comparable" companies were excessive.

4. *Calculation of what the company must do in absolute performance terms to be worth a certain P-E ratio.* To reach such a conclusion, management must first assess the reasonableness of its P-E ratio in such terms.

Exhibit 8 shows the P-E ratios that should prevail, based on profitability over time, ability to reinvest earnings, and a cost of equity of 15%. To develop the tables, we calculated the dividends per share for each set of assumptions about profitability and future reinvestment rates. We discounted the dividends to their present value at the assumed cost of equity, then divided the present value by the EPS in the first year to arrive at the theoretically appropriate P-E ratio. For example, the ratio for the sample company illustrating the dividend valuation model is 5.5 ($4.44 ÷ $.80).

Some patterns in the exhibit, being counterintuitive, could lead to erroneous conclusions as to the cheapness or dearness of a stock. It may be surprising that a company trapped in a low-return business for the next five years should sell at a higher multiple than a company able to reinvest 30% of its earnings at a 30% return on book equity. The explanation is that investors expect the first company to show a great improvement in profitability, earnings per share, and dividends per share at the end of five years, so they are pricing the stock in part on that basis. The high P-E ratio reflects a market price based on better prospects for profitability, divided by the low current earnings.

Price-earnings ratios are helpful, but only if used with considerable care. Part of that care should be an understanding of what must happen in fundamental terms to justify a particular P-E multiple. Tables similar to those in Exhibit 8 can help management gain that understanding.

Implications for the CFO

Outguessing the market obviously is not an easy game—the performance of institutional investors bears testimony to that. A conclusion by corporate management that the market is valuing the company's stock incorrectly

Exhibit 8. Theoretically Appropriate P-E Ratios Based on Cost of Equity of 15%

Years in Which Returns Will Continue[a]	30% of Earnings Reinvested				
	Return Earned on Book Equity				
	10%	15%	20%	25%	30%
5	8.2	6.7	5.9	5.5	5.3
10	7.2	6.7	6.5	6.6	6.8
20	6.3	6.7	7.2	7.9	8.8
30	6.0	6.7	7.5	8.6	10.0

Years in Which Returns Will Continue	70% of Earnings Reinvested				
	Return Earned on Book Equity				
	10%	15%	20%	25%	30%
5	8.1	6.7	6.1	5.8	5.7
10	6.8	6.7	7.1	7.8	8.9
20	5.2	6.7	9.0	12.6	18.0
30	4.5	6.7	10.8	18.5	33.3

Years in Which Returns Will Continue	100% of Earnings Reinvested				
	Return Earned on Book Equity				
	10%	15%	20%	25%	30%
5	8.0	6.7	6.2	6.1	6.2
10	6.4	6.7	7.7	9.2	11.4
20	4.1	6.7	11.7	21.2	38.7
30	2.6	6.7	17.9	48.8	132.0

[a]The company is assumed to earn a return on book equity equal to its cost of equity after the initial 5-, 10-, or 15-year period.

should be backed up either by the existence of information not publicly available or by evidence of a breakdown in the processing of the information.

There have been periods of market inefficiency, however, caused in part by the unwillingness of portfolio managers to hold portfolios that differ substantially from those of other managers, their competitors. On occasion, insiders also have obtained information that permitted some profitable market timing. Thus, second-guessing the market can be profitable for the corporation. It warrants working through a fundamental valuation of the stock based on the dividend valuation model. But it is a tough game wherein one is well advised to assume that the market price is right until the chief financial officer proves otherwise.

The payoff from a careful, fundamental valuation is not limited to those occasions when a stock is found to be incorrectly priced. Often the CFO's problem is to convince fellow managers that the market price is reasonable or to explain why forecasts of stock market prices are highly uncertain.

Absolute valuation, based on a full understanding of the fundamentals as seen by the better outside analysts and by the inside planners, can be an important input to those discussions.

Notes

1. For a review of the evidence, see Irwin Tepper, "Empirical Data Pertaining to the Efficiency of the Stock Market," #9-279-070 (Boston, Intercollegiate Case Clearing House).

2. For an account of the valuation models in use at leading institutional research and investment firms, see David F. Hawkins and Walter J. Campbell, *Equity Valuation: Models, Analysis and Implications* (New York, Financial Executives Research Foundation, 1978).

3. For a discussion of how to determine the cost of equity capital for a company, see David W. Mullins, "Diversification, the Capital Asset Pricing Model, and the Cost of Equity Capital," #9-276-183 (Boston, Intercollegiate Case Clearing House).

4. Daniel Seligman, "The Terrible Two-Tier Market (cont'd)," *Fortune*, October 1973, p. 106.

5. William E. Fruhan, Jr., *Financial Strategy: Studies in the Creation, Transfer, and Destruction of Shareholder Value* (Homewood, Ill., Richard D. Irwin, 1979), p. 24.

6. See John Lintner, "Inflation and Security Returns," *Journal of Finance*, May 1975, p. 259; also Franco Modigliani and Richard A. Cohn, "Inflation, Rational Valuation and the Market," *Financial Analysts Journal*, March-April 1979, p. 24.

Appendix. Developing a Dividend Forecast

A forecast of a company's dividend stream cannot be made in isolation. It must start with the goals for the company that management has set and revises periodically, and with management's portfolio of product-market choices and strategies.

This process coalesces eventually into an operating and financing plan over a period of, say, three to five years. One part of the plan is a determination of the need that the company may have for additional financing for the investments to support its product-market strategies.

Another part of the plan is a determination of the segments of the capital markets that the company plans to tap and the terms it would accept—which, of course, depend to a greater extent on its near-term competitive and financial performance.

Once management has settled on an operating and financing plan for the next several years, it can make a forecast of financial performance that includes a dividend stream. In tabular form the forecast could look like this:

	Years					
	1	2	3	4	5	. . .
Net income	$	$	$	$	$	$
Cash dividends						
Number of shares of common stock						
Earnings per share						
Dividends per share						
Debt as a percentage of capital						
Times interest earned						

At the end of the period of estimated dividends per share, it can be assumed that dividends *per share* grow from that point on at a constant rate equal to the expected return on book equity times the percent of earnings reinvested (assuming no future new equity issues). The value of a stream growing at a constant rate is equal to the beginning dividend per share divided by (the discount rate minus the growth rate).

13

How to Negotiate a Term Loan

JASPER H. ARNOLD III

Despite the proliferation of services available to finance ongoing operations, the fundamental source of capital for all companies remains banks. And negotiations with banks always boil down to a contract between those who have the money and those who need it. Most growing companies need to seek external financing at some point, and a very common form of this financing is the bank term loan. These loans often carry with them restrictive covenants that can unduly hamper management and increase the risk of a default.

Unfortunately, for many managers these negotiations are pitted with more uncertainties and difficulties than other types of contracts. The responsibility weighs heavily on a small company manager who may lack financial expertise, especially if the company's future is uncertain. An officer in a more financially sophisticated corporation may understand the process—but not know how to best protect the diverse interests of one part of the company from the demands of the others.

Talks with participants on both sides of the loan process, coupled with his own banking experience, give the author a knowledgeable perspective on how to turn the process around to the company's advantage. His advice for the manager is to plan a negotiating strategy. By learning to think like a banker, you will be better able to obtain a loan agreement that meets your needs without putting a stranglehold on your business.

Financial managers responsible for negotiating term loans from commercial banks often feel confronted by a stone wall—the banker's restrictions (*restrictive covenants*) on the company to ensure repayment. While the ultimate

---

Author's note. Bankers' restrictions are imposed via a formal, written loan agreement, which typically contains two distinct types of covenants, affirmative and negative. I review both, as well as the structure of a typical agreement, in the Appendix. Throughout the article, I deal solely with negative covenants, since they are the most restrictive and vigorously debated.

objectives are easily understood (getting the least expensive funds under the fewest restrictions), achieving them is not. Since the first caveman loaned a spear to a friend only to have it returned the next day broken into little pieces, lenders have been cautious in dealing with borrowers. Moreover, lenders know they have a certain power over borrowers and have turned it into a mystique. Unlike the case in other contract negotiations, many borrowers feel they have few, if any, cards to play—that is, they have to take most of what the banker decides to dish out.

After years of participating in the loan negotiation process, I have found it not as one-sided as it appears. The banker does *not* always win; savvy companies realize that, as in every other aspect of the business, success depends on negotiating strategy.

To help companies devise an an effective negotiating strategy, I studied 50 requests for term loans made at eight New York and regional banks. The study, a review of the borrower's financial statements and the final loan agreements, confirms that managers winding up with the best (least restrictive) loan package:

- ☐ Learn to think like the banker and identify the bank's objectives.
- ☐ Meet the banker's objectives in making the loan with the least damage to their own position.
- ☐ Set a list of priorities on the restrictions wanted by the banker, so that they can give in on one or two of them without hindering the company's strategy.
- ☐ Influence the banker to relax or withdraw noncrucial restrictions.

Inside the Banker's Head

First, let's look at the two sides in this contest. At the outset the bank's perspective is built on an objective and subjective analysis of the borrowing company's financial position. The analysis rests on that well-established tenet—permanent asset needs should be financed with permanent capital. When permanent capital takes the form of long-term debt, the lender wants to find out how healthy the borrower's long-term earning power is. So the bank asks for financial information as a start—historical financial statements (typically five years) as well as a forecast of your company's income statement, balance sheet, and the sources and uses of funds statements for each year.

The bank's principal and interest will be returned from the future stream of earnings before interest and taxes (EBIT). (Normally, a bank calculates EBIT as *sales* less *cost of sales* less *selling, general, and administrative expenses*.) Consequently, the bank wants to learn the extent of business risk—in other words, how much the future EBIT stream could vary. Another important element is understanding the borrower's industry—both the company's strengths and weaknesses and its overall strategy. (Although EBIT is available to cover interest expense, principal payments, not being tax deductible, must be paid out of the net income stream. Moreover, annual principal payments cannot be made out of "cash flow" [net income + depreciation] unless the borrower can forego replacing depreciated fixed assets.)

Banks consider some lines of business inherently risky and this will influence the analysis, but the financial forecast becomes the primary basis on which the banker quizzes the manager to determine the degree of business risk. The banker also uses the forecast to establish how restrictive the loan will be.

Bankers also put considerable emphasis on the company's historical earnings record as an indicator of business risk. Wide fluctuations in profits or net losses—or consistently thin profit margins—usually lead to an assessment of high business risk.

After the EBIT stream, the company's balance sheet is the most important financial indicator because the assets are the bank's secondary source of repayment if earnings are not adequate to repay the loan. Therefore, the assessment of balance sheet strength or weakness hinges on the extent to which the banker thinks the loan is recoverable if assets must be sold.

Judgment is largely based on a few key ratios. For example, the current ratio or net working capital position represents the amount of liquid assets the company has available to repay debts. The banker also investigates fixed asset liquidity, important in the event of financial distress or bankruptcy.

Another key balance sheet variable is the company's margin of safety (i.e., the extent to which it is leveraged). To a banker, a company with a total liabilities-to-equity ratio of one to one can suffer a 50% deterioration in asset value and still repay a loan. If leverage is at a three-to-one ratio, however, creditors can only tolerate a 25% shrinkage in asset value. Moreover, since the size of annual principal and interest payments increases as leverage rises, the greater the leverage the greater the chance EBIT will not cover these payments.

The Making of Restrictions

Bankers use these simple financial indicators to determine the scope and severity of the restrictions placed on a potential borrower. The five possible types of restrictions include cash flow control, strategy control, the default "trigger," balance sheet maintenance, and asset preservation.

Cash Flow Control

The first source of restrictions comes directly from an analysis of cash flow. A company may want to build its assets so rapidly or pay such excessive dividends that the banker questions whether the EBIT stream will be sufficient to service the loan. In this case, repayment must come from a refinancing by another creditor or an equity sale. If the bank is confident that the company's earnings record and balance sheet will be strong enough to permit refinancing, it will not seek to control the company's cash flow. However, even when refinancing appears possible, bankers will usually limit excessive dividends and stock repurchases to preserve the company's equity base.

Strategy Control

Lenders may try to control future strategy if they believe that the company's resources are ill-matched with the opportunities and risks present in the environment—or when a particular strategy requires an imprudent degree of leverage or illiquidity. Resulting covenants either prohibit managers from implementing the strategy or force them to modify it. In such cases, bankers usually want to reduce the total amount of money invested in a particular product market or spread the investment out over a longer time period, either by limiting capital expenditures and acquisitions or by writing in a debt-to-equity test.

The Infamous Trigger

One of the most feared aspects of restrictions is the bank's right to call the loan, or trigger a default. The readiness of the trigger depends on the strength of the balance sheet and the degree of business risk—that is, the potential variability in EBIT. Losses erode company assets by reducing the net working capital and the equity base. In that event (or possibly if profitability declines), the banker wants the right to call the entire loan for repayment before deterioration advances. If the company cannot repay the loan, the bank has legal recourse on the assets.

Banks, however, seldom pull the dreaded trigger. Such action usually means bankruptcy for the company, adverse publicity for the bank, and a time-consuming, costly legal proceeding for both parties. In most cases, if the restrictions trigger a default, the loan is not called; instead, this imminent possibility forces the borrower to return to the bargaining table. The banker then wants a proposal for corrective action. In return for continuing the loan, the bank can boost the interest-rate demand collateral as compensation for the risk or else rewrite the covenants.

Balance Sheet Maintenance

A company can harm its balance sheet by excessive leveraging or by financing fixed assets with short-term loans, both of which reduce its net working-capital position and liquidity. To keep the borrower from wantonly employing short-term credit, lenders impose a current ratio and/or net working-capital minimum. Also included is a debt-to-equity limit or even a prohibition on additional borrowings.

Asset Preservation

Because bankers regard assets as the ultimate source of repayment, they do not want to see a significant portion sold or pledged to other creditors. So, unless the loan is secured, lenders will write in a limit on the extent to which companies can pledge assets (a "negative pledge clause").

Even if the company can put up sufficient collateral, the bank will restrict the sale of assets to forestall disposal for less than their value or for securities that could prove worthless. The bank will place limits on asset sales or require that any sale be made at fair market value in cash and that the proceeds be used to reduce the loan or to acquire replacement assets.

How the Restrictions Are Set

Using this general information, you can see how to chart your initial negotiating strategy. Exhibit 1 illustrates the minimum objectives the banker must achieve, depending on the degree of a particular company's business risk and balance sheet strength. Six principal rules of loan negotiation hold.

- ☐ *The banker will always require certain balance sheet standards.* At a minimum, management will be unable to leverage assets too highly or use excessive short-term liabilities to finance long-term assets.
- ☐ *There will always be a trigger.* Despite the fact that the banker will probably never call the loan, the presence of a trigger gives the bank the power to take over the company's assets as a result of poor earnings performance.
- ☐ *Assets will be preserved.* No banker wants to see the assets of a company sold—or pledged to another creditor.
- ☐ *Restrictions on cash flow vary.* Bankers feel comfortable when companies with good prospects and healthy balance sheets can call on outside capital to service debt. Yet they are concerned lest management authorize excessive dividends or buy back large amounts of stock, so they include a very loose limit on dividends or rely on a debt-to-equity or a net working-capital test for control. A company with a weak balance sheet or high business risk will encounter demands to ensure that most of the cash it generates is used for repayment instead of dividends or capital expenditures.
- ☐ *Tightness of restrictions depends on the level of business risk and strength of the balance sheet.* "Tightness" is the degree to which the balance sheet and income statement tests track existing and forecast levels. The tighter the covenant, the more restrictive the control on management's freedom to pay cash out, leverage the company, or incur losses.
- ☐ *Strategy control applies across the board.* With a company having a high degree of business risk and a weak balance sheet, the bank

Exhibit 1. Determinants of the Objectives and Tightness of Restrictive Covenants

Covenant objectives		
	1 Cash flow control	4 Balance sheet maintenance
	2 Strategy control	5 Asset preservation
	3 Trigger	

Quadrant 4	Quadrant 1
Moderate covenants	**Loose covenants**
Relevant objectives: 1, 3, 4, and 5	Relevant objectives: 1, 3, 4, and 5 but limited to controlling excessive dividend payments or stock repurchases

Low business risk (↑) / **High business risk** (↓)

Weak balance sheet (←) / **Strong balance sheet** (→)

Quadrant 3	Quadrant 2
Relevant objectives: 1, 3, 4, and 5	Relevant objectives: 1, 3, 4, and 5
Tight covenants	**Moderate covenants**

Note:
If the banker believes that the borrower intends to pursue an inappropriate strategy, he will make the covenants restrictive—possibly, in the case of Quadrant 3 borrowers, even prohibiting or modifying the strategy.

will try to restrain strategic movement that it deems inappropriate. More credit-worthy candidates will suffer fewer restrictions if the banker does not like the corporate strategy, but will be faced with more sensitive triggers that can be quickly set off if the strategy fails.

Some examples of different negotiations help illustrate the various possibilities.

An oil field pump manufacturer (Quadrant II) wanted a five-year term loan of several million dollars to double the size of its manufacturing facility and to provide working capital to expand sales. The company had been plagued with low profit margins, inventory control problems, and operating inefficiencies. To retain market share, however, the expansion was necessary even though the added production and sales capacity might exacerbate the problems.

The banker thought the balance sheet was reasonably strong. To maintain that strength, she set a long-term debt-equity limit and a current ratio minimum. Because the borrower's strategy exposed it to much business risk, however, the banker wanted a quick default triggered if losses occurred. So she set a minimum net worth covenant that increased every year and closely tracked the forecast levels. The banker also thought that the company's ultimate profitability was too uncertain for her to risk refinancing as a source of required principal payments, so she imposed capital expenditure, investment, and dividend restrictions. The bank included a negative pledge clause and a prohibition on asset sales of more than $1 million in any fiscal year.

Most of the successful companies in Quadrant 1 were members of the *Fortune* "1000" industrials. The lenders were willing to let these companies do as they pleased if balance sheet ratios remained within certain bounds and profits did not drop. Therefore, they set debt-to-equity maximums and current ratio or working capital restrictions well outside of the forecast levels. These covenants, taken together with either a net worth minimum or a coverage test, also provided a trigger. Negative pledge clauses were always used and asset sales were limited.

A regional chain of steak houses wanted financing to open up several new restaurants within one year in a distant market where it was unknown. The expansion, which would more than double the chain's size, required high leveraging, and management wanted to expand at a time when some of the new restaurants had not yet realized satisfactory profits. Further, restaurant business assets are viewed as highly illiquid if sold under distress conditions. Thus the bank saw a rapid growth strategy as too risky—and set restrictions to slow growth.

A moderate debt-to-equity ratio would curtail expansion until the existing restaurants generated enough new equity to support the borrowings necessary to open the new units. This test simultaneously ensured holding the company's leverage to a satisfactory level. Unwilling to rely on a refinancing for repayment and determined to control the company's cash, the banker prohibited dividends and long-term investments. The creditor used a debt-to-equity test as a trigger if losses occurred and added a cash-flow-coverage ratio. The loan agreement did not restrict the company's extension of collateral to other creditors, but it did restrict excessive asset sales.

Forge Your Own Strategy

You can use the model in Exhibit 1 to determine what will influence the banker in your particular case and what restrictions the banker is likely to impose. Keep in mind the following guidelines:

1 Consider your earnings history over the past five years. Losses, consistently low profit margins, or very volatile earnings usually indicate a great degree of business risk.
2 Ask yourself whether the variables that determine EBIT (e.g., raw material costs, sales volume, product price, foreign exchange rates)

will change over the life of the loan and cause severe declines in earnings.

3 After taking into account the loan, look at the existing and forecast balance sheet ratios such as the debt-to-equity ratio and the current ratio. Do they indicate an illiquid or highly leveraged condition? (If a company's forecast is based on assumptions that are overgenerous in view of historical results, a banker will frequently draw up a forecast with more conservative assumptions. Try it yourself. In that case, can the debt be serviced? What happens to the leverage and liquidity ratios?)

4 Considering the types of assets the company owns, the net working capital level, and the margin of safety for creditors (leverage), could the bank get repayment if the company's assets were liquidated? If the answer is yes, then yours is a strong-balance-sheet company. If the answer is no or maybe, then yours is a weak-balance-sheet company.

Supplement this analysis by questioning the banker before negotiations start. First ask about the bank's preliminary judgments on the balance sheet, historical earnings performance, and the business risk of the company. Then inquire about the soundness of your proposed strategies.

Be careful. Probe responses and always read between the lines. Following initial conversations, make sure the banker receives any additional information necessary about the company—its products, markets, and strategy.

Once you have a good idea as to the banker's objectives, evaluate each possible restriction. To do this properly, you must understand how the more popular restrictive covenants are used and how they can simultaneously accomplish one or more objectives. Appendix A gives a good example of their versatility.

For example, the current ratio and minimum net-working-capital tests give the bank a broad range of control. They simultaneously provide a trigger, control cash flow, and maintain the balance sheet. These covenants, particularly the current ratio minimum, are the most often violated—simply because almost every financial event or managerial action affects the company's working capital.

Identify Costly Restrictions

During negotiations the manager must try to minimize the impact of restrictions that might unduly hamper management or easily trigger a violation before the company's financial situation has seriously deteriorated. The most useful tool to determine whether restrictions are too tight is your financial forecast. For example, suppose the bank wants to impose a long-term debt-equity limit of .75 to 1, and you forecast that next year's profit will be $3 million; long-term debt, $15 million; and equity, $21 million. You can figure that a drop greater than $1 million in anticipated net income would cause a default (.75 = $15 million/X; X = $20 million; necessary decline in net income = $21 million − $20 million, or $1 million). In light of that margin, you must decide how likely such earnings performance is.

A Basic Negotiating Posture

At the outset, the banker will try to impose as many tight restrictions as possible, especially if yours is a small company or one that has traditionally dealt with one bank. Address each proposed restriction individually and push for its elimination, or at least its relaxation, by using an appropriate mix of the following arguments:

- ☐ Management needs strategic flexibility to avoid default.
- ☐ Even if the restriction is dropped, the banker will still achieve the objectives with the remaining covenants.
- ☐ A strong balance sheet shows that company assets provide a secure, secondary source of repayment if earnings deteriorate.
- ☐ A strong earnings outlook means the bank can tolerate a weaker balance sheet. Large payouts of cash are acceptable because strong future earnings make it possible to service the bank debt by refinancing.
- ☐ The banker can tolerate large payouts of cash or other managerial actions because, if earnings deteriorate, a trigger covenant will be violated and the bank can then demand tighter covenants that closely control management.

Watch out for unnecessarily tight dividend restrictions or capital expenditure limits. You can have them dropped or relaxed if your balance sheet is strong enough or if you can point to a low amount of business risk. To the extent that you can, stress: (1) your high margin of safety (low leverage); the liquidity of the balance sheet (high current ratio), and the availability of your assets as a secondary source of repayment even if earnings are used for something else; and/or (2) that your strong earnings will permit a refinancing if they are used for something other than debt servicing.

A borrower with a strong balance sheet and a low level of business risk can usually convince the banker that a very loose dividend restriction (e.g., "cumulative dividends and stock repurchases shall not exceed 45% of cumulative net income") is acceptable. Or you can maintain that the debt-to-equity ratio and the current ratio (or net working capital minimum) adequately protect the bank from excessive payouts of the company's equity.

If you are not so fortunate, try to make trade-offs among covenants. For example, bankers will reduce controls on cash flow if you agree to an easily released trigger. If you start losing money, the trigger will cause a default and allow the banker to demand a tightening in the controls to stop the cash drain.

Eliminate Duplication

The smart manager will insist that the banker can achieve many objectives through a single covenant. For example, the debt-equity ratio restriction can control management's use of leverage and also serve as the yardstick for a trigger if the company incurs losses.

If the banker proposes a net worth minimum as a trigger and a debt-equity ratio as a brake on leverage, the manager can argue for elimination of the trigger because the debt-equity ratio is a sufficient control. The banker may counter by maintaining that he wants to safeguard loss control directly, but the borrower may at least get the restrictions relaxed somewhat.

Relax the Trigger

When a trigger is too restrictive, you may be able to show that even though future earnings might be less than planned, this would not necessarily reflect a fundamental or long-lasting deterioration in the company's earning power. In the previous example (where more than a $1 million fall in net income, from the forecast of $3 million to less than $2 million, would have violated the .75-to-1 long-term debt-equity limit), you might argue that such a profit decline could be caused by temporary factors beyond your control, such as bad weather or strikes. Or make the point that an exact forecast is impossible and you need a wide enough margin for error to properly test decisions.

You will have better luck with this appeal if you show that your company's assets will still provide an assured, secondary source of repayment if the banker relaxes the covenant from .75 to 1 to, say, 1 to 1. Prospects for strong earnings also may help you bargain for more flexibility on the use of debt financing.

Dealing with Strategy Control

A strategy restriction often leads corporate executives to seek a more "enlightened" bank. Unfortunately, if one bank thinks this kind of control necessary, usually most others will agree.

Rather than shopping around, find out why the banker objects to a strategy; then point out your thinking behind it and the importance of flexibility. After all, success here should guarantee future earnings power. Then agree to other restrictions—for example, a tight trigger that allows the bank to put a stop to the strategy if it results in losses. If, after considerable discussion, the bank officer continues to regard the plan as inappropriate, consider financing from a source less averse to risk than a commercial bank.

A Competing Note

Some *Fortune* "1000" companies shop for the best terms by requesting several banks to bid on a loan. They instruct bidders to quote the interest rate, the compensating balance arrangement, the repayment provisions, and a set of restrictive covenants. Such a procedure—or even the *threat* of it—influences some banks to propose more acceptable terms.

I do not suggest that all companies, particularly small ones, use this technique. Before negotiating a term loan, however, you should obtain some information on the types of covenants that might be demanded either by visiting with financial officers in companies that have recently raised bank debt or by talking with lending officers to get a feel for the types of covenants that might be required. Armed with this knowledge, you can mention the requirements of other banks when the potential lender is unduly restrictive.

. . . and a Concluding One

Covenants set at the time a loan is negotiated that allow you free rein still may prove restrictive in light of future opportunities. However, compliance can be—and nearly always is—waived or the covenant amended if the bank's review of a project shows it to be strategically appropriate without drastically altering the risk picture.

Appendix A. Examples of the Versatility of Covenants

Debt-equity ratio

Limits the ability of management to leverage the company.

Restricts expansion of assets in traditional or new markets if this expansion must be financed with debt.

Limits dividend payments.

Triggers a default in the event of losses.

Current ratio or minimum net working capital

Keeps management from borrowing short term to finance long-term assets.

Limits dividend payments, capital expenditures, and investments because such cash outflows are a use of working capital in the flow-of-funds sense.

Triggers a default in the event of losses because losses are a use of working capital.

Net worth minimum

Causes a default if losses occur.

Restricts dividend payments.

Interest coverage ratio

Causes a default if losses occur.

Limits the ability of management to leverage the company.

Capital expenditure restrictions

Conserves cash within the company.

Keeps the borrower from expanding in particular markets or product lines.

Appendix B. The Typical Bank Loan Agreement

Bank loan agreements contain a *representation and warranties section* normally stipulating that the borrower:	**The *affirmative covenants section*, considered "boilerplate covenants," includes promises that the borrower will:**	**The *negative covenants section* stipulates any number of the following promises that the borrower will not:**
Is properly incorporated.	Submit annual, audited financial statements.	Permit some type of debt-to-equity ratio (e.g., total liabilities-to-equity or long-term debt-to-equity) to exceed a specified maximum.
Has the power and authority to enter into the loan agreement and the promissory note.	Submit periodic (usually quarterly or monthly) unaudited, interim financial statements.	Permit the interest coverage ratio (EBIT/interest expense) to be less than a specified minimum. (Other coverage tests are also used; *cash flow coverage: net income + depreciation/current maturities* of long-term debt shall be no less than a specified minimum.)
Is current on its taxes.	Submit periodic certificates signed by an officer of the company stating whether the company is in compliance with the loan agreement.	Permit additional borrowings.
Is not the subject of any litigation except as disclosed.	Maintain its corporate existence.	Permit guarantees of third-party obligations to exceed a specified dollar amount.
Has good title to its assets.	Maintain adequate insurance.	Permit the current ratio to fall to less than a specified minimum.
Has not pledged any of its assets except as disclosed.	Maintain its corporate assets in good condition.	Permit net working capital to fall to less than a specified minimum.
Is not in violation of any other credit agreement.	Pay all taxes unless contested in good faith.	Permit annual capital expenditures to exceed specified dollar amounts.
Has made full disclosure of its financial condition in its most recently submitted financial statements.		Permit dividend payments and stock repurchases to exceed a specified cumulative or annual dollar amount.
		Pledge its assets to another creditor (a variation is to pledge its assets unless the bank is equally secured by the assets).

Appendix B. (*Continued*)

Bank loan agreements contain a *representation and warranties section* normally stipulating that the borrower:	**The *affirmative covenants section*, considered "boilerplate covenants," includes promises that the borrower will:**	**The *negative covenants section* stipulates any number of the following promises that the borrower will not:**
		Merge with or acquire another company (a variation is to merge with or acquire another company unless the borrower is the surviving company and no violation of a covenant would result). Sell its assets (except inventory in the ordinary course of business and obsolete or fully depreciated equipment), unless the money received is used to retire the bank loan or to buy replacement assets. Permit investments (such as the purchase of common stock or bonds of other companies), loans, or advances to exceed a specific dollar amount outstanding.

Occasionally a banker will tailor a restriction. For example, one institution recently prohibited an agricultural commodities trader from incurring a loss that exceeded a certain amount on closing out all long and short positions. Loan agreements also list *events of default*, including failure to pay principal or interest when due, failure to comply with an affirmative covenant after notice of the violation has been given by the bank, violation of a negative covenant, discovery that a representation or warranty was incorrect, a default in the payment of money owed to another lender, and bankruptcy of the company. The *remedies section* states that should a default occur, the lender may declare the entire principal of the note, together with accrued interest, immediately due and payable.

14

Does It Pay to Shop for Your Bond Underwriter?

DENNIS E. LOGUE and RICHARD J. ROGALSKI

How can corporate financial executives sift through the claims of investment bankers who clamor for their business? None of them is reticent about the advantages of doing business with one's particular firm. Putting aside the matter of the credibility of these claims, is there any way of scientifically distinguishing the product of one investment bank from that of another? Here is an attempt to measure the corporate debt underwriting performance of leading Wall Street firms (accounting for about 90% of the total business in the two years these authors studied). The authors gauged the results of negotiated bond underwritings in two dimensions—the cash spread and the degree of underpricing of the securities. They have come up with exceedingly interesting findings.

The financial officers of most successful companies are visited by streams of investment bankers trying to sell their capital-raising services. Despite the importance of investment banks in raising capital for corporations (and governments), the performance of the industry has been subjected to very little scrutiny. Reputations vary widely among firms, but does performance fit the reputations?

Are there significant differences among investment banks in underwriting costs and in post-offering price action of underwritten issues (i.e.,

Authors' note. The research support for this study came from the Tuck Associates Research Program at the Amos Tuck School of Business Administration, Dartmouth College. We gratefully acknowledge the helpful comments and suggestions of Richard Bower and Bulent Gultekin and especially those of J. Peter Williamson.

in the amount of underpricing)? Or do all firms in the industry price more or less alike? To put it more pragmatically, does it pay corporate treasurers to shop among investment bankers, or can they assume that charges are about equal, regardless of which house handles the service? Does the choice make much difference, even in the short run? Is the decision worth agonizing over?

Suppose your company plans to issue straight, secured debt. How does it proceed to choose the best firm to handle the financing? The investment banking community has suggested several criteria:

- ☐ Certain firms that view themselves as market-timers tell you that, by carefully selecting the offering date, they can sell an issue at a lower interest rate than would otherwise be feasible. This is not a testable boast, but bear in mind that anyone who could time the market's turning points would probably make more money by doing that full time than by providing corporate financial services.
- ☐ Some firms argue that their imprimatur on a new issue will gain a higher rating from the bond-rating agencies and thus a lower coupon interest rate. This contention could be valid, but there is no way to test it either.
- ☐ Some firms claim to have better securities distribution. The interpretation of *better* is quite subjective, and judgment concerning this assertion cannot be made outside special circumstances.
- ☐ Some firms contend that their financial advice on, say, dividend policy and acquisition strategy is so good that they ought to get your business. This is also a judgment call, not amenable to careful analysis.

So how do corporate financial officers choose? A selection on the basis of cost of underwriting service is an economically sensible way to proceed unless they have compelling reasons for giving weight to subjective factors.

In regard to the pricing of new equity issues, research shows a pattern of initial underpricing. By pricing lower, of course, investment bankers aim to sell the securities quickly, thus reducing their risk and making up for the lower compensation.[1]

This research also reveals differences in the performance of unseasoned stock issues underwritten by prestigious and "unprestigious" investment banking houses. Prestigious firms' equity offerings perform less well than those of less prestigious firms, but is it the underwriter or the company whose securities are underwritten that makes the difference? Naturally, prestigious Wall Street firms do business with larger, well-known corporations, even for initial offerings, whereas less prestigious investment banks tend to deal with smaller, riskier companies whose issues are more difficult to price and sell.

In any event, investment banks do differ from category to category. What happens within categories has not been well examined. To find an answer in one broad category, we investigated issues of bonds in two consecutive years. We did not address the sale of common stocks because nonutility companies that are seasoned in the market float more bond issues than equity issues.

Spreads and Underpricing

We measured the performance of prestigious investment banking firms in two dimensions of negotiated bond underwritings—the cash spread (the difference between the price at which they buy and the price at which they subsequently sell the securities) and the degree of underpricing of new securities (the difference between the interest rate on the price at which the securities are sold and the true, equilibrium price).

Moreover, since investment bankers evidently often "trade off" these two elements—that is, accept a smaller spread if the underpricing is greater—we also computed a combined measure. A record of lower underwriter spreads plus underpricing costs appears to be a good indicator of investment bank performance. The benefits of a correct choice of bank by a corporate financial officer would consequently be immediate, measurable, and possibly substantial.

We drew our sample from *Institutional Investor's* listings of all negotiated debt issues in 1975 and 1976. All such offerings by 11 investment banking firms, excluding notes and convertible debt, comprise the data. The sample is quite representative; it contains about 89% of the 1975 volume and about 91% of the 1976 volume.[2] (To avoid biasing the results toward the hypothesis that all investment banks are similar, we gave only the lead firm—the manager or first-named comanager—credit for an issue.)

We selected these two periods because they are recent (hence should yield insight into contemporary industry structure) and because they represent two very different market periods. Interest rates fluctuated little in 1975 but greatly in 1976. These years appear to be representative of a wide variety of conditions. The principal criterion for including an investment house in the sample was to have had at least five offerings in each of these two years and at least three bond issues rated A by Standard & Poor (S&P) in each year.

The distribution of new negotiated bond issues by underwriter and by rating is shown in Exhibit 1. Morgan Stanley and Goldman Sachs accounted for the most bond deals regardless of rating, whereas First Boston and Merrill Lynch underwrote the most A-rated issues. The large quantity of bonds in a single-risk category (A) allowed testing for differences among the investment houses where the riskiness of the bonds could be held constant.

Exhibit 1. Data on Bond Samples

Year	MS	FB	GS	SB	LB	KL	ML	BE	KP	DR	WW	Total
By investment bank[a]												
1975	27	20	23	11	15	9	14	17	14	13	6	169
1976	17	11	14	16	8	5	15	8	7	8	7	116
By investment bank (A-rated only)												
1975	10	16	12	5	13	6	11	9	5	5	4	96
1976	4	6	4	8	3	4	6	4	4	3	3	49

By bond rating	AAA	AA	A	BBB	Total
1975	18	34	96	21	169
1976	9	36	49	22	116

Source: Institutional Investor, June 1976 and June 1977.

Note: Since 1976 Lehman Brothers and Kuhn Loeb have merged, and Merrill Lynch has acquired White Weld.

[a]The names of the 11 firms are Morgan Stanley (MS), First Boston (FB), Goldman Sachs (GS), Salomon Brothers (SB), Lehman Brothers (LB), Kuhn Loeb (KL), Merrill Lynch (ML), Blyth Eastman Dillon (BE), Kidder Peabody (KP), Dillon Read (DR), and White Weld (WW).

Underwriting Spreads

The first comparison focuses on spreads measured as a percent of proceeds to the issuers—that is, the difference between underwriter selling price and net price to the issuer as a percentage of that net. In 1975 the average underwriting spread for all corporate bonds underwritten by the 11-firm sample was .9142% (with a standard deviation of .13%). Among the investment firms, the average spread varied from a low of .8728% to a high of .975%. In 1976 the spread averaged .9389% (with a standard deviation of .188%), and it varied among investment houses from .8329% to 1.0292%.

For A-rated bonds in 1975, the average spread was .8964% (with a standard deviation of .087%), and the range among investment banks was narrower than for all bonds. For A-rated bonds in 1976, the average spread was .8857% (with a standard deviation of .055%). This variation also was smaller than for all bonds. (For details on the calculations, see the Appendix.)

Statistical analysis of the underwriters' spreads reveals no significant difference among investment banks. This is true for both 1975 and 1976 and for A-rated as well as for all other bonds. It is also true whether or not one adjusts for the size of the issue. On the basis of this evidence, we conclude that none of these Wall Street firms was significantly more or less expensive to deal with than the others in 1975 or 1976.

To analyze the second component of underwriting cost, the amount of underpricing of a security, we examined the yield spread—that is, the difference between the offering yield on a particular issue and the yield on the

S&P bond index for that quality bond on about the same date as the offering date of the bond. (Inasmuch as the S&P indexes are available only on a weekly basis, a perfect match between the two was impossible.) To approximate the yield spread, we subtracted the index yield for the appropriate week from the offering yield of the new issue.

The difference between offering yield and the yield on an index of comparably risky bonds can be substantial; in 1975 the overall difference averaged 42.7 basis points, and the average underpricing ranged from 8.87 basis points to 69.04. Underpricing for A-rated bonds averaged 51.37 basis points and ranged among the investment banks from 23.42 to 84.29.

In 1976 Wall Street priced bonds much more aggressively. The underpricing averaged −1.42 basis points, which means that offering yields were on balance lower than the yields on indexes of comparable-quality bonds. In the group of 11, the yield spread ranged from −30.93 to 20.80 basis points. For A-rated bonds, the overall average was 1.45 basis points and the differences in the group extended from −48.27 points to 27.33.

Statistical analysis of the yield spreads revealed no significant differences among the 11 houses in both 1975 and 1976. This finding applies to all bonds and also to A-rated bonds only, with or without an adjustment for the size of the issue. Moreover, no similarity in yield spreads between years was evident; the firm with the smallest underpricing for all bonds in 1975 ranked third lowest in 1976, and the largest underpricer in 1975 was only third highest in 1976. These rankings also change as one considers just the A-rated offerings.

The yield spread may be interpreted as extra compensation for the underwriter. If a company allows its investment bank to sell securities to yield more than comparably risky securities are yielding, the bank has a much easier selling job. Although the issuers thereby reduce the investment bank's cost, they pay not only the underwriter spread, but also a higher interest rate than investors could get by purchasing comparable government securities.

We made a final comparison using total underwriting cost, which can be obtained by combining the direct cost of issuance with the indirect cost of underpricing (i.e., adding the underwriting spread to the yield spread). Statistical analysis of the total cost figures in the sample confirmed our earlier finding that no differences exist in each cost taken alone.

Underpricing Action

Admittedly, the cost data we used in this analysis can be questioned on the ground that the newly issued bonds may have been rated incorrectly. A poor evaluation of the quality of a bond by the rating agency can bias the yield spread.

Also, the bond yield index may have been inaccurate. This is a distinct possibility because all bonds in the index may not have been traded on the day of index compilation (every Wednesday). Moreover, in a period of rapidly changing yields, an index that reflects historical yield quotations can be misleading. Finally, the average maturity of the new bonds may differ significantly from the index maturity.

For these and other reasons we calculated a more robust measure of bond performance. This measure entails dividing the offering yield on the new bond by the yield on a government security of the same maturity and coupon on the day of offering and then subtracting the result from a corresponding measurement at various time intervals. In other words, this yardstick reflects the degree of rise or fall of a new bond yield for a time after issuance compared with a similar government security. To the extent that the spread between the yields on government and corporate securities remains roughly constant, this measure of bond performance is meaningful.

Exhibits 2 and 3 show the mean of the performance measures in 1975 and 1976 segmented by investment banks over selected intervals after the offerings. (The variances of the results are given in the Appendix.)

A look at the mean performance measures reveals both positive and negative numbers. A negative number indicates that the yield on new bonds issued by that underwriter fell, on average, relative to the government bond yield. In other words, a negative number shows a narrowing of the spread in that the difference between yields on the corporate securities and comparable government bonds declined between the day of offering and the end of the particular period. A positive mean performance measure indicates, of course, a rise in the relative yield on the corporate bonds.

If a banker underprices a security, the yield spread between it and a government security usually narrows by the end of the offering month, or at least by the end of the third month thereafter. Obviously, bond offerings are subject to the same economic forces that operate to enlarge or narrow risk premiums. To the extent that the narrowing of premiums in offerings of one investment banker is consistently smaller than that in the offerings of others, one can assume that he is doing a better job of pricing because his securities' prices are closer to the market than theirs.

In the first month of 1975, with respect to all bonds the offerings of every investment firm appreciated in price relative to their government counterparts. In the same period of 1976, however, nearly all corporate offerings depreciated in price relative to the corresponding government bonds. In 1976 only one investment bank—Morgan Stanley—underpriced securities consistently; the others priced quite aggressively.

Admittedly, a technical sampling difficulty could have caused this finding. For 1975, we obtained price and yield quotations at the end of each offering month on 156 out of 169 issues. For 1976, however, we could get one-month quotes on only 52 of 116 securities because many issues remained in syndication at the close of the first month. This fact suggests that the selling of securities was much more difficult in 1976 than in the previous year. The one investment bank that seemingly priced securities poorly in 1976 compared with the others also was one of the few firms all of whose

Exhibit 2. Mean Price Action of 1975 Issues over Time

Investment Bank	1 Month	3 Months	6 Months	12 Months
All bonds				
MS	−.0185	−.0335	−.0419	−.0491
FB	−.0389	−.0356	−.0431	−.0479
GS	−.0199	−.0299	−.0396	−.0307
SB	−.0196	−.0297	−.0395	−.0438
LB	−.0052	−.0184	−.0142	−.0051
KL	−.0101	−.0269	−.0227	−.0253
ML	−.0136	−.0262	−.0237	−.0469
BE	−.0091	−.0307	−.0293	−.0438
KP	−.0255	−.0258	−.0214	−.0296
DR	−.0196	−.0449	−.0355	−.0413
WW	−.0032	−.0388	−.0431	−.0538
All	−.0184	−.0308	−.0332	−.0382
A-rated bonds only				
MS	−.0210	−.0212	−.0422	−.0439
FB	−.0473	−.0454	−.0557	−.0592
GS	−.0133	−.0240	−.0229	−.0130
SB	−.0127	−.0229	−.0292	−.0373
LB	−.0005	−.0128	−.0085	−.0076
KL	−.0163	−.0390	−.0323	−.0347
ML	−.0138	−.0270	−.0233	−.0516
BE	.0140	−.0138	−.0115	−.0191
KP	.0369	−.0313	−.0213	−.0528
DR	−.0123	.0027	.0010	.0042
WW	−.0051	−.0228	−.0299	−.0210
All	−.0173	−.0250	−.0273	−.0323

Sources: Corporate bond yields. *Standard & Poor's Bond Guide*, government securities yields, and *Wall Street Journal*.

Note: The sample size for one-month performance was 156 for all bonds and 87 for A-rated bonds. For other performance measures, the sample sizes shown in Exhibit 1 prevail.

issues were being quoted at the end of each month of offering. Morgan Stanley was the most successful house in selling out its clients' debt.

Statistical analysis of the performance measurement data in Exhibits 2 and 3 reveals no significant differences among investment banks in terms of security underpricing in either year. In respect to A-rated bonds, where risk differences pose a less serious comparability problem, the tests over-

Exhibit 3. Mean Price Action of 1976 Issues over Time

Investment Bank	1 Month	3 Months	6 Months	12 Months
All bonds				
MS	−.0189	−.0186	.0035	−.0157
FB	.0084	.0048	−.0023	−.0262
GS	.0028	.0090	−.0186	−.0055
SB	.0040	−.0103	−.0054	−.0275
LB	.0082	−.0062	−.0029	−.0036
KL	.0030	−.0079	−.0026	−.0160
ML	.0057	.0096	.0070	−.0040
BE	.0051	−.0238	−.0120	−.0297
KP	.0049	.0002	−.0094	−.0216
DR	.0544	.0313	.0200	.0078
WW	.0075	−.0151	.0085	−.0231
All	−.0032	−.0047	−.0016	−.0149
A-rated bonds only				
MS	−.0018	−.0155	.0393	−.0200
FB	.0139	−.0020	−.0093	−.0343
GS	−.0112	−.0092	−.0069	−.0220
SB	.0039	−.0083	−.0030	−.0234
LB	−.0097	−.0020	−.0091	−.0099
KL	−.0030	−.0100	.0005	−.0174
ML	−.0107	−.0028	−.0163	−.0183
BE	−.0551	−.0565	−.0386	−.0511
KP	.0110	−.0028	−.0044	−.0194
DR	.1075	.0801	.0506	.0159
WW	.0132	−.0046	.0809	.0027
All	−.0015	−.0051	.0031	−.0203

Note: The sample size for one-month performance was 52 for all securities and 28 for A-rated securities. For other performance measures, the sample sizes shown in Exhibit 1 prevail.

whelmingly support the contention that no measurable performance differences exist among the firms examined.

We conducted two more tests. In the first we added the underwriter's spread to the one-month yardstick. This sum represents a different approach to measurement of the total cost of issuing new bonds.

We took this approach to check the possibility that a comparatively low- or high-spread underwriter was also a comparatively low or high underpricer and therefore so low or high across the board that the combined amount would be significantly lower or higher than others. This proved not to be the case. Combinations of underwriter spread and underpricing measures showed no differences.

In the second test we sought to discover whether any investment bank was more consistent in determining underwriter spread or pricing. If all the issues of one firm always experienced a yield spread of the same magnitude (say 25 basis points), a corporate treasurer might prefer to deal with that underwriter. The treasurer would be reasonably confident of never doing badly with that firm, unlike others whose issues showed yield spread swings from 70 down to 2. Here also our tests failed to discriminate differences among the firms. (Details about this test can be found in the Appendix.)

Does It Pay to Shop?

In sum, it appears that none of the prominent Wall Street firms, either on average or over time, priced new bond issues better or worse than the others in the period when we examined them. This conclusion holds true even if various kinds of risk and the size of issue are held constant. Our findings support the view that it probably does not pay corporate issuers of bonds to shop for investment banking services. This rather unsurprising conclusion gives no comfort to corporate financial officers who have agonized over the selection of the "right" firm to sell their companies' securities.

The investment banking industry is intensely competitive, and prices do not remain out of line for long. The choice of an investment banker must rely on judgment and belief regarding the ancillary benefits of dealing with one rather than another. Indeed, for many companies, the main criterion is not price, but the excellence and reliability of the financial advice and other services rendered. Unfortunately, these factors cannot be quantified.

Notes

1. See Dennis E. Logue, "On the Pricing of Unseasoned Equity Issues: 1965–1969," *Journal of Financial and Quantitative Analysis*, January 1973, p. 91; and Dennis E. Logue and John R. Lindvall, "The Behavior of Investment Bankers: An Econometric Investigation," *Journal of Finance*, March 1974, p. 203.

2. For an analysis of concentration and competition in the industry, see Samuel L. Hayes III, "The Transformation of Investment Banking," *HBR*, January-February 1979, p. 153.

Appendix. Study Methodology

Most of the conclusions drawn in this article are based on a Kruskal-Wallis test to determine whether differences exist among investment banks. It is an all-purpose test that is nonparametric concerning the underlying distribution. Because it is distribution free, the test does not depend on normality and equal variances—unlike the usual one-way analysis of variance.

A Kruskal-Wallis statistic can be computed from ranks of the quantitative measure being analyzed and subjected to a chi-square test. The null hypothesis is that a given measure for investment banks is drawn from identically distributed populations. For our purposes, this is the same as concluding that no discernible differences in costs or performance exist among investment firms.

We supplemented the nonparametric analysis with standard equality-of-means and equality-of-variance tests. To test the equality of means, we performed an analysis of variance. The null hypothesis to be considered is that all of the means are equal for all investment firms, regardless of the measure of performance. An F test can be used. The means in Exhibits 2 and 3 are the basis for the F tests.

We made comparisons of firms with respect to consistency by evaluating the equality of variances for a given measure using Bartlett's test. A chi-square test can be used. The Bartlett test is an all-purpose test that can be employed for unequal sample sizes. The variances shown in Tables A and B provide rough measures of the consistency of individual investment banks' pricing performance. These variances are the basis for the Bartlett test.

We conducted all three of these tests with and without size. That is, for each measure of difference among investment banks, we computed the three test statistics with and without holding constant the effect of the size of the offering. We also experimented on risk. Among other things, we held investment bank measures constant for the influence of such variables as the variance of the rates of return on investment by issuer and issuers' betas.

A note on the cost comparisons: Averages may not indicate clearly the central tendency of the sampled spreads. Extremely large or small spreads can distort comparisons using averages, especially when sample sizes are small, as in this case. Evidence of this behavior is apparent in the erratic variations around the spreads.

Therefore, the median may be a better gauge for comparing spreads. A close look at the data supports this notion. For example, the median spread of A-rated bonds in 1975 for all 11 firms was .875. In fact, 72 of the 96 bonds had a .875 spread. Much the same picture emerges in 1976, when 20 of the 49 A-rated securities had a .875 spread. Medians are the basis for the Kruskal-Wallis test.

A note on the underpricing computations: It is important to note that the interval headings in Exhibits 2 and 3 are not exact. The one-month performance measures are actually computed from the date of issue to the end of the month during which the security was offered—on average, about 15 days after offering. The other headings are similarly off by an average of 15 days—that is, they measure about 2½, 5½, and 11½ months from the date of issuance.

Table A. Variance of Price Action of 1975 Issues over Time

Investment bank	1 Month	3 Months	6 Months	12 Months
All bonds				
MS	.002600	.005402	.008052	.009800
FB	.002362	.003792	.003788	.006459
GS	.000516	.002139	.003199	.002465
SB	.000886	.001359	.000715	.001462
LB	.000853	.002575	.002742	.002834
KL	.000446	.001450	.001533	.002597
ML	.000238	.002305	.001173	.003230
BE	.001201	.001609	.002219	.003058
KP	.000964	.001683	.001718	.001355
DR	.000340	.005015	.004546	.009141
WW	.000310	.002345	.002441	.004266
All	.001282	.002998	.003535	.004864
A-rated bonds only				
MS	.002339	.001916	.001569	.004746
FB	.002642	.003958	.003858	.006891
GS	.000384	.001626	.001271	.001650
SB	.001485	.000771	.000492	.002150
LB	.000725	.002727	.002915	.002806
KL	.000188	.001719	.001954	.003222
ML	.000214	.002904	.001294	.003906
BE	.001163	.000668	.001508	.001867
KP	.001162	.003559	.002755	.000848
DR	.000043	.001614	.001262	.000912
WW	.000502	.000427	.001318	.000949
All	.001404	.002420	.002340	.003718

Note: For sample size, see Exhibit 2.

For some purposes, it might be desirable to measure performance on a calendar basis rather than from time of issuance. However, obtaining yields for newly issued bonds on particular dates from a constant source is very difficult. One advantage of making the calculations as we have is the consistency of the data source for postoffering yields, *Standard & Poor's Bond Guide*.

In addition, the statistical tests we used deal with central tendencies of investment houses, not of any particular bond. As long as the issuance dates cluster around the middle of the issue month, our results can be in-

Table B. Variance of Price Action of 1976 Issues over Time

Investment bank	1 Month	3 Months	6 Months	12 Months
All bonds				
MS	.001768	.000216	.002878	.000620
FB	.000293	.001068	.000887	.001039
GS	.000286	.001174	.001278	.001304
SB	.000273	.001087	.001175	.000942
LB	.000002	.000145	.000871	.000963
KL	.000092	.000219	.001097	.001606
ML	.001385	.001133	.004559	.001709
BE	.003416	.001638	.003862	.002188
KP	.000466	.000363	.000665	.001103
DR	.002814	.003319	.001528	.000328
WW	.000261	.002544	.008235	.001634
All	.001279	.001300	.002528	.001298
A-rated bonds only				
MS	.000025	.000080	.007533	.000687
FB	.000293	.001590	.001258	.001689
GS	.000029	.000246	.001360	.000076
SB	.000454	.000653	.000648	.000268
LB	.000000	.000031	.000348	.000049
KL	.000092	.000252	.001323	.001998
ML	.001126	.001621	.002815	.002906
BE	.003416	.000296	.005339	.003147
KP	.000037	.000417	.000440	.001594
DR	.000000	.004516	.001521	.000178
WW	.000000	.000973	.009331	.000504
All	.001423	.001619	.003447	.001487

Note: For sample size, see Exhibit 3.

terpreted on average to be ½-, 2½-, 5½-, and 11½-month performance measures relative to the date of issuance.

Statistical analysis of the dates of issuance in a given month reveals no significant differences. This fact implies that the typical security in the sample was issued around the middle of the month in both years.

Further details of the statistical tests, plus additional tables, can be obtained by writing to the authors.

PART FOUR
MAKING GOOD INVESTMENT DECISIONS

AN OVERVIEW

There is growing recognition in the field of corporate finance that it is cash flows that matter in capital investment decisions. Managers and shareholders have a natural interest in earnings per share, but too much focus on reported earnings contributes to a short-term perspective that may be detrimental to the long-run strategic interests of the firm. Thus corporations create value for shareholders, not by investing in projects with high current earnings, but by investing in projects that have a positive cash value, or more technically, a positive net present value. This occurs when the cash flows generated by a project or investment strategy have a value that exceeds the value of cash put into it. Because the cash flows occur at different times, the present, or current, values of the inflows and outflows are computed using an appropriate discount rate. Then the value of cash received can be compared to the required cash outflows.

This concept is easy to illustrate in a textbook, but it poses a host of issues to be resolved when attempts to implement it in practice are made. What is the correct discount rate? How can cash flows be estimated, particularly when they occur at some distance in the future? How can this kind of analysis be integrated with the strategic thinking of the company?

These issues are clearly important. If the discount rate used is too high, a company will underinvest in labor-saving machinery and in important strategic moves. Similarly, a firm might not undertake a project that had strategic importance if long-term cash flow benefits were not incorporated in the analysis, or if insufficient attention were paid to nonquantifiable factors.

These and other issues involved in capital investment decisions are addressed in the articles of Part 4. First, Rappaport in "Selecting Strategies That Create Shareholder Value" illustrates the basic conceptual approach of discounting cash flows and discusses why this approach is the best method for evaluating projects. Furthermore, he shows how discounted cash flow techniques can be used to evaluate strategic business units. In "Cash Flow Analysis: More Important Than Ever," Gale and Branch recognize the importance of a strategic point of view in investment decisions, but point out the need to understand key links between strategies and cash flows. These links are illustrated by drawing on a large data base supplied by more than 200 companies.

The uncertainty of future cash flows has always been a troublesome point in capital investment decisions. Hertz addresses this issue in a classic article, "Risk Analysis in Capital Investment." He proposes a simulation methodology that provides explicit information about the uncertainty in future cash flows and the rate of return on a project. The first step is to estimate a probability distribution for each of several key factors, such as market size, share of market, and selling prices. Then a computer simulation model is used to draw information from these distributions and compute the distribution of outcomes that might occur if the project were undertaken.

What is the correct discount rate to use? Hayes makes two important points on this question in "Capital Commitments and the High Cost of Money." First, the discount rate used should reflect the opportunities and expectations of bond and equity security holders, not a past return the company has achieved on its assets or book equity. Second, returns desired by security holders go up in an inflationary environment and thus the discount rate should be increased with inflation. These two ideas are important for a company to maintain an attractive stock price and to continue to attract funds from the capital markets.

Developments in the theory of capital markets have also had important implications for selection of a discount rate. One of them is that the discount rates used in some firms may be too high. This occurs if a corporation uses a high discount rate for risky projects and the rate is set high enough to compensate for the total risk involved. Shareholders do not need such a high return if they hold diversified portfolios that diversify away some of the risk. This and other aspects of the new capital market theory are summarized in Mullins' article, "Does the Capital Asset Pricing Model Work?"

Leaving theory aside, the last two articles in Part 4 address the practical issue: Should corporations invest funds to gain market share? Biggadike in "The Risky Business of Diversification" acknowledges that it is indeed risky, but that the long-term rewards are worth the risk. Fruhan's "Pyrrhic Victories in Fights for Market Share" provides an interesting counterpoint by describing some important attempts that failed after substantial investments. He concludes by indicating three key questions a company needs to address before attempting a market share fight.

15
Selecting Strategies That Create Shareholder Value

ALFRED RAPPAPORT

Although accounting ratios such as earnings per share and return on investment continue to enjoy great popularity for evaluating company strategy, such measures fall short in basic ways, according to this author. Since the ultimate test of a corporate plan is whether it creates value for shareholders, what is needed is a reliable index for assessing plans by this criterion. With discounted cash flow analysis as a basis, the shareholder value approach uses readily available data to determine the value-creating prospects for alternative strategies at the business unit and corporate levels.

In today's fast-changing, often bewildering business environment, formal systems for strategic planning have become one of top management's principal tools for evaluating and coping with uncertainty. Corporate board members are also showing increasing interest in ensuring that the company has adequate strategies and that these are tested against actual results. Although the organizational dynamics and the sophistication of the strategic planning process vary widely among companies, the process almost invariably culminates in projected (commonly five-year) financial statements.

This accounting format enables top managers and the board to review and approve strategic plans in the same terms that the company reports its performance to shareholders and the financial community. Under current practice the projected financial statements, particularly projected earnings-per-share performance, commonly serve as the basis for judging the attractiveness of the strategic or long-term corporate plan.

Author's note. I wish to thank Carl M. Noble, Jr., and Robert C. Statius Muller for their many helpful suggestions.

The conventional accounting-oriented approach for evaluating the strategic plan does not, however, provide reliable answers to such basic questions as the following:

- ☐ Will the corporate plan create value for shareholders? If so, how much?
- ☐ Which business units are creating value and which are not?
- ☐ How would alternative strategic plans affect shareholder value?

My chief objective here is to provide top management and board members with a theoretically sound, practical approach for assessing the contributions of strategic business unit (SBU) plans and overall corporate strategic plans toward creating economic value for shareholders.

Limitations of EPS

A principal objective of corporate strategic planning is to create value for shareholders. By focusing systematically on strategic decision making, such planning helps management allocate corporate resources to their most productive and profitable use. It is commonly assumed that if the strategic plan provides for "satisfactory" growth in EPS, then the market value of the company's shares will increase as the plan materializes, thus creating value for shareholders. Unfortunately, EPS growth does not necessarily lead to an increase in the market value of the stock. This phenomenon can be observed empirically and explained on theoretical grounds as well.

Of the Standard & Poor's 400 industrial companies, 172 achieved compounded EPS growth rates of 15% or better during 1974 to 1979. In 27, or 16%, of these companies stockholders realized *negative* rates of return from dividends plus capital losses. For 60, or 35%, of the 172 companies, stockholders' returns were inadequate to compensate them just for inflation. The returns provided no compensation for risk. Exhibit 1 gives a more complete set of statistics. Additional evidence of the uncertain relationship between EPS growth and returns to shareholders is offered by the 1980 *Fortune* "500" survey of the largest industrial corporations. Forty-eight, or almost 10%, of the companies achieved positive EPS growth rates, whereas their stockholders realized negative rates of return for the 1969–1979 period. Thirteen of these companies had EPS growth rates in excess of 10% during this period.

EPS and related accounting ratios, such as return on investment and return on equity, have shortcomings as financial standards by which to evaluate corporate strategy for the following six reasons:

1 Alternative and equally acceptable determinations are possible for the EPS figure. Prominent examples are the differences that arise from LIFO and FIFO approaches to computing cost of sales and various methods of computing depreciation.

Exhibit 1. EPS Growth Rates versus Rates of Return to Shareholders for Standard & Poor's 400 Industrial Companies

	1976–1979	1975–1979[c]	1974–1979
Companies with annual EPS growth of 10% or greater[a]			
Total	**259 (100%)**	**268 (100%)**	**232 (100%)**
Negative rates of return to shareholders	32 (12%)	7 (3%)	39 (17%)
Rates of return inadequate to compensate shareholders for inflation[b]	65 (25%)	36 (13%)	89 (38%)
Companies with annual EPS growth of 15% or greater[a]			
Total	**191 (100%)**	**205 (100%)**	**172 (100%)**
Negative rates of return to shareholders	14 (7%)	2 (1%)	27 (16%)
Rates of return inadequate to compensate shareholders for inflation[b]	33 (17%)	20 (10%)	60 (35%)

Note: EPS growth and rate-of-return calculations prepared by CompuServe, Inc. using Standard & Poor's Compustat data base.

[a]Restated primary EPS excluding extraordinary items and discontinued operations.

[b]The annual growth rates in the consumer price index for 1976–1979, 1975–1979, and 1974–1979 are 7.7%, 7.6%, and 8%, respectively.

[c]The small number of companies with negative rates of return to shareholders for this period is due to low level of market at the end of 1974. Standard & Poor's stock index at the close of 1974 was 76.47 and, in subsequent years, 100.88, 119.46, 104.71, 107.21, and 121.02.

2 Earnings figures do not reflect differences in risk among strategies and SBUs. Risk is conditioned both by the nature of the business investment and by the relative proportions of debt and equity used to finance investments.
3 Earnings do not take into account the working capital and fixed investment needed for anticipated sales growth.
4 Although projected earnings, of course, incorporate estimates of future revenues and expenses, they ignore potential changes in a company's cost of capital both because of inflation and because of shifting business and financial risk.

5 The EPS approach to strategy ignores dividend policy. If the objective were to maximize EPS, one could argue that the company should never pay any dividends as long as it expected to achieve a positive return on new investment. But we know that if the company invested shareholders' funds at below the minimum acceptable market rate, the value of the company would be bound to decrease.
6 The EPS approach does not specify a time preference rate for the EPS stream, that is, it does not establish the value of a dollar of EPS this year compared with a year from now, two years from now, and so on.

Shareholder Value Approach

The economic value of any investment is simply the anticipated cash flow discounted by the cost of capital. An essential feature of the discounted cash flow technique, of course, is that it takes into account that a dollar of cash received today is worth more than a dollar received a year from now, because today's dollar can be invested to earn a return during the intervening time.

Although many companies employ the shareholder value approach using DCF analysis in capital budgeting, they use it more often at the project level than at the corporate strategy level. Thus, we sometimes see a situation where capital projects regularly exceed the minimum acceptable rate of return, whereas the business unit itself is a "problem" and creates little or no value for shareholders. The DCF criterion can be applied not only to internal investments such as additions to existing capacity but also is useful in analysis of opportunities for external growth such as corporate mergers and acquisitions.

Companies can usefully extend this approach from piecemeal applications to the entire strategic plan. An SBU is commonly defined as the smallest organizational unit for which integrated strategic planning, related to a distinct product that serves a well-defined market, is feasible. A strategy for an SBU may then be seen as a collection of product—market-related investments and the company itself may be characterized as a portfolio of these investment-requiring strategies. By estimating the future cash flows associated with each strategy, a company can assess the economic value to shareholders of alternative strategies at the business unit and corporate levels.

Steps in Analysis

The analysis for a shareholder value approach to strategic planning involves the following sequential steps:

- ☐ Estimation for each business unit and the corporation of the minimum pretax operating return on incremental sales needed to create value for shareholders.

☐ Comparison of minimum acceptable rates of return on incremental sales with rates realized during the past five years and initial projections for the next year and the five-year plan.

☐ Estimation of the contribution to shareholder value of alternative strategies at the business unit and corporate levels.

☐ Evaluation of the corporate plan to determine whether the projected growth is financially feasible in light of anticipated return on sales, investment requirements per dollar of sales, target capital structure, and dividend policy.

☐ A financial self-evaluation at the business unit and corporate levels.

(Before proceeding to the case illustration in the next section, the reader may wish to refer to the Appendix to examine the basis for estimating the minimum pretax operating return on incremental sales needed to increase shareholder value, as well as the calculation of the absolute shareholder value contributed by various strategies.)

Case of Econoval

Econoval, a diversified manufacturing company, divides its operations into three lines of business—semiconductors, energy, and automotive parts (see Exhibit 2).

Before beginning their detailed analysis, Econoval managers must choose

Exhibit 2. Strategic Overview of Econoval's Lines of Business

Business Unit	Product Life Cycle Stage	Strategy	Risk	Current Year's Sales (in $ millions)
Semiconductors	Embryonic	Invest aggressively to achieve dominant market position	High	$50
Energy	Expanding	Invest to improve market position	Medium	75
Automotive parts	Mature	Maintain market position	Low	125

appropriate time horizons for calculating the value contributed by each business unit's strategy. The product life cycle stages of the various units will ordinarily determine this choice. If we were to measure value creation for all businesses arbitrarily in a common time horizon, say five years, then embryonic businesses with large capital requirements in early years and large payoffs in later years would be viewed as poor prospects even if they were expected to yield exceptional value over the life cycle. Therefore, in this case, I have extended the projections for the semiconductor unit to 10 years and have limited projections for the energy and auto parts units to five years in the company's long-term financial plan.

Step 1. Estimation of minimum return on incremental sales needed to create value for shareholders.

The basis for calculating the minimum acceptable return on incremental sales appears as Equation (4) in the Appendix. For each business unit, four parameters need to be estimated: capital expenditures per dollar of sales increase; cash required for working capital per dollar of sales increase; the income tax rate; and the weighted average cost of capital. Exhibit 3 summarizes the results.

Before proceeding, I should comment on how to estimate these variables. To estimate the recent values for capital investment required per dollar of sales increase, one simply takes the sum of all capital expenditures less depreciation over the preceding 5 or 10 years and divides this amount by the sales increase during the period. Note that if a business continues to replace existing facilities in kind and if the prices of these facilities remain constant, then the numerator (i.e., capital expenditures less depreciation) approximates the cost of real growth in productive capacity.

However, the costs for capital expenditures usually rise each year owing to inflationary forces and regulatory requirements such as environmental control. These cost increases may be partially offset by advances in

Exhibit 3. Minimum Pretax Operating Return on Incremental Sales Based on Initial Planning Projections

	Investment Requirements Per Dollar of Sales Increase			
Business Unit	Capital Expenditures	Working Capital	Cost of Capital	Minimum Return on Incremental Sales
Semiconductors	.40	.20	.15	.145
Energy	.20	.20	.14	.091
Automotive parts	.15	.20	.13	.075

technology. Thus the numerator reflects not only the cost of real growth, but price changes in facilities as well as the impact of product mix changes, regulation, and technological improvements. Whether the historical value of this variable is a reasonable basis for the projection period depends significantly on how quickly and to what extent the company can offset increased fixed capital costs by higher future selling prices, given the competitive structure of the industry.

The increase in required working capital should reflect the cash flow consequences of changes in (1) minimum required cash balance, (2) accounts receivable, (3) inventory, and (4) accounts payable and accruals.

The appropriate rate for discounting the company's cash flow stream is the weighted average of the costs of debt and equity capital. For example, suppose a company's aftertax cost of debt is 6% and its estimated cost of equity 16%. Further, it plans to raise capital in the following proportion—20% by way of debt and 80% by equity. It computes the average cost of capital at 14% as follows:

	Weight	Cost	Weighted cost
Debt	.20	.06	.012
Equity	.80	.16	.128
Average cost of capital			.140

Is the company's cost of capital the appropriate rate for discounting the cash flow projections of individual business units? The use of a single discount rate for all parts of the company is valid only in the unlikely event that they are identically risky.

Executives who use a single discount rate companywide are likely to have a consistent bias in favor of funding higher-risk businesses at the expense of less risky businesses. To provide a consistent framework for dealing with different investment risks and thereby increasing shareholder value, management should allocate funds to business units on a risk-adjusted return basis.

The process of estimating a business unit's cost of capital inevitably involves a substantial degree of executive judgment. Unlike the company as a whole, ordinarily the business unit has no posted market price that would enable the analyst to estimate systematic or market-related risk. Moreover, it is often difficult to assign future financing (debt and equity) weights to individual business units.

One approach to estimating a business unit's cost of equity is to identify publicly traded stocks in the same line of business that might be expected to have about the same degree of systematic or market risk as the business unit. After establishing the cost of equity and cost of debt, the analyst can calculate a weighted-average cost of capital for the business unit in the same fashion as for the company.

The cost of equity or minimum return expected by investors is the risk-free rate (including the expected long-term rate of inflation) as reflected in current yields available in long-term government bonds plus a premium for accepting equity risk. The overall market risk premium for the last 40 years has averaged 5.7%.[1] The risk premium for an individual security can be estimated as the product of the market risk premium and the individual security's systematic risk, or beta coefficient.[2]

Following is the estimate for Econoval's semiconductor unit's cost of equity:

Risk-free rate + average beta coefficient for selected similarly financed semiconductor companies × market risk premium for equity investments = cost of equity

$$9.25\% + 1.5\ (5.7\%) = \underline{\underline{17.8\%}}$$

Assuming an aftertax cost of debt of 6.5% and financing proportions of 25% debt and 75% equity, the semiconductor unit's risk-adjusted cost of capital is estimated to be 15%. Risk-adjusted rates for the energy and auto parts units are 14% and 13%, respectively.

Step 2. Comparison of minimum acceptable rates of return on incremental sales with recently realized rates and initial planning projections.

Having developed some preliminary estimates of minimum return on incremental sales, Econoval now wishes to compare those rates with past and initially projected rates for each business unit's planning period. This comparison (Exhibit 4) provides both a reasonable check on the projections and insights into the potential of the various business units for creating shareholder value.

From Exhibit 4, we can determine that the semiconductor unit is projecting substantial improvement over historical margins on the basis of a continuing product mix shift toward higher-margin proprietary items and substantial R&D expenditures to maintain competitiveness in the learning curve race.

Exhibit 4. Econoval's Rates of Return on Incremental Sales

	Historical			
Business Unit	Last Year	Past Five Years	Minimum Acceptable	Initial Forecast
Semiconductors	.115	.110	.145	.155
Energy	.100	.120	.091	.110
Automotive parts	.070	.080	.075	.080

If the planned margins materialize, the semiconductor unit will contribute to shareholder value. At this initial stage, the company is concerned with the reasonableness of the projections and the small distance between projected and minimum acceptable margins. The energy unit is projecting a rate of return on incremental sales in line with its recent experience, and this 11% rate is comfortably over the 9.1% minimum acceptable rate.

The problem business unit is the automotive parts division. Margins have been eroding steadily, and the projected five-year margin is just above the acceptable minimum. Econoval managers are thus committed to investigating a full range of strategic alternatives for the automotive unit.

Step 3. Estimation of shareholder value contribution for alternative strategies at the business unit and corporate levels.

Once the company has developed and analyzed its initial planning projections, SBU managers and the corporate planning group can prepare more detailed analyses for evaluating alternative planning scenarios. Exhibit 5 shows the semiconductor unit's planning parameters for conservative, most likely, and optimistic scenarios.

The worst case or conservative scenario assumes significant market penetration by Japanese producers via major technological advances coupled with aggressive price cutting. The most likely scenario assumes the semiconductor group's continued dominance in the metal-oxide-semiconductor (MOS) market, substantial R&D expenditures to enable the semiconductor group to maintain its competitiveness in the learning curve race, and gradual Japanese technological parity, which will place pressure on sales margins. The optimistic scenario projects more rapid industry growth and great success in the unit's effort to carve out high-margin proprietary niches.

Exhibit 6 presents the shareholder value contribution for each of these three scenarios and for a range of discount rates.

Econoval expects the semiconductor unit's ten-year plan for the most likely scenario to contribute $10.60 million to shareholder value. The range of shareholder values from conservative to optimistic scenarios is from $4.87 million to $29.93 million for the estimated cost of capital or discount rate of 15%.

An assessment of the likelihood of each scenario will provide further insight into the relative riskiness of business unit investment strategies. For example, if all three scenarios are equally likely, the situation would be riskier than if the most likely scenario is 60% probable and the other two are each 20% probable.

Econoval performed similar analyses for the energy and automotive parts units. Exhibit 7 summarizes the results for most likely scenarios. To ensure consistency in comparing or consolidating scenarios of various business units, it is important that the corporate planning group establish that such scenarios share common assumptions about critical environmental factors such as inflation and energy prices.

Exhibit 5. Semiconductor Unit's Planning Projections for Various Scenarios

	Year									
	1	2	3	4	5	6	7	8	9	10
Conservative										
Sales growth rate	.25	.25	.20	.20	.18	.18	.18	.18	.18	.18
EBIT/sales	.115	.12	.125	.13	.135	.135	.135	.135	.135	.135
Working capital per dollar of sales increase	.20	.20	.20	.20	.20	.20	.20	.20	.20	.20
Capital expenditures per dollar of sales increase	.42	.42	.42	.40	.40	.35	.35	.35	.35	.35
Cash income tax rate	.41	.41	.41	.41	.41	.41	.41	.41	.41	.41
Most likely										
Sales growth rate	.30	.28	.25	.22	.20	.20	.20	.20	.20	.20
EBIT/sales	.12	.125	.13	.135	.14	.145	.15	.15	.15	.145
Working capital per dollar of sales increase	.20	.20	.20	.20	.20	.20	.20	.20	.20	.20
Capital expenditures per dollar of sales increase	.45	.45	.44	.42	.42	.40	.38	.38	.35	.35
Cash income tax rate	.40	.40	.40	.40	.40	.40	.40	.40	.40	.40
Optimistic										
Sales growth rate	.32	.30	.30	.25	.25	.25	.25	.25	.25	.25
EBIT/sales	.125	.13	.14	.145	.15	.15	.15	.15	.15	.15
Working capital per dollar of sales increase	.18	.18	.18	.18	.18	.18	.18	.18	.18	.18
Capital expenditures per dollar of sales increase	.40	.38	.38	.36	.36	.35	.35	.35	.35	.35
Cash income tax rate	.39	.39	.39	.39	.39	.39	.39	.39	.39	.39

On closer inspection, we see that the analysis in Exhibit 7 provides support for management's concern about the automotive unit's performance. Although the unit now accounts for 50% of Econoval's sales, the company expects it to contribute only $3.57 million, or about 15% of the total increase in shareholder value.

On the basis of traditional criteria such as sales and earnings growth rates, the semiconductor unit clearly emerges as the star performer. However, its high investment requirements and risk vis-à-vis its sales margins combine to limit its value-creating potential. Despite the fact that the semiconductor unit's sales and earnings growth rates are substantially greater than those of the energy unit, the semiconductor unit is expected to contribute only marginally more shareholder value in 10 years than the energy unit in five years.

Exhibit 6. Semiconductor Unit's Shareholder Value Contribution for Different Scenarios and Discount Rates (in $ millions)

Scenario	Discount Rate				
	.140	.145	.150	.155	.160
Conservative	$ 9.30	$ 6.96	$ 4.87	$ 2.99	$ 1.30
Most likely	16.92	13.59	10.60	7.91	5.48
Optimistic	39.64	34.53	29.93	25.79	22.05

The shareholder value increase per discounted dollar of investment provides management with important information about where it is realizing the greatest benefits per dollar of investment. Indeed, this *value* return on investment (VROI), rather than the traditional accounting ROI, enables management to rank various business units on the basis of a substantive economic criterion.

The numerator of the VROI is simply the shareholder value increase of a strategy and the denominator, the present cost or investment. When the VROI ratio is equal to zero, the strategy yields exactly the risk-adjusted cost of capital, and when VROI is positive, the strategy yields a rate greater than its cost of capital. Note that the semiconductor unit ranks last, even behind the auto parts unit, in this all-important performance measure.

Ranking units on the basis of VROI can be particularly helpful to corporate headquarters in capital-rationing situations where the various parts of the business are competing for scarce funds. In the final analysis, however, corporate resources should be allocated to units so as to maximize the shareholder value of the company's total product-market portfolio.

Exhibit 7. Shareholder Value, Sales Growth, and Earnings Growth Rates by Business Unit for Most Likely Scenarios

		Shareholder Value Increase			Growth Rates	
Business Unit	Years in Plan	$ millions	Per Discounted $ of Sales Increase	Per Discounted $ of Investment	Sales	Earnings
Semiconductors	10	10.60	.077	.128	22.4%	26.1%
Energy	5	8.79	.175	.438	15	17.7
Automotive parts	5	3.57	.068	.194	10	11.9
Consolidated		**22.96**				

Step 4. Evaluation of the financial feasibility of the strategic plan.

Once the company has established a preliminary plan, it should test its financial feasibility and whether it is fundable. This involves integrating the company's planned investment growth strategies with its dividend and financing policies. A particularly effective starting point is to estimate the company's maximum affordable dividend payout rate and its sensitivity to varying assumptions underlying the strategic plan.

To illustrate, Econoval calculates the maximum dividend payout for the first year of the five-year plan. On a consolidated basis, Econoval projects sales growth of 15.5%, earnings before interest and taxes (EBIT) to sales of 9.56%, an investment of $.481 per dollar of incremental sales, a cash income tax rate of 42.2%, and a current and target debt-to-equity ratio of 45.2% and 44.3%, respectively. Econoval can pay out no more than 6.3% of its net income as dividends. At the 6.3% payout rate, the earnings retained, plus added debt capacity, are just equal to the investment dollars required to support the 15.5% growth in sales from $250 million to $288.75 million.

It is easy to demonstrate this result. At $.481 per dollar of incremental sales, investment requirements (net of depreciation) on the projected $38.75 million sales increase will total $18.63 million. This amount will be financed as follows:

Aftertax earnings on sales of $288.75 million	**$13.34 million**
Less 6.3% dividend payout	.84
Earnings retained, i.e., increase in equity	12.50
Added debt capacity	5.08
Increase in deferred taxes	1.05
	$18.63 million

The maximum affordable dividend payout rate table (Exhibit 8) shows how sensitive this rate is to changes in growth, profitability, investment intensity, and financial leverage. Note, for example, that if sales growth is increased from 15.5% to 16.5%, the maximum affordable dividend payout rate decreases from 6.3% to 1.1%, whereas a 1% increase in EBIT/sales raises the maximum affordable rate from 6.3% to 16.6%.

Exhibit 9 presents Econoval's strategic funds statement for its five-year planning period. The cash required for investment in working capital and fixed capital exceeds the cash sources from operations in each year. This difference is reflected in the "net cash required" line. Another source of funds is, of course, debt financing.

The increase in debt capacity is established by reference to the target debt-to-equity ratios of Econoval's three principal businesses. Adding the increase in debt capacity to the net cash required provides the maximum

Exhibit 8. Maximum Dividend Payout Rate Analysis

Sales Growth		Investment Requirements per Dollar of Sales Increase								
		.431 Debt/Equity			.481 Debt/Equity			.531 Debt/Equity		
		.393	.443	.493	.393	.443	.493	.393	.443	.493
.145										
EBIT ÷ sales	.086	−9.6%	10.1%	28.5%	−20.8%	−0.7%	18.1%	−31.9%	−11.5%	7.6%
	.096	3.8	21.2	37.4	−6.1	11.7	28.2	−15.9	2.2	19.0
	.106	14.4	29.9	44.4	5.6	21.4	36.2	−3.2	12.9	28.0
.155										
EBIT ÷ sales	.086	−15.1	4.7	23.1	−26.9	−6.7	12.1	−38.7	−18.1	1.1
	.096	−1.0	16.4	32.6	−11.4	6.3	22.9	−21.9	−3.7	13.2
	.106	10.1	25.7	40.2	0.7	16.6	31.5	−8.6	7.6	22.8
.165										
EBIT ÷ sales	.086	−20.4	−0.6	17.8	−32.8	−12.6	6.2	−45.3	−24.7	−5.4
	.096	−5.7	11.7	28.0	−16.7	1.1	17.7	−27.7	−9.5	7.5
	.106	5.8	21.4	36.0	−4.0	11.9	26.8	−13.8	2.4	17.6

Book tax rate = .460, cash tax rate = .422
Current debt/equity = .452
Current equity = $53.550 million

Exhibit 9. Econoval Strategic Funds Statement for Five-Year Planning Period (in $ millions)

	Year					
	1	2	3	4	5	Total
Net income	13.34	15.74	18.54	21.75	25.44	94.81
Depreciation	3.84	4.74	5.82	7.03	8.32	29.74
Increase in deferred taxes	1.05	1.29	1.56	1.88	2.23	8.02
Sources of funds	**18.23**	**21.77**	**25.92**	**30.66**	**35.99**	**132.57**
Capital expenditures	14.71	17.58	20.22	22.55	25.66	100.72
Increase in working capital	7.76	8.97	10.16	11.33	12.66	50.88
Uses of funds	**22.47**	**26.55**	**30.38**	**33.88**	**38.32**	**151.60**
Net cash provided (required)	(4.24)	(4.78)	(4.46)	(3.22)	(2.33)	(19.03)
Increase in debt capacity	5.08	5.89	6.60	7.20	8.02	32.79
Maximum affordable dividend	**0.84**	**1.11**	**2.14**	**3.98**	**5.69**	**13.76**
Maximum affordable dividend payout rate	6.3%	7.1%	11.5%	18.3%	22.3%	14.5%

affordable dividend, which, as seen earlier, is $.84 million or 6.3% in the first year and rises annually to 22.3% in the fifth year.

In Exhibit 10, strategic funds statements for each of Econoval's main lines of business provide improved insights into product portfolio balancing opportunities. The semiconductor group places a substantial burden on corporate funds. Over the next five years it will require more than $26 million of cash while the energy and auto parts units will throw off about $7 million in cash. Even after taking into account the estimated debt capacity contribution of semiconductors, corporate headquarters will still have to transfer $11 million to the unit.

After some further analysis, Econoval managers concluded that the strategic plan was financially feasible. The analysis did, however, raise two concerns. First, Econoval had a low affordable dividend payout rate and was vulnerable to sales margins lower than those projected. Of immediate concern was that the current year's dividend is larger than next year's projected affordable dividend.

Also, the strategic funds statement underscored the risk associated with the semiconductor group's aggressive competitive positioning and the

Exhibit 10. Strategic Funds Statement for Five-Year Planning Period by Business Units (in $ millions)

	Semiconductors	Energy	Automotive Parts	Consolidated
Net income	$34.53	$30.92	$29.36	$ 94.81
Depreciation	17.95	6.07	5.72	29.74
Increase in deferred income taxes	4.21	2.55	1.26	8.02
	56.69	**39.54**	**36.34**	**132.57**
Capital expenditures	62.31	21.24	17.17	100.72
Increase in working capital	20.45	15.17	15.26	50.88
	82.76	**36.41**	**32.43**	**151.60**
Net cash provided (required)	(26.07)	3.13	3.91	(19.03)
Increase in debt capacity	15.05	9.26	8.48	32.79
Maximum affordable dividend	**($11.02)**	**$12.39**	**$12.39**	**$ 13.76**

related high level of investment requirements. This group's large cash requirements, coupled with its modest VROI, prompted Econoval managers to launch a study of alternative product portfolio strategies.

Step 5. A financial self-evaluation at the business unit and corporate levels.

Increasingly, companies are adding financial self-evaluation to their strategic financial planning process.[3] A financial evaluation poses two fundamental questions: How much are the company and each of its major lines of business worth? How much would each of several plausible scenarios involving various combinations of future environments and management strategies affect the value of the company and its business units?

The following types of companies would especially benefit from conducting a financial evaluation:

- ☐ Companies that wish to sell and need to establish a minimum acceptable selling price for their shares.
- ☐ Companies that are potential takeover targets.
- ☐ Companies considering selective divestments.

- ☐ Companies evaluating the attractiveness of repurchasing their own shares.
- ☐ Private companies wanting to establish the proper price at which to go public.
- ☐ Acquisition-minded companies wanting to assess the advantages of a cash versus a stock offer.

The present equity or shareholder value of any business unit, or the entire company, is the sum of the estimated shareholder value contribution from its strategic plan and the current cash flow level discounted at the risk-adjusted cost of capital less the market value of outstanding debt. Exhibit 11 summarizes these values for Econoval and its three major business units. For example, the semiconductor unit's current cash flow perpetuity level is \$2.97 million, which, when discounted at its risk-adjusted rate of 15%, produces a value of \$19.8 million. Subtracting the \$5 million of debt outstanding provides the \$14.8 million prestrategy equity value. To obtain the total equity or shareholder value of \$25.40 million for the semiconductor unit, simply add the \$10.60 million value contributed by the strategic plan.

The sum of the three business unit values is \$83.79 million. Combining the cash flows of the individual businesses and discounting them at the 14% risk-adjusted corporate cost of capital yields a value of \$87.57 million. In this case, the difference between the value of the whole and the sum of the parts is minor. However, this may not always be true.

Aggregating the values of the company's business units is consistent with the assumption that the riskiness of each unit must be considered

Exhibit 11. Business Unit and Corporate Financial Evaluation Summary—For Most Likely Scenario (in \$ millions)

	Semiconductors	Energy	Automotive Parts	Consolidated
Risk-adjusted prestrategy equity value	\$14.80	\$20.93	\$25.10	\$60.83
Shareholder value contribution from strategic plan (see Exhibit 8)	10.60	8.79	3.57	22.96
Total equity value	**\$25.40**	**\$29.72**	**\$28.67**	**\$83.79**
Percent of total equity value	30.3%	35.5%	34.2%	
Econoval equity value at corporate cost of capital of 14%				\$87.57

separately. If, however, the company's entry into unrelated businesses reduces the overall variability of its cash flows, then the lower expected probability of bankruptcy can decrease its cost of debt and increase its debt capacity.

What happens to the company's overall cost of capital naturally depends on any changes in the cost of equity capital as well as on the cost of debt. Analysis of the impact of business units on the total risk of the company is at best extremely difficult and subjective.

A more attractive alternative is to (1) assume risk independence in establishing cost of capital for business units and (2) interpret the difference between the value of the company and the aggregate value of its individual businesses as a broad approximation of the benefits or costs associated with the company's product portfolio balancing activities.

Econoval's corporate financial evaluation gave management not only an improved understanding of the relative contribution to shareholder value coming from each business but also the basis for structuring the purchase of an acquisition currently being negotiated. Econoval's market value was then about 25% less than its own estimate of value. Because the cash and exchange-of-shares price demanded by the selling shareholders was not materially different, Econoval management decided to offer cash rather than what it believed to be its undervalued shares.

Meeting the Fiduciary Duty

A fundamental fiduciary responsibility of corporate managers and boards of directors is to create economic value for their shareholders. Despite increasing sophistication in strategic planning applications, companies almost invariably evaluate the final product, the strategic plan, in terms of earnings per share or other accounting ratios such as return on investment or return on equity.

Surprisingly, the conventional accounting-oriented approach persists despite compelling theoretical and empirical evidence of the failings of accounting numbers as a reliable index for estimating changes in economic value. How should the board member of a company that has reported a decade of 15% annual EPS growth and no increase in its stock price respond when asked to approve yet another five-year business plan with projected EPS growth of 15%? The shareholder value approach to strategic planning would enable the board to recognize that despite impressive earnings growth projections, the company's increasing cost of capital, rising investment requirements per dollar of sales, and lower margins on sales are clear signs of value erosion.

A number of major companies are now using the shareholder value approach to strategic planning. The method requires virtually no data not already developed under current financial planning systems; moreover, an interactive computer program such as the "strategy valuator" (used in preparing the numerical illustrations) can help implement all of the steps I have outlined. Use of this approach should improve companies' prospects of creating value for their shareholders and thereby contribute to the long-run interests of the companies and of the economy.

Notes

1. Roger G. Ibbotson and Rex A. Sinquefield, "Stocks, Bonds, Bills and Inflation: Updates," *Financial Analysts Journal,* July–August 1979, p. 40.

2. For a method of predicting beta, see Barr Rosenberg and James Guy, "Prediction of Beta from Investment Fundamentals," *Financial Analysts Journal,* May–June 1976, p. 60 and July–August 1976, p. 62.

3. For a more detailed description of how to conduct a corporate financial self-evaluation, see my article, "Do You Know the Value of Your Company?", *Mergers and Acquisitions,* Spring 1979.

Appendix. Calculation of Value Contributed by Strategy

The present value of a business is defined simply as the anticipated aftertax operating cash flows discounted by the weighted average cost of capital. The present value of the equity claims or shareholder value is then the value of the company (or business unit) less the market value of currently outstanding debt. The value of equity for a business that expects no further real sales growth and also expects annual cost increases to be offset by selling price increases is given by the following formula:

$$E_t = \frac{p\,(1 - T)S}{k} - D_t \qquad \textbf{(1)}$$

where:

E_t = value of the equity at time t

p = earnings before interest and taxes divided by sales

T = income tax rate

S = sales

k = weighted average cost of capital

D_t = market value of debt outstanding at time t

The change in shareholder value (ΔE) for a given level of sales increase (ΔS) is then:

$$\Delta E_t = \frac{p_t'(1 - T)\Delta S_t}{k} - \frac{(f_t + w_t)\Delta S_t}{(1 + k)} \tag{2}$$

where:

$p' = \Delta EBIT/\Delta$ sales, that is, incremental operating margin on incremental sales.
f = capital expenditures minus depreciation per dollar of sales increase.
w = cash required for net working capital per dollar of sales increase.

The change in equity or shareholder value is the difference between the aftertax operating cash flow perpetuity and the required investment outlay for fixed and working capital. Since all cash flows are assumed to occur at the end of the period, the outlays for working capital and fixed assets are discounted by (1 + k) to obtain the present value. There is neither an increase nor a decrease in shareholder value for a specified sales increase whenever the value of the inflows and outflows is identical. Specifically, when

$$\frac{p_t(1 - T)}{k} = \frac{(f_t + w_t)}{(1 + k)} \tag{3}$$

From Equation (3) the break-even operating return on sales or the minimum pretax operating return on incremental sales (p_{min}) needed to create value for shareholders is derived as

$$p_{min} = \frac{(f + w)k}{(1 - T)(1 + k)} \tag{4}$$

Minimum acceptable returns on incremental sales for a range of investment requirements per dollar of sales and costs of capital are presented below.

Minimum pretax operating return on incremental sales to create value for shareholders[a]

	Investment requirements per dollar of incremental sales						
Cost of capital	.20	.30	.40	.50	.60	.70	.80
.12	.040	.059	.079	.099	.119	.139	.159
.14	.045	.068	.091	.114	.136	.159	.182
.16	.051	.077	.102	.128	.153	.179	.204
.18	.056	.085	.113	.141	.169	.198	.226
.20	.062	.093	.123	.154	.185	.216	.247

[a]Assumed income tax rate, 46%.

The shareholder value contributed by any strategy can be estimated by taking the capitalized value of the difference between the projected and the minimum acceptable operating return on incremental sales. More specifically, the change in shareholder value for time t is given by the following equation, which assumes book and cash income tax rates are identical. If they are not, another term must be added.

$$\Delta E_t = \frac{(p_t - p_{tmin})(1 - T_t)\Delta S_t}{k(1 + k)^{t-1}} \tag{5}$$

To illustrate, consider a business with sales of $50 million for its most recent year and the following assumptions for its five-year plan: sales growth rate = 15%; pretax operating margins on incremental sales = 13.5% for the first two years and 14.5% for the remaining three years; book and cash tax rate = 46%; working capital per dollar of sales = .20; capital expenditures per dollar of sales = .35; and cost of capital = 14%. Applying Equation (4) for the minimum return on incremental sales (p_{min}), we obtain 12.5%. A summary of the shareholder value contributed by the five-year plan is presented below.

Shareholder value contributed by five-year plan (in $ millions)

	Years					
	1	2	3	4	5	Total
Sales	$57.50	$66.12	$76.04	$87.45	$100.57	$387.68
Sales increase	7.50	8.62	9.92	11.41	13.12	50.57
Projected return on incremental sales minus minimum return	.01	.01	.02	.02	.02	
Shareholder present value increase[a]	$.29	$.29	$.59	$.59	$.60	$2.36

Note: The present value of the five-year plan is $2.36 million.

[a]Computed by using Equation (5).

16

Cash Flow Analysis: More Important Than Ever

BRADLEY T. GALE and BEN BRANCH

You won't find many executives arguing the importance of cash flow to the future success of their businesses, especially as inflation increases the already high cost of capital. Most will admit, however, that they tend only to monitor their cash—that they have few ideas about how to control it or use it to their strategic advantage.

Based on information culled from their extensive data base, Bradley Gale and Ben Branch of the Strategic Planning Institute have found that cash flow can be manipulated and can serve as an effective tool in business strategies. In this article, they demonstrate that a business's competitive position, the growth rate of its market, and its current strategic moves have a predictable effect on cash flow. By understanding how these factors impinge on cash supplies, the manager of a single business unit can evaluate the trade-offs among alternative strategies that use cash. Also, managers of groups of businesses can improve their ability to allocate cash supplies among their individual businesses.

Managers sometimes think that their strategies are tied to the tail of a very erratic cash kite and that fluctuations in cash supplies are too irregular and unpredictable to manage properly.

In fact, the reverse is true. Cash flow is predictable and manageable. A company's strategy and market position directly affect it. The recognition

Authors' note. We gratefully acknowledge the contribution of colleagues at the Strategic Planning Institute—Mark Chussil, Donald F. Heany, Sidney Schoeffler, and Donald J. Swire—to the research for this article, and we thank Ruth G. Newman for her editorial guidance.

of this fact is as calming as it is essential—not only to the manager of a single business unit but also to a CEO or group vice-president.

The single business unit needs cash to grow, modernize, and finance normal day-to-day operations. But managers must analyze the cash potential of each business unit in order to decide which can be relied on as cash sources and which require heavy investment to grow.

In the 1980s, companies face increasing requirements for funds even as they deplete their resources by allocating more to energy conservation and environmental protection (so-called unproductive uses of cash). Moreover, skyrocketing inflation menaces their cash supplies. And lagging U.S. productivity compounds the problem of cash availability because it underscores the need for many businesses to reindustrialize at great expense.

We have used the PIMS data base (see Appendix A for a more detailed description of PIMS) to discover some important facts about cash generation and cash use, about how companies use and abuse this vital resource, and about ways in which they can restructure cash flow.

- ☐ *Growth drains cash.* Being in a strong market is exciting, but keeping up with the fast pace requires cash. Even when real market growth is zero, inflation drains cash.
- ☐ *A high relative market share generates cash.* But building a future market position requires large expenditures for marketing programs or new product development.
- ☐ *Aggressive asset management is vital to ensure sufficient cash.* Increased investment relative to sales can be threatening because it always strains cash supply.

In this article, we examine these findings and their implications for all companies.

Cash Producers versus Cash Users

A large percentage of the businesses we studied consume more cash than they generate; in fact, more than a third have a negative operating cash flow before interest expenses (see Exhibit 1). After we subtract interest expenses and dividend payments from cash flow, about two-thirds of the businesses are cash drains.

That so many businesses are cash drains suggests that control is a slippery and complex problem. There are wide differences in the *rate* at which particular businesses use or generate cash. For example, 26% generate cash at a yearly rate above 10% of investment. On the other hand, nearly 15% of them *consume* cash at the 10% rate or beyond. Since businesses may show such divergent cash flow results, it is rational to assume that successful cash control demands systematic study and the careful attention of senior management.

Exhibit 1. Cash Flow Level of PIMS Businesses, 1970–1979

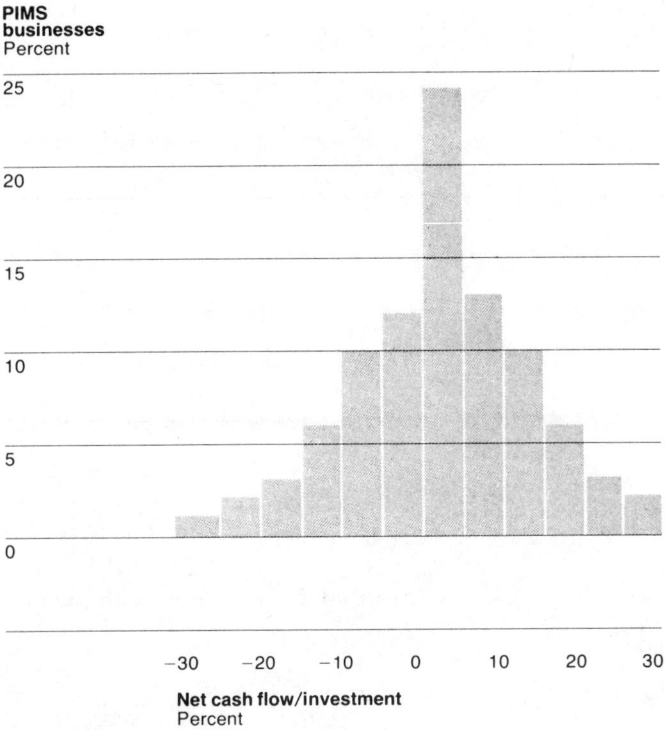

PIMS businesses
Percent

25
20
15
10
5
0

−30 −20 −10 0 10 20 30

Net cash flow/investment
Percent

Note:
8% of all PIMS businesses are beyond these bounds.

Businesses in fast-growth markets usually absorb cash unless corporate policy directs that they break even; businesses in slow-growth markets usually throw off cash unless they are allowed to keep and reinvest it.

Cash flow is lowest when sales growth (in current dollars) is rapid (see Exhibit 2A). When growth is slow or negative, cash flow is very positive. In fact, at a moderate growth rate, all a company needs is an average ROI to generate positive cash flow (before dividend or interest payments). At rapid growth rates, however, average ROI no longer suffices.

The algebraic relationship between growth and ROI needed to generate a break-even cash flow is positive and dramatic. But the correlation between growth and *actual* ROI is only moderate. When actual ROI exceeds that required to break even (growth rate below 15%), cash flow is positive. When it falls short, cash flow is negative. (Exhibit 2B shows ROI needed for a business to finance break-even cash flow at various rates of growth.)

We have observed how cash flow decreases with growth in current dollar sales. Such a decrease depends on growth in real market and selling price, as well as basic market share strategy.

Exhibit 2A. Rapid Growth Drains Cash

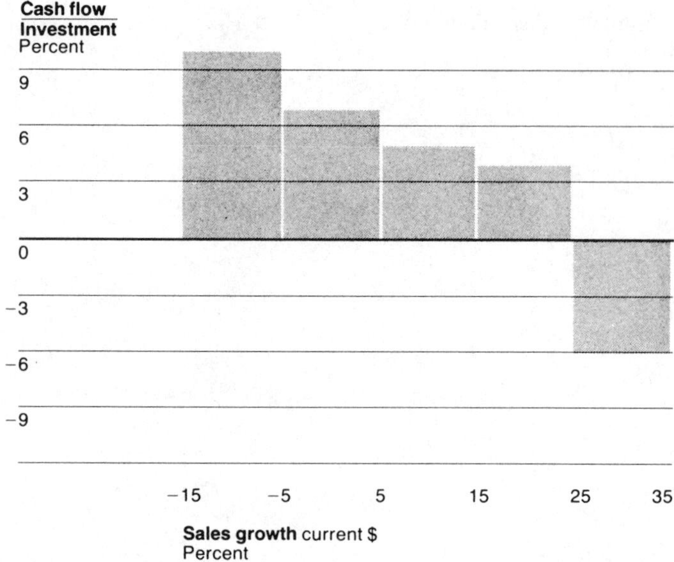

Exhibit 2B. ROI for Break-Even Cash Flow Increases with Sales Growth

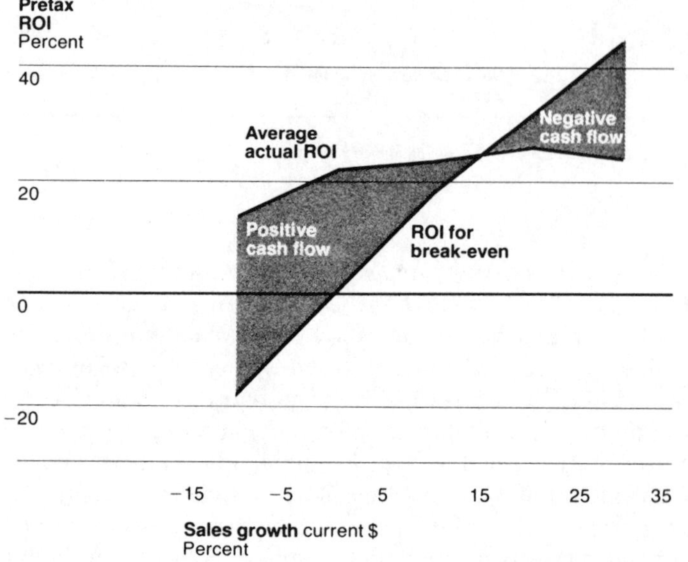

Note: Break-even ROI (pretax, preinterest) = 2g/(1 + g), where g is the rate of growth expressed as a decimal. If g = .10, ROI for break-even cash flow rate = .2/1.1 = 18%. See S.J.Q. Robinson, "What Growth Rate Can You Achieve?" *Long-Range Planning*, August 1979. Also, readers will note that the crossover points between positive and negative cash flow rates shown in Exhibits 2A and 2B differ. The ROI for the break-even rate assumes that investment will grow at the same rate as sales over-time. But during the 1970s the ratio of investment to sales declined. Because investment did not keep pace with sales, the ROI actually needed to break even during the 1970s was less than that shown in Exhibit 2B.

When real market growth is rapid, maintaining share may require considerable cash for working capital and for additional plant and equipment.

Inflation also takes its toll. Although one might expect that a rise in the selling price would generate cash, it generally does not. Indeed, a company finds its cash depleted as rising prices are either accompanied by (or are prompted by) rising costs. In addition, as prices rise, the need of most companies to tie up larger amounts of money in inventory and accounts receivable exacerbates cash requirements.

Thus cash flow varies *inversely* with both the real market growth rate and the rate of increase in selling prices. Our data base shows that businesses with slow rates of selling price and real market growth generate an average cash flow rate of 6%, whereas those with the highest growth in both average only 2%.

One caveat: A low rate of cash flow year after year does not carry the same stigma as recurrent low ROI. Even negative cash flow is not necessarily a serious problem. As long as a business establishes the strategic position required to earn an attractive return, it generates cash when the market ultimately slows down. But, while rapid growth continues, the company may still require additional resources (see Exhibit 3).

If your business is in a slow-growth market, chances are you find it relatively easy to generate enough cash to meet your needs. But whether your market grows, shrinks, or stands still, a large relative share produces cash.

Large-share businesses in slow-growth markets (called "cash cows" in terminology coined by the Boston Consulting Group) have the highest cash flow, whereas small-share businesses in rapidly growing markets have the lowest. In our data base, the former generates an average positive cash flow of 9%, whereas the latter generates a negative 3%. Exhibit 4 shows cash flow contour lines emanating from an empirical model that captures the joint impact of real market growth and relative market share on cash flow.

These contour lines are smooth and systematic because they represent the *average* cash flow rate for a locus of growth/share positions. But we need to remember that growth and share together account for only about one-tenth of the dispersion in cash flow rates illustrated in Exhibit 1. An individual business may be above or below the cash flow value on its contour line because several key factors other than growth and share also affect its cash flow rate. Exhibit 5 presents some of the key factors that affect cash generation and cash use. They are selected from a cash flow model that explains about two-thirds of the dispersion in cash flow rates among business units.

In addition to market growth and share, a change in either market share or investment intensity can affect cash *flow* by influencing cash *use*. As we have seen, businesses often consume cash when attempting to maintain share in a growing market. Gaining or attempting to build share can also be expensive.

Exhibit 3. Cash Needs Are Determined by Environment and Strategy

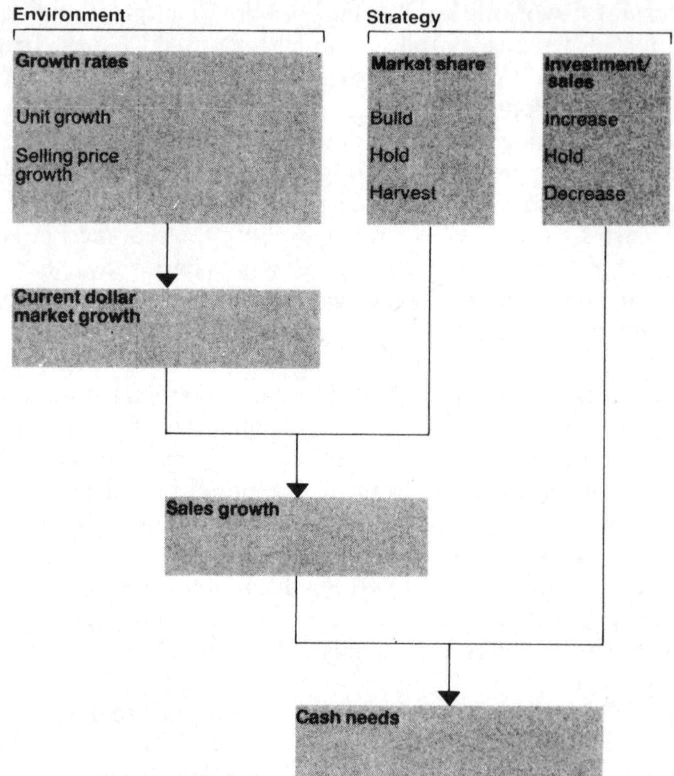

In addition to the normal jockeying for market share against domestic competitors, businesses also endure the pressures of world-class competition. Confrontations lead to shakeouts and fewer competitors. By definition, the survivors realize a net gain in share and a drain on their cash supplies.

Whether management decides to build share or capitalize on the business's present position, the decision should be based on the conscious realization of the impact of the decision on cash flow. If a company wishes to strengthen its future market position by increasing marketing expenditures or introducing new products, it will have to withstand higher costs in the short run.

Similarly, managers can generate cash by harvesting the business's present market position, reducing marketing expenditures, and withholding introduction of new products. Those businesses in our data base that aggressively put out a lot of new products and increase marketing expense show a negative cash flow of 4%, compared with a positive 5% for less aggressive companies.

Companies that increase investment intensity usually face a dramatic

Exhibit 4. Cash-flow-rate Contour Lines for the Growth-Share Matrix

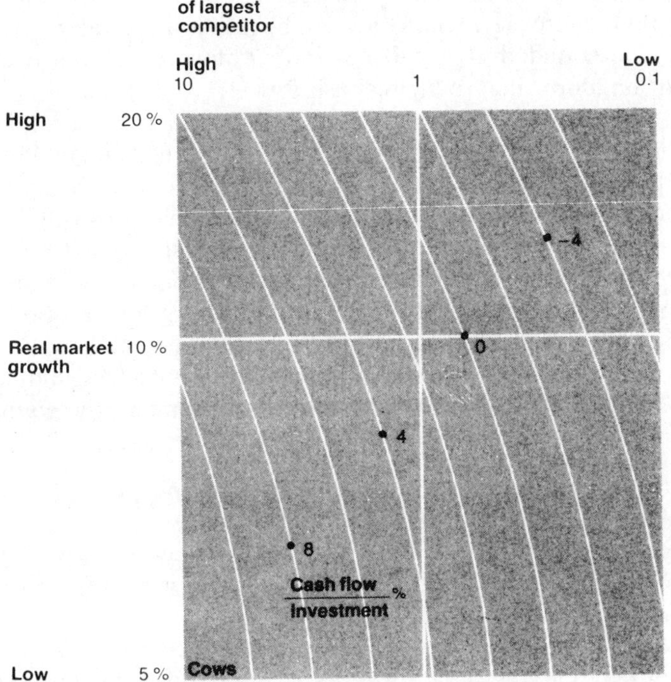

Exhibit 5. Summary of Factors Affecting Cash Generation and Use

Cash Generation		Cash Use	
Factor	Impact	Factor	Impact
Long-run		Real market growth	–
Market share	+	Selling price growth	–
Investment intensity	–	Percentage change in share	–
Short-run			
Rate of new product introductions	–	Point change in investment/sales	–
Marketing expense growth	–		

reduction in their cash flow. For example, management may decide to boost investment relative to sales and value added in order to push capacity ahead of the market, increase inventories, or liberalize receivables policy. This tactic may be sound, but it will cut into profits and increase the rate of investment buildup, thus reducing cash flow.

More serious may be circumstantial shifts, such as an unplanned rise in inventories or accounts receivable, the need to replace quickly plant and equipment at inflated costs, or a sales slump that reduces capacity utilization.

Although it is difficult to predict when circumstances will force a business to consume cash, world-class competition certainly acts as a catalyst. Foreign competitors with up-to-date technology, plant, and equipment put pressure on executives to reindustrialize, and soaring construction costs hike up the price tag of reindustrialization. Because the stakes are usually high, a miscalculation in the attempt to rebuild a single business unit can cripple an entire company. Without rigorous asset management, the equity built up over 40 or 50 years can dissipate in two or three years.

Aggressive asset management has two principal goals:

1 Reduce the amount of cash required to keep pace with growth.
2 Reduce excess capital and thereby improve profits.

Managers *can* reduce investment relative to sales without harming (and in fact they may *enhance*) the business's competitive position, but success requires careful strategic planning.

Cash Allocation and Portfolio Balance

A business unit's market environment, competitive position, and strategy all affect its rate of cash flow. In a portfolio context, the multibusiness general manager will want to turn the relationship around to focus on the effects of cash allocation on the strategy of individual business units.

The manager can find the ratio of cash reinvestment by dividing cash used (increase in gross plant and equipment plus increase in net working capital) by cash generated (aftertax income plus depreciation). Businesses with a cash flow rate of zero reinvest as much cash as they generate—that is, a cash reinvestment ratio of one.

Businesses in rapidly growing markets usually have cash reinvestment ratios greater than one, whereas those in declining or slow-growth markets have ratios much less than one.

The portfolio of an entire company will balance if the cash used by rapidly growing businesses roughly equals the cash generated by businesses with declining or slow growth. The same balancing effect can be achieved if the company requires each business unit to have a cash reinvestment ratio of one (see Exhibit 5).

This second balancing act may backfire. A business in a rapidly growing market may not keep pace and may be strangled. Its share of the market slips, and it cannot generate cash. If the cash generated by a business supplying a slow-growth market is not invested elsewhere, that business may overinvest in its basic product line. Such a business does not compensate for the cash flow needs of the company's high-growth businesses. Instead it becomes investment intensive; profits fall, as does its ability to generate cash.

By understanding that the welfare of the portfolio depends as much on capital allocation among businesses as on project selection within business units, managers can guarantee a more profitable equilibrium between present needs and long-term goals and begin to allocate assets strategically across the portfolio. With the increasing demands of high inflation, lagging productivity, and the need to reindustrialize, only astute companies that understand the link between strategy and cash will survive and prosper.

Appendix A. What Is PIMS?

The empirical evidence supporting our findings comes from the data base assembled by the Strategic Planning Institute (SPI), a nonprofit, tax-exempt organization in Cambridge, Massachusetts.

Called PIMS (profit impact of market strategy), the data base includes the business experiences, both good and bad, of more than 1,700 product and service businesses operated by SPI's more than 200 member companies in North America, Europe, and Australia. Each business is defined as a division, product line, or other profit center within its parent company, selling a distinct set of products or services to an identifiable group of customers in competition with a well-defined set of companies.

For each business, the data separate revenues, operating costs, investments, and strategic plans. Before making information in the data base available to member companies, SPI disguises and summarizes the collected data.

SPI collects data not only on traditional balance sheets and income statements, but also on each company's market share, investment intensity, productivity, product quality, and unionization. The data base describes more than 200 such characteristics for each business and, in addition, documents its actions, the market it serves, its competitive environment, and its financial results.

Appendix B. Alternative Measures of Net Cash Flow Rates

So far, we assume that interest expenses are zero. Typically, interest expenses are about 4% of investment (say, the ratio of debt to investment equals .4 and the interest rate equals 10%). Interest expenses are subtracted before taxes. Assuming the tax rate is 50%, we need to adjust our cash flow figures by 2% (.5 of 4%) to reflect interest expenses. Since the average net cash flow rate (preinterest expense) is 4%, the average cash flow rate after interest and taxes (but before dividend payments) would be about 2%.

If dividend payments are about 5% of investment (say ROI after interest expenses and taxes equals 10%, and half of profits is paid out as dividends), the average net cash flow rate after dividend payments will be about −3%.

The PIMS average for different measures of net cash flow (NCF) rates can be summarized as follows:

NCF Measure	PIMS Average, 1970–1979	Percentage of PIMS Business with Negative NCF Rates
(a) NCF rate, assuming interest expense = 0	4%	33%
(b) NCF rate, assuming interest expense = 4% of investment	2%	50%
(c) NCF rate, after interest expenses and assuming dividends = 5% of investment	−3%	67%

The exhibit shows NCF rates based on measure (a). To obtain rough NCF rates that reflect interest expenses (b), subtract 2 points from the NCF figures shown in the exhibit.

Simply subtracting an additional five points from after-interest cash flow rates will not yield a good approximation of the true after-dividend NCF rates. The dividend payout ratio usually declines as growth increases, and most of the exhibit shows the effects of growth-related factors. In very rapid growth situations, the additional subtraction could be as low as 0 to 2 points. In slow growth or declining environments, it could be as much as 8 to 9 points.

17
Risk Analysis in Capital Investment

DAVID B. HERTZ

How can business executives make the best investment decisions? Is there a method of risk analysis to help managers make wise acquisitions, launch new products, modernize the plant, or avoid overcapacity? "Risk Analysis in Capital Investment" takes a look at questions such as these and says "yes"—by measuring the multitude of risks involved in each situation. Mathematical formulas that predict a single rate of return or "best estimate" are not enough. The author's approach emphasizes the nature and processing of the data used and specific combinations of variables like cash flow, return on investment, and risk to estimate the odds for each potential outcome. Managers can examine the added information provided in this way to rate more accurately the chances of substantial gain in their ventures.

In a retrospective commentary, the author discusses the now routine use of risk analysis in business and government, emphasizing that the method can—and should—be used in any decision-requiring situations in our uncertain world.

Of all the decisions that business executives must make, none is more challenging—and none has received more attention—than choosing among alternative capital investment opportunities. What makes this kind of decision so demanding, of course, is not the problem of projecting return on investment under any given set of assumptions. The difficulty is in the assumptions and in their impact. Each assumption involves its own degree—often a high degree—of uncertainty; and, taken together, these combined uncertainties can multiply into a total uncertainty of critical proportions. This is where the element of risk enters, and it is in the evaluation of risk that the executive has been able to get little help from currently available tools and techniques.

There is a way to help executives sharpen key capital investment decisions by providing them with a realistic measurement of the risks involved. Armed with this gauge, which evaluates the risk at each possible level of return, they are then in a position to measure more knowledgeably alternative courses of action against corporate objectives.

Need for New Concept

The evaluation of a capital investment project starts with the principle that the productivity of capital is measured by the rate of return we expect to receive over some future period. A dollar received next year is worth less to us than a dollar in hand today. Expenditures three years hence are less costly than expenditures of equal magnitude two years from now. For this reason we cannot calculate the rate of return realistically unless we take into account (1) when the sums involved in an investment are spent and (2) when the returns are received.

Comparing alternative investments is thus complicated by the fact that they usually differ not only in size but also in the length of time over which expenditures will have to be made and benefits returned.

These facts of investment life long ago made apparent the shortcomings of approaches that simply averaged expenditures and benefits, or lumped them, as in the number-of-years-to-pay-out method. These shortcomings stimulated students of decision making to explore more precise methods for determining whether one investment would leave a company better off in the long run than would another course of action.

It is not surprising, then, that much effort has been applied to the development of ways to improve our ability to discriminate among investment alternatives. The focus of all of these investigations has been to sharpen the definition of the value of capital investments to the company. The controversy and furor that once came out in the business press over the most appropriate way of calculating these values have largely been resolved in favor of the discounted cash flow method as a reasonable means of measuring the rate of return that can be expected in the future from an investment made today.

Thus we have methods that are more or less elaborate mathematical formulas for comparing the outcomes of various investments and the combinations of the variables that will affect the investments. As these techniques have progressed, the mathematics involved has become more and more precise, so that we can now calculate discounted returns to a fraction of a percent.

But sophisticated executives know that behind these precise calculations are data that are not that precise. At best, the rate-of-return information they are provided with is based on an average of different opinions with varying reliabilities and different ranges of probability. When the expected returns on two investments are close, they are likely to be influenced by intangibles—a precarious pursuit at best. Even when the figures for two investments are quite far apart, and the choice seems clear, there lurk memories of the Edsel and other ill-fated ventures.

In short, the decision makers realize that there is something more they ought to know, something in addition to the expected rate of return. What is missing has to do with the nature of the data on which the expected rate of return is calculated and with the way those data are processed. It involves uncertainty, with possibilities and probabilities extending across a wide range of rewards and risks. (For a summary of the new approach, see the Appendix.)

The Achilles Heel

The fatal weakness of past approaches thus has nothing to do with the mathematics of rate-of-return calculation. We have pushed along this path so far that the precision of our calculation is, if anything, somewhat illusory. The fact is that, no matter what mathematics is used, each of the variables entering into the calculation of rate of return is subject to a high level of uncertainty.

For example, the useful life of a new piece of capital equipment is rarely known in advance with any degree of certainty. It may be affected by variations in obsolescence or deterioration, and relatively small changes in use life can lead to large changes in return. Yet an expected value for the life of the equipment—based on a great deal of data from which a single best possible forecast has been developed—is entered into the rate-of-return calculation. The same is done for the other factors that have a significant bearing on the decision at hand.

Let us look at how this works out in a simple case—one in which the odds appear to be all in favor of a particular decision. The executives of a food company must decide whether to launch a new packaged cereal. They have come to the conclusion that five factors are the determining variables: advertising and promotion expense, total cereal market, share of market for this product, operating costs, and new capital investment.

On the basis of the "most likely" estimate for each of these variables, the picture looks very bright—a healthy 30% return. This future, however, depends on whether each of these estimates actually comes true. If each of these educated guesses has, for example, a 60% chance of being correct, there is only an 8% chance that all five will be correct (.60 × .60 × .60 × .60 × .60). So the "expected" return actually depends on a rather unlikely coincidence. The decision makers need to know a great deal more about the other values used to make each of the five estimates and about what they stand to gain or lose from various combinations of these values.

This simple example illustrates that the rate of return actually depends on a specific combination of values of a great many different variables. But only the expected levels of ranges (worst, average, best; or pessimistic, most likely, optimistic) of these variables are used in formal mathematical ways to provide the figures given to management. Thus predicting a single most likely rate of return gives precise numbers that do not tell the whole story.

The expected rate of return represents only a few points on a continuous curve of possible combinations of future happenings. It is a bit like trying to predict the outcome in a dice game by saying that the most likely outcome is a seven. The description is incomplete because it does not tell us about all the other things that could happen. In Exhibit 1, for instance, we see the odds on throws of only two dice having six sides. Now suppose that each of eight dice has 100 sides. This is a situation more comparable with business investment, where the company's market share might become any one of 100 different sizes and where there are eight factors (pricing, promotion, etc.) that can affect the outcome.

Nor is this the only trouble. Our willingness to bet on a roll of the dice depends not only on the odds, but also on the stakes. Because the probability of rolling a seven is one in six, we might be quite willing to risk a few dollars on that outcome at suitable odds. But would we be equally willing to wager $10,000 or $100,000 at those same odds, or even at better odds? In short, risk is influenced both by the odds on various events occurring and by the magnitude of the rewards or penalties that are involved when they do occur.

To illustrate again, suppose that a company is considering an investment of $1 million. The best estimate of the probable return is $200,000 a year. It could well be that this estimate is the average of three possible returns—a one-in-three chance of getting no return at all, a one-in-three chance of getting $200,000 per year, a one-in-three chance of getting $400,000 per year. Suppose that getting no return at all would put the company out of business. Then, by accepting this proposal, management is taking a one-in-three chance of going bankrupt.

If only the best-estimate analysis is used, however, management might go ahead, unaware that it is taking a big chance. If all of the available

Exhibit 1. Describing Uncertainty—A Throw of the Dice

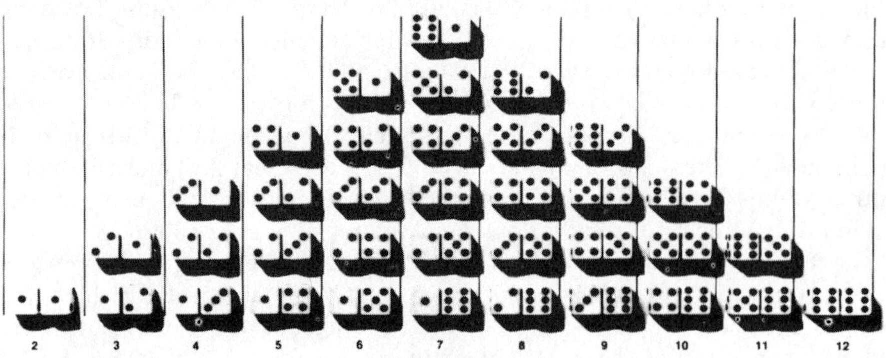

information were examined, management might prefer an alternative proposal with a smaller, but more certain (i.e., less variable) expectation.

Such considerations have led almost all advocates of the use of modern capital-investment-index calculations to plead for a recognition of the elements of uncertainty. Perhaps Ross G. Walker summed up current thinking when he spoke of "the almost impenetrable mists of any forecast."[1]

How can executives penetrate the mists of uncertainty surrounding the choices among alternatives?

Limited Improvements

A number of efforts to cope with uncertainty have been successful up to a point, but all seem to fall short of the mark in one way or another:

1. *More accurate forecasts.* Reducing the error in estimates is a worthy objective. But no matter how many estimates of the future go into a capital investment decision, when all is said and done, the future is still the future. Therefore, however well we forecast, we are still left with the certain knowledge that we cannot eliminate all uncertainty.

2. *Empirical adjustments.* Adjusting the factors influencing the outcome of a decision is subject to serious difficulties. We would like to adjust them so as to cut down the likelihood that we will make a "bad" investment, but how can we do that without at the same time spoiling our chances to make a "good" one? And in any case, what is the basis for adjustment? We adjust, not for uncertainty, but for bias.

For example, construction estimates are often exceeded. If a company's history of construction costs is that 90% of its estimates have been exceeded by 15%, then in a capital estimate there is every justification for increasing the value of this factor by 15%. This is a matter of improving the accuracy of the estimate.

But suppose that new-product sales estimates have been exceeded by more than 75% in one-fourth of all historical cases and have not reached 50% of the estimate in one-sixth of all such cases? Penalties for such overestimating are very real, and so management is apt to reduce the sales estimate to "cover" the one case in six—thereby reducing the calculated rate of return. In so doing, it is possibly missing some of its best opportunities.

3. *Revising cutoff rates.* Selecting higher cutoff rates for protecting against uncertainty is attempting much the same thing. Management would like to have a possibility of return in proportion to the risk it takes. Where there is much uncertainty involved in the various estimates of sales, costs, prices, and so on, a high calculated return from the investment provides some incentive for taking the risk. This is, in fact, a perfectly sound position. The trouble is that the decision makers still need to know explicitly what

risks they are taking—and what the odds are on achieving the expected return.

4. *Three-level estimates.* A start at spelling out risks is sometimes made by taking the high, medium, and low values of the estimated factors and calculating rates of return based on various combinations of the pessimistic, average, and optimistic estimates. These calculations give a picture of the range of possible results, but do not tell the executive whether the pessimistic result is more likely than the optimistic one—or, in fact, whether the average result is much more likely to occur than either of the extremes. So, although this is a step in the right direction, it still does not give a clear enough picture for comparing alternatives.

5. *Selected probabilities.* Various methods have been used to include the probabilities of specific factors in the return calculation. L. C. Grant discussed a program for forecasting discounted cash flow rates of return where the service life is subject to obsolescence and deterioration. He calculated the odds that the investment will terminate at any time after it is made depending on the probability distribution of the service-life factor. After having calculated these factors for each year through maximum service life, he determined an overall expected rate of return.[2]

Edward G. Bennion suggested the use of game theory to take into account alternative market growth rates as they would determine rate of return for various options. He used the estimated probabilities that specific growth rates would occur to develop optimum strategies. Bennion pointed out:

> Forecasting can result in a negative contribution to capital budget decisions unless it goes further than merely providing a single most probable prediction. . . . [with] an estimated probability coefficient for the forecast, plus knowledge of the payoffs for the company's alternative investments and calculation of indifference probabilities . . . the margin of error may be substantially reduced, and the businessman can tell just how far off his forecast may be before it leads him to a wrong decision.[3]

Note that both of these methods yield an expected return, each based on only one uncertain input factor—service life in the first case, market growth in the second. Both are helpful, and both tend to improve the clarity with which the executive can view investment alternatives. But neither sharpens up the range of ''risk taken'' or ''return hoped for'' sufficiently to help very much in the complex decisions of capital planning.

Sharpening the Picture

Because every one of the many factors that enter into the evaluation of a decision is subject to some uncertainty, executives need a helpful portrayal of the effects that the uncertainty surrounding each of the significant factors has on the returns they are likely to achieve. Therefore, I use a method combining the variabilities inherent in all the relevant factors under consideration. The objective is to give a clear picture of the relative risk and the probable odds of coming out ahead or behind in light of uncertain foreknowledge.

A simulation of the way these factors may combine as the future unfolds is the key to extracting the maximum information from the available forecasts. In fact, the approach is very simple, by using a computer to do the necessary arithmetic. To carry out the analysis, a company must follow three steps:

1. Estimate the range of values for each of the factors (e.g., range of selling price and sales growth rate) and within that range the likelihood of occurrence of each value.

2. Select at random one value from the distribution of values for each factor. Then combine the values for all of the factors and compute the rate of return (or present value) from that combination. For instance, the lowest in the range of prices might be combined with the highest in the range of growth rate and other factors. (The fact that the elements are dependent should be taken into account, as we shall see later.)

3. Do this over and over again to define and evaluate the odds of the occurrence of each possible rate of return. Because there are literally millions of possible combinations of values, we need to test the likelihood that various returns on the investment will occur. This is like finding out by recording the results of a great many throws what percent of sevens or other combinations we may expect in tossing dice. The result will be a listing of the rates of return we might achieve, ranging from a loss (if the factors go against us) to whatever maximum gain is possible with the estimates that have been made.

For each of these rates we can determine the chances that it may occur. (Note that a specific return can usually be achieved through more than one combination of events. The more combinations for a given rate, the higher the chances of achieving it—as with sevens in tossing dice.) The average expectation is the average of the values of all outcomes weighted by the chances of each occurring.

We can also determine the variability of outcome values from the average. This is important because, all other factors being equal, management would presumably prefer lower variability for the same return if given the choice. This concept has already been applied to investment portfolios.

When the expected return and variability of each of a series of investments have been determined, the same techniques may be used to examine the effectiveness of various combinations of them in meeting management objectives.

Practical Test

To see how this new approach works in practice, let us take the experience of a management that has already analyzed a specific investment proposal by conventional techniques. Taking the same investment schedule and the same expected values actually used, we can find what results the new method would produce and compare them with the results obtained by conventional methods. As we shall see, the new picture of risks and returns is different from the old one. Yet the differences are attributable in no way to changes in the basic data—only to the increased sensitivity of the method to management's uncertainties about the key factors.

Investment Proposal

In this case, a medium-size industrial chemical producer is considering a $10 million extension to its processing plant. The estimated service life of the facility is 10 years; the engineers expect to use 250,000 tons of processed material worth $510 per ton at an average processing cost of $435 per ton. Is this investment a good bet? In fact, what is the return that the company may expect? What are the risks? We need to make the best and fullest use of all the market research and financial analyses that have been developed to give management a clear picture of this project in an uncertain world.

The key input factors management has decided to use are market size, selling prices, market growth rate, share of market (which results in physical sales volume), investment required, residual value of investment, operating costs, fixed costs, and useful life of facilities. These factors are typical of those in many company projects that must be analyzed and combined to obtain a measure of the attractiveness of a proposed capital facilities investment.

Obtaining Estimates

How do we make the recommended type of analysis of this proposal? Our aim is to develop for each of the nine factors listed a frequency distribution or probability curve. The information we need includes the possible range of values for each factor, the average, and some idea as to the likelihood that the various possible values will be reached.

It has been my experience that for major capital proposals managements usually make a significant investment in time and funds to pinpoint information about each of the relevant factors. An objective analysis of the values to be assigned to each can, with little additional effort, yield a subjective probability distribution.

Specifically, it is necessary to probe and question each of the experts involved—to find out, for example, whether the estimated cost of production really can be said to be exactly a certain value or whether, as is more likely, it should be estimated to lie within a certain range of values. Management usually ignores that range in its analysis. The range is relatively easy to determine; if a guess has to be made—as it often does—it is easier to guess with some accuracy a range rather than one specific value. I have found from experience that a series of meetings with management personnel to discuss such distributions are most helpful in getting at realistic answers to the a priori questions. (The term *realistic answers* implies all the information management does not have as well as all that it does have.)

The ranges are directly related to the degree of confidence that the estimator has in the estimate. Thus certain estimates may be known to be quite accurate. They would be represented by probability distributions stating, for instance, that there is only 1 chance in 10 that the actual value will be different from the best estimate by more than 10%. Others may have as much as 100% ranges above and below the best estimate.

Thus we treat the factor of selling price for the finished product by asking executives who are responsible for the original estimates these questions:

- ☐ Given that $510 is the expected sales price, what is the probability that the price will exceed $550?
- ☐ Is there any chance that the price will exceed $650?
- ☐ How likely is it that the price will drop below $475?

Managements must ask similar questions for all of the other factors until they can construct a curve for each. Experience shows that this is not as difficult as it sounds. Often information on the degree of variation in factors is easy to obtain. For instance, historical information on variations in the price of a commodity is readily available. Similarly, managements can estimate the variability of sales from industry sales records. Even for factors that have no history, such as operating costs for a new product, those who make the average estimates must have some idea of the degree of confidence they have in their predictions, and therefore they are usually only too glad to express their feelings. Likewise, the less confidence they have in their estimates, the greater will be the range of possible values that the variable will assume.

This last point is likely to trouble businesspeople. Does it really make sense to seek estimates of variations? It cannot be emphasized too strongly that the less certainty there is in an average estimate, the more important it is to consider the possible variation in that estimate.

Further, an estimate of the variation possible in a factor, no matter how judgmental it may be, is always better than a simple average estimate, since it includes more information about what is known and what is not known. This very lack of knowledge may distinguish one investment possibility from another, so that for rational decision making it must be taken into account.

This lack of knowledge is in itself important information about the proposed investment. To throw any information away simply because it is highly uncertain is a serious error in analysis that the new approach is designed to correct.

Computer Runs

The next step in the proposed approach is to determine the returns that will result from random combinations of the factors involved. This requires realistic restrictions, such as not allowing the total market to vary more than some reasonable amount from year to year. Of course, any suitable method of rating the return may be used at this point. In the actual case, management preferred discounted cash flow for the reasons cited earlier so that method is followed here.

A computer can be used to carry out the trials for the simulation method in very little time and at very little expense. Thus for one trial 3,600 discounted cash flow calculations, each based on a selection of the nine input factors, were run in two minutes at a cost of $15 for computer time. The resulting rate-of-return probabilities were read out immediately and graphed. The process is shown schematically in Exhibit 2.

Data Comparisons

The nine input factors described earlier fall into three categories:

1 *Market analyses.* Included are market size, market growth rate, the company's share of the market, and selling prices. For a given combination of these factors sales revenue may be determined for a particular business.
2 *Investment cost analyses.* Being tied to the kinds of service-life and operating-cost characteristics expected, these are subject to various kinds of error and uncertainty; for instance, automation progress makes service life uncertain.
3 *Operating and fixed costs.* These also are subject to uncertainty but are perhaps the easiest to estimate.

These categories are not independent, and for realistic results my approach allows the various factors to be tied together. Thus, if price determines the total market, we first select from a probability distribution the price for the specific computer run and then use for the total market a probability distribution that is logically related to the price selected.

We are now ready to compare the values obtained under the new approach with those obtained by the old. This comparison is shown in Exhibit 3.

Exhibit 2. Simulation for Investment Planning

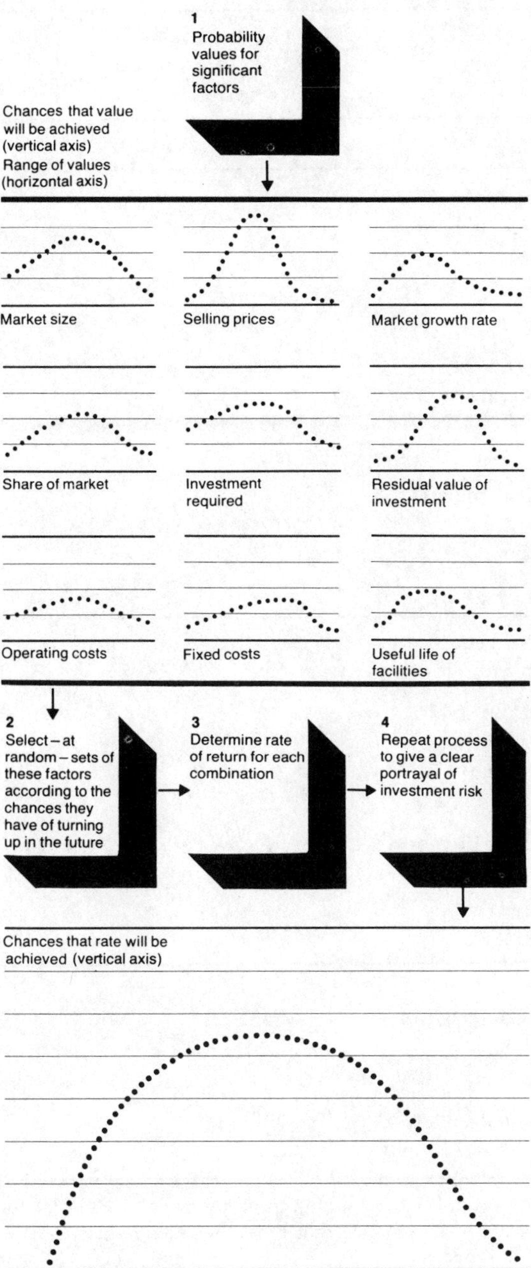

Exhibit 3. Comparison of Expected Values under Old and New Approaches

	Conventional "Best Estimate" Approach	New Approach
Market analyses		
1. Market size		
Expected value (in tons)	250,000	250,000
Range	—	100,000–340,000
2. Selling prices		
Expected value (in dollars/ton)	$510	$510
Range	—	$385–$575
3. Market growth rate		
Expected value	3%	3%
Range	—	0–6%
4. Eventual share of market		
Expected value	12%	12%
Range	—	3%–17%
Investment cost analyses		
5. Total investment required		
Expected value (in $ millions)	$9.5	$9.5
Range	—	$7.0–$10.5
6. Useful life of facilities		
Expected value (in years)	10	10
Range	—	5–15
7. Residual value (at 10 years)		
Expected value (in $ millions)	$4.5	$4.5
Range	—	$3.5–$5.0
Other costs		
8. Operating costs		
Expected value (in dollars/ton)	$435	$435
Range	—	$370–$545
9. Fixed costs		
Expected value (in $ thousands)	$300	$300
Range	—	$250–$375

Note: Range figures in right-hand column represent approximately 1% to 99% probabilities. That is, there is only a 1-in-100 chance that the value actually achieved will be respectively greater or less than the range.

Valuable Results

How do the results under the new and old approaches compare? In this case, management had been informed, on the basis of the one-best-estimate approach, that the expected return was 25.2% before taxes. When we run the new set of data through the computer program, however, we get an expected return of only 14.6% before taxes. This surprising difference results not only from the range of values under the new approach, but also from the weighing of each value in the range by the chances of its occurrence.

Our new analysis thus may help management to avoid an unwise investment. In fact, the general result of carefully weighing the information and lack of information in the manner I have suggested is to indicate the true nature of seemingly satisfactory investment proposals. If this practice were followed, managements might avoid much overcapacity.

The computer program developed to carry out the simulation allows for easy insertion of new variables. But most programs do not allow for dependence relationships among the various input factors. Further, the program used here permits the choice of a value for price from one distribution, which value determines a particular probability distribution (from among several) that will be used to determine the values for sales volume. The following scenario shows how this important technique works:

Suppose we have a wheel, as in roulette, with the numbers from 0 to 15 representing one price for the product or material, the numbers 16 to 30 representing a second price, the numbers 31 to 45 a third price, and so on. For each of these segments we would have a different range of expected market volumes—for example, $150,000 to $200,000 for the first, $100,000 to $150,000 for the second, $75,000 to $100,000 for the third. Now suppose we spin the wheel and the ball falls in 37. This means that we pick a sales volume in the $75,000 to $100,000 range. If the ball goes in 11, we have a different price, and we turn to the $150,000 to $200,000 range for a sales volume.

Most significant, perhaps, is the fact that the program allows management to ascertain the sensitivity of the results to each or all of the input factors. Simply by running the program with changes in the distribution of an input factor, it is possible to determine the effect of added or changed information (or lack of information). It may turn out that fairly large changes in some factors do not significantly affect the outcomes. In this case, as a matter of fact, management was particularly concerned about the difficulty in estimating market growth. Running the program with variations in this factor quickly demonstrated that for average annual growth rates from 3% to 5% there was no significant difference in the expected outcome.

In addition, let us see what the implications are of the detailed knowledge the simulation method gives us. Under the method using single expected values, management arrives only at a hoped-for expectation of 25.2% after taxes (which, as we have seen, is wrong unless there is no variability in the many input factors—a highly unlikely event).

With the proposed method, however, the uncertainties are clearly portrayed, as shown in Exhibit 4. Note the contrast with the profile obtained under the conventional approach. This concept has been used also for evaluation of product introductions, acquisition of businesses, and plant modernization.

Exhibit 4. Anticipated Rates of Return Under Old and New Approaches

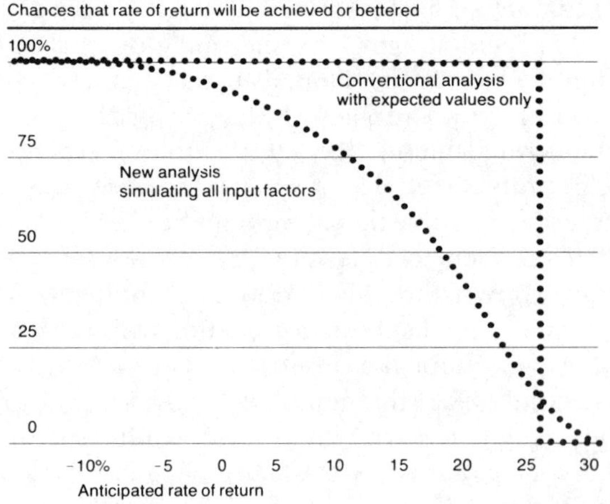

Percent return	Probability of achieving at least the return shown
0%	96.5%
5	80.6
10	75.2
15	53.8
20	43.0
25	12.6
30	0

Comparing Opportunities

From a decision-making point of view one of the most significant advantages of the new method of determining rate of return is that it allows management to discriminate among measures of (1) expected return based on weighted probabilities of all possible returns, (2) variability of return, and (3) risks.

To visualize this advantage, let us take an example based on another actual case but simplified for purposes of explanation. The example involves two investments under consideration, A and B. With the investment analysis, we obtain the tabulated and plotted data in Exhibit 5. We see that:

- ☐ Investment B has a higher expected return than Investment A.
- ☐ Investment B also has substantially more variability than Investment A. There is a good chance that Investment B will earn a return quite different from the expected return of 6.8%—possibly as high as 15% or as low as a loss of 5%. Investment A is not likely to vary greatly from the anticipated 5% return.
- ☐ Investment B involves far more risk than does Investment A. There is virtually no chance of incurring a loss on Investment A. However, there is 1 chance in 10 of losing money on Investment B. If such a loss occurs, its expected size is approximately $200,000.

Clearly, the new method of evaluating investments provides management with far more information on which to base a decision. Investment decisions made only on the basis of maximum expected return are not unequivocally the best decisions.

Concluding Note

The question management faces in selecting capital investments is first and foremost: What information is needed to clarify the key differences among various alternatives? There is agreement as to the basic factors that should be considered—markets, prices, costs, and so on. And the way the future return on the investment should be calculated, if not agreed on, is at least limited to a few methods, any of which can be consistently used in a given company. If the input variables turn out as estimated, any of the methods customarily used to rate investments should provide satisfactory (if not necessarily maximum) returns.

In actual practice, however, the conventional methods do not work out satisfactorily. Why? The reason, as we have seen earlier in this article and as every executive and economist know, is that the estimates used in making the advance calculations are just that—estimates. More accurate

Exhibit 5. Comparison of Two Investment Opportunities

Selected Statistics	Investment A	Investment B
Amount of investment	$10,000,000	$10,000,000
Life of investment (in years)	10	10
Expected annual net cash inflow	$ 1,300,000	$ 1,400,000
Variability of cash inflow		
1 chance in 50 of being *greater than*	$ 1,700,000	$ 3,400,000
1 chance in 50 of being *less than*[a]	$ 900,000	$ (600,000)
Expected return on investment	5.0%	6.8%
Variability of return on investment		
1 chance in 50 of being *greater than*	7.0%	15.5%
1 chance in 50 of being *less than*[a]	3.0%	(4.0%)
Risk of investment		
Chances of a loss	Negligible	1 in 10
Expected size of loss	Negligible	$200,000

[a]In the case of negative figures (indicated by parentheses) *less than* means *worse than*.

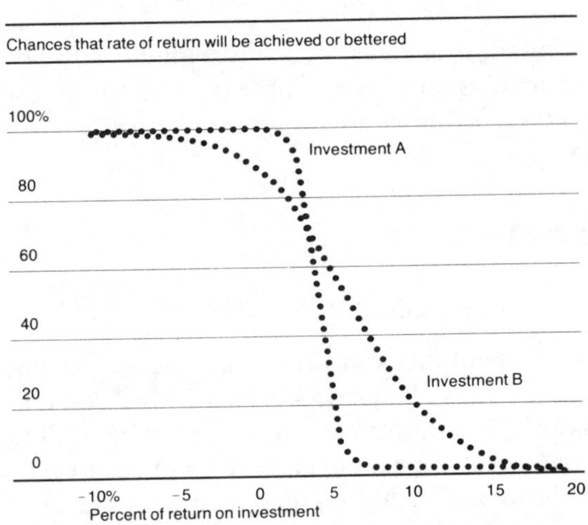

estimates would be helpful, but at best the residual uncertainty can easily make a mockery of corporate hopes. Nevertheless, there is a solution. To collect realistic estimates for the key factors means to find out a great deal about them. Hence the kind of uncertainty that is involved in each estimate can be evaluated ahead of time. Using this knowledge of uncertainty, executives can maximize the value of the information for decision making.

The value of computer programs in developing clear portrayals of the uncertainty and risk surrounding alternative investments has been proved. Such programs can produce valuable information about the sensitivity of the possible outcomes to the variability of input factors and to the likelihood of achieving various possible rates of return. This information can be extremely important as a backup to management judgment. To have calculations of the odds on all possible outcomes lends some assurance to the decision makers that the available information has been used with maximum efficiency.

This simulation approach has the inherent advantage of simplicity. It requires only an extension of the input estimates (to the best of our ability) in terms of probabilities. No projection should be pinpointed unless we are certain of it.

The discipline of thinking through the uncertainties of the problem will in itself help to ensure improvement in making investment choices. For to understand uncertainty and risk is to understand the key business problem—and the key business opportunity. Because the new approach can be applied on a continuing basis to each capital alternative as it comes up for consideration and progresses toward fruition, gradual progress may be expected in improving the estimation of the probabilities of variation.

Lastly, the courage to act boldly in the face of apparent uncertainty can be greatly bolstered by the clarity of portrayal of the risks and possible rewards. To achieve these lasting results requires only a slight effort beyond what most companies already exert in studying capital investments.

Retrospective Commentary

When this article was published almost 20 years ago, there were two recurrent themes in the responses of the management community to it: (1) how the uncertainties surrounding each key element of an investment decision were to be determined; and (2) what criteria were to be used to decide to proceed with an investment once the uncertainties were quantified and displayed.

I answered the latter question in an *HBR* sequel, "Investment Policies That Pay Off," describing the relationships of risks and stakes to longer term investment criteria. This article, published in 1968, showed how risk analyses can provide bases for developing policies to choose among a variety of investment alternatives. Similar approaches were subsequently developed for investment fund portfolio management.

The analysis of uncertainty in describing complex decision-making situations is now an integral part of business and government. The elements of an investment decision—private or public—are subject to all the uncertainties of an unknown future. As the 1964 article showed, an estimated probability distribution paints the clearest picture of all possible outcomes. Such a description contains considerably more information than simplistic combinations of subjective best estimates of input factors. Best estimates are point estimates (there may be more than one—high, medium, low) of the value of an element of the investment analysis used for determining an outcome decision criterion, such as internal rate of return or present value of the investment.

Thus even where the conventional approach was used for the best estimate in a single-point determination for the statistically estimated expected values from a distribution of an element, the single-point approach was shown to be exceedingly misleading. In Exhibit 3, a single-point best-estimate analysis gave an internal rate of return of 25.2%. And a risk analysis employing estimated frequency distributions of the elements showed that an average of possible outcomes, weighted by the relative frequency of their occurrences at 14.6%, was more realistic as well as significantly different. It presented a truer picture of the actual average expectation of the result of this investment (if it could be repeated over and over again).

The case was thus made, and the point of this result—that risk and uncertainty were more accurately defined by a simulation of input variables—was little questioned thereafter. Managements began to adopt some form of this procedure to examine some, if not all, significant investments where doubt existed about the risk levels involved. My sequel article attempted to demonstrate that if enough investments were chosen consistently on the basis of criteria related to these kinds of risk portrayals, the overall outcomes would stabilize around the desired expected value or best estimate of the criterion.

All this now seems simple and straightforward. Earlier it was falsely thought that risk analysis was aimed at *eliminating* uncertainty, which was not worth doing at all since the future is so desperately uncertain. Thus in 1970 the *Financial Times* (of London) published an article intended to show the futility of risk analysis. It concerned a baker of geriatric biscuits who made an investment only to go bankrupt when his nursing home market precipitately disappeared with the death of its founder. The author cited as a moral, "Don't put all your dough in one biscuit."

It took a while for the points to diffuse through executive circles that (1) exactly such an analysis would have been just as bad, or worse, done via single-point subjective estimates, and (2) no one analytical technique could control future events, even with sensitive inputs and requirements for follow-up control to improve the odds as projected by the original risk analyses. But in the end, judgment would be required in both input estimation and decision.

I did not intend the article to be an argument in methodology but rather a cautionary note to examine the data surrounding an investment proposal in light of all the pervasive uncertainties in the world, of which business is simply one part. The years since 1964 have made it clear to me that this message should have been amplified and more emphatically insisted on in the article.

Had this point been clearer, the issue whether to take the risk and proceed with an investment might have been less troublesome. Had I been able to look with more prescience, I might have seen that the area of risk analysis would become routine in business and virtually universally adopted in public cost-benefit issues.

Cost-benefit analysis for public decisions is, of course, only a special form of investment analysis. Government issues that require decisions involving significant uncertainty are too numerous to catalog fully—energy, from both fossil and nuclear sources; chemical, drug, and food carcinogen hazards; DNA manipulation and its progeny of gene splicing.

The Three Mile Island nuclear accident brought home the fallibility of stating a risk analysis conclusion in simplistic terms. The well-known Rasmussen report on nuclear reactor safety, commissioned by the Nuclear Regulatory Commission, undertook what amounted to a risk analysis that was intended to provide a basis for investment decisions relating to future nuclear energy production. The Nuclear Regulatory Commission, in January 1979, disclaimed the risk estimates of that report; new studies to estimate risk are now underway. But there is also a school of thought saying we face too many risks each day to worry about one more.

A commonly stated estimate of the risk of a major nuclear power plant accident is 1 chance in 1 million years. In the 1964 article, I portrayed the image of risk with a chart of the throws of two dice that would be required to give various outcomes—from two ones to two sixes, each of these having a 1-in-36 chance of occurring. There should be no problem in visualizing or testing the meaning and the chances of any of the events pictured by these dice. And, although 1 in 1 million is somehow presented as "mind boggling" compared with 1 in 36, and so unlikely to occur as to be beyond our ken, I suggest that it is just as simply visualized.

We simply need to use eight dice at once. If we chart all the possible outcomes for eight dice, as we did for the two, we find that the sum of eight (or 48) can occur just one way—via all ones (or all sixes). The odds of this occurring are roughly 1 in 1,680,000. Thus the visualization of such odds, and more important, the lesson we must learn about risk—which incidents like Three Mile Island should teach us—is that *what can happen will happen if we just keep at it long enough*. Any of us can simulate a statistical picture of the estimated risks or even the complexities of the Rasmussen analysis with enough patience and enough dice (or a computer).

Incidentally, to make the eight dice act more like the odds of 1 in 1 million, simply mark any two "non-1" sides with a felt pen and count them as ones if they turn up; the odds of getting all ones become a little less than 1 in 1 million. And the chances of human error can be included by similarly marking other dice in the set. The difficulty is not in constructing such a simulation to portray the odds but in determining events that may lead to these odds and estimating the frequencies of their occurrence.

Risk analysis has become one with public policy. Without it, any important choice that leads to uncertain outcomes is uninformed; with it, properly applied and understood, the decision maker—business executive, government administrator, scientist, legislator—is better able to decide why one course of action might be more desirable than another.

Notes

1. "The Judgment Factor in Investment Decisions," *HBR*, March-April 1961, p. 99.
2. "Monitoring Capital Investments," *Financial Executive*, April 1963, p. 19.
3. "Capital Budgeting and Game Theory," *HBR*, November-December 1956, p. 123.

Appendix. Summary of New Approach

After examining present methods of comparing alternative investments, the author reports on his firm's experience in applying a new approach to the problem. Using this approach, management takes the various levels of possible cash flows, return on investment, and other results of a proposed outlay and gets an estimate of the odds for each potential outcome.

Currently, many facilities' decisions are based on discounted cash flow calculations. Management is told, for example, that Investment X has an expected internal rate of return of 9.2%, whereas for Investment Y a 10.3% return can be expected.

By contrast, the new approach would put in front of the executives a schedule that gives them the most likely return from X, but also tells them that X has 1 chance in 20 of being a total loss, 1 in 10 of earning from 4% to 5%, 2 in 10 of paying from 8% to 10%, and 1 chance in 50 of attaining a 30% rate of return.

From another schedule they learn what the most likely rate of return is from Y, but also that Y has 1 chance in 10 of resulting in a total loss, 1 in 10 of earning from 3% to 5% return, 2 in 10 of paying between 9% and 11%, and 1 chance in 100 of a 30% rate of return.

In this instance, the estimates of the rates of return provided by the two approaches would not be substantially different. However, to the decision maker with the added information, Investment Y no longer looks like the clearly better choice, since with X the chances of substantial gain are higher and the risks of loss lower.

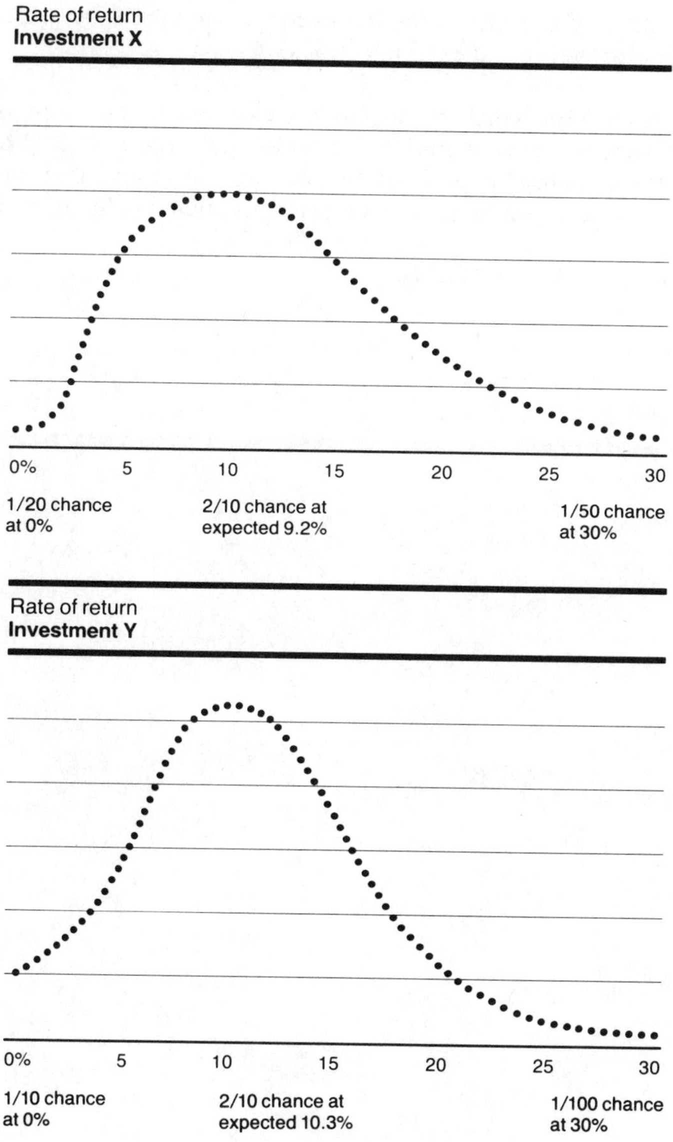

Two things have made this approach appealing to managers who have used it:

1 Certainly in every case it is a more descriptive statement of the two opportunities. And in some cases it might well reverse the decision, in line with particular corporate objectives.
2 This is not a difficult technique to use, because much of the information needed is already available—or readily accessible—and the

validity of the principles involved has, for the most part, already been proved in other applications.

The enthusiasm with which managements exposed to this approach have received it suggests that it may have wide application. It has particular relevance, for example, in such knotty problems as investments relating to acquisitions or new products and in decisions that might involve excess capacity.

18
Capital Commitments and the High Cost of Money

SAMUEL L. HAYES III

What do equity funds cost nowadays? According to this article, the current inflation rate of 5% or more has boosted the cost to an average of 14 to 15%. When examining projected capital commitments, have U.S. corporations routinely made adjustments for the sharply higher cost of money? In two studies, the author of this article found to his dismay that a great many corporate financial officers exhibited a curious rigidity in this regard. Although many of them used advanced methods to measure the needed project funds, such as discounted cash flow, few of them had sufficiently weighted the cost of debt and equity in their calculations. This article analyzes the corporate response to the eroding effects of inflation and offers some cautionary words about what the future holds.

> For which of you, intending to build a tower, sitteth not down first, and counteth the cost, whether he have sufficient to finish it? Lest haply, after he hath laid the foundation, and is not able to finish it, all that behold it begin to mock him. [The Gospel according to St. Luke, 14, 28–29.]

Although this biblical admonition suggests the agelessness of capital budgeting, the modern practice of corporate financial management is really a creature of the post–World War II period. During that time the groundbreaking work of scholars like J. B. Williams in the 1930s was extended by succeeding generations of theorists and interpreters until it provided a quite complete prescription for the financial management of capital.

Wave on wave of MBA students learned increasingly refined and sophisticated applications of this theory. One naturally would assume that with steady infiltration of better-trained managers the U.S. corporate community has become more and more skillful at measuring the profitability of its ventures and selecting the investments that offer the best returns.

Surveys of practice during the 1960s appeared to confirm business' success in this regard and suggested that this new religion of financial analysis was nearly dominating the U.S. corporate decision-making process.[1] Indeed, a recent study of the capital allocation process of 33 large U.S. corporations reported that almost all of the sample used some form of discounted cash flow analysis and that 61% of them used the weighted average cost of capital as the minimum acceptable rate of return on new project commitments.[2]

Some additional research I have supervised suggests that return-on-investment analysis may have been less rigorous than many observers have supposed. The bases for this assertion are a 1975 field study of more than three-score large U.S. companies and a personal survey of 53 senior financial officers participating in a financial management seminar at the Harvard Business School. IBM sponsored the field study out of a desire to increase understanding of the process by which its major customers make capital commitments.

The company drew the sample from its largest customers with an eye to diversifying industry representation. The great majority of them appear in the *Fortune "500"* compilation of industrials. There is almost no overlap between this sample and that in the Brigham analysis. In the field study, research assistants with financial training interviewed financial officers as well as executives concerned with investment decisions in data-processing equipment.

Inadequate Yardsticks

Although much of the data collected did not lend itself to rigorous statistical analysis, the field researchers made two disquieting observations:

1 The process of capital allocation often appeared to be highly politicized. Despite the widespread use of DCF analysis during the project proposal stages, organizational politics often dictated the selection of investments. Then the results of the profitability analysis were either subordinated to these subjective factors or the cash flows "adjusted" to yield results consistent with the conclusion.
2 The operating and financial assumptions built into the project analyses tended to be inflexible. Such important variables as capital costs and the impact of inflation on project cash flows were not easily modified or changed.

These observations corroborate a great deal of research on the decision-making structure in large organizations presenting evidence that the process often becomes highly politicized and is carried on at the expense of the more rigorously defined profit maximization dictated by financial analysis.[3] Scholars of analytical finance have long taken comfort from their conviction that the discipline imposed by capital markets corrects any sustained deviation from the path of long-term profit maximization. The widespread familiarity with sophisticated methods of project analysis demonstrates that top management has not completely lost sight of the power of that discipline.

Therefore, the inflexibility of managerial assumptions in analyzing project profitability, which the researchers noted, is very disturbing. If the financial inputs sometimes misled corporate decision makers, were they getting the right signals about the profit potential of particular projects? And how could a misleading decision process be used year after year without tripping up the company?

These questions led me to the additional survey mentioned earlier in which I polled senior corporate financial officers who attended a three-week financial management program during the summer of 1975. The 53 U.S. and Canadian companies they represented were as diversified by industry as those in the IBM-sponsored study. They were also diversified in size, ranging in sales from about $10 million to several billion dollars. (Four of the 53 companies were included in the Brigham poll.)

This second study revealed that although discounted cash flow analysis was widely used in one form or another in the companies that these executives represented, the *inputs* to that calculative procedure were often inadequate in regard to profitability yardsticks and the cash flow estimates of both revenues and costs.

Exhibit 1 shows that although three-quarters of the responding firms

Exhibit 1. Methods of Establishing ROI in 53 Companies

Criteria	Number of Companies with Sales Less Than $500 Million	Number of Companies with Sales More Than $500 Million
Average cost of capital only	5	7
Average cost of capital with other criteria	1	6
Historical company standards	3	7
Industry standards	3	4
Other criteria only	2	3
No criteria	10	2
Total	24	29

(77%) had established a minimum ROI hurdle rate of one form or another for projects of average risk, only slightly more than one-third (36%) based it in whole or in part on their average or weighted cost of money—a profit standard that is widely acknowledged to be superior to more traditional yardsticks (see the Appendix). The proportion of the larger companies in the sample employing an average cost of money was 45%, which is still substantially lower than the 61% reported by Brigham.

About a third of the sample relied on the less refined and often misleading historical rates of return earned by their own companies or by composites of companies in their industries. And almost 25% of the respondents used no minimum return standard for any projects, let alone those of average risk.

Many were also slow in making changes in response to an altered business environment. Between 1970 and mid-1975, 28 of the respondents (evenly divided between small and large companies) had seen no need to adjust their capital-budgeting procedures in response to accelerating inflation.

This was a striking piece of information. Between mid-1969 and the beginning of 1975 the Consumer Price Index rose on an annualized basis from 5.5% to 11.7%. Accompanying this rise was an unsurprising "lead" in cost escalation and a "lag" in price adjustments, which reduced profit margins in many sectors of the economy.

Among the roughly one-half of the sample that had taken inflation into account in their capital project selection procedures, only a handful mentioned adjusting cost and revenue estimates over the projected life of the investment. And yet both prices and costs would be *expected* to rise sympathetically with future inflation and, under ideal conditions, to maintain stable percentage margins over time. As mentioned earlier, some problems naturally occur when the different cash flows rise at uneven rates and (at least temporarily) either squeeze or balloon profit margins inordinately.

A much larger number prescribed an increase in the minimum hurdle rate as the remedy. A higher hurdle rate is a poor way of getting at dislocations in cash flows caused by inflation. It can, however, be an appropriate way to reflect an increase in the cost of capital for projects of average risk when used along with cash flow inflation adjustments. During the 1970–1975 period the cost of borrowed funds rose dramatically above the levels prevailing in the 1960s. The yield on single-A long-term bonds climbed from 6.7% at the beginning of 1969 to 9.1% by June 1975.

The cost of equity capital, crudely associated in the eyes of many executives with sharply declining stock prices, undoubtedly rose as well. The much-quoted University of Chicago calculation of the combined annual returns (dividends plus capital gains) over a 40-year period, ending in 1965, from a composite of all securities listed on the New York Stock Exchange was 9.3%.[4] The average annual inflation rate was less than 2%, so investors obtained a real return of between 7% and 8%. By the end of 1974, however, the CPI-measured rate of inflation had accelerated to approximately 12%,

Exhibit 2. Recalculation of Weighted Cost of Capital

	Ratio	Aftertax Cost	Weighted Cost
Debt	.30	.045	.0135
Equity	.70	.14	.0980
			.1115

and many economists were warning businesspeople to build a hard-core 6 to 7% rate of inflation into their strategic planning.

Therefore, equity capital suppliers in the mid-1970s might logically require an overall annual return of at least 14 to 15% in order to end up with a real return of 7 to 8% after the higher anticipated inflation adjustment. (It could be argued that this is only the gross return to the equity supplier and that adjustment for an investor's personal taxes would require an even more startling hike in equity returns due to inflationary pressures.) Besides, what rational investor would knowingly commit his money to the uncertain prospect of a 9 to 10% return when debt instruments issued by companies of similar quality are offering a comparable yield on a senior and *contractual* basis?

If the U.S. corporate community had been fully reflecting this increase in the cost of long-term capital by the middle of the 1970s, we might have expected the weighted (or average) cost of money to have increased substantially. The 8.1% aftertax figure calculated in the Appendix would have to be adjusted upward to the 11.15% calculated in Exhibit 2.

Instead, I found in the survey of senior financial officers that of the 19 corporations employing the weighted cost of money to determine the minimum acceptable return on their typical projects, only 10 had made an upward adjustment in the cost calculation (see Exhibit 3). Even then, the larger

Exhibit 3. Response to Inflation of Companies Using Weighted Cost of Capital

	Companies with Sales Less Than $500 Million	Companies with Sales More Than $500 Million
Number of companies adjusting upward	3	7
Mean ROI hurdle rate in these companies		
1970	12.8%	11.5%
1975	14.5%	13.6%
Mean increase	1.7%	2.1%

companies making a change had averaged only a 2.1% adjustment, whereas moderate-sized companies making a change had averaged only 1.7%.

The reasoning behind the changes was sometimes obscure. In several cases it was clear that the adjustment had come in response to an increase in the cost of borrowed funds and/or to reflect a change in the mix of debt and equity funds. In almost none of the cases did the respondent mention a perceived increase in the returns expected by *equity* investors.

It was surprising that a large number of companies in the sample had made absolutely no adjustment in their hurdle rate during the first half of the 1970s. Even among those that had made such a recalculation, the adjustments were usually inadequate and, moreover, were insensitive to the escalation in equity costs—the most expensive and most heavily weighted part of their capital structures.

The Benign '60s—and After

In the past, how did these companies sustain themselves with such rough-and-ready approaches to measuring the profit of investment commitments and the costs of funds needed to implement them? On the basis of contacts with many corporate executives, I speculate that these decision makers were lulled into a state of complacency.

For one thing, the post-World War II expansion, with its moderate rate of inflation, may have helped insulate top executives from the adverse consequences of rough, rule-of-thumb capital-budgeting techniques. Some poorly conceived capital investments were probably bailed out by buoyant demand.

In addition, the slow rate of inflation reduced the potential for error in estimating plant and equipment replacement costs as well as the working capital necessary to implement projects. Moderate inflation also provided a stable base for estimating the magnitude and timing of revenues and operating costs associated with new projects.

The availability of cheap capital was another very important factor. Various corporate executives with whom I have talked in recent years viewed borrowed funds, even though cyclically growing in cost during the 1960s, as relatively cheap; because of the government subsidy through the tax deductibility of interest expense, they felt they could easily increase their debt-equity ratios.

When called on to sell stock in order to redress the capital structure balance between debt and equity, corporate managers often measured the perceived "cost" of new equity in terms of immediate dilution of earnings-per-share. If the stock was selling at 40 times current earnings, an aftertax return of 2.5% was sufficient to avoid immediate dilution in EPS. Although executives were quite sensitive to EPS growth rates, they seldom made the connection between a growth rate and the provision of an adequate total return to the equity investor.

Once the economic boom had run its course at the end of the 1960s and pulled the equity market down with it, the conditions that may have cushioned management from the impact of sloppy investment decision making began to deteriorate. Consider the following developments:

- ☐ Without an ebullient economy, the need for more accurate measurement of revenues and cost on new projects became more pressing. A miscalculation of the real cash profit was more likely to cut profits and drain the company's financial strength, since managers no longer enjoyed a constantly rising demand to rescue them from the consequences of misplaced optimism on project performance.
- ☐ The high rate of inflation in the 1970s caused a sharp rise in the working capital necessary to support a unit of production output as well as an escalation in the cost of replacing plant and equipment. On the operating side, the classic assumption that price increases outpace wage and materials costs, thus maintaining or even enhancing profit margins, proved to be the reverse; prices (aided by controls) remained sluggish while labor and materials costs exploded. Consequently, profit margins declined and real earnings shrank (after inventory profits and underdepreciation adjustments had been factored in).
- ☐ The cost of borrowed capital rose dramatically in 1969–1970 and, for some companies, funds were hard to obtain at any price. The sharp drop in stock prices and in accompanying P-E multiples severely tested the conviction of those managers who had viewed the cost of equity as the reciprocal of the P-E multiple. (Did a multiple of 5× *now* mean that new equity capital must earn 20% after tax or 40% before tax?) Moreover, the real return on U.S. corporate assets dropped from a rate of 10% after taxes in 1965 to 5.4% in 1970.[5] This decline in profitability, not surprising in light of the capital allocation procedures described earlier, may have contributed to the collapse of equity prices in 1969–1970.

My research suggests, however, that even in the face of these dramatic changes, many corporations made at best only modest changes in how they evaluated their capital sources and cash flows. My interviews indicate that executives in these companies evidently considered inflation pressures a passing phenomenon; most of the managers I interviewed did not know how to factor the impact of inflation into investment calculations. Therefore, even those executives who were sensitive to inflation tended either to ignore the possibility of a lead-lag effect on the cost-revenue pattern of their projected cash flows or to compensate for it subjectively in their decisions.

Top management also apparently reasoned that the long slide in equity prices would eventually reverse itself. Then the companies could come to the equity market at a much better price and therefore at capital costs more in line with those perceived in the pre-1970 period. In the meantime, many companies with further borrowing capacity relied on debt (often short term) to supplement internally generated cash for financing of growth.[6]

What of the Future?

These observed patterns in capital-budgeting procedures are of special interest for what they imply about the future. I believe that many U.S. corporations will become increasingly dependent on outside funding for their investment needs. The market also will increasingly demand evidence of management's past skill in selecting really profitable investments. Let us briefly examine some evidence that leads in that direction.

Strong pressures to maintain, and even increase, the pace of business investment are likely to continue. Many economists believe that U.S. corporations have generally been underspending on new plant and equipment for some years, when viewed either in comparison with earlier periods or with other industrialized nations (see Exhibit 4). Thus even greater capital outlays are probable.

Moreover, a recent Department of Commerce study concludes that in order to reach certain national goals by 1980—namely, achieve a 4.7% unemployment rate, meet the mandated clean environment standards, and measurably reduce our foreign energy dependence—fixed business investment must rise sharply from 10.1% of GNP during 1971 through 1975 to 12.4% during the years 1976 through 1980. In constant dollars, annual investment must grow from $596 billion to nearly $875 billion in the 1976 to 1980 period, when the Carter administration will have completed its term of office.[7]

To complicate this picture, continuing inflationary pressures are likely to be a disconcerting variable in corporate financial planning. Greater erosion of purchasing power will swell the capital needed to produce each unit of capacity, add to the cost of that capital, and complicate the effort to measure its profitability.

Exhibit 4. Spending in Major Industrial Nations for Plant as a Percentage of Total Output (adjusted for inflation), 1960 to 1973

Japan	29.0%
West Germany	20.0
France	18.2
Canada	17.4
Italy	14.4
United Kingdom	15.2
United States	13.6

Source: U.S. Treasury.

Despite the problems that this prospect presents, financial executives will not be permitted the luxury of throwing up their hands at the difficulty of measuring ROI and reverting to a subjective rule of thumb to make a selection among investment projects. As Exhibit 5 shows, their dependence on outside (and more profit-demanding) fund sources has been growing (although it was temporarily interrupted in 1975 to 1976 by a sharp decline in capital investments, probably linked to the 1974 recession). This trend is due partly to the inadequacy of *real* profits and to the higher per-unit cost of new capacity resulting from inflation. Pressures to invest more in plant, to rebuild the U.S. manufacturing base, may well accelerate this dependency.

Moreover, U.S. corporations may feel that they need to pay out more of their profits in dividends, thus depriving themselves not only of these funds, but also of the greater debt capacity that the larger equity base usually generates. Investors' preferences seem to be shifting away from earnings retention, with its accompanying future earnings growth expectation, toward cash dividend yield.

A review of recent equity offerings and the dividend adjustments of

Exhibit 5. Gross Internal Funds as a Percentage of Capital Expenditures among Nonfinancial Corporations, 1960 to 1976 (in billions of dollars)

Year	Gross Internal Funds	Capital Expenditures	Percent
1960	$ 34.4	$ 38.7	88.9%
1961	35.6	36.3	98.0
1962	41.8	43.6	95.9
1963	43.9	45.2	97.1
1964	50.5	51.6	97.9
1965	56.6	62.3	90.9
1966	60.5	76.0	79.6
1967	61.3	72.6	84.4
1968	62.3	77.6	80.3
1969	61.7	85.0	72.6
1970	58.9	80.6	73.1
1971	68.6	86.2	80.0
1972	80.8	101.0	80.0
1973	83.8	124.4	67.4
1974	77.6	134.6	57.6
1975	103.4	95.7	107.9
1976	122.4	138.4	88.4

Source: Federal Reserve Board of Governors, *Flow of Funds*.

some of the classic growth-stock companies supports the conclusion that cash dividends are now perceived as a more important buttress of share values. In the context of security analysis, when current alternative investment opportunities are particularly lucrative, dividend payments *now* are more likely to produce a higher stock price than massive reinvestment of earnings to enhance the EPS growth rate.

Sharp Pencil Needed

These factors are likely to erode further the mentality of the "fortress corporation," with its defensive strategy of maintaining cash flow self-sufficiency and thus its insulation from the critical scrutiny and profit demands of outside capital suppliers, particularly equity investors. And because lenders' coverage and equity cushion requirements will limit debt funds, corporations must inevitably come to grips with the problem of attracting and holding more new equity capital.

It has been argued that new equity capital will require a higher total return (dividends plus capital appreciation) than previously because of more attractive opportunities for investors, particularly in high-yield bonds. (Partly because of the *recurring* need to tap these equity investors, many corporations will run a special risk if they lure money with promises of more profits than they can hope to deliver.) Equity funds must be invested to earn a return high enough not only to pay the expected dividend, but also to allow the flow-back of profits sufficient to create a growing earnings stream and ultimately higher dividends and stock values.

What does this mean for the corporation employing new capital? It means that its managers will have to wield a sharp pencil to measure the actual, time-adjusted cash flows their projects will throw off. And equally important, they must ensure that the net operating profit, adjusted for time, is sufficient to provide the composite of capital suppliers with a competitive "rent" for the commitment of their money.

The not-unreasonable calculation in Exhibit 2 suggests that a moderate-risk project should be able to earn more than 11% on an aftertax basis—or more than 22% on a pretax basis! Many corporate executives may protest that they do not *have* many moderate-risk projects returning that much, so implementation of this decision rule would cause a substantial cutback in their capital projects.

I would respond that if, after adjustment for the impact of inflation on cash flows and on capital costs, a project looks unattractive from a risk-adjusted profit point of view, reject it. If there is insufficient real demand to permit the project's output to yield an adequate return, it has no place in the company's future asset structure. It is possible, therefore, that when some companies apply these more rigorous project selection standards, they may find themselves with a shortage of sufficiently profitable investment opportunities rather than a shortage of available capital.

Corporate officers would be well advised to review their capital allocation procedures and determine whether their companies can meet this stiffer capital profitability test. Jesus of Nazareth may not have had a vision of the twentieth-century corporation when He preached to the multitudes 2000 years ago, but He nonetheless was on target in warning of the postaudit wrath that visits a sloppy financial planner or a corporation that lures in new equity with false promises on which it cannot deliver.

Notes

1. See Thomas P. Klammer, "Empirical Evidence of the Adoption of Sophisticated Capital Budgeting Techniques," *Journal of Business,* July 1972, p. 387.

2. Eugene F. Brigham, "Hurdle Rates for Screening Capital Expenditure Proposals," *Financial Management,* Fall 1975, p. 17.

3. Joseph L. Bower, *Managing the Resource Allocation Process: A Study of Corporate Planning and Investment* (Boston, Division of Research, Harvard Business School, 1970).

4. Lawrence Fisher and James H. Lorie, "Rates of Return on Investment in Common Stocks: The Year-by-Year Record, 1926 to 1965," *Journal of Business,* July 1968, p. 291.

5. "Profitability and Investment," *The Morgan Guaranty Survey,* Morgan Guaranty Trust Co., September 1974, p. 10.

6. Federal Reserve Board of Governors, *Flow of Funds.*

7. U.S. Department of Commerce, *Study of Fixed Capital Requirements of the U.S. Business Economy, 1971–80,* 1975.

Appendix. Calculating the Hurdle Rate

Conceptually, corporate financial management is based on the premise that capital committed to investment projects is intended to yield the maximum amount of profit, with adjustments for the timing of the various cash flows to reflect the time value of money. Allowance must also be made for the risks and uncertainties surrounding the flows, since investors insist on higher expected returns when asked to assume higher levels of risk. Underpinning these decisions is a strategy for raising the required funds that will yield the highest risk-adjusted return to the corporation's residual owners (the shareholders) and thus maximizing the value of their stock in combination with the dividends paid. From here on I shall concentrate on measuring the profit standard (hurdle rate) appropriate for a typical project with risks equal to the average risk of all of the company's assets.

To pursue these profit goals, there are analytical tools to measure the magnitude and timing of cash flows (revenues and costs) for each prospective project and their impact on project profitability. This approach, labeled discounted-cash-flow analysis or present-value analysis, is recognized by most students of finance as superior to the traditional cash-payback calculation or accounting rate of return.

The annual profit standard typically recommended to evaluate these cash flows is the weighted cost of the various debt and equity monies used to underwrite the projects.

Debt funds carry relatively low explicit costs because of their senior claim against the corporation and the deductibility of their interest expense for tax purposes. For example, a 7% term loan would cost a profit-making corporation only about 3½% after a tax offset of approximately 50%.

Equity funds, whose suppliers want a higher return because they are assuming more risk, are also more expensive because their cost is not a tax deductible expense. If investors expect a total annual return of 10% (made up of dividend yield plus growth in future dividends and share value), the aftertax cost is a full 10%.

The temptation should be resisted to measure investment returns directly against the cost of the capital source employed for each project. Otherwise, when new debt funds are available, the manager might be misled into accepting low-yield projects that barely cover the aftertax cost of debt. Once it exhausted the borrowed funds, the company would have to revert to equity capital, which is more expensive, and consequently reject some relatively profitable investments that nonetheless failed to return the aftertax "cost" of equity.

To avoid these problems, sophisticated financial executives typically use an average or "weighted" cost of money reflecting their costs and the proportions in which the company expects to draw on investment funds in the foreseeable future. Assume that a company expects to maintain a capital structure of 30% debt and 70% equity and therefore adds new capital in approximately this proportion. With an aftertax debt cost of 3½% and an aftertax equity cost of 10%, the company's weighted cost of capital can be calculated as shown below.

This weighted cost calculation signals the *minimum* acceptable return on an average-risk project, since it represents the least "rent" the company must pay to each class of capital suppliers to compensate them for the risk they are assuming. If the company can earn more than this minimum, the "surplus" will further enhance the returns to the equity holders.

	Ratio	**Aftertax cost**	**Weighted cost**
Debt	.30	.035	.011
Equity	.70	.10	.070
			.081

19

Does the Capital Asset Pricing Model Work?

DAVID W. MULLINS, JR.

An important task of the corporate financial manager is measurement of the company's cost of equity capital. But estimating the cost of equity causes a lot of head scratching; often the result is subjective and therefore open to question as a reliable benchmark. This article describes a method for arriving at that figure, a method spawned in the rarefied atmosphere of financial theory. The capital asset pricing model (CAPM) is an idealized portrayal of how financial markets price securities and thereby determine expected returns on capital investments. The model provides a methodology for quantifying risk and translating that risk into estimates of expected return on equity.

A principal advantage of CAPM is the objective nature of the estimated costs of equity that the model can yield. CAPM cannot be used in isolation because it necessarily simplifies the world of financial markets. But financial managers can use it to supplement other techniques and their own judgment in their attempts to develop realistic and useful cost of equity calculations.

Although its application continues to spark vigorous debate, modern financial theory is now applied as a matter of course to investment management. And increasingly, problems in corporate finance are also benefiting from the same techniques. The response promises to be no less heated. CAPM, the capital asset pricing model, embodies the theory. For financial executives, the proliferation of CAPM applications raises these questions: What is CAPM? How can they use the model? Most important, does it work?

CAPM, a theoretical representation of the behavior of financial markets, can be employed in estimating a company's cost of equity capital. Despite limitations, the model can be a useful addition to the financial manager's analytical tool kit.

The burgeoning work on the theory and application of CAPM has produced many sophisticated, often highly complex extensions of the simple model. But in addressing the above questions I shall focus exclusively on its simple version. Even so, finding answers to the questions requires an investment of time to understand the theory underlying CAPM.

What Is CAPM?

Modern financial theory rests on two assumptions: (1) securities markets are very competitive and efficient (i.e., relevant information about the companies is quickly and universally distributed and absorbed); (2) these markets are dominated by rational, risk-averse investors who seek to maximize satisfaction from returns on their investments.

The first assumption presumes a financial market populated by highly sophisticated, well-informed buyers and sellers. The second assumption describes investors who care about wealth and prefer more to less. In addition, the hypothetical investors of modern financial theory demand a premium in the form of higher expected returns for the risks they assume.

Although these two assumptions constitute the cornerstones of modern financial theory, the formal development of CAPM involves other, more specialized limiting assumptions. These include frictionless markets without imperfections like transaction costs, taxes, and restrictions on borrowing and short selling. The model also requires limiting assumptions concerning the statistical nature of securities returns and investors' preferences. Finally, investors are assumed to agree on the likely performance and risk of securities, based on a common time horizon.

The experienced financial executive may have difficulty recognizing the world postulated by this theory. Much research has focused on relaxing these restrictive assumptions. The result has been more complex versions of the model that, however, are quite consistent with the simple version of CAPM examined in this article.

Although CAPM's assumptions are obviously unrealistic, such simplification of reality is often necessary to develop useful models. The true test of a model lies not just in the reasonableness of its underlying assumptions, but also in the validity and usefulness of the model's prescription. Tolerance of CAPM's assumptions, however fanciful, allows the derivation of a concrete, although idealized, model of the manner in which financial markets measure risk and transform it into expected return.

Portfolio Diversification

CAPM deals with the risks and returns on financial securities and defines them precisely, if arbitrarily. The rate of return an investor receives from buying a common stock and holding it for a given period of time is equal to the cash dividends received plus the capital gain (or minus the capital loss) during the holding period divided by the purchase price of the security.

Although investors may expect a particular return when they buy a particular stock, they may be disappointed or pleasantly surprised, because fluctuations in stock prices result in fluctuating returns. Therefore common stocks are considered risky securities. (In contrast, because the returns on some securities, such as Treasury bills, do not differ from their expected returns, they are considered riskless securities.) Financial theory defines risk as the possibility that actual returns will deviate from expected returns, and the degree of potential fluctuation determines the degree of risk.

An underpinning of CAPM is the observation that risky stocks can be combined so that the combination (the portfolio) is less risky than any of its components. Although such diversification is a familiar notion, it may be worthwhile to review the manner in which diversification reduces risk.

Suppose there are two companies located on an isolated island whose chief industry is tourism. One company manufactures suntan lotion. Its stock predictably performs well in sunny years and poorly in rainy ones. The other company produces disposable umbrellas. Its stock performs equally poorly in sunny years and well in rainy ones. Each company earns a 12% average return.

In purchasing either stock, investors incur a great amount of risk because of variability in the stock price driven by fluctuations in weather conditions. Investing half the funds in the suntan lotion stock and half in the stock of the umbrella manufacturer, however, results in a return of 12% regardless of which weather condition prevails. Portfolio diversification thus transforms two risky stocks, each with an average return of 12%, into a riskless portfolio certain of earning the expected 12%.

Unfortunately, the perfect negative relationship between the returns on these two stocks is very rare in the real world. To some extent, corporate securities move together, so complete elimination of risk through simple portfolio diversification is impossible. However, as long as some lack of parallelism in the returns of securities exists, diversification will always reduce risk.

Two Types of Risk

Some of the risk investors assume is perculiar to the individual stocks in their portfolios—for example, a company's earnings may plummet because of a wildcat strike. On the other hand, because stock prices and returns move to some extent in tandem, even investors holding widely diversified portfolios are exposed to the risk inherent in the overall performance of the stock market.

So we can divide a security's total risk into *unsystematic risk,* the portion peculiar to the company that can be diversified away, and *systematic risk,* the nondiversifiable portion that is related to the movement of the stock market and is therefore unavoidable. Examples of systematic and unsystematic risk factors appear in Exhibit 1.

Exhibit 2 graphically illustrates the reduction of risk as securities are

Exhibit 1. Some Unsystematic and Systematic Risk Factors

Unsystematic risk factors

A company's technical wizard is killed in an auto accident.

Revolution in a foreign country halts shipments of an important product ingredient.

A lower-cost foreign competitor unexpectedly enters a company's product market.

Oil is discovered on a company's property.

Systematic risk factors

Oil-producing countries institute a boycott.

Congress votes a massive tax cut.

The Federal Reserve steps up its restrictive monetary policy.

Long-term interest rates rise precipitously.

added to a portfolio. Empirical studies have demonstrated that unsystematic risk can be virtually eliminated in portfolios of 30 to 40 randomly selected stocks. Of course, if investments are made in closely related industries, more securities are required to eradicate unsystematic risk.

The investors inhabiting this hypothetical world are assumed to be risk averse. This notion, which agrees for once with the world most of us know, implies that investors demand compensation for taking on risk. In financial markets dominated by risk-averse investors, higher-risk securities are priced to yield higher expected returns than lower-risk securities.

A simple equation expresses the resulting positive relationship between risk and return. The risk-free rate (the return on a riskless investment such as a T-bill) anchors the risk/expected return relationship. The expected return on a risky security, R_s, can be thought of as the risk-free rate, R_f, plus a premium for risk:

$$R_s = R_f + \text{risk premium}$$

Exhibit 2. Reduction of Unsystematic Risk Through Diversification

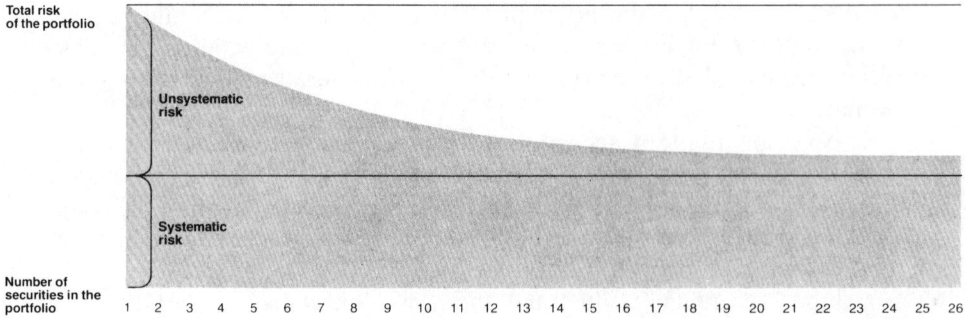

The reward for tolerating CAPM's unrealistic assumptions is in having a measure of this risk premium and a method of estimating the market's risk/expected return curve. These assumptions and the risk-reducing efficacy of diversification lead to an idealized financial market in which, to minimize risk, CAPM investors hold highly diversified portfolios that are sensitive only to market-related risk.

Because investors can eliminate company-specific risk simply by properly diversifying portfolios, they are not compensated for bearing unsystematic risk. And because well-diversified investors are exposed only to systematic risk, with CAPM the relevant risk in the financial market's risk/expected return trade-off is systematic risk rather than total risk. Thus an investor is rewarded with higher expected returns for bearing only market-related risk.

This important result may seem inconsistent with empirical evidence that, despite low-cost diversification vehicles such as mutual funds, most investors do not hold adequately diversified portfolios.[1] Consistent with CAPM, however, large investors such as the institutions that dominate trading on the New York Stock Exchange do typically hold portfolios with many securities. These actively trading investors determine securities prices and expected returns. If their portfolios are well diversified, their actions may result in market pricing consistent with the CAPM prediction that only systematic risk matters.

Beta is the standard CAPM measure of systematic risk. It gauges the tendency of the return of a security to move in parallel with the return of the stock market as a whole. One way to think of beta is as a gauge of a security's volatility relative to the market's volatility. A stock with a beta of 1.00—an average level of systematic risk—rises and falls at the same percentage as a broad market index, such as Standard & Poor's 500-stock index.

Stocks with a beta greater than 1.00 tend to rise and fall by a greater percentage than the market—that is, they have a high level of systematic risk and are very sensitive to market changes. Conversely, a stock with a beta less than 1.00 has a low level of systematic risk and is less sensitive to market swings.

The Security Market Line

The culmination of the sequence of conceptual building blocks is CAPM's risk/expected return relationship. This fundamental result follows from the proposition that only systematic risk, measured by beta (β), matters. Securities are priced such that:

$$R_s = R_f + \text{risk premium}$$
$$R_s = R_f + \beta_s (R_m - R_f)$$

where:

R_s = the stock's expected return (and the company's cost of equity capital).
R_f = the risk-free rate.
R_m = the expected return on the stock market as a whole.
β_s = the stock's beta.

This risk/expected return relationship is called the security market line (SML). I have illustrated it graphically in Exhibit 3. As I indicated before, the expected return on a security generally equals the risk-free rate plus a risk premium. In CAPM the risk premium is measured as beta times the expected return on the market minus the risk-free rate. The risk premium of a security is a function of the risk premium on the market, $R_m - R_f$, and varies directly with the level of beta. (No measure of unsystematic risk appears in the risk premium, of course, for in the world of CAPM diversification has eliminated it.)

In the freely competitive financial markets described by CAPM, no security can sell for long at prices low enough to yield more than its appropriate return on the SML. The security would then be very attractive compared with other securities of similar risk, and investors would bid its price up until its expected return fell to the appropriate position on the SML. Conversely, investors would sell off any stock selling at a price high enough to put its expected return below its appropriate position. The resulting reduction in price would continue until the stock's expected return rose to the level justified by its systematic risk.

(An arbitrage pricing adjustment mechanism alone may be sufficient to justify the SML relationship with less restrictive assumptions than the traditional CAPM. The SML, therefore, can be derived from other models than CAPM.[2])

One perhaps counterintuitive aspect of CAPM involves a stock exhib-

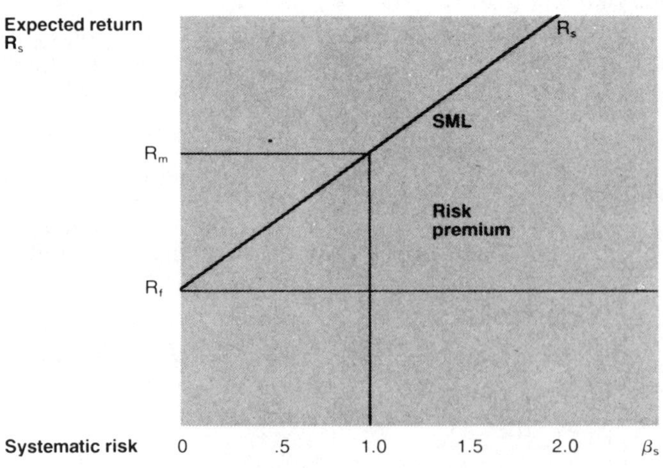

iting great total risk but very little systematic risk. An example might be a company in the very chancy business of exploring for precious metals. Viewed in isolation the company would appear very risky, but most of its total risk is unsystematic and can be diversified away. The well-diversified CAPM investor would view the stock as a low-risk security. In the SML the stock's low beta would lead to a low risk premium. Despite the stock's high level of total risk, the market would price it to yield a low expected return.

In practice, such counterintuitive examples are rare; most companies with high total risk also have high betas and vice versa. Systematic risk as measured by beta usually coincides with intuitive judgments of risk for particular stocks. There is no total risk equivalent to the SML, however, for pricing securities and determining expected returns in financial markets where investors are free to diversify their holdings.

Let me summarize the conceptual components of CAPM. If the model correctly describes market behavior, the relevant measure of a security's risk is its market-related, or systematic, risk measured by beta. If a security's return bears a strong positive relationship with the return on the market and thus has a high beta, it will be priced to yield a high expected return; if it has a low beta, it will be priced to yield a low expected return.

Because unsystematic risk can be easily eliminated through diversification, it does not increase a security's expected return. According to the model, financial markets care only about systematic risk and price securities such that expected returns lie along the security market line.

How Can It Be Used?

With its insight into the financial markets' pricing of securities and the determination of expected returns, CAPM has clear applications in investment management. Its use in this field has advanced to a level of sophistication far beyond the scope of this introductory exposition.

CAPM has an important application in corporate finance as well. The finance literature defines the cost of equity as the expected return on a company's stock. The stock's expected return is the shareholders' opportunity cost of the equity funds employed by the company.

In theory, the company must earn this cost on the equity-financed portion of its investments or its stock price will fall. If the company does not expect to earn at least the cost of equity, it should return the funds to the shareholders, who can earn this expected return on other securities at the same risk level in the financial marketplace. Because the cost of equity involves market expectations, it is very difficult to measure; few techniques are available.

Cost of Equity

This difficulty is unfortunate in view of the role of equity costs in vital tasks such as capital-budgeting evaluation and the valuation of possible acquisitions. The cost of equity is one component of the weighted average cost of capital, which corporate executives often use as a hurdle rate in evaluating investments. Financial managers can employ CAPM to obtain an estimate of the cost of equity capital.

If CAPM correctly describes market behavior, the security market line gives the expected return on a stock. Because this expected return, R_s, is by definition the company's cost of equity, k_e, the SML provides estimates of equity costs as well. Thus:

$$k_e = R_s = R_f + \beta_s (R_m - R_f)$$

Arriving at a cost of equity for evaluating cash flows in the future requires estimates of the future values of the risk-free rate, R_f, the expected return on the market, R_m, and beta, β_s.

Over the past 50 years, the T-bill rate (the risk-free rate) has approximately equaled the annual inflation rate. In recent years, buffeted by short-term inflationary expectations, the T-bill rate has fluctuated widely. Although sophisticated techniques could be employed to estimate the future inflation and T-bill rates, for the purposes of this exposition let us make a rough estimate of 10%.

Estimating the expected return on the market is more difficult. A common approach is to assume that investors anticipate about the same risk premium ($R_m - R_f$) in the future as in the past. From 1926 to 1978, the risk premium on the Standard & Poor's 500-stock index averaged 8.9%.[3] Benchmark estimates of 9% for the risk premium and 10% for the T-bill rate imply an estimated R_m of 19%.

This is substantially higher than the historical average of 11.2%. The difference reflects the long-term inflation rate of 10% incorporated in our estimated T-bill rate. The future inflation rate is assumed to be 7.5% higher than the 2.5% average rate over the 1926–1978 period. Expected returns (in nominal terms) should rise to compensate investors for the anticipated loss in purchasing power. As elsewhere, more sophisticated techniques exist, but an estimate of 19% for R_m is roughly consistent with historical spreads between stock returns and the returns on T-bills, long-term government bonds, and corporate bonds.

Statistical techniques that gauge the past variability of the stock relative to the market can estimate the stock's beta. Many brokerage firms and investment services also supply betas. If the company's past level of systematic risk seems likely to continue, beta calculations from historical data can be used to estimate the cost of equity.

Plugging the assumed values of the risk-free rate, the expected return on the market, and beta into the security market line generates estimates of the cost of equity capital. In Exhibit 4, I give the cost of equity estimates of three hypothetical companies.

The betas in Exhibit 4 are consistent with those of companies in the three industries represented. Many electric utilities have low levels of sys-

Exhibit 4. Examples of Estimating the Cost of Equity Capital

Security market line

$$k_e = R_s = R_f + \beta_s (R_m - R_f)$$
$$= 10\% + \beta_s (19\% - 10\%)$$
$$= 10\% + \beta_s (9\%)$$

Electric utility	**Airline**	**Chemical company**
$\beta_u = .75$	$\beta_A = 1.55$	$\beta_c = 1.10$
$R_u = 10\% + \beta_u (9\%)$	$R_A = 10\% + \beta_A (9\%)$	$R_c = 10\% + \beta_c (9\%)$
$= 10\% + .75 (9\%)$	$= 10\% + 1.55 (9\%)$	$= 10\% + 1.10 (9\%)$
$= 16.75\%$	$= 23.95\%$	$= 19.9\%$
$k_e = 17\%$	$k_e = 24\%$	$k_e = 20\%$

Assumptions

$R_f = 10\%$, $R_m = 19\%$

tematic risk and low betas because of relatively modest swings in their earnings and stock returns. Airline revenues are closely tied to passenger miles flown, a yardstick very sensitive to changes in economic activity. Amplifying this systematic variability in revenues is high operating and financial leverage. The results are earnings and returns that vary widely and produce high betas in these stocks. Major chemical companies exhibit an intermediate degree of systematic risk.

I should stress that the methodology illustrated in Exhibit 4 yields only rough estimates of the cost of equity. Sophisticated refinements can help estimate each input. Sensitivity analyses employing various input values can produce a reasonably good range of estimates of the cost of equity. Nonetheless, the calculations in this exhibit demonstrate how the simple model can generate benchmark data.

Exhibit 5 shows the SML risk/expected return spectrum employing the average betas for companies in more than three dozen industries. The result is a pricing schedule for equity capital as a function of risk. The spectrum represents shareholders' risk/expected return opportunities in the financial markets and, therefore, shareholder opportunity costs to the particular company.

Employment of CAPM

Applications of these concepts are straightforward. For example, when a manager is calculating divisional costs of capital or hurdle rates, the cost of equity component should reflect the risk inherent in the division's operations rather than the parent company's risk. If the division is in one of the risky businesses listed in Exhibit 5, a cost of equity commensurate with this risk should be employed even though it may be much higher than the parent's cost of equity.

One approach to estimating a division's cost of equity is to calculate CAPM estimates of the cost of equity for similar, independent companies

Exhibit 5. Risk/Expected Return Spectrum

Estimated Cost of Equity (%)	Beta	Industry	Methodology and Assumptions: $k_e = R_s = R_f + \beta_s (R_m - R_f) = 10\% + \beta_s (19\% - 10\%)$					
High-risk stocks								
26.20%	1.80	Air transport						1.80
								1.75
		Real property						1.70
			Travel, outdoor recreation					1.65
24.40	1.60	Electronics	Miscellaneous, finance					1.60
								1.55
			Nondurables, entertainment					1.50
23.05	1.45	Consumer durables						1.45
			Business machines	Retail, general	Media			1.40
					Insurance	Trucking freight		1.35
21.70	1.30	Producer goods	Aerospace	Business services	Apparel	Construction	Motor vehicles	1.30
			Photographic, optical		Chemicals	Energy, raw materials	Tires, rubber goods	1.25
20.80	1.20	Railroads,			Forest			1.20

		shipping			products, paper		
20.35	1.15	Miscellaneous, conglomerate		Drugs, medicine		Domestic oil	1.15
				Soaps, cosmetics			1.10
					Steel	Containers	1.05
Medium-risk stocks							
19.00	1.00	Nonferrous metals	Agriculture, food				1.00
							.95
					Liquor		.90
17.65	.85	International oil	Banks				.85
					Tobacco		.80
Low-risk stocks							
16.75	.75		Telephone				.75
							.70
							.65
15.40	.60		Energy utilities				.60
							.55
							.50
							.45
							.40
13.15	.35		Gold				.35

Source of betas: Barr Rosenberg and James Guy, "Prediction of Beta from Investment Fundamentals," *Financial Analysts Journal*, July–August 1976, p. 62.

operating in the same industry. The betas of these companies reflect the risk level of the industry. Of course, refinements may be necessary to adjust for differences in financial leverage and other factors.

A second example concerns acquisitions. In discounted cash flow evaluations of acquisitions, the appropriate cost of equity should reflect the risks inherent in the cash flows that are discounted. Again, ignoring refinements required by changes in capital structure and the like, the cost of equity should reflect the risk level of the target company, not the acquiror.

Does CAPM Work?

As an idealized theory of financial markets, the model's assumptions are clearly unrealistic. But the true test of CAPM, naturally, is how well it works.

There have been numerous empirical tests of CAPM. Most of these have examined the past to determine the extent to which stock returns and betas have corresponded in the manner predicted by the security market line. With few exceptions the major empirical studies in this field have concluded that:

- ☐ As a measure of risk, beta appears to be related to past returns. Because of the close relationship between total and systematic risk, it is difficult to distinguish their effects empirically. Nonetheless, inclusion of a factor representing unsystematic risk appears to add little explanatory power to the risk/return relationship.
- ☐ The relationship between past returns and beta is linear—that is, reality conforms to what the model predicts. The relationship is also positively sloped—that is, there is a positive trade-off between the two (high risk equals high return, low risk equals low return).
- ☐ The empirical SML appears less steeply sloped than the theoretical SML. As illustrated in Exhibit 6, low-beta securities earn a return somewhat higher than CAPM would predict, and high-beta stocks earn less than predicted. A variety of deficiencies in CAPM and/or in the statistical methodologies employed have been advanced to explain this phenomenon.

Although these empirical tests do not unequivocally validate CAPM, they do support its main implications. The systematic risk measure, beta, does appear to be related to past returns; a positive risk/return trade-off does exist; and this risk/return relationship does appear to be linear. The contradictory finding concerning the slope of the SML is a subject of continuing research. Some researchers suggest using a more gradually sloped "empirical market line" based on these findings instead of the theoretical SML.

Recent work in the investment management field has challenged the

Exhibit 6. Theoretical and Estimated Security Market Lines

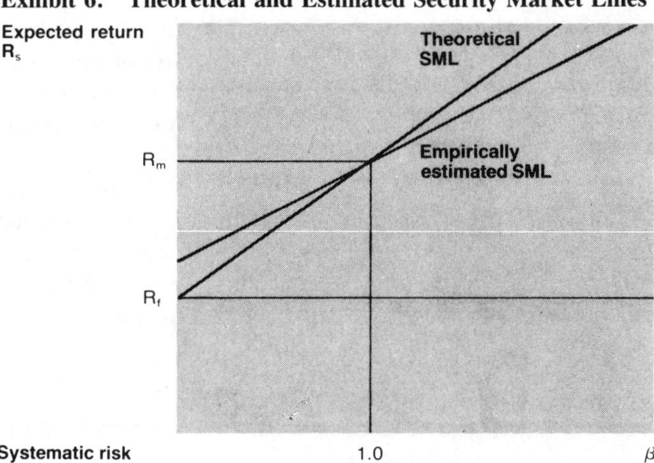

proposition that only systematic risk matters. In a complex world it would be unlikely to find only one relevant type of risk—market risk.

Much progress has been made in the development of richer asset-pricing models. As of yet, however, none of these more sophisticated models has proved clearly superior to CAPM. This continues to be a fertile area of research, focused primarily on investment management applications.

Application Problems

In corporate finance applications of CAPM, several potential sources of error exist. First, the simple model may be an inadequate description of the behavior of financial markets. (As I just noted, empirical work to date does not unequivocally support the validity of CAPM.) In attempts to improve its realism, researchers have developed a variety of extensions of the model.

A second problem is that betas are unstable through time. This fact creates difficulties when betas estimated from historical data are used to calculate costs of equity in evaluating future cash flows. Betas should change as both company fundamentals and capital structures change. In addition, betas estimated from past data are subject to statistical estimation error. Several techniques are available to help deal with these sources of instability.

The estimates of the future risk-free rate and the expected return on the market are also subject to error. Here, too, research has focused on developing techniques to reduce the potential error associated with these inputs to the SML.

A final set of problems is unique to corporate finance applications of CAPM. There are practical and theoretical problems associated with employing CAPM, or any financial market model, in capital-budgeting decisions involving real assets. These difficulties continue to be a fertile area of research.

Dividend Growth Model

The deficiencies of CAPM may seem severe. They must be judged, however, relative to other approaches for estimating the cost of equity capital. The most commonly used of these is a simple discounted cash flow (DCF) technique, which is known as the dividend growth model (or the Gordon-Shapiro model).

This approach is based on the proposition that the price of a company's stock equals the present value of future dividends per share discounted by the company's cost of equity capital. With the assumption that future dividends per share are expected to grow at a constant rate and that this growth rate will persist forever, the general present value formula collapses to a simple expression:

$$P = \frac{dps}{k_e - g}$$

where:

P = the current price of the stock.
dps = next year's dividends per share.
g = the perpetuity growth rate in dividends per share.
k_e = the company's cost of equity capital.

If the market is pricing the stock in this manner, we can infer the cost of equity impounded in the stock price. Solving for the cost of equity yields

$$k_e = \frac{dps}{P} + g$$

The cost of equity implied by the current stock price and the assumptions of the model is simply the dividend yield plus the constant growth rate.

Like CAPM, two of the model's assumptions limit the dividend growth technique. One is the assumption of a constant perpetual growth rate in dividends per share. Second, to permit the general present value formula to collapse to the simple stock price equation I gave, the perpetual constant growth rate must be less than the company's cost of equity. If this is not the case, the equation is not valid.

These two assumptions sharply limit the applicability of the dividend growth model. The model cannot be used in estimating costs of equity for companies with unstable dividend patterns or for rapidly growing companies where g is likely to be greater than k_e. (Obviously, the model also does not apply to companies paying no dividends.) Unlike CAPM, the model is limited mainly to companies enjoying slow, steady growth in dividends. More complex DCF techniques can, however, handle a wider range of companies.

Another problem with using the dividend growth model to estimate costs of equity is in gauging g. To derive a sound cost of equity figure, one must estimate the growth rate investors are using to value the stock. Thus it is the market's current estimate of g that matters, not the company's. This is a major source of error in the dividend growth model.

In contrast, the only company-specific input to the SML is the beta, which is derived by an objective statistical method. Even more sophisticated DCF techniques require as an input the market's estimate of the company's future dividends per share.

When compared with the dividend growth model and other DCF approaches, CAPM's deficiencies do not appear so severe. There is no reason, however, to consider CAPM and the dividend growth model as competitors. Very few techniques are available for the difficult task of measuring the cost of equity. Despite the shortcomings, investors should use both the DCF and CAPM models as well as sound judgment to estimate the cost of equity.[4]

Imperfect, but Useful

Investment managers have widely applied the simple CAPM and its more sophisticated extensions. CAPM's application to corporate finance is a recent development. Although it has been employed in many utility rate-setting proceedings, it has yet to gain widespread use in corporate circles for estimating companies' costs of equity.

Because of its shortcomings, financial executives should not rely on CAPM as a precise algorithm for estimating the cost of equity capital. Nevertheless, tests of the model confirm that it has much to say about the way returns are determined in financial markets. In view of the inherent difficulty in measuring the cost of equity, CAPM's deficiencies appear no worse than those of other approaches. Its key advantage is that it quantifies risk and provides a widely applicable, relatively objective routine for translating risk measures into estimates of expected return.

CAPM represents a new and different approach to an important task. Financial decision makers can use the model in conjunction with traditional techniques and sound judgment to develop realistic, useful estimates of the costs of equity capital.

Notes

1. See Marshall E. Blume, Jean Crockett, and Irwin Friend, "Stock Ownership in the United States: Characteristics and Trends," *Survey of Current Business*, November 1974, p. 16.

2. See Stephen A. Ross, "The Arbitrage Theory of Capital Asset Pricing," *Journal of Economic Theory*, December 1976, p. 341.

3. See Roger G. Ibbotson and Rex A. Sinquefeld, *Stocks, Bonds, Bills, and Inflation: Historical Returns (1926–1978)*, 2nd ed. (Charlottesville, Virginia, Financial Analysts Research Foundation, 1979). The rates I have used are arithmetic means. Arguments can be made that geometric mean rates are appropriate for discounting longer-term cash flows.

4. For an exposition of the dividend growth model, see Thomas R. Piper and William E. Fruhan, Jr., "Is Your Stock Worth Its Market Price?" *HBR*, May–June 1981, p. 124.

Appendix. For Further Reading

The development and testing of capital market theory have been fertile areas of research over the past 15 years. This work has produced an extensive body of literature exploring the issues raised in this introductory exposition.

Early Development of the Model

A number of researchers contributed to the development of CAPM. Harry M. Markowitz did the early work on diversification, summarized in his *Portfolio Selection: Efficient Diversification of Investment,* Cowles Foundation Monograph 16, Yale University Press, 1959. Jack L. Treynor ("Toward a Theory of the Market Value of Risky Assets," unpublished manuscript, 1961) conducted early work on equilibrium asset pricing. CAPM was developed independently in seminal papers by William F. Sharpe ("Capital Asset Prices: A Theory of Market Equilibrium under Conditions of Risk," *Journal of Finance,* September 1964, p. 425; and John V. Lintner ("The Valuation of Risk Assets and the Selection of Risky Investments in Stock Portfolios and Capital Budgets," *Review of Economics and Statistics,* February 1965, p. 13. Franco Modigliani and Gerald A. Pogue provide a useful introduction to CAPM in "An Introduction to Risk and Return," *Financial Analysts Journal,* March–April 1974, p. 68 and May–June 1974, p. 69.

Assumptions and Extensions

The assumed competitive efficiency of financial markets has been the subject of much empirical work. Classic references include two works by Eugene F. Fama, "Efficient Capital Markets: A Review of the Theory and Empirical Work," *Journal of Finance,* May 1970, p. 383 and *Foundations of Finance,* Basic Books, 1976; see chapter 5. The June–September 1978 issue of *Journal of Financial Economics* reviews recent evidence apparently contrary to the efficient markets hypothesis. Extensions of CAPM are examined in Michael C. Jensen, "Capital Markets: Theory and Evidence," *Bell Journal of Economics and Management Science,* Autumn 1972, p. 357, as well as in chapters 8 and 9 of Fama's book.

Empirical Evidence

The risk-reducing efficacy of diversification is demonstrated in John L. Evans and Stephen H. Archer, "Diversification and the Reduction of Dispersion: An Empirical Analysis," *Journal of Finance,* December 1968, p. 761; and W.H. Wagner and S.C. Lau, "The Effect of Diversification on Risk," *Financial Analysts Journal,* November–December 1971, p. 48.

Researchers have extensively examined the stability of betas and have found past betas to be useful predictors of future betas. For discussion and references, see James C. Van Horne, *Financial Management and Policy,* fifth edition, Prentice-Hall, 1980, pp. 61–62.

The major empirical studies of CAPM include Irwin Friend and Marshall E. Blume, "Measurement of Portfolio Performance under Uncertainty," *American Economic Review,* September 1970, p. 561; Merton H. Miller and Myron Scholes, "Rates of Return in Relation to Risk: A Reexamination of Some Recent Finds"; and Fischer Black, Michael C. Jensen, and Myron Scholes, "The Capital Asset Pricing Model: Some Empirical Tests," both in Michael C. Jensen, editor, *Studies in the Theory of Capital Markets,* Praeger, 1972; Marshall E. Blume and Irwin Friend, "A New Look at the Capital Asset Pricing Model," *Journal of Finance,* March 1973, p. 19; Eugene F. Fama and James D. MacBeth, "Risk, Return and Equilibrium: Empirical Test," *Journal of Political Economy,* May–June 1973, p. 607. For an example of the recent evidence suggesting the relevance of unsystematic risk, see Irwin Friend, Randolph Westerfield, and Michael Granito, "New Evidence on the Capital Asset Pricing Model," *Journal of Finance,* June 1978, p. 903.

Richard Roll wrote an important article on the empirical tests of CAPM in "A Critique of the Asset Pricing Theory's Tests," *Journal of Financial Economics,* March 1977, p. 129. For a critique of Roll's critique see David Mayers and Edward M. Rice, "Measuring Portfolio Performance and the Empirical Content of Asset Pricing Models," *Journal of Financial Economics,* March 1979, p. 3.

Corporate Finance Applications

For a detailed analysis of the role of CAPM in estimating capital costs and in capital budgeting, see the discussion and references in Richard A. Brealey and Stewart C. Myers, *Principles of Corporate Finance,* McGraw-Hill, 1981, chapters 7–9; Thomas E. Copeland and J. Fred Weston, *Financial Theory and Corporate Policy,* Addison-Wesley, 1979, chapters 10–12; and James C. Van Horne's previously mentioned *Financial Management and Policy,* chapters 7–9.

20

The Risky Business of Diversification

RALPH BIGGADIKE

On the basis of a sample from the top 200 of the *Fortune* "500" and data from the PIMS (Profit Impact of Market Strategies) project, this author gives some guidelines for established companies on what to expect from new ventures. He points out that it takes an average of 10 to 12 years before the ROI of ventures equals that of mature businesses. He advocates rapid share building despite the adverse effect that this apparently has on current financial performance and thus advises large-scale entry for the company that wants to grow through the addition of a new business.

One way companies grow is to launch new businesses into product markets where they have not previously competed. For example, GE, starting with an incandescent lamp business, has moved to businesses covering more than 700 product markets. Recent examples of corporate diversification include the entries of Gillette into manufacture of felt-tip pens, John Deere into snowmobiles, and Texas Instruments into pocket calculators.

Corporate growth through the addition of new businesses has received further impetus from the "product portfolio" concept, which argues that if a company is both to grow and to allocate resources wisely it must mix established with new businesses. Growth and a balanced portfolio are attractive objectives, but, for some companies, their pursuit has produced big problems. NCR reported losses of $60 million in 1972, primarily because of its entry into the computer field. General Foods took a $39 million write-off in 1972 on its entry into the business of fast food chains. Rohr Industries, Inc. announced a $59.9 million write-off in 1976 on its mass transit venture.

Author's note. Parts of this article are drawn from my previous research reported in *Corporate Diversification* (Boston, Division of Research, Harvard Business School, forthcoming).

Results such as these suggest that launching new businesses is risky. Achieving a balanced product portfolio appears to be more difficult in practice than in theory. Articles on the product portfolio concept reinforce this perception of risk by referring to new businesses as "wildcats," "sweepstakes," or "question marks"—hardly the most reassuring of terms. From this viewpoint, corporate diversification resembles Russian roulette.

Conversely, some executives and economists argue that big losses are rare events. Venturing by established companies, they suggest, is much less risky than venturing by individuals. Some of the problems of individual ventures, such as acquiring capital, a brand reputation, and economies of scale, are less severe for established companies.

Another question concerning negative results is, "How long do we have to put up with losses?" Although most managers do not expect immediate profits, few accept several years of losses. Indeed, any corporate venture that promises losses for a period longer than the job horizon of most managers seems unlikely to survive. One company has a firm rule: "Kill new businesses if they are not profitable at the end of year 3."

The problem is that, with current knowledge of corporate ventures, one just does not know whether large losses for several years are the common experience or the exception. There is no known rationale for saying that new ventures should be profitable at the end of three years. In addition, it is not clear how much cash, on the average, a wildcat business will demand and over what time period.

This article deals with these issues. First, I present data on the performance of a sample of corporate new ventures. I seek to evaluate their initial performances and to determine the average length of time needed to achieve profitability. Second, I will address the question, "How might performance be improved?" and suggest some guidelines for future management of corporate ventures.

The Sample

The data in this article are from a sample of corporate ventures launched in the United States by the top 200 companies in the *Fortune* "500" and a sample of established businesses in the PIMS project.[1] A corporate venture is defined as a business marketing a product or service that the parent company has not previously marketed and that requires the parent company to obtain new equipment or new people or new knowledge. A business is defined as a division, product line, or other profit center within its parent company selling a distinct set of products or services to an identifiable group or groups of customers in competition with a well-defined set of competitors. Corporate acquisitions were included in the venture sample only if the acquiring company had committed significant resources to the business and altered its strategy after purchase.

The sample included 68 ventures launched by 35 companies that supplied data on their first two years of operations. Of these ventures, 47 had been operating for four years, allowing analysis of the second two-year period of operation as well. The sample consisted mainly of industrial goods businesses. Data were provided by managers of the parent company and of the venture and were disguised by the managers, thus limiting analysis to ratios only, not absolute dollar values.

All these ventures entered existing markets. Markets were defined at a segment level, a more narrowly defined market than those identified by, say, the Bureau of the Census. Thus the data used to measure market size and growth rates cover only the specific products or services, customer types, and geographic areas in which each corporate venture actually operates.

The population from which this sample was derived can be summarized as surviving corporate ventures, launched in the late 1960s and early 1970s by a subset of the *Fortune* top 200 companies mentioned earlier and characterized by a high degree of diversification. These results probably do not apply to ventures that individuals launched or that had to create entirely new markets (e.g., the first business to introduce penicillin).

The data base does, however, embrace entrants that entered existing markets with incremental innovations (e.g., the first business to introduce electronic calculators) and that had a "me too" technology. It also includes entrants to concentrated and fragmented markets and entrants to rapid growth and mature markets. Participating executives describe the ventures as typical examples of the new businesses that their parent companies have launched.

Financial Performance

The sample indicates that corporate ventures, on average, suffer severe losses through their first four years of operations. Exhibit 1 shows that the ROI for the median business was −40% in the first two years and −14% in the second two years.

A few businesses achieved profits in the first two years—specifically, 12 out of 68, or 18% of the sample. The most profitable venture recorded an ROI of +80%; the lowest ROI was −442%. By the end of year four, of the 47 ventures with four years of data, 18, or 38%, had made a profit. These 18 do not include seven of the 12 businesses profitable in year two. Early profitability in a venture, therefore, does not necessarily guarantee continued profitability.

One can now more precisely assess new businesses' appetite for cash. The ratio of cash flow to investment was −80% in the first two years and −29% in the second two years. No business had a positive cash flow in the first two years; six businesses had a positive cash flow in the second two years.

The ratio of gross margin to sales revenue showed the most favorable

Exhibit 1. Financial Performance in the First Four Years of Operations

Performance Ratio	Median Value[a]	
	Years 1 and 2	Years 3 and 4
Return on investment[b]	−40%	−14%
Cash flow—investment[c]	−80	−29
Pretax profit—sales	−39	−10
Gross margin—sales[d]	+15	+28
Number of businesses	68	47

[a]I show performance of the median business because the sample performance was spread over a wide range. The median is not affected by extreme cases and therefore is less likely to mislead.

[b]The ratio of net pretax income to average investment. Income is calculated after deduction of corporate expenses but prior to interest charges. Investment is calculated as working capital plus fixed capital (valued at net book value).

[c]Cash generated by aftertax earnings *minus* cash absorbed by increased working capital and increased *net* investment in plant and equipment.

[d]Sales revenues *minus* purchases, manufacturing, and depreciation as a ratio to sales revenues.

picture. Of the 68 ventures, 48, or 70%, reported a positive gross margin in their first two years, which points to marketing and R&D expense as contributors to the negative income statements. Exhibit 2 shows that the median marketing expense to sales revenue ratio, at 38%, was the second highest operating ratio in the first two years; R&D expense to sales revenue ratio was a hefty 19%.

Most operating and capital ratios showed some improvement in the second two years. For example, Exhibit 2 shows that marketing-sales rev-

Exhibit 2. Operating and Capital Ratios in the First Four Years of Operations

	Median Value	
Operating Ratios	Years 1 and 2	Years 3 and 4
Purchase—sales	46%	44%
Manufacturing—sales	28	25
Marketing—sales	38	22
R&D—sales	19	8
Capital Ratios		
Inventory—sales	24	22
Receivables—sales	16	12
Investment—sales	98	73
Number of businesses	68	47

enue ratio improved to 22% and investment-sales revenue ratio improved from 98% to 73%. However, these ratios did not improve because of any declining outlays on operating and capital items. In fact, outlays continued to rise in the second two years. Rather, growth in sales revenues—at 45% per year for the median venture—rose faster than outlays.

The key to improving financial statements, then, is to obtain rapid sales growth with a less than proportionate increase in outlays. Although not surprising, this perspective is in contrast to the common approach of forecasting improvement because of declines in initial launch outlays. According to this sample, both expenses and capital items go only one way—up.

Another common view, that the problem with new businesses is that initial returns are low because of high capital requirements, is also wide of the mark. Rather, in this sample the problem is that there is no return at all—net income is negative. The appellations "wildcats" or "sweepstakes" thus appear uncomfortably accurate descriptions of corporate new ventures.

Losses for How Long?

Severe losses over the first four years of operations raise the question, "How long, on the average, do corporate new ventures take to improve performance?" I estimated an answer to this question by extracting from the PIMS data base two groups of businesses in more advanced stages of development. One group of businesses, termed "adolescents," had data on their fifth through their eighth year of operations. The other group of businesses are, on average, 18 years old and describe their product or service as mature; these businesses can be regarded as established and were called "mature." These groups allow us to compare performance over three stages of business development: start-up, adolescence, and maturity.

It appears that new ventures need, on the average, eight years before they reach profitability. Note in Exhibit 3 that ROI did not become positive until the seventh and eighth years, with the median business earning 7%. However, the adolescents still have some way to go before attaining the 17% reported by mature businesses. In fact, a simple time projection of the results in the first eight years suggests that 10 to 12 years elapse before the ROI of ventures equals that of mature businesses.

Figures drawn from this comparison must be regarded as estimates because we cannot be sure that the businesses in the adolescent and mature samples were, in *their* first four years, structurally similar to the businesses in the venture sample. However, even if we limit accuracy to plus or minus two to three years, this length of time to reach profitability is not encouraging.

Cash flow does not become positive for the median business in the first eight years. A similar time projection suggests that 12 years are needed before ventures generate cash flow ratios similar to those of mature businesses.

Some executives previewing these results were initially astonished. This reaction led them, and me, to review personal experiences with cor-

Exhibit 3. Median Performance in Start-Up, Adolescent, and Mature Stages

	Start-Up		Adolescence		Maturity
Performance Ratio	Years 1 and 2	Years 3 and 4	Years 5 and 6	Years 7 and 8[a]	Average Age about 18 Years
Return on investment	−40%	−14%	−8%	+7%	+17%
Cash flow—sales	−90	−29	−5	−4	+ 3
Pretax profit—sales	−39	−10	−5	−4	+ 9
Gross margin—sales	+15	+28	+19	+22	+26
Number of businesses	68	47	61	61	454

[a]Profit to sales is negative while ROI is positive because these averages are medians, not means (mean ROI is +5% and mean profit to sales is +1%).

porate ventures. The overriding question was, "Could the financial results be that bad for that long?" Managers found that the sample data were so provocative that they had to test them against their own venture experiences.

Although these personal recollections cannot be used analytically, the executives eventually concluded that the sample results squared with many of their companies' venture experiences. I cannot reveal these recollections, but I can cite examples from the public domain:

- ☐ Around 1970, Xerox started work on two new businesses—duplicators and electronic typing systems. In 1977, both were still unprofitable, although reports suggested that profitability was near.
- ☐ Singer tried to build a business machines venture for 10 years, but finally quit in 1975. The venture was still unprofitable.
- ☐ GE tried for 13 years, from 1957 to 1970, to establish its computer venture. The company's nuclear venture took about 15 years to reach profitability.[2]

Market Performance

Although the median corporate venture in the first four years increased sales revenues at 45% per year, this sales growth did not lead to a strong market position. The median venture achieved 7% share in the first two years and 10% in the second two years. Relative share (defined as the venture share divided by the combined share of the three largest competitors) is a more relevant measure of competitive position. The medium corporate venture held 11% and 13% in the first and second two-year periods, respectively.

Although the low initial share level might be expected for a new business, the apparent difficulty in improving share is disturbing. Although 39 of the 47 businesses with four years of share data gained share in the second two years, one-third gained less than a single point and only one-quarter gained more than four points. The impressive sales revenue growth for many ventures was negligible in the context of a market growing slightly faster and a starting position of zero share.

Market Share and Financial Performance

Persuasive theoretical arguments and a good deal of concrete evidence suggest that high market share improves financial performance.[3] Although this previous research was done on established businesses, it seems likely that share will similarly benefit new businesses. However, few researchers have discussed the financial impact of building share. One can argue from common sense that building share should damage financial performance in the same time period.

Building share can require higher quality, broader marketing, lower prices, and extended capacity—all expensive items that damage both income statements and balance sheets. Furthermore, some rapid share builders are starting from both a low share position and an inferior cost position. Their financial results will thus experience a "double whammy."

Earlier research leads one to expect a positive relationship between financial performance and share for new ventures. Conversely, in the same time period, a negative relationship between financial performance and share building should be expected. Although the small sample size and the wide variability in the data prevent rigorous testing of these relationships, one can say that the evidence of this sample supports them.

Effect of Market Share

To get the data on these relationships, I divided the venture sample into three approximately equal-sized groups—low, medium, and high relative market share ventures in their first and second two years. Exhibit 4 shows data on the first relationship: businesses with low relative share reported—93% ROI, and businesses with high relative share reported −21% ROI in the first two years—a difference of 72 points. The impact of relative share on profit margin and cash flow/investment was similar. The advantages of high relative share continued in the second two years of operations. The benefits of share are similar to those cited for established businesses: profit margin increases sharply, and the purchases-to-sales and marketing-to-sales ratios decline.[4]

Effect of Building Share

Having share and building it produce quite different effects on financial performance. Exhibit 5 shows that the greater the rate of gain in relative share, the poorer the financial performance. Rapid share builders reported a median ROI of −20% for the first four years of operations compared to −4% ROI for those who were not building share. That is to say, a strategy

Exhibit 4. Relationship between Financial and Market Performance

	First Two Years Median Value Relative Share[a]			Second Two Years Median Value Relative Share[a]		
Performance Ratio	Low (below 4%)	Medium (4% to 42%)	High (over 42%)	Low (below 7%)	Medium (8% to 33%)	High (over 50%)
Return on investment	−93%	−40%	−21%	−20%	−5%	−6%
Cash flow—investment	−110	−67	−74	−39	−22	−23
Pretax profit—sales	−95	−35	−21	−29	−2	−5

[a]Relative share is the venture share divided by the combined share of the three largest competitors.

Exhibit 5. Financial Performance and Change in Relative Share, First Four Years

	Median Value		
Performance Ratio	Rapid Share Builders	Moderate Share Builders	Holders or Losers of Share
Return on investment	−20%	−10%	−4%
Cash flow—investment	−58	−20	−19
Pretax profit—sales	−24	−6	−2

of rapid relative share building carried a short-term penalty of 16 percentage points in ROI over the alternative of holding relative share.

As might be expected, the penalty on the cash flow-to-investment ratio was even more severe. Rapid relative share builders reported a median cash flow—investment ratio of −58%, whereas share holders reported −19%, a difference of 30 points.

On the average, the market share of rapid share builders was lower than that of the shareholders throughout the first four years of operations. Gaining share from a low share base was doubly handicapping. Rapid share builders, on the average, had price-cost margins worse than those of the shareholders. That is, they charged lower prices and carried higher direct costs than did their competitors. To gain share from a low share position, several ventures had to offer customers a better bargain, at the same time bearing the financial disadvantages of low share. This combination is surely the quintessence of the "double whammy."

Share before Profits

The foregoing findings demonstrate that ventures cannot report both good financial and good market performance in the same time period: These two aspects of performance conflict. But we know from other studies that the highest ROI for established businesses goes to the highest market shareholder. If a business can have both good financial and good market performance only when share is established, the management implication is clear: a venture's objective for its early years should be to build share, regardless of short-run financial performance.

If we accept this objective, it follows that corporate ventures should enter on a large scale for the best results. Obviously, only a business with a large capacity relative to the size of the market has the potential to gain a large market share. This approach is often referred to as building capacity ahead of demand. But it is a controversial strategy and, some executives have argued, counterintuitive, because it raises the required investment and therefore the risk. Yet my findings here suggest the opposite: Perhaps the biggest risk is entering too small. It may be true, in corporate venturing as in love, that faint heart never won fair lady.

Entry Scale

To obtain further evidence for the idea that to enter on a large scale is the best strategy, I analyzed these ventures according to the size of their entry. I used two measures of scale: production and market scales. Production scale is defined as the initial production capacity of the business, expressed as a percentage of the market size. Market scale is defined as the number of customers served and the breadth of product line offered by the venture, relative to its competitors. Production and market scale together represent the maximum potential share a business can obtain. We need both measures of scale because economies of a large plant can be realized only if the output is continuously sold.

Exhibit 6 shows the distribution of this sample on these measures. Just over half the sample, 37 businesses, entered with a capacity less than 20% of the size of the market. Similarly, about half the sample offered product lines less broad than their competitors'; more than one-third served fewer customers than did their competitors. Thus, on the average, our sample consists of small-scale entrants.

When we look at performance by different sizes of entry scale, we see that the small-scale strategy failed to reduce losses. And neither did it build share. Exhibit 7 shows performance in the first two years by an index of entry scale, which is simply production and market scales combined. The big losers were those ventures with the smallest entry scale: These had a median ROI of −41%, compared with −24% for those with the largest entry scale. The second two years showed similar performances.

Exhibit 7 also returns us to relative share: The large-scale entrants achieved the highest relative share as well as the least negative financial performance. For a few businesses, therefore, the conflict between financial and market performance was less severe. Although these ventures still sustained losses, they were at least building market position.

These findings provide persuasive support for the argument that entering on a large scale is likely to lead to better financial results earlier than does the intuitively obvious approach, that is, entering on a small scale. In fact, small-scale entries are doubly handicapped. Their immediate financial performance is terrible, and satisfactory market position remains undeveloped.

Managers' Intentions

I asked managers whether they had deliberately chosen the small-scale entry strategy. Most venture managers had indeed targeted a low initial market

Exhibit 6. Distribution of Sample on Entry Scale, First Two Years

Production scale: capacity as percentage of market size		
Less than 10%	21	31%
10%–19%	16	24
20%–29%	5	7
30%–39%	4	6
40%–49%	4	6
50%–59%	2	3
60% +	15	22
	67	99%
Median = 19%		
Marketing scale product line breadth		
Less broad[a]	44	65%
Same breadth	13	19
Broader	11	16
	68	100%
Segment size		
Fewer customers[a]	25	37%
About the same	36	54
More customers	6	9
	67	100%

[a]Relative to competitors

share. Exhibit 8 shows that 34 entrants, half the sample, set for the first two years a market share objective below 10%. Therefore, I judge that the poor performance of this sample was largely self-inflicted. In effect, these entrants obtained the market share they deserved, and this share in turn contributed to their financial losses. They could not generate enough revenue to cover their entry costs and to overcome their relative direct cost disadvantage.

An important management question here is, "Why would executives seek a low share?" At least four explanations come to mind:

1. Perhaps there is still a widespread lack of awareness of the relationship between profitability and share. I suggest this explanation because, if executives were aware of this relationship, they would realize that they must build share in the start-up phase of a venture—ideally, reaching the number one position.

Exhibit 7. Performance by Index of Entry Scale, First Two Years

	Median Value		
	Small Scale	Medium Scale	Large Scale
Return on investment	−41	−47	−24
Relative share	1	12	64

2. Perhaps middle managers (presumably the proposers of new businesses) fear that, if they ask for too much capital and launching expenses, their idea will not be approved by top management. Thus they plan a small-scale entry to minimize their financial demands. Maybe capital-budgeting criteria emphasize financial results prematurely, thus fostering the practice of taking several small dips at the corporate well rather than one large scoop.

3. Venture managers probably expect to be evaluated more on their own goals than on the long-run success of the particular venture. Therefore, they project a small share because they are more likely to attain it.

Iroquois Brands Ltd. seems to have deliberately overturned such standard capital-budgeting and evaluation criteria when it introduced a revolving venture capital fund. Iroquois hopes to encourage a long-term focus:

> Neither short-term earnings nor executive bonuses are penalized when the new ventures are started up. . . . The fund supplies 75% of the cost of approved projects, with the subsidiary putting up the remaining 25%. . . . Repayment, plus a 10% charge, starts one year after the new product goes to market or becomes profitable.[5]

4. Another explanation could be that executives believe that starting small is prudent. After all, seeking high share requires larger investment for capacity and more marketing expenses to generate the sales to fill that capacity—all for a new business in an unknown, often still-evolving market.

Exhibit 8. Market Share Objectives, First Two Years

Share Objective	Businesses	Percentage	
5% or less	24	36%	51%
6%–10%	10	15	
11%–15%	8	12	
16%–20%	8	12	
20% +	17	25	
	67[a]	100%	

[a]One venture did not provide data.

As one executive put it, "Far better to enter small, learn as you go, and expand with experience."

If the small-scale approach were to work, it would seem most appropriate to the electronics industry—surely one of the most uncertain industries in the economy. Often, strategists cannot even be sure which of several competing production technologies is most efficient or profitable. Yet electronics executives argue strongly that "if you're going to get into a market, you'd better do it big." One of the major reasons for this view is an experience curve in which costs drop 15 to 30% each time accumulated volume doubles. In the face of such a cost-volume relationship, it is foolhardy to enter small, because the inevitable result must be an inferior relative cost position.

Not just in fast-growth markets do we hear executives saying, "Do it big." John A. Murphy, president and chief executive officer of Miller Brewing Company, said recently, "Ours is a simple objective; it is to become Number One."[6] Pursuing this objective, Miller and its owner since 1970, Philip Morris, have invested $500 million to increase capacity from about 5 million barrels to 34.8 million (in an industry growing at about 3% per year) and have spent $3 per barrel on advertising, almost three times the industry average. The results of Miller's strategy are shown in Exhibit 9.

One might argue that it is too early to evaluate the financial success of Miller's strategy. And, of course, the strategy has not been fully implemented. Miller spent $250 million in 1978 to add more capacity. But one cannot deny that Miller and its parent company have built a strong market position in an industry that is likely to enjoy many more years of life.

Management Implications

The clearest recommendation from this study is the need for large-scale entry. Such a recommendation might appear foolhardy in view of the financial results of this sample. Recall from Exhibit 7, however, that large-scale entrants reported the least negative results. I suggest that the eight years, on average, taken to reach positive net income would be reduced if higher relative share were achieved in the early years. Larger-scale entries might require less managerial patience.

Exhibit 9. One Company's Results with Large-Scale Entry

	1970	1971	1972	1973	1974	1975	1976	1977
Sales (in millions of dollars)	$198	$204	$210	$276	$404	$658	$983	$1,323
Profit (in millions of dollars)	$11.4	$1.3	$0.2	$(2.4)	$6.3	$28.6	$76.1	$106.5
Share	4%	4%	4%	5%	6%	9%	12%	15%
Market position	7	7	7	5	5	4	3	2

Source: *Business Week*, *New York Times*, and annual reports.

One might argue that market segmentation would allow profitable small-scale entries. However, as I explained while describing the sample, markets for the PIMS program are defined narrowly, at least compared with census definitions. Segmentation, therefore, has already occurred. We have been examining the performance of corporate ventures into parts of industries, rather than into entire industries. To illustrate this point, a venture marketing hospital pharmacy equipment confined the definition of its market to pharmacy equipment only, not to all types of hospital equipment. Therefore, its market share was its share of pharmacy equipment sales, not of hospital equipment sales.

I do not, however, recommend large spending on every opportunity in sight. Corporate diversification should not be played like Russian roulette. I do recommend that fewer ventures be launched, so that each can have the advantage of adequate resources to achieve a good market position, right from year one. Starting too many ventures at the same time diffuses the company's effort.

The recommendation for fewer ventures leads to another: One should back a new business and its managers as long as they continue to build share. Similarly, one should withdraw resources from a profitable venture if profits have been gained at the cost of share. It may be hard to realize in the heat of today's decisions, but a profitable corporate venture sitting on a low share is in fact tomorrow's dog. Conversely, the unprofitable venture gaining share and demanding ever more cash is tomorrow's winner.

The recommendation to enter on a large scale means that middle-level managers should "call it as they see it." I have seen too many corporate venture plans with, for example, marketing-sales ratios only slightly higher than those for established businesses and profits forecast for the second year. According to this sample, such a corporate venture rarely exists.

Middle-level executives must estimate what it will take to build a successful business and see that top executives know what they are getting into. This sample tells us that share points are gained only slowly and after the commitment of substantial resources. Middle managers should study the most recent venture pro forma they have been working on. If its operating and capital ratios are better than those shown in Exhibit 2, they should ask themselves, "Why will *this* venture outperform the median venture in a sample of corporate ventures?"

Similarly, if profits are forecast early in the life of the venture, they should ask, "What is relative market share in the first year of profitability?" It is quite probable that early profitability has been forecast at the expense of a long-term market position.

Conclusion

The data in this article tell us, more precisely than we knew before, about the risks in corporate ventures. The odds are unattractive. Indeed, many managers will find them daunting. But, at the same time, managers know that they have to build a balanced corporate product portfolio. I believe that the way to improve the odds and build the portfolio is to commit substantial resources to each venture and to defer immediate financial performance in favor of market position. Launching new businesses takes large scale entry and continual commitment; it is not an activity for the impatient or for the fainthearted.

Notes

1. See Sidney Schoeffler, Robert D. Buzzell, and Donald F. Heany, "Impact of Strategic Planning on Profit Performance," *HBR*, March–April 1974, p. 137; and Robert D. Buzzell, Bradley T. Gale, and Ralph G.M. Sultan, "Market Share—A Key to Profitability," *HBR*, January—February 1975, p. 97.

2. "GE's New Strategy for Faster Growth," *Business Week*, July 8, 1972, p. 52.

3. See Buzzell, Gale, and Sultan, "Market Share—A Key to Profitability."

4. Ibid., p. 99.

5. "Iroquois Brands: An Aggressive Search for the Unique," *Business Week*, February 27, 1978, p. 112.

6. *Milwaukee Journal*, September 22, 1977.

21

Pyrrhic Victories in Fights for Market Share

WILLIAM E. FRUHAN, JR.

United States business has a way of growing compulsively; companies tend to want "in" where a lively market is concerned, and once they are in, they want first place. There are times, as the author shows, when a little self-restraint is an admirable thing. When a company can be sure that moving into a new area or moving up the ladder is going to cost it its lifeblood; when a company can see the hand of government writing restrictive legislation on the wall; when a company must race an established competitor to exhaustion just to get a foothold in a new market—these are times when management should put the ceiling of realism on its ambitions. The author cites examples of disasters stemming from overambition of this kind, from the computer industry, the food business, and the airline companies.

In many U.S. industries, profitability is closely linked to market share. ROI statistics demonstrate this characteristic quite clearly for automobile manufacturing, for example, as Exhibit 1 illustrates.

Since profits can jump impressively in many industries as a company's position in the market-share pecking order advances, market-share battles are often waged with energy; but unfortunately, in spite of the tremendous stakes involved, companies tend to launch their campaigns for building market share without much foresight.

Specifically, they tend to ignore three basic questions:

Question 1. Does the company have the financial resources necessary to win—and then support—the level of sales implied by its market-share target; or, if it does not have these resources, can it acquire them at acceptable cost?

Question 2. Will the company find itself in a viable position if its drive for an expanded market share should be thwarted—by antitrust action, say—before it has reached its market-share target?

Exhibit 1. Return on Equity for Automobile Manufacturers Ranked by Market Share

Company	Market Share Rank	1960	1962	1964	1966	1968	1970
General Motors	1	16.9%	21.3%	23.5%	21.2%	18.2%	6.1%
Ford	2	15.6	14.6	12.9	13.3	13.0	9.4
Chrysler	3	4.6	8.8	20.4	11.4	14.1	−0.3

Question 3. Will regulatory authorities permit the company to achieve its objective *with the strategy it has chosen to follow*?

To demonstrate the importance of these questions to expansion strategies, let me review the experiences of a number of companies, operating in quite separate industries, that fought, by-and-large disastrously, to increase their market shares.

Main-Frame Computers

Recently, two companies opted out of the main-frame computer manufacturing industry. Prior to their exit from the business, both of these companies had committed themselves to increasing their market shares:

- ☐ According to press reports during September 1970, General Electric's studies indicated that it had to have a 15% market share if the company were to become competitive in the industry.[1]
- ☐ About the same time, RCA concluded that it needed a 10% share to become competitive; and the company committed itself, publicly, to meeting that goal by the mid-1970s.[2]

Modest as they might first appear, these market-share objectives represented a more than threefold advance from these companies' 1969 industry standings, which are given in Exhibit 2. Further, both companies planned to meet these objectives solely through internal growth. Both probably felt that antitrust regulations ruled out a strategy for expansion through acquisition of other domestic computer manufacturers, and hence decided to seek their expanded shares through internal means.[3]

A strategy of internal growth in the computer industry, however, demands a major financial commitment. Since a large fraction of manufacturers' output is marketed via leases, operations are capital intensive. For example, in 1969 IBM required a capital base of about $5.9 billion to support shipment estimated at $4.95 billion, as indicated in Exhibit 2. These figures suggest

Exhibit 2. Competitors' Standings in the 1969 Main-Frame Computer Market (dollar figures in millions)

Company		Sales Value of Computers Shipped	Market Share	Total Corporate Capital[a] 1969	Total Corporate Revenue 1969	Percent of Total Revenues from Computers
IBM		$4,950	69.0%	$5,906	$7,197	83%
Sperry Rand		400	5.6	977	1,710	36
Honeywell		340	4.7	956	1,281	27
Burroughs		305	4.3	907	759	36
GE		290	4.0	3,554	8,448	3
Control Data		255	3.6	984	1,084	53
RCA		230	3.2	1,875	3,222	7
NCR		195	2.7	1,104	1,255	16
Xerox		75	1.1	1,099	1,483	8
Others		130	1.8	—	—	—
Industry total for year	1969	$ 7,170	100.0%			
Projections of industry shipments	1970	$ 7,720				
	1971	8,940				
	1972	10,300				
	1973	11,800				
	1974	13,400				

Source: International Data Publishing Co., annual reports, and author's estimates.

[a]Includes short-term loans, long-term debt, and shareholders' equity.

that, given a stable market share, $1 in annual shipments requires the support of about $1.20 of firm capital in this industry.

This degree of capital intensity, coupled with the absolute size of the computer industry and the speed with which RCA (and presumably GE, too) wished to reach its market-share objectives, leads to one inescapable conclusion: The market-share aspirations of GE and RCA required a capital commitment quite out of proportion to their capital-generating ability.

Exhibit 3 shows this clearly. The combined retained earnings and the additions to debt capital that the earnings retentions of GE and RCA might have supported at their debt/equity ratios in the late 1960s were insufficient to meet the future capital needs arising solely from the *computer divisions* of these diversified companies. Yet, in 1969, the computer divisions' revenues accounted for less than 10% of total corporate revenues in the two companies.

The implications are clear. The debt/equity ratios of GE and RCA

Exhibit 3. Severe Capital Intensity in the Main-Frame Computer Industry (dollar figures in millions)

A. All-industry figures

Year	Projected industry computer shipments	Industry capital/ shipments ratio	Total capital required by industry
1969	$ 7,170	1.2	$ 8,600
1970	7,720	1.2	9,270
1971	8,940	1.2	10,710
1972	10,300	1.2	12,350
1973	11,800	1.2	14,200
1974	13,400	1.2	16,100

B. RCA projected goals

Year	Share of market projection	Total capital required	New capital required
1969	3.2%	$ 276	—
1970	4.0	371	$ 95
1971	5.0	536	165
1972	6.3	778	242
1973	8.0	1,135	357
1974	10.0	1,610	475

C. GE projected goals

Year	Share of market projection	Total capital required	New capital required
1969	4.0%	$ 344	—
1970	5.2	482	$138
1971	6.8	730	248
1972	8.9	1,100	370
1973	11.5	1,635	535
1974	15.0	2,420	785

D. Capital generation

	RCA (1969)	GE (1968)
Profit after taxes	$151	$357
Dividends	68	235
Earnings retentions	$ 83	$122

Exhibit 3. ***(Continued)***

D. Capital generation

	RCA (1969)	GE (1968)
Debt/equity ratio[a]	× .45	× .27
Debt potential at D/E ratio	37	33
Total capital generation potential	$120	$155

[a]Includes long-term debt only; in the case of RCA, does not include debt of the Hertz Corporation.

(already high by IBM standards) would have had to be raised sharply, or equity securities would have had to be sold (at low P/E ratios by IBM standards) before these companies could have come close to achieving their market-share objectives. Exhibit 4 gives the statistics for the competing companies.

As *this* exhibit implies, the prospects for GE and RCA were not always quite this dim. Back in 1955, both companies had sufficient corporate resources (in terms of total profit or cash flow) to challenge IBM. By 1961, however, this ability, even for GE, was somewhat questionable. By the mid-1960s, and certainly after the IBM System 360 became a demonstrated success, the contest was over. IBM had so far outdistanced its nearest competitors, and its markets had grown to enormous size so rapidly, that the simple passage of time was raising market-entry barriers to insurmountable heights.

All that remained were the acknowledgements—which finally came in 1970 and 1971—that neither GE nor RCA could marshal the resources necessary to achieve, without domestic acquisitions, even a marginal market share in the computer industry at acceptable cost. Had they asked my *Question 1* somewhat earlier than 1970, both GE and RCA might have greatly reduced their losses in the computer business.

Retail Groceries

The retail grocery trade is a second industry in which the fight for market share is well worth examining.

In food retailing, the Federal Trade Commission has found a high correlation between the *profit contribution* of chain stores in a given geographic market area—usually a city or metropolitan area—and the *market share* achieved by those chain stores in the same market area. (Exhibit 5 demonstrates the strength of this correlation.) Indeed, in reference to one company operating in this industry, the FTC's chief economist has stated,

Exhibit 4. Financial Statistics for Major Computer Manufacturers, 1955–1969

Company	1955	1957	1959	1961	1963	1965	1967	1969
A. Debt/equity ratio								
Burroughs	33%	70%	62%	61%	65%	56%	48%	58%
Control Data	—	—	0	0	103	78	163	39
GE	0	25	19	14	11	17	31	27
Honeywell	18	28	24	28	35	42	65	77
IBM	102	60	50	36	27	15	13	10
NCR	50	59	24	41	51	38	69	61
RCA	97	85	76	52	48	43	50	45
Sperry Rand	—	65	60	62	70	58	31	36
Xerox	38	23	28	59	64	72	52	35
B. Average P/E ratio								
Burroughs	13.1	24.0	22.4	21.3	24.5	15.7	32.4	43.1
Control Data	—	—	32.6	95.3	49.9	55.1	53.3	43.2
GE	22.3	21.9	25.8	25.5	26.7	27.1	24.5	28.4
Honeywell	19.2	29.8	30.6	42.2	23.3	26.3	29.6	32.7
IBM	22.7	31.0	42.0	54.9	34.6	35.8	43.5	40.4
NCR	14.3	17.7	23.0	27.0	27.6	22.8	26.3	32.1
RCA	14.3	13.3	23.6	29.8	20.5	22.2	23.5	17.8
Sperry Rand	13.7	22.0	18.7	32.6	18.3	14.4	23.7	18.6
Xerox	30.6	27.4	45.8	78.5	43.8	54.7	62.3	45.7
C. Profit after taxes (in millions of dollars)								
Burroughs	$ 12	$ 10	$ 11	$ 11	$ 9	$ 18	$ 35	$ 55
Control Data	—	—	—	1	3	8	8	52
GE	201	248	280	242	271	355	361	278
Honeywell	19	21	29	25	35	38	42	63
IBM	73	111	176	253	363	477	652	934
NCR	18	23	22	30	22	29	35	44
RCA	48	39	40	36	66	101	148	151
Sperry Rand	46	28	37	24	27	32	64	81
Xerox	1	1	2	5	23	62	100	161

Source: Annual reports; *Moody's Industrial Manual,* 1970; *Value Line Investment Survey.*

Exhibit 5. Market Shares Charted Against Store Contribution to Corporate Profit, by Groups of Cities (1958)

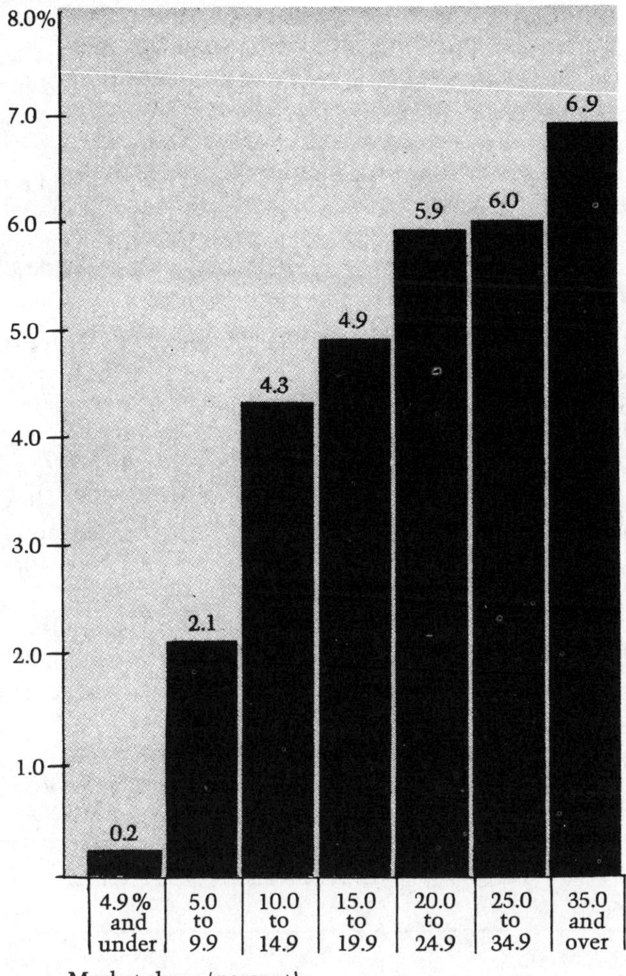

"I have never seen a closer relationship between the market dominance of a firm in an individual market, or group of markets, and its profitability. . . ."[4]

Stated another way, the profitability of an individual company in grocery retailing depends not so much on its total industry market share, but rather on its weighted-average market share in the various city-market areas in which it participates. This relationship between profitability and city-market share suggests that a growth-minded retail company planning to expand its market position rapidly faces a strategic dilemma: Should it gain toehold positions in a large number of city-market areas (e.g., via acquisitions), and then build its share in each city from this limited base later? Or should it devote its resources to building a dominant position in one city-market area at a time?

Many large chains operating in the industry faced precisely this dilemma between 1948 and 1958, a period when the retail food industry was consolidating itself rapidly through mergers. (Exhibit 6 shows the trend toward consolidation in those years.) In that decade, the most active acquirer in the field, National Tea, opted for the "toehold" strategy on a nationwide basis, as did many of its competitors. These companies found themselves spread quite thin in numerous markets just at the critical moment in 1958 when (1) the last of the large-store independents were disappearing via merger into competitive chain operations and (2) the FTC was taking decisive action to halt the consolidation movement by blocking future mergers in this industry.

In short, these companies found themselves in disadvantaged competitive positions and without usable strategies. The detrimental effect on ROI, in the case of National Tea, is clear from the figures in Exhibit 7. What National Tea and many of the others in the group had failed to do was adequately test their strategies against my *Questions 2* and *3:* They had failed to consider their positions, should they have to shelve their strategies midway to their goals, and they had failed to prepare themselves for restrictive government regulation.

In contrast, Winn-Dixie—the second most active acquirer in the retail grocery field—appears to have tested its strategies well, judging by the figures given in Exhibit 7. And, in fact, in planning its acquisitions in the

Exhibit 6. Percentage Distribution of Food Store Sales, by Type of Retailer, for 1948, 1954, and 1958

	Percentage of Food Store Sales		
Type of Retailer	1948	1954	1958
Top 20 chains	24.0%	30.1%	34.0%
Other chains	5.2	6.7	9.8
Cooperative members[a]	7.7	12.7	18.8
Voluntary members[a]	4.6	10.0	12.0
Unaffiliated independents	58.5	40.5	25.4
Total	100.0%	100.0%	100.0%

[a]Arrangements between wholesalers and independents have assumed two basic forms: the retailer-owned cooperative food wholesaler and the wholesaler-sponsored voluntary retail group. Groups of independents so affiliated with a particular wholesaler commonly are referred to as voluntary or cooperative groups or chains.

Exhibit 7. ROI and Acquisition Activity of Three Retail Grocery Companies

Company	Share of U.S. Food Store Sales in Countries where Company Operates, 1958	ROI				Number of Stores Acquired, 1949–1958	Share of U.S. Food Store Sales, 1958
		1955	1960	1965	1970		
Winn-Dixie	17.2%	17.7%	19.8%	20.6%	18.3%	306	1.3%
A&P	12.6	10.5	12.1	8.8	7.4	0	9.7
National Tea	8.6	9.5	9.1	8.4	5.5	485	1.6

1948–1958 period, Winn-Dixie drove for market depth in a limited geographic area, namely, the Southeast. The company continues to reap the benefits of this bit of foresight in strategy formulation even today. Clearly, there can be an enormous profit payoff in keeping a relatively modest exposure to adverse regulatory responses that might be expected to occur in the middle of a share expansion drive.

Air Transport

My third and final example of a heroic but less-than-successful fight for market share is taken from the air transportation industry.

In this field, consumer buying habits and basic industry economics seem to have entered into a conspiracy to make market-share duels look like very attractive investment opportunities. In making plans, first of all, many air travelers initially contact the air carrier that they believe has the most daily flights to their destination city, which is a natural thing to do. But because of this customer trait, the frequency of a carrier's flight departures in relation to those of its competitors often becomes the crucial factor determining the carrier's share of the passenger traffic in a particular city-pair market. Just as a relatively larger allocation of shelf space in a supermarket might help a cereal manufacturer gain an edge over one's competitors, so an added round-trip flight each day between Boston and Chicago might help an airline boost its share of the passenger traffic moving between these cities.

In air travel, the relationship between product availability and market share is especially dramatic. In a city-pair market served by only two air carriers, for example, a carrier with 70% of the "daily flight frequencies" might attract 80% of the passenger traffic (see Exhibit 8).

Equally, the carrier with only 30% of the flights in this situation might get only 20% of the traffic. This relationship between frequency share and market share is, of course, moderated by differences in carrier promotion and quality of service; but it seems to hold true where competitors can be distinguished only be service frequency.

Now, what are the economics in this situation? Because most flights operate at a loss unless passengers occupy at least 40% of the seats available, the minority carriers on many routes operate at a significant loss. In the example I just mentioned, where one carrier has 70% of capacity and 80% of the business, and his competitor has only 30% of the capacity and 20% of the business, the competitor is almost certain to lose money on his operation. The dominant carrier, on the other hand, often achieves the very substantial profits implied by relatively high load factors. (Exhibit 9 presents the details of this situation.)

Thus, in the long run, the air carrier with sufficient financial resources to purchase the extra aircraft and fly the extra flight frequencies necessary

Exhibit 8. Market Share and Capacity Share on a Two-Carrier Route

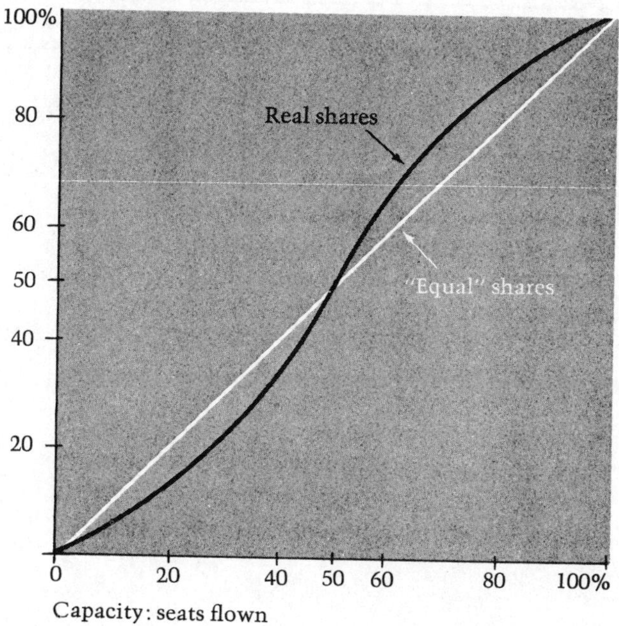

to achieve a dominant capacity share in particular city-pair markets is almost bound to come out ahead.

If my analysis is correct, one might expect the history of the airline industry to reflect (1) chronic capacity competition, (2) poor profitability, and (3) frequent failures among the smaller carriers, as the larger carriers built their market shares by overwhelming smaller rivals via capacity competition.

Although one does indeed find the first two characteristics, a closer look at the record (see Exhibits 10 and 11) illustrates the market shares of

Exhibit 9. Hypothetical Market Shares of Two Carriers Competing in a City-Pair Market

Carrier	Seats Flown per Year	Share of Seats on Route	Share of Market	Total Passengers Flown	Passenger Load Factor
Dominant	70,000	70%	80%	44,000	62.8%[a]
Minority	30,000	30%	20%	11,000	36.7%[a]
Total	100,000			55,000	

[a]Overall passenger load factor on route—55%.

Exhibit 10. Average Market Shares for the 11 Domestic Trunk Air Carriers (domestic operations), 1954–1970

Airlines	1954	1958	1962	1966	1970
Big 4					
American	23.7%	22.3%	20.5%	19.0%	17.4%
Eastern	16.9	17.1	12.3	12.6	13.0[a]
Trans World	16.0	14.8	13.7	14.1	12.8
United	20.2	20.9	24.5[b]	21.9	23.7[a]
Little 7					
Braniff	3.7%	4.2%	3.8%	3.8%	3.8%
Continental	1.3	1.9	3.1	4.0	4.6
Delta	5.1	6.1	8.3	9.3	10.1
National	4.1	4.0	4.2	4.8	3.9
Northeast	1.0	1.6	2.4	1.6	2.1
Northwest	5.0	4.5	4.1	5.1	4.7
Western	2.7	2.7	3.3	3.7	3.9
Total for Big 4	76.8%	75.0%	70.9%	67.7%	66.9%
Total for Little 7	23.2	25.0	29.1	32.3	33.1

[a]Data for 1970 show a rising market share for two of the Big 4 carriers. This was due to strikes at National and Northwest that temporarily but significantly reduced their market shares during the year.

[b]Includes Capital Airlines that merged into United in 1961 and that accounted for 5.6% of domestic trunk revenues in 1960.

the largest carriers shrinking over the past 15 years and the highest level of profitability among the smallest carriers. Frequent failures among the smaller carriers have just not taken place—quite the reverse. Hence, on this point, either my analysis has led us down a blind alley, or something must have intervened in the competitive environment to reverse neatly the anticipated and the actual outcomes. The "something" is, of course, the Civil Aeronautics Board (CAB). This government regulatory body has become, in practice, an allocator of market shares and relative profitability for the domestic trunk air carriers.

Regulatory Inversion

The CAB has been able to accomplish this rather remarkable inversion of free market results for two principal reasons. First, it has the power to grant

Exhibit 11. ROI for the 11 Domestic Trunk Air Carriers, 1954–1970

Airlines	1954	1958	1962	1966	1970
Big 4					
American	15.6%	12.4%	5.7%	20.2%	− 7.8%
Eastern	13.1	6.3	−16.7	7.4	− 1.1
Trans World	18.7	2.7	−20.2	7.4	−33.9
United	10.8	11.2	1.9	8.8	− 7.2
Little 7					
Braniff	28.4%	10.5%	11.4%	33.0%	−10.1%
Continental	11.3	−1.7	6.9	31.7	3.9
Delta	15.7	9.9	26.5	37.2	16.1
National	10.7	4.5	24.5	22.6	− 4.9
Northeast	3.0	–	–	0	–
Northwest	9.7	8.4	6.4	20.2	8.7
Western	13.1	7.3	11.7	23.3	− 3.4
Big 4	14.0%	8.9%	− 3.2%	11.5%	−11.0%
Little 7	13.4	4.5	12.6	27.3	5.2
Industry	13.9	7.7	1.3	17.2	− 4.5

or withhold licenses permitting air carriers to fly in various markets. Second, it can control the number of participants in any given city-pair market. This power is significant because the number of carriers competing in a city-pair market has a very heavy impact on that market's profit potential. So pronounced is the impact of competition, in fact, that one carrier's monopoly routes, although they generated less than 10% of its revenue, supported the fraction of its traffic—more than 50%—that was carried at a loss.

Thus the CAB exercises tremendous profit control over the individual carrier. By making the largest new-route awards to smaller carriers, it can, over a long period of time, regulate a carrier's market share of the total industry traffic.

How has the CAB used this great regulatory power? Exhibits 10 and 11 show that since the carriers were removed from government subsidy in the mid-1950s, the air carrier market shares have slowly been leveling out. Even at that early date, the CAB may well have looked at the air transportation industry in the context of my *Question 1* and come to the conclusion that, without its intervention, small carriers would simply be unable to withstand market-share battles waged by bigger rivals with greater financial resources.

Hence, to avoid capacity duels that might end in small-carrier bankruptcy, and to offset the advantages large carriers have in raising expansion capital, the CAB has tended to give the small carriers a dramatic edge in relative profitability.

Exhibits 10 and 11 point out a meaningful contrast between the growth and profit opportunities of the smallest large carrier (Eastern) and the largest small carrier (Delta). The essence of this contrast was exquisitely penned by Paul H. Frankel 24 years ago, in his study of the petroleum industry:

> There is no more enthusiastic satellite than the biggest operator outside the ring—But the more successful he becomes the greater his danger of cutting off the branch upon which he is sitting. For, beyond a certain point . . . he is faced with . . . joining the inner circle himself. Thus, while the position of the biggest "outsider" is the most desirable, the lot of the smallest "insider" is the most uncomfortable.[5]

The game rules for profitability apply very differently to companies on the two sides of the regulatory fence; and companies that plan to climb that fence had better recognize the fact explicitly.

Further, the intent of the CAB's regulations is to maintain the number of competitors for market share, both large and small; and its resulting regulations may have created, in effect, a no-win market environment for the Big Four carriers.

Unfortunately, this no-win environment does not seem to have muted the willingness of the Big Four carriers to wage wasteful and expensive capacity wars. Indeed, these firms seem quite unwilling to address the implications of *Question 3*—their need to devise more creative and effective strategies for gaining larger shares.

Word of Warning

Most companies have committed themselves to fight for larger market shares. I contend that companies often make this commitment before they have adequately considered my three basic questions:

1 Are company financial resources adequate?
2 If the fight is stopped short for any reason, will the company's position be competitively viable?
3 Will government regulators permit the company to follow the strategy it has chosen?

In computer manufacturing, GE and RCA both pursued dramatic increases in their market shares long after the evidence indicated that their goals were financially impossible. In choosing an internal-growth rather than an acquisitions strategy, these companies showed they had considered the antitrust aspects of *Question 3*, but they were quite late in acknowledging the relevance of *Question 1*.

In grocery retailing, National Tea and many of its competitors evidently neglected *Questions 2* and *3*. As a result, halfway to their market-share goals, they were trapped in competitively disadvantaged positions. Winn-Dixie's strategy dealt more successfully with *Questions 2* and *3*, and this company remains a consistent leader in terms of industry profitability.

Finally, in the air transport industry, the CAB has structured a no-win environment for the larger carriers. These companies are simply not permitted to build their market shares through the traditional avenue of internal expansion. For their part, the larger carriers have yet to identify a market-share expansion strategy that recognizes my *Question 3*—the *feasibility* question—as the capacity wars and eroded profits of recent years demonstrate; yet their taste for doing battle with losing strategies seems undeterred.

Here, as in all the examples I have cited earlier, the cost of ignoring or failing to gather evidence relating to the three questions I posed initially has been frightfully high.

I could continue to add examples, but let me recommend some points for thought instead:

- ☐ Are you operating in an industry where extremely heavy financial resources are required?
- ☐ Are you in an industry where an expansion strategy might be cut off abruptly by a regulatory agency?
- ☐ Are you in an industry where some agency is even now planning some new regulatory hurdles?

If the answer to any of those questions is *yes*, and if yours is the kind of company that fights for market shares, reassess your battle plan.

Notes

1. "Honeywell Tries to Make Its Merger Work," *Business Week*, September 26, 1970, p. 93.

2. Gene Smith, "RCA Profits Topple, Kodak Sets Mark," *The New York Times*, October 15, 1970.

3. Allan T. Demaree, "G.E.'s Costly Ventures Into Futures," *Fortune*, October 1970, p. 158.

4. United States Federal Trade Commission, *In the Matter of National Tea Co., Findings as to the Facts, Conclusions, and Order*, Docket #7453, March 4, 1966, p. 57.

5. Essentials of Petroleum (London, Chapman & Hall, Ltd., 1946), p. 86

PART FIVE
MERGERS AND ACQUISITIONS

AN OVERVIEW

Acquisition decisions are among the most important "capital expenditure" decisions made by a corporation. They can have a major impact on the strategic direction of the firm; they frequently involve large amounts of money or large numbers of shares; and they can attract a significant amount of public attention and interest, sometimes too much from the perspective of the acquiring company. Do shareholders of acquiring firms benefit from corporate decisions to expand by this method, particularly when large premiums are paid to target company shareholders?

Research work in corporate finance indicates a way to think about this question. It suggests that shareholders of an acquiring firm benefit only when the value of cash flows received from the acquired company exceeds the price paid. It is difficult to achieve this objective, particularly when a substantial premium is paid, unless there is some basis for improving either the target company or the acquiring company by putting the two firms together. For example, the profitability of the target company might be substantially improved when given access to the national distribution system of the acquiring firm.

Although this way of thinking about the value of an acquisition is straightforward, it has implications that go against some of the traditional reasons given for mergers. To take one example, a merger undertaken for the sake of diversification can reduce the riskiness to which shareholders are exposed. If diversification is the only objective, however, it is not a very valuable service to shareholders, since they can diversify their own portfolio by purchasing shares in the same target company. Furthermore, they can purchase shares in such companies at current market prices, thus achieving diversification without paying the premium an acquiring company would probably have to pay. To be sure, the individual shareholders would not realize any economies of scale or synergy that might be obtained by putting the two companies together, but then the purpose of the acquisition would be to obtain these economies, not diversification per se.

This point of view toward mergers and acquisitions is explained and illustrated well in the first article by Salter and Weinhold, "Diversification via Acquisition: Creating Value." They indicate some myths about acquisitions that need to be rethought and then suggest some key factors that have the potential to create value for shareholders. In "Strategic Analysis for More Profitable Acquisitions," Rappaport adopts a similar view. He goes on to provide a specific methodology that can be used to value an acquisition target.

Regardless of any numerical value estimated for a target company, qualitative factors will always be important in an acquisition decision. Salter and Weinhold address these issues in their second article. In "Choosing Compatible Acquisitions," they propose a screening approach that integrates qualitative criteria, such as the integration potential of a target company, with a quantitative estimate of its value.

22
Diversification via Acquisition: Creating Value

MALCOLM S. SALTER and WOLF A. WEINHOLD

When debating whether to try to acquire a business that will take their company into either a related or an unrelated field, top corporate officers must answer this vital question: Will it create value for our shareholders? The interest of top management is in improving operating results, which, it hopes, will eventually be reflected in a higher value for the company's stock. Unless management has good reason to believe that the transaction can produce a market value higher than investors could obtain themselves by diversifying their own portfolio, the company should not make the acquisition. The authors discuss the misconceptions that maintain the popularity of corporate diversification programs (many of them unsuccessful) and then outline ways in which a merger can create value for stockholders.

During the past 25 years an increasing proportion of U.S. companies have seen wisdom in pursuing a strategy of diversification. Between 1950 and 1970, for example, single-business companies comprising the *Fortune* "500" declined from 30% to 8% of the total. Acquisition has become a standard approach to diversification.

In recent years the productivity of capital of many multibusiness companies has lagged behind the economy. Nevertheless, diversification through acquisition remains popular; between 1970 and 1975, acquired assets of large manufacturing and mining companies averaged slightly more than 11% of total new investment in those companies, and most of that activity was diversifying acquisition.[1] In the past few years the pace of activity has been slower than in the hectic 1967–1969 period, but the combination of high corporate liquidity, depressed stock prices, and slow economic growth has meant that for many companies acquisitions are among the most attractive investment alternatives. Since mid-1977, hardly a week has gone by without at least one major acquisition being announced by a diversifying corporation.

In light of this continuing interest and the apparent economic risks in following such a strategy, we present a review of the theory of corporate diversification. We begin by discussing seven common misconceptions about diversification through acquisition. We then turn to the basic question facing companies wanting to adopt the strategy: How can a company create value for its shareholders through diversification?

Our consideration of value creation leads to an examination of the potential benefits of the alternatives available—related-business diversification and unrelated-business diversification. Businesses are related if they (1) serve similar markets and use similar distribution systems, (2) employ similar production technologies, or (3) exploit similar science-based research.[2]

Common Misconceptions

There are seven common misconceptions about diversification through acquisition that we can usefully highlight in the context of recent history. They relate to the economic rationale of this strategy and to the management of a successful diversification program.

1. *Acquisitive diversifiers generate larger returns (through increased earnings and capital appreciation) for their shareholders than nondiversifiers do.* This notion gained a certain currency during the 1960s, in part because of the enormous emphasis that securities analysts and corporate executives placed on growth in earnings per share (EPS). Acquisitive diversifiers that did not collapse at once from ingesting too many businesses often sustained high levels of EPS growth.

However, once it became apparent that a large proportion of this growth was an accounting mirage and that capital productivity was a better indicator of management's performance and a business's economic strength, the market value of many acquisitive companies plunged.

Many widely diversified companies have had low capital productivity in recent years. Exhibit 1 shows the performance of a sample originally selected by the Federal Trade Commission in 1969 as representative of companies pursuing strategies of diversification and not classifiable in standard industrial categories. Although the average return on equity of the sample was 20% higher than the average of the *Fortune* "500" in 1967, it was 18% below the *Fortune* average in 1975. Even the surge in profits in 1976 and 1977 and the impact of nonoperating, accounting profits in several corporations failed to bring the sample average up to the *Fortune* average. What is even more telling than the return on equity figures is that the sample's return on assets was 20% or more below the *Fortune* "500" average throughout the 10-year period.

Thus it is not surprising that acquisitive diversifiers have had low price-earnings ratios. On December 31, 1977, the average P/E of the sample, which includes many busy diversifiers, was 30% below that of the New York Stock Exchange stocks as a whole. This discount has changed little over several years. Even high return-on-equity performers like Northwest Industries, Teledyne, and Textron have P/Es well below the market's average.

Such low market values imply great uncertainty about the size and variability of future cash flows. And when they are uncertain about a company's cash flow, investors and stock analysts view them as less valuable than reliable and predictable earnings streams, so they are inclined to discount the company's future earnings heavily. The high discount rates of acquisitive diversifiers produce growth with less capital appreciation than that of nondiversifiers whose earnings streams appear to be more predictable. What will create value is growing cash flows with little uncertainty about their size or variability.

2. *Unrelated diversification offers shareholders a superior means of reducing their investment risk.* Unrelated diversification may be attractive from an investor's point of view—its use is frequently offered to justify or defend conglomerate mergers—but it is not a superior means of reducing investment risk. (By *investment risk* we mean the variability of returns over time, *returns* being defined as capital appreciation plus dividends paid to investors.)

According to contemporary financial theory, a security's risk and return can be decomposed into two elements: (1) what is specific to each company and called "unsystematic" because it can be diversified away and (2) what is "systematic" because it is common to all securities (the securities market) and hence nondiversifiable.[3] Since the unsystematic risk of any security can be eliminated through simple portfolio diversification, the investor does not need widely diversified companies like Litton Industries and Gulf & Western Industries to eliminate the risk for him.

Contemporary financial economists believe that prices of securities reflect the consensus of many knowledgeable buyers and sellers concerning a company's prospects. This consensus leads to an efficient capital market, where the investor finds it extremely difficult to consistently make risk-adjusted profits in excess of those the market realizes as a whole. Although it does not claim that the price of every security always accurately reflects its underlying (systematic) risk, the theory does suggest that when one views all securities over time, the "overvaluations" and "undervaluations" by the market balance out.[4]

Several researchers have extended this efficient capital market concept to the analysis of conglomerate mergers. Their studies suggest that unrelated corporate diversification has little to offer investors with respect to risk reduction over a diversified portfolio of comparable securities.

They also suggest that if diversified companies cannot increase returns or reduce risks more than comparable portfolios do, these companies can

Exhibit 1. Performance Data of 36 Diversified Manufacturers (1967, 1973, 1975, 1977)

	1967			1973		
Company	Year-End Total Assets (in millions of dollars)	Return on Assets	Return on Equity	Year-End Total Assets (in millions of dollars)	Return on Assets	Return on Equity
Avco	$1,618.5	3.4%	14.7%	$ 1,412.2	(1.3)%	(3.6)%
Bangor Punta	144.4	4.0	13.6	328.1	0.5	1.3
Bendix	833.4	5.5	11.3	1,427.0	4.1	11.1
Boise Cascade	865.2	3.3	11.3	1,585.4	9.0[a]	21.1[a]
City Investing	338.9	4.0	18.5	3,622.8	2.0	10.3
Colt Industries	197.1	6.1	16.7	266.0	4.0	10.0
FMC	931.8	6.6	13.6	680.5	5.7	11.6
GAF	473.5	4.1	6.9	627.0	4.6	8.7
General Tire	741.7	4.1	8.4	1,233.9	6.2	12.9
W.R. Grace	1,578.4	3.4	8.6	2,003.8	4.2	11.3
Gulf & Western	749.4	6.4	26.8	2,364.1	3.8	13.4
ICI	865.5	2.3	4.0	1,736.6	3.0	6.0
ITT	2,961.2	4.0	11.4	10,133.0	5.2	14.1
Walter Kidde	253.1	7.0	14.7	739.5	5.1	12.5
Koppers	326.5	4.3	7.7	520.3	5.7	11.2
LTV	845.1	4.8	18.3	1,829.1	2.7[a]	23.7[a]
Litton	945.0	7.4	19.0	2,116.2	2.0	5.2
Martin Marietta	527.2	7.0	11.9	1,074.0	5.3	11.4
3M	1,034.7	14.2	19.9	2,280.9	13.0	20.6
NL Industries	576.4	8.9	13.4	987.8	4.8	10.9
Northwest Industries	1,286.3	3.0	6.0	964.8	5.9[a]	13.4[a]
Norton Simon	463.8	3.3	6.7	1,120.0	7.0	15.5
Ogden	381.7	5.3	14.1	713.6	3.7	12.9
Rapid-American	337.8	4.8	14.9	1,755.5	1.7	13.7
SCM	451.4	5.6	19.7	552.7	3.3	7.8
Signal	1,090.3	4.5	9.1	1,378.1	4.2	8.7
Singer	1,049.2	4.8	11.1	1,897.0	5.0	11.9
Sperry Rand	1,095.2	5.9	11.9	1,840.6	4.9	10.6
Studebaker-Worthington	561.0	5.9	12.1	995.1	3.3	10.5
TRW	710.9	7.6	17.3	1,446.1	6.6	15.1
Teledyne	337.7	6.4	15.8	1,229.6	5.3	12.6
Tenneco	3,589.3	4.1	11.8	5,127.3	4.5	12.3
Textron	669.7	9.2	20.4	1,310.4	7.7	16.1
U.S. Industries	162.3	7.4	20.5	1,033.5	6.5	12.7
White Consolidated	277.3	3.8	14.7	597.4	5.9	15.1
Whittaker	118.0	7.4	29.3	589.4	(1.0)[a]	(3.3)[a]
Sample average		5.3	13.9		4.0	12.2
Fortune "500"		7.8	11.7		5.0	12.4

Criteria for the selection of companies in the Federal Trade Commission sample:
1. Each company in 1969 had total assets of $250 million or more.
2. Each company had 50% or more of its total sales derived from manufactured products.

1975			1977			
Year-End Total Assets (in millions of dollars)	Return on Assets	Return on Equity	Year-End Total Assets (in millions of dollars)	Return on Assets	Return on Equity	EPS Growth Rate (1967–1977)
$ 1,250.4	4.9%[a]	12.1%[a]	$ 4,125.6	2.8%[a]	18.6%[a]	3.6%
234.9	3.6	8.7	395.4	4.6	13.9	2.1
1,567.6	5.1	11.1	1,810.6	6.5	14.1	7.7
1,569.5	4.1	7.5	1,799.0	6.4	12.1	7.8
3,938.0	0.8	5.0	4,721.0	1.8	10.2	14.7
866.3	6.0	14.8	1,112.2	6.3	13.8	9.3
1,843.9	5.9	13.7	2,141.5	5.6	12.7	6.8
705.4	4.4	8.4	762.4	(6.2)	(14.2)	—
1,427.3	4.4	9.1	1,587.3	7.3	13.3	12.9
2,523.8	6.6	18.8	2,941.0	4.8	11.4	3.0
3,305.7	4.2	17.5	4,159.1	3.6	12.2	8.0
2,241.7	2.2	5.3	2,613.2	3.0	7.1	6.5
10,408.0	3.8	9.6	12,285.5	4.5	10.7	4.8
854.9	5.1	12.3	1,107.2	5.1	11.0	3.2
679.7	8.9	17.6	851.9	7.8	14.1	14.2
1,962.8	0.7	3.9	2,067.0	(1.9)[a]	(10.1)[a]	—
2,185.7	1.6	4.4	2,063.8	2.7	6.5	(4.1)
1,139.0	4.9	9.4	1,376.8	7.4	14.1	8.5
3,016.8	8.7	15.0	3,529.6	11.7	18.2	10.0
1,059.5	4.3	9.1	1,325.8	5.0	9.4	(1.2)
1,184.1	8.6	18.6	1,764.6	7.3	18.2	13.4
1,355.7	6.1	11.9	1,487.2	6.9	12.4	12.9
926.0	5.1	14.8	1,021.7	4.9	15.4	6.1
1,481.0	(0.6)	(4.9)	1,485.3	3.2[a]	22.5[a]	7.8
704.1	4.0	10.1	767.9	4.9	10.9	0.0
1,866.8	2.2	5.3	2,152.8	4.7	11.6	6.0
1,797.1	(25.2)	(96.0)	1,461.9	6.5[a]	20.6[a]	0.8
2,533.1	5.2	12.9	2,841.5	5.5	12.1	10.1
883.6	3.4	9.1	915.2	7.6	15.5	12.1
1,686.5	6.2	14.1	2,056.7	7.5	16.7	8.0
1,141.9	8.9	20.5	1,420.1	13.7	28.4	32.3
6,584.2	5.2	15.0	8,278.3	5.2	13.9	8.4
1,433.3	6.7	13.1	1,738.3	7.9	14.8	5.5
941.7	1.1	2.1	837.4	5.1	8.4	(3.8)
858.2	5.5	16.0	934.2	5.9	15.5	13.1
508.9	0.6	1.6	481.2	3.3	9.7	1.6
	3.6	9.5		5.3	12.4	
	5.7	11.6		6.5	13.3	

3. Each company had less than 50% of its total sales in any one industry and was engaged in three or more product lines.

[a]Extraordinary items included.

at best offer the investor only value comparable to that of a mutual fund. Indeed, widely diversified companies with systematic risks and returns equivalent to those of a mutual fund may actually be *less* attractive investment vehicles because of their higher management costs and their inability to move into or out of assets as quickly and as cheaply as mutual funds do.[5] For a specific case involving systematic risk, see the Appendix comparing Gulf & Western Industries with a portfolio having like assets.

3. *Adding countercyclical businesses to a company's portfolio leads to a stabilized earnings stream and a heightened valuation by the marketplace.* This misconception is an extension of the previous one. For decades, proponents of unrelated or conglomerate diversification have argued that when a company diversifies into an industry with a business cycle or a set of economic risks different from its own, it enhances the "safety" of its income stream. In essence, this sense of safety is a very simple form of the "risk pooling" concept underlying insurance.

In light of the poor performance of many diversified companies, it should be obvious that safety is difficult to attain. Because of the complex interactions of the United States and other nations' economies, finding genuinely countercyclical businesses is very hard. At the most, there are industry cycles that either lead or lag behind the general economy (e.g., housing and capital goods, respectively) or that are less cyclical than the general economy (e.g., consumer goods and tobacco products).

Even if diversifying companies can identify the countercyclical businesses, diversifiers find it difficult to construct balanced portfolios of businesses whose variable returns balance one another. Moreover, inasmuch as businesses grow at various rates, widely diversified companies face the continual challenge of rebalancing their business portfolios through very selective acquisitions.

Quite apart from this argument, the low stock market values of widely diversified companies during the past eight years indicate that the marketplace has heavily discounted the future cash returns to investors in companies consisting of purportedly countercyclical businesses. Although there are undoubtedly many reasons for this situation, it suggests that the market may be more interested in growth and the productivity of invested capital than in earnings stability per se. In addition, investors have little incentive to bid up the prices of diversified companies because an investor can obtain the benefits of stabilizing an income stream through simple portfolio diversification.

4. *Related diversification is always safer than unrelated diversification.* This misconception rests on the notion of corporate executives that they reduce their operating risks when they stick to buying businesses they think they understand. They want to limit their diversification to businesses with similar marketing and distribution characteristics, similar production technologies, or similar science-based R&D efforts.

Although this presumption often has merit, making related acquisitions does not guarantee results superior to those stemming from unrelated diversification. For example, Xerox's entry into data processing via its acquisition of Scientific Data Systems, which Xerox justified on the ground of technological, marketing, and manufacturing compatibility, led to a great drain on earnings for years. The management of Singer decided to take advantage of the company's competence in electromechanical manufacturing as the basis for its diversification program. The result was dramatic failure, leading to a $500 million write-off of assets.

A close reading of the Xerox and Singer cases suggests that successful related diversification depends on both the quality of the acquired business and the organizational integration required to achieve the possible benefits of companies exchanging their skills and resources. Such exchange has been called *synergy*.

Even more important, the perceived relatedness must be real, and the merger must give the partners a competitive advantage. Unless these conditions are met, related diversification cannot be justified as superior or even comparable to unrelated diversification as a means of reducing operating risks or increasing earnings.

5. *A strong management team at the acquired company ensures realization of the potential benefits of diversification.* Many companies try to limit their pool of acquisition candidates to well-managed companies. This policy is rarely the necessary condition for gaining the potential benefits of diversification.

As we shall stress later in this article, the potential benefits of related diversification stem from augmenting the effective use of the surviving company's core skills and resources. Usually such improvement requires an exchange of core skills and resources among the partners. The benefits of unrelated diversification are rooted in two conditions: (1) increased efficiency in cash management and in allocation of investment capital; and (2) the capability to call on profitable, low-growth businesses to provide the cash flow for high-growth businesses that require significant infusions of cash.

Whether pursuing related or unrelated diversification, it is often the acquiring company's management skills and resources—not those of the acquired company—that are critical to achieving the potential benefits of diversification. Indeed, if the acquired company is well managed and priced accordingly by the capital market, the acquirer must exploit the potential synergies with the acquiree to make the transaction economically justifiable.

6. *The diversified company is uniquely qualified to improve the performance of acquired businesses.* During the height of the merger and acquisition activity of the 1960s, executives of conglomerates often argued that they could improve the profitability of acquired companies by "modernizing" administrative practices and exerting more operating discipline than that demanded by the marketplace.

Consider the testimony of Harold S. Geneen, then chairman and president of International Telephone & Telegraph Corporation, at a government hearing concerning how ITT provided "constructive bases for merger."

"We can afford to price fairly," Geneen said, "and to exchange our own equity stocks with the shareholders of an incoming company. We can improve operating efficiencies and profits sufficiently to make this valuation worthwhile to both sets of shareholders." In a document outlining ITT's acquisition philosophy and submitted to the hearing, Geneen wrote that from 1960 to 1965 the company had "developed the ability through management skills, routines, and techniques to set and progressively meet higher competitive standards and achieve them in practically every line and product that we have undertaken."[6]

The claims that Geneen and many other successful diversifiers have invoked are not benefits of diversification per se but simply the benefits of that nebulous factor, "good management." Single-business companies pursuing vertical integration or horizontal expansion through acquisition can achieve identical results. To gain the benefits Geneen claimed, a company needs only to allow managers with the requisite skills to implement their desired improvements in the organization.

Rarely, it may be argued, does an organization willingly take steps that could alter its traditional administrative and managerial practices. Under these circumstances, change will occur only when forced from the outside, and diversifying companies often represent such a force. Nevertheless, the benefits achieved are not, strictly speaking, benefits of diversification.

7. *Great deals are made by professional "deal makers."* The most potentially dangerous misconception on our list is the one that credits the imaginative work of investment bankers and other brokers with the success of a diversifying acquisition. The investment banker's role is to provide attractive ideas, but it is the company's role to select the ideas that have the greatest strategic and economic value.

This role involves developing diversification objectives and acquisition guidelines that fit a carefully prepared concept of the corporation. It also involves the company's ability to recognize and exploit the potential for creating value through diversifying acquisitions. Every experienced corporate diversifier has learned, often painfully, that he must live with an acquisition long after it has ceased being a "great deal."

Ways to Create Value

A company following a diversification strategy can create value for its shareholders only when the combination of the skills and resources of the two businesses satisfies at least one of the following conditions:

☐ An income stream greater than what could be realized from a portfolio investment in the two companies.

☐ A reduction in the variability of the income stream greater than what could be realized from a portfolio investment in the two businesses—that is, reduced systematic risk.

Included in both conditions is explicit comparison of corporate diversification on the shareholder's behalf with independent portfolio diversification on the investor's part. This comparison deserves comment.

Most benefits derived from reducing unsystematic corporate risk through diversification are, of course, equally available to the individual investor. Diversified companies can achieve trade-offs between total risk and return that are superior to the trade-offs available to single-business companies. Diversified companies cannot create value for their stockholders merely by diversifying away unsystematic risk.

Inasmuch as investors can diversify away unsystematic risk themselves, in efficient capital markets unsystematic risk is irrelevant in the equity valuation process. A diversifying company can create value for its shareholders only when its risk-return trade-offs include benefits unavailable through simple portfolio diversification.

There are seven principal ways in which acquisition-minded companies can obtain returns greater than those obtainable from simple portfolio diversification. The first four are particularly relevant to related diversification, whereas the last three are more relevant to unrelated diversification.

1. *A diversifying acquisition can raise the productivity of capital when the particular skills and one merger partner's knowledge of the industry are applied to the competitive problems and opportunities facing the other partner.* When the reinforcement of skills and resources critical to the success of a business within the combined company leads to higher profitability, value is created for its shareholders. This reinforcement is the realization of synergy.

The acquisition by Heublein, Inc. of United Vintners in 1968 is a good case in point. Heublein's strategy during the 1960s was to obtain high margins in marketing liquor and specialty food products through intensive, innovative advertising. At the time, Heublein stood out in this respect because the industry was production- and distribution-oriented. The company's liquor products division accounted for more than 80% of 1965 sales. Its principal product was the premium-priced Smirnoff vodka, the fourth largest and fastest growing liquor brand in the United States.

The 1968 acquisition of United Vintners, the marketing arm of a large grape growers' cooperative that owned two of California's best-known wine brands, gave Heublein the opportunity to raise its investment in an industry where it had some experience (it was the U.S. distributor for Lancers wine) and to extend the application of its proven skills in promoting specialty products. By identifying and then exploiting an emerging consumer preference for lighter-bodied, often slightly flavored products, Heublein helped

United Vintners launch two new products—Cold Duck (a champagne-sparkling burgundy combination) and Bali Hai (a fruit-flavored wine).

By the end of 1969, one year after its acquisition of United Vintners, Heublein had increased sales by over 2.5 million cases and augmented the subsidiary's profitability. Heublein's marketing strategy was so successful that during the 1960s and early 1970s its return on equity averaged over 30% and the marketplace valued Heublein at over 35 times its earnings. Heublein discovered in its diversification efforts, however, that its strategy of aggressive advertising was not the key success factor in either brewing (Hamm's beer) or fast foods (Kentucky Fried Chicken), and its market valuation suffered accordingly. By 1977, Heublein had seen its P/E fall to 10 and its stock price to one-third of its previous high.

2. *Investments in markets closely related to current fields of operation can reduce long-run average costs.* A reduction in average costs can accrue from scale effects, rationalization of production and other managerial efforts, and technological innovation. For example, a marketing department's budget as a percent of sales will decline if existing resources can be used to market new or related products. Similarly, a large company like Procter & Gamble can expect its per-unit distribution costs to decline when it augments the use of its existing distribution system to move products to the marketplace. This notion has been the basis of many acquisitions made by consumer products companies.

3. *Business expansion in an area of competence can lead to the generation of a "critical mass" of resources necessary to outperform the competition.* In many industries, companies have to achieve a certain size, or critical mass, before they can compete effectively with their competitors.

For example, the principal way many small laboratory instrumentation companies hope to offer sustained competition against such entrenched companies as Hewlett-Packard, Tektronix, Beckman Instruments, and Technicon is to attain a size giving them sufficient cash flow to underwrite competitive research and development programs. One way to reach this size is to make closely related diversifying acquisitions.

4. *Diversification into related product markets can enable a company to reduce systematic risks.* Many of the possibilities for reducing risk through diversification are implicit in the previous three ways to increase returns because risk and return are closely related measurements. However, diversifying by acquiring a company in a related product market can enable a company to reduce its technological, production, or marketing risks. If these reduced business risks can be translated into a less variable income stream for the company, value is created.

Although there is no evidence that General Motors's strategy was developed with this notion in mind, an important result of GM's diversification within the motor vehicle industry has been its ability to easily absorb changes in demand for any one automotive product. GM's extensive related-product line reduces the company's marketing risk and enables GM's managers to concentrate on production efficiencies. As a result, GM's income stream tends to be less volatile than those of its competitors and of portfolios of discrete investments in unassociated, although automotive-related, companies.

5. *The diversified company can route cash from units operating with a surplus to units operating with a deficit and can thereby reduce the need of individual businesses to purchase working capital funds from outside sources.* Through centralizing cash balances, corporate headquarters can act as the banker for its operating subsidiaries and thus can balance the cyclical working capital requirements of its divisions as the economy progresses through a business cycle or as its divisions experience seasonal fluctuations. This type of working capital management is, of course, an operating benefit completely separate from the recycling of cash on an investment basis.

6. *Managers of a diversified company can direct its currently high net cash flow businesses to transfer investment funds to the businesses in which net cash flow is zero or negative but in which management expects positive cash flow to develop. The aim is to improve the long-run profitability of the corporation.* This potential benefit is a by-product of the U.S. tax code, which imposes double taxation of dividends—once via corporate profits taxes and once via personal income taxes. By reinvesting its surplus cash flow, the company defers taxes that stockholders otherwise would have to pay on the company's dividends.

In November 1975, Genstar, Ltd. of Canada justified this way of creating value in a submission to the Royal Commission on Corporate Concentration. There Genstar argued that the well-managed, widely diversified company can call on its low-growth businesses to maximize net cash flow and profits in order to enable it to reallocate funds to the high-growth businesses needing investment. By so doing, the company will eventually reap benefits via a higher ROI and the public will benefit via lower costs and, presumably, via lower prices.

As Exhibit 2 shows, two of Genstar's major business areas—cement as well as chemicals and fertilizers—used far less cash (for working capital and reinvestment) in 1971–1974 than they generated (*cash generated* being defined as net income after taxes plus depreciation and deferred taxes). Genstar recycled the excess cash flow into its housing and land development, construction, and marine activities. So Genstar was able not only to employ its assets more productively than before, but also to reap economic benefits beyond those possible from a comparable securities portfolio.

Genstar's argument for cross-subsidization has an important extension. Diversified companies have access to information that is often unavailable

Exhibit 2. Relationship between Cash Used and Cash Generated by Business Areas of Genstar, 1971–1974

Area	Cash Use Ratio[a]
Building supplies	1.01
Cement	.31
Housing and land development	1.72
Construction	1.67
Chemicals and fertilizers	.38
Marine activities	1.87
Imports and exports	.46
Investments	.52
Total for the company	1.02

[a]The cash use ratio is cash used divided by cash generated. A business area's cash use ratio is determined by comparing its cash used with its cash generated. A cash use ratio higher than 1 indicates that the business area is a net cash user, while a ratio of less than 1 indicates a net cash generator. Cash generated is defined as net income after tax plus depreciation and deferred tax.

to the investment community. This information is the internally generated market data about each industry in which it operates, data that include information about the competitive position and potential of each company in the industry.

With this inside information, diversified enterprises can enjoy a significantly better position in assessing the investment merits of particular projects and entire industries than individual investors can. Such access enables the companies to choose the most attractive projects and thereby to allocate capital among "their" industries more efficiently than the capital markets can.

7. *Through risk pooling, the diversified company can lower its cost of debt and leverage itself more than its nondiversified equivalent. The company's total cost of capital thereby goes down and provides stockholders with returns in excess of those available from a comparable portfolio of securities.* As the number of businesses in the portfolio of an unrelated diversifier grows and the overall variability of its operating income or cash flow declines, its standing as a credit risk should rise. Because the company pools its own divisions' risks and supports any component threatened with bankruptcy, theoretically (at least) the company should have a somewhat lower cost of debt than that of companies unable to pool their risks. More importantly, the reduced variability of the diversified company's cash flow improves its ability to borrow.

This superior financial leverage enables the corporation's shareholders to shift some risk to government and thereby reduce the company's total cost of capital. (Since interest, in contrast to dividends, is tax deductible, the government shoulders part of the cost of debt capitalization in a business venture.) These benefits become significant, however, only when the enterprise aggressively manages its financial risks by employing a high debt-equity ratio or by operating several very risky, unrelated projects in its portfolio of businesses.

Although this type of company can enjoy a lower cost of capital than a less diversified company of comparable size, it can also have a higher cost of *equity* capital than the other type. This possibility stems from the fact that part of the financial risk of debt capitalization is borne by the equity owners. In addition, investors' perceptions of risk are not solely conditioned by the degree of diversification in corporate assets. Indeed, the professional investor may be unwilling to lower the rate of return on equity capital just because a company has acquired a well-balanced or purportedly countercyclical collection of businesses.

The risks and opportunities the investors perceive for a company greatly depend on the amount and clarity of information that they can effectively process. As a company becomes more diversified, its business can become less clearly defined and its investors' uncertainty about its risks and opportunities can rise. The greater this uncertainty, of course, the higher the risk premium the equity investor demands and the higher the company's cost of equity capital becomes.

Diversification Strategies

An unrelated-business diversifier is a company pursuing growth in product markets where the main success factors are unrelated to each other. Such a company, whether a conglomerate or simply a holding company, expects little or no transfer of functional skills among its various businesses. In contrast, a related-business diversifier uses its skills in a specific functional activity or product market as a basis for branching out.

The most significant benefits to the stockholder occur in related diversification when the special skills and industry knowledge of one merger partner apply to the competitive problems and opportunities facing the other. Shareholders' benefits from unrelated or conglomerate diversification can occur where more efficient capital and asset management leads to a better return for investors than that available from a diversified portfolio of securities of comparable systematic risk. Exhibit 3 summarizes the benefits that are attainable from the two types of diversification.

Unfortunately, the benefits that offer the greatest potential are usually the ones least likely to be implemented. Of the synergies usually identified to justify an acquisition, financial synergies are often unnoted, whereas op-

Exhibit 3. Potential Benefits of Diversification

	Related-Business Diversification	Unrelated-Business Diversification
Product-market orientation	Diversification into business with similar marketing and distribution characteristics, similar production technologies, or similar science-based research activities.	Diversification into product markets with key success variables unrelated to the key success variables of the acquirer's principal business.
Transferable resources	Operating and/or functional skills; excess capacity in distribution systems, production facilities, or research operations.	General management skills; surplus financial resources.
Nature of potential benefits	Increased productivity of corporate resources through operating synergy, improved competitive position accruing from greater size of business and lower long-run average costs, all leading to reduction in the variability of the income stream and/or a larger income stream than that available from simple portfolio diversification.	Efficient cash management and allocation of investment capital, reduced cost of debt capital, and growth in profits through cross-subsidization, all leading to a larger income stream than that available from simple portfolio diversification; unlikely reduction of systematic (market-related) risk.
Relative ease of achieving potential benefits	Difficult because of organizational problems associated with integrating formerly self-sufficient companies into the acquiring company.	Easy-to-achieve capital efficiencies and benefits from cross-subsidization.

erating synergies are widely trumpeted. Yet our experience has been that the benefits most commonly achieved are those in the financial area.

It is not hard to understand why. Most managers would agree that the greatest impediment to change is the inflexibility of the organization. The realization of operating benefits accompanying diversification usually requires significant changes in the company's format and administrative behavior. These changes are usually slow to come, and so are the accompanying benefits.

Nevertheless, diversification does offer potentially significant benefits to the corporation and its shareholders. When a company has the ability to export or import surplus skills or resources useful in its competitive environment, related diversification is an attractive strategic option. When a company possesses the skills and resources to analyze and manage the strategies of widely different businesses, unrelated diversification can be the best strategic option. Finally, when a diversifying company has both of these abilities, choosing a workable strategy will depend on the personal skills and inclinations of its top managers.

Notes

1. Bureau of Economics, Federal Trade Commission, *Statistical Report on Mergers and Acquisitions* (Washington, D.C., November 1976), p. 93.

2. Richard P. Rumelt first articulated this useful definition in his *Strategy, Structure, and Economic Performance* (Boston, Division of Research, Harvard Business School, 1974).

3. William F. Sharpe, *Portfolio Theory and Capital Markets* (New York, McGraw-Hill, 1970), p. 96.

4. For summaries of empirical evidence supporting the efficient market theory, see Eugene F. Fama, "Efficient Capital Markets: A Review of Theory and Empirical Work," *Journal of Finance*, May 1970, p. 383; and Michael C. Jensen, "Capital Markets: Theory and Evidence," *Bell Journal of Economics and Management Science*, Autumn 1972, p. 35.

5. See Keith V. Smith and John C. Shreiner, "A Portfolio Analysis of Conglomerate Diversification," *Journal of Finance*, June 1969, p. 413; J. Fred Weston and Surenda K. Mansinghka, "Tests of Efficiency Performance of Conglomerate Firms," *Journal of Finance*, September 1971, p. 919; and R. Hal Mason and Maurice B. Gondzwaard, "Performance of Conglomerate Firms: A Portfolio Approach," *Journal of Finance*, March 1976, p. 39.

6. Hearings before the Antitrust Subcommittee of the Committee of the Judiciary, U.S. House of Representatives, November 20, 1969.

7. A more thorough presentation of this method of making a comparative risk analysis is available from the authors at Harvard Business School, Soldiers Field, Boston, Mass. 02163.

Appendix. Analysis of Systematic Risk

Since portfolio theory tells us that reducing systematic risk is impossible through portfolio diversification, let us analyze a portfolio of assets against a diversified company's assets similar in size and allocation. This risk analysis requires three kinds of information: (1) the investment composition, by industry, of the diversified company; (2) the size of the investment the company has made in each industry; and (3) the systematic risk of each of those industries.

Summing the industries' systematic risks, weighted by their relative size in the portfolio, results in a measure of the portfolio's systematic risk. The last step before comparing the portfolio's systematic risk with the diversified company's systematic risk is to adjust for differences in financial risk. Once this is done, the analyst can determine, within statistical limits, whether the diversifying corporation has reduced its systematic risk.

The results of a risk analysis of Gulf & Western Industries, a high return-on-equity performer for over a decade, are presented in Table A. An analysis of a comparable portfolio for G&W is given in Table B. Both tables reflect a five-year period ending in July 1975. The businesses of G&W's eight divisions overlap very little. Grouping these divisions with Gulf & Western's investment portfolio produces a well-diversified comparable portfolio.

As Table A indicates, Gulf & Western's systematic risk, adjusted for financial leverage, differs insignificantly from that of a comparable portfolio. All three systematic risk measurements are within one standard deviation of each other. Whatever benefits Gulf & Western provides its shareholders, reduction of investment risk apparently is not one of them.[7]

Table A. Portfolio Comparison

	Systematic Risk (beta)	Standard Deviation
Gulf & Western's portfolio statistics		
Leverage = .37[a]		
Systematic risk (according to Merrill Lynch, Pierce, Fenner & Smith)	1.15	.20
Systematic risk (according to Value Line)	1.35	.20
Comparison portfolio's statistics		
Weighted average leverage = .30[b]		
Weighted average systematic risk[b]	1.15	
Systematic risk when leverage = .37	1.26	.15

[a]Market value of debt divided by the sum of the market values of debt and equity.

[b]Taken from Table B.

Table B. Systematic Risk Analysis of a Portfolio Similar to That of Gulf & Western Industries (dollars in millions)

Group	Standard & Poor's Industry Category	Industry Average: Sales/ Assets	Industry Average: Debt/ Assets	G&W's 1974 Sales	Assets of a Company Comparable to G&W Group	Debt of a Company Comparable to G&W Group	Comparable Company's Assets as Percentage of Portfolio's Assets	Industry's Systematic Risk	Weighted Systematic Risk of Comparable Companies in Portfolio
Food and agricultural products	Sugar	2.1	.45	$ 175	$ 85	$ 37	4.3%	.6	.026
Natural resources	Lead and zinc	1.2	.1	178	150	15	7.5	.72	.054
Paper and building products	Paper	2.1	.4	405	190	75	9.5	.9	.085
Financial services	Small loan finance	.6	.15	494	446	70	22.4	1.35	.302
Leisure time	Movies	1.8	.3	298	165	50	8.3	1.65	.137
Automotive replacement and parts	Automotive replacement and parts	3.0	.1	225	75	7	3.8	1.7	.063

Table B. *(Continued)*

Group	Standard & Poor's Industry Category	Industry Average: Sales/ Assets	Industry Average: Debt/ Assets	G&W's 1974 Sales	Assets of a Company Comparable to G&W Group	Debt of a Company Comparable to G&W Group	Comparable Company's Assets as Percentage of Portfolio's Assets	Industry's Systematic Risk	Weighted Systematic Risk of Comparable Companies in Portfolio
Consumer products	Tobacco	2.1	.3	212	100	30	5.0	.85	.042
Manufacturing	Automotive OEM	2.3	.3	327	140	45	7.0	1.25	.104
	Capital goods: machinery	1.8	.25	285	160	40	8.0	1.3	.068
	Electrical	2.0	.2	195	100	20	5.0	1.3	.088
Operating group's total				$2,794	$1,611	$389	80.8%		.969
Intangibles					100		5.0	.969[a]	.048
Investments					284	211	14.2	.95	.135
Total					$1,995[b]	$600	100.0%		1.15

[a]Intangibles arise from an excess investment over the equity acquired. Its risk matches that of the underlying assets (operating portfolio).

[b]G&W's 1974 annual report listed this investment as $1,983 million (within 1% of the comparison portfolio).

23
Strategic Analysis for More Profitable Acquisitions

ALFRED RAPPAPORT

As more and more corporations see acquisitions and mergers as an important part of their growth strategy, the acquisitions market has become intensely competitive, and buyers are paying a substantial premium for target companies. This author describes a framework for acquisitions analysis that evaluates both the buying and the selling company and helps the buyer decide, among other things, the maximum price the buyer should pay for a particular company as well as the best way to finance the acquisition.

Less than a decade after the frantic merger activity of the late 1960s, we are again in the midst of a major wave of corporate acquisitions. In contrast to the 1960s, when acquirers were mainly freewheeling conglomerates, the merger movement in the 1970s includes such long-established giants of U.S. industry as General Electric, Gulf Oil, and Kennecott Copper. Because of the decline in the value of the dollar and the greater political stability of the United States, foreign companies also have become increasingly active buyers of U.S. companies during the past few years.

Most acquisitions are accomplished with cash today, rather than with packages of securities as was common in the 1960s. Finally, the current merger movement involves the frequent use of tender offers that often lead to contested bids and to the payment of substantial premiums above the premerger market value of the target company. In 1978, cash tender offer premiums averaged more than 70% above premerger market values.

The popular explanation for the recent merger rage is that the market is "undervaluing" many solid companies, thus making it substantially cheaper to buy rather than to build. Couple this belief with the fact that many corporations are enjoying relatively strong cash positions and the widely held view that government regulation and increased uncertainty about the economy make internal growth strategies relatively unattractive, and we see why mergers and acquisitions have become an increasingly important part of corporate growth strategy.

Despite all of the foregoing rationale, more than a few of the recent acquisitions will fail to create value for the acquirer's shareholders. After all, shareholder value depends not on premerger market valuation of the target company but on the actual acquisition price the acquiring company pays compared with the selling company's cash flow contribution to the combined company.

Only a limited supply of acquisition candidates is available at the price that enables the acquirer to earn an acceptable return on investment. A well-conceived financial evaluation program that minimizes the risk of buying an economically unattractive company or paying too much for an attractive one is particularly important in today's seller's market. The dramatic increase in premiums that must be paid by a company bidding successfully calls for more careful analysis by buyers than ever before.

Because of the competitive nature of the acquisition market, companies not only need to respond wisely, but often must respond quickly as well. The growing independence of corporate boards and their demand for better information to support strategic decisions such as acquisitions have raised the general standard for acquisition analysis. Finally, sound analysis convincingly communicated can yield substantial benefits in negotiating with the target company's management or, in the case of tender offers, its stockholders.

Malcolm S. Salter and Wolf A. Weinhold outlined seven principal ways in which companies can create value for their shareholders via acquisition in Article 22. In my article, I will show how management can estimate how much value a prospective acquisition will in fact create. In brief, I will present a comprehensive framework for acquisition analysis based on contemporary financial theory—an approach that has been profitably employed in practice. The analysis provides management and the board of the acquiring company with information both to make a decision on the candidate and to formulate an effective negotiating strategy for the acquisition.

Steps in the Analysis

The process of analyzing acquisitions falls broadly into three stages: planning, search and screen, and financial evaluation.

The acquisition planning process begins with a review of corporate objectives and product-market strategies for various strategic business units. The acquiring company should define its potential directions for corporate growth and diversification in terms of corporate strengths and weaknesses and an assessment of the company's social, economic, political, and technological environment. This analysis produces a set of acquisition objectives and criteria.

Specified criteria often include statements about industry parameters, such as projected market growth rate, degree of regulation, ease of entry, and capital versus labor intensity. Company criteria for quality of management, share of market, profitability, size, and capital structure also commonly appear in acquisition criteria lists.

The search and screen process is a systematic approach to compiling a list of good acquisition prospects. The search focuses on how and where to look for candidates, and the screening process selects a few of the best candidates from literally thousands of possibilities according to objectives and criteria developed in the planning phase.

Finally comes the financial evaluation process, which is the focus of this article. A good analysis should enable management to answer such questions as:

- ☐ What is the maximum price that should be paid for the target company?
- ☐ What are the principal areas of risk?
- ☐ What are the earnings, cash flow, and balance sheet implications of the acquisition?
- ☐ What is the best way of financing the acquisition?

Corporate Self-Evaluation

The financial evaluation process involves both a self-evaluation by the acquiring company and the evaluation of the candidate for acquisition. Although it is possible to conduct an evaluation of the target company without an in-depth self-evaluation first, in general this is the most advantageous approach.[1] The scope and detail of corporate self-evaluation will necessarily vary according to the needs of each company.

Two fundamental questions posed by a self-evaluation are: (1) How much is my company worth? (2) How would its value be affected by each of several scenarios? The first question involves generating a "most likely" estimate of the company's value based on management's detailed assessment of its objectives, strategies, and plans. The second question calls for an assessment of value based on the range of plausible scenarios that enable management to test the joint effect of hypothesized combinations of product-market strategies and environmental forces.

Corporate self-evaluation viewed as an economic assessment of the value created for shareholders by various strategic planning options promises potential benefits for all companies. In the context of the acquisition market, self-evaluation takes on special significance.

First, although a company might view itself as an acquirer, few companies are totally exempt from a possible takeover. During 1978 alone, 80 acquisitions exceeding $100 million were announced. The recent roster of acquired companies includes such names as Anaconda, Utah International, Babcock & Wilcox, Seven Up, Pet, Carborundum, and Del Monte. Self-evaluation provides management and the board with a continuing basis for responding to tender offers or acquisition inquiries responsibly and quickly. Second, the self-evaluation process might well call attention to strategic divestment opportunities. Finally, self-evaluation provides acquisition-minded companies a basis for assessing the comparative advantages of a cash versus an exchange-of-shares offer.

Acquiring companies commonly value the purchase price for an acquisition at the market value of the shares exchanged. This practice is not economically sound and could be misleading and costly to the acquiring company. A well-conceived analysis for an exchange-of-shares acquisition requires sound valuations of *both* buying and selling companies. If the acquirer's management believes the market is undervaluing its shares, then valuing the purchase price at market might well induce the company to overpay for the acquisition or to earn less than the minimum acceptable rate of return.

Conversely, if management believes the market is overvaluing its shares, then valuing the purchase price at market obscures the opportunity of offering the seller's shareholders additional shares while still achieving the minimum acceptable return.

Valuation of Acquisitions

Recently *Business Week* reported that as many as half of the major acquisition-minded companies are relying extensively on the discounted cash flow (DCF) technique to analyze acquisitions.[2] Although mergers and acquisitions involve a considerably more complex set of managerial problems than the purchase of an ordinary asset such as a machine or a plant, the economic substance of these transactions is the same. In each case, there is a current outlay made in anticipation of a stream of future cash flows.

Thus the DCF criterion applies not only to internal-growth investments, such as additions to existing capacity, but equally to external-growth investments, such as acquisitions. An essential feature of the DCF technique is that it explicitly takes into account that a dollar of cash received today is worth more than a dollar received a year from now, because today's dollar can be invested to earn a return during the intervening time.

To establish the maximum acceptable acquisition price under the DCF approach, estimates are needed for (1) the incremental cash flows expected to be generated because of the acquisition and (2) the cost of capital—that is, the minimum acceptable rate of return required by the market for new investments by the company.

In projecting the cash flow stream of a prospective acquisition, what should be taken into account is the cash flow contribution the candidate is expected to make to the acquiring company. The results of this projection may well differ from a projection of the candidate's cash flow as an independent company. This is so because the acquirer may be able to achieve operating economies not available to the selling company alone. Furthermore, acquisitions generally provide new postacquisition investment opportunities whose initial outlays and subsequent benefits also need to be incorporated in the cash flow schedule. Cash flow is defined as

(earnings before interest and taxes [EBIT]) × (1-income tax rate) + depreciation and other noncash charges − capital expenditures − cash required for increase in net working capital

In developing the cash flow schedule, two additional issues need to be considered: (1) What is the basis for setting the horizon date—that is, the date beyond which the cash flows associated with the acquisition are not specifically projected? (2) How is the residual value of the acquisition established at the horizon date?

A common practice is to forecast cash flows period by period until the level of uncertainty makes management too "uncomfortable" to go any farther. Although practice varies with industry setting, management policy, and the special circumstances of the acquisition, 5 or 10 years appear to be an arbitrarily set forecasting duration used in many situations. A better approach suggests that the forecast duration for cash flows should continue only as long as the expected rate of return on incremental investment required to support forecasted sales growth exceeds the cost-of-capital rate.

If for subsequent periods one assumes that the company's return on incremental investment equals the cost-of-capital rate, then the market would be indifferent whether management invests earnings in expansion projects or pays cash dividends that shareholders can in turn invest in identically risky opportunities yielding an identical rate of return. In other words, the value of the company is unaffected by growth when the company is investing in projects earning at the cost of capital or at the minimum acceptable risk-adjusted rate of return required by the market.

Thus, for purposes of simplification, we can assume a 100% payout of earnings after the horizon date or, equivalently, a zero growth rate without affecting the valuation of the company. (An implied assumption of this model is that the depreciation tax shield can be invested to maintain the company's productive capacity.) The residual value is then the present value of the resulting cash flow perpetuity beginning one year after the horizon date. Of course, if after the horizon date the return on investment is expected to decline below the cost-of-capital rate, this factor can be incorporated in the calculation.

When the acquisition candidate's risk is judged to be the same as the acquirer's overall risk, the appropriate rate for discounting the candidate's cash flow stream is the acquirer's cost of capital. The cost of capital or the minimum acceptable rate of return on new investments is based on the rate investors can expect to earn by investing in alternative, identically risky securities.

The cost of capital is calculated as the weighted average of the costs of debt and equity capital. For example, suppose a company's aftertax cost of debt is 5% and it estimates its cost of equity to be 15%. Furthermore, it plans to raise future capital in the following proportions: 20% by way of debt and 80% by equity. Exhibit 1 shows how to compute the company's average cost.

It is important to emphasize that the acquiring company's use of its own cost of capital to discount the target's projected cash flows is appropriate only when it can be safely assumed that the acquisition will not affect the riskiness of the acquirer. The specific riskiness of each prospective candidate should be taken into account in setting the discount rate, with higher rates used for more risky investments.

If a single discount rate is used for all acquisitions, then those with the highest risk will seem most attractive. Because the weighted average risk of its component segments determines the company's cost of capital, these high-risk acquisitions will increase a company's cost of capital and thereby decrease the value of its stock.

Case of Alcar Corporation

As an illustration of the recommended approach to acquisition analysis, consider the case of Alcar Corporation's interest in acquiring Rano Products. Alcar is a leading manufacturer and distributor in the industrial packaging and materials handling market. Sales in 1978 totaled $600 million. Alcar's acquisition strategy is geared toward buying companies with either similar marketing and distribution characteristics, similar production technologies, or a similar research and development orientation. Rano Products, a $50 million sales organization with an impressive new-product development record in industrial packaging, fits Alcar's general acquisition criteria particularly well. Premerger financial statements for Alcar and Rano are shown in Exhibit 2.

Exhibit 1. One Company's Average Cost of Capital

	Weight	Cost	Weighted Cost
Debt	.20	.05	.01
Equity	.80	.15	.12
Average cost of capital			.13

Exhibit 2. Premerger Financial Statements for Alcar and Rano (in millions of dollars)

	Alcar	Rano
Statement of income (year ended December 31)		
Sales	$600.00	$50.00
Operating expenses	522.00	42.50
EBIT	78.00	7.50
Interest on debt	4.50	.40
Earnings before taxes	73.50	7.10
Income taxes	36.00	3.55
Net income	$37.50	$ 3.55
Number of common shares outstanding (in millions)	10.00	1.11
Earnings per share	$3.75	$3.20
Dividends per share	1.30	.64
Statement of financial position (at year-end)		
Net working capital	$180.00	$7.50
Temporary investments	25.00	1.00
Other assets	2.00	1.60
Fixed assets	216.00	20.00
Less accumulated depreciation	(95.00)	(8.00)
Total	$328.00	$22.10
Interest-bearing debt	$56.00	$5.10
Shareholders' equity	272.00	17.00
Total	$328.00	$22.10

Acquisition for Cash

The interactive computer model for corporate planning and acquisition analysis used in the Alcar evaluation to follow generates a comprehensive analysis for acquisitions financed by cash, stock, or any combination of cash, debt, preferred stock, and common stock. In this article, the analysis will concern only the cash and exchange-of-shares cases. In the cash acquisition case, the analysis follows six essential steps:

- ☐ Develop estimates needed to project Rano's cash flow contribution for various growth and profitability scenarios.

☐ Estimate the minimum acceptable rate of return for acquisition of Rano.

☐ Compute the maximum acceptable cash price to be paid for Rano under various scenarios and minimum acceptable rates of return.

☐ Compute the rate of return that Alcar will earn for a range of price offers and for various growth and profitability scenarios.

☐ Analyze the feasibility of a cash purchase in light of Alcar's current liquidity and target debt-to-equity ratio.

☐ Evaluate the impact of the acquisition on the earnings per share and capital structure of Alcar.

Step 1. Cash Flow Projections. The cash flow formula presented earlier may be restated in equivalent form as

$$CF_t = S_{t-1}\,(1+g_t)\,(p_t)\,(1-T_t) \;-\; (S_t - S_{t-1})\,(f_t + w_t)$$

where:

CF = cash flow.
S = sales.
g = annual growth rate in sales.
p = EBIT as a percentage of sales.
T = income tax rate.
f = capital investment required (i.e., total capital investment net of replacement of existing capacity estimated by depreciation) per dollar of sales increase.
w = cash required for net working capital per dollar of sales increase.

Once estimates are provided for five variables, g, p, T, f, and w, it is possible to project cash flow.

Exhibit 3 shows Alcar management's "most likely" estimates for Rano's operations, assuming Alcar control; Exhibit 4 shows a complete projected 10-year cash flow statement for Rano.

Before developing additional scenarios for Rano, I should make some brief comments on how to estimate some of the cash flow variables. The income tax rate is the effective cash rate rather than a rate based on the accountant's income tax expense, which often includes a portion that is deferred. For some companies, a direct projection of capital investment requirements per dollar of sales increase will prove a difficult task.

To gain an estimate of the recent value of this coefficient, simply take the sum of all capital investments less depreciation over the past 5 or 10 years and divide this total by the sales increase from the beginning to the end of the period. With this approach, the resulting coefficient not only represents the capital investment historically required per dollar of sales increase, but also impounds any cost increases for replacement of existing capacity.

Exhibit 3. Most Likely Estimates for Rano's Operations under Alcar Control

	Years		
	1–5	6–7	8–10
Sales growth rate (g)	.15	.12	.12
EBIT as a percentage of sales (p)	.18	.15	.12
Income tax rate (T)	.46	.46	.46
Capital investment per dollar of sales increase (f)	.20	.20	.20
Working capital per dollar of sales increase (w)	.15	.15	.15

Employing the cash flow formula for year 1:
$CF_1 = 50(1+.15)(.18)(1-.46) - (57.5-50)(.20+.15) = 2.96$

One should estimate changes in net working capital requirements with care. Actual year-to-year balance sheet changes in net working capital may not provide a good measure of the rise or decline in funds required. There are two main reasons for this: (1) the year-end balance sheet figures may not reflect the average or normal needs of the business during the year; and (2) both the accounts receivable and inventory accounts may overstate the magnitude of the funds committed by the company.

To estimate the additional cash requirements, the increased inventory investment should be measured by the variable costs for any additional units of inventory required and by the receivable investment in terms of the variable costs of the product delivered to generate the receivable rather than the absolute dollar amount of the receivable. (For an illustration of this calculation, see my Article 8.)

In addition to its most likely estimate for Rano, Alcar's management developed two additional (conservative and optimistic) scenarios for sales growth and EBIT-sales ratio. Exhibit 5 gives a summary of all three scenarios. Alcar's management may also wish to examine additional cases to test the effect of alternative assumptions about the income tax rate and capital investment and working capital requirements per dollar of sales increase.

Recall that cash flows should be forecast only for the period when the expected rate of return on incremental investment exceeds the minimum acceptable rate of return for the acquisition. It is possible to determine this in a simple yet analytical, nonarbitrary, fashion. To do so, we compute the minimum pretax return on sales (P_{min}) needed to earn the minimum acceptable rate of return on the acquisition (k) given the investment requirements for working capital (w) and fixed assets (f) for each additional dollar of sales and given a projected tax rate (T). The formula for P_{min} is:

$$P_{min} = \frac{(f+w)\,k}{(1-T)\,(1+k)}$$

Exhibit 4. Projected 10-Year Cash Flow Statement for Rano (in millions of dollars)

	Years									
	1	2	3	4	5	6	7	8	9	10
Sales	$57.50	$66.12	$76.04	$87.45	$100.57	$112.64	$126.15	$141.29	$158.25	$177.23
Operating expenses	47.15	54.22	62.36	71.71	82.47	95.74	107.23	124.34	139.26	155.97
EBIT	$10.35	$11.90	$13.69	$15.74	$18.10	$16.90	$18.92	$16.95	$18.99	$21.27
Income taxes on EBIT	4.76	5.48	6.30	7.24	8.33	7.77	8.70	7.80	8.74	9.78
Operating earnings after taxes	$5.59	$6.43	$7.39	$8.50	$9.78	$9.12	$10.22	$9.16	$10.25	$11.48
Depreciation	1.60	1.85	2.13	2.46	2.84	3.28	3.74	4.25	4.83	5.49
Less capital expenditures	(3.10)	(3.57)	(4.12)	(4.74)	(5.47)	(5.69)	(6.44)	(7.28)	(8.22)	(9.29)
Less increase in working capital	(1.13)	(1.29)	(1.49)	(1.71)	(1.97)	(1.81)	(2.03)	(2.27)	(2.54)	(2.85)
Cash flow	$2.96	$3.41	$3.92	$4.51	$5.18	$4.90	$5.49	3.86	$4.32	$4.84

Exhibit 5. Additional Scenarios for Sales Growth and EBIT/Sales

	Sales Growth			EBIT/Sales		
Scenario	Years 1–5	6–7	8–10	Years 1–5	6–7	8–10
1. Conservative	.14	.12	.10	.17	.14	.11
2. Most likely	.15	.12	.12	.18	.15	.12
3. Optimistic	.18	.15	.12	.20	.16	.12

Alcar's management believes that when Rano's growth begins to slow down, its working capital requirements per dollar of additional sales will increase from .15 to about .20 and its effective tax rate will increase from .46 to .50. As will be shown in the next section, the minimum acceptable rate of return on the Rano acquisition is 13%. Thus:

$$P_{\min} = \frac{(.20 + .20)\,(.13)}{(1 - .50)\,(1 + .13)} = .092.$$

Alcar's management has enough confidence to forecast pretax sales returns above 9.2% for only the next 10 years, and thus the forecast duration for the Rano acquisition is limited to that period.

Step 2. Estimate Minimum Acceptable Rate of Return for Acquisition. In developing a company's average cost of capital, measuring the aftertax cost of debt is relatively straightforward. The cost of equity capital, however, is more difficult to estimate.

Rational, risk-averse investors expect to earn a rate of return that will compensate them for accepting greater investment risk. Thus, in assessing the company's cost of equity capital or the minimum expected return that will induce investors to buy the company's shares, it is reasonable to assume that they will demand the risk-free rate as reflected in the current yields available in government bonds plus a premium for accepting equity risk.

Recently, the risk-free rate on government bonds has been in the neighborhood of 8.8%. By investing in a portfolio broadly representative of the overall equity market, it is possible to diversify away substantially all of the unsystematic risk—that is, risk specific to individual companies. Therefore, securities are likely to be priced at levels that reward investors only for the nondiversifiable market risk—that is, the systematic risk in movements in the overall market.

The risk premium for the overall market is the excess of the expected return on a representative market index such as the Standard & Poor's 500-stock index over the risk-free return. Empirical studies have estimated this market risk premium (representative market index minus risk-free rate) to average historically about 5 to 5.5%.[3] I will use a 5.2% premium in subsequent calculations.

Investing in an individual security generally involves more or less risk than investing in a broad market portfolio; thus one must adjust the market risk premium appropriately in estimating the cost of equity for an individual security. The risk premium for a security is the product of the market risk premium times the individual security's systematic risk, as measured by its beta coefficient.

The rate of return from dividends and capital appreciation on a market portfolio will, by definition, fluctuate identically with the market, and therefore its beta is equal to 1.0. A beta for an individual security is an index of its risk expressed as its volatility of return in relation to that of a market portfolio.[4] Securities with betas greater than 1.0 are more volatile than the market and thus would be expected to have a risk premium greater than the overall market risk premium or the average-risk stock with a beta of 1.0.

For example, if a stock moves 1.5% when the market moves 1%, the stock would have a beta of 1.5. Securities with betas less than 1.0 are less volatile than the market and would thus command risk premiums less than the market risk premium. In summary, the cost of equity capital may be calculated by the following equation:

$$k_E = R_F + B_j (R_M - R_F)$$

where:

k_E = cost of equity capital.
R_F = risk-free rate.
B_j = the beta coefficient.
R_M = representative market index.

The acquiring company, Alcar, with a beta of 1.0, estimated its cost of equity as 14% with the foregoing equation:

$$\begin{aligned} k_E &= .088 + 1.0\ (.052) \\ &= \underline{\underline{.140}} \end{aligned}$$

Since interest on debt is tax deductible, the rate of return that must be earned on the debt portion of the company's capital structure to maintain the earnings available to common shareholders is the aftertax cost of debt. The aftertax cost of borrowed capital is Alcar's current beforetax interest rate (9.5%) times one minus its effective tax rate of 46%, which is equal to 5.1%. Alcar's target debt-to-equity ratio is .30, or, equivalently, debt is targeted at 23% and equity at 77% of its overall capitalization as Exhibit 6 shows Alcar's weighted average cost of capital. The appropriate rate for discounting Alcar cash flows to establish its estimated value is then 12%.

For new capital projects, including acquisitions, that are deemed to have about the same risk as the overall company, Alcar can use its 12%

Exhibit 6. Alcar's Weighted Average Cost of Capital

	Weight	Cost	Weighted Cost
Debt	.23	.051	.012
Equity	.77	.140	.108
Average cost of capital			.120

cost-of-capital rate as the appropriate discount rate. Because the company's cost of capital is determined by the weighted average risk of its component segments, the specific risk of each prospective acquisition should be estimated in order to arrive at the discount rate to apply to the candidate's cash flows.

Rano, with a beta coefficient of 1.25, is more risky than Alcar, with a beta of 1.0. Employing the formula for cost of equity capital for Rano:

$$\begin{aligned} k_E &= .088 + 1.25\ (.052) \\ &= \underline{\underline{.153}} \end{aligned}$$

On this basis, the risk-adjusted cost of capital for the Rano acquisition is as shown in Exhibit 7.

Step 3. Compute Maximum Acceptable Cash Price. This step involves taking the cash flow projections developed in Step 1 and discounting them at the rate developed in Step 2. Exhibit 8 shows the computation of the maximum acceptable cash price for the most likely scenario. The maximum price of $44.51 million, or $40.10 per share, for Rano compares with a $25 current market price for Rano shares. Thus, for the most likely case, Alcar can pay up to $15 per share, or a 60% premium over current market, and still achieve its minimum acceptable 13% return on the acquisition.

Exhibit 9 shows the maximum acceptable cash price for each of the three scenarios for a range of discount rates. To earn a 13% rate of return, Alcar can pay at maximum $38 million ($34.25 per share), assuming the conservative scenario, and up to $53 million ($47.80 per share), assuming

Exhibit 7. Risk-Adjusted Cost of Capital for Rano Acquisition

	Weight	Cost	Weighted Cost
Debt	.23	.054[a]	.012
Equity	.77	.153	.118
Average risk-adjusted cost of capital			.130

[a]Beforetax debt rate of 10% times one minus the estimated tax rate of 46%.

Exhibit 8. Maximum Acceptable Cash Price for Rano—Most Likely Scenario, with a Discount Rate of .130 (in millions of dollars)

Year	Cash Flow	Present Value	Cumulative Present Value
1	$ 2.96	$ 2.62	$ 2.62
2	3.41	2.67	5.29
3	3.92	2.72	8.01
4	4.51	2.76	10.77
5	5.13	2.81	13.59
6	4.90	2.35	15.94
7	5.49	2.33	18.27
8	3.86	1.45	19.72
9	4.32	1.44	21.16
10	4.84	1.43	22.59
Residual value	11.48	26.02[a]	48.61
Plus temporary investments not required for current operations			1.00
Less debt assumed			5.10
Maximum acceptable cash price			$44.51
Maximum acceptable cash price per share			$40.10

[a] $\frac{\text{Year 10 operating earnings after taxes}}{\text{Discount rate}} \times \text{year 10 discount factor} = \frac{11.48}{.13} \times .2946 = 26.02$

the optimistic scenario. Note that as Alcar demands a greater return on its investment, the maximum price it can pay decreases. The reverse is, of course, true as well. For example, for the most likely scenario, the maximum price decreases from $44.51 million to $39.67 million as the return requirement goes from 13% to 14%.

Step 4. Compute Rate of Return for Various Offering Prices and Scenarios. Alcar management believes that the absolute minimum successful bid for Rano would be $35 million, or $31.50 per share. Alcar's investment bankers estimated that it may take a bid of as high as $45 million, or $40.50 per share, to gain control of Rano shares. Exhibit 10 presents the rates of return that will be earned for four different offering prices, ranging from $35 million to $45 million for each of the three scenarios.

Under the optimistic scenario, Alcar could expect a return of 14.4% if it were to pay $45 million. For the most likely case, an offer of $45 million would yield a 12.9% return, or just under the minimum acceptable rate of 13%. This is as expected, since the maximum acceptable cash price as calculated in Exhibit 8 is $44.51 million, or just under the $45 million offer.

Exhibit 9. Maximum Acceptable Cash Price for Three Scenarios and a Range of Discount Rates

	Discount Rates				
Scenarios	.11	.12	.13	.14	.15
1. Conservative					
Total price ($ millions)	$48.84	$42.91	$38.02	$33.93	$30.47
Per share price	44.00	38.66	34.25	30.57	27.45
2. Most likely					
Total price ($ millions)	57.35	50.31	44.51	39.67	35.58
Per share price	51.67	45.33	40.10	35.74	32.05
3. Optimistic					
Total price ($ millions)	68.37	59.97	53.05	47.28	42.41
Per share price	61.59	54.03	47.80	42.59	38.21

If Alcar attaches a relatively high probability to the conservative scenario, the risk associated with offers exceeding $38 million becomes apparent.

Step 5. Analyze Feasibility of Cash Purchase. Although Alcar management views the relevant purchase price range for Rano as somewhere between $35 and $45 million, it must also establish whether an all-cash deal is feasible in light of Alcar's current liquidity and target debt-to-equity ratio. The maximum funds available for the purchase of Rano equal the postmerger debt capacity of the combined company less the combined premerger debt of the two companies plus the combined premerger temporary investments of the two companies. (Net working capital not required for everyday operations of the business is classified as "temporary investment.")

In an all-cash transaction governed by purchase accounting, the acquirer's shareholders' equity is unchanged. The postmerger debt capacity is then Alcar's shareholders' equity of $272 million times the targeted debt-to-equity ratio of .30, or $81.6 million. Alcar and Rano have premerger debt

Exhibit 10. Rate of Return for Various Offering Prices and Scenarios

		Offering Price			
	Total ($ millions)	$35.00	$38.00	$40.00	$45.00
Scenarios	Per share	$31.53	$34.23	$36.04	$40.54
1. Conservative		.137	.130	.126	.116
2. Most likely		.152	.144	.139	.129
3. Optimistic		.169	.161	.156	.144

balances of $56 million and $5.1 million, respectively, for a total of $61.1 million.

The unused debt capacity is thus $81.6 million minus $61.1 million, or $20.5 million. Add to this the combined temporary investments of Alcar and Rano of $26 million, and the maximum funds available for the cash purchase of Rano will be $46.5 million. A cash purchase is therefore feasible within the tentative price range of $35 to $45 million.

Step 6. Evaluate Impact of Acquisition on Alcar's EPS and Capital Structure. Because reported earnings per share (EPS) continue to be of great interest to the financial community, a complete acquisition analysis should include a comparison of projected EPS both with and without the acquisition. Exhibit 11 contains this comparative projection. The EPS stream with the acquisition of Rano is systematically greater than the stream without acquisition. The EPS standard, and particularly a short-term EPS standard, is not, however, a reliable basis for assessing whether the acquisition will in fact create value for shareholders.[5]

Several problems arise when EPS is used as a standard for evaluating acquisitions. First, because of accounting measurement problems, the EPS figure can be determined by alternative, equally acceptable methods—for example, LIFO versus FIFO. Second, the EPS standard ignores the time value of money. Third, it does not take into account the risk of the EPS stream. Risk is conditioned not only by the nature of the investment projects a company undertakes, but also by the relative proportions of debt and equity used to finance those investments.

A company can increase EPS by increasing leverage as long as the marginal return on investment is greater than the interest rate on the new debt. However, if the marginal return on investment is less than the risk-adjusted cost of capital or if the increased leverage leads to an increased cost of capital, then the value of the company could decline despite rising EPS.

Primarily because the acquisition of Rano requires that Alcar partially finance the purchase price with bank borrowing, the debt-to-equity ratios with the acquisition are greater than those without the acquisition (see Exhibit 11). Note that even without the Rano acquisition, Alcar is in danger of violating its target debt-to-equity ratio of .30 by the ninth year. The acquisition of Rano accelerates the problem to the fifth year. Whether Alcar purchases Rano or not, management must now be alert to the financing problem, which may force it to issue additional shares or reevaluate its present capital structure policy.

Acquisition for Stock

The first two steps in the acquisition-for-stock analysis, projecting Rano cash flows and setting the discount rate, have already been completed in connection with the acquisition-for-cash analysis developed in the previous section. The remaining steps of the acquisition-for-stock analysis are:

Exhibit 11. Alcar's Projected EPS, Debt-to-Equity Ratio, and Unused Debt Capacity—without and with Rano Acquisition

	EPS		Debt/equity		Unused Debt Capacity (in millions of dollars)	
Year	Without	With	Without	With	Without	With
0	\$ 3.75	\$ 4.10	.21	.26	\$25.60	\$20.50
1	4.53	4.89	.19	.27	34.44	9.42
2	5.09	5.51	.17	.28	44.22	7.00
3	5.71	6.20	.19	.29	40.26	4.20
4	6.38	6.99	.21	.30	35.45	.98
5	7.14	7.87	.24	.31	29.67	−2.71
6	7.62	8.29	.26	.31	22.69	−7.77
7	8.49	9.27	.27	.32	14.49	−13.64
8	9.46	10.14	.29	.33	4.91	−22.34
9	10.55	11.33	.31	.34	−6.23	−32.36
10	11.76	12.66	.32	.35	−19.16	−43.88

Note: Assumed cash purchase price for Rano is \$35 million.

- ☐ Estimate the value of Alcar shares.
- ☐ Compute the maximum number of shares that Alcar can exchange to acquire Rano under various scenarios and minimum acceptable rates of return.
- ☐ Evaluate the impact of the acquisition on the earnings per share and capital structure of Alcar.

Step 1. Estimate Value of Alcar Shares. Alcar conducted a comprehensive corporate self-evaluation that included an assessment of its estimated present value based on a range of scenarios. In the interest of brevity, I will consider here only its most likely scenario.

Management made most likely projections for its operations, as shown in Exhibit 12. Again using the equation for the cost of equity capital, the minimum EBIT as a percentage of sales needed to earn at Alcar's 12% cost of capital is 10.9%. Since management can confidently forecast pretax return on sales returns above 10.9% for only the next 10 years, the cash flow projections will be limited to that period.

Exhibit 13 presents the computation of the value of Alcar's equity. Its estimated value of \$36.80 per share contrasts with its currently depressed market value of \$22 per share. Because Alcar management believes its shares to be substantially undervalued by the market, in the absence of other compelling factors it will be reluctant to acquire Rano by means of an exchange of shares.

Exhibit 12. Most Likely Estimates for Alcar Operations without Acquisition

	Years		
	1–5	6–7	8–10
Sales growth rate	.125	.120	.120
EBIT as a percentage of sales	.130	.125	.125
Income tax rate	.460	.460	.460
Capital investment per dollar of sales increase	.250	.250	.250
Working capital per dollar of sales increase	.300	.300	.300

Exhibit 13. Estimated Present Value of Alcar Equity—Most Likely Scenario, with a Discount Rate of .120 (in millions of dollars)

Year	Cash Flow	Present Value	Cumulative Present Value
1	$ 6.13	$ 5.48	$ 5.48
2	6.90	5.50	10.98
3	7.76	5.53	16.51
4	8.74	5.55	22.06
5	9.83	5.58	27.63
6	10.38	5.26	32.89
7	11.63	5.26	38.15
8	13.02	5.26	43.41
9	14.58	5.26	48.67
10	16.33	5.26	53.93
Residual value	128.62	345.10[a]	399.03
Plus temporary investments not required for current operations			25.00
Less debt outstanding			56.00
Present value of Alcar equity			$368.03
Present value per share of Alcar equity			$ 36.80

[a] $$\frac{\text{Year 10 operating earnings after taxes}}{\text{Discount rate}} \times \text{year 10 discount factor} =$$

$$\frac{128.62}{.12} \times .32197 = 345.10$$

Exhibit 14. Calculation of Loss by Alcar Shareholders (in millions of dollars)

Alcar receives 86.27% of Rano's present value of $44.51 million (see Exhibit 8)	$38.4
Alcar gives up 13.73% of its present value of $368.03 million (see Exhibit 13)	(50.5)
Dilution of Alcar shareholders' value	$12.1

To illustrate, suppose that Alcar were to offer $35 million in cash for Rano. Assume the most likely case, that the maximum acceptable cash price is $44.51 million (see Exhibit 8); thus the acquisition would create about $9.5 million in value for Alcar shareholders. Now assume that instead Alcar agrees to exchange $35 million in market value of its shares in order to acquire Rano. In contrast with the cash case, in the exchange-of-shares case Alcar shareholders can expect to be worse off by $12.1 million.

With Alcar shares selling at $22, the company must exchange 1.59 million shares to meet the $35 million offer for Rano. There are currently 10 million Alcar shares outstanding. After the merger, the combined company will be owned 86.27%—that is, (10.00)/(10.00 + 1.59)—by current Alcar shareholders and 13.73% by Rano shareholders. The $12.1 million loss by Alcar shareholders can then be calculated as shown in Exhibit 14.

Step 2. Compute Maximum Number of Shares Alcar Can Exchange. The maximum acceptable number of shares to exchange for each of the three scenarios and for a range of discount rates appears in Exhibit 15. To earn a 13% rate of return, Alcar can exchange no more than 1.033, 1.210, and 1.442 million shares, assuming the conservative, most likely, and optimistic scenarios, respectively. Consider, for a moment, the most likely case. At a market value per share of $22, the 1.21 million Alcar shares exchanged would have a total value of $26.62 million, which is less than Rano's current market

Exhibit 15. Maximum Acceptable Shares to Exchange for Three Scenarios and a Range of Discount Rates (in millions)

	Discount Rates				
Scenarios	.11	.12	.13	.14	.15
1. Conservative	1.327	1.166	1.033	0.922	0.828
2. Most likely	1.558	1.367	1.210	1.078	0.967
3. Optimistic	1.858	1.630	1.442	1.285	1.152

value of \$27.75 million—that is, 1.11 million shares at \$25 per share. Because of the market's apparent undervaluation of Alcar's shares, an exchange ratio likely to be acceptable to Rano will be clearly unattractive to Alcar.

Step 3. Evaluate Impact of Acquisition on Alcar's EPS and Capital Structure. The \$35 million purchase price is just under 10 times Rano's most recent year's earnings of \$3.55 million. At its current market price per share of \$22, Alcar is selling at about six times its most recent earnings. The acquiring company will always suffer immediate EPS dilution whenever the price-earnings ratio paid for the selling company is greater than its own. Alcar would suffer immediate dilution from \$3.75 to \$3.54 in the current year. A comparison of EPS for cash versus an exchange-of-shares transaction appears as part of Exhibit 16. As expected, the EPS projections for a cash deal are consistently higher than those for an exchange of shares.

However, the acquisition of Rano for shares rather than cash would remove, at least for now, Alcar's projected financing problem. In contrast with a cash acquisition, an exchange of shares enables Alcar to have unused debt capacity at its disposal throughout the 10-year forecast period. Despite the relative attractiveness of this financing flexibility, Alcar management recognized that it could not expect a reasonable rate of return by offering an exchange of shares to Rano.

Exhibit 16. Alcar's Projected EPS, Debt-to-Equity Ratio, and Unused Debt Capacity—Cash vs. Exchange of Shares

	EPS		Debt/Equity		Unused Debt Capacity (in millions of dollars)	
Year	Cash	Stock	Cash	Stock	Cash	Stock
0	\$ 4.10	\$ 3.54	.26	.21	\$20.50	\$25.60
1	4.89	4.37	.27	.19	9.42	35.46
2	5.51	4.93	.28	.17	7.00	46.62
3	6.20	5.55	.29	.18	4.20	48.04
4	6.99	6.23	.30	.20	0.98	46.37
5	7.87	7.00	.31	.21	−2.71	44.29
6	8.29	7.37	.31	.23	−7.77	40.90
7	9.27	8.22	.32	.24	−13.64	36.78
8	10.14	8.98	.33	.26	−22.34	29.90
9	11.33	10.01	.34	.27	−32.86	21.79
10	12.66	11.17	.35	.29	−43.88	12.29

Note: Assumed purchase price for Rano is \$35 million.

Conclusion

The experience of companies that have implemented the approach to acquisition analysis described in this article indicates that it is not only an effective way of evaluating a prospective acquisition candidate, but it also serves as a catalyst for reevaluating a company's overall strategic plans. The results also enable management to justify acquisition recommendations to the board of directors in an economically sound, convincing fashion.

Various companies have used this approach for evaluation of serious candidates as well as for initial screening of potential candidates. In the latter case, initial input estimates are quickly generated to establish whether the range of maximum acceptable prices is greater than the current market price of the target companies. With the aid of a computer model, this can be accomplished quickly and at relatively low cost.

Whether companies are seeking acquisitions or are acquisition targets, it is increasingly clear that they must provide better information to enable top management and boards to make well-conceived, timely decisions. Use of the approach outlined here should improve the prospects of creating value for shareholders by acquisitions.

Notes

1. For a more detailed description on how to conduct a corporate self-evaluation, see my article, "Do You Know the Value of Your Company?", *Mergers and Acquisitions*, Spring 1979.

2. "The Cash-Flow Takeover Formula," *Business Week*, December 18, 1978, p. 86.

3. For example, see Roger G. Ibbotson and Rex A. Sinquefield, *Stocks, Bonds, Bills, and Inflation: The Past (1926–1976) and the Future (1977–2000)* (New York, Financial Analysts Research Foundation, 1977), p. 57. They forecast that returns on common stocks will exceed those on long-term government bonds by 5.4%.

4. For a discussion of some of the problems in estimating beta as a measure of risk, see Eugene F. Brigham, *Financial Management: Theory and Practice* (Hinsdale, Ill., The Dryden Press, 1977), p. 666.

5. See William W. Alberts and James M. McTaggart, "The Short-Term Earnings Per Share Standard for Evaluating Prospective Acquisitions," *Mergers and Acquisitions*, Winter 1978, p. 4; and Joel M. Stern, "Earnings Per Share Don't Count," *Financial Analysts Journal*, July–August 1974, p. 39.

24
Choosing Compatible Acquisitions

MALCOLM S. SALTER and WOLF A. WEINHOLD

In today's low-growth yet volatile environment, many companies choose to diversify through acquisition. An acquisition candidate with high potential will be one that can create economic value by leading to a free cash flow for the combined company that is either larger or less risky than that of a comparable investment portfolio. Candidates with the greatest promise for value creation will be those offering a good fit with the acquirer's unique set of skills and resources. The authors examine how an assessment of these skills and resources can help companies decide (1) whether related or unrelated acquisitions make sense, (2) which economic, strategic, and managerial variables should be stressed in evaluating an acquisition candidate's risk-return profile, and (3) what potential exits for successful integration with the acquiring company.

Although some view large-scale acquisitions primarily as the province of adventurous conglomerates, in fact many old-line conservative giants are actively involved in such activities. General Electric, for instance, paid \$2 billion in stock for Utah International, Exxon paid \$1.2 billion in cash for Reliance Electric, and Allied Chemical and Kennecott Copper each paid more than \$500 million for their respective acquisitions of Eltra and Carborundum.

When such corporate acquisitions succeed, it is often because the acquirers have a mechanism for identifying candidates that offer the greatest potential for creating value for the company's shareholders. In a previous article, we pointed out that value is created when diversifying acquisitions lead to a free cash flow for the combined company (1) that is greater than could be realized from a portfolio investment in the two companies or (2) whose variability is smaller than it would be with a portfolio investment in the two companies. (See Article 22 by us.)

Effective systems for identifying and screening acquisitions have four important properties. First, they must provide means of evaluating a candidate's potential for creating value for the acquirer's shareholders. Second, they must be able to reflect the special needs of each company using the system. Relying on checklists or priorities with supposed universal applicability is the surest possible way of placing an entire acquisition program in jeopardy. Third, they must be easy to use—but not overly rigid. Because most structured frameworks of analysis run the risk of promoting mechanical solutions to complicated policy issues, formal screening and evaluation procedures must not be allowed to crowd out more informal, spontaneous contributions to the decision-making process.

Fourth, and perhaps most important, an effective acquisition screening system must serve as a mechanism for communicating corporate goals and personal knowledge among the parties involved. The analytic concepts and language inherent in such a system can significantly aid managers in implementing an acquisition program that is conceptually sound, internally consistent, and economically justifiable.

This article will focus on guidelines for screening acquisitions that diversify the acquirer's operations. Our interest in such acquisitions is prompted by two considerations.

First, in today's low-growth yet volatile environment, most companies with high-growth goals or an imbalanced portfolio of businesses find diversification necessary. Only a few companies have both the organizational and the technological traits for successful diversification through internal development and thus acquisition becomes the only alternative.

Second, large companies seeking expansion opportunities often find significant antitrust barriers in their pursuit of those acquisition candidates that make the greatest strategic and business sense. These high-potential acquisitions are companies closely related to existing businesses. However, the company that reaches for the benefits of scale economies, production efficiencies, or market rationalizations will, in many cases, run afoul of antitrust legislation.

Acquisitions for diversification can be related or unrelated to the original business. Each type has important variants.

Related acquisitions that might be called "supplementary" involve entry into new product markets where a company can use its existing functional skills or resources. Such acquisitions are typically most valuable to companies with a strong competitive position and a desire to extend their corporate competence to new areas of opportunity. The base on which this form of diversifying acquisition is built can either be a proprietary functional skill, as is the case for many of the major pharmaceutical and chemical companies, or a more general corporate capability, such as Gillette showed in disposable consumer products or United Technologies in capital goods.

Related acquisitions that are "complementary" rather than supplementary involve adding functional skills or resources to the company's existing distinctive competence while leaving its product-market commitment relatively unchanged. This type of acquisition is most valuable to companies in attractive industries whose competitive or strategic position could be strengthened by changing (or adding to) their value-added position in the commercial chain.

A classic example would be an original-equipment automotive parts manufacturer expanding into the distribution of replacement parts to secure a more stable, controllable market. Such a strategy often leads to a form of vertical integration as these new functional skills and/or resources are more closely linked to the diversifying company's core businesses. The acquisitions of American Television and Communications by Time, Inc. or Cardiac Pacemakers by Eli Lilly represent this complementary type of strategy.

Unrelated acquisitions involve entry into businesses with product markets or key success factors unrelated to existing corporate activities. These unrelated businesses can be managed either actively or passively. In active management, the corporate office becomes heavily involved in evaluating the new division's objectives and in establishing a highly competitive internal market for capital funds. Conglomerates such as Teledyne, Gulf & Western, and International Telephone and Telegraph typify companies pursuing this approach. In passive management, corporate headquarters usually limits its involvement to investment reviews, but there may be a centralized financing or banking function. The recent U.S. acquisitions by Thomas Tilling, Thyssen, and the Flick Group are all examples of this strategy. Diversified U.S. companies like U.S. Industries, IU International, and Alco Standard have historically followed this strategy, although recent economic events have forced the corporate office in each of these instances to take a more active management role.

The choice of a particular acquisition strategy largely depends on identifying the route that best uses the company's existing asset base and special resources. When a company can export (or import) surplus functional skills and resources relevant to its industrial or commercial setting, it should consider related acquisitions as an attractive strategic option. On the other hand, a company that has a special capacity to (1) analyze the strategies and financial requirements of a wide range of businesses, (2) tolerate—and even encourage—a lack of uniformity in the organization's structure, and (3) transfer surplus financial resources and general management skills among subsidiaries when necessary can exploit the potential benefits of unrelated acquisitions.

Acquisition Guidelines

The decision to pursue a specific type of diversifying acquisition provides the context for drawing up precise guidelines. Although every acquisition-minded company should undertake an audit of corporate strengths and weaknesses as well as an analysis of its risk-return profile and cash flow characteristics, the process of developing acquisition guidelines for related diversification should differ in focus and in content from what is used for unrelated diversification.

Related Diversification

The most significant shareholder benefits from related acquisitions accrue when the special skills and industry knowledge of one merger partner can help improve the competitive position of the other. It is worth stressing again that not only must these special skills and resources exist in one of the two partners, but they must also be transferable to the other. Thus, acquisition guidelines would describe those companies with functional skills and resources that would either add to or benefit from the company's resource package.

Lest such identification appear too obvious or elementary, consider the dilemma that Ciba-Geigy Corporation faced in its 1974 acquisition of Airwick Industries. Ciba-Geigy's products were almost entirely specialty chemicals and pharmaceuticals. Its corporate objectives were to continue to improve its long-term profits through new products derived from its extensive research program and from acquisitions in related fields. An attractive acquisition, according to Ciba-Geigy's acquisition task force, should:

- ☐ Participate in growing markets.
- ☐ Have a proprietary position in its markets.
- ☐ Have operations likely to be favorably affected by Ciba-Geigy's know-how in both research and development and the manufacture and marketing of complex synthetic organic chemicals.
- ☐ Be product rather than service oriented.
- ☐ Have sales of $50 million or more.
- ☐ Earn a good gross profit margin on sales.
- ☐ Have the potential for a return on investment of 10% or more.
- ☐ Be involved in such activities as specialty chemicals; proprietary pharmaceuticals; cosmetic and toiletry products; animal health products; proprietary household and garden products; medical supplies; products and services related to air, liquid, and solid waste treatment; or photochemicals and related products.

The search—a model of intelligent acquisition behavior—involved reviewing more than 18,000 companies in-house, along with an outside computer review. In addition, the company circulated the acquisition criteria among commercial and investment banking firms for their suggestions, and the task force worked with the company's divisions to identify attractive candidates. All told, about 100 companies came through this screen and were scrutinized more closely. Among these was Airwick Industries.

Airwick had 1973 sales of $33.5 million, net earnings of $2.7 million, and a return on shareholders' investment of 22.5%. The company's principal products were air fresheners and a full line of sanitary maintenance items (such as disinfectants, cleansers, insecticides with odor-counteracting features, and some swimming pool products). Over the previous five years, the rapidly growing air freshener market had become extremely competitive. Bristol-Myers, American Home Products, and S. C. Johnson had all entered the market. Although Airwick's financial performance had been good, it was clearly facing financial pressures in meeting the marketing onslaught of these major consumer products companies.

After several weeks of extensive interviews and analysis, Ciba-Geigy's task force concluded that Airwick was a sound company that had numerous potential synergies with Ciba-Geigy. The task force reported that acquisition of Airwick would be an attractive way of entering the household products business, *if* Ciba-Geigy had a strategic interest in this area. The tentativeness of this conclusion suggests that the acquisition guidelines failed to provide sufficient criteria for a final choice of the acquisition candidate.

Related diversification requires that new businesses or activities have a coherence or "fit" with the existing businesses of the acquirer. Achieving this fit involves exploring a range of possible choices. A quick review of Ciba-Geigy's eight acquisition guidelines finds only two that express any notion of strategic fit (third and fourth). The company's distinctive skills lay in its sophisticated research in organic chemicals and its technologically advanced production skills. Relative to many other companies, Ciba-Geigy did not require nor perhaps encourage an advanced marketing program.

If Ciba-Geigy's objectives were to build on these skills and talents a strategy of related-supplementary diversification, attractive acquisition candidates would have similar critical success variables. Specifically, such businesses would:

1. Require high levels of chemically based research and development skills.
2. Manufacture products by chemical processes requiring a high degree of engineering or technical know-how.
3. Sell principal products on technically based performance specifications.
4. Not require heavy advertising or expensive distribution systems that would take resources away from the maintenance of distinctive R&D and manufacturing capabilities.

Ciba-Geigy would have steered away from businesses that were either marketing intensive or involved in the production of commodity chemicals, including many of those businesses it had targeted.

Alternatively, if Ciba-Geigy had wished to add important skills and resources in new functional activities—a related-complementary diversification strategy—attractive acquisition candidates would have experience in large-scale manufacturing, marketing, and distribution of chemically based products. They would be businesses:

1 Whose resource inputs could include Ciba-Geigy's specialty chemicals.
2 Whose success depends highly on chemical usage or application.
3 Whose production and/or distribution involve chemically based products.
4 Whose key success factor is marketing oriented. This may include, but is not limited to, companies with extensive distribution systems, well-known brand names, and/or a tradition of customer acceptance.

These quite different sets of acquisition guidelines, although both seeking related diversification, help explain the task force's dilemma with Airwick. Lacking precise diversification objectives and acquisition guidelines, the task force analyzed Airwick according to related-supplementary criteria, which required skills similar to those of Ciba-Geigy. However, Airwick's key success factors were quite different from Ciba-Geigy's, and Ciba-Geigy's functional strengths were largely irrelevant to Airwick's future. Naturally, the task force felt the need to hedge its recommendations until it had more meaningful acquisition guidelines for marketing-oriented companies.

The lesson of this case is simple but fundamental. Companies pursuing a strategy of growth into related fields must decide whether to expand existing skills and resources into new product markets or whether to add new functional skills and resources.

Unrelated Diversification

The principal benefits for companies pursuing unrelated acquisitions stem from improved corporate management of working capital, resource allocation, or capital financing and lead to a cash flow for the combined company that is either larger or less risky than its component parts. A company pursuing unrelated acquisitions therefore can usefully focus its acquisition criteria on the size and riskiness of a business's cash flow and the compatibility of this cash flow pattern with its own cash flow profile. Once again, lest this appear too obvious, consider the uncertainty faced by General Cinema Corporation.

General Cinema, the nation's largest operator of multiple-auditorium theater complexes and largest soft drink bottler, has compiled an enviable financial record. Both return-on-equity and earnings growth have exceeded 20% for the last decade. By the mid-1970s, the company had reduced the large amount of debt it had incurred while actively acquiring soft drink bottlers. It then began an acquisition search for a "third leg of the stool."

General Cinema's acquisition guidelines indicated a preference for well-run small- to medium-sized companies ($5 million to $20 million in pretax earnings) whose consumer- or leisure-oriented products had unique characteristics that protected them against competition. Senior managers spoke of using the company's competence in any new acquisition. All this suggests some very general related-diversification strategy.

General Cinema's actions suggest, however, that this strategy was not followed. Its soft drink bottling business is not closely related to the multiple-auditorium theater business in either a product-market or a functional skill sense, nor were several of its previous diversification attempts, which involved bowling alleys, FM radio stations, and furniture retailing.

Thus, in General Cinema's case, the difference between the company's espoused theory of diversification and its actual behavior is clear. Assuming, therefore, it had a realistic interest in unrelated diversification, what additional acquisition guidelines could usefully structure General Cinema's search for an attractive unrelated acquisition candidate?

Turning first to General Cinema's risk profile, one finds a high level of risk at the corporate level (its stock had a beta in excess of 1.8) but relatively low levels of risk at the operating subsidiary level. This divergence in risk levels was due to management's policy of aggressive financial leverage with a debt-to-equity ratio (including capitalized leases) exceeding 3 to 1. By incurring high levels of financial leverage to increase its risk level, rather than assuming either operating or competitive risk, General Cinema was creating value for its shareholders.

A cash flow analysis of General Cinema's product-market portfolio reinforces these conclusions. All of General Cinema's divisions were classic cash cows—the largest competitors in mature, low-growth industries. In addition, the competitive positions of both the theater and bottling divisions were especially strong due to the franchise nature of both markets. Because both movie theaters and bottling operations are capital-intensive businesses, their cash flows, relative to many industries, were high. General Cinema's cash flow strength was likely to increase as continued growth in revenues and financial leverage interacted to generate an increasing surplus of cash funds.

In short, General Cinema showed many of the characteristics of a well-managed, unrelated diversifier. In fact, the distinctive competence General Cinema's senior managers often referred to consisted of well-developed planning and control skills in the corporate office, a key success variable for many such companies. Thus, additional acquisition guidelines for General Cinema, reflecting an unrelated-active strategy, could be as follows:

1 The acquisition candidate should be asset intensive. The assets could either be fixed, such as buildings and equipment, or intangible, such as trademarks, franchises, or goodwill. In either case, they should be well established with significant on-going value in order to be "bankable."

2 Since high levels of debt would be used, the acquisition's assets should create high barriers to entry. This implies products relatively immune to technological obsolescence or markets not exposed to significant levels of internal competition or external pressure.

3 Since General Cinema's surplus cash flow is increasing, an attractive acquisition should have significant growth potential over an extended period of time.

4 The acquisition candidate may have a low pretax return on invested capital (say 16%). However, total invested capital (debt, leases, and equity) should be at least three times the equity investment. Reflecting this (potential) leverage, the pretax return on equity should be high (at least 30%).

5 The requirements for relative immunity to market change and a high growth rate imply that the acquisition would be service oriented rather than technology based.

6 For senior managers to feel comfortable with the acquisition, they should market or distribute products or services to the consuming public.

7 Because General Cinema lacks surplus general managers, the acquisition should have good operating managers. Successful integration into General Cinema requires that the acquisition be adaptable to intensive planning and financial controls.

Most of the guidelines are as applicable to companies managing unrelated acquisitions passively as to companies operating actively. However, the criteria requiring integration into an intensive planning and financial control system and a corporate-managed resource allocation process embody those elements found in most actively managed portfolios of unrelated businesses.

The Ciba-Geigy and General Cinema cases clearly show how closely tied acquisition guidelines should be to overall corporate strategy. Effective acquisition guidelines must reflect carefully thought-out corporate objectives. In situations where the objectives (and especially diversification objectives) lack specificity or relevance, acquisition guidelines will be vague and have limited use in structuring a process for productive acquisition search and screening.

Screening the Candidates

Once an acquisition-minded company has established detailed and comprehensive guidelines, it can develop its own system for identifying promising candidates. This screening system should identify candidates with the greatest potential of creating value for the acquiring company's shareholders.

As we said earlier, economic value is created only when diversifying acquisitions lead to a free cash flow for the combined company (1) that is greater than could be realized from a portfolio investment in the two companies or (2) whose variability is smaller than would occur from a portfolio investment in the two companies.

We have identified eight principal ways in which one or both of these conditions can be met through diversifying acquisitions as well as several additional ways that are not, strictly speaking, due to diversification.[1] Each involves the way in which the two companies' resource structures can be successfully integrated to form a more efficient business unit.

The following list briefly outlines those economic, strategic, and managerial variables that have the greatest potential impact on value creation. These variables can be divided into two broad categories—those dealing with the candidate's risk-return profile and those dealing with the candidate's integration potential.

Risk-Return Variables

Return characteristics principally concern the size and timing of an acquisition's prospective cash flows. Although such characteristics are often thought of as company specific, many industries show readily identifiable cash flow patterns over their business cycles and/or their life cycles.

Size and Period of Cash Flow. These variables focus on the pattern of free cash flows into and out of the acquisition over time. Generally, a period of investment (negative cash flow) during industry growth is followed by a period of return (positive cash flow) during maturity. A specific acquisition's cash flow pattern will reflect its capital intensity, profitability, growth rate, and stage of maturity.

Noncapitalized Strategic Investments. These are investments in assets that are not reflected on the company's balance sheet, but are nevertheless important to its competitive success. Such assets as R&D skills, production technology, and market power (through advertising or distribution presence) are typically highly illiquid, but are often the most effective competitive weapons and market entry barriers a company has.

Returns Due to Unique Characteristics. Returns from the intangible assets developed through "strategic expenses" are often high, because along with specialized management skills they usually represent a company's distinctive competence. Alternatively, high returns may reflect entrepreneurial talents or access to one-of-a-kind sources of supply. Care should be given to distinguishing between company characteristics that can be developed and unique characteristics such as entrepreneurial talent, government franchises, or access to low-cost natural resources.

Investment Liquidity. Liquidity primarily depends on the marketability of the investment's underlying assets. Generally, the less risky an asset and the higher its collateral value, the easier it is to convert into cash. Highly liquid assets seldom provide distinct competitive advantages, however, or yield high rates of return.

Every return (or cash flow) has some level of risk; normally, the greater the potential returns, the greater the risks. A critical part of management's job is to control these risks so that the risk-return trade-off becomes more attractive than otherwise.

Vulnerability to Exogenous Changes in Supply or Demand. These risks arise from exposure to changes outside the company's control or, alternatively, the inability of managers to influence their business environment. The risks faced by a company depend on how critical a specific environmental factor is to the company, how readily available substitutes are, and how specialized the company's internal resources are. The greater the company's ability to lay off or pass on these environmental risks in the marketplace, the more stable its cash flow and the lower its risk.

Ease of Market Entry and Exit. Generally, the easier market entry or exit is, the more likely it is that industry rates of return will be driven toward normal or risk-adjusted levels. Entry-exit barriers can include capital requirements, specialized skills and resources, market presence, and government licenses or permits. Michael E. Porter described how knowledge about and use of entry and exit barriers can be critical in corporate strategy and competitive rivalry.[2]

Excess Productive Capacity. The risk of excess capacity is directly linked to market growth and the nature of capital investment to meet that growth. If it is most efficient to add new productive capacity in large increments of fixed investment (with corresponding sunk costs) and if these assets are long-lived (or with similar technological efficiencies), significant incentives to maintain volume through price cutting will exist whenever one competitor's relative demand falls off. Where market demand is relatively price inelastic, everyone in the industry will suffer revenue losses and reduced profitability.

Gross Margin Stability. This is closely related to production capacity risks and the ease of market entry and exit. Gross margins are good indicators of profitability and the availability of cash flow to support the development of more competitive technological, marketing, or administrative systems. The stability of gross margins also indicates the relative attractiveness of increasing operating leverage by substituting capital investment (with its fixed costs) for variable costs in the production process.

Competitive Strength. This depends on market share position, vulnerability to external forces in the marketplace, and position vis-à-vis suppliers and purchasers. Substantial evidence shows that in many industries companies with high market share have higher cash flows and higher returns on investment than those with low market share. If, however, a high market share position requires large investments in relatively specialized assets (fixed or intangible), these companies may also be highly vulnerable to major changes in the marketplace. Such external market risks include technological obsolescence, swift changes in consumption patterns, and new distribution or marketing systems accompanying changing demographics or technology. Finally, shifts in the bargaining strengths, or competitive positions, of suppliers or purchasers may substantially alter the costs or benefits of internal market share positions.

Societal Liabilities. The increasing legislation concerning social issues and the public welfare has altered the costs and rates of returns of many companies. Driving forces behind this legislation include environmental concerns, consumer protectionism, and employee safety and benefits.

Political Risk. Many companies have discovered that political and environmental risks may be significantly greater than the strategic, competitive, or technological risks faced in day-to-day business. The Mideast crisis and the continued turbulence in much of the Third World are only the most obvious instances. Unstable economic and monetary policy in the United States and trade policy in Japan are other, equally important, facets. Failure to assess and manage these risks correctly may render an otherwise successful corporate strategy irrelevant.

Each of these risk measures reflects one particular aspect of an asset's or a company's risk profile. How managers handle these risks as well as the inherent economic characteristics of the asset can be summarized through the following two capital market risk measures:

- ☐ *Financial risk.* This refers to the burden of fixed contractual payments incurred to own an asset. The greater this fixed burden (usually through debt or lease payments), the greater the financial risk. Skilled managers often use financial risk as an integral part of corporate strategy.
- ☐ *Systematic and unsystematic risk.* These measure the volatility (or the riskiness) of the returns of an asset or a business relative to the returns of all other assets in the marketplace. Systematic or market-related risk, which is most relevant to equity investors because it directly influences market value, reflects a company's inherent cash flow volatility and financial risk relative to the volatility of the economy in general. Unsystematic risk measures the risk specific to a particular company or asset. It can be reduced or eliminated by investors through portfolio diversification.

Integration Potential

The second set of criteria a diversifying company should consider in developing its screening program concerns the acquisition's potential for successful integration. Such criteria are often much more important for a related diversifier than for an unrelated diversifier. In fact, a related diversifier may well focus most of its efforts in this area, because its corporate strategy and business commitments will render many risk-return criteria meaningless. Nevertheless, issues of organizational compatibility and the availability of general management skills are critical to the success of all diversifying companies.

Supplementary Skills and Resources. These criteria principally reflect a related-supplementary diversification strategy. Consequently, they focus on a company's ability to transfer and effectively use the skills and resources of one partner to the competitive advantage of the other. Generally, the potential benefits of this type of merger increase as the shared skills and resources constitute an increasingly larger element in the cost of doing business.

Complementary Skills and Resources. These criteria reflect a related-complementary diversification strategy. They focus on improving the competitive position of the business by adding new functional skills and resources to the existing resource base.

Financial Fit-Risk Pooling Benefits. These criteria are more important in unrelated than in related diversification. They focus on developing an internal capital market that is more efficient than the external capital marketplace. These benefits can arise out of improved working capital (cash) management, improved investment management (cross-subsidization), improved resource allocation, or more aggressive financial leverage.

Availability of General Management Skills. Talented general managers are essential whenever value creation depends on the revitalization of underused assets. A surplus of general management resources in either partner must always be considered an extremely positive feature.

Organizational Compatibility. As any experienced diversifier will know, this is a critical issue. All of the previous criteria identify the potential for value creation, which can be realized only by an organization that can effectively exploit this potential and thereby create a more competitive enterprise.

Meeting Individual Corporate Needs

An acquisition screening system should reflect a company's specific objectives. For example, a currently cash-rich company expecting to face substantial capital investment demands in five years might articulate its size and period of investment criteria as: "The most favorable investment pattern (purchase price plus subsequent infusion of funds into the acquisition) is a maximum of $100 million over the next three-year period. The acquired company should become financially self-sufficient by the end of the third year and generate surplus cash flow by the fifth year.''

By composing such statements, a company can tailor generic guidelines often found in acquisition screening grids to its own unique needs. Where guidelines or screening criteria are complex or especially important to the acquiring company, any particular measure may require more than one statement. Similarly, the desired characteristics of industries and companies may be expressed in either positive or negative terms depending on the acquiring company's resources and objectives.

Developing these criteria should involve all members of the group or task force responsible for formulating and implementing the acquisition program. Each should generate descriptive statements based on one's understanding of the company's objectives and needs. Subsequent discussions among these persons can then lead to a single set of generally accepted and explicit screening criteria.

Once formal statements or criteria have been developed, it is sometimes useful to establish weightings or scoring ranges for each measure. These scoring ranges will reflect the importance of each item to the acquiring company.[3] Specific designation of the value of each measure forces managers to discuss the entire acquisition in terms of corporate objectives, resources, and skills.

Such a discussion also ensures internal consistency of the program. Wide discrepancies may signal that managers differ in their perceptions of the company's objectives, strategy, or distinctive competence or, alternatively, that they have either overlooked or understood only implicitly key elements in the diversification strategy.

As the acquisition task force screens industries, industry subgroups, and individual companies, the process will typically be iterative, reducing the potential acquisition universe to a smaller and smaller size. Industry subgroups (companies sharing the same key success factor or similar products and/or markets) will replace industries, and companies will replace industry subgroups until a limited set of candidates exists.

At each step in the screening process, the managers involved should individually evaluate the potential candidates and then meet to analyze their evaluations and discuss any major differences. Managers should ask: Do the results make intuitive sense? Why is there such a wide (or narrow) spread in the point scores? Has some critical element been overlooked?

As the screening process develops, company strategists should modify both the explicit screening criteria and their scoring ranges as new information about the potential acquisition and/or the environment emerge. Some diversifiers may also be useful to make the statements more detailed as the screening process narrows attention to fewer candidates or to eliminate certain criteria altogether. Generally, the need to revise statements will be less for related diversifiers than for unrelated diversifiers, since the former typically have a smaller universe of candidates to choose from. Clear communication of objectives and differences of opinion is particularly important since, once an acquisition decision has been made, a company can reverse itself only with very high financial and organizational costs.

This procedure should stimulate the flow of information and judgments among those responsible for the acquisition program and lead to a questioning of assumptions, provide a critical analysis of differences of opinion, and improve the consistency between corporate objectives and resources. Just as the capital budget or the operating budget can be used as a communications tool, so too can the acquisition screening grid serve an important communications function.

Potential for Value Creation

The last step in the screening process is determination of the candidate's potential for value creation for the shareholders of the acquiring company. This potential should then be compared to the cost of the acquisition as well as to the company's other investment opportunities (including the repurchase of its own stock).

In many ways, this procedure is similar to capital budgeting exercises that use the notion of net present value or discounted cash flow, but the analysis of a potential acquisition is significantly more complex than most capital budgeting decisions. Whereas the typical investment project involves assets with risks reasonably similar to those already in the company's portfolio and under the control of familiar managers, this is not the case with many acquisition candidates. Not only may the acquired asset's risks be different but the managers of an acquired company are often of unknown quality. Even where some familiarity exits, the managers' attitudes and motivation can change radically after the acquisition is consummated.

Another significant difference between an acquisition and the typical investment project is that the capital marketplace acts as a pricing mechanism to equate the value of a company with its risk-return characteristics. A lucky acquirer may well find a bargain or, more precisely, a company whose intrinsic value is greater than its market value plus the transaction costs necessary to acquire it.

Much more likely, however, is the case where an acquisition candidate is not undervalued relative to its existing level of cash flow and risk but rather is underusing its asset base. In this case, the acquirer will have to make extensive changes in the acquired company's management and/or use of assets for the acquisition to be economically justifiable. These changes will result typically in a company whose risk and expected cash flow are vastly different from what they previously were. Historic measures of this asset's performance may well be useless in the evaluation of future prospects.

The specific mechanics of net present value (or the discounted cash flow valuation process) appear in almost any financial handbook and are in the repertoire of most investment bankers or management consultants. (For a good summary of this evaluation process, see Article 23 in this book by Alfred Rappaport.) For discounted cash flow to be useful in acquisition analysis, it should be readily adaptable in the following three areas:

1 Developing detailed cash flow projections (including additional capital investments) over the acquired company's period of ownership.
2 Establishing relevant rates of return for the acquired company (and its constituent parts) based on its prospective risk characteristics and its capital structure.
3 Performing sensitivity analyses under the various economic, operating, and financial scenarios likely to be faced.

While this approach seems straightforward and objective, it is in practice much more complex and intuitive. Wherever operating, financial, or strategic changes are to be made in the acquired company's businesses, simple extrapolation or projection of current performance is, at best, risky. Similarly, if integration with the acquirer is to occur, as in related diversification, managers must evaluate changes in the cash flows and risk levels of both acquirer and acquired. Virtually every attempt to achieve one of the several potential benefits of diversification will lead to subtle yet important changes in the combined company's cash flow and risk characteristics. Careful use and a thorough understanding of the valuation process are of paramount importance, for slight errors in estimating these cash flows or risk levels can lead to valuation prices that differ by 30% or 40%.

Nevertheless, a careful application of the method we have outlined will force a company to be as concrete as possible in its assessment of future risks and returns. No one formula or method, least of all a simplified discounted cash flow analysis, should be expected to reveal by itself the best option or decision. The worth of any screening and evaluation system will vary according to both the quality of information used and the ability of managers to use this tool without crowding out important intuitive judgments about the compatibility of corporate cultures, the quality of an acquisition candidate's management, and the long-term strength of a candidate's competitive position.

The room for error in making these judgments is considerable. The anticipated benefits of an acquisition are often greater than those finally realized. Reaping benefits that stem from operating synergies requires considerable time and management effort. The knowledge of which benefits are achievable and at what costs comes from both prior experience and a strong sense of administrative feasibility. These personal characteristics of decision makers, along with the ability to value future returns accurately, lie at the base of a successful acquisition screening system.

Preparing the Ground

Executives often ask why they should have elaborate acquisition guidelines when such decisions must often be made without sufficient time for detailed, comprehensive analysis or when candidates best suited to their company's needs are not available. To summarize, formal acquisition guidelines can help companies prepare themselves for swift action in three ways:

First, working through a formal process in periods of relative calm tends to reinforce a broad understanding among executives of the company's objectives. Given the complexities of organizational life in the modern corporation, this benefit is not trivial.

Second, experience with a structured process, such as articulating acquisition guidelines or writing specific screening criteria, leads to widely shared assumptions about the company's strengths and weaknesses and its special needs and to a general agreement on what is most important for future profitability and corporate development.

Third, working within a formal system develops a common language or set of concepts relevant to the acquisition decision. This language system and the analytic framework it represents serve to ensure that key decision makers follow similar logic when acquisition opportunities suddenly appear and quick decisions are necessary.

The issue concerning the availability of acquisition candidates is often overemphasized. Most companies, especially those that are publicly owned, are available at a price. In the capital markets, where there is a continual auction of corporate securities, companies change hands every day. The real question is not whether attractive candidates are available but whether the company's potential to create value for the acquirer's shareholders is sufficient to justify the purchase price.

Notes

1. See our book, *Diversification Through Acquisition: Strategies for Creating Economic Value* (New York, Free Press, 1979).

2. Michael E. Porter, "How Competitive Forces Shape Strategy," *HBR*, March–April 1979, p. 137.

3. See our book, *Diversification Through Acquisition*, p. 194, for a detailed explanation of how to develop a weighting system.

PART SIX
PENSION FUND MANAGEMENT

AN OVERVIEW

Corporate pension fund management does not capture the public eye as do mergers and acquisitions, but contributions to pension funds represent a major spending item for business firms and this subject poses a number of key issues for corporate executives. Like other important capital expenditures, regular decisions must be made concerning how much money to invest, how to manage the assets over time, and how to withdraw funds from the investment, that is, how to design and reach agreement on benefit and eligibility provisions. Moreover, unlike most other capital expenditures, the time period involved is very long (perpetuity), and there are numerous legal, tax, and actuarial complexities.

One critical issue is the need to make assumptions about future salaries and investment returns. In "Pension Plan Sponsors: Open the Actuarial Black Box," Dreher suggests that assumptions used in a pension plan be made explicit. In particular, an explicit inflation assumption should be made and then it should be incorporated in projected salary growth and investment returns. In a survey of 180 firms, he found virtually no correlation between salary and return assumptions even though both are influenced heavily by the inflation rate.

Tepper's article, "Risk vs. Return in Pension Fund Management," describes a computer-based model that can be usefully employed to simulate the operation of a pension fund. It was used in the article to study the implications of different portfolio mixes of stocks and bonds, but it also incorporates other key aspects of a pension plan, such as work force projections and actuarial assumptions. Thus it can tie together all the important factors of a pension plan. In "How Much Funding for Your Company's

Pension Plan?,'' Tepper and Paul point out that it makes sense in some situations for companies to make more than the minimum required pension contributions. This results from the fact that earnings in the pension fund are tax-free. Situations favoring above-minimum pension funding are identified in the article.

The last two articles in Part 6 provide some practical advice by corporate executives. In Figgie's article, ''Defusing the Pension Liability Bomb,'' he explains his company's approach to funding pension plans. He argues for full funding of pension plans and for not letting employee retirement benefits run ahead of the company's funding ability. Kent focuses on a different area, describing Honeywell's approach to management of the assets in his article, ''Team Management of Pension Money.'' It is an interesting description of the process his company went through to develop a portfolio strategy, select a team of fund managers, and design a management process.

25
Pension Plan Sponsors: Open the Actuarial Black Box

WILLIAM A. DREHER

Dreher suggests that pension plan assumptions be made explicit and used consistently. For example, an explicit inflation assumption should be incorporated in projections of both salary growth and investment returns.

What would you say the U.S. inflation rate will average over the next 20 years—3%? 5%? 7%? Would you believe 1%? No? Well, that's what the sponsors of 180 pension plans, included in a 1979 survey my firm conducted, are assuming. The survey strongly suggests that actuaries may be recommending, and their clients adopting, assumptions that have only remote connection with reasonable expectations.

For the 180 plans, all having final-pay benefit formulas, the average investment return assumption has been slightly under 6%. At a glance, one might conclude that the funding of these plans is quite conservative. But that is only part of the story: Their salary increase assumptions have averaged only about 4.25%. After allowing for productivity wage gains and merit and seniority increases, these actuarial assumptions are, in the aggregate, implying a future inflation rate of about 1%.

Today few forecasters seriously suggest that the long-term inflation rate will fall below 3%.

Although salaries and wages always have to fight to stay even with inflation, over a typical employee's career his or her real income will probably rise at an average rate of 3 to 4% per year—depending on the real growth rate of GNP and other economic elements. If inflation averages 4%

or 5% over the long term, 7 to 9% average annual salary increases are much more likely than 4.25%.

Do the two understatements in the 180 pension plans trade off? Is the typical pension plan underfunding or underaccruing pension expense? If salary projections are 3 to 5% lower than they ought to be, how much more investment return than 6% is required to compensate for the error on the salary side?

The answer varies from plan to plan, of course, but a rough guess is that 2 to 3% of additional investment return will offset the 3 to 5% understatement of salaries and enable the plan sponsor to keep costs level as a percentage of payroll. This adjustment raises the required investment return from 6 to 8% or 9%.

Our survey shows no consistency between the investment return assumptions and the salary increase assumptions. The correlation coefficient between the two variables is −.02, indicating a purely random relationship. The spread between the investment return assumption and the salary increase assumption ranges from +5% to −2.5%.

It is difficult to draw a conclusion about the quality of pension funding represented by this cross section of plans; their benefit and eligibility provisions, their investment policies, and the demographic characteristics of the working and retired participants all differ considerably. A judgment from only two actuarial assumptions implies that all the other assumptions—for mortality, retirement, and employee turnover, to name only a few—are collectively appropriate.

With these hazards in mind, I have estimated the funding adequacy of these 180 plans and assumed that future salary increases would average between 7% and 8.5% and that nominal investment returns, after management fees and trading costs, would fall in the 8 to 9% range.

I have concluded that about 15% of the plans are underfunding their current obligations, about 40% are fairly realistic, and the remaining 45% are overfunding the current level of plan benefits. The sponsors in the last group are pessimistic about the outlook for our country's economic and financial markets or want to fund for future plan amendments in advance of their formal adoption, or both.

Influencing my judgment was Peat Marwick's latest survey of economists. It produced a consensus that the long-term rate of inflation will average 6%, that real wage gains for the work force will average 2%, that bond returns will approximate 8.5%, and that equities will yield about 12.5%.

One may ask why actuaries and their clients take such a myopic view of the future, particularly when the American Academy of Actuaries has stated: "The greater impact of inflation on pension costs . . . has led to increasing use of explicit recognition of inflation in each actuarial assumption, the preferred approach." (The FASB defines *explicit* as "incorporating a realistic estimate of the future impact of inflation directly into the relevant actuarial assumption.")

In the selection of actuarial assumptions, there is no sensible alternative to the explicit approach. In this atmosphere of realism, plan sponsors can participate actively in the assumption-setting dialogue. They will understand the consequences and rationale of the methods and assumptions underlying the plan's costs and liabilities.

Investment Policies

Pension fund investment policies have become much more conservative in recent years. The shift from equities to debt securities was mainly a reaction to the bitter stock market lessons of 1973 and 1974 as well as an overreaction to ERISA's fiduciary standards, which became law within weeks of the 1974 market bottom. The use of implicit (i.e., not explicit) actuarial assumptions greatly affected this trend.

In recent years many plan sponsors have asked, "Why shouldn't we buy 9% (or 10% or 11%) bonds or an insurance-company-guaranteed investment contract? That way we can lock in our 6% investment return assumption." The question is sensible, but the answer is wrong unless the sponsor understands the relationship between the actuarial assumptions and the plan's investment policy. Plans that use implicit assumptions encourage the illusion that an all-bond investment policy will meet the funding requirements.

The shift of pension funds from 70% equity exposure in 1974 to 50% currently has cost them terribly. For the six years ended September 30, 1980, the typical pension fund had an equity return of 15.3%, whereas the average fixed-income portfolio had a total annual return of 6.9%.

Such a conservative investment policy may continue to be costly. Our 1979 survey of economists indicates that per-share earnings would suffer a decline of about 8.2% in 1980, but then would grow at an average rate of 10.3% from 1981 through 1986. This group of economists estimated a cash yield of 4.9% on stocks and a price/earnings multiple of 9.2 at the end of 1986.

We took these market assumptions and applied capital asset pricing theory to develop a projected total return on stocks for the 1981–1986 period. The result was 18% compounded.

The economists anticipate an average total return on diversified corporate bond portfolios of about 11% per year over the next five years. In this environment, companies with pension funds should reexamine their asset mix guidelines and consider raising the maximum equity exposure available to their investment managers.

When setting the benchmarks against which their investment managers will be tested, too many pension plan sponsors look to the actuarial investment return assumption. Even if a plan has explicit assumptions, it is dangerous to expect the portfolio's investment return to track the actuarial assumptions year by year. It is dangerous because of the different time horizons. The funding policy of a pension plan is usually focused on projections over at least 20 or 30 years; investment policies and the investment managers' expectations are focused on much shorter time spans—three to five years at most.

Two additional reasons that investment policies and performance goals should not be tied to the actuarial investment return assumption are:

- ☐ The actuary may be incorporating large safety margins into the investment assumption to provide for the possibility of adverse economic and investment results, to accelerate tax deductions, or (if the company is regulated) to increase its cost structure.
- ☐ The client may be disguising a program of advance funding for future plan amendments by adopting an actuarial assumption that understates reasonable expectations for returns on the plan's portfolio.

The sponsors of the pension plan (even if it is final-pay related) may need to improve early retirement benefits, add a spouse's pension feature, or provide cost-of-living increases for retirees. The long-term cost of a COLA provision for retirees may require another 2 to 2.5% return on plan assets. Therefore, the "true" investment return objective—of a plan needing an 8% or a 9% return to fund its final pay benefits and to keep its annual costs from rising—may be closer to an 11% than it is to a 6% actuarial assumption.

Learning from History

Bonds are no longer the safe solution to the investment problem. The odds have changed, and it is now necessary to accept equity risk and to hope that the incremental return on equities will bring total portfolio returns into the 10 to 12% range.

A wise pension plan sponsor will base decisions on a realistic outlook toward the future and will coordinate the economic, financial, and demographic assumptions underlying the plan's actuarial basis and its investment policy.

Too many plan sponsors and too many of their actuaries have failed to recognize this commonsense requirement. In choosing actuarial assumptions, they have presumed that the recent past is the best predictor of long-term expectations. Doing this is as unwise as driving a car with both eyes on the rearview mirror.

They have also planned for the asset side of the pension fund balance sheet by basing the investment policy on economic and financial assumptions that bear little or no relationship to the assumptions underlying the measurement of the plan's liabilities and costs.

We cannot rewrite the history of the 1970s, but we can absorb its message and attempt to deal with the challenges and opportunities that the 1980s present to pension plan sponsors. As a corporate manager, you can deal with the issue by:

- ☐ Developing an opinion about the near-term and long-term real growth of the economy, about inflation rates, and about how all these will affect your company and industry.
- ☐ Considering the potential for changes in the size and composition of your work force.
- ☐ Making realistic forecasts of wage and salary increases and identifying the prospects for amending your plan's benefits.
- ☐ Keeping in mind your criteria for estimating the cost of debt and the required return on equity.
- ☐ Integrating the assumptions underlying your plan's investment policy with the comparable elements in its actuarial basis.

Remember that the key for plan sponsors is to set sensible funding targets, based on defensible actuarial assumptions, and to choose accounting (read "actuarial") methods that appropriately allocate pension costs and funding obligations to current and future accounting periods. You may find that pension costs are not an extreme burden on corporate resources and that unfunded plan liabilities are less onerous than unrealistic actuarial appraisals have suggested.

26
Risk vs. Return in Pension Fund Investment

IRWIN TEPPER

Pension liabilities and corporate contributions to pension funds, as everybody knows, have been growing at a great rate. So there is no more important goal in pension management than seeking the investment policy that provides the highest yield without, at the same time, causing undue risk of unfunded liabilities. This article outlines one technique for determining the proper investment mix in view of the organization's financial goals, the condition of its pension plan, and the situation of its participants. A computer model simulates how the pension plan will fare in a range of investment policies and actuarial conditions, and lays out the results clearly for the benefit of the organization's financial planners. By means of a case study, the author shows how a company actually went through the process and ultimately arrived at a decision that has proved right for it.

What pension plan investment policy should we have? Because pension plans are no longer a negligible factor in the financial picture of most companies, this question is now being addressed at the highest levels of corporate management. A recent study of 40 companies, selected as representative of U.S. industry, reveals that pension costs account for 18% of pretax profits and that unfunded pension liabilities approach 19% of net worth.[1] Furthermore, the pension burden probably will continue to escalate.

The investment policy question dominates the list of management's thinking about pensions because the ultimate decision determines the long-run costs of the plan. Obviously, the higher the fund's rate of return, the less money a company must lay out to meet its escalating pension obligations.

Unfortunately, as the events of 1973 and 1974 demonstrated, the converse is also true. The 40% decline in the stock market in those two years severely reduced pension fund values. Because no offsetting reduction in the value of pension liabilities took place, the bear market dramatically increased unfunded liabilities.

The Employee Retirement Income Security Act of 1974 (ERISA) prescribes that such deficiencies must be made up out of corporate funds, although recognition of the loss may be spread over a 15-year period. (Under ERISA, the full market decline in a pension portfolio does not, of course, have to be recognized in the year of its occurrence. Under the permissible smoothing procedures in asset valuation, recognition of the loss can be spread over several years.) In a typical plan, the contributions in each of those years would approximate 10% of the loss.

The impact on net earnings depends on the circumstances. It is safe to say, however, that for most mature companies the 1973–1974 experience added significantly to the financial burden of their pension plans.

Other provisions of ERISA have clarified the link between a pension plan's investment policy and the sponsor's finances. In the event of termination of the plan, the sponsor is accountable for any unfunded vested liability up to 30% of corporate net worth. (In the study I have referred to, the unfunded vested liability averaged 5% of net worth.) Because this claim has the status of a tax lien, banks and other creditors are now factoring any unfunded vested liability into the lending decision.

The law also contains a fiduciary responsibility provision applicable to trustees, money managers, and all other parties involved in the asset management function. Its intent is to ensure that the company sets the plan's investment policy with due regard for future financial requirements and the sponsor's ability to meet them. This provision has formalized the concept of pension fund financial planning as an integral part of arriving at investment policy.

The optimal stock-bond mix is the single most important element of the investment policy decision. It is widely accepted that, on the average, equities will continue to yield higher long-run returns than bonds; but equities will also remain much more volatile. How can this prospect be factored into investment policy?

By means of a case study, this article analyzes a technique that allows corporate sponsors to measure the effects of various asset mixes directly and in the terms most meaningful to them—pension costs and unfunded pension liabilities. By factoring pension costs into the income statement and unfunded pension liability into the balance sheet, a company can set pension fund investment policy with the same criteria it employs to control other elements of its finances.

In focusing on investment policy, I do not consider the analysis of other important matters affecting a pension plan—that is, inflation, actuarial assumptions, or the funding policy. But the framework I discuss in this article is capable of handling many of these issues.

Planning Framework

The relationship between investment policy and the future financial burden of a pension plan is influenced by many factors. Playing an important role are:

- ☐ The future population of the plan's participants (active employees, retirees, and vested terminated employees).
- ☐ The plan's benefit provisions, such as vesting and early retirement.
- ☐ The actuarial cost method, the asset valuation procedure, and the assumptions established by the plan's actuary.
- ☐ Future capital market conditions.

How can the sponsor bring all these factors together in order to see the net effect of investment policy in its broadest context? The most direct way is to simulate the operation of the pension fund over the spectrum of bond-stock mixes and generate a set of pro forma financial statements for the plan. Exhibit 1 is a diagram of one model used to do this. A computer-based simulation model performs all the calculations.

For each prospective investment policy, the computer projects pension costs and unfunded liability for each of the next 20 years. The steps it goes through include (1) projecting the entries and departures of the work force and retiree pools; (2) projecting salary increases; (3) calculating the plan's normal cost (i.e., the cost of benefits created in the current year); (4) amortizing the plan's past service liability, as required by ERISA; (5) estimating the benefit payments to be made to retirees in the current year; (6) determining the earnings on the pension fund; (7) analyzing the investment experience of the plan; and (8) setting up the 15-year amortization schedules. (Some cost methods permit experience gains and losses to be built into future costs, and the computer model is modified to accommodate this factor.)

The computer model that does all this must, of course, be complex. It contains a package that analyzes the dynamics of the work force, the complete actuarial system established for the plan, and a technique for "sampling" the investment experience that the fund will encounter. Once constructed and verified, however, it is easy to use. As I shall demonstrate, the output comes in a form well suited for its intended use.

The plan's investment experience is derived from a set of forecasts of the returns that the sponsors and their money managers expect to obtain in the stock and bond markets. A realistic assessment of the manager's ability to deal with capital market uncertainties should be factored into these projections.

No one who could have anticipated the performance of the stock market in 1973 and 1974—the worst in 40 years—would have invested in equities. Yet pension funds on the whole were saddled with substantial equity investment during that period. Since most of these funds were in the hands

Exhibit 1. A Pension Fund Financial Planning Framework

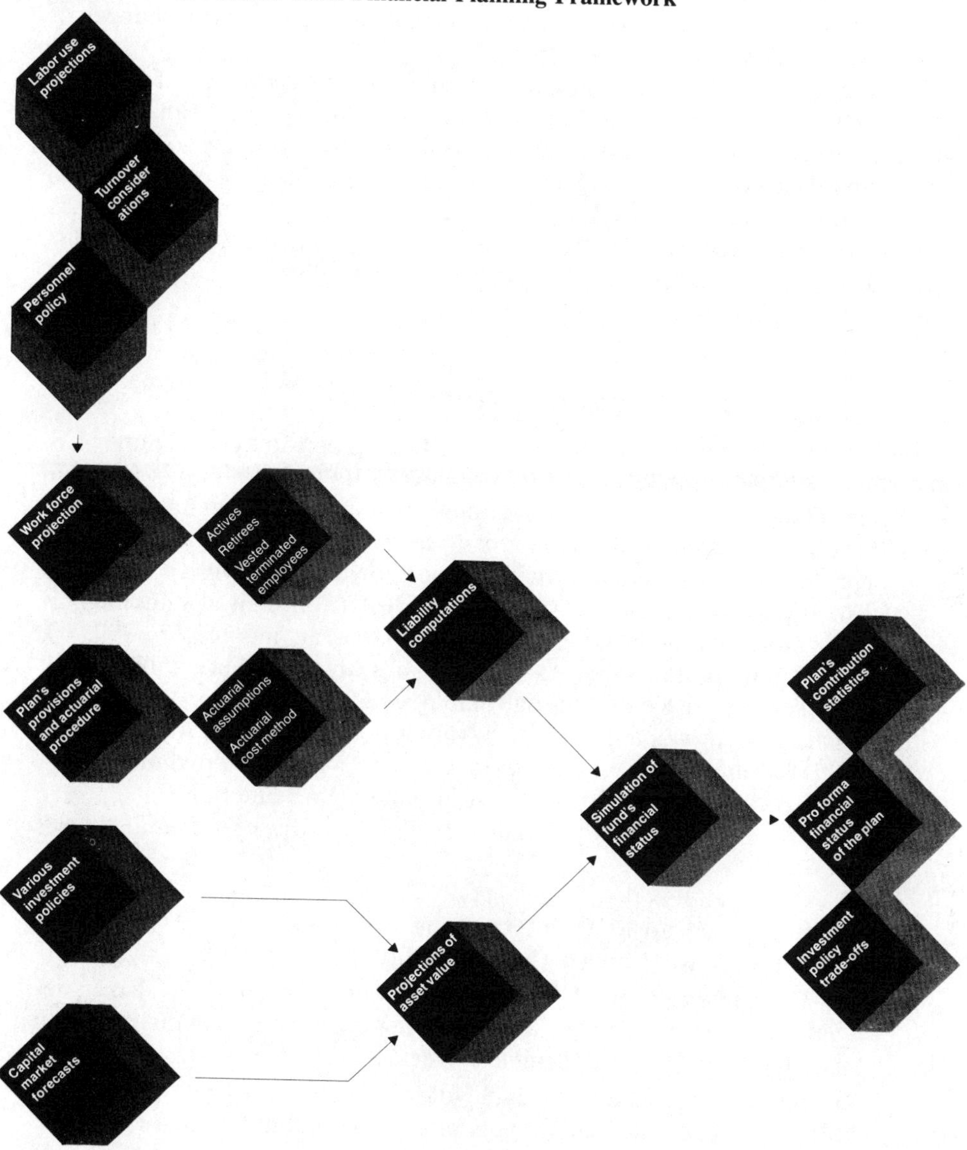

of money managers, it is obvious that even the professionals in the business cannot penetrate the uncertainties in the capital markets.

Of course, the 1973–1974 period is not the only one in which the stock market failed to perform according to expectations. The lesson to be learned from history is that the investment process must be accepted as a statistical phenomenon in which expected returns and risks go hand in hand. Mere point estimates of annual returns make up an incomplete and unrealistic description of the capital markets. The sponsor must specify the chances of earning each possible level of return.

The computer model simulates the investment experience of the pension fund over the 20-year period. Instead of making a point estimate of the fund's earnings, it constructs a random sample drawn from a pool of all the possible returns of the plan's investment experience. The pool is constructed so that the chances of obtaining any one occurrence depend on the odds specified by the sponsor. In the case that follows (an actual, although disguised, case), I elaborate on this procedure and other aspects of pension fund financial planning.

Super Investment Policy

Prompted by the enactment of ERISA and rising pension costs, Super Co. is using a planning model to aid in a review of its pension plan's financial policies. The plan covers some 600 employees, many of whom have become eligible only recently as the result of a change in the company's benefit package. Super management anticipates no growth in the work force.

The company's profits in 1976 slipped 30% from their all-time high of two years before. The company's pension costs last year amounted to $600,000, or about 22% of pretax income. The plan has an unfunded liability of $2 million (assets equal $7 million and liabilities $9 million). In ordering the study, management wanted to know whether it could realistically expect to reduce this liability with a change in investment policy, by how much if so, and what trade-offs would be involved in pursuing a reduction.

In launching the study, Super established these actuarial policy parameters:

- ☐ It adopted an 8½% interest rate assumption for the plan. This figure is somewhat higher than is usually found.
- ☐ It assumed an annual salary growth rate of 7%, a figure also somewhat higher than average, for projecting retirement benefits (the plan has a final-average pay formula for establishing benefits).
- ☐ It forecast for the foreseeable future a 5½% to a 6% rate of inflation, which would be reflected not only in the payroll, but also in the nominal returns the plan earned on its investments. In other words, the sponsor assumed that the relationship between inflation and the returns in each sector of the capital market would *not* continue their abnormal pattern of the last decade.
- ☐ It expected the bond market to yield a lower average return and to exhibit much less volatility than stocks.

Super's bond portfolio was to be actively managed—that is, its manager would trade when he saw incremental profit opportunities. The sponsor expected this approach to result in a modest improvement in the results that would be achieved by a buy-and-hold strategy. A different person ran the equity portfolio, which was to be diversified. He was expected to shift funds into and out of cash equivalents when he felt confident that such timing decisions would, on the average, enhance the return.

Taking into account historical relationships, forecasts of economic and financial scenarios, and the portfolio administration characteristics of each manager, Super came up with the statistical forecasts of returns on its stock and bond portfolios that can be seen in Exhibit 2. The simulation model uses these probability distributions to extract random samples of the plan's investment experience.

The exhibit shows two probability distributions, one for 100% of the stocks invested and one for 100% of the bonds purchased. This histogram indicates that, for example, there is a 13% chance of obtaining a bond return between 3% and 5%, and a 7% chance of losing between 5% and 10% of its money invested in equities.

Super was in the process of changing its asset valuation scheme, which provides the basis for determining if the plan's investment return is matching the actuarial assumption or whether a gain or a loss has actually occurred. Super had been using a formula designed to smooth fluctuations in its equity investment experience. Now the company decided to experiment with a method whereby bonds would be kept at amortized (i.e., book) value and equities would be maintained at full market value. This procedure is sanctioned under ERISA.

Exhibit 2. Forecasts of Annual Returns on Stocks and Bonds

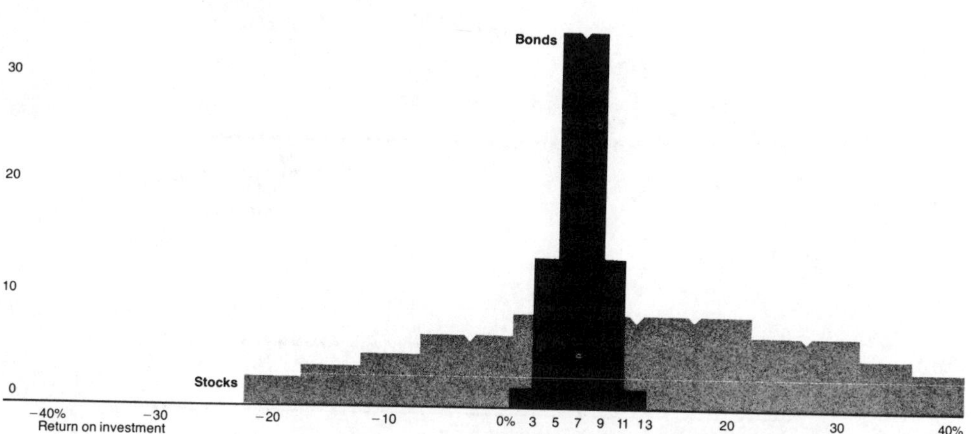

Financial Analysis

Exhibit 3 shows how Super's investment policy affects its pension costs and unfunded liability. The data come from a simulated look at the twentieth year into the future; years 1 to 19 exhibit similar financial profiles on a somewhat smaller scale.

The percentile lines incorporate the data on the volatility, or risk, inherent in the future financial condition of the plan. For example, there is a 95% chance that the value of the quantity on the vertical axis will fall below the 95th percentile line. On the other hand, there is a 5% chance that pension costs will exceed this value. The median (50th percentile line) is a measure of the trend in the data, because the chance of being on either side of this line is 50/50. The distances from the median to the 5th and the 95th percentiles are measures of the risk inherent in achieving results close to the statistical tendencies (that is, the median). The "bumps" in the percentiles are a product of the simulation process rather than a discontinuity in the pension finances.

The actuarial projection of costs (the dashed line) includes such estimates as the plan's normal costs and unfunded liability amortization but excludes the impact of investment experience. This projection assumes that

Exhibit 3. Impact of Investment Policy on Pension Costs in the Twentieth Year

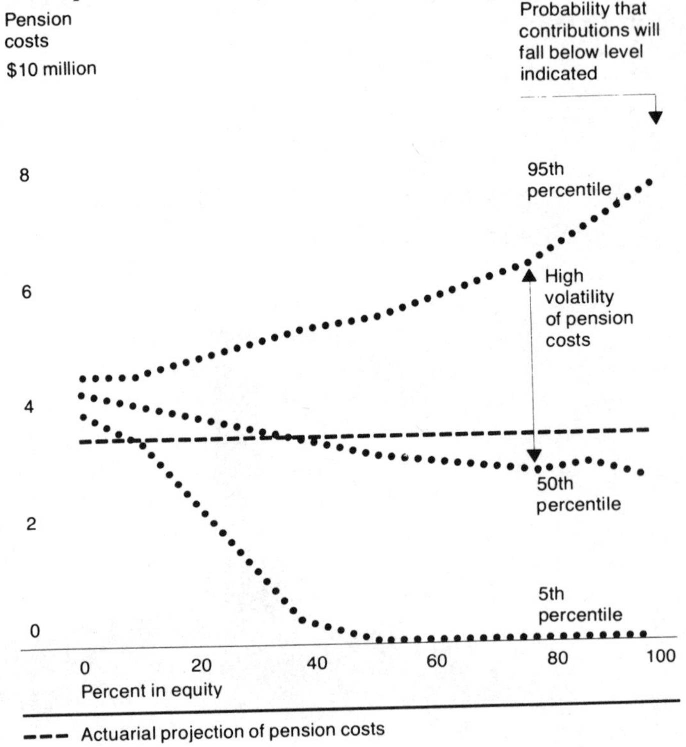

Pension costs $10 million

Probability that contributions will fall below level indicated

8
6
4
2
0

95th percentile

High volatility of pension costs

50th percentile

5th percentile

0 20 40 60 80 100

Percent in equity

--- Actuarial projection of pension costs

the pension fund will earn the plan's actuarial interest rate every year. The differences between the dashed line and the dotted lines are attributable solely to the impact of investment experience (i.e., all other factors in the pension system are held constant). In this manner, Super can determine whether the plan's interest rate assumption is appropriate for the investment policy selected.

Looking at the left side of Exhibit 3, Super's financial vice-president observed that if the company selected an investment policy that had little equity investment, the pension contributions would be highly predictable, but the plan also would incur the highest average cost over the range of possibilities. The contributions would exceed the actuarial projection because portfolios dominated by long-term bonds are incapable of producing returns as high as the plan's 8½% interest rate assumption. As a result, the plan would experience a series of actuarial losses on investments, amortizable over 15 years. Therefore, if an all-bond investment policy is chosen, the company should reduce the plan's interest rate assumption.

Increasing the proportion of stocks relative to bonds, he noticed, would reduce the average level (the 50th percentile) of pension costs. At the same time, however, the unpredictability would increase greatly, reflecting the volatility of the stock market. Eventually, the marginal benefits of rising equity investment would almost disappear as the potential risk became insupportable.

Super had figured that the actuarial projection of $3.3 million in pension costs would approximate 22% of pretax earnings in the twentieth year. That proportion was the same as the company's experience in 1976. Super was anticipating no significant growth and was assuming that its revenues and costs would grow more or less in proportion to the inflationary movement of the economy.

Using 22% as a rough benchmark, the financial staff estimated that an all-bond portfolio would lead to an average level of pension costs equal to 26% of pretax profits, whereas an all-equity portfolio would result in an 18% level. Therefore, Super could adjust the average level of pension costs, as a percentage of pretax profits, within a plus or minus 4% band around the current figure. Naturally, in pursuing a cost reduction, the company would have to accept higher risk. For example, an all-equity portfolio would expose Super to a 5% chance that pension costs would amount to 63% of pretax income 20 years hence.

The relationship between investment policy and the projected financial status of the pension plan—that is, its asset-liability balance—appears in Exhibit 4. It is evident that the investment policies stressing equities tend to move the plan toward a fully funded status. This favorable funding trend accompanies the declining level of average contributions, which, of course, reflects the superior returns anticipated in the stock market.

Because the stock market is so unpredictable, however, a significant deterioration in the plan's unfunded liability may develop as soon as the manager makes any major equity investment. Equity investments in excess

Exhibit 4. Pension Plan Asset Value and Liabilities in the Twentieth Year

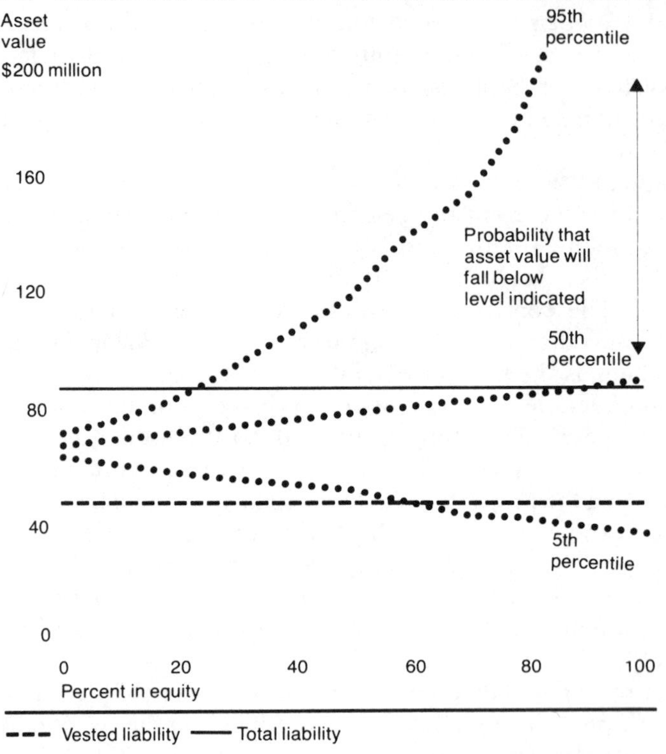

of 60% present troubling possibilities of unfunded vested liabilities—a critical concern for stockholders, creditors, and the Pension Benefit Guaranty Corporation. That corporation, of course, is the termination insurance fund administered by the Department of Labor, which steps in when a pension plan fails and imposes a lien on the employer of up to 30% of his assets.

Ultimate Decision

From these graphs, the financial VP could see that equity-oriented investment strategies would significantly reduce pension costs and the unfunded liability, and at the same time make pension finances unstable. The investment policy trade-offs are present throughout the spectrum of asset mixes; the appropriate one depends on the sponsor's circumstances and financial goals.

But there seemed to be little point in further consideration of the two ends of the spectrum—either at the low-risk end, with a maximum equity commitment of 10%, or at the other end, where equity investments of 70 to 80% offer little reward for taking extra risks. In the intermediate range, there is a relatively constant trade-off between expected contributions and volatility.

In the five years prior to 1975, Super had experienced steady growth, and the relationships among salaries, pension contributions, and profits before taxes had been stable. In 1975 and 1976, however, the failure of revenues to rise at previous rates, while salaries and other operating expenses climbed, had disrupted these stable relationships. Therefore, the company concluded, the near-term uncertainty in the business overshadowed the risks inherent in a pension policy heavily commited to equity.

Another factor was the executives' feeling that the capital markets would be more volatile than originally assumed. They ordered a simulation rerun for a pessimistic view of the market. The results indicated that pension contributions would *rise* rather than fall as the investment in stocks increased beyond the level of 50% equities. Yet the volatility continued to rise.

On the ground that the potential rewards were justified, the financial VP and his associates decided to adopt a 50 to a 70% range in the stock-bond mix for the next few years. At the end of that period, the decision was to come under review.

Integrating the Analysis

The financial planning model I have described is useful for examining a range of pension problems broader than the investment policy question. It can assist sponsors in projecting pension costs, in testing their actuarial model against experience, and in determining the cost of proposed benefit liberalization. The analysis helps managers make explicit their assumptions about the future.

The development of a pension fund financial planning model is an interdisciplinary task requiring the participation of the plan's actuaries and money managers. Usually, these professionals have operated independently. Although this stance may be acceptable at the level of policy implementation, it is intolerable in policy setting. Happily, ERISA has been responsible for a new-found interest in integrating into policymaking the analysis of the plan's assets and liabilities. Corporate sponsors should follow this lead in promoting a cooperative atmosphere among the pension planning participants.

It is fair to say that much of the extraordinary growth of pension liabilities, the associated corporate costs, and the attendant asset accumulation could have been predicted, and the companies that did project them knew what to expect. It is also fair to say that, given the policies their sponsors have followed, the current difficulties of many pension plans are understandable.

Despite the limitations imposed by ERISA, pension plan sponsors still enjoy broad discretion in the way they comply with the newly augmented regulations. An effort to improve pension trust management along the lines I have suggested should pay off.

Note

1. Jack L. Treynor, Patrick J. Regan, and William W. Priest, *The Financial Reality of Pension Funding Under ERISA* (Homewood, Illinois, Dow Jones–Irwin, 1976).

27
How Much Funding for Your Company's Pension Plan?

IRWIN TEPPER and ROBERT D. PAUL

Tepper and Paul point out in their article that it makes sense, in some situations, for companies to contribute more than the minimum required to their pension program. This results from the fact that pension fund earnings are tax free.

Corporations are breaking with tradition in pension funding policy. No longer do they automatically make merely the minimum contributions determined by their actuaries in order to comply with the Employment Retirement Income Security Act of 1974 (ERISA). For example, here is a statement in a Joy Manufacturing Co. annual report:

> In fiscal 1976, the company elected to fund $2,044,000 in addition to pension costs accrued. The additional contribution, which had no effect on fiscal 1976 pension expenses, is included in prepaid expenses and deposits at September 24, 1976.

ERISA has changed the picture. The minimum funding level has been raised. Now actuarial assumptions have to be certified as being reasonably related to expected experience. Experience losses have to be amortized over 15 years and, most important, the corporation remains liable for vested benefits of up to about $12,068 annually per participant even if the plan is ended. The stockholders have at risk at least 30% of their net worth if the plan is terminated or the company goes out of business.

These considerations have led a growing number of pension plan sponsors to view pension funding in a new light. If a corporation's plan obligates it to pay out certain benefits, and not simply make contributions at a certain minimum level, then the question of funding is not one of "if" but of "when." This question is similar to a capital-budgeting problem in that a higher initial financial commitment produces future returns in the form of reduced cash outlays to fund the pension plan.

The poor performance of the stock market in recent years also has contributed to the reexamination of pension funding policy. As a result, many sponsors have concluded that the pension fund is no longer an attractive investment opportunity, especially compared with the company's cost of capital.

Pension costs in the long run equal the benefits paid out plus administrative expenses less earnings on invested assets. Clearly the higher the percentage of costs covered by the earnings on investments, the lower the company's out-of-pocket costs.

On the other hand, any contributions made to the pension fund in excess of the minimum required by statute deprive the stockholders of capital that might be better employed in the business. The instinctive feeling of many corporate managers that removing dollars from the treasury earlier than the law requires could be detrimental to the stockholders has influenced the pension funding strategy of many corporations. This assumption deserves reexamination.

Investment Alternative

The earnings on money in the pension fund are not, of course, subject to tax. Therefore, a company's pension fund gives it the chance to earn a tax-free rate of return.

When compared on a rate-of-return basis, other corporate investments obviously must be twice as attractive as the pension fund on a beforetax basis in order to yield equivalent aftertax benefits. If pension fund assets are invested in, say, 8% bonds of another corporation, it would take a pretax return of nearly 16% to match this rate of return. But few corporations enjoy a pretax rate of return on assets of more than 16%.

It can be argued that the marginal return on internal investment exceeds the pension fund benchmark. Certainly some investments promise benefits that greatly exceed pension fund opportunities. Unless the economy is facing a period of capital shortage, however, it is unlikely that pension funding will be noncomparable to other outlays. Periods of corporate illiquidity and unfriendly capital markets, such as we have had recently, do not last forever, and any corporation that perceives itself to be in a perpetual state of capital shortage is likely to be ignoring valuable capital-budgeting opportunities, including funding for its pension plan.

Financing the Investment

Borrowing to fund the investment in the pension plan is a sound, reasonably risk-free step. A company can use the proceeds from a debt offering to buy equivalent bonds for the pension fund, at presumably identical yields. This arbitrage approach lets the fund earn tax-free interest while the sponsor pays the same amount of interest and gets a tax deduction.

Using borrowed money to finance an *equity* investment in the pension fund produces the same tax advantage, but introduces a possibly undesirable element of risk. Unless some investments in the pension fund are unavailable to shareholders, or the sponsor believes that the fund's money manager invests better than the shareholders, there is no justification for investment in the pension fund on their behalf.

Financing the pension fund with a mix of debt and equity will, of course, provide a tax benefit to the extent of the debt component of the funds employed.

Negative Aspects

The tax benefits that make the pension fund a good investment alternative must be balanced against some negative factors. One is the impact of funding on corporate liquidity. Obviously it is hard, if not impossible, for the company to draw on its pension fund assets because they are held in trust as collateral for pension liabilities.

The illiquidity of the pension fund, however, does not make it a totally inflexible source of funds. Let us return to the Joy Manufacturing illustration. At the time the company made the $2 million contribution in excess of the ERISA floor, the plan's minimum funding requirement was approximately $8 million. The minimum probably would have continued at about $8 million annually. This means that in the near term, barring some drastic and unexpected event, the company would be funding substantially greater amounts than the excess $2 million.

Under the ERISA funding accounting system that Joy uses, the company kept the $2 million on the pension fund books as a credit to be used to meet future pension expenses, whereas on the corporate financial statements it appears as a prepaid expense. (The company could have elected an accounting system under which the full $10 million would have been the required pension expense.) Hence Joy has the flexibility to use the $2 million credit in a time of financial need as an offset against future funding requirements.

Another negative factor stems from the event of termination of a pension plan. Its assets then are allocated to the beneficiaries based on a priority of claims scheme, whereas the sponsor is liable only for deficiencies in meeting the claims of beneficiaries with a vested right to benefits guaranteed by the Pension Benefit Guaranty Corporation (PBGC).

Other beneficiaries receive money only if any remains after senior claims are met. Therefore, the larger the investment of corporate assets in the pension fund, the greater the loss is likely to be in a termination situation if the assets exceed the amount required to match the PBGC-guaranteed benefits and the excess turns out to be irrecoverable.

When one considers the multitude of reasons for termination other than bankruptcy or severely adverse business circumstances, it becomes apparent that termination possibilities are not always remote. Pension plans are often dissolved as a result of change in ownership, liquidation, closing of a subsidiary, a division, or a plant, a consolidation of the company's pension plans, or conversion or a profit-sharing plan.

In the absence of any implicit moral obligation, sponsors should be cautious in funding beyond their legal obligation—the guaranteed vested liability benchmark—if even a small chance of termination exists. Corporate exposure in the pension fund is probably the single most important factor to be considered in deciding where to limit contributions.

Still another often-discussed negative factor is inflation. Because of the late failure of rates of return in pension fund portfolios to keep up with climbing inflation rates, many sponsors question the logic of funding tomorrow's benefits with today's dollars. In this view, investing in the pension fund beyond the minimum is a poor decision if management cannot rely on the fund's rate of return to at least maintain the purchasing power of corporate funds.

It can be argued, however, that sponsors who take a dim view of the future investment climate are overreacting to their recent experience. A number of singular events coincided to produce the inflationary explosion. The level of the capital markets today reflects the consensus of investors' expectations for inflation. The anticipated returns on portfolios have a built-in inflation premium and, unless inflation fails to materialize in accordance with expectations, pension fund portfolios will allow sponsors to finance future benefits with today's dollars with no bias in the real outcome.

The economic incentives to fund the pension plan are present even for sponsors distressed over the outlook for a balance between investment returns and inflation. They can hedge fully with a debt-financed investment in a pension portfolio consisting of bonds. Thus any purchasing power losses (gains) in pension fund assets would be offset by purchasing power gains (losses) on the corporate balance sheet. In other words, if the company winds up with cheap dollars in the pension fund, at the same time it can pay off its own debt obligations in equally cheap dollars.

If a company has recently provided extra funding for its pension plan, the company's labor negotiators may be subjected, during the next collective bargaining sessions, to pressure to improve benefits. To these negotiators there is an asymmetry at work in labor relations: The company is asked to raise benefits when the pension plan is well funded, but benefits are not easily negotiated downward if the asset-liability balance deteriorates.

To rebut their opposite numbers in bargaining sessions, company representatives can point out that the employer has increased the rate of funding in order to make the benefits more secure. The improvement in funding has occurred not from a windfall in the stock market but through assets financed by the company and transferred from it.

Setting a Policy

Pro forma analysis is well suited for analyzing the effects of various funding policies. Discounted cash flow analysis can aid in estimating the present value of the economic benefits of advance funding.

As a rule of thumb, the present value of making a contribution now, as opposed to some time in the future, is equal to the product of the corporate tax rate and the amount that is funded. The economic benefit decreases as the interval over which the contribution is accelerated decreases. The impact of the other pros and cons is difficult to quantify, so the sponsor must choose a point along the spectrum of possibilities.

To help the public and the securities analysts understand the implication of the funding policy, the company should take care with the accompanying accounting and disclosure decisions. The accounting issues should not affect the policy decision but should reflect its intended impact.

The company need not treat any funding in excess of the minimum requirement as an expense that will depress reported earnings; as Joy Manufacturing has done, the company can carry it as a prepaid expense on the balance sheet to be amortized in the future. Disclosure of details of the transactions will help understanding of the rationale for the decision and will be reflected in the public's assessment of the company.

Actuarial policy can be varied widely to accommodate the funding decision. The actuary can select from a number of acceptable funding methods, each generating a different value for allowable funding limits. The manner in which actuaries treat inflation, the method they use to value the assets of the plan, and the degree of conservatism they employ in the valuation

Exhibit 1. Factors Favoring Above-Minimum Pension Funding

Other large investments planned	Few
Availability of debt capital	Good
Cost of capital	Low
Projected ERISA minimum contributions	Constant or increasing
Current unfunded present value of benefits for vestees	High
Chance of termination	Low

are parameters that can legitimately be varied to accommodate the company's funding policy.

Perhaps the biggest mistake in advance funding is matching it with an ill-conceived investment policy. As we indicated, the benefits of funding can be locked in with a bond portfolio. Few pension funds are invested in this manner, however, mainly because equities promise higher average returns and may offer a better hedge against inflation uncertainties.

But equities are also riskier. Therefore, the company should choose the mix based on analysis of the acceptable level of risk in the fund.

The corporate situations that should influence the decision-making process on advance funding of the pension plan are listed in Exhibit 1. For companies that have these characteristics, funding more than the minimum required by ERISA makes a lot of sense.

28
Defusing the Pension Liability Bomb

HARRY E. FIGGIE, JR.

As unfunded pension liabilities mount to huge proportions, companies and their labor unions are failing to heed the ticking of the time bomb that such liabilities may represent. Using the example of Figgie International (formerly A-T-O, Inc.), this author shows how a sound plan can be built up. He points out that government must change its requirements to encourage companies to fund their plans sooner, business must be content to accept a few cents less profit in order to put its plans on a better footing, and labor must not press for ever-larger commitments until the danger is past.

Unfunded pension liabilities today comprise a long-term debt of staggering dimensions. Although no one knows exactly how much money is involved, the debt runs to the tens of billions of dollars, and it is growing every year. This future debt represents a time bomb in our economy.

At best, pension obligations can undermine the stability of corporations; at worst, they could eventually cause business and industry to lose their right to manage pension funds. Surveys show that current assets of private and public pension systems are about $500 billion. Congress, which has already enacted the Employee Retirement Income Security Act and Multi-Employer Pension Plan Amendments Act, cannot be expected to long ignore and leave unregulated such an aggregation of assets. Should this happen, and one of the largest groups of investors in our stock market be moved from private to government control or regulation, the country's capital structure could be imperiled.

Of course, the underpinning of any policy to rehabilitate pension plan funding has to be prudent management of the fund itself. I have long believed that corporate chief executives should, wherever possible, involve themselves in all facets of pension funding. If this responsibility is not at the topmost level, it should be delegated near there. The pension plan represents a major business in which the company is engaged, whether it wants to be or not. It may already be equal to 50% or more of the company's net worth.

Because a pension plan usually has a life in perpetuity, it is probably the longest-term business in which corporations are engaged. This makes managing it especially challenging. Adding to the difficulty is the fact that managers are not dealing with plants and products that have predictable returns but with financial assets over which they have less control.

It is my experience that chief executives in business are not giving this problem the attention it warrants. Often just the opposite occurs. As liabilities mount, some top officers appear to be saying, in effect: "After me, the deluge. Let my successor worry about it."

Management, labor, and government all have a responsibility in this dilemma. With unions on one side pressing for past-service benefit increases and the Treasury Department on the other not allowing tax-deductible funding of such obligations in fewer than 10 years after the commitment is assumed, any corporation is, to a certain extent, caught in the middle. Yet, if their managements have the will, most companies can find a way to get out from under the burden of unfunded liabilities.

Management must be willing to accept, for the time being, a few cents less per share of increase in earnings. Labor must wake up to the fact that its long-term interest requires that it cooperate. In addition, the Internal Revenue Service must change its regulations to encourage companies to fund their plans promptly in a businesslike way.

None of us has a crystal ball, but projections make it clear that prompt and continued funding of past-service liabilities, as rapidly as the company can possibly do so, is essential. Everyone is aware of the toll that inflation is taking on fixed incomes and of the pressure this has generated to continually enlarge pension benefits. The problem for industry is not so much that pensions are being liberalized—Figgie International has been steadily improving its salary and hourly plans—but that so many plans are being liberalized in ways and under conditions that all but guarantee future financial disaster for possibly both the plan and the company.

A recent survey of 100 major U.S. corporations' unfunded vested benefits showed that these obligations increased by 14% between 1978 and 1979. General Motors' unfunded vested liability totaled $6.1 billion, almost a third of the corporation's net worth. The figure for Bethlehem Steel was $1.19 billion, more than 46% of its net worth; for Chrysler, $1.2 billion.

If such practices remain unchanged, it seems certain that some major plans will go under. If they do, thousands of workers could find themselves without continuing pension coverage. This disaster could also bankrupt the government-run pension insurance program, leaving it with billions of dollars of liabilities. Chrysler alone could do this, because the Pension Benefit Guaranty Corporation (PBGC) has a $1.46 million deficiency in assets to be made up by future insurance premiums (1979 fiscal year figures).

Many multiemployer plans have long been in trouble. If such plans fail, the employers will face years of liability, which could extend decades beyond any bargaining agreement affecting the plan. The liability of a single multiemployer plan, Central States Teamsters Plan, was $3.5 billion in unfunded vested liabilities as of December 31, 1980.

Sources of the Problem

Why are so many company plans locked into a spiral of ever-deepening liability? Typically, what happens is this: A manufacturer has a so-called $5 pension plan. This means a worker gets a $5 credit for every year she works. Thus, if she works 30 years, on retirement she receives $150 a month for the rest of her life. The manufacturer decides to grant employees future service credits of $6, $7, and $8 over the next three years because his industrial relations people tell him that this represents only so many cents per hour. He makes this settlement and technically should be able to manage it with increased contributions to the pension fund.

Simultaneously, however, unions will insist on and management will grant retroactive benefits to the same levels. This means the company is now agreeing that within the next three years all *past* service will be treated in the same manner, or at $6, $7, and $8. Thus a pension fund that usually has an unfunded liability to begin with adds a tremendous extra obligation, generally without anyone recognizing the impact beforehand.

At this point, even if the company wants to fund this added amount in a sound manner, the IRS discourages it from doing so by a rule precluding tax-deductible funding in fewer than 10 years. Admittedly, most corporations choose 20- to 30-year funding, putting off the problem into some never-never land. But even with the 10-year goal, pension plans that continue to grant past-service benefit increases cannot expect to improve their unfunded position. In fact, the situation will inevitably continue to deteriorate.

Improving the Plan

Even if prompt funding precludes adding to short-term profits (always an appealing temptation), such a policy will ultimately benefit shareholders. Analysts and brokers are now scrutinizing those unfunded liability footnotes in the annual reports more closely than ever before. A recent survey by Professor Martin Feldstein of Harvard, who heads the National Bureau of Economic Research, shows that stock prices go down as unfunded liabilities go up. Also, because the sooner money is put into the fund the longer it has to generate tax-free funds, present employees and pensioners can derive greater security, assuming prudent investment policies and a reasonable investment climate.

Still another advantage of keeping pension plans fully funded with regard to accrued benefits is that, in certain situations, full funding can free management to make beneficial decisions. For example, some companies have wanted to close or sell a lagging plant, but have been unable to do so because the pension plan termination costs were so high it was cheaper to continue operating on a marginal basis. Certainly, neither the company nor the shareholder benefits when bad economic decisions are made on the basis of a poorly funded pension plan.

Two Types of Plans

For salaried employees, the defined benefit plans—those that promise a specific benefit tied to number of years of service—traditionally come in one of two types: "career average" or "final pay." The former bases the pension on a person's average earnings over his or her entire career with the company. The latter usually takes the consecutive best five of the last 10 years of employment as the basis, or sometimes the consecutive best three of the last five years.

Generally, career-average plans offer lower pensions than final pay, which also more closely reflect the impact of inflation. Final-pay plans, however, make it all but impossible for actuaries to estimate true costs. How does one know whether an actuary is providing too much or too little for a plan based on a salary 20 years from now? Such final-pay plans generally result in much higher annual contributions because the actuaries must anticipate an employee's level of pay at the time of retirement.

Compensating for Inflation

Because of the toll inflation takes on fixed incomes, there is considerable pressure today to tie pensions to the consumer price index or some other gauge. Very few companies, I believe, are indexing benefits for employees after retirement. In my view, any such unquantifiable obligation is risky and unbusinesslike.

Even the government is encountering grave problems trying to link benefits to inflation for social security. I do not believe that private enterprise, which has neither blanket taxing powers nor infinite resources, should undertake such an open-ended obligation. It would jeopardize the security of all employees.

Example of Figgie

I need not cite other companies as examples. The experience of my own company, Figgie International (formerly A-T-O, Inc.), proved this. We took over an operation in 1966 that had pension assets of roughly $400,000, an unfunded liability of $990,000, and a pension level of $2. We wanted to fund the plan as quickly as we could and so adopted the IRS minimum period of 10 years, which was consistent with our company policy in our other divisions.

For 12 years we funded on a 10-year basis. Meanwhile, in every union negotiation, despite occasional strikes, we granted pension increases both forward and backward. The increases were not outlandish. At the end of 12 years, the pension level was up to $6. Furthermore, we limited retroactivity to the date that we had acquired the company, which was 1966, and therefore did not accept liability for service before that. This tended to reduce even more the amount of unfunded liability that could accrue.

Yet, at the end of 12 years of funding to the maximum allowed, while our assets in the plan had risen from $400,000 to $1.6 million for a 400% increase, our unfunded amount had *gone up* from $990,000 to $1.09 million—a $100,000 increase.

In 1977 we decided to stand firm on policies that would turn around our hourly plans, using an approach we had developed for our main salaried employee plan seven years earlier. We felt we could put the hourly plans on a sound basis in spite of government constraints.

The four of us on the pension committee at Figgie International meet regularly with our investment advisers. We select our advisers not only on their track records, but also because their thinking is compatible with our corporate philosophy and goals. They review with us their performance and the position of the plan, directions of the economy, and prospective and current investments.

It is important, of course, to make a conservative assumption about the plan's investment return and a realistically liberal one about employee's pay raises. We assumed a 6% return on investments, and last year our assets rose in value 24%. But the counterbalancing assumptions for salary levels were too low. At one time, it would have been appropriate to assume that a 4% or 5% annual increase would be adequate for the long term, but lately, of course, compensation has been going up 8%, 9%, and 10%.

Our salaried plan, which we acquired when we started the corporation in 1964, was very sick. It had roughly $333,000 in assets and $3.5 million in unfunded liabilities. We recognized that, to nurse our pension plan back to good health, we had to adopt practices that would give us a chance of catching up financially. We also recognized that we had to enhance the plan benefits periodically because we were behind comparatively.

Throughout our 37 divisions and subsidiaries, hourly pension plans, as opposed to those for salaried workers, differ in details because they were developed through negotiations with our local work-force analysts. To a certain extent we have tailored the plans to the needs and wishes of individual divisions. For example, younger workers are more interested in current pay than in higher pensions, whereas other groups with perhaps an older work force put greater emphasis on long-term benefits.

Since 1977 one general corporate policy decision has governed almost all agreements: past-service benefit increases are granted when accrued benefits are fully funded. We said to each of our hourly employee groups in effect: "When we inherited your plan, it was rather unhealthy. If you will work with us and let us get into a fully funded position with regard to accrued benefits, we will begin granting past-service increases when we get overfunded. In that way, you will always know that when you retire there will be funds available to take care of you.'' This approach has been successful in all but two locations. Incidentally, these two locations currently have the worst unfunded problems in our corporation.

As a result of the cooperation of the employees and unions, where applicable, the great majority of our hourly plans are now either fully funded or only marginally underfunded with regard to accrued benefits. We take a slide presentation to the 27 locations that are overfunded to show exactly how we are making past-service pension adjustments to use these extra amounts.

At one of our divisions in the Midwest we did only future service in 1977. We told our employees that if they cooperated with us we would start retroactive benefits as soon as we could. By 1981 we were able to make substantial increases and brought all the early years up to a $4-per-year service credit. By now, anyone with, for example, 30 years of service has received a 32% increase in benefits. Even with these increases, we have maintained the integrity of the plan and stayed fully funded for all accrued benefits. We will adjust again when we are sure the plan can handle it.

In those instances where we are not yet able to bring the past-service benefits fully up to the current level, we tend to put the heaviest weight on long service to help those employees who are closest to retirement.

By starting early to put our salary plan on a sound basis first, we gained credibility with the hourly personnel. In the salaried plan we start with a contributory career average. Then as the plan becomes overfunded with respect to accrued benefits, we increase the pension benefit step by step until it recognizes the current salary level. Subsequently, we periodically seek to keep it current. Employees now know that their plan reflects their total compensation increases and any improvement in their job classification. Since 1964 we have adjusted our plan and/or its benefits 10 times.

To use an oversimplified example, suppose someone started working for us 10 years ago for $10,000 and is now making $20,000. The person's career average would be roughly $15,000. Once our actuarial review said we were overfunded for accrued benefits and could afford to do it, we would raise the level, until today the pension would be based on $20,000. We include in this figure total compensation—which means base, plus incentive, bonus, or overtime pay, whichever is applicable. As of now our employees are current through 1979.

If this kind of revision takes place every three or four years, the company will have given the employee a pension that generally exceeds the average of the final-pay plans. Yet the process has taken place on a controlled basis. When we make commitments, everyone knows the money is there to make good on them.

Although ours is a contributory plan—each employee puts up to 3%

of one's pay into the fund—we periodically reserve the employees' contributions for them by setting up a separate account in a guaranteed income contract with an insurance company. We started doing this as soon as our plan became overfunded, and we hope to continue as long as it remains in this condition. The tax-deferred fund in each employee's name accrues at about 9.5% or better until retirement. This fund will supplement the normal benefit and should add from 10% to 15% to the pension itself, if the employee chooses an annuity at retirement. But employees can receive the money in a lump sum at retirement or even draw on it, in an emergency, during their years of employment.

We compensate for inflation in the best way we know how. We have improved and are continuing to upgrade our benefits. With the salaried retirement plan, we have not only moved up to the total earnings of a recent year as the base for the pension, but have also improved the benefit formula.

When I took over at A-T-O, the salaried plan had assets of $330,000 and an unfunded liability of $3.5 million. The largest pension anyone could get—even the president—was $122.50 a month after 35 years of service. Today, we believe we have one of the best salary pension plans in the United States. It has several advantages over most.

Defects of Public Policy

Corporations seeking to put their pension finances on a sound basis will not get much help from public policy as it is now constituted. With its openhandedness toward military and federal service employees—including congressmen—the government has not made it any easier for private companies to exercise prudence. Taxpayers are supporting pensions for government retirees that are adjusted for cost of living twice a year and that, by and large, are more generous than most of the privately employed citizenry could ever hope for.

The Employee Retirement Income Security Act of 1974 (ERISA), well intentioned as it was, backfired in its early years. Its costly requirements, red tape, and punitive provisions induced many small companies to drop their defined-benefit pension plans altogether. In the first two years of ERISA, companies ended about 5,000 pension programs affecting 160,000 employees—more than four times the number of plans federal officials had anticipated would be dropped. Some of these went to a profit-sharing or defined plan instead. ERISA administrators have now succeeded in reducing the number of regulations and in streamlining the reporting requirements, but there is still too much red tape. Further, the potential punitive claim on 30% of the company's net worth by the Pension Benefit Guaranty Corporation is too much for a small company, or any company, to risk if it has a choice.

By far the most important single reform the government could undertake would be to stop discouraging companies from funding their pension plans promptly. Instead, it should encourage them—or even compel them—to do so. There should be no time limit on how quickly this funding could be accomplished. Moreover, any company that grants a past-service benefit increase should be required to pay for the increase in the same year it is granted and should receive a full tax deduction for the payment.

Such a change requires a turnabout of philosophy in Washington. At present, the government's rationale for disallowing tax-deductible funding in fewer than 10 years is that companies would then shelter their profits in good years, thus depriving the government of millions of dollars in tax revenue. If money is not put into pension funds early to build interest or dividend income, there will have to be even greater infusions of money later that would escape taxation. Whatever tax income the government would lose now it would pick up eventually. Further, this infusion of new capital, by strengthening the securities markets, would be an additional aid to America's financial recovery. Even though some business executives would reject early funding as hurting their "per-share earnings," such a policy could encourage sound business practices and improve the health of the private sector.

Even more important, it would seem, from Washington's point of view, early funding would help avert what could easily become a disaster for the government pension insurance program. If a few corporate giants, such as Chrysler, should fold, the federally operated PBGC could come under tremendous strain or face bankruptcy. The PBGC can take up to 30% of net worth of a failed company to help meet the pension liability. But where would any shortfall between that amount and the sum needed to pay off the employees and pensioners come from? It would have to be made up by the premiums member companies are compelled to pay. Already, the existing premium system penalizes prudent businesses for the follies of others since the prudently managed pension funds must pay the same premium per participant.

In addition, because the federal insurance does not provide full coverage, the failure of large pension plans anywhere would be a catastrophe for many of the employees involved who are not vested. Employees with nonvested pensions are guaranteed nothing by the federal insurance. And for all employees, ancillary benefits that the plan might have offered would be nullified.

I would be remiss if I did not point out the potential enormity of the future problems facing industry and the government. If these are allowed to remain unsolved, pension liabilities over the next 30 years could grow almost beyond our comprehension. Let me explain. If you hired an employee in 1972, aged 22, for $9,000 and gave him annual raises of 8%, by 1980 his salary would have been $16,700. If he works for you until age 65, or the year 2015, and he receives 8% annual raises, his salary will be $246,300. Given industry's present modus operandi, unfunded liabilities will run into the trillions.

Multiemployer Pension Plans

No review of the unfunded liability problem would be complete without consideration of multiemployer pension plans. Almost a quarter of American workers in private industry with defined benefits are covered by these programs, and many of the larger ones are reported to be in bad financial shape. They are found mostly in such labor-intensive industries as construction, trucking, mining, and apparel.

Typically, a union will say to each of these companies something like: "You are not large enough to operate your own plan. It makes sense for you, then, to join our industry plan. It will only cost you a few cents an hour."

Hundreds of other such small companies in this industry may be members of the same plan. If a company prefers to adopt its own program, chances are it will risk a long and catastrophic strike.

Although the committees formed to run these plans are nominally split—often with three union members and three members representing management—some management trustees frequently, for one reason or another, find it advantageous to vote with the union bloc. Traditionally, participating companies have had little input in the decision-making process, since multiemployer plans have generally been viewed by management and labor as an exclusive province of the union.

Nevertheless, even after ERISA went into effect in 1974, the liability of a participating company was fairly limited. The company had a financial obligation if the plan exhausted its funds and terminated, but any single employer could withdraw from the plan without incurring any further obligation whatsoever if the plan continued in effect for five additional years after the company's withdrawal.

In the fall of 1980 the Multi-Employer Pension Plan Amendment Act (MEPPAA) was signed into law as a "corrective" measure. The new rules require that if a company withdraws from the plan, it becomes liable for fully funding a portion of all of the benefits for present and retired participants—that is, the benefits of its own employees. Under MEPPAA the plan may take up to 100% of a company's net worth to satisfy this liability if the company withdraws from the plan. But the term *withdraw* is interpreted so broadly that it covers a host of contingencies—for example, the sale of company assets or the closing of a marginal plant. If a union is decertified, a company might have to change pension plans and thus face a withdrawal liability. Even a reduction in the work force can be interpreted as a partial withdrawal.

Figgie International has several subsidiaries that are involved in multiemployer plans. We inherited most of them. Despite periodic requests, we have had difficulty in securing financial statements for these plans. Yet representatives of any of them can walk in tomorrow and say, "You have 100 workers with an unfunded liability of $8,000 each. So you have a potential withdrawal liability of $800,000."

Even if a company sells a plant and the buyer takes over that liability, the seller is not free from obligation for five years. Any time within that period the government can come back to the former owner and say something like, "When you sold the company three years ago, there was an $800,000 liability. The buyer has gone out of business (or dropped the plan). You now owe $800,000, and you have 20 years in which to clear it up." As more and more business executives become aware of the far-reaching implications of MEPPAA, the backlog of litigation challenging the act is growing. Some of these cases are questioning the basic constitutionality of the statute itself.

Most employers will now stay out of these shared plans if they possibly can. Even when a multiemployer program appears to be in good shape today, its financial stability could fall apart tomorrow if the trustees start granting retroactive benefits. Unions themselves are concerned about these changes because they know that selling such plans will be very difficult unless the law is altered.

A Concluding Note

Whether a plan is sponsored by multiple employers or a single employer, its funding must be put on a sound basis. Not only does it make good business sense; ultimately it is the only humane course to follow. Businesspeople must understand the seriousness of the pension problem and assume their share of the responsibility for resolving it. Union officials should join them in an intelligent and committed approach. Most importantly, the government must change its philosophy and permit tax deductions for early funding so that these liabilities will not grow beyond control.

29
Team Management of Pension Money

GLENN H. KENT

Companies that employ several managers to operate slices of the pension fund pie typically use an "isolation booth" approach and pit each against the others. A few companies have departed from this custom and conduct periodic meetings with all the managers present—such as New Jersey Bell Telephone, which gathers its nine managers together occasionally to discuss long-term fund goals and consider projects of asset growth. The idea is to focus on specific objectives rather than on the performance of other managers. Honeywell, Inc. has taken this idea further, perhaps, than any other company. Since mid-1977 the big manufacturer, whose pension assets total about $400 million, has engaged its six money managers in a quarterly dialogue whose agenda includes market performance and risk exposure of all aspects of the portfolio, innovative investment approaches, and allocation of the next quarter's pension contributions to particular managers. Each manager receives a fee based on an unvarying percentage of total assets, no matter what percentage the manager controls at a given time. Although it is much too early, of course, to make a definitive statement about the success of this cooperative procedure, so far it is working well.

In the stock market of 1973–1974 nearly all corporate sponsors of pension funds, including Honeywell, Inc., had a rude awakening. During that 13-month period Honeywell's fund managers doggedly maintained their positions in growth stocks and our fund depreciated dramatically.

After that experience, the company decided that the pension investment mechanism must be managed more as Honeywell's divisions are managed—that is, with carefully established objectives and closely monitored performance, and with emphasis on diversification.

This decision, coupled with the looming regulatory environment and accelerating inflation that threatened to water the pensioners' ultimate benefits, led Honeywell's board of directors to act to safeguard the interests of the plan participants and maintain plan funding on a sound basis.

That action, taken in early 1976, was the creation of the Corporate Pension and Retirement Committee (CPRC), composed of four senior corporate officers and a senior vice-president of a major operating group, and delegation to it of the entire pension funding and benefit administration responsibility. The board of directors retained only the approval of committee-recommended benefit and actuarial changes, and annual contributions to the pension fund.

The committee's work has created an approach to directing pension fund investment that is unusual among corporations employing a multimanager arrangement. Its two main features are (1) supervision of a fixed portion of the whole portfolio by each manager, no matter how much one has invested at any given time, and (2) frequent consultation in a give-and-take atmosphere.

In 1976 Honeywell, like most companies, had full-discretion investment managers—three banks and two investment advisory firms. The composite of these five independent investment judgments represented the investment policy for the funds. The CPRC commissioned a long-range pension liability and funding study with the purpose of formulating a comprehensive funding policy. The study consisted of three phases:

1 A 20-year projection of plan liabilities.
2 Development of an investment policy to satisfy those liabilities.
3 Building an investment management structure to implement that policy.

Analysis and Conclusions

The 20-year plan liability projections covered participant projections, total accrued and future liabilities, prior service costs, vested liabilities, and pension payments; and they included population census data, benefit improvement projections, and participant growth rates based on corporate long-range plans. These data, integrated with actuarial assumptions, provided the CPRC with 20 simulated annual actuary reports for the plan liabilities.

We made several projections from these to incorporate varying inflation trend and level assumptions. The projections, which revealed substantial liabilities over time, alerted the committee to the magnitude of the task to be undertaken during the second phase of the study.

In that phase, the objective of the CPRC was to form an investment policy that not only prudently satisfied the projected liabilities, but also stayed well within Honeywell's financial capabilities to fund. For each of the 20 periods the committee's staff made capital market assumptions in terms of rates of return and risk parameters for various types of equity and debt instruments, plus the same inflation assumptions used for the liability projections.

These market assumptions formed the basis of an analysis of asset mix choices ranging in degree of risk from 100% Treasury bills to a 100% aggressive equity portfolio. The committee simulated rate of return, market value, and cost probability distributions, which enabled it to compare different risk/return combinations with the liabilities and corporate revenue and earnings projections.

From these results the committee selected the optimal investment mix strategy that satisfied the various liability requirements and cash flow needs of the plans, that maintained an acceptable risk level, and that appeared financially manageable from a corporate earnings standpoint. The mix selected was 70% equity and 30% debt. (But it can vary as high as 80% to 20% and as low as 55% to 45% without interference from the CPRC.)

A basic and important insight evolved from this part of the study. In developing an investment policy to meet the long-range plan liabilities, the committee members gradually became aware of the importance of maintaining the integrity of the total investment objective throughout the investment process. If Honeywell reverted to the "isolation booth" approach in dealing with individual money managers and in measuring their performance, the company could not guarantee attainment of the overall rate-of-return objective within the established risk parameters.

The committee therefore concluded that it must carefully control the asset allocations underlying the total investment policy objective, both between and within the debt and equity segments. And the committee established within the 70% to 30% equity-debt mix the asset allocations that are illustrated in Exhibit 1.

Dividing Responsibilities

In thinking about the establishment of an investment management structure capable of implementing the agreed-on policy, the committee naturally decided to base it on the investment segments of the total portfolio. On the active side of the equity portion, the committee concluded, two managers should be chosen to handle the aggressive (appreciation-oriented) part and two to handle the conservative (income-oriented) part. Each would be responsible for 10½% of the total portfolio.

The purpose of splitting each of the active halves of the equity holdings was to obtain a greater balance of viewpoint and diversification in investment. In the active aggressive area, one manager was expected to follow a "traditional" style of investment, whereas the other was to be more quantitatively oriented. The same division of interest was planned in the active conservative portion. These splits would also minimize the tendency toward manager-by-manager comparisons, which are characteristic of corporate pension management performance "horse races."

Exhibit 1. Total Portfolio and Its Segments

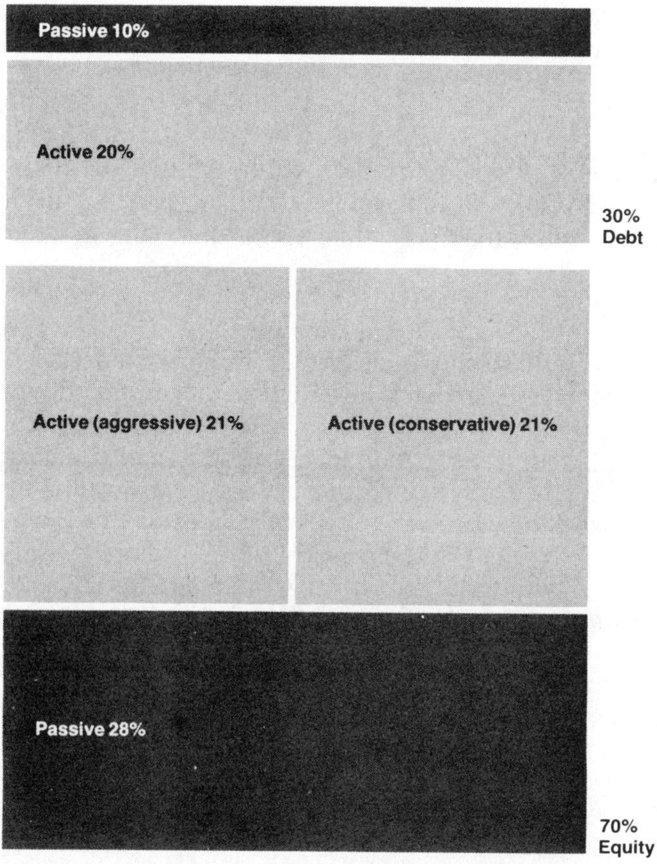

Six Managers

The criteria for manager selection included the usual considerations—type of organization, past performance, the quality of the persons who were to handle the account. Also high on our list were some less typical qualifications:

☐ A consistent competence in one of the specific investment styles we had identified.

☐ A business purpose consisting primarily of management of pension assets in one of the special styles we needed.

☐ A demonstrated emphasis on and dedication to improving the state of the art in pension fund investment.

☐ A willingness to accept certain administrative or procedural requirements: meeting jointly with the other managers on a quarterly basis, reducing transaction costs, giving up or accepting more assets in the interest of better total portfolio performance, and agreeing to special fee arrangements.

We narrowed the large initial list to 36 firms, including the current managers. We informed each prospect of our needs by slide presentations showing the plan liabilities, the investment policy, and the administrative requirements. Our reasoning behind this procedure was to make sure that the money managers fully understood what had to be done and how it had to be accomplished.

The procedure also enabled each firm to determine if (and if so, where) its expertise fit in the structure and whether Honeywell's requirements and approach were acceptable. The investment styles of some finalists did not fit any of the requirements and several others of the 36 candidates were uncomfortable with either the investment or the administrative approach.

After an intensive three-month search, Honeywell selected six managers, five to handle the equity portion and one to handle the debt portion. (Later, the passive debt segment of 10% was placed in an insurance investment contract.) Four of the managers are investment advisory firms; the other two are banking institutions that place a strong emphasis on the investment function and on finding new and better ways of investing.

Operating Approach

To focus on achieving the total investment objective, the six managers must perform as a unit. Each must view one's investment performance as a function of how it contributes to the overall objective, with the goal of synergistically achieving a total result exceeding that of a composite of independently run segments.

The managers are all in the same basket; the more successful they all are, the more total assets will grow. Then all benefit, because they are paid on the basis of a percentage of total assets. From time to time, as market conditions fluctuate, particular managers may have under their control a portion of the total assets amounting to more or less than their fixed allocation. But the percentage basis of their fee remains the same. If, over a long period of time, managers retain an amount larger than their fixed percentage of the total, their fee would still be based on the lesser fixed percentage; but at the outset the managers accepted the arrangement with the understanding that such an irregularity could happen. The converse, of course, could also occur.

So far, no conflicts have surfaced among the managers. The only matter that has arisen is some debate concerning the modern portfolio theories underlying the Barr Rosenberg fundamental risk measurement technique. The group has been studying the application of the University of California professor's system for measuring risk and return to the Honeywell multiple-manager structure.

Because Honeywell from the start intended to use the portfolio managers as consultants on an ongoing basis, and because it is important for each manager to know where the fund is going, the managers hold quarterly meetings. The group, formally identified as the Investment Advisory Board, consists of a principal member of the investment staff of each firm and myself serving as chairman.

At each meeting, which typically lasts a day, we analyze all aspects of the total portfolio and each segment. We look at the rates of return, beta exposure parameters and the volatility within the portfolio, and the R^2 (extent to which the returns are being influenced by the market).

We also analyze transaction costs and consider any matters concerning the reduction of these costs that a manager may bring up. Through a directed brokerage program, in which stock sales and purchases are directed by Honeywell to certain brokers who rebate to the fund a portion of their commissions, the company has realized a saving of about $300,000 to date.

The next step is to review an intratrust stock transfer procedure that is also designed to reduce transaction costs. If one of the active equity managers wants to sell a stock that is one of Standard & Poor's 500, she must give it to the diversification fund (index fund) manager, who pays her in cash. The fund must also give up any issue selected by an active manager, who pays the fund for the stock. In a year and a half of operation of the new procedure, about 250 transfers of this kind have been made (with only a single case in which one manager sold and another manager bought the same issue). Honeywell estimates conservatively a saving of $1.2 million for this period.

Every six months to a year the Investment Advisory Board updates the capital market assumptions for the planning model. (The board is also chartered to recommend, when circumstances are unusual, a major asset adjustment to the CPRC.)

During the individual manager meetings, either before or after the group meeting, each manager is asked to bring up any new investment ideas that might affect one's portfolio operation or be adopted for use in it. At each session we also have a guest speaker. The most recent guest speaker was the economist Arthur Laffer, deviser of the well-known Laffer curve.

Asset Allocation

Finally, at the meeting we develop a contribution allocation plan for the next three months. Last year the group allocated each quarter some $8 million to $9 million—the residual after pension deductions—and this year the amount will average about $10 million.

Our objective is to match the assets to the managers within the basic policy mix. We do this in two ways: via the joint manager recommendation process just described and via transactions between the fixed-income manager and the active equity managers—that is, withdrawal of assets from one of the latter and assignment of them to the former or vice versa.

The responsibilities of the fixed-income manager include the investment of all cash equivalents. For example, if one of the aggressive equity managers decides that it is not the time to be in the market, he pulls out and the fixed-income manager gets the proceeds of the assets sold.

At each meeting a representative of a consulting service lays out the broad economic and market picture and recommends in what area, longer term, the funds are most likely to realize favorable performance. This counsel includes not only whether debt or equity appears more attractive but also such considerations for equity as the attractiveness of high versus low risk, liquidity versus illiquidity, high capitalization versus medium or low, and other current aspects of the equity market that may have a positive or negative bias away from more basic market expectations.

The managers critique the consultant's recommendations as well as each other's views. These critiques form the basis for determining how the contributions in the next quarter will be allocated. Obviously, to make this dialogue productive, the members of the group must have developed confidence in each other's capabilities—an added benefit of the frequent meetings and the policy of rotating the meetings around managers' offices.

As the reader can see, Honeywell's objective is not to play a short-term timing game but to make use of the multimanager structure as if one super investment consultant were responsible for the total portfolio and for achieving an optimal long-term mix of assets.

Results So Far

Since Honeywell adopted this approach in mid-1977, the managers have exceeded the policy objectives in each quarter and in total. Exhibit 2 illustrates this relationship for the total fund for the 18 months ended December 31, 1978. Total return for that period, net of fees and transaction costs, happened to fall right on the capital market line that runs through the T-bill rate on the vertical axis and the S&P return where it intersects with 1.0 beta. (In the long run, the slope of this line should be positive, but in this particular 18 months T-bills outperformed stocks.)

The policy performance expectation represents a return weighted 70% by the S&P return and 30% by the Lehman Brothers, Kuhn Loeb (LKL) composite bond index. The trapezoid represents the risk parameters set by the CPRC; it is bounded by beta on the horizontal and the portfolio standard deviation on the vertical. In the long term, the CPRC expects the total return to fall approximately in the center of the trapezoid; in the short term, the committee expects the return to fall within or near these boundaries.

From the outset, the managers have been fully and constructively involved and have suggested a number of new or innovative performance analysis and investment ideas that are under consideration for use or have been implemented. Manager inputs to the asset allocation process have been

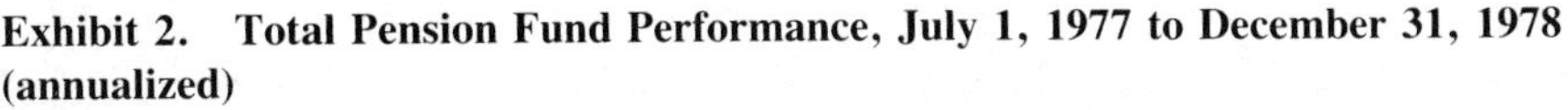

Exhibit 2. Total Pension Fund Performance, July 1, 1977 to December 31, 1978 (annualized)

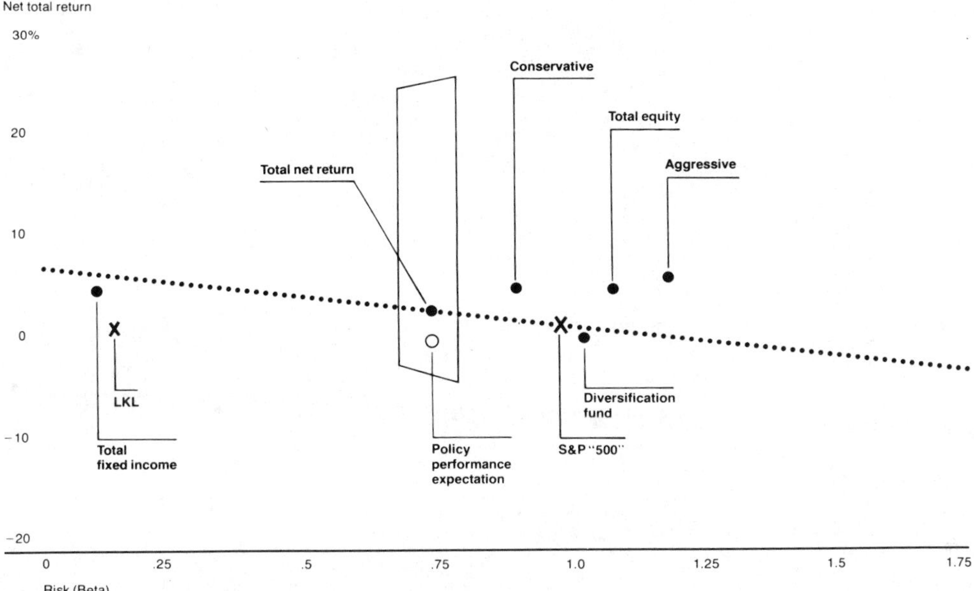

invaluable in helping to determine how to channel the new money into the fund.

The involvement of the managers as a team has added a new and very beneficial dimension to the investment process that cannot be achieved in the more typical one-on-one meetings. It has also changed the meeting atmosphere from routine "score keeping" and oversight sessions to an intellectually stimulating and productive process for the benefit of the pension fund.

Of course, we do not know yet whether the results of this system over the long term will meet the goals for the fund that the CPRC has set. But we are encouraged by a good start.

Although I do not suggest that the Honeywell approach to satisfying the liabilities to our plan participants can or should be adopted by others, every corporate sponsor employing a multimanagement structure does have certain investment responsibilities that cannot be delegated. Use of some disciplined method to identify plan liabilities and to establish a compatible investment policy and management structure to satisfy those liabilities is a far more prudent approach than permitting the aggregate result of a fully discretionary multimanaged fund to become the investment "policy" by default.

PART SEVEN
NEW DEVELOPMENTS IN FINANCIAL MARKETS

AN OVERVIEW

Financial conditions were very different in the early 1980s from what they were even a few years earlier. Wilkins points out some of the key changes in his article, "Financial Flexibility in the 1980s." Among the differences he mentions are higher rates of inflation, higher interest rates, greater debt burdens, and increased volatility in the financial markets. Wilkins goes on to discuss some of the developments that have occurred in the financial markets, particularly the greater freedom of action exercised by corporations. An example is the increase in direct placement of corporate securities and less reliance on financial intermediaries. His final admonition to corporations is to maintain their financial soundness and flexibility in the face of substantial uncertainty.

Even if one has a more optimistic view of the world than Wilkins, it is clear that the changes he mentions have had a major impact on financial markets and financial instruments. In an era of volatile interest rates and concern about inflation, it has become more difficult to attract investors to long-term securities with fixed interest rates. It is not surprising, therefore, that floating-rate securities have emerged and increased in importance. Marks and Law document this growth of floating-rate notes in the United States and analyze their use in their 1980 article, "Hedging Against Inflation with Floating-Rate Notes." Although the cost of floating-rate debt to the corporation will increase if inflation and interest rates do, they point out that some companies have revenues that are more sensitive to inflation than their costs. For these companies, floating-rate securities may provide a useful earnings hedge.

For other corporations and many governmental borrowers, floating-rate securities pose a problem because of their uncertain cost and cash flow requirements for debt service. Two articles in this section suggest ways to reduce this problem. Boettcher and Sotelino ("A Look at the Variable-Maturity Loan") suggest that loans to corporations and governments be structured so that the regular debt service payments to lenders would be held constant, as in traditional home mortgages. The interest rate would be allowed to change as in floating-rate notes, but the principal payment would be adjusted to keep the total payment constant. Under this approach, the total number of payments would vary with interest rates, but the borrower would not have to be concerned about uncertain cash flow requirements each period. In the second article, "Hedging on Loans Linked to the Prime," Krasker proposes an approach that can be implemented by U.S. corporations borrowing under conventional loan terms. He shows how the financial futures market can be used to hedge increases in the cost of borrowing.

Just as fluctuating interest rates affect the motivations and concerns of financial market participants, high interest rates also have implications for the types of financial instruments desired. In a high rate environment, for example, some investors want to "lock up" the high yield for a long time. In other words, they don't want to receive substantial interest payments that they may not be able to reinvest at high rates. They would prefer to leave their money "in the investment," and have it compound at a high rate. This is one of the key features of the original-issue discount bonds that began to be issued in the early 1980s. With these bonds, purchasers received little or sometimes no interest during the life of the bond. Much or all of the return is provided by the difference between the low purchase price of the bond when issued and the face value of the bond at maturity. Tax and other factors are also important to an understanding of these bonds, as explained in the article by Woolridge and Gray, "Are Original-Issue Discount Bonds Here to Stay?"

One new financing technique that has been refined and has grown in importance over the past several years is project financing. The extremely high cost of many natural resources and other projects around the world, combined with the rising debt burdens of major companies, have encouraged substantial ingenuity in the design and structure of these major financings. Wyant discusses these developments in his article, "Essential Elements of Project Financing."

Stetson in "The Reshaping of Corporate Financial Services" provides an appropriate conclusion to this book. There has been an important evolution in the demand for financial services, spurred in part by inflation and high interest rates. This development along with an increased competitiveness on the part of financial institutions have helped to break down traditional barriers among institutions. Stetson documents these important shifts and provides some thoughts on how the future financial industry might develop.

30 Financial Flexibility in the 1980s

MAURICE G. WILKINS, JR.

Long gone are the days when a large company needing an infusion of money merely weighed the options involving equity and debt and, if debt was the answer, whether it should be a bank loan, private placement, or public issue. Now inflation and the uncertainties injected by a diluted dollar are big elements in the decision. And a variety of financing wrinkles from an increasingly competitive group of lenders and brokers has been introduced for tailoring to the borrower's particular needs. Flexibility is the key. A veteran financial officer here outlines the changed situation at the outset of a new decade.

Henry Kaufman, the economist at Salomon Brothers, calls it "the new era of economic discontinuity." Whatever you wish to call it, we are without doubt in a much different economic environment from that which existed before. The 1950s and 1960s were typified by moderate cyclical swings, low rates of inflation, and few structural changes in the financial and economic system. It was a tranquil setting for making long-range corporate financial plans.

Those times ended in the 1970s. They have been replaced by persistent erosion of our system. Although the business cycles we have experienced have varied in intensity, they have never deviated from long-term movement toward:

- ☐ Higher rates of inflation.
- ☐ Declining liquidity in the banking system.
- ☐ Higher interest rates.
- ☐ Greater debt burdens in all sectors of the economy.
- ☐ Increasing volatility in the financial markets.
- ☐ Growing political instability.

These discontinuities are producing fundamental social, political, and economic changes, the results of which probably cannot be foreseen. Corporate financial planners, therefore, must be able to react quickly to events as they occur and yet refrain from irrevocably committing themselves to a plan. In this way they can avoid being hemmed in by events outside their ability to control.

Corporate strategists, choosing from all the financing possibilities available, have to emphasize maximum flexibility. The variety of these choices on the domestic scene has increased substantially in recent years (see the Appendix). In this article I shall focus on some of the innovations whose use will probably become more widespread in the 1980s.

Commercial Banking Trends

Bank relationships are changing. The great amount of U.S. dollars held on deposit outside the United States (the equivalent of domestic M_1A), plus the absence of barriers between this source of funds and the domestic money supply, has opened the doors to large foreign banks wanting to enter our market. And they have done so very aggressively. These banks are larger than most U.S. banks and have no base of profitable business to protect in their pricing policies. As a result they have gone after the cream of the U.S. market, the larger multinational company, on a basis that is different, more flexible, and generally cheaper.

As an example, Textron recently obtained Eurocurrency credit lines aggregating $150 million. These are available for a two-year period on a fully committed basis with the provision that, as long as the banks are satisfied with our credit-worthiness, they will automatically extend the lines at the end of the eleventh month of the initial term and annually thereafter.

In effect, this "evergreen revolver" permits borrowings that will never have a maturity of less than 13 months or more than 25 months. Therefore the loans qualify for treatment as long-term debt for balance sheet purposes even though the credit facilities are essentially for short-term uses. In addition, currencies other than U.S. dollars can be drawn at our option as available, although the binding commitment for the banks is only in U.S. dollars.

All this we obtained for commitment fees and borrowing spreads that totaled only one-half of what Textron paid for similar provisions in the early 1970s. The competition in banking that this transaction signals will, I believe, continue in the 1980s and spread to the next tier of corporate borrowers.

The European method of pricing, based on the supposition that a bank buys its money to fund its loans in an interbank market for a certain period and that the borrower pays this cost plus a spread, will become the norm in the 1980s. It is with us right now in the domestic market via money market loans in which most big banks lend funds for short periods at rates based on the Federal Funds rate plus a spread. The spread is determined by how aggressive the bank is on that particular day or what its liquidity position is.

Traditionally companies have kept balances with banks that, in return, would extend short-term credit on request. These "confirmed" lines of credit (confirmed by letter) are, of course, not legally binding commitments on the part of the banks or the corporations to keep the balances with them.

The recent trend has been toward legally binding, committed credit facilities, on which the company pays a fee and receives a firm commitment from the bank to supply the funds. This commitment to lend runs for a certain period, and payments for it are billed just like interest.

When everything is defined in dollars and cents, it is only natural that price competition heightens. And in this case it has brought innovation. In addition to a straightforward commitment to lend, there are now variations whereby the banks tailor their commitments to customers' particular operating needs. Textron's captive finance company, for example, was recently offered a line of credit it could keep available in its off-season periods by paying a fee of only one-half of what it paid during the part of the year when it was most likely to borrow. You might call this a "commitment to commit," but anyway it represents a saving for a seasonal borrower.

There are also lots of other bank-financing variations that are emerging, like commercial paper back-up lines. These will proliferate in the 1980s.

Underwritten vs. Direct Borrowing

As the role of the commercial banker is changing, so too is that of the investment banker. In the past, an investment banker was on the board of every sizable corporation, and all its long-term borrowing or equity financing was directed by or through his firm. There has been a slow but steady trend away from that practice. It was fostered at least in part by the required annual disclosure of corporate payments for such services.

Some of the largest companies—Exxon, as an example—have successfully sold their debt securities directly to the public through "Dutch auctions." The largest of the captive finance companies, like GMAC and Sears Acceptance, now regularly sell intermediate-term (two to six years) notes directly to institutional investors.

The last long-term borrowing that my company undertook was a $100 million private placement that we negotiated and placed entirely ourselves. We thereby saved about $1 million in fees and commissions. Because we manage the bulk of our pension funds internally, we are in constant contact with the securities markets and we feel quite comfortable working both sides of the street, as a lender and as a borrower, without the need of a middleperson or an adviser. In the financial markets of the 1980s, more of the larger corporations will learn to do their own thing in like manner.

Corporations will also make more financing arrangements directly among themselves. So far the largest area of this activity has of course been the commercial paper market, which has roughly doubled in size, from $50 billion to $100 billion, in the past five years. A lot of money in this market is supplied by financial institutions, but a lot also represents the "haves" among the nonfinancial corporations lending directly to the "have nots."

Another area where new developments are possible is in the borrowing and lending of pension funds directly between companies. Under ERISA, lending from a company's pension trust to the company itself is either prohibited or severely limited. There is no law, however, against Textron's pension fund lending directly to Gillette, or against Gillette's pension fund providing the debt for a leverage lease of a Textron-built helicopter. This type of intercompany financing could open direct access to the largest pools of long-term capital that will be available in the 1980s.

Most large corporations have traditionally tapped the public debt and equity markets for their external funds on at least a periodic basis. This practice will certainly continue, for Wall Street has shown real talent for melding the needs of corporations with the desires of investors.

Recent innovations in the corporate debt markets have been numerous. The floating-rate notes, as an example, originated by financial institutions like Citibank, have now evolved into "floating rate droplock" debentures issued by industrials like Gulf Oil. The interest rates on these long-term debentures float at a spread over the going yield on U.S. Treasuries, unless (or until) those yields drop to certain levels, at which time the interest rate "locks in" at a fixed rate until maturity. At the moment it is difficult to tell who might benefit the most from this innovation, the issuer or the investor. In any event, it represents another step in an evolutionary trend that we shall see in the 1980s unless, for some reason, inflation subsides.

The impact of inflation on the willingness of investors to acquire debt will probably lead to the gradual disappearance of long-term, fixed-rate borrowing in the public market. Corporate borrowing at a fixed interest rate for 30 to 40 years has been a phenomenon confined almost entirely to the U.S. capital markets. To a large extent it is a product of the volume of contractual savings available in the insurance industry plus the investment philosophy of those institutions.

Both of these are changing, particularly the philosophy. In their ability to borrow at a fixed rate, corporations in the 1980s will probably be limited to 10 years or less—as they are in other countries—or they will have to develop new ways to compensate the investor for the ravages of inflation.

Speaking of "ravages," at this time major industrial companies are doing very little equity financing, primarily because the relationship of market prices to book or replacement values makes such financing among the most expensive. This situation will probably not change dramatically, at least in the early 1980s; but you have to be prepared to take what the market gives you when it wants to give it to you.

A Concluding Note

The 1980s will offer tremendous challenges to top management in financing. Their task is to enable their companies, on the one hand, to compete effectively in a strongly inflationary environment and, on the other hand, to protect themselves if the financial apocalypse really does come.

Appendix. Internal Financial Soundness

Maintaining a high credit rating must be in the forefront of any corporate strategy. A high credit rating (A or better) is an absolute prerequisite for a company seeking external financing. A weak credit posture means few available choices and very high financing costs.

It is also vitally important that a company mobilize its internal cash balances for its own use. The "good old boy" relationships of yesteryear, when you left balances with your friendly banker in the hope that he would give you preference when times were tough, have largely disappeared, particularly for larger corporations.

Today they use every device available to mobilize those balances for their continual use, and bank credit as well as services are paid for in cash on a contractual and businesslike basis. This trend probably will continue and expand to smaller companies in the 1980s.

31

Hedging against Inflation with Floating-Rate Notes

KENNETH R. MARKS and WARREN A. LAW

In these turbulent, inflation-beset times, how can a company raise debt so as to maintain financial flexibility and limit the burden it must carry for many years, and at the same time attract investors who are concerned about *their* return over that period of time? One way is through the floating-rate note, whose variety and adaptability provide certain advantages for both issuer and purchaser. One recent industrial floating-rate note issue is that of Georgia-Pacific Corporation, which embodies "puttable, callable, and convertible" features. FRNs constitute one illustration of the innovative techniques that corporations may find necessary these days.

For both borrowers and lenders, 1979 was a traumatic year. The speed and magnitude of interest rate changes were unprecedented in U.S. history. For example, during Eisenhower's first term the largest single monthly change in Moody's composite average of yields on corporate bonds was 13 basis points. During October 1979 the corresponding move was 125 basis points. Long-term Treasury bond yields moved 100 basis points in two weeks. At the same time, during much of the year economists debated whether a recession was likely, already under way, or almost over.

"The market hates uncertainty" is an old and sensible maxim. But financing decisions have to be made. When interest rates are high by conventional yardsticks, borrowers hesitate to raise long-term debt. But in 1979, they had no assurance that rates that seemed high at the time might not turn out to have been low.

In this environment some borrowers of long-term money have sought to increase their financial flexibility through provisions permitting them to take advantage of any declines in interest rates. A borrower can accomplish this goal through sinking fund payments that begin in the early years (that are coupled with options allowing the company to make additional sinking fund payments) and through the use of lower call price schedules. For example, when IBM offered its 25-year debentures in October 1979, it structured the issue to provide for sinking fund payments that begin at the end of the sixth year (and that carry an option to increase the mandatory payment by 150%) and a call price of $102.50 at the first call date.

Undoubtedly, IBM hopes that in 6 to 10 years interest rates will be significantly lower than in 1979, so that the company will be able to exercise all the sinking fund options and redeem the remaining debentures at a slight premium at the first call date. In this case the issue would have an average life of only 8¾ years and a 9.65% borrowing cost.

At almost the same time as IBM, another major industrial corporation, Georgia-Pacific, raised long-term funds by selling a much less conventional debt instrument—floating-rate notes described as "puttable, callable, and convertible." This $150 million issue attracted little attention, but deserved more because it illustrates the lengths to which corporate borrowers and their investment bankers are going to tailor debt instruments that hedge an issuer's risks in a world of volatile and uncertain interest rates, while at the same time attracting buyers who are also trying to limit *their* uncertainties. We shall discuss the Georgia-Pacific offering later.

Not A New Security

Floating-rate notes (FRN) originated in Europe and first appeared in the United States in 1974, when Citicorp sold $650 million of its 15-year notes (still the largest floating-rate issue ever sold in the United States). The rate on these notes was set at a minimum of 9.7% for the first 10 months and thereafter at 1% above the three-month Treasury bill rate and adjusted semiannually.

The success of the Citicorp offering, which was increased from an original size of $250 million, attracted other borrowers. Within a few months, six other issues, ranging in size from $40 million to $200 million, were sold. All but one were sold by financial institutions, which could hedge against the uncertain interest costs by putting the proceeds into floating-rate earning assets.

Floating-rate notes had obvious attractions for such borrowers in 1974. Interest rates were at historically high levels and expected to decline, so FRN borrowing over the longer term would cost less on average than fixed-rate, long-term debt. At the time of the Citicorp issue, commercial paper rates were well above Treasury bill yields; in July 1974 the three-month prime commercial paper rate was 11.9%, whereas T-bills of similar maturity yielded 7.6%. Since Citicorp's FRN rates were based on T-bill yields, the floating-rate note initially promised a cheaper and more assured source of funds than commercial paper.

Any attraction for a borrower, of course, usually represents a disadvantage to the lender. In this case, however, the 1974 FRN borrowers were able to find lenders to whom commercial paper or other short-term, money market instruments did not represent a realistic alternative investment opportunity—individual savers. With one exception, each of the 1974 FRNs had a "put" feature that allowed holders to redeem the notes at their face value and at their discretion, beginning about two years after the time of issue.

The put feature made FRNs extremely attractive to individuals who, because they enjoyed little access to the higher rates of return available in large-denomination securities, were often limited to rates paid by savings institutions (which, in turn, were limited by Regulation Q). In essence, FRNs served to disintermediate savings deposits.

Even so, as each new issue appeared, the demand for FRN issues in 1974 declined—a fact which suggests that the "retail" market for such issues was rather limited.

The put feature, however, turned out to be a fatal flaw in the 1974 FRNs. When short-term Treasury rates declined precipitously in 1975–1976, interest rates on FRNs were no longer attractive to savers, and a majority of investors "put" the notes to the issuers. Citicorp, for example, was obliged to redeem 56% of its issue in 1976, and by the end of 1978 only 27% remained outstanding. As a result the 1974 FRNs provided their issuers with funds for only a short time.

Revival in 1978

By mid-1978 money market conditions were beginning to resemble those of 1974. Yields on six-month Treasury bills rose from less than 5% in January 1977 to about 7.5% in July 1978, and many economists were forecasting double-digit interest rates by the year's end. As a result, lenders again became wary of long-term, fixed-rate commitments.

Once more, Citicorp led the way in raising long-term funds via a floating-rate note, issuing in July a $200-million, 20-year security with the interest rate set at a spread of 1.2% above the six-month T-bill rate for the first five years (having a minimum rate of 7.5%) and with spreads and minimum rates ratcheted downward in later years.

This time, however, the issue was clearly designed for sale to institutional investors. The features that distinguished it from 1974 issues were (1) deletion of the put feature, to ensure a long-term source of funds; (2) a "floor," or minimum interest rate, to protect the investor; and (3) a sinking fund, beginning in 1989, that would retire 90% of the notes before maturity.

The absence of the put device was only one reason individuals were not expected to be major buyers of the new Citicorp FRN. More important was the availability of alternative investments that did not exist in 1974, especially certificates issued by savings institutions that also offered yields keyed to T-bill rates and the money market funds with high, and floating, yields.

By January 1979 the forecasts of 1978 were realized. Six-month Treasury bills were yielding almost 10% and many forecasters were predicting even higher rates. The yield curve was sharply inverted, providing incentive for institutional investors to remain "short" until they sensed that long-term rates were peaking. In addition, many institutions with substantial losses in their fixed-income portfolios, arising from the interest rate increases in 1978, were reluctant to expose themselves to further losses. As a consequence, they sought investments whose market prices would stay close to purchase prices if interest rates continued to rise.

For these reasons, both buyers and sellers found FRNs attractive. In 1979, 18 issues totaling $2.7 billion were completed.

As demand for these issues rose in early 1979, terms became more aggressive and new options were added. In April Continental Illinois Corporation came out with an FRN that could be converted at any time before May 1986 at the *holder*'s option into fixed-rate (8½%), long-term debentures. (This was, incidentally, the first debt security of any kind to be convertible into another debt obligation instead of into an equity offering.) This convertibility feature was used by several subsequent issuers. At the time of offering, the interest rate on the debenture was usually set 125 to 150 basis points below the current rate at which the issuer could have sold long-term, fixed-rate securities.

In May Gulf Oil Corporation offered $250 million in floating-rate notes with still other new features. The fact that the issuer was not a financial institution was unusual in itself. Previously only one nonfinancial concern had issued floating-rate debt—Standard Oil (Indiana) in 1974. The Gulf issue was a 30-year debenture with a coupon floating 35 basis points over the *long-term* U.S. Treasury bond rate—that is, the rate on the 30-year "constant maturity" series published by the Federal Reserve Board.

The issue had an imaginative "drop lock" feature, under which the rate on the security would cease to float and would convert to a fixed rate of 8⅜% at any time the Treasury bond series had a yield equal to or less than 8% for three consecutive days. The initial rate on the Gulf issue was 9.55%, which was 35 basis points above the latest Treasury bond index. This was approximately the spread that would have been required, at the time of pricing, for Gulf to issue a fixed-rate debenture.

Even more complex is the Mellon National Corporation FRN issue sold in June 1979. As was the case in the Continental offering, holders have the option to convert their notes into fixed-rate debentures at an 8½% rate. Unlike Continental, however, Mellon retains the right to convert the securities, at its option, to a fixed-rate debenture whose rate would be set at the higher of 8½% or 65 basis points over the then-prevailing rate on Treasury bonds.

In its $150 million offering due October 1987, Georgia-Pacific incorporated certain features of the Mellon issue, such as the option of the issuer to convert, and added other features to heighten its attractiveness to investors.

The interest rate on the Georgia-Pacific issue is 12% for the first six months, the higher of 12% or 75 basis points over T-bills for the next six months, and it floats thereafter at a spread over T-bill rates that gradually declines from 75 basis points in 1980 to 50 basis points after October 1984 (with a minimum interest rate of 6%). Georgia-Pacific can convert the FRNs at any time between October 1, 1980 and April 1, 1987 into debentures due in 2009, with a fixed interest rate equal to the higher of 8½% or at least 40 basis points over long-term U.S. Treasuries.

In turn, the *holder* has the right at any time before October 1, 1987 to convert into 8½% debentures. Moreover, the holder has the right to put the FRNs to Georgia-Pacific at face value on October 1, 1984, or at any time within 15 days after the company has given notice it intends to convert the FRNs into fixed-rate debentures.

The Georgia-Pacific issue is so complex that it seems to have temporarily exhausted the ingenuity of investment bankers; at this writing, no further innovations have appeared. Perhaps none is needed, for by now the existing number of permutations and combinations of puts, calls, conversion features, drop locks, and so on, should be adequate to meet the needs of any issuer. Moreover, overly complex terms could be a drawback in attracting investors, who may be reluctant to buy a security that they find difficult to assess.

Analysis of the FRN

The increasingly intricate nature of the later FRNs reflects the increasingly uncertain environment in which financial decisions have to be made. Many corporations that need long-term money are understandably hesitant to lock themselves into interest costs that, in most cases, are higher than any they have ever faced. In the past they have borrowed short term at such times and refunded the loans when long-term rates declined. But who today can be comfortable predicting when, if, and by how much long-term rates will decline and whether short-term funds will always be available until then?

As we have noted, most FRNs have been issued by financial institutions that have floating-rate earning assets and are therefore less concerned about the cost of money than about the spread between its cost and its selling price. In fact, the revenues of some financial institutions are more interest-rate sensitive than their costs, and floating-rate financing provides them with greater earnings stability.

But in conditions as uncertain as those of 1980, even nonfinancial corporations should consider floating-rate debt. If, as many argue, interest rates in the long run merely reflect inflation rates, then any company that expects its revenues to vary with inflation to a greater extent than its costs should consider a floating-rate liability as an earnings hedge. Some capital-intensive companies fit this description, since a major cost component (depreciation) is little affected by current inflation.

Others may also find FRNs attractive depending on their expectations of interest rates and the costs of alternative financing vehicles. Companies that had long-term requirements, and wanted to fund them short term until long rates fell to an acceptable level, would have found FRNs to be attractive, at least initially, in 1974 and 1979. In both periods, FRNs were cheaper than bank loans or commercial paper, as Exhibit 1 shows.

When interest rates decline, this advantage may disappear, as it did in 1975. Presumably, however, if borrowers had a convertibility option, they would choose to convert the FRN into fixed-rate, long-term debt. For this reason it is important that the issuer retain the ability to convert the FRN, provided that the market does not charge an excessive premium for this right.

In comparison with long-term, fixed-rate financing, floating-rate notes turn out to be more cost effective than fixed-rate debt if interest rates decline appreciably. However, with the inverted yield curve that characterized 1974 and 1979 (and that characterizes most tight-money periods), the current cost of floating-rate debt tied to short-term rates is much higher than fixed-rate borrowing.

If this condition continues long enough, FRNs tied to short-term rates could be more expensive during their lives than long-term, fixed-rate debt—even if we assume that the short rates will eventually decline. But the borrower's strategy of selling floating-rate notes may still have been superior to using commercial paper or bank credit as a temporary source of funds while the company waited for easier money to fund its capital requirements.

Long-Term Floaters

The Gulf issue, as we have mentioned, has a coupon rate that floats at a spread of 35 basis points over the long-term Treasury bond rate. Such a long-term floater offers certain advantages. First, the interest cost is considerably more stable than in the case of short-term floaters. From 1974 through 1978, for example, monthly average Treasury bond rates moved in

Exhibit 1. Borrowing Rates in Two Tight-Money Periods

	Prime Rate	Prime Commercial Paper[a]	T-bill +1%[a]
September 1974	11.25%	12.05%	10.00%
November 1979	15.25	14.50	13.10

[a]Expressed as interest rate equivalents for comparability.

a range of 160 basis points (7.30 to 8.90%), whereas the comparable range for six-month T-Bills was 525 basis points (4.60 to 9.85%).

In addition, in periods when the yield curve is inverted, a long-term floater will probably have a lower initial coupon rate than an FRN tied to short-term rates. Gulf's initial rate was 9.55%. In contrast, rates on straight short-term floaters were about 11.1% at the time of the Gulf offering, and rates on convertible short-term floaters were about 10.7%.

As credit tightened in late 1979, this advantage (reflecting the inverted yield curve) became even greater. When money becomes easier, however, short-term rates fall faster than long rates until the yield curve assumes the usual upward slope. At that time the long-term floater becomes more expensive.

The overall cost saving of a long-term floater, compared with a short-term one, therefore depends on the average spread between T-bill and Treasury bond rates during the period before conversion of the issue. If, for example, the long-term floater is priced at 35 basis points over long Treasuries and the short-term floater at 100 basis points over T-bills, the long-term floater will be cheaper if, on average, long Treasuries do not yield 65 basis points more than T-bill rates (adjusted to an "interest yield equivalent"). During 1974–1978 the differential between these rates was 130 basis points. (An adjustment to this comparison would be necessary if the floaters have minimum-rate floors.)

Put Feature

As experience with the 1974 FRNs illustrates, a put feature is generally undesirable if the borrower needs long-term money. One could argue that the issue will be put to the borrower only if interest rates decline, thereby enabling the borrower to refund the issue at low fixed rates.

But the timing of the funds requirements is so uncertain as to make this strategy impractical. This defect can be partly overcome by specification of a date at which the issue can be put, but uncertainty might still prevail as this date approached—if, for example, the level of money rates made it difficult for investors to decide whether to put their securities.

Other possible objections to the put device arise from its classification as short-term debt once it becomes puttable within one year. When assessing the financial flexibility of a company and the quality of its securities, rating agencies consider its short-term indebtedness. Many issuers are also subject to debt covenants that limit such indebtedness. Also, in the case of banks, funds received from securities that are puttable within seven years of issue do not qualify as capital for regulatory purposes.

Convertibility

The choice of a straight FRN or one convertible into a fixed-rate security depends on several factors, including the borrower's expectations of interest rates (both short and long) throughout the life of the security, the maximum interest rate acceptable to the company on fixed-rate financing, and the initial savings available from offering holders the convertibility feature. Since the spread over Treasury bills is lower for FRNs convertible at the holder's option and the minimum rate is usually lower, the issuer will benefit in comparison with straight FRNs if conversion does not occur.

If conversion does occur, the company will have long-term, fixed-rate financing at an interest rate lower than the fixed rate available at the time of original sale. By selecting the fixed interest rate now, however, the issuer may forgo the opportunity to get an even lower rate later. Moreover, a convertible FRN may prevent the company from benefiting from a prolonged period at the bottom of an interest rate cycle.

By structuring the security to be convertible at its option, the issuer eliminates a serious risk: The possibility that interest rates may rise after the date of the offering and thereby weaken the company's control over its future borrowing costs. If the company ascertains at some point that higher interest rates are coming, it can elect to convert the issue and cut its losses. The ability of the issuer to convert, of course, reduces the attractiveness of a convertible FRN to buyers.

With these considerations in mind we can illustrate some of the trade-offs in offering an FRN like Georgia-Pacific's. The company provided investors with the right to put the security at its principal value if the company later elected to convert the FRN. To ensure that investors would find conversion more attractive than putting the FRNs, Georgia-Pacific retained the right to set the rate on the debenture at the greater of 8½% or at least 40 basis points over 30-year Treasuries. The "at least" provision enables the company to use a rate high enough to cause the debentures to trade at a premium, thereby encouraging conversion.

Clearly the company, faced with near-record interest rates at the time of the issue, hoped to convert it in a reasonable length of time at lower rates. Under these market conditions, the company could have offered a fixed-rate, 30-year debenture at about 9.70%.

Recall that these FRNs have a rate of 12% for the first six months and the higher of 12% or 75 basis points over T-bills for the second six. If you assume payment of 12% interest in the first year, the breakeven interest rate in October 1980 (the earliest time at which the company can exercise the conversion option) is 9.42%. That is, if Georgia-Pacific successfully converts the FRNs into debentures with an interest rate of less than 9.42% in October 1980, it will have obtained a lower overall cost of borrowing than by issuing 9.70% debentures. To achieve the 9.42% rate, long-term Treasury rates will have to fall below 9.02%—a reasonable hope at the time of the Georgia-Pacific offering.

But at that time, many forecasters were predicting that interest rates would rise significantly. By October 1980, they expected short-term rates to be substantially higher than a year before and to stay at a high level for some time. If this rise occurs, the company may choose to convert the FRNs in order to get out from under the onerous short-term rates.

As an alternative to early conversion, the company can wait in the hope that short-term interest rates will decline substantially. Exhibit 2 shows how the cost of borrowing for Georgia-Pacific's FRN varies depending on the level of interest rates prior to conversion, the period of time to conversion, and the assumed rate at conversion.

"Indexing" Debt Rates

To the investor, FRNs may be considered a form of indexing—a direct reaction to, and flight from, inflation. One investment banker has described the pressures leading to their invention as "no different from those that led unions to demand cost-of-living clauses." Because the "second generation" FRNs had minimum interest rate provisions, the analogy with wage contracts is apt.

Borrowers' concerns are in some respects the mirror image of lenders'. However uncertain corporate financial officers may be about future interest rates, they must have *some* opinion. An obvious rule: Companies whose managements are most pessimistic about the direction of interest rates should issue fixed long-term debt; those most optimistic should consider having some floating-rate notes in their capital structures. Convertibility offers a partial hedge against being wrong.

Of course, companies considering the issuance of floating-rate securities will want to assess the potential financing costs under various interest rate projections—and certainly a company's own interest rate expectations will play a significant role in this process. But the company must also consider

Exhibit 2. Cost-of-Borrowing Analysis of Georgia-Pacific FRN

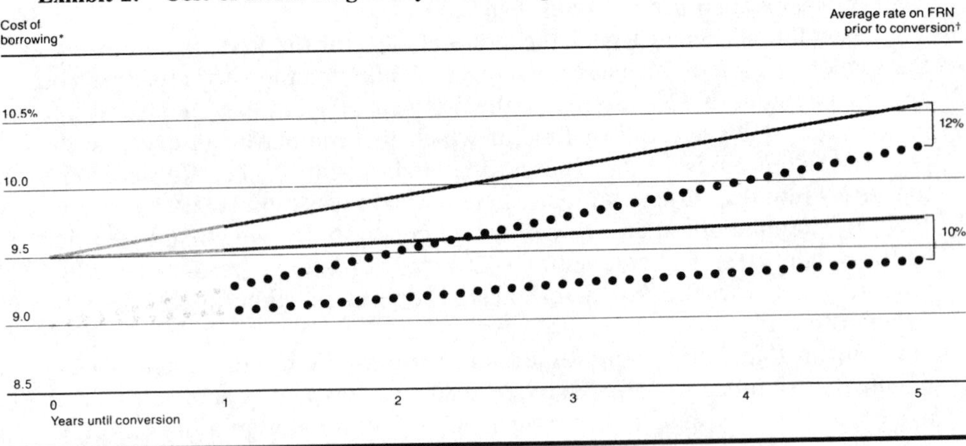

Assumed rate on conversion: dotted lines indicate 9.0%, solid lines 9.5%.

*Excludes underwriting costs.

†Equal to T-bill rate plus spread.

its basic objectives, its views toward its capital structure, and its attitudes toward uncertainty in its borrowing costs.

Companies whose revenues are more interest-rate sensitive than its costs may find that floating-rate securities provide a valuable earnings hedge. Other companies may find that the addition of a small amount of floating-rate securities in their capital structures is cost effective and provides a useful compromise between issuing short-term debt and issuing long-term, fixed-rate debt, especially in today's volatile markets.

32
A Look at the Variable-Maturity Loan

JAMES H. BOETTCHER AND FERNANDO B. SOTELINO

Economic uncertainty makes innovation a necessary component for survival in any aspect of business—from research and development to financing. But that's difficult for a company when faced with the entrenched attitudes of financial institutions. Banks seem more content to pass the ills of the uncertainty (reflected in high interest rates) on to their customers rather than offer innovative yet realistic alternatives. Most financial officers will attest that companies have to accept the entire burden of interest risk or they simply do not get the funds.

Two bankers with the Crocker National Bank in the USA and Hong Kong have been working on a financing technique, the fixed-payment, variable-maturity loan, in which the bank shares some of the burden of interest risk with the company. Although FPVM is not a totally new concept, Mr. Boettcher was the first banker to conceptualize and develop it for application with large-scale government and corporate loans. In this article, he and Mr. Sotelino explain the usefulness of the technique, where it can be applied, and how it is best evaluated by an interested corporate or government borrower.

Given the volatility of borrowing costs in the past few years, corporate financial managers may well long for the economically halcyon days of the 1950s. But the days when politics were stable and both interest rates and inflation were low are long gone. Even if rates decline, recent crashes in the bond market, continuing expectations of inflation, and the likely ebb and flow of the political will to fight inflation will curtail the issue of fixed-rate, long-term debt for some time.

Instead, lenders pass virtually all the interest-rate risk in this "floating" environment to the corporate customer, who is increasingly reluctant to finance capital-intensive projects. Corporate financial managers tell us:

Debt-service uncertainty means we can't accurately forecast the cost of capital in order to prepare meaningful feasibility studies.

We've had to put off new acquisitions to avoid being locked into such high interest rates.

Unless we keep our percentage of capitalization low (about 10%), we are concerned that heavy reliance on floating-rate debt will adversely affect our bond ratings in the future.

We've had to reduce our debt-equity ratio to maintain acceptable financial risk; that will probably result in a lower return on equity as well as a lower sustainable growth rate.

Although we cannot turn back the clock, there is a compromise approach to lending: the fixed-payment, variable-maturity loan (FPVM). FPVMs allow for a fixed debt-service schedule that substitutes an agreed-on fixed periodic payment with a variable maturity for the month-to-month cash flow uncertainty of the standard floating-rate loan. Such loans have been used before for some debt reschedulings and real estate financing, but we do not know of any case in which either corporate or government borrowers have taken systematic advantage of this financing opportunity.

That is too bad, because an FPVM can (1) spread the risk of interest-rate fluctuations between borrower and lender; (2) accommodate virtually any payment schedule the borrower wants; (3) allow the borrower flexibility in designing an all-inclusive debt service schedule to meet particular cash flow requirements; and (4) reduce significant cash flow problems during the early years of a capital-intensive project start-up.

From the bank's perspective, the FPVM loan is somewhat more operationally complex than a standard floating-rate loan, and depending on how actual interest rates compare with those anticipated when the FPVM terms were agreed on, the final maturity of such a loan may be lengthened. These drawbacks are, we believe, outweighed by the facts that for the bank (1) more "financially viable" borrowers (i.e., better credit risks) result from the predetermined month-to-month debt service certainty; (2) the final maturity could be shortened as well as lengthened; (3) the profitability of such a loan is at least as high as, or often higher than, for a standard floating-rate loan; and (4) in case the maturity is lengthened, the floating-rate nature of the FPVM loan allows the bank to continue to earn an interest greater than the cost of funding the outstanding principal.

What Does It Look Like?

The FPVM loan falls between two more standard loan options: the floating-rate, fixed-maturity loan (i.e., a standard London InterBank Offered Rate or prime-priced loan) and the fixed-rate, fixed-maturity loan (i.e., a fixed-rate private placement or bond issue). By accommodating a fixed debt-service schedule, the loan has a variable maturity. For a given debt-service schedule, the higher the interest rate, the longer the maturity because the period necessary to amortize the amount borrowed will be longer.

Exhibit 1 shows two amortization schedules for a \$10 million loan priced at a 1% spread over LIBOR (London InterBank Offered Rate)—one for a current and standard floating-rate loan, the other for an FPVM loan. If it takes out the standard floating-rate loan, a company will make 10 annual payments of \$1 million each, as well as variable interest payments, beginning at the end of the first year. For the FPVM loan, the company will remit annual payments of \$1.843 million until the loan principal is repaid in full.

Working through the loan repayment, you can see that the principal amortized by each fixed payment depends on the actual interest rate for that period. The higher the interest rate, the greater the proportion of the fixed payment that will go toward interest and the lower the principal amortized. As LIBOR falls, the principal amortized increases; the principal declines as LIBOR increases and then, in this example, continually increases as the interest expense shrinks. The final maturity extends slightly beyond the expected 10 years; even though the actual *average* LIBOR rate was the expected 12%, the interest rate in the early years was higher than expected and delayed initial amortization of principal.

Establishing the FPVM Payment Schedule

So far we have been discussing the most straightforward version of FPVM. The annual payment of \$1.843 million used in Exhibit 1 is the same as that of a fixed-rate, fixed-maturity \$10 million loan at 13%. One major advantage of FPVM, however, is that it can accommodate virtually any payment schedule requested by a borrower—level, stepped, increasing, or decreasing—depending on, for example, a project's cash flow characteristics.

To design an acceptable payment plan, the lender and borrower must first decide on the payment profile desired, on "first cut" payment amounts for each step if the profile is not level, and on interest-rate assumptions. With this input, a computer model we developed calculates the final maturity. If the lender finds the length of the final maturity unacceptable given its assumptions about future interest-rate trends, it will raise the payment level until the model forecasts an acceptable final maturity.

Exhibit 2 illustrates three alternative payment profiles that, for the same interest rates, produce about the same final maturity of 10 years. The first and second graphs in that exhibit show what happens when, in the first two years, actual interest rates exceed the expected rates used to determine the payment schedule. Situations such as these are handled by allowing for *limited* "negative principal" payments—in other words, adding the current interest due to the outstanding principal.

The payment options offer the borrower remarkable flexibility. The

Exhibit 1. Amortization Schedules for Floating-Rate and FPVM Loans

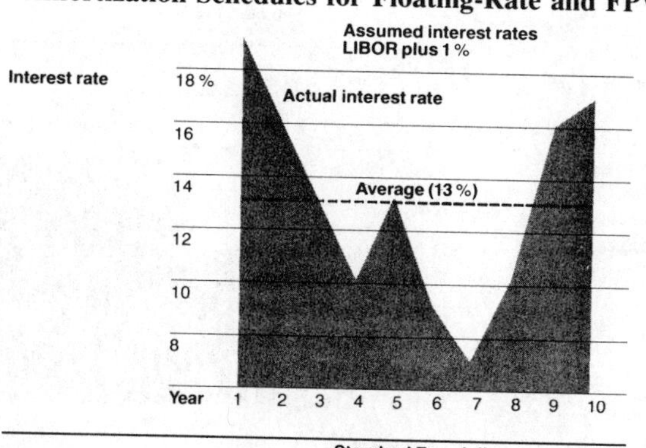

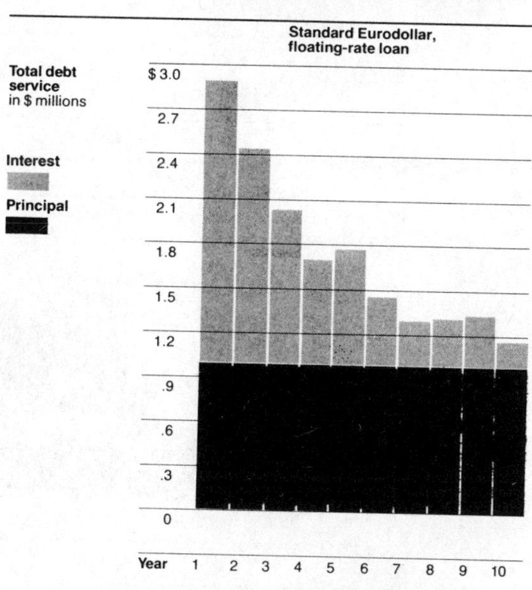

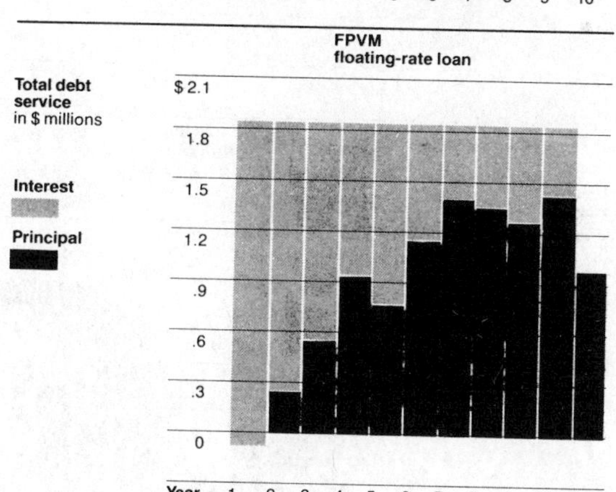

Exhibit 2. Alternative Debt-Service Profiles with Approximately the Same Maturities [in $ millions]

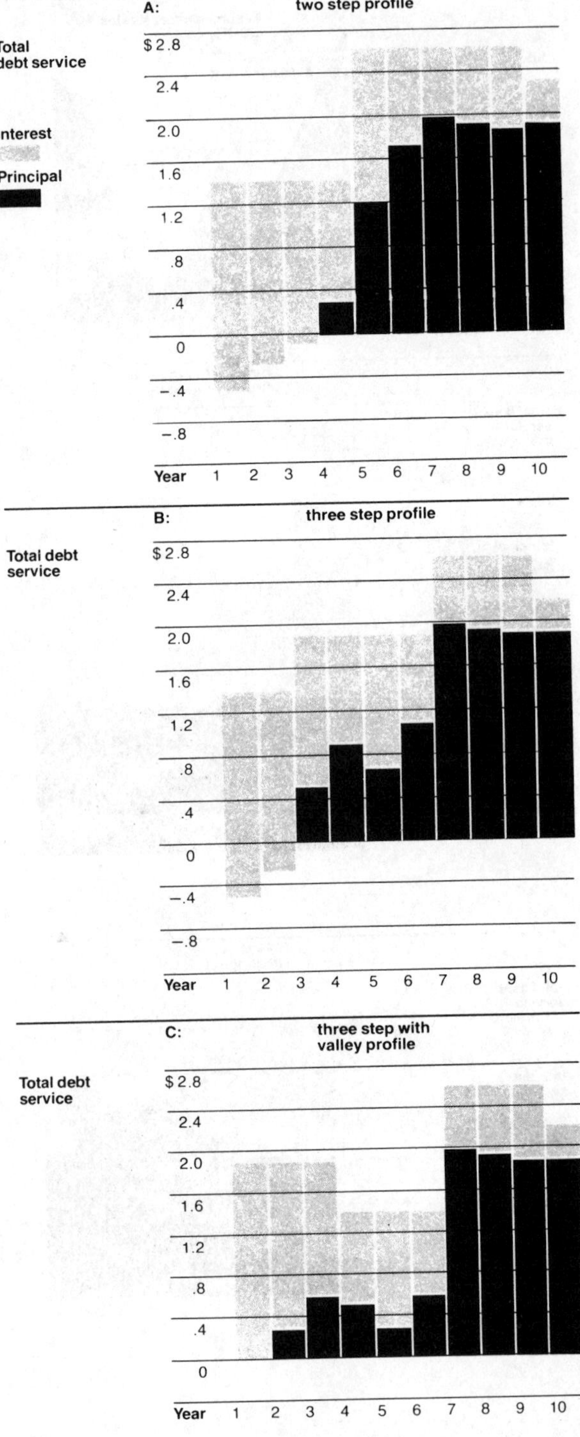

chief financial officer of an Asian company, undertaking a major factory expansion, sought from our bank a low payment level for the first two years (a grace period) followed by one step up for the remainder of the loan (see Exhibit 3). We were ready to agree to this profile, but when he expressed concern about the change of government expected in four years, we decided to alter the payment schedule. Although the country was politically stable, such governmental changes historically resulted in economic disruptions and drops in sales for 12 to 18 months before and after the change.

To limit the mandatory cash outflows during the transition period, we suggested a reduction in the debt-service payment level for a two-year period, as shown in the lower half of Exhibit 3. This change meant we had to raise payment levels elsewhere to realize the same expected final maturity.

Impact of Different Interest Rates

In an FPVM, the lender and borrower share, in a manner acceptable to both, the risk of changing interest rates. The actual rates undoubtedly will differ from those agreed on. The final maturity will be longer if average rates are higher; it will be shorter if they are lower.

Exhibit 3. Debt-Service Profiles Before and After Adjustment for Periods of Political Transition [in $ millions]

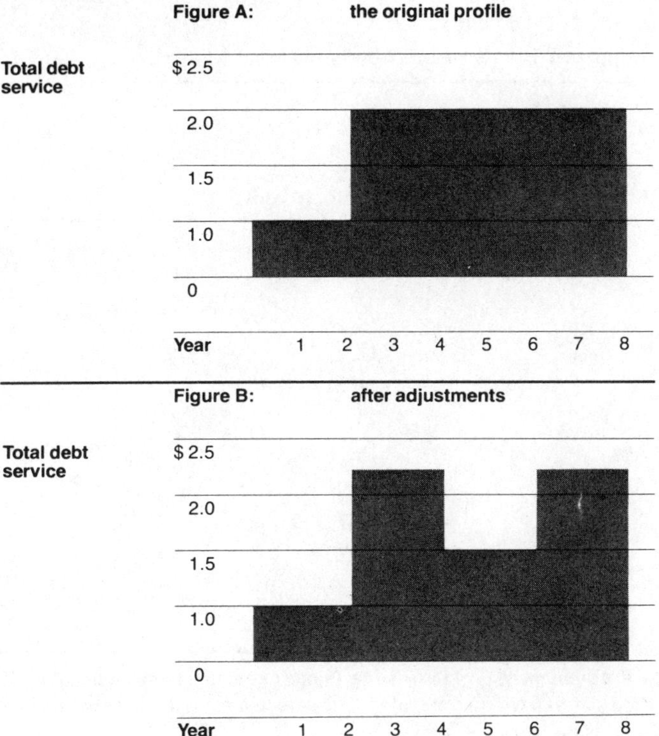

The three fixed-payment scenarios in Exhibit 4 illustrate the impact of different interest-rate levels on the final maturity of an FPVM loan. In the cases of the $902,000 payment at 13% and the $981,000 at 15%, you can see that if the actual interest rate equals the expected rate, final maturity is 10 years. Interest rates that turn out lower or higher than expected translate into final maturities of less or more than 10 years, respectively. The closer the originally estimated interest-rate scenario is to the actual average rates, the closer the final maturity will be to the expected maturity forecast in the loan agreement.

We want to emphasize that the uncertainty surrounding final maturity should not prevent either lenders or borrowers from using FPVM loan transactions. Both sides can approximate final maturity of an outstanding FPVM loan one year or more in advance. Borrowers, then, have sufficient time to roll over or refinance the debt, and lenders can plan to redeploy assets being paid off. And by negotiating a date on which all the outstanding principal will be paid off, the lender is protected against the possibility of an unreasonably long final maturity.

How Volatile Rates Affect Maturity

Throughout this article, our examples assume an average, constant rate of interest for the life of the loan instead of a cyclical pattern that more closely

Exhibit 4. Impact of Interest-Rate Levels on Final Maturity

Fixed Payment and Assumed Interest Rate	Actual Interest Rate	Years to Maturity
$902,000	11%	8.7
(13%)	13	10.0
	15	12.0
	17	16.7
$944,000	11%	8.2
(14%)	13	9.3
	15	11.1
	17	14.4
$981,000	11%	7.7
(15%)	13	8.6
	15	10.0
	17	12.4

Note: These fixed-payment profiles assume equal, semiannual payments of a $10-million, 10-year annuity-type loan at fixed interest rates. The actual interest rates are assumed to be constant for the life of the loan.

tracks reality. This assumption not only helps simplify our explanation of the concept, but also, we have found, helps us zero in on a mutually agreeable payment profile with a potential borrower.

Of course, a computer can easily handle any combination of interest rates as well as absolute average rate levels. But such complexity is not necessary, because assuming an average constant rate does not result in final maturities that are materially different from those obtained using floating rates. Even if the actual rate cycles differ from those expected, as long as the *average* rate is close to the average used to derive the original payment schedule the final maturity will be close to that expected.

Exhibit 5 shows the resulting final maturities for four actual interest-rate cycles, each of which averages 13%, using the $10 million FPVM loan repaid with equal annual payments of $1.843 million. All scenarios assume a 4½-year cycle, which approximates that which has occurred over the past 10 to 12 years. Such history is, of course, no assurance of future interest-rate cycles, but it does provide a starting point for simulation. The exhibit shows three interesting facts.

Exhibit 5. Alternative Interest-Rate Cycles and Their Final Maturities

	Interest-Rate Scenarios Each Averages 13%	Years to Maturity
A	Level at 13%	10.00
B	Narrow fluctuation (14 to 12%)	10.12
C	Wide fluctuation (19 to 7%), starting at 19%	10.62
D	Wide fluctuation (19 to 7%), starting at 7%	9.31

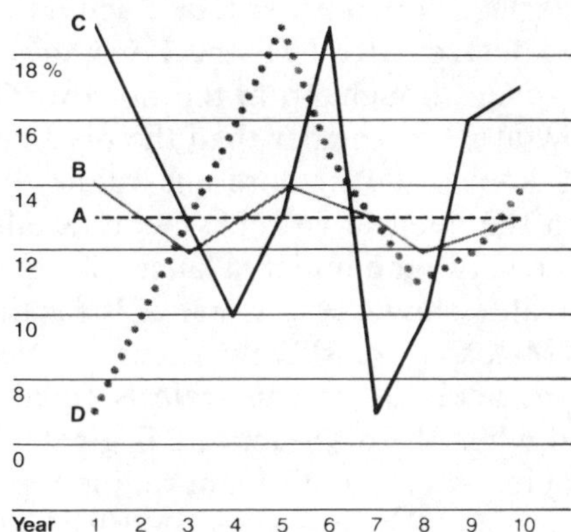

1 The impact of interest-rate fluctuation on final maturity is relatively small. For the case considered, an interest-rate cycle with amplitude of almost 50% (13% plus or minus 6%) led to final maturity variation of less than 10% (.6 to .7 of one year).
2 As expected, other things being equal, wider interest-rate fluctuation results in a larger impact on final maturity.
3 For the scenarios with wide fluctuations, final maturity was longer or shorter than expected, depending on whether the actual floating rate prevailing in the early years of debt repayment was greater or smaller than the expected interest rate.

Net Present Value Comparison

An FPVM loan gives the borrower a certain debt-service cash flow while retaining the advantage of floating-rate pricing, with interest being paid at the same rate as the standard term loan. When making their borrowing decisions, however, most companies would also like to consider the effective cost of the financing. Typically, this cost is found by making discounted cash flow calculations in which the timing of cash inflows (such as drawdowns) and outflows (such as commitment and front-end fees, and interest and principal payments) is taken into consideration. Therefore, the merits of each type of loan on a net present value (NPV) basis have to be examined.

In Exhibit 6, we compare the NPVs of a level FPVM without a grace period of a corresponding Eurodollar loan with and without one, and of a stepped loan for three actual interest-rate scenarios: actual interest rate is equal to, greater than, and less than the expected 13% interest rate.

We assume all of the following: that the initial balance of the loan is $10 million; target maturity is 10 years; expected interest rate is 13%; payments are semiannual; grace period in the stepped-payment case is 5 years. This results in fixed-payment schedules of $910,000 for the level case. For the stepped-payment case, it creates $650,000 payments for the first nine semiannual payments and $1.3 million due for the remaining ones. Interest rates are equal to 11% for the lower actual interest-rate cases and 15% for the higher scenarios. We consider four discount-rate scenarios—two higher than the 13% expected rate (15% and 17%), one equal to it, and one lower than it (11%)—even though, from the borrower's standpoint, it makes no sense to borrow at a cost higher than the discount rate.

Exhibit 6 shows the net present value of each debt-service profile associated with the alternative repayment schedules, actual interest rates, and discount rates *less* the initial balance of the loan. For a given scenario, the higher the value shown, the worse it is for the borrower.

The FPVM loans are slightly superior to standard Eurodollar alternatives when the actual borrowing rate is equal to or greater than the expected rate and when the discount rate is greater than the actual borrowing rate. For example, when the discount rate is 17% and the actual borrowing rate 13%, the level and the single-stepped FPVM loans are superior by NPVs

Exhibit 6. Comparison of Net Present Value of an FPVM and a Standard Eurodollar Loan

		Type of Loan											
		Level FPVM $910,000 in U.S. Dollars: No Grace Period			Standard Eurodollar: No Grace Period			Stepped FPVM $650,000 and $1.3 Million in U.S. Dollars: Five-Year Grace Period			Standard Eurodollar: Five-Year Grace Period		
Actual interest rate		11%	13%	15%	11%	13%	15%	11%	13%	15%	11%	13%	15%
Discount rate	11%	0	0.87	1.97	0	0.73	1.46	0	1.02	2.77	0	0.99	1.98
	13	−0.7	0	0.91	−0.69	0	0.69	−0.85	0	1.1	−0.93	0	0.93
	15	−1.33	−0.72	0	−1.31	−0.65	0	−1.6	−0.89	0	−1.74	−0.87	0
	17	−1.89	−1.39	−0.93	−1.86	−1.24	−0.62	−2.26	−1.67	−0.94	−2.46	−1.64	−0.82

Assumptions: Loan is for $10 million; target maturity is 10 years; expected interest rate is 13%; payments are made semiannually.

of $150,000 and $30,000, respectively. Even when the actual falls below the expected borrowing rate, the net present values of the FPVM loans are not much below those of the Eurodollar alternatives.

Because a company won't fund operations at a cost higher than the discount rate, both the level and the stepped FPVM loans are superior to their standard Eurodollar alternatives in terms of NPV. Of course, if the actual borrowing rate is significantly lower than expected, the FPVM alternative will show a lower net present value than the Eurodollar loan. We think this is a small price to pay for the benefits of debt-service certainty, especially since interest would be paid at the same rates as under a standard floating-rate loan.

How FPVM Can Help

We initially refined FPVM for companies wishing to finance capital-intensive start-up projects that have as much as 50 to 75% of funding in the form of floating-rate debt. The biggest problem occurs during the one to four years when a project gradually increases its capacity (as in the case of a mining or chemical project), trains staff and managers to run a new facility, and gradually builds up market share to a sustainable level. In virtually all cases, serious cash flow problems can arise if interest rates climb to 18% or 20% for an extended period when a 10%, 14%, or even 16% average rate was used to establish the financial viability of the project. The FPVM loan can help, since the cash flow required for debt service during this period is fixed and therefore independent of interest rates.

But what happens if actual rates fall below those agreed to in the FPVM payment schedule? Then the company will pay back the loan faster than it would have under a normal floating-rate loan. Such a situation is usually not the problem because the initial payment schedule is based on conservatively forecast cash flows likely to be generated by the project. Even in a case of a significantly lower than anticipated interest rate, the company can usually prepay and refinance the loan or arrange extra borrowing to maintain the same amount of principal outstanding. If you consider this ability to prepay and/or borrow additional amounts to maintain some target level of debt, the FPVM loan becomes a tool for managing ongoing corporate or government debt.

Several government officials we talked to view an FPVM loan as a better way to budget and manage the foreign exchange reserves of their countries; because they can predict the foreign exchange requirements for as many as two years out, they can develop a budget that will not require unplanned borrowing, will not draw down reserves, and will not necessitate the cutback of budgeted programs.

Many managers believe that an FPVM loan can lessen financial risk by reducing vulnerability to a liquidity crisis caused by large swings in short-term rates (often in tandem with a downturn in sales).

In addition, several financial planners have commented to us that the FPVM approach would enable them to concentrate their efforts more on the operational end and strategic aspects of their industries by reducing the year-to-year cash flow uncertainty caused by large amounts of floating-rate debt.

Bridging the Gap

Although the FPVM loan alternative for corporate or government borrowers is new and not yet widely accepted, we believe that the continued volatility and uncertainty of worldwide inflation (and consequently of interest rates) will accelerate its acceptance.

On the one hand, commercial and even institutional lenders are reluctant to provide the kind of fixed-rate loans that many borrowers used to rely on to finance their fixed-asset investments. On the other hand, inflation has increased the cost of many projects to the point where companies often must borrow heavily from commercial banks in order for their projects to proceed.

The FPVM is a loan mechanism that bridges these two poles. It ensures the availability of capital by giving lenders a floating-rate return that varies with inflation and avoids the potential loss of principal inherent in, for example, the fixed-rate bond. At the same time, it enhances the viability of projects by reducing interest-rate risk and allowing debt-service schedules that better match the cash flow requirements of a given situation. In this way, we believe, FPVM loans can help to ensure the continued flow of funds from savers to investors in a manner that is helpful to both.

33
Hedging on Loans Linked to the Prime

WILLIAM S. KRASKER

Krasker shows how corporations can use the financial futures market to hedge possible increases in the cost of borrowing.

Until the late 1970s the risk of unanticipated interest rate changes was small for a company that had borrowed money at an interest level linked to the prime rate. Interest rates fluctuated very little, and the largest portion of a company's debt typically consisted of fixed-rate obligations.

In the last few years, as everybody knows, interest rates have become much more volatile. Moreover, banks often insist on lending at variable rates.

Although the growth of futures markets has been phenomenal in recent years, no prime rate futures markets exist in which businesses can directly hedge the risk of unanticipated changes in the prime. If, however, the prime is correlated with other rates, as intuition and data suggest, it is possible partly to hedge this risk. Analysis reveals an interesting application here of a statistical method, regression analysis, that has many applications in and out of business.

Let us look at a hypothetical small company, Pint Size Corporation, which borrowed $5 million from a bank in mid-1979. Under the terms of the loan, PS pays interest each March 1, June 1, September 1, and December 1 at an annualized rate two percentage points above the prime rate prevailing on that date. Exhibit 1 shows the sequence of these payments over the next two years; the wild fluctuations reflect the wide swings in the prime. The

---

**Author's Note.* I obtained the coefficients of the regression not by ordinary least squares but by a method that exploits the first-order serial correlation of the error terms.

Exhibit 1. Pint Size's Quarterly Payments

September 1979	$161,250
December	191,250
March 1980	228,875
June	157,875
September	152,875
December	254,375
March 1981	225,000

unprecedented levels of the prime in March 1980 and December 1980 forced PS to make particularly high interest payments in those quarters.

The company could have used the financial futures markets to reduce the risk of such high outlays. To hedge its September 1979 payment, for example, PS might have sold 90-day Treasury bills for September delivery. If interest rates rose unexpectedly in the interim, the increase in the payment to the bank would have been offset by a profit on the short sale of the T-bills.

This hedging strategy is fine in principle, but it does not tell PS *how many* Treasury bills to sell short. PS would have no problem if changes in the prime and T-bill rates corresponded exactly. As Exhibit 2 shows, PS could hedge perfectly by selling five September futures contracts, each for $1 million of Treasury bills. (In my calculations I ignore the hedger's transaction costs, but they are small.)

In reality, of course, interest rates do not move in unison, and without further information PS management cannot be sure that this short sale would reduce the risk rather than add to it. The extra information needed concerns

Exhibit 2. "Perfect" Hedging Illustrated

June 1
PS anticipates a 15% prime rate on September 1 and sells five Treasury bill futures contracts for September delivery at 10%.

Scenario A: September 1
Actual prime rate equals 18%. Unanticipated cost = ¼ × .03 × $5 million, or $37,500. Actual Treasury bill rate equals 13%. Profit on futures contracts = ¼ × .03 × $5 million, or $37,500.

Scenario B: September 1
Actual prime rate equals 13%. Unanticipated saving = ¼ × .02 × $5 million, or $25,000. Actual Treasury bill rate equals 8%. Loss on futures contracts = ¼ × .02 × $5 million, or $25,000.

Note: The ¼ fraction appears in these calculations because the prime rate and the 90-day T-bill rate are quoted at annual rates.

the correlation between the prime and T-bill rates—and regression analysis provides it.

To Find the Appropriate Hedge

Through regression analysis you can estimate the relationship between the prime rate and other interest rates. For example, using monthly data from mid-1977 to mid-1979, PS could have estimated the following regression equation:

$$R = 1.63 + .83T + E$$

Here R is the prime rate, T is the annualized rate on new 90-day Treasury bills, and E is a random error term reflecting the fact that we cannot perfectly forecast the prime rate.*

The regression equation says that on average a rise of 100 basis points (one percentage point) in the T-bill rate is associated with an 83 basis-point rise in the prime rate. The actual rise will be more or less than 83 basis points, depending on the value of the random term E. The constant term in the regression, 1.63, is related to both the average values of the variables during the sample period and to the coefficient on T. This term plays no part, however, in determining the hedging strategy.

The regression equation shows that we can think of the prime rate as having two independent components, one related to the T-bill rate and the other a random component about which the T-bill rate gives us no information. Intuition correctly suggests that the best that Pint Size could do would be to sell futures to neutralize the risk associated with the first component.

Not surprisingly, the regression coefficient .83 on the Treasury bill rate is the information PS needs: to best hedge its September payment, the company should sell $.83 \times 5$, or 4.15 September contracts. Since a fraction of a contract cannot be sold, PS rounds off to 4.

Exhibit 3 shows how the company would have fared if, in mid-1979, it had simultaneously hedged its next seven payments in the way just described. Despite the large swings in the prime, the net payments (interest paid less profit on the corresponding futures contract) would have remained quite stable. In fact, for this seven-quarter period PS would have gained much more than stability; as the chart shows, it would have made a tidy profit on the contracts because, beginning in late 1979, interest rates were generally higher than expected.

Had rates been lower, PS would have lost money on the futures, but of course in this case its interest payments would also have been lower. On average, hedging should neither make nor lose money (except for brokers' fees); its advantage is in reducing uncertainty.

Exhibit 3. Effect of Hedging Over Seven Periods

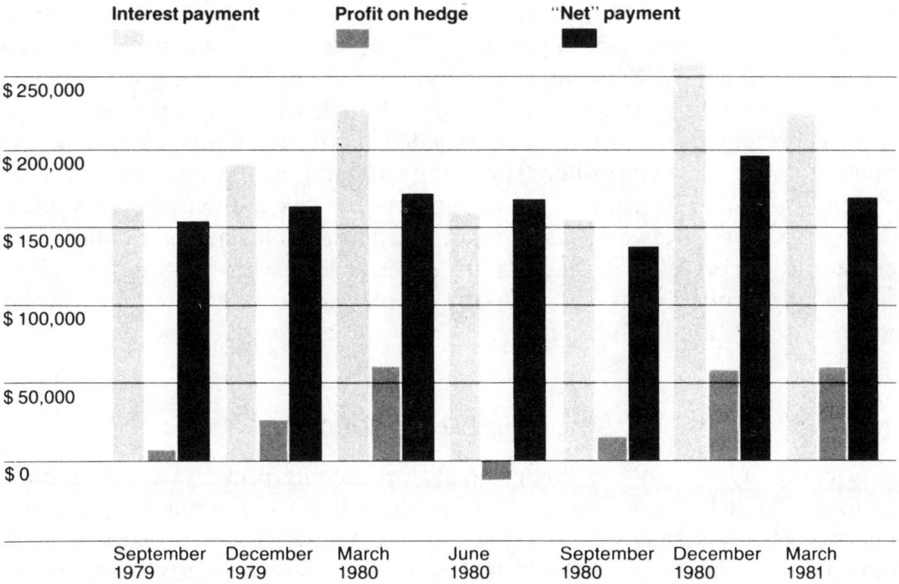

Interest payment
Profit on hedge
"Net" payment

$250,000
$200,000
$150,000
$100,000
$50,000
$0

September 1979
December 1979
March 1980
June 1980
September 1980
December 1980
March 1981

Multiple Regression Analysis

Pint Size, being unrestricted in trading in futures markets, should be able to hedge more effectively by trading simultaneously in two or more markets. In addition to T-bills, futures are traded in long-term Treasury bonds, Ginnie Maes, and commercial paper. As an illustration, let us consider hedging strategies using both T-bills and commercial paper.

With data from the same two-year period as before, PS could obtain this multiple regression:

$$R = 1.32 + .25T + .63P + E$$

P is the interest rate on 90-day commercial paper loans and E again represents random error. According to this regression, if the Treasury bill rate rises 100 basis points and the commercial paper rate stays constant, the prime will rise 25 basis points on average. Similarly, if the commercial paper rate rises 100 basis points and the Treasury bill rate remains unchanged, the prime will rise 63 basis points on average.

Why is the T-bill coefficient so much smaller in this regression than in the previous one? Because the Treasury bill rate and the commercial paper rate are correlated. In the first regression, T served partly as a proxy for the commercial paper rate; when the Treasury bill rate rises, the commercial paper rate generally rises also, and the coefficient on T in the first equation has to reflect the effect of both. The proxy effect disappears when the commercial paper rate is included.

For the reasons stated earlier, the best PS could do would be to hedge away the component of the uncertainty in the prime rate that is related to the T-bill and commercial paper rates. To do this, the company decides to sell .25 × 5, or 1.25 T-bill contracts and .63 × 5, or 3.15 commercial paper contracts, rounding off the sales to 1 and 3 contracts, respectively.

Theoretically, one can always hedge more effectively using two (or more) futures markets rather than one, provided all the regression coefficients are different from zero. In the present case, however, very little difference exists between one market and more than one, particularly because the effects of rounding off are more severe with two markets. Pint Size would probably prefer to use the simpler strategy: hedging only in the more widely traded T-bill futures.

Smoothing Fluctuations

Any company can follow this strategy for hedging prime rate-linked obligations. Because there is evidence that the relationship among the various interest rates has changed since the Federal Reserve Board adopted a more monetarist position in 1979, let us estimate a regression based on recent data. Using monthly observations from January 1981 through April 1982, we obtain this estimated regression equation:

$$R = 11.27 + .51T + E$$

This regression says that to best hedge a particular quarterly interest payment using T-bill futures, a company should sell, for delivery on the month of that payment, .51 contract for each $1 million of loan principal. For example, to hedge a March 1 interest payment on a $10 million loan, the company would sell .51 × 10, or 5.1 March contracts (in practice, 5).

Hedging in this way obviously cannot eliminate all the risk, since changes in the T-bill rate do not correspond exactly with those in the prime. But the data suggest that this method can cut the fluctuations by better than half. For many companies that have suffered through the recent interest rate gyrations, that would be welcome relief.

34

Are Original-Issue Discount Bonds Here to Stay?

J. RANDALL WOOLRIDGE and GARY GRAY

Newly issued bonds with little or no coupon interest were a new development in the United States and international bond markets in the early 1980s. Woolridge and Gray explain their key features and who benefits from this type of bond.

The economic climate of recent years has spawned many financial innovations in the capital markets as companies seek to reduce the cost of raising money. One popular item is the original-issue discount bond (although the concept is not brand new).[1]

The OIDs of J. C. Penney, Cities Service, General Motors Acceptance, and Aluminum Company of America, among others—with coupons ranging from 0% to 7%—were met with overwhelming enthusiasm in the financial markets when issued in 1981. More than $10 billion in principal amount and $4 billion in bond proceeds were raised last year through this medium.

The popularity of OIDs is linked, of course, to economic conditions. When interest rates are high, OIDs not only offer great savings to issuers over full-coupon bonds, but also hold great attraction for investors. When interest rates eventually return to lower levels, the financial benefits to issuers may decline but will not disappear. The major question at that juncture will be whether investors still want them.

Editor's Note. Readers who want to see the calculations on which the ADM bond comparison is based may obtain a short addendum to the article. Send a stamped, self-addressed envelope to Amanda Touche Bowler, *Harvard Business Review*, Boston, Massachusetts 02163.

Seasoned deep-discount bonds, which had been issued at par before the acceleration in interest rates, have always enjoyed an active market because investors in high-income brackets benefit from the preferential tax treatment of the capital gains accruing from the accretion of the discount from par. Thus seasoned deep discounts sell at lower yield-to-maturity levels than comparable higher-coupon bonds.

New-issue OIDs, of course, do not carry this tax benefit. The original-issue discount is amortized on a level basis over the life of the debt. As the discount is amortized, the investor must declare it as ordinary gross income even though the income is not received until maturity or prior sale.

This tax treatment has generated a "clientele effect" because only certain classes of investors find it advantageous to buy the security. The investors in recent OID issues are nontaxable entities, notably pension funds and foreign individuals and institutions.

Because it greatly reduces the universe of potential investors, the clientele effect may have profound secondary market implications for OIDs. The appetite of the huge pension fund industry, however, is enormous. Time will tell.

ADM Issue

To illustrate the attractiveness of the OID in a volatile economic climate, let us look at one case where a company sold a package of full-coupon and original-issue discount debentures. Since both issues were nearly identical except for the coupon rates and the sinking-fund provision, we are provided with a well-equipped laboratory.

On May 12, 1981, Archer-Daniels-Midland Company sold two bond issues, both due on May 15, 2011: a 16% full-coupon, $125 million principal amount of sinking-fund debentures and a 7%, $250 million principal amount of original-issue discount debentures. The company offered the original-issue discount debt to investors at 46.246% of face value for a yield of 15.35%, if held to maturity, and 15.14% on a current basis. The full-coupon debentures were offered at 99.50% of face value, with a 16.08% yield, both current and to maturity. On the OIDs Archer-Daniels received $115,615,000, less the cost of issuance, and of course will repay the full $250 million to holders at maturity.

For federal income tax purposes ADM will amortize the original discount on the OIDs as ordinary interest payments on a level annual basis over the 30-year life of the issue. The debenture holders must also declare this amount, $4,479,500 per year, as ordinary income for federal tax purposes. ADM will carry this debt initially on its balance sheet at $115,615,000. As the original discount is amortized, the value of the OIDs will increase linearly on the balance sheet to $250 million in 2011.

The primary monetary benefit to the issuer of an OID financing comes from the tax treatment for accounting purposes of the original discount. Annual amortization of the discount means tax treatment similar to that of a normal interest payment. Thus the company can take generous interest write-offs annually while avoiding payment of the lump-sum discount until the OIDs mature. The time value of money thus produces a considerable saving. For the ADM issue, using a cost of capital equaling the yield of the full-coupon bond (16.08%), the tax-adjusted present value of the saving is $12,613,511.

A second financial benefit may arise from lower cash outflows for interest payments. The lower OID coupon rate, however, does not guarantee a lower interest payment because OID interest must be paid on the entire principal amount of the issue. For the ADM debenture the annual saving in interest payments is $1,091,351. After adjustment for taxes and discounting by the cost of capital, the present value of the cash flow saving is $3,621,644.

A third benefit, compared with full-coupon bonds, comes from the initial pricing. On a yield-to-maturity basis, OIDs have been priced as much as 100 basis points below the yield levels of full-coupon bonds that are comparable in quality and maturity. This pricing differential will be greatest in periods of high interest rates when OIDs offer investors the most benefits.

The lack of an effective optional refunding call provision on OIDs is the main reason for the pricing differential. The noncallability feature provides great upside price movement potential for OIDs in declining interest rate environments because, if interest rates fall to the point where it is advantageous to refinance callable debt, the prices of callable bonds will stay below those of noncallable bonds.

This gap reflects investor expectations that the bond will be redeemed at the first optional call date. Therefore, a noncallable bond has a much greater upside trading potential than a callable bond and is worth more to an investor.

A second reason for the pricing differential results from the compounding of the yield to maturity in the purchase price. A yield calculation holds an implicit assumption that, as semiannual interest payments are received, the payments will be reinvested at an interest rate equivalent to the bond's yield to maturity. This assumption is usually unrealistic; the investor must reinvest cash at yields available in the market at the time.

This phenomenon, known as reinvestment rate risk, is greatly reduced in OIDs. In fact, it is eliminated in a zero-coupon OID. For example, J. C. Penney's zero-coupon debentures, which sold for $332.46, guarantee a return of 14.25% when they mature in 1989 at $1,000.

The pricing of the ADM issues revealed a yield differential on the full-coupon bonds, compared with the OID's, of 73 basis points (16.08% vs. 15.35%). Consequently, the OID issue sold for $5,422,125 more than if it were priced at the full-coupon yield.

Because much of the interest paid in an OID issue is in the form of the amortized discount, a much larger principal amount of OIDs than full-coupon debt must be sold to obtain the same amount of dollars. The present value of this difference in principal amounts that must be paid at maturity has to be subtracted from the present value of total issuer savings to obtain the net issuer financial benefit. For the ADM issue, after the adjustment of the principal, the net financial benefit was $20,132,146.

When Interest Rates Fall

Will a decline in interest rates mean the demise of OIDs? This seems possible but not probable. Such an environment affects issuer benefits in several ways:

- ☐ The original-issue discount may fall owing to the smaller difference in the coupon rates. Consequently, tax treatment benefits may drop. Lower interest rates, however, also trim a company's cost of capital, which means that tax treatment benefits will be discounted at a lower rate—thereby increasing their present value.
- ☐ The difference in interest payment cash flows will likely be lessened if not erased.
- ☐ The initial pricing advantage of OIDs will be less, if not eliminated or reversed, because of the lower value of call and reinvestment-rate risk protection to investors.
- ☐ The present value of the difference in principal amounts to be paid at maturity will be greater due to the lower discount rate in the form of the cost of capital.

But the net financial benefit to the issuer need not decline and may even increase. As interest rates subside, the reduction in the company's cost of capital dramatically raises the present value of tax treatment benefits. For example, suppose interest rates decline and ADM can issue a full-coupon bond at 10% or an OID at 3%. Assuming that the net proceeds of both issues are $125 million, that both 30-year issues sell to yield 10% to maturity (no pricing differential), and that ADM's cost of capital is 10%, the net present value of the saving to ADM would exceed $28 million.

The key assumptions here concern the initial pricing and the cost of capital; but the levels to which the initial price would have to drop, or to which the cost of capital would have to rise, to eliminate the saving to ADM would force a yield to maturity on the OID that would far exceed that of the full-coupon security.

Other Issuer Perspectives

Potential issuers must be aware of other factors when considering a deep-discount financing.

On the positive side, OIDs have longer duration than full-coupon bonds. *Duration*, a term coined by Frederick Macauley in 1938, is the period of time elapsing before a stream of payments generates one-half of its present value. Inherent in the calculation of duration are the bond's maturity, coupon rate, and yield characteristics. A lengthier period means that a company has longer use of its borrowed funds, thereby reducing future interest rate uncertainties, and will be obliged to tap the financial markets less often.

On the negative side, OIDs virtually eliminate the opportunity for using optional call provisions. The present value of a future refunding decision to the issuing company, however, is small due to the high cost of capital that must be employed to discount future cash flows in today's markets. (This is especially significant because of the long period that prevails in call protections in industrial issues—10 years.)

A second disadvantage of OIDs is the dependence of much of the benefit on the cash flows generated by the tax treatment of the amortization of the original-issue discount. The recent reduction in corporate income tax rates also cuts the cash flow benefits.

The third problem area is subtle and, because OIDs have no history, impossible to evaluate. An original-issue discount financing injects a growing leverage factor into the issuer's balance sheet. All else being equal, as the original-issue discount is amortized and long-term corporate liabilities rise, the company's debt-equity ratio also rises.

The market believes that a higher debt-equity ratio means a greater credit risk. With increased risk, investors expect a higher return. So the company may find that raising funds in the marketplace becomes more costly.

Finally, the lack of sinking-fund or refunding provisions means that an issuer must plan for the huge balloon payments it will be obliged to make at maturity. This is a serious consideration not only for the company but, also for the marketplace; in view of the large number of 30-year issues sold in 1981, for example, the markets could feel enormous pressure in 2011.

Note

1. See William K. Harper, Paul D. Berger, and Earl M. Foster, "How about Original-Issue, Deep-Discount Bonds?", *HBR*, September-October 1975, p. 8.

35
Essential Elements of Project Financing

LARRY WYNANT

When undertaking a mammoth venture such as a mine, whose functioning could be differentiated from other corporate operations and whose financing might tax its resources, many a U.S. and Canadian company in recent years has elected to proceed on a project-financing basis. The parties assuming the financial and general operating risks for the sponsor can be lending institutions, government agencies, customers who contract to buy the output, and suppliers. In the case of a project abroad, local government and international agencies may take on part of the financial (and political) risks. Usually the financial obligation entails limited recourse, if any, to the sponsoring corporation. At a time when mounting inflation and large debt burdens can inhibit the ability of capital-intensive companies to replace or update plant, the project-financing technique has decided advantages.

In recent years numerous industrial projects have been undertaken around the world that have consumed enormous amounts of capital. Rapid inflation, novel technological characteristics, and (often) a remote location have combined to require sums that tax the financial capacity of even the largest corporations.

Four years ago a survey of ongoing nuclear power, mining, and natural resource projects found more than 200 with anticipated capital costs exceeding $500 million.[1] Since then inflation has, of course, accelerated sharply. Moreover, the developmental nature and foreign location of many of these ventures involve such enormous monetary risks that the outcome of a project has a tremendous impact on the sponsoring company.

The companies and their investment bankers have devoted considerable ingenuity to designing ownership structures and financing packages that cope with these capital demands and risk pressures. Joint venture arrangements and government support for projects are two avenues that they have followed.

At a time when U.S. business is already constrained by high leverage ratios and high interest rates, the prospect of further inflation and stepped-up spending requirements influences the capital-intensive company to seek imaginative ways of obtaining funding. My research (see the Appendix) suggests that project financing can be a very effective vehicle for enlarging the amount of debt available to a new undertaking as well as for managing the sponsor's exposure to the associated risks.

This technique is usually applied to extremely large natural resource and energy investments costing hundreds of millions of dollars. The same strategy, however, can be useful in cases where capital needs are manageable but risks are great. The transportation, power, chemicals, and agribusiness sectors in particular have used project financing for all sizes of investments.

It is easy to see why. Exhibit 1 indirectly traces the investment required for a unit of capacity in several capital-intensive industries by measuring assets to revenues during the 1955 to 1975 period. Metal mining and primary metals have been especially pressured by rising capacity costs.

For many companies in these industries faced with the necessity of replacing or updating plant, debt financing naturally has been the main recourse. Exhibit 2 illustrates the increased reliance on leverage over the past two decades.

Capital needs could mushroom in the near future; many U.S. corporations will have to search for new funding to cover their needs for strategically and economically attractive investments. A counter-response to the warnings 10 years ago of a capital crunch for the 1975–1985 decade argued

Exhibit 1. Ratios of Total Assets to Total Sales in Selected Industries, 1955–1975

	1955	1960	1966	1971	1975
Manufacturing					
Chemicals	.85	.90	.85	.89	.85
Machinery	.75	.79	.74	1.02	1.00
Paper and allied products	.81	.88	.89	.95	.83
Petroleum refining	.95	1.06	1.07	1.09	[a]
Primary metals	.78	.98	.88	1.20	1.01
Rubber and plastic products	.58	.66	.71	.75	.72
Mining					
Metal mining	1.45	1.96	1.48	2.32	2.20
Crude petroleum and natural gas	1.39	1.62	1.29	1.21	[a]
Agriculture, forestry, and fishing	1.01	.92	.88	.82	.79
Construction	.47	.47	.47	.51	.54

Source: Internal Revenue Service, *Statistics of Income, Corporation Income Tax Returns*, for the particular years.

[a]Ratios are unavailable because of changes in industry definition.

Exhibit 2. Use of Leverage in Selected Manufacturing Industries, 1960–1978 (ratio of short- and long-term debt to stockholders' equity)

	1960	1965	1970	1975	1978
All manufacturing	.25	.28	.45	.42	.41
Chemicals	.23	.32	.41	.43	.46
Machinery	.27	.28	.45	.39	.37
Paper and allied products	.25	.34	.59	.56	.53
Petroleum refining[a]	.19	.19	.29	.19	.27
Primary metals	.24	.29	.52	.49	.56
Rubber and plastic products	.32	.38	.66	.53	.55

Source: Federal Trade Commission, *Quarterly Financial Report for Manufacturing and Trade Corporations* (for the particular years).

[a]Ratios are not strictly comparable because of changes in industry definition.

that demand and supply mechanisms in the capital markets and innovative financing techniques would avert a crisis. In my opinion, project financing—a major innovation of the recent past—offers considerable promise for meeting these challenges.

The definitions of this approach run the gamut, depending on the advantage or objective that the financing package is designed to achieve. The following summary, however, captures the basic elements: Project financing is a financing of a major independent capital investment that the sponsoring company has segregated from its assets and general purpose obligations. The economic prospects of the project, combined with commitments from the sponsor and third parties, provide the support for extensive borrowings carrying limited financial recourse to the parent company.

Several characteristics distinguish project financing from traditional arrangements:

- ☐ The undertaking is established as a separate entity and relies heavily on leverage, generally for 65% to 75% of its capital needs.
- ☐ The borrowing is linked directly to the assets and cash flow potential of the venture.
- ☐ Commitments by third parties (suppliers, customers, and government agencies) and the sponsor make up important elements of the credit support.
- ☐ The sponsor's guarantees to lenders usually do not cover all the risks involved.
- ☐ The debt of the project is differentiated, at least for balance-sheet purposes, from the parent company's direct obligations.

Structuring the Venture

Tailoring this kind of enterprise requires a trade-off between the sponsor's desired risk exposure and the economics of the venture, including commitments by the sponsor and other parties to satisfy lenders' concerns that it can support a wide base of debt financing. Accomplishing this balance for projects that involve large front-end investments and great marketing, technology, and political uncertainties demands considerable time, cost negotiations, and financial expertise.

The extent of financial engineering needed calls for the services of an experienced adviser. Many of the larger U.S. commercial and investment banks have established project-financing departments and participate regularly in lending syndicates. A handful of the largest international commercial banks and an equally small number of investment houses have gained dominance as advisers in extremely large and complex project undertakings.

No one financing package, of course, would suit the needs of all projects. Each new development carries unique risks and capital needs and will have access to different funding sources. However, negotiating an underwriting of any project venture demands the corporate financial staff's attention to these key elements of the task:

1 Assessment of the start-up and operating risks and the range and likelihood of negative consequences.
2 Identification of the major lending sources and the terms for obtaining funds.
3 Analysis of the opportunities for reducing or laying off the risks.
4 Achieving the leverage targets through special fund sources and support arrangements.
5 Structuring of the ownership and credit arrangements to allow flexibility for future financing.

Assessment of the Risks

Each player in a major project—sponsor, lending institution, government agency, customer for the output, and host government in the case of a foreign venture—will view its prospects and characteristics with different objectives and considerations. Consequently, the negotiations necessary to design the financing package are complex and lengthy.

The initial task confronting the financial officer of the parent company, of course, is to investigate the feasibility of underwriting the investment on a project basis. This would call for creation of a separate company with clearly delineated operating and financial prospects: estimated capital requirements, anticipated output levels, technology or production requirements, raw materials sources, expected customers and future market conditions, and the structural and operating relationships between the project and the parent.

Designing a financing package that reduces the sponsor's risk exposure and presents the lenders with a strong proposal is of primary importance. With the aid of computer simulation to estimate the impact of such variables as market prices and operating costs on profitability and return on investment, the corporate financial staff can get an idea of the potential risks.

Start-Up Cost Overruns. The long start-up period for a major venture (sometimes 10 years in an exploration project) obviously adds to the potential for serious underestimation of costs. Many recent projects have entailed capital expenditures as high as 200% of original estimates.

Inflation, inaccurate engineering and design studies, and large operating deficits during the start-up phase are the usual reasons cited. All three of these underlay the problems of one company that had arranged $120 million of financing for an Indonesian copper mining development requiring inland construction in a remote mountainous region and a novel pipeline system for carrying the ore in slurry to the coast. By completion time three years later, modification of the site had pushed costs to more than $200 million.

Unexpectedly High Operating Costs. Incorrect estimates of operating costs can result from many factors: inaccurate assessment of the production or recovery process, poor engineering to meet product quality and quantity specifications, low productivity of foreign labor, unexpectedly high equipment replacement, inflation or unexpected price hikes for certain production components, and changes in parity of currencies for international projects.

The sponsors of a joint nickel-mining venture in Australia in the mid-1970s, for example, had negotiated long-term sales contracts in U.S. dollars. Operating expenses began climbing dramatically as the Australian dollar was revalued. The production process used oil as a fuel source, and the price of that commodity soared. The combination of cost pressures caused the sponsors to eventually write off their equity investment in the project.

Volatile Market Conditions. A venture producing a commodity product is likely to encounter changing market prices over its expected life. Therefore, an estimate of future prices at the planning stage is subject to considerable error.

In Foreign Ventures, High Political Risks. The political uncertainties surrounding foreign projects have become very serious during the past decade as developing countries and industrialized nations alike have adopted a more hostile posture toward foreign investments. Instances of outright expropriation by developing nations, such as Peru, Chile, and Cuba, as well as industrialized countries, such as Canada's nationalization of the potash industry in the mid-1970s, have been well publicized. But indirect actions by host governments—including foreign exchange restrictions, currency inconvertibility, increases in local taxes or royalties, demands for equity participation—can destroy or at least impair the economic attractiveness of a project.

Executives of the companies I studied all related incidents of intervention by foreign governments. One case involved increased royalties imposed on the project's output; in another, a sudden change in permitted depletion allowances resulted in a tax levy on past income of more than $25 million.

Identification of Loan Sources

Depending on the nature and location of the undertaking, potential sources for financing include export credits, international financing agencies, private lenders, and customers.

During the past two decades, many of the industrialized nations have established export credit and loan insurance programs. In the United States, the Export-Import Bank (Ex-Im) grants loan financing and gives guarantees to stimulate the exports of U.S. manufacturers, while the Overseas Private Investment Corporation (OPIC) provides insurance against risks of expropriation, currency inconvertibility, and war damage, as well as strictly business risks, for projects in some 90 developing nations. Similar funding and insurance can be obtained from other government agencies, such as the Export Insurance Division in Japan and the Export Credit Guarantee Department in Great Britain.

Theoretically, all the OECD countries will match terms and rates offered by their export credit agencies. But the agencies of some industrialized countries, particularly France, Britain, and Japan, have offered more competitive rates through "mixed" credits that combine concessionary aid lending with normal, market-related rates. Ex-Im has recently adopted a more aggressive posture by matching competing rates and offering more financing on an ad hoc basis and by pushing for fuller export financing agreements with other governments.

The terms for and costs of export financing and insurance are generally very attractive. Loans are usually provided with a long maturity on a fixed-price basis at rates somewhat better than free market conditions would permit. Similarly, private lenders are granted low-cost insurance protection.

Other politically sponsored funding sources available for industrial projects are the World Bank and regional lending organizations such as the Inter-American Development Bank and the Asian Development Bank. These entities generally emphasize development projects in Third World countries and may offer certain advantages in rates and loan maturities.

Loans from commercial banks are available through their participation in export credit programs as well as on the strength of the project's repayment capacity. Inasmuch as any loan proposal to a lending institution must meet the tests of a normal credit risk, the financial executive of the sponsoring company will be obliged to ascertain the costs involved as well as the level and types of risks that are acceptable to the lending groups.

Project financing was an outgrowth of the expansionary mood that pervaded the banking industry in the late 1960s and early 1970s. In their eagerness to get into an exciting new area and secure a position in international lending, bankers took on many project loans without fully recognizing the risks in nonrecourse or limited-recourse arrangements.

Many loans were granted that lacked, for example, completion agreements by the parent companies or assessments by the lenders of the sponsors' capacity or willingness to produce more equity if necessary. The loan agreements for a $600 million project in Peru in the early 1970s, for instance, were silent as to stockholders' responsibilities for cost overruns of more than $20 million. The ultimate project costs exceeded $725 million, which forced the lending group to renegotiate its financing support.

Borrowers no longer have such freedom. Problem projects, rampant inflation, and concerns about the risks of foreign loans—not to mention the cost overruns—have caused the banking industry to insist on much tighter agreements and stronger loan support from sponsors. The completion agreement for a recent $100 million Wyoming coal project committed the owners to meet volume and cost specifications for a minimum period of continuous operation and to provide all additional equity needed for completion of the undertaking.

The large international banks, however, still remain prepared to assume the political risks for foreign projects. In a venture abroad nowadays, the political climate often presents the most serious hazards.

Customer credits should also be explored as a source of loans. United States utility companies, for example, increasingly subsidize exploration and development through advance payments to oil companies in return for secured sources of gas or petroleum. The market for the output of the project may be tight enough to permit the sponsors to bargain for low-cost financing from customers. In nickel, copper, and other metals, market conditions have obliged Japanese and West German companies to seek long-term sources of supply. For many new projects the companies were willing to provide financing directly or solicit support from their government funding agencies.

To obtain the most favorable deal, the financial executive and financing specialist must search out all lending sources. As one financial vice-president said: "It's essential that the financial officer know the credit market thoroughly and design the financing to fit existing demand and supply conditions. It's important to know lenders around the world—their preferences, needs, and idiosyncrasies—and what one lender is prepared to do that others won't."

His company had engineered two successful overseas financings, each tailored to take advantage of the opportunities at the time. In one, the company obtained credit from U.S. commercial banks anxious to get involved in international business of this sort. In the other, the company was able to tap local banks because the host government gave incentives to them in order to aid industrial development in outlying regions of the country.

Reducing the Risks

As I have indicated, the growing popularity of project financing is in great part a consequence of cost escalations that surpass normal corporate resources. But even in the case of a small venture, or in the absence of capital restraints in underwriting a large venture, the project may involve risks that are unacceptable to the parent company.

Linking the financing to the fortunes of the project, however, can permit transfer of some hazards to other parties. In the case of foreign developments, for instance, credit and insurance programs offered by the industrialized nations provide nonrecourse financing and transfer some of the commercial and political risks to the funding agencies.

If demand and supply conditions for the eventual output are favorable, the sponsor can negotiate with customers to provide debt financing or absorb greater price risks in return for an assured future supply. Floor prices and price escalation clauses enable the sponsor to shift the consequences of price uncertainties to the project's "offtakers." Direct financial participation by customers reduces the other major element of market risk—the possibility that the sales agreements will not be honored.

During the past decade, two major foreign mining developments by one U.S. company received the go-ahead largely because (1) the governments involved were ready to provide export credit financing or loan guarantees to ensure raw materials sources for domestic needs and (2) the smelters and metal processors wanted to lock in supplies. These projects represented roughly 70% of the company's total assets, so it could not finance them alone.

The willingness of the large international banks to assume political risk is a reflection of their diversified loan portfolios, through which they can spread the hazards of foreign projects. (Of course, the banks charge risk premiums on these loans.) Furthermore, an institution's position and influence as a large international banker may cause the host government to think twice about expropriation or other actions that would jeopardize the project's success, thereby alienating an important segment of the credit market.

The companies whose executives I interviewed had employed a number of measures to minimize the political risks for large foreign ventures. Among these measures were agreements with lenders to carry the risks, purchase of political risk insurance for the equity investment, and formation of large lending consortia to include institutions from countries that were either trading partners or major creditors of the host governments.

This type of strategy unfolded in 1976 when Peru sought a $300 million balance-of-payments loan from a syndicate of U.S. money center banks.

They granted the loan on condition of satisfaction of two matters concerning U.S. customers of the banks—namely, a back-tax dispute with Southern Peru Copper Co. (owned by AMAX, Inc.) and compensation for Peru's expropriation in 1975 of Marcona Mining Co. (a joint venture of Cyprus Mines and Newmont Mining Corp.).

Achieving the Leverage Target

A project financing typically obtains debt funding equivalent to 65 to 75% of total capital needs. To procure such extensive support, the financial officer has to structure the agreements (1) to satisfy the demands of private lenders who are only prepared to assume normal credit risks and (2) to lay off any additional risks to partners, customers, or government institutions.

A study of 17 completed financings for new mines and related developments found that more than half had serious problems and could not generate sufficient cash flow to cover debt servicing.[2] Only one project, however, resulted in a loss to lenders. All of these projects were highly leveraged, yet they had satisfied the banks' requirements of being within the boundaries of normal credit risks.

The lenders must be provided with complete, detailed estimates of the project's risks and return potential, including feasibility studies, engineering reports, and particulars of commitments by the contractors, suppliers, and customers. In a loan to the sponsoring company, the lenders are much less concerned with the economic prospects of the particular investment than with the parent's credit worthiness and ability to meet debt obligations.

A project-financing proposal forces lenders to revise their assessment of the parent's debt-service capacity to include the forecasted cash flow for the undertaking. Investment bankers use the term "lenders' psychology" to suggest that lending institutions are locked in by traditional debt-equity ratios in the particular industry. By setting up the project as a separate borrowing entity, however, the sponsor can better demonstrate its prospects and debt-servicing capacity.

In trying to maximize borrowing capacity, one financial vice-president had pursued a "sum of the parts is greater than the whole" strategy. On a project basis the company had financed two overseas developments totaling $400 million and a domestic expansion program of roughly the same size.

On the strength of the projects, management had succeeded in making risk-sharing arrangements with major banks and, in the case of the foreign investments, similar arrangements with customers. The executive was convinced that the direct and indirect borrowings, equivalent to about 85% of the total investment, greatly exceeded the level of debt financing that the rating agencies or major lenders would have considered reasonable if financed by the parent. The company's debt ratio at the time averaged about 30%.

Preserving Financial Flexibility

Corporate financial officers aim to achieve a balance between the company's risk exposure and the amount of project leverage that they can negotiate—while retaining the parent company's financial flexibility. Top management must decide the level of commitment the company can afford to undertake as well as the form of that commitment.

The aspect of project financing that has received the greatest promotion is the ability of the proposal to raise funds solely on its own merits, without parent company guarantees. Such instances, however, are rare. Two of them, both undertaken by Freeport Minerals in the late 1960s, were a $120 million copper project in Indonesia and a $305 million nickel mine and processing plant in Australia. The initial equity investment in each case amounted to less than 25%, and the loans were totally nonrecourse to Freeport. However, full credit support had been offered by Ex-Im and OPIC to the U.S. lenders in the Indonesian project, and a considerable amount of purchasing financing had been used for both ventures.

The sponsors are usually required to provide *some* form of credit support. The level of support may, however, amount to only limited guarantees. Lenders view with alarm the prospect of a project unfinished due to engineering or technical problems or a large cost overrun. Hence bankers generally ask the owners beforehand to sign an agreement stipulating tests of physical and/or economic completion. After the completion provisions are met, the project loans become nonrecourse, thereby returning autonomy to the sponsor in financing any new projects.

High-risk ventures can normally get credit only if the parent gives general guarantees to the lenders. Full guarantees show up as direct liabilities on the sponsor's balance sheet.

But a host of financing arrangements have emerged that provide indirect credit. Long-term purchase commitments, a very common medium, commit sponsors to payments sufficient to service the debt. "Take or pay" contracts are often used to support the borrowing. A recent coal project of roughly $100 million was financed off the balance sheet on the strength of such a contract with a utility. For the promise of an assured supply, the customer agreed to pay, even in the absence of output, enough to cover interest and principal payments.

Other examples of indirect credits are cost-sharing arrangements, where sponsors are obliged to provide their pro rata shares of all costs including debt-service payments and parent indirect guarantees, such as working capital maintenance clauses.

The nature of the sponsor's loan support can critically affect its flexibility for two reasons:

1 A limited-recourse arrangement can free up the parent's borrowing capacity for future expansion. A completion agreement, as opposed

to a full guarantee of the project loans, enables the sponsor to piggyback its credit from project to project. Therefore, the financial officer should try to negotiate a minimum credit support in terms of the types of risks covered and the length of the guarantee period.

2 The manner in which the project loans are reported in financial statements can affect the parent's borrowing strength. The off-balance-sheet treatment of most project loans is promoted as a great benefit, although the advantage has not reduced over time. In the wake of recent changes in lease accounting to permit fuller disclosure of underlying financial obligations, the balance-sheet treatment of indirect liabilities is receiving more attention from the SEC and accounting bodies.

Even so, the indirect nature of typical sponsor guarantees, joint ownerships, and (often) a foreign location are factors that still permit a project loan to be unconsolidated or reported on the parent's balance sheet under a caption other than long-term debt—usually in a footnote. Suppose that a U.S. manufacturer has established many of its affiliated ventures as separate borrowing entities, backed by completion agreements. Viewing its completion guarantees simply as part of doing normal business, the company might not report them as contingent liabilities in its financial statements.

The rating agencies tend to look on off-balance-sheet obligations more favorably than direct debt. One investment banker I talked to employed this rule of thumb: The rating agencies generally ignore an off-balance-sheet financing unless the obligations amount to more than 5% to 10% of the parent's assets. Moreover, project financings typically fall outside the debt restrictions in loan indentures.

To test whether the benefits from such maneuvering are real or illusory, I sent 140 mail questionnaires to the largest commercial banks and life insurance companies as well as to pension and mutual fund managers and security analysts at the major investment houses. The responses suggest that for most institutions, indirect liabilities are not formally or at least not fully included in their analysis of a company's financial position.

Exhibit 3 summarizes the evaluation procedures used by analysts for some off-balance-sheet financing techniques. For the most familiar indirect liability—leases—the bulk of the respondents had developed formal evaluation techniques such as equating leases with debt for calculating balance-sheet ratios or estimating the company's fixed-charge coverage. However, contingency guarantees and long-term purchase commitments, which are less-understood liabilities, are either ignored because of inadequate disclosure or treated informally as a separate factor.

It is dangerous to conclude that informal procedures are ineffective. But a likely tendency by the respondents to indicate what they felt was the desired answer, regardless of the practices actually employed, and analysis

Exhibit 3. Lenders' and Analysts' Evaluation of Off-Balance-Sheet Obligations

Method of Evaluation	Percent of Respondents Indicating Treatment For		
	Leases	Contingency Guarantees	Long-Term Service of Purchase Commitments
1. Treated as a separate factor to be weighed in the credit evaluation	11%	34%	–
2. Impact of the contract on future operations assessed	–	–	51%
3. Included as a form of debt in balance-sheet ratios	15	30	21
4. Required payments included in calculating fixed-charge coverage ratios	14	–	–
5. Both No. 3 and No. 4	53	–	–
6. Generally ignored	4	–	–
7. Given minor consideration because guarantee is limited	–	4	–
8. Given minor consideration because of inadequate information	–	30	36
9. Not specified	3	2	2

of their added written responses suggest that an informal procedure may really mean that the liability escapes adequate recognition.

Close to 90% of the survey group expressed belief that leasing, purchase agreements, contingency guarantees, and other special financing arrangements enhance a company's borrowing capacity. The respondents offered balance-sheet treatment as the most popular explanation. The group also noted that the typical obligations in a project financing are seldom controlled by private or public loan agreements. (Answers to industry-specific questions, such as those concerning production-payment financing confirm the general results shown in Exhibit 3.)

Financing Costs

In addition to risk reduction and borrowing capacity advantages, project financing can serve other ends. Tax considerations and concerns over common liabilities in a joint venture arrangement can make a strong case for this kind of structure in many situations.

The benefits obviously are not without cost. Most large ventures involve multiple lending groups and undertakings by numerous parties, and the additional management, legal, and syndication activities translate into high front-end fees. A range of .5 to 1.5% on a deal of $200 million is normal. To an extent the charge depends on the amount of work that the commercial or investment bank has to put into the financing. Also, of course, a smaller company will be obliged to lay out a higher percentage than, say, a prime rate borrower.

The process of spreading risks to produce a limited-recourse financing may also entail significant costs, depending on which parties are asked to shoulder the risks. Private lenders are generally unwilling to assume equity positions and, in the case of a foreign venture, the political risk premium or project loan usually equals the rate differential charged the particular country. But since commercial banks have a comparative advantage in assuming risks abroad, the expected returns from the undertaking (net of interest charges) will actually increase in the case of project financing.

Projects can also obtain funding or risk insurance from government agencies at favorable rates. As to securing financial commitments from customers, if demand and supply conditions are unfavorable, customer participation may require substantial price concessions.

Most of the financings undertaken by the companies included in my study involved an overall loan premium of one to two percentage points above the parent company's borrowing rate. However, these premiums were minor considering the high leverage and minimal recourse in the agreements.

But project financing is not always a cheap form of financing; many proposals have been abandoned or, ultimately, underwritten conventionally because the costs of project financing became prohibitive. One copper producer, for example, opted to underwrite a $200 million domestic refinery itself, despite the massive capital requirements. The project was to be integrated so closely into the company's operations that a limited-recourse financing would have provided few benefits. If difficulties had arisen, the company would have been forced to bail out the refinery anyway. As the financial vice-president explained later, "Since the financing would use up our overall credit capacity, why not do it in the simplest and least costly fashion?"

Future Financing Needs

Although the capital shortage widely heralded a few years ago has not materialized, the needs of U.S. industry for larger infusions of capital are nevertheless enormous. As economists and other members of the financial community have pointed out, the level of spending on plant and equipment has fallen considerably behind that of other large industrialized nations.[3] How much funding is needed depends, of course, on how rapidly business pushes ahead with an overhaul of its basic plant and how inflation affects the costs of new or replaced capacity.

In addition, companies are facing project costs that tax their financial capacities on a scale basis or because of the high risks involved—or both. A complicating element is the fact that many corporations, handicapped by an already high level of debt financing, will be forced to seek outside funding. So in many cases project financing is a feasible strategy.

The nature of project financing will continue to evolve as structuring techniques are further developed in response to new capital projects and changing moods in the financial community. For the foreseeable future, however, loan proposals that do not protect institutional lenders through provision for substantial recourse to either the parent companies or other third parties will not meet with much success. Nevertheless, project financing remains a highly effective strategy for sharing risks and increasing the debt-financing capacity of the venture.

Notes

1. *The Banker*, January 1976, p. 77.

2. Grover R. Castle, "Project Financing—Guidelines for the Commercial Banker," *Journal of Commercial Bank Lending*, April 1975, p. 14.

3. See, for example, George E. Cruikshank, "Capital Shortage May Shortchange Development," *Nation's Business*, April 1979, p. 84.

Appendix. Research Procedure

My conclusions grew from a close study of the experiences of investment houses and major companies that have used project financing structures. I conducted field interviews with specialists at the American and Canadian commercial and investment banks that are widely acknowledged to be leaders in this field.

Through a mail questionnaire sent to 140 commercial banks, life insurance companies, money managers, and investment firms, I investigated the attitudes of financial institutions toward project loans. In addition, I explored in depth the motives and financial strategies behind roughly a dozen domestic and foreign projects, initiated from 1967 to 1976, that had employed this type of funding. The bulk of the cases chosen were mineral exploration ventures simply because escalating capital demands for such undertakings have forced this industry to innovate with the project-financing technique.

36
The Reshaping of Corporate Financial Services

CHARLES P. STETSON, JR.

Whether in the form of a crumbling bond market, the fight over acquisitions of U.S. banks by foreign ones, or the seesawing price of gold, the turmoil in the world's financial markets is apparent to almost every manager. But few may know (because much of the industry itself does not) that the turmoil will probably result in more imaginative and varied services offered from a host of different types of companies and, importantly, at lower costs to the corporate customer.

What is happening is that a once protected industry is now being subjected to free market principles for a number of reasons. In this article, the author demonstrates that the change is inevitable and that it will not necessarily be a bad thing. In the end, a more sophisticated, mature, and, in a sense, dynamic industry will emerge to serve the financial needs of corporate America.

The different businesses, collectively known as corporate financial services, used to be separated into easily identifiable sectors—through a combination of regulation, tradition, and superstition; in the past 10 years, the barriers among them have begun to disappear. Deals and reorganizations that might have been "unthinkable" are now being sought. Already, we are seeing the following "extraordinary" things happen:

- ☐ Major U.S. industrial companies, once the primary customers of the banks and securities firms, have become their biggest competitors in many areas.
- ☐ In the unregulated overseas market, Merrill Lynch has entered the commercial banking business, and the major U.S. money center commercial banks have begun underwriting and trading securities.

☐ Aetna Life Insurance Company is directly competing with J. P. Morgan Interfunding, a subsidiary of Morgan Guaranty Bank, for intermediate-term loan credits.

☐ Pension funds are lowering quality standards for their bond purchases, sometimes resulting in direct competition with insurance companies; and insurance companies are getting into the securities business.

Incidents like these illustrate the tremendous transformation of the corporate financial services industry. Once divided into separate market niches or subindustries by type of service or product offered, the industry is changing; lines are beginning to blur and competition is becoming fierce. The biggest push is coming from the federal government. It used to maintain the separate and distinct nature of the industry but now is eroding protection through a new wave of deregulation.

This new wave will benefit most U.S. companies. A mature, highly unified industry will emerge as competition accelerates. Financial institutions will bear little resemblance to their former selves, but they will offer companies a wider range of financing possibilities.

Because the changes are just in the beginning stages, many financial institutions do not yet perceive their extent, or, at least, they do not acknowledge the pervasiveness or long-range implications. Most securities firms and commercial banks, for example, tend to view themselves as being able to cope and exist as they always have. A few innovators, like Citicorp and Merrill Lynch, however, are placing themselves in a real position to compete.

In order for companies to better understand the changes and extract the greatest number of benefits from them, this article examines the current turmoil in the industry and projects the shape of things to come in the 1980s.

Traditional Lineup

In the more traditional services, both commercial banks and securities firms tended to view the large industrial company as their bread and butter. Because of the size and needs of the larger firms, opportunities for developing specific financial services appeared frequently, and pricing for risks undertaken generally seemed attractive because of the lack of competition. Services were divided into short-term loans and deposit receipts at commercial banks and long-term financing from securities firms. In the 1960s, securities firms became a competitive threat to the banks, expanding into the commercial paper market as agents for the larger industrial organizations.

The pension funds, both public and private, however, continued to play a more passive role. Most were managed by the trust departments of commercial banks and to a lesser extent by investment advisors. Insurance companies managed their own investments; they provided long-term debt financing, although occasionally they bought new issues of equity. Pension funds tended to invest in a high-quality debt, whereas insurance companies emphasized medium levels. For the most part, neither pension funds nor insurance companies showed much ability—or interest—in the generation of new business.

Captive finance companies, such as General Electric Credit Corporation, provided financing of their parent company's receivables. Typically, this financing also has been provided to smaller companies that have poor credit ratings and few alternative sources of funding.

This traditional lineup did not last, however. Actually, the picture has been changing since the end of World War II, although very slowly—and with few aware of it. As we can see in Exhibit 1, commercial banks experienced a drop of 16% in market share of financial assets between 1946 and 1972. Life insurance companies were close behind. Securities firms remained constant, but the biggest gains were made by pension funds and, to a lesser extent, by finance companies. All that was necessary to provoke fundamental change was a slight push—from the right direction.

First Thawing-Out

In the mid-1970s, the executive and legislative branches of government became strong proponents of economic deregulation and competition. Congress passed the Securities Amendments Act of 1975, which, among other things, mandated a national securities market with greater access for nonsecurities firms. This act formalized an end to price fixing on securities brokerage, unleashing declines of 40 to 50% in institutional brokerage.

The commercial bank sector has also been deregulated. After the Hunt Commission study, Congress enacted the Financial Institutions Act of 1975, which created more competition for commercial banks from thrift institutions by allowing short-term certificates and NOW accounts.

Another major proponent of deregulation on banking has been the Federal Reserve, which has supported commercial banks' entry into related financial areas such as private placement and acquisition advisory services. Further, it has allowed commercial banks to greatly increase their assets-to-equity ratio in the last 10 years by adding substantial loan assets.

The increased disclosure required by government agencies has also helped break down barriers. For example, the Securities and Exchange Commission requirement of detailed financial information from public companies has significantly increased the amount of information available not only about financing, but also about techniques, strategies, and pricing. With more information available, the number of regular financial publications, including *Corporate Finance Week, The Bank Letter,* and *Novicks' Corporate Finance Report*, has mushroomed. Part of the "mystique" surrounding the business, a mystique that helped support a formidable fee structure, is now gone.

Exhibit 1. U.S. Corporate Financial Services Industry Financial Assets Owned by Sectors (in $ billions)

	1946		1972		1977		Market Shares 1946–1972	Changes 1972–1977
Insurance companies	$ 54.6	26%	$ 299.9	23%	$ 437.7	21%	− 3	
Pension funds	6.5	3	237.3	18	321.6	15	+15	−3
Finance companies	4.9	2	79.1	6	124.8	6	+ 4	
Securities firms	3.4	2	21.8	2	28.5	1		−1
Domestic commercial banks	134.2	66	657.9	50	1,068.2	52	−16	+2
Foreign banking firms			23.0	2	83.0	4	+ 2	+2
Total	**$203.6**		**$1,319.0**		**$2,063.8**			

Source: Data derived from 1978 Citicorp and Federal Reserve Bulletin, "Financial Competition and the Public Interest."

Similarly, the fuller disclosure of rates of return on the savings function of whole life insurance urged by the Federal Trade Commission has caused customers increasingly to switch to term life, which does not generate a future cash value. But this trend now places a major constraint on traditional asset growth for insurance companies.

Increased disclosure means corporations are more willing to buy services from other vendors. In fact, more knowledge about financings allows interested shareholders to closely examine the performance of top management. For their part, corporate management now accepts the best bid for major financing and manages relationships on a deal-by-deal basis. The education process reduces the proprietary exclusiveness of many services and the premium pricing it produces.

Worldwide capital markets initially created by the interest equalization tax, which limited the raising of capital in the United States, evolved at first with dollars outside the United States and later with a variety of other currencies. The pool grows larger due to increased flows of petrodollars. And in the wake of the capital shortages of 1970 and 1975, companies increasingly have used these markets, becoming multinational in their financing as well as in their marketing.

In the opposite way, the phasing out of the interest equalization tax in the early 1970s resulted in the return to the U.S. capital markets of many European companies. They were closely followed by foreign banks, which now have begun to compete for a market share of domestic and overseas financings of U.S. companies.

Response to Changes

Most financial services firms have responded to change by trying to compete harder in their own sector of the industry. Casting aside the former understanding that they not call on a competitor's clients, many firms have developed highly organized programs to actively solicit new business. In the securities business, the programs of Merrill Lynch and Goldman Sachs have been widely studied and, in some instances, emulated. Further, firms have begun cutting rates or adding services. In commercial banking, for example, Morgan Guaranty and Wells Fargo developed their "super prime" rate to compete against other commercial banks.

And it is no longer possible to ignore "outside threats" from new rivals. One principal new competitor for a commercial bank, for example, is the captive finance company. The finance companies of General Motors and Ford have net receivables and capital funds ranking first and second, respectively, among U.S. financial institutions. Although many captive finance subsidiaries of manufacturing companies started out by financing their parent company receivables—and continue to do so—some, such as Westinghouse Credit, are developing an organizational base and awareness of profit opportunities in related areas such as inventory equipment financing and leasing. Because of the nature of their financing, they have tended to concentrate on the smaller industrial companies.

There are many other potential entrants into this market. For example, Sears, Roebuck, which has expanded its consumer finance business, could offer corporate financial services to small- and medium-sized companies.

Once Passive, Now Active

Insurance companies have begun to shorten maturities; so, Aetna Life Insurance Company occasionally competes with commercial banks for intermediate-term credits. Furthermore, many insurance companies have aggressively sought to add pension management to their list of services, placing it in separate accounts where additional fees can be earned.

Several of the largest insurance companies have established regional offices to actively seek smaller loans. Equitable Life Assurance has five such outlets for processing, negotiating, and closing loans from $750,000 to $10 million. In 1977, Equitable generated $100 million in private placements alone. Metropolitan Life apparently is following suit. Other insurance companies are actively identifying nonsecurities firms as sources of potential loans either brokered through banks or other institutions or directly placed.

Another thrust of insurance companies is into the securities industry to diversify and help generate new business. In the early 1970s, INA purchased Blyth, later added Eastman Dillon, and now, through merger, has a minority ownership in Paine Webber. In the securities industry, Prudential purchased a minority interest in Hambros; Equitable, in Schroder's—both securities firms in England. These latter two insurance companies also have purchased leasing companies.

Securities firms have, by and large, been slow to recognize the need for diversification. Their market share dropped from 2% to 1% between 1972 and 1977. One exception is Merrill Lynch; by its entry into commercial banking overseas and de facto commercial banking domestically through its cash management account, it has sought to forge a new presence.

Pension funds, like insurance companies, have become buyers of intermediate-term debt. In some instances, they have lowered quality standards for bond purchases even to the point of buying unrated debt securities that have been purchased mostly by insurance companies.

Commercial Banks Reverse Decline

Realizing the need to reverse their market share decline, commercial banks have been mounting an aggressive response. It has begun to work, as the general level of market share decline was arrested in the period from 1972 to 1977. Many banks expanded their geographical presence by adding new offices in major U.S. cities for international loans and domestic loans. (The McFadden Act restriction on multistate banking does not apply to these offices.)

Commercial banks have begun to move into intermediate-term debt financing of receivables, inventory, and equipment. Recognizing the importance of the medium- to smaller-sized company, Citibank's restructured commercial finance subsidiary built assets reportedly in excess of $1.9 billion, almost 50% of which are outside of New York.

In addition, Citibank was one of the first to establish a corporate finance department that offers private placements, strategic planning, and acquisition analysis. The bank also sought to add revenues by successfully marketing dividend reinvestment plans with no brokerage charges to corporate shareholders. In the overseas market, Citicorp has become a major securities underwriter for multinational U.S. companies.

Biggest Long-Term Threats

Almost unnoticed, two formidable competitors have entered into the industry: foreign banks and large U.S. corporations. Foreign banks doubled their overall market from 1972 to 1977. They seized significant portions of the commercial and industrial loans market; in California, the penetration is already 30%. For total commercial and industrial loans of large banks reporting weekly, the market share by 1978 was 20%.

In New York alone, there are more than 210 representative foreign bank offices. Furthermore, foreign banks have purchased several significant U.S. commercial banks, including Franklin National, Marine Midland, Union Bank, and the New York City branches of Bankers Trust Company. Foreign banks have begun moving in on finance companies; Barclays Bank has acquired American Credit.

Foreign banks are aggressively seeking corporate business from a distinct competitive advantage—they are not subject to certain reserve requirements of the U.S. Federal Reserve, thus giving them a lower cost of capital than their U.S. counterparts. To compete, U.S. commercial banks now must reduce their spreads even further or grant more generous terms. In fact, the influence of European pricing has been so strong that U.S. banks have recently been offering companies the choice of a rate based on a spread over U.S. prime or a spread over the London interbank rate. This has exerted even more downward pressure on beleaguered profit margins. Moreover, foreign banks have developed significant positions in several states; U.S. commercial banks may not, under the McFadden Act.

Over the long haul, however, commercial banks may feel the greatest pressure from large U.S. industrial companies, once their principal source of revenue. These companies now compete through their Treasury staffs in the issuance of commercial paper, private placements, acquisition analysis, and pension fund management. There is no reason why industrial companies could not make public offerings like those announced by two large financial companies—Sears, Roebuck for $500 million and Citicorp for $1 billion. Public offerings could even be done in concert with securities firms, similar to a proposed offering of Associates Corporation of North America, a division of Gulf & Western. It is important to note that the financial services performed by large industrial companies can frequently be accomplished at lower cost and with greater internal control.

Deregulation in the 1980s

The major government forces pushing for deregulation are still hard at work. Congress is holding hearings on many facets of the problem; it has already studied and called for hearings on the national securities market and numerous reports from the SEC, beginning with a special study in 1963, and on the banking industry, starting with the Hunt Commission study.

In addition to a natural inclination for deregulation, Congress will feel pressure from commercial banks that are under increasing competitive attack as foreign banks further increase the size and scope of their U.S. operations. The U.S. banks want to be able to operate under the same rules as foreign banks. In fact, they already have done as much as they can. Any action Congress takes will probably only recognize the fact that commercial banks have already developed a national infrastructure, except for taking local deposits. Many have forecasted the change. In fact, in a 1977 report on the securities industry, the Stanford Research Institute projected that Congress would amend the McFadden Act by 1981 and eliminate a number of restrictions on branch banking.[1]

One other remaining regulatory block is the Glass-Steagall Act. Although its original restrictions have been eased, much of the division established between commercial banking and securities firms remains. The act gives securities firms exclusive rights to market making, that is, trading and domestic underwriting of securities including corporate debt and equity. But current events make it unlikely that they can keep these rights.

Since the early 1970s, securities firms have suffered significant net outflows of equity capital and increased liabilities due to larger working-capital requirements and trading inventories. (At the end of 1977, the New York Stock Exchange member firms had equity capital of $3.1 billion; that compares with the $85 billion of equity capital of commercial banks.) Volatile markets, a declining equity base, and increasingly larger-sized issues (such as the unprecedented $1 billion financing for IBM) have made underwriting precarious for securities firms.

It would take only several unsuccessful offerings or a severe downturn in debt or equity markets to prevent securities firms from taking the needed risks in capital raising. Alternatively, the SEC, as it proceeds with establishing the rules for a national market for common stocks, could make it necessary for securities firms to take on significant additional common-stock inventory. That would take away already limited capital available for underwriting, thus provoking an underwriting crisis. Commercial banks, with their vastly larger capital base and domestic and international expertise in underwritings, might logically "come to the rescue." And Congress would have to change the act.

The timing of both changes is difficult to predict. There is considerable pressure to maintain the status quo from various powerful lobbying groups such as the smaller commercial banks and the Securities Industry Association. However, as it becomes clear that outside assistance is needed to complete underwritings successfully, the resistance to change will break down as it did in the earlier deregulation of brokerage commissions.

What Will It Take to Succeed?

During this decade, the corporate financial services industry will have to learn that the factors critical for success will be quite different from traditional ones. Attitudes will have to adjust, for example, to the new importance of the medium- to smaller-sized companies.

For these smaller companies, typically between $5 million and $200 million in sales and no debt ratings, factoring of accounts receivables alone is a $20 billion industry, and leasing about $65 billion.[2] The need for other types of financing will be even greater. In general, premium pricing through brand differentiation can be maintained by proper positioning in this market. Even after taking into account increased administrative costs, the margins could be nearly double those of large corporate accounts, where margins have been greatly reduced.

As the markets change, however, so will required resources. Capital will be more essential than knowledge of the market. For example, commercial banks and captive finance companies will need funds to increase the volume of their loan business. Securities firms will have to call on more capital for a number of reasons, including industry outflow of equity, larger public underwritings, and increased securities inventory and accounts receivables due to expanded market trading activities.

Insurance companies will also feel the pinch; if the trend from whole life to term insurance continues, they will have to find a new source of capital. The sole exceptions to this bleak picture are pension funds; because of accruing employee liabilities and recent government legislation, including ERISA, they are reasonably assured of significant future cash flow.

Access to low-cost capital will be vital for all subindustries. During the transitional period, there will be a number of one-time opportunities for acquisition. Furthermore, capital will also be needed for opening new offices, investing in equipment and technology to deliver services at lower long-term costs, and training personnel.

Foreign banks with good access to low-cost capital overseas and captive finance companies with their call on parent company capital will be in the best competitive position. At a disadvantage will be securities firms with their limited access to capital, due to lack of existing "seasoned" public debt and lack of investment-grade debt ratings.

New competition will require new flexibility. If a commercial bank can act as principal in a loan, it can better generate business. General Motors Acceptance Corporation recently awarded a European debt financing to

Chemical Bank's international subsidiary instead of to GM's traditional securities firm because Chemical was in a position to guarantee the offering terms by taking a major portion as principal, whereas securities firms have been unwilling to date to take on securities as a long-term investment.

Another example is the European Investment Community's recent auction of $100 million in bonds. Somewhat similar in concept to Exxon's "dutch auction" (where securities firms, either independently or in groups, bid for the bonds), there is no reason why this type of financing or similar-type financings, such as competitive bids used by utility companies, could not be done more frequently in the future by U.S. industrial companies to obtain lower interest rates.

The financial services industry will pay more attention to its client base and ability to generate new business. More active interface with companies by financial firms will help preserve market share. Also required will be a disciplined new business program as well as a certain geographic presence. To maintain profitability, the industry will have to keep its marketing and delivering costs low.

Shape of the Industry in the 1980s

In an atmosphere of change and motion, the corporate financial services industry will become much more uniform (see Exhibit 2). The evolution will mean a complete breakdown of boundaries; no business will be safe from competition.

A period of acquisitions will probably occur as money-centered banks buy up small regional banks to fill in their national infrastructure. Foreign banks will vie directly with their U.S. counterparts and offer substantially the same services. Insurance companies will establish local offices and fur-

Exhibit 2. Corporate Financial Services Industry Financial Assets Owned by Sector, circa 1985 (in $ billions)[a]

			Market Share Changes 1977–1985
Commercial banks	$2,143.1	53%	+1
Foreign banks	356.9	9	+5
Securities firms	42.1	1	
Insurance companies	697.6	17	−4
Pension funds	552.6	14	−1
Finance companies	244.2	6	
Total	**$4,036.5**	**100%**	

[a]Author's estimates.

ther expand into the commercial finance and securities subindustries. Captive finance companies, such as Westinghouse and General Electric, will begin direct unsecured lending to higher-quality credits; in essence, they will become banks.

Because they will be the hardest hit and are the least prepared to cope, securities firms will suffer the greatest damage. Some will enter the traditional areas of commercial banking and offer to finance short- and intermediate-term loans as principals. (Salomon Brothers has already considered this move.) Others will concentrate on less capital-intensive areas such as consulting on long-range strategy, acquisitions, and large project financings. Smaller firms will be absorbed by larger ones or by commercial banks, foreign banks, or insurance companies. For their part, pension funds will begin to generate more business on their own or perhaps pay finders' fees.

The organizational revolution will require the finance industry to reevaluate itself fundamentally. It will be forced to realize that it is like any other industry—that it must market to survive. Many financial institutions that have had little or no interest in planning now will have to develop long-range planning and analysis departments similar to those in industrial companies.

In developing the strategic plan, those companies in a dominant market position will probably be most concerned with the entry, if any, of new competitors. For example, Merrill Lynch, with a dominant position in the securities industry, has moved into commercial banking overseas. Commercial banks, such as Citibank, with a dominant position internationally must be aware of and respond to such a powerful new market entrant.

One crucial decision for firms with less than dominant market shares will be the area in which they can afford to compete against the larger firms. In the securities industry, the profitability of Lehman Brothers was significantly increased when it stopped competing in underwriting for nonclient companies, a highly competitive area with low profitability and large volatility.

Specialization will be the key note: Firms will have to look for market niches, just as Lazard Frères has become proprietary in initiating acquisitions for major companies, and Republic National Bank has specialized in international loan credits.

If a financial institution is going to implement its strategy, it must look to its customer base. Should it try to generate new business by starting more local offices? Should it seek to acquire businesses in other sectors?

It will be important to have the right management resources in place. When Citicorp entered the private placement business, it hired a seasoned and well-regarded investment banker away from a securities firm. Now insurance companies compliment Citicorp on its sensitivity to their needs.

Strategic Kickoff Points

To ensure increased return on assets and equity, there are several useful approaches:

☐ The new business effort could be structured to increase income, and nonproprietary services repackaged to create product differentiation, allowing premium pricing. (A financial institution, for example, could offer corporations a package of long- and short-term financing for their expansion program. Alternatively, an acquisition could be prepackaged with financing.)

☐ The institution could increase the number of products sold to one customer, perhaps by marketing financial consulting services, particularly to smaller companies. (Commercial banks have implemented this strategy, in part, by offering their customers private placements and acquisition studies.)

☐ The importance of commodity products must be played down; they should be viewed as incremental sources of income, emphasized only when favorable margins can be achieved. (A financial institution might have a separate unit to manage this market so as to monitor profitability, following the lead of securities firms which typically have a department devoted to competitive bidding.)

☐ New business for others could come from medium- and smaller-sized industrial companies, since the leading competitors for remaining large corporate businesses will be the top U.S. commercial and foreign banks and several diversified financial services companies, including Citibank, Merrill Lynch, Deutsche Bank, and Barclays Bank. (Those firms that develop innovative new products and adapt present products and services to the medium- and smaller-sized industrial market will be the major beneficiaries.)

Effects on Corporate America

In order to profit from the new wave, corporations must learn to understand the evolving finance industry—what services are available from which sources? S.R.I. projects that by 1981, 15 to 20% of private placements might be provided by firms other than securities firms.[3] Although exact numbers are difficult to project, it is interesting to note how rapidly market share can be obtained. One nonbanking financial services company projected a 4% market share in 1979, which would have made it fourth in terms of all firms, including investment banking firms, as sole lead agent for private placements.

The key questions will be: What services are needed? What is the best firm for these services? How can the company negotiate the fees under the existing price structures that, in many cases, are still fixed by tradition?

If more services are needed than can be paid for through these pricing structures, additional fees will be required. If fewer services are needed, corporations will probably want to internalize services that they had previously purchased outside and/or upgrade the quality of valuable existing services. For example, if a corporation generates $300,000 in fees for a long-term debt financing and needs an estimated $400,000 in services, the company should be prepared to direct the business to institutions that will offer some added incentive to make the deal.

Overall, financial officers will have to rethink existing relationships and turn more toward an "open door" policy, in order to obtain the greatest value for fees paid. They will have to rely more on internal assessments as advice and suggestions from financial institutions become more transaction oriented, self-serving, and less oriented to the long-term benefits of the company.

In companies with sales of over $200 million, there will be an accelerated move to bring in-house many important services such as acquisition studies, commercial paper, and private placements. Some, like pension management and investor relations, will still be provided by a combination of outside vendors and in-house resources. The degree to which services are internalized will depend on the degree of financial activity of the company. However, there should be no limitations on what large companies can do for themselves.

Large companies will also move toward competitive bidding for outside services, with the most capital-intensive companies, such as utilities, railroads, and finance companies, providing leadership. It would not be surprising, however, with the new short-form registration for public offerings established by the SEC, to see some industrial companies move toward competitive bidding for securities.

Medium-sized corporations will not have the internal resources and will continue to seek outside expertise; financial institutions will increasingly focus more services and sources of finance on these corporations. In outside relationships, medium-sized organizations should establish direct relationships with insurance companies which can provide private placements of debt and, in some instances, equity-related securities and pension fund management. Also, they can turn to finance companies for inventory, accounts receivable, and equipment financing, and to nontraditional services of commercial banks, such as private placement. In some cases, bank services in these new areas might be paid through compensating balances.

Smaller corporations, like their medium-sized counterparts, will have a greater number of services available, like asset financing through leasing, inventory, and accounts receivable financing. Furthermore, although public offerings of equity on the stock market have not always been favorable in the past several years, there is now an increasing amount of institutional money around.

Pension funds, insurance companies, and commercial banks have made significant equity investments through venture capital in start-up companies, bridge financings (which allow a company to delay a public offering in hopes of a more favorable market later), and sometimes existing companies purchased by leverage buyout. Captive finance companies, in a similar fashion, have been more active in acquisition financing and leverage buyouts. Thus, a case can be made that there is more capital available to smaller corporations today than attractive investment opportunities.[4]

Overall, corporate America in the 1980s will benefit from the lower costs and better services that competition has created. However, within the corporate organization, the industry changes will have to be analyzed, and senior management and boards of directors will have to become comfortable with these changes. Policy decisions in the finance area should be made internally. The advice of the company's traditional financial services firm must be reviewed more carefully in light of both interim- and long-term goals of the corporation.

The responsibility falls principally on chief financial officers to take a "hands on" approach to the financial direction of the company in determining which financial institutions will be used for each service. Their position will take on greater importance as it is necessary to manage multiple relationships with different financial firms. There will be a testing and exploration phase that companies will go through to evaluate new services and new firms. Chief financial officers will have to be wary of firms that are "low balling" to get the business or making unrealistic proposals. An evaluation process needs to be established to measure performance. Those corporations that perceive and understand the changes occurring in the financial services industry will be in the best position to take advantage of them.

It will be important to monitor the industry in the next few years, assess new developments, and test the factors essential for success mentioned earlier. New factors may become evident during this transition, and those firms which best understand the changing marketplace will make the most successful adaptation. By the mid-1980s, the evolution of the industry will have slowed. A new and more mature structure will be in place, and stability will be achieved in the industry as a whole.

Notes

1. "Outlook for the U.S. Securities Industry" (Stanford, Calif., Stanford University Press, January 1977).

2. Lawrence R. Fuller, "Citicorp—Elements of a Corporate Strategy" (New York, Drexel Burnham Lambert, October 1978).

3. "Outlook for the U.S. Securities Industry," op. cit.

4. For further information, see my article, "SEC's Regulation Discourages Equity Capital Financing," *California Business*, June 8, 1978, p. 13.

About the Authors

Jasper H. Arnold III *is a senior vice president and manager of the credit department at First City National Bank of Houston where he has had considerable experience in the field of term lending. He has taught corporate financial management in the MBA program at the University of Houston and frequently conducts seminars on finance and accounting for the non-financial executive. Mr. Arnold is a graduate of the University of Texas at Austin and received the doctor of business administration degree from the Harvard Business School. His other publications include "Banker's Acceptance: A Low-Cost Financing Choice" in the* Financial Executive, *and "Warrants and Convertible Debt as Financing Vehicles in the Private Placement Market," which he wrote with Thomas R. Piper in* Explorations in Economic Research.

Ralph Biggadike *is the Paul M. Hammer Professor of Business Administration at the University of Virginia. He is currently writing a text and casebook on business policy and has published in* The Academy of Management Review. *Mr. Biggadike's research interests center around the implementation aspects of strategy, particularly the role of systems, culture, and managerial style in successful implementation. He consults on corporate new venture selection, strategy and management, and strategy implementation.*

James H. Boettcher *is vice president of Crocker National Bank. He is currently located in Jakarta as manager of Crocker's Asian merchant banking activities. His responsibilities include financial advisory work for governments and companies, project financing, and corporate finance as well as arranging equity and debt placements. Mr. Boettcher holds an MBA in finance and an MA in economics from Stanford University in addition to a BS in electrical engineering from the University of Wisconsin. He has lectured on project financing and risk sharing at Stanford University and the Colorado School of Mines and has presented numerous financial papers at meetings of the American Institute of Mining Engineers. His most recent* *paper, published in the AIME's* Mineral Resources of the Pacific Rim, *was entitled "A Triumvirate Approach for LDC Natural Resource Projects."*

***Ben Branch** is professor of finance, University of Massachusetts, Amherst and a research associate at the Strategic Planning Institute. He is the author of* Fundamentals of Investing *and many articles on economics and finance.*

***Gordon Donaldson** is the Willard Prescott Smith Professor of Corporate Finance at the Harvard Business School. His academic and professional career has been focused on the problems of financial management of the individual firm. He is past president of the Financial Management Association. His publications include* Basic Business Finance *(with Hunt and Williams),* Corporate Debt Capacity, *and* Strategy for Financial Mobility. *His forthcoming publications include* Decision Making at the Top: The Shaping of Strategic Direction *(with Jay Lorsch) and* The Management of Corporate Wealth. *Both books draw on a field study of corporate strategic and financial goals.*

***William A. Dreher** is the partner in charge of the human resources consulting group of Peat, Marwick, Mitchell & Co. Mr. Dreher has extensive consulting experience with public employee retirement systems, corporations, and eleemosynary organizations. Mr. Dreher holds a BA from the University of Iowa. He is a Fellow of the Society of Actuaries; a member of the American Academy of Actuaries; and an Enrolled Actuary under the provisions of ERISA. He has served on the Board of Governors of the Society of Actuaries, on the Board of Directors of the American Academy of Actuaries, as a member of the Advisory Board, BNA Pension Reporter, as a member of the Academy of Actuaries Committee on Actuarial Principles and Practices in Connection with Pension Plans, and on the Investment Performance Committee of the International Foundation for Employee Benefit Plans. He is a Trustee of the Employee Benefits Research Institute.*

***John J. Dyment** is a director in the office of the chairman of Arthur Young & Company, responsible for strategic and long-range planning for his firm. Prior to returning to the United States in July of 1979 to join the office of the chairman, he was responsible for the management consulting practice of Arthur Young in Europe. He is a graduate of McGill University and the Harvard Business School, is a Canadian Chartered Accountant, and has had some 25 years of management consulting experience, most of it in the international field. He is the author of numerous articles on business and financial subjects.*

***Harry E. Figgie, Jr.** is chairman and chief executive officer of Figgie International.*

***William E. Fruhan, Jr.** is a professor of business administration at the Harvard Business School. He received his SB degree from Yale University and* *his MBA and DBA from Harvard University. Mr. Fruhan is the author of* Financial Strategy *and* The Fight for Competitive Advantage. *He is co-editor of* Case Problems in Finance. *In 1980 Mr. Fruhan won the Financial Analysts Federation's Graham & Dodd Award for his feature article entitled "Levitz Furniture: A Case History in the Creation and Destruction of Shareholder Value." Mr. Fruhan has served as course head for finance in the first year of Harvard's MBA program and as faculty chairman for the Corporate Financial Management executive education program.*

Bradley T. Gale *is the director of research of the Strategic Planning Institute (SPI) and a member of its Board of Trustees. Mr. Gale has designed analytical tools on profitability, cash flow, and productivity improvement which are widely used by North American and European companies. He also undertakes major consulting assignments focused on business strategy, productivity, and profitability. Mr. Gale holds a BSEE from Worcester Polytechnic Institute and a PhD in economics from Rutgers University. He has published in* Planning Review *and* The Antitrust Bulletin *as well as the* Harvard Business Review.

Gary Gray *is a vice president of E. F. Hutton and a PhD candidate in finance at the Pennsylvania State University. He has published articles in* The Journal of Bank Research, The Journal of Commercial Bank Lending, The Banker's Magazine, *and* The Municipal Finance Journal.

Helmut Hagemann *is director of the McKinsey and Company office in Munich. He is the author of numerous articles and the co-author of several books dealing with the topics of finance, management of financial institutions, and information technology. Mr. Hagemann has a doctorate in economics from Harvard University.*

Samuel L. Hayes III *is the Jacob Schiff Professor of Investment Banking at the Harvard Business School. He received his AB from Swarthmore College and his MBA (with Distinction) and DBA from Harvard University. From 1965 to 1972 he taught at Columbia University, and he has been teaching at Harvard Business School since then. He is the author or co-author of numerous articles and working papers and is the co-author of* Competition in the Investment Banking Industry. *He has also served as a director or consultant to a variety of private and government sector organizations.*

David B. Hertz *is a retired partner of McKinsey and Company. He is the author of* New Power for Management: Computer Systems and Management Science *and is working on a book dealing with the use of artificial intelligence in business decision making.*

Robert W. Johnson *is professor of management in the Krannert Graduate School of Management and director of the Credit Research Center at Purdue University. He holds an MBA degree from the Harvard Business School* *and a PhD from Northwestern University. He is the author of* Capital Budgeting *and co-author of* Financial Management *(5th ed.) and* Self-Correcting Problems in Finance *(3rd ed.). He has numerous publications in the area of consumer credit and financial management. He was a presidential appointee to the National Commission on Consumer Finance and serves on the Policy Board of the* Journal of Retail Banking. *In 1970 he was elected as the first president of the newly formed Financial Management Association.*

Glenn H. Kent *is vice president of pension fund investment with Honeywell, Inc. He is chairman of Honeywell's Investment Advisory Board and is a member of the Investment Advisory Board of the Minnesota State Board of Investments. Mr. Kent is also on the Board of Advisors of The Sentinel Pension Institute, Inc. He has an MBA from the University of Denver and graduated* cum laude *from the William Mitchell College of Law in St. Paul, Minnesota.*

William S. Krasker *is a professor of business administration at the Harvard Business School, where he teaches managerial economics in the MBA program. He has specialized in econometrics and macroeconomics and is currently doing research in finance.*

Warren A. Law *is Edmund Cogswell Professor of Banking and Finance at the Harvard Business School. He is a director of E. F. Hutton Group, among other companies.*

Wilbur G. Lewellen *is professor of management at the Graduate School of Management of Purdue University. He has been a faculty member at Purdue since 1964 and has held visiting appointments at Harvard, MIT, and Duke University during that period. He holds a BS degree in engineering from Penn State and an MS and PhD in management from MIT. Mr. Lewellen is the author or co-author of three books and approximately 60 articles in professional journals, in the areas of corporate financial management, investments, taxation, and executive compensation. He is on the editorial boards of several professional journals, has extensive consulting experience with both private industry and government, and is a Research Associate of the National Bureau of Economic Research.*

Dennis E. Logue *taught at the Amos Tuck School of Business Administration of Dartmouth University when he wrote "Does It Pay to Shop for Your Bond Underwriter?"*

Kenneth R. Marks *is a vice president of Morgan Stanley & Co., where he specializes in project finance. Prior to this, Mr. Marks was a member of Morgan Stanley's public utility group and its general corporate finance group. Mr. Marks has a PhD in finance from New York University and has taught at NYU's Graduate School of Business Administration.*

David W. Mullins, Jr. *received a BS in administrative sciences from Yale University and an SM in finance from the Sloan School of Management at the Massachusetts Institute of Technology. After completing his PhD in finance and economics at MIT, he joined the faculty of the Harvard Business School, where he is currently associate professor of business administration and teaches finance in the MBA, executive, and doctoral programs. He is the author of several articles appearing in scholarly publications such as the* Journal of Finance *and the* Journal of Business, *is co-author of a book on cash management, and is co-editor of the eighth edition of* Case Problems in Finance. *He has been a consultant to a wide variety of firms and has taught in numerous executive training programs in the United States and abroad. In teaching, research, and consulting, he specializes in the theory and practice of corporate financial management.*

Robert D. Paul, *a graduate of the University of Michigan, has over 30 years' experience in the employee benefits field, most of it gained while working at the Martin E. Segal Company where he is now vice chairman. Mr. Paul's articles in the area of employee benefits have appeared in* The New York Times, Financial Executive, *and* Sloan Management Review *as well as the* Harvard Business Review.

Thomas R. Piper *is a professor of business administration at the Harvard Business School. He received his BA from Williams College and his MBA and DBA from Harvard University. He is the author of numerous articles, including several on inflation and financial strategy written for the National Bureau of Economic Research. Mr. Piper is also the author of* The Economics of Acquisitions by Registered Bank Holding Companies *and a co-editor of* Case Problems in Finance. *He has served as faculty chairman for the Corporate Financial Management executive education program, course head for finance in the first year of the MBA program, and chairman of the MBA Policy Committee.*

Andreas R. Prindl *has a BA degree from Princeton, an MA and PhD from the University of Kentucky, and conducted a year of postgraduate research at the London School of Economics. In 1964 he joined Morgan Guaranty Trust Company of New York and in 1970 established in London an international money management consulting program for the bank's clients. The group dealt with over 300 of the world's multinationals on exchange risk and liquidity management. In 1976 he became general manager of the Tokyo office of Morgan Guaranty, returning to London in 1980 to become executive director of the Saudi International Bank. In April 1982 he established a mergers and acquisitions advisory group within Morgan Guaranty's London office. Mr. Prindl has written a number of journal articles on international money management. He is co-author of* International Money Management *and author of* Foreign Exchange Risk *and* Japanese Finance.

***Alfred Rappaport** is the Leonard Spacek Professor of Accounting and Information Systems and director of the Accounting Research Center at the J. L. Kellogg Graduate School of Management, Northwestern University. The author of books and many articles on a broad range of accounting, finance, and managerial topics, Mr. Rappaport is best known for his writings on strategic financial planning, executive incentives, and mergers and acquisitions. His articles have appeared in* The Accounting Review, Journal of Accounting Research, Harvard Business Review, Financial Management, Financial Analysts Journal, Financial Executive, Mergers and Acquisitions, Business Week *and* The Wall Street Journal. *He is a consultant to corporations and investment banks on financial planning and merger-acquisition analysis.*

***Malcolm S. Salter** is professor of business administration at the Harvard Business School, where he teaches business policy. Mr. Salter is co-author of* Policy Formulation and Administration, Diversification Through Acquisition, *and many articles addressing general management issues. Mr. Salter received his AB, MBA, and DBA degrees from Harvard University.*

***Frederick Wright Searby** was elected a member of The Bendix Corporation board of directors and president of the company's industrial group in June 1982. He assumed his post as industrial group president on July 1. Mr. Searby joined Bendix after a 20-year career with McKinsey & Company, an international management consulting firm. He served as managing director of McKinsey's Cleveland office, as a member of the firm's board of directors, and as chairman of its directors' committee. He is a graduate of Dartmouth College (*cum laude*) and the Harvard Business School (with distinction). Mr. Searby is the author of a number of articles on strategy, acquisition, and corporate finance published in the United States and in European business journals.*

***William D. Serfass, Jr.** is a certified public accountant. He is a former manager of Price Waterhouse & Co., serving in that position from 1967 to 1971. He has also served as vice president of various affiliates of Laird, Inc., New York City investment bankers, and as a director of various companies. Mr. Serfass joined HMW Industries in May 1971 as a vice president and chief financial officer. In May 1973, he was elected to the board of directors and to executive vice president. Mr. Serfass has been a frequent speaker and contributor of articles to professional publications.*

***Fernando B. Sotelino** is vice president of Crocker Bank's Merchant Banking Division in San Francisco, where he is responsible for the generation, negotiation, and management of advisory engagements in the areas of project and corporate finance. Prior to joining Crocker in 1979, he was professor of finance of the Graduate School of Business of the Federal University of Rio de Janeiro and management consultant for IEAD–Rio. Mr. Sotelino* *holds an MBA in finance and an MA in economics from Stanford University, and an MSc in industrial engineering and BSc in civil engineering from the Federal University of Rio de Janeiro.*

James McNeill Stancill *teaches at the Graduate School of Business of the University of Southern California. He makes a specialty of corporate financial management, particularly as it relates to the developing firm. Using the real world of business as his "laboratory," Mr. Stancill teaches a rigorous yet pragmatic approach to business—a spirit he attempts to integrate into his writings. He is a graduate of the Wharton School, University of Pennsylvania, where he was also an instructor before joining USC in 1964. In addition to his academic and consulting experience, he also has work experience in electronics research and development and university administration.*

Charles P. Stetson, Jr. *is president of Davis Skaggs Capital, a venture capital and investment banking firm in San Francisco. He has worked for a major New York investment banking firm and has prepared two case studies taught as part of the finance program at the Stanford University Graduate School of Business.*

Irwin Tepper *taught at the Harvard Business School when he wrote "Risk vs. Return in Pension Fund Management."*

Wolf A. Weinhold *is a private investor. He divides his free time between research at the Harvard Business School and management consulting. A graduate of MIT's Sloan School of Management, Mr. Weinhold is co-author (with Malcolm Salter) of* Diversification Through Acquisition: Strategies for Creating Economic Value *and numerous articles on issues of corporate strategy and financial economics.*

Maurice G. Wilkins, Jr. *has been vice president and treasurer of Textron Inc. since 1978. Mr. Wilkins joined Textron in 1974 as director of investment management and was appointed treasurer in 1976. As vice president and treasurer, he is responsible for all corporate treasury functions, including cash management, capital financing, pension trust investment, and the Textron Financial Corporation. Before joining Textron, Mr. Wilkins was vice president–investment of the Paul Revere Life Insurance Company and, prior to that, was associated with the Mechanics National Bank of Worcester, Massachusetts. He is a trustee of the Citizens Bank in Providence. A former U.S. Marine pilot, Mr. Wilkins was graduated from Dartmouth College and the Stonier Graduate School of Banking at Rutgers University.*

J. Randall Woolridge *is assistant professor of finance at Pennsylvania State University. Mr. Woolridge holds a PhD in finance from the University of Iowa. His articles have appeared in the* Journal of Finance, *the* Journal of Financial and Quantitative Analysis, *the* Journal of Financial Research, *and* *other academic and professional journals. He consults in the areas of corporate finance, commercial bank management, and utility rate setting.*

Larry Wynant *is an associate professor of finance at the School of Business Administration, the University of Western Ontario in London, Canada. He received an MBA degree from the University of Western Ontario and a doctor of business administration degree from the Harvard Business School. Before entering academic life, Mr. Wynant gained experience in credit and general banking with a major Canadian chartered bank. Through his research, teaching, and consulting activities, Mr. Wynant has for several years investigated strategies for financing large-scale ventures. He has written extensively on the topic of project financing.*

Author Index

Subject Index